JOHANN CHRISTOPH BLUMHARDT

Johann Christoph Blumhardt (1805–1880)

The Blumhardt Source Series

Christian T. Collins Winn and Charles E. Moore, editors

Johann Christoph Blumhardt

A Biography

FRIEDRICH ZÜNDEL

EDITED BY

Christian T. Collins Winn and Charles E. Moore

Translated by Hugo Brinkmann

PLOUGH PUBLISHING HOUSE

Published by Plough Publishing House
Walden, New York
Robertsbridge, England
Elsmore, Australia
www.plough.com

Translated from Friedrich Zündel, *Johann Christoph Blumhardt: Ein Lebensbild*, 4th edition (Zürich: S. Höhr, 1883).

ISBN: 978-0-87486-241-6
23 22 21 20 19   1 2 3 4 5 6 7 8

A catalog record for this book is available from the British Library.
Library of Congress Cataloging-in-Publication Data pending.

Contents

Series Foreword by Christian T. Collins Winn and Charles E. Moore | ix
Foreword by Dieter Ising | xi
Acknowledgments | xv

PART ONE: Years of Growth and Preparation

FIRST SECTION: INTRODUCTION—CHILDHOOD AND YOUTH

  1 The Native Soil | 3
  2 Birth and Childhood | 9
  3 At the University | 20

SECOND SECTION: THE CANDIDATE

  4 Dürrmenz | 33
  5 Basel | 36
  6 Iptingen | 50

PART TWO: Möttlingen

FIRST SECTION: INTRODUCTION—THE EARLY DAYS

  7 Previous Rectors of Möttlingen | 91
  8 Installation, Wedding, Beginning of Ministry | 101

SECOND SECTION: THE STRUGGLE

  9 The Illness of Gottliebin Dittus | 117

THIRD SECTION: THE AWAKENING

  10 The Movement of Repentance | 158
  11 The Miracles | 205
  12 Blumhardt's Message and Expectant Hopes | 246
  13 Expectancy as Expressed in Blumhardt's Writings | 298
  14 Worship Services and Christian Fellowship | 327

FOURTH SECTION: A PRIVATE INDIVIDUAL WITH A UNIVERSAL VOCATION

15 Blumhardt as a Private Person | 342
16 The Time of Transition | 383

PART THREE: Bad Boll

FIRST SECTION: HISTORY OF THE HOUSE

17 Bad Boll | 405
18 Bad Boll's Inner Circle | 412

SECOND SECTION: THE PASTOR OF BAD BOLL

19 The Housefather | 434
20 The Spiritual Guide and Counselor | 454
21 Answered Prayer | 476
22 The Preacher | 487
23 Journeys | 494
24 The Author | 501

THIRD SECTION: CONCLUSION

25 Pastoral Care in a Smaller Circle—Fresh Hopes | 512
26 Death | 520
27 Epilogue | 525

Scripture Index | 531
Subject Index | 536

Photographs follow page 398

Series Foreword

T HE BLUMHARDT SOURCE SERIES seeks to make available for the first time in English the extensive oeuvre of Johann Christoph Blumhardt (1805–1880) and his son Christoph Friedrich Blumhardt (1842–1919), two influential religious figures of the latter half of the nineteenth century who are not well known outside their native Germany. Their influence can be detected in a number of important developments in nineteenth- and twentieth-century Protestantism: the recovery of the eschatological dimension of Christianity and the kingdom of God; the recovery of an emphasis on holistic notions of spirituality and salvation; the rise of faith healing and later, Pentecostalism; the convergence of socialism and the Christian faith; and the development of personalist models of pastoral counseling.

Their collected works make available their vast body of work to scholars, pastors, and laypeople alike with the aim of giving the Blumhardts a full hearing in the English language for the first time. Given the extent of their influence during the theological and religious ferment of the late nineteenth and early twentieth centuries, we believe that these sources will be of great interest to scholars of that period across various disciplines. It is also true, however, that there is much spiritual and theological value in the witness of the Blumhardts. We hope that by making their witness more widely known in the English-speaking world the church at large will benefit.

The project outline is flexible, allowing for volumes that aim either in a scholarly direction or towards the thoughtful lay reader. The emphasis will be to reproduce, with only slight modifications, the various German editions of the Blumhardts' works that have appeared since the late nineteenth century. A modest scholarly apparatus will provide contextual and theologically helpful comments and commentary through introductions, footnotes, and appendices.

During their long ministries, the elder and younger Blumhardt found themselves called to serve as pastors, counselors, biblical interpreters, theologians, and even politicians. No matter the vocational context, however, both understood themselves as witnesses to the kingdom of God that was both already present in the world, and also breaking into the current structures of the world. Together they represent one of the most powerful instances of the convergence of spirituality and social witness in the history of the Christian church. As series editors, it is our conviction that their witness continues to be relevant for the church and society today. We hope that the current series will give the Blumhardts a broader hearing in the English-speaking world.

Christian T. Collins Winn and Charles E. Moore

Foreword

FRIEDRICH ZÜNDEL (1827–1891) WAS from Schaffhausen, Switzerland, and wanted to become an engineer or architect. But in 1845 his attention was drawn to a newspaper article critical of events in Möttlingen, a small village on the edge of the Black Forest. After reading about the prayer-healings and the awakening that had touched the village there, he wanted to see for himself, first hand, what was actually happening. So he undertook a hefty hike to Möttlingen and became personally acquainted with the village congregation and with its pastor, Johann Christoph Blumhardt (1805–1880). What impressed him? First, he found no fanatic excesses or "public shrieking of repentance," as had been rumored, but, instead, "upright fruits of repentance." Furthermore, he was struck by Blumhardt's hopes regarding the imminent events in the kingdom of God: the biblical promises regarding the return of Jesus Christ and the outpouring of the Holy Spirit.

So struck, Zündel gave up his engineering studies and enrolled as a student of theology in Erlangen and Berlin. By 1859 he became the pastor in Sevelen in the Rhine Valley (Canton St. Gallen, Switzerland), followed by a short time in Oberglatt (Canton Zurich). In 1874 he was pastor of the "minority congregation" in Winterthur, Switzerland, which had seceded from the State Church. Bypassing doctrinal differences, Zündel concentrated on developing a working relationship with the pastors of the State Church, in keeping with Blumhardt's own "inter-confessional" approach. It was said of Zündel, "In State Church circles he spoke Free Church; in Free Church circles he spoke State Church."[1]

---

1. Georg Merz, "Forward," in Friedrich Zündel, *Aus der Apostelzeit*, 2nd ed. (Munich: Kaiser, 1923), vi. This saying was based on information gathered from Zündel's widow, Emilie Zündel-Pestalozzi.

All the while, Zündel maintained close contact with the Blumhardt family, who in 1852 moved to Bad Boll to spearhead a center for pastoral counseling. He became a close friend of Blumhardt's son Christoph, who succeeded his father as leader of Bad Boll, after his father's death in 1880. At Johann Christoph Blumhardt's funeral, Zündel reminded his listeners that God's promises were still valid, even after Blumhardt's death!

It was natural then for Zündel to become Johann Christoph Blumhardt's first biographer. The first edition of this book appeared in the very year of 1880. He thus found little time for extensive research. Blumhardt's youth, school years, vicariate, and the Basle period thus remained largely in the dark. Even by the fifth edition in 1887 (the last from Zündel's own hand) Zündel limited himself to relatively few of Blumhardt's letters and spoken sermons. He simply relied on his own personal knowledge of Blumhardt and the accounts related by the Blumhardt family and guests at Bad Boll.

But what personal knowledge! Zündel's biography gives a moving portrayal of the events surrounding Gottliebin Dittus and the spiritual renewal of the people of Möttlingen that followed. He was the first person not only to recount the stories of the awakening and the healings that followed, but to show their inner connection to each other. He also successfully conveyed how it was that prayer leads to healing; how prayer is not a feverish state of mind, drummed-up artificially, but a calm and grateful receiving of the "blooms in the field of everyday life." That his account is not exaggerated is proved by what became known only after Zündel's death: a far more extensive collection of Blumhardt's correspondence (together with other handwritten sources, such as diary entries, comprising nearly 4,000 documents).

These extraordinary accounts of struggle, awakening, faith-healing and hope, the "testimony of that which God desires to become in this world"—all this was written down by Zündel at that time when such an account was an offense to many and a source of refuge for others. For this reason, Blumhardt's son, Christoph, offered Zündel his deepest thanks: "He dared to relieve me of what we experienced, to write it in a book and sling it in the face of the entire world to spite the people: you have it right here!"[2]

---

2. Meditation for June 11, 1891, the day of Zündel's burial. In Christoph Blumhardt, *Ansprachen, Predigten, Reden, Briefe 1865–1917*, vol. 2 (Neukirchen-Vluyn: Neukirchner Verlag, 1978), 14.

One man, in particular, proved fertile soil for the book's message: the influential Religious Socialist Hermann Kutter. In a letter to Lydia Rohner on March 1, 1892, he wrote, "So it is good that you are making Zündel your spiritual possession. This will create kingdom ground under your feet and lays the base for our life of fellowship.—From the concepts in it, as they are expressed in Zündel's book, I have constructed my present life, which stands and falls with them more and more."[3]

Although Zündel wrote two other books, both of which found an appreciative readership, *Jesus* (1884) and *In the Apostles' Times* (1886), his most significant work remains this biography. With this book Zündel shaped Blumhardt's portrait for generations. "May it take the blessing God placed on Blumhardt," he writes in his preface, and "cause something of that air to waft to the reader, the air of an approaching lovely time of grace that might be sensed in the presence of the blessed, and may it fill him with assurance of the certainty of all those great and beautiful matters that this life portrait recounts."

Zündel's work stands in the tradition of those "lives" that not only instruct but, above all else, also aim to "edify." His aim is to help the reader be led to a life oriented to the kingdom of God. The critical questions that appear in the text serve chiefly as only a negative foil to the glorious figure of Blumhardt. Zündel's account, in short, is a Protestant hagiography.

The immediacy of Zündel's experience is invaluable. When one lays Zündel's biography aside—inspired, perhaps, or with a critical frown— one cannot help, in any case, be impressed. It also becomes clear that there was something which Zündel did not aim to do and was not able to do: to conduct a conversation with Blumhardt, a real conversation that poses questions, listens and is prepared to learn and to contradict, a conversation conducted with awareness of the limitations of one's own thinking, but also of the limits of the other. Zündel's biography, this unique work whose portrayal cannot be duplicated, has found its own limits in its very nearness to Blumhardt.

Dieter Ising
Stuttgart, June 2009

---

3. *Hermann Kutter in seinen Briefen*, ed. by Max Geiger and Andreas Lindt (Munich: Kaiser, 1983), 122.

Acknowledgments

T HE EDITORS WISH TO thank Tait Hoglund and Brian Bauernfeind for their help in the initial stages of preparing the manuscript, Miriam Mathis for her tireless work in copyediting, Dieter Ising for his help in clarifying several obscure references, and the Church Communities International Archives and Records Center in New York for providing photographs and original translated material.

PART ONE

Years of Growth and Preparation

First Section

1

The Native Soil

IT IS CUSTOMARY, WHEN starting a person's biography, to describe his parents, grandparents, etc., and the immediate family in which he grew up. In the case of a man like Blumhardt it is all the more important to depict his spiritual and intellectual forebears, background, and surroundings, for he influenced many contemporaries in their religious life and in fact left a rich spiritual legacy to the Protestant church.

Early in the nineteenth century the upper classes in Germany had been inundated by Voltaire's unbelief and the faith of the lower classes was undermined by the French Revolution. But here and there, particularly in Württemberg and above all in Stuttgart, there were quiet circles with a fresh, youthful faith in the Gospel. Christianity in Württemberg owes its well-known health and vigor mainly to a number of outstanding men. While gratefully embracing the movement of awakening in the Protestant church known as Pietism, these men earnestly resisted the excessive emotionalism that soon became the bane of Pietism in many other places. Among these men we especially mention J. A. Bengel and his pupil Oetinger.[1] Pietism before long paid little heed to the call "Back

1. Editors' Note: Johannes Albrecht Bengel (1687–1752), a prolific and influential Lutheran New Testament scholar, was a pioneer in the field of textual criticism of the New Testament. His exegesis in the *Gnomon Novi Testimenti* (1742) influenced figures like John Wesley and continued to be used into the nineteenth and twentieth centuries. Bengel's greatest student was Friedrich Christoph Oetinger (1702–1782). Oetinger's theosophical theories gave inspiration to the celebrated German Idealist Hegel. Bengel,

3

to the Bible!" which its founding father Spener[2] had raised, and instead gave itself to the cultivation of emotions as the sole way to salvation. Bengel, on the other hand, took the call seriously and threw himself into the study of the Bible with enormous diligence and great inner freedom. In many quarters the cult of feeling led to a suspicious and disparaging attitude toward the official church and to a tendency to regard informal sociability as the main expression of Christian fellowship. It was different with Bengel. He combined his own joy in such sociable gatherings with a deep reverence for the Church and found a way of bringing these two forms of Christian life into mutual harmony. It is largely due to his clear, Christ-centered perception that such gatherings are flourishing in Württemberg even today—doubtless also because of their continuing contact with the established church, whereas elsewhere they have for the most part disappeared when that contact was missing.

What Bengel did for a deeper understanding of the New Testament is well known. The same holds true, at least in scholarly circles, for his courage and diligence in using the oldest available manuscripts in his endeavor to correct mistakes in Luther's Bible translation. He needed all his innate conscientiousness to stand up for the apostolic Bible against the ingrained prejudices of his own fellow believers, attached as they were to the familiar Luther translation.

Another endeavor of Bengel's, again showing his free-ranging spirit, exerted an even greater influence upon Christian people. By a diligent study of Revelation he sought to learn more about the course that the history of God's kingdom and the Church of Christ could be expected to take. While his revision of Luther's translation tended to give cold shivers to believers, this second undertaking earned him the ridicule of the world. To be sure, the way he found the history of Christendom reflected in Revelation is untenable, and so is his attempt to calculate the time of the Lord's return. This actually led him to predict the latter for the year 1836, though he left open the possibility of an error. With respectful silence we note his words: "Neither in time nor in eternity will I need to regret my apocalyptic labors."

Oetinger, and Nikolaus Ludwig Graf von Zinzendorf (1700–1760), founder of the Moravian Brethren, together constitute the three central figures in the formation of Württemberg Pietism.

2. Editors' Note: Philipp Jakob Spener (1635–1705), author of the *Pia Desideria* (1675), is widely considered the "father of Pietism."

On the other hand, precisely that side of his work was a courageous deed, with rich blessings in its train. The whole Bible, one might say, testifies that human history has an ultimate goal, and to proclaim that this goal deserves and needs serious and scholarly study was a worthy reply to wild enthusiasts whose lips were full of "revelation" and "The Lord is coming." But what was of importance for the church itself was Bengel's authoritative pointing to the great and sure goal of the kingdom of God. For it almost seemed as if God's kingdom had been reduced to an arrangement enabling humanity to live a godly life and die a blessed death. The course of world events was perceived as something totally unrelated to the kingdom. It was seen as a process that Jesus Christ, though still acknowledged as the Son of God, would never meddle with—or if at all, merely to bring it to an abrupt conclusion. Bengel's was a mighty summons, which re-echoed strongly throughout his homeland, Württemberg, and gave a robust character to the piety of the circles mentioned above. It awakened in them a grateful, expectant readiness for God's kingdom. Even among the devout it makes a difference whether one thinks: The world will go on, but we pass away, or: The world passes away, but we stand for evermore (cf. 1 John 2:17). Awareness that the Lord will come has made people gird their loins and have their lamps burning.

This great, free, and bold style of Christian thinking was further developed by Bengel's pupil Oetinger. While Bengel was a churchman through and through, Oetinger's characteristic was the urge to think, study, and know; his thirst for clarity and truth could never be stilled. Philosophy, theology, medicine, chemistry: which of these was his favorite field? The first and second most likely. In order to reach down to absolute rock bottom in these subjects, however, he kept bringing in new and original material from all sides. He found inward refreshment in Ignatius of Loyola and schooled himself in the subtleties of learned rabbis; yet with the same delight he delved into the works of the unbelieving philosopher Shaftesbury, whose spirit-filled writings he translated in order to publicize one of his own great ideas: the importance of common sense. He called it the "plain man's wisdom" and recommended it as a rich store of helpful guidance for the perception of truth in general and for the understanding of Holy Scripture in particular. He also considered it a bulwark of true piety, since it helps to preserve the truthfulness and originality of genuine piety from being perverted by human bigotry into something artificial or trivial.

The second concept that Oetinger implanted firmly and deeply into present-day Christian thinking is that of reality as a living unity of matter and spirit. That concept on the one hand sees matter—the visible—as permeated by spirit; on the other hand, it rescues from oblivion and brings to light the actual existence of an invisible world of spirit. By that concept of the oneness of body and spirit Oetinger helped to halt the translating of scriptural ideas into modern ways of thinking, at the expense of their original content and to have them understood as they are meant in the Bible.

In that way, the circles from which our Blumhardt stemmed had received a rich spiritual inheritance from their forebears, and this left its stamp on their whole tone of life. For the most part they were humble artisans, ranging from well-to-do to poor (Blumhardt's father being among the latter), but they also included schoolmasters, pastors, merchants, and even higher-up government officials, all seeking inward refreshment and deepening in that brotherly circle. Here, the hopes and goals of the kingdom of God were discussed on a high inner plane. Their thoughts and expectations concerning the kingdom found living expression when they participated in the founding of the Basel Mission Society. More than one might think, it was hopes for the victory of the kingdom, such as Bengel's vision of the future had kindled in them, that awakened in these men—who had never caught so much as a glimpse of the ocean—the longing to take the Gospel to their heathen brothers across the seas. We shall get more closely acquainted with the Basel Mission later on, when we accompany "candidate" Blumhardt into the Mission Institute at Basel.

Two forms of church life that were linked with the above circles ought to be briefly mentioned here: the Moravian Church and the Korntal community. Bengel, severe and sober-minded, sternly opposed the brotherly society that Zinzendorf had founded, while Oetinger at least cold-shouldered it. They took exception to the Bible's being used merely for edification, instead of being earnestly studied as a whole—a tendency they seemed to detect particularly in Count Zinzendorf. As time went on, though, the contrasts evened themselves out, and the network of orderly fellowships, which the Moravian Church had spread over the Protestant areas proved to be a decided help to scattered groups of the faithful. The itinerant Moravian preachers in particular rendered a valuable service by blazing new trails, as well as by acting as good Samaritans and leading strays and stragglers back to the main body.

But there was and still is one Moravian institution that was generally acclaimed—their book of daily texts, called *Losungsbüchlein*. Annually, the Moravian Church selects two Bible texts for every day of the year— one text picked by lot from the Old Testament, the other a matching passage selected from the New Testament. Each text has added to it a stanza from a hymn. The widespread distribution and extraordinary popularity of this little book, designed for daily family devotion, can be ascribed to the rich variety of the material. As the year rolls by, the reader is guided to this or that book of the Bible. Thousands upon thousands all over the globe read and take to heart the same text on the same day; so it is easy to understand how widely circulated and how beloved the little book is. We are greatly indebted to the Moravian Church for that gift. Some, along with me, also gratefully acknowledge the fact that in the selection of the hymn stanzas the feeling of mainstream church members has lately been taken more into consideration.

The Korntal community is a splendid testimony to the dedication and the creative urge of the above-mentioned circles as well as to the wise liberalism of the king of Württemberg. When the Württemberg church hymnal, introduced in 1791 and watered down by rationalistic influences, was joined in 1809 by a prayerbook (collection of church prayers) breathing the same spirit, the faithful lost their sole remaining chance of giving vocal expression to their faith. In the circles we have spoken about, this led to an irresistible urge to leave the country. This urge was nourished not only by a longing to live out their Christian ideas in an autonomous fellowship, but also by the expectation of a great turning point in the history of God's kingdom. As the prevailing notions of political economy made such plans highly distasteful to the government, the mayor of Leonberg, Gottlieb Wilhelm Hoffmann, submitted to the authorities a brilliant suggestion. He proposed to let the would-be emigrants move from their various places of residence to a sanctuary assigned to them within their own fatherland; there they would be allowed to give concrete form, at their own discretion, to their religious and moral convictions. Some decades earlier, the young poet Schiller, while attending the *Karlsschule* (Charles's School) on the grounds of the ducal palace called Solitude, in his drama *Die Räuber* (The Robbers) had dreamed of a community freed of the barriers of tradition. He had no idea that on the estate named Korntal basking in the sunshine at his very feet the germ of truth in his ideas would one day become reality in a holy yet sensible way. For it so happened that the Württemberg government readily acceded to Hoffmann's proposal, and it was possible to acquire the Korntal estate, then belonging to Count Gorlitz, for the purpose. Hoffmann, together with Michael Hahn (a remarkable peasant and head of the religious society called *Michelianer* (Michaelites), who even today are numbered in tens of thousands, drafted the ecclesiastic and civic order of the new congregation, taking as their model the Moravian settlement at Königsfeld. Hoffmann became its first overseer.

2

Birth and Childhood

GODLINESS, IT SEEMS, WAS an outstanding trait of the stock from which Blumhardt came. Ostertag[1] for example tells of a Blumhardt who was coachman to the ducal court of Württemberg. He tells of the time when this man's son Matthäus got married. After the wedding dinner the father of the bridegroom, together with master shoemaker Volker, the bride's father, knelt down in a cornfield and prayed that the young couple and their future children and grandchildren might all find salvation and that "not a hoof might be left behind" (Exodus 10:26). One of the descendants thus interceded for—the son[2] of this shoemaker Matthäus Blumhardt—was Christian Gottlieb Blumhardt, first inspector of the Basel Missionary Society. Our Blumhardt is not strictly one of these descendants; his line goes back to a brother of the above-mentioned Matthäus, Johann Christoph Blumhardt, *famulus* (or attendant) at the Blaubeuren monastery; so he is a grandson of the inspector's uncle. But that coachman ancestor will surely have included also that other line in his prayer. Blumhardt's father, Johann Georg Blumhardt, started out as a baker and flour merchant and later

---

1. Ostertag, *Entstehungsgeschichte der evangelischen Missiongesellschaft in Basel* (Basel: Verlag des Missionshaus, 1865), 63.

2. Translator's Note: Zündel actually says "grandson," but that appears to be a mistake, for in two other places (pp. 10 and 39) Christian Gottlieb Blumhardt, the mission inspector, is described as the *son* of the shoemaker Matthäus Blumhardt. That agrees with the statements that "our" Blumhardt is the "grandson of the inspector's uncle" (p. 9) and that the inspector is a cousin of "our" Blumhardt's father (p. 39).

was a wood measurer in Stuttgart. His mother, Johanna Luise, was the daughter of Christoph Deckinger, a master tailor. So it is among humble trades-people that we find ourselves—a class that has often been a main focus of spiritual life in Germany.

Ostertag's book tells yet another incident—again taken from that other line of the Blumhardt family—of the fine Christian spirit at work in those circles. At the age of twenty-one, Christian Gottlieb Blumhardt (the later mission inspector) had been asked to preach a Good Friday sermon in the neighborhood of Stuttgart. He was about to decline the request, because his father Matthäus, mentioned above, lay close to death. But the father ordered him to preach, saying he would surely live through his son's sermon. Returning home after this solemn Good Friday sermon, preached at the behest of the dying father and "greatly blessed," according to a sister's account, the young preacher finds family and friends gathered around the dying father, who lay festively dressed in a clean gown. It was the father's express wish that he might take leave of his dear ones at a meal of remembrance, after the Savior's example. An earnest prayer spoken by the dying man was followed by a simple, festive meal. After it he blessed each of his children with laying on of hands. Among other things, he said to Christian Gottlieb, "The Savior will so bless you and so equip you with the power of his spirit that you will be a blessed instrument of his grace among the heathen." Thus even in death this man's heart went out to the heathen, and his heart's desire to see his beloved son Gottlieb consecrated to their salvation turned out to be prophetic foresight. A few hours later he passed away peacefully.

Our Blumhardt was born on July 16, 1805. "That was a difficult time in Germany," as he told later (*Täglich Brod* 1879, July 16).[3] "I experienced that right at my birth, on July 16, 1805. On that day foreign troops marched into Stuttgart, and my mother with me, her baby, was in extreme danger, for there was no limit to the violence and brutality of the soldiers, who also entered her house. My mother had to hide and pray for the baby to keep still, lest he be heard by the soldiers. Our father was away; he had gone to the town hall, to seek help against the violence of the military. But the baby did keep quiet and help came."

---

3. Editors' note: *Täglich Brod aus Bad Boll, bestehend in einem Bibelwort mit kurzur erbaulicher Betrachtung auf alle Tage des Jahres, nach stenographischen Aufzeichnungen*, edited by Theophil Blumhardt, vols 1–4 (Bad Boll and Heilbronn, 1878–1881). [*Daily Bread from Bad Boll*] Cited throughout as *Täglich Brod*, year, and day.

An hour after his birth, Blumhardt tells, his mother was once more standing at the cooking stove.

Johann Christoph was his parents' second child, but as his older brother died at the age of eleven, he was from then on the oldest of six children. As early as his fourth year he began to attend school. "History is silent about how the three-year-old boy got to school," a reliable source tells us, "but we have documentary evidence that he did." If the "how" is taken literally, "history" has *not* really remained silent about it. Blumhardt himself tells us that his father used to carry him to school in his arms, and at times he returned home in a similar way, that is, in the arms of the good schoolmaster, who looked after him with tender care. According to Ostertag, that teacher (named Gundert) was a lively, spirit-filled, believing member of those Christian circles that Blumhardt's father also belonged to. He was the grandfather of Dr. Gundert, the missionary who succeeded Dr. Barth as director of the *Calwer Verlagsverein* (Calw Publishing Association). This early schooling had a marked influence on Blumhardt's character. It was, so to speak, natural for him to be a man of culture, not so much in the sense of intellectual refinement, but in the sense that school learning and discipline had become part of his very nature.

Having one day carried home the boy, still quite tiny, one of Christoph's[4] later teachers said to the father, "Here is your son; he is not meant to be a tradesman. You must let him study; the boy has special gifts and could be destined for greatness." The father replied, "But how can I do that? Where am I to find the means to let my son study?" "The means will be found," said the teacher. "I am firmly convinced that something great may become of this boy. He must study, and God will surely find the means. Just have faith!"

From that time on Christoph attended the *Gymnasium* (high school preparing for university)—before long, free of charge.

From an early age the boy found joy in the Bible; it also comforted and quickened him amid manifold tribulations caused by poverty and other difficulties. In the evenings, when the children were in bed, Christoph would stand on his bed in his nightshirt and tell his younger brothers and sisters with lively enthusiasm the stories he had

4. Editors' Note: Before the authorial career of Christoph Friedrich Blumhardt (1842–1919), the famous son of Johann Christoph Blumhardt, Johann Christoph Blumhardt published under the name Christoph Blumhardt.

found in the Bible. By the time he was eleven, he had read the whole Bible through twice. Thus the spirit pervading the Bible shaped and nourished the boy's spirit into the very depths of his subconscious. His thinking became instinctively biblical; from now on, he took the biblical view of things for granted; any other way of thinking seemed alien. In particular, the loving nearness of a personal God, as one who truly manifests his presence to the soul, was to him a deeply felt need and also a sure fact. In view of this, he found it painful, strange, and saddening that not only he, but also the venerable, devout men around him, seemed to lack the nearness to God that he saw in the Bible. Even at that time it puzzled him that the gifts of grace of the apostolic age had so receded into the background.

The distress and tribulation that clouded Christoph's early years was due in part to the general need of the times—the war and the famine of 1815 and 1816—and in part to the specific needs of his family. At one time every member of the family—father, mother, and six children—came down one after the other with typhoid fever. Every morning a concerned uncle ventured into the contaminated house as far as the foot of the stairs and inquired of the mother in a loud shout how her family was getting on. Those were hard times, and Christoph, while studying diligently, also had to pitch in with the manifold chores around the house.

As we have but little information on Christoph's childhood, I would like to cite here an experience of those years that remained important to him.

> When I was nine, our professor at the Stuttgart *Gymnasium* once asked me to supervise a small group of my classmates for an hour. It was remarkable, by the way, that it occurred to me to say to the other boys, all of the same age as I, "Children, not so loud!" Then the boys really let me have it for calling them "children." I found that strange, for I thought, "What else are they if not children, and how should I address them?" But even children don't want to be children nowadays. To come to the point, however: While I kept walking to and fro among the boys, I overheard one of them, who was leafing through a Bible reader, ask another, "Listen, can you tell me which story moved you to tears the most?" The other answered promptly, "Yes, the story of Jesus' suffering! Whenever I read that, it makes me cry." The first boy became thoughtful, and I too, felt struck in my heart, because

I had never yet felt it so deeply. What that boy said moved me to tears. That happened sixty years ago now, but I have still not forgotten that sensitive boy, and every time I read out the story of Jesus' suffering, he helps me to see it in all its seriousness.

Even here a trait of Christoph's character—as felicitous as it is beautiful—comes to the fore that explains in large measure the influence he exerted on people and his ready access to their hearts. It is the reverence he felt for the other person, his warm, appreciative way of placing the other above himself, and his thankful acceptance of the good in the other. This may have become less noticeable toward the end of his life. In those last years he stood largely alone and stubbornly held aloft the banner of his hopes. Yet the reader may still perceive this appreciative reverence for others shining forth from this account of his life.

At an early age his love of singing and his musical talent awakened. Unable to wait for the time when the school curriculum would introduce him to the noble art of singing, he would edge his way close to the precentor (directing singer) in church, and by closely watching the music in front of that man as well as the notes that issued forth, he learned to read music. Before long, he had to take his share in the choral singing of the *Stiftskirche* (collegiate church) in Stuttgart. Once, when bread was being distributed in that church, these young bearers of the future had to officiate as singers, and one of them had to be the speaker. Christoph was chosen to be the speaker, and the singers missed him greatly!

Because of his father's great poverty, from a very early age the boy had to help support the family. Many times he carried home heavy chunks of wood from the wood market, and he was especially keen to split the firewood for his mother's household needs. In later life his small but sturdy hands bore witness that he had done more than just push a pen in his younger years.

Blumhardt tells how seriously his father took the education of his children:

> He was deeply concerned to lead his children to Christ. He gathered us children regularly for prayer and Bible reading, had us sing spiritual songs together, and encouraged us in all kinds of ways. I shall never forget the moment one evening when he spoke to us of the possible persecutions that might be in store for those confessing to the name of Jesus. I felt a thrill run through my

whole body when at the end he exclaimed with lively gestures, "Children, rather let your heads be cut off than deny Jesus!" Such an education, supported by equal care on the part of a tenderly loving mother and a sympathetic uncle, awakened the good within me at an early age, and I consider it my particular good fortune to have still many a lively childhood memory of special workings of God's grace in my heart.

On their mutual visits, Blumhardt often heard the older men speak of impending great developments in God's kingdom, such as his father had spoken of—of the approaching "end time," and the solemn impression that made on him remained with him throughout his life.

Unfortunately we have no detailed information about his confirmation at the age of thirteen, an important period in his life. From the extremely high value he set on that time and especially on the festive occasion concluding it, we may infer that it was a time of rich blessing for him. Still, to tally with Blumhardt's character and the course of his inner development, it must have been an experience of a steady, simple, and organic nature.

In Württemberg, for a boy who wants to devote himself to the ministry of the Protestant state church, confirmation is followed at once by the so-called *Landexamen*, a state-wide examination in which pretty well all boys of that age group who desire to study theology—between sixty and a hundred or more in number—compete for the thirty (forty at that time) scholarships annually available at the four "lower" seminaries or "monasteries": Schönthal, Blaubeuren, Urach, and Maulbronn. These are former monasteries, which during the Reformation were dissolved and transformed into schools preparing prospective ministers for the study of theology at Tübingen University. The entire further theological training of the thirty lucky winners is taken care of by the State of Württemberg. After four years they advance from the lower to the upper seminary, called the *Stift*, at Tübingen, a celebrated breeding-ground for writers. In Blumhardt's time the seminary student had to pass three more successive examinations (one a year), the last one being the decisive one. It was on only his second try, at the age of fourteen, that Blumhardt succeeded in gaining one of the thirty scholarships. In various ways his poverty had stood in the way of an immediate success. The "monastery" whose gates now opened to him was Schönthal. It is situated in a pleasant valley on the Jaxt River. The ground on which it

stands belonged at one time to the lords of Berlichingen; in the nearby
castle of that name the students could marvel at the iron hand of the
celebrated Götz von Berlichingen.[5] It was only at the beginning of
the nineteenth century, when through the Napoleonic mediatization
(i.e. annexation to one of the larger German states of lands formerly
immediately subject to the Holy Roman Empire) it became part of
Württemberg, that the Schönthal monastery was dissolved and transformed into a Protestant seminary.

In the Protestant church of Württemberg a freshly installed minister usually gives his new congregation a short description of his life
and development. To this pleasant custom we owe a brief account of
Blumhardt's life until then, as he told it to his Möttlingen parishioners.
Beginning here, its several parts will serve us as introductions as we
consider the successive stages of his life. For instance, Blumhardt tells
the following about his time at Schönthal:

> I had faithful teachers at Schönthal.[6] The short time that the late
> Prelate von Abel was principal of the seminary was a particular
> blessing to me. That venerable old man took a special interest in
> me, and some of his long and truly fatherly talks with me im-
> pressed me deeply.
>
> Among my fellow students I found several of like mind,
> whose company was of great value to me. Above all, I cannot
> leave unmentioned Wilhelm Hoffmann, son of the founder and
> director of Korntal, now assistant at Winnenden. (Later he was
> Gottlieb Blumhardt's successor as inspector of the Basel Mission
> and died in 1873 as court preacher in Berlin.) With him I formed

5. Hero (and title) of a drama by Goethe.

6. The biography of Hoffmann written by his son tells us more about these teach-
ers, as follows. Abel, later "prelate" (i.e., superintendent general in the Württemberg
Protestant church), had been Friedrich Schiller's—the playwright—teacher at
Karlsschule (Charles's School) and was the first to call his attention to Shakespeare.
He was subsequently professor at Tübingen University, where he taught psychology to
Schelling and Hegel. Abel's fellow teachers at Schönthal were Hauber, an outstanding
mathematician, as well as expert in Latin and Oriental Languages; Fischer, known for
his skillful translation into Latin of Voss's *Luise* and Goethe's *Hermann and Dorothea*;
Hermann, later prelate at Ludwigsburg; Wunderlich, later superintendent, esteemed
as a clever mathematician and as a watchful overseer. Together, these teachers represented a rich store of knowledge and experience with which to prepare their pupils
during the four-year course at Schönthal for entry into university. Finally, mention
should be made of Kern, a beloved teacher, who as rector of Dürrmenz later on had
Blumhardt as his curate. His "simply exquisite" sermons were published by Wilhelm
Hoffmann jointly with L. Völter.

a most intimate friendship during my very first days at Schönthal. For nine years I shared with him all my youthful concerns, and God let this association become a source of inestimable benefit for my heart and my studies.

Blumhardt's tribute to his friend just after the latter's death in 1873 in the periodical *Der Christenbote* (Christian Messenger)[7] was hailed by Hoffmann's son and biographer as the best and most faithful extant account of Hoffmann's time in Schönthal. There Blumhardt depicts that unique and fruitful friendship as follows:

> I have always considered it a particularly gracious leading of the Lord that on my entry into the Schönthal "monastery" in October 1820, when we were fourteen years old, my very first new acquaintance was the late Wilhelm Hoffmann. Already on the way to Schönthal, especially at the last coach stop, we two boys, as yet unknown to each other, caught sight of and eyed one another from our respective chaises. The one in which he rode with his father, which was drawn by the two ponies, so well-known later on, mostly followed closely behind the one in which I was traveling with the late minister of state, Herr von Schmidlin, and his son, who had the kindness to thus facilitate my journey. On arrival in Schönthal, we scurried about looking for rooms and places for ourselves and, with an eye to the future, tried to find what seemed best. A remark made then by Wilhelm's father challenged and impressed me. Seeing how avidly we looked around, he said to him and to me, as if I, too, were his son, "Whoever wants to live like a Christian must not take the best for himself, but leave it for the others." That one word gave me a keynote that kept resonating within me throughout my life. On many occasions I also found it reverberating in my dear Wilhelm.
>
> We immediately became close friends, who could also share with one another the finer and higher things of life. Our friendship was not an ordinary one, for it had a mutually elevating influence on us both, especially since Wilhelm's father, with his vast experience and an eye to the practical even in spiritual matters, served as a link between us, also later during the holidays. For nine years we could be seen together daily, arm in arm. As Wilhelm was much taller than I, who was among the shortest

---

7. Editors' note: "Erinnerungen an Wilhelm Hoffmann, Generalsuperintedenten in Berlin, aus seiner Jugendzeit," *Der Christenbote* 39 (1873), 305–8. ["Reminiscences Concerning Wilhelm Hoffmann, General Superintendent in Berlin, From His Youth"].

in the class, we would stroll along, his arm around my neck and my arm around his waist. Generally bareheaded (as was then the custom among students), we were constantly talking and at times arguing, but always about matters that in some way nourished our spirit. To be sure, with my friend the preferred subject of conversation—attractive and stimulating though it was to both of us and also pursued by both—tended to be an intellectual one, while in my case it was more likely to be a concern of the heart, and he was well aware of that. Yet whatever it was, it was there in both of us and filled us both inwardly.

It is a rare thing for two friends and fellow students to give to each other as much as we did, and yet I have to say that he was almost wholly the giver and I the avid recipient. His brilliant mind, searching for the truth, lighted on everything noble and drew me along with him, yet never so that our individual personalities merged or got lost in each other. Each in his own way, we retained our independence and individuality. Yet we were so firmly bound together inwardly that we never let each other go, and if now and then, especially during the middle period of our time in Tübingen, the divergent courses of our lives led us apart for a while, we always came back together as eagerly as ever and completely understood each other. My friend was gifted in every direction, especially in linguistics. Together we practiced reading the Greek and Roman classics, especially the poets. Because of building work in the seminary we had eleven weeks of vacation in 1821; that was our first autumn vacation. I spent that time mostly in Korntal, and the two of us worked at a written translation of Horace's letters and satires. But of course, all I could do was look up to him and admire his speed and skill at grasping what Horace had to say and rendering it with such insight. By myself I would at that time have been quite incapable of understanding Horace the way he did.

While still at Schönthal, we also began to learn and practice English and French together, and before long my friend and I plunged into the literature of those languages. During our free time we would often go out, sit in a meadow or wood, and read and study these writings, again with him doing everything and me being at the receiving end. Now and then he would also give vent to his youthful imagination in poetry, and what he shared with me showed me sufficiently how high he could soar and how little I was able to follow him. At other times we would pick up this or that thoughtful and uplifting little booklet, and some of what we read there left a deep impression on us. He loved literature altogether, and whatever was outstanding in any of its branches would not remain unknown to him. With his excellent memory he could instantly remember the names of all the books in a list and could also quickly and very distinctly recall passages that were original or witty or apt to lead one deeper. He sought to obtain this or that book that would enlighten him on subjects he did *not* have at his disposal, and it often seemed to me as if from the mere title of a book its content would flash into his mind.

As he was most ready to share his thoughts with me, I benefited greatly from all this, for through him my mind, too, was ever drawn to what was real, spirit-filled, and original, but it also pleased him when here and there I showed a liking for simple things as well, as long as they seemed right otherwise. Even though I could not really keep up with him in all that, something of it did remain with me, and for that I feel grateful to him to this day. This is how it was already at Schönthal, where, instruction being somewhat inadequate in those days, the students had to pick up most by studying on their own. And it was even more so in Tübingen, where we occupied ourselves with philosophy and theology.

What a vivid picture that gives of those halcyon days of the two friends' school years! How it shows us their joyous urge to achieve, their delight in growing, their youthful forays into the land of knowledge! It is also worth noting that Blumhardt was more than a year older than his friend and mentor. While the courses of their lives diverged, they continued to have one thing in common: a wide horizon, coupled with an inner urge to have what had come to them from God in quiet become reality and a common possession of all humankind. As regards the divergence of the ways they followed, a humorous brotherly word to Hoffmann is remembered, which has been ascribed either to Dr. Barth or, perhaps more correctly, to Blumhardt. When Hoffmann moved from Tübingen to take up his new post as court preacher in Berlin, one of the two, it is said, saw him off with this farewell warning: "Watch out that you don't lose your second 'f'!" To explain: *Hoff*mann means "man of hope" (*Hoffnung*), while Hofmann signifies a courtier (court = *Hof*).

A fellow student of those days describes Blumhardt as a steady character, who studied diligently, though without distinguishing himself, morally pure and always very modest. He tells that "when encountering coarseness or attacks on his reverence for God, Blumhardt would indeed react, yet without being moralistic. When his patience was exhausted, he would say, 'Now listen, that's enough of that; it's going the wrong way.'"

It was during his time at Schönthal, in 1822, that he lost his father. He had spent the fall vacation the year before in his parental home. On the day when he left to go to Korntal with his friend Hoffmann, his sick father, driven by his great love for his son, accompanied the two, notwithstanding his chest ailment. But it went beyond his strength. At a certain place, which Blumhardt was always to remember, his father took leave of him in tears, sensing correctly that he would not see him again on this earth. Neither at his father's death nor at his burial was Blumhardt able to be with him. The father's passing made it even more imperative for him to support his mother and his brothers and sisters. He took this obligation very seriously. For example, to carry it out he made use of an existing arrangement at Schönthal that entitled each seminary student to a daily allowance of a pint of wine, with the understanding that he actually received the wine only on special occasions and that in general he was simply credited each month with "wine money," that is, the monetary value of that allowance (fluctuating with the current price of wine). Blumhardt managed to save a considerable part of his wine money for his mother's household expenses.

3

At the University

IN THE FALL OF 1824 Blumhardt entered the University of Tübingen; in other words, the top class of the "lower seminary" at Schönthal advanced to the "higher" theological seminary or *Stift* in Tübingen. The *Stift* is governed by a superintendent (*Ephorus*) who is surrounded by a staff of tutors (*Repetenten*)—younger theologians who have passed their exam with distinction. In this way the best and ablest graduates of previous classes extend with gentle authority a helping hand to succeeding students. It is to this wise arrangement that the Tübingen seminary owes its high rank among Protestant schools of theology and its reputation as an inexhaustible source of eminent writers.

About his time in Tübingen Blumhardt tells his Möttlingen parishioners the following:

> My stay at Tübingen, from 1824 to 1829, was no less blessed. I cannot tell here in greater detail about my studies, which became the more important to me, the more deeply I immersed myself in them. With gratitude to God I must give praise and thanks for the countless ways I was helped, partly by the seminary institution itself, partly by the faithful assistance of various teachers, and partly also by a brotherly relationship with many friends. In outer things it was a struggle for me now and then, but God helped me through in ways that are still a marvel to me. My prayers were frequently answered in memorable ways, which could not help strengthening all the more my living trust in God.
>
> Especially dear to me was the contact with several new friends that the Lord let me find in Tübingen. Two of them have long

since gone to their rest. The one, Rudolf Flad of Stuttgart, who worked with much blessing as a curate (*Vikar*) in Oβweil and died in Stuttgart, stood by me with counsel and warning through his maturity and Christian experience. The other was Mosmann from Schaffhausen. A brief biography of him has appeared in print. He was one of the truest and most childlike souls I ever met and has been of unspeakable benefit to me through his tender conscience, his deep faith, and his warm, brotherly love. In a special way, my participation in the association of Christian students became a blessing to me, and I feel touched in my heart as I remember the intimate conversations we had together.

A decidedly unusual account of one's university days! Blumhardt refers briefly to his studies and speaks with more warmth and at greater length of his economic straits and how relief and divine help had been forthcoming. But when he comes to thinking of his friends, he really bursts into lively eloquence.

That he devotes so few words to his studies is sufficiently explained, as he indicates himself, by the educational level of his Möttlingen parishioners, to whom the account was addressed. Nevertheless, it also reflects a peculiarity of his education, namely that none of his university teachers had a creatively transforming influence on him, nor did any kindle his enthusiasm. Blumhardt always remembered with gratitude his university teachers—Steudel and others—but what he appreciated above all was that instead of being so-called geniuses, trail-blazers, powerful heads of parties, or founders of schools they were plain, conscientious, capable teachers.[1] In those days, he said, it was a matter of *learning*, not of *speculating*. To be sure, a certain amount of "speculating" or theorizing *was* being done (as we shall see later on), but not by him.

Instead, he studied theology in a way that was in tune with his own conviction, already mature by then. Holy Scripture and the revelation set forth in it occupied a higher place for him than it did for others, as he discovered. Both his mind and his heart, acting in harmony, urged him to study it. And to judge by his sermons of that time, he knew even then how to read it with the "enlightened eyes of the heart" (an expression that Luther, departing from the original text, rendered as "eyes of

1. True, Baur [Ferdinand Christian Baur (1792–1860)] was already one of the younger teachers at that time. But his type of biblical criticism, like that of others, was not to Blumhardt's taste, for he sensed in it a half-conscious tendency to cast aspersions on the Bible, and for that reason he did not in his own heart expect that kind of scholarship to bear much fruit.

understanding")—that is, with that harmony of head and heart that Paul wishes for his readers (Ephesians 1:18). Hence the exactitude with which Blumhardt later on could fathom the meaning of individual passages, as well as the breadth of vision with which he saw the grand interrelatedness of it all. This, too, is noticeable already in his first sermons.

Next to the Bible, he delved with delight into Reformation writings, especially those of Luther, whose whole thought he assimilated once and for all, with great decidedness and clarity. To judge from his later talks and writings, he must have diligently studied religious doctrine as well. Two things were very apparent in him later on: on the one hand, a jurist's liking for exactness, springing from a well-trained logical mind. He would use it to test whether a certain idea was really the faithful expression of a divinely revealed truth. On the other hand, his manner was one of childlike simplicity and just for that reason one of extreme clarity. "Simplicity is the hallmark of the divine," he said. He felt the need for a conviction that was well rounded, firmly integrated, and dogmatically coherent. He strove to fit each new spiritual insight like a new building block into the whole, and this gave his entire thinking that imprint of completeness, sobriety, and certainty that distinguished him favorably from many another popular preacher.

Another characteristic of his theological thinking should be mentioned here: He was an enemy of empty phrases and clichés as well as of a supposedly "spiritual" understanding, if meant in the sense that the spirit is in some way credited with a curiously rarefying and dissolving power. He understood everything in its literal, natural sense, "just as it stands." This imparted a solidity to his perception and thinking that was almost unique. His way of reckoning with none but extremely massive factors repelled many persons initially and misled them into forming a low opinion of his intellectual power in general. Strangely enough, however, those under the influence of his pastoral care would unawares shed, however much they might resist, those shadowy, supposedly "spiritual" concepts mentioned above. Like a healing power there would dawn on them the realization how much we let ourselves be mystified by those "spiritual" notions—in other words: led up the garden path and tricked out of perceiving the real truth and the true reality. So much about Blumhardt's theological studies.

As for the rest, he somewhat resembled his friend Hoffmann in the way he chose his subjects. Like him he subscribed to the principle:

my pasture is everywhere. He went wherever he hoped to learn something *factual*. He sat in on medical lectures, for instance, and later on he
displayed such broad and detailed knowledge of world history, physics,
astronomy, and other subjects that we may assume earlier forays into
these fields too. He went in for music as well, practicing the piano without a teacher, also copying pieces by Beethoven. In addition, in order to
help out with his mother's household needs, he, together with Hoffmann
and others, translated English writings into German for a Stuttgart
publisher.

As a student at the theological seminary he could not sidestep philosophy but like everybody else was obliged to acquaint himself with the
works of Kant, Fichte, and Schelling, since according to regulations the
first two years at the university had to be devoted to philosophy. Besides,
the brilliant philosophical achievements being published just then attracted the students more than theology, feebly represented as it was. It
was a time when the ideas of Schelling and Hegel electrified students, especially in Tübingen, and Blumhardt's friend Hoffmann was also swept
along for a while by the current of Schelling's thought. Blumhardt was
protected from this not only by his biblical way of thinking but also by
his antipathy toward everything merely "assumed." But he did do some
work in this field, and independent work at that, as we see from an essay he wrote on the human will—its freedom and unfreedom. That is a
problem closely related to Schelling's greatest thoughts. The essay earned
him these words of praise from his tutor, "Well, well, our little Blumhardt
has original ideas—very original indeed!"

As Hoffmann's biographer tells us, the common interest in philosophy and literature drew together a little circle of students. Among
the older members of this circle were Hoffmann and Blumhardt, and
some of its younger members later became well known for their contributions in those areas: David Friedrich Strauss, the esthetician Vischer,
and Gustav Pfitzer. Somebody writing about Blumhardt has rightly
pointed out that the all-round character of his university studies stood
Blumhardt in good stead later on; it laid the foundation for the wealth
of general knowledge so well befitting the later "pastor in Bad Boll" and
contributed to making conversation with him so attractive and fruitful
for all, including highly cultured persons.

It could sadden us to note in Blumhardt's account of his life how, after just briefly referring to his studies, he on the one hand speaks warmly

of the many instances of "relief" that came to him from the seminary, from teachers, and friends, on the other hand of the wonderful help of God. This is an obvious reference to his economic straits. He entered the university in utter poverty and felt inwardly obligated and constrained to help support his orphaned family. This filial loyalty brought him rich blessing through the manifold experiences of help it earned him, both from people and from God. The further delving into the English language that it led to also bore him good fruit later on. English being the *lingua franca* of the world's islands and coastlands, his proficiency in it enabled him later on to gain an unequaled encyclopedic knowledge of the state of affairs in God's kingdom all over the earth—knowledge this man, whose priestly heart beat for all nations, hungered for.

As we have seen, it is of his friends that he speaks most warmly of all in his report. The first of his close friends is already known to us from his time at Schönthal. Wilhelm Hoffmann, fair-haired and Germanic in type, great in height and equally great in spirit, at that time full of enthusiasm "for everything and more," and by his side the short, swarthy, quiet Blumhardt—the two of them looked downright comical, we are told, as they strolled along arm in arm. Yet they were a real blessing to each other. In 1830, for example, Hoffmann wrote to Blumhardt, "Dear friend, apart from my love to you and the time we spent together, all my proud aspirations in Tübingen strike me as so many aberrations." The inward, spiritual, and fruitful character of his relationship to the other two friends he mentions, especially Mosmann, becomes sufficiently clear from what he reports.

Blumhardt actually was not one to be monopolized by a few friends; he had a heart for all, and in the same way as there are flower-lovers, he was a lover of humanity in the true sense. One of his younger fellow students reports: "Blumhardt was popular and well-liked by all kinds of students. Because of his genial and companionable ways he never managed, until just before the due date, to write the two term papers that had to be submitted every semester, but then he would buckle down to it, work day and night, and come up with something good."

Already in his student days he had a way of making use of every minute, even such as are commonly considered lost, to get on with some work. He also knew how to stay away from his friends altogether during hours when work had to be done. Looking for a place where he would not be disturbed, he sometimes (probably only during the summer) moved into a little-used woodshed at a distance from the rooms of his companions. During one summer his fellow student Hauber (later Prelate von Hauber) lived there with him. To keep the many bedbugs at bay, they kept a starling, which Blumhardt, rising with the sun, would greet every morning with "Hänsle, Hans!" Hauber recalls Blumhardt's tireless diligence, sincere humility, and his way of getting on with his work quietly and steadily. These qualities are also remembered in a poem written by a friend, entitled "To Christoph Blumhardt in the Woodshed." The affectionate address, "Dear heart" is followed in lofty and highly mythological language by words of praise for a certain little bird. The bird has settled, with a sunbeam (actually a blade of straw) in its beak, on a tree opposite the woodshed, in order to lighten up the hermit's cave.

Blumhardt disliked exclusive groups because of the barriers they set up between members and nonmembers. Scarcely anybody ever felt rebuffed by him on account of his standpoint. He was, for instance, on familiar terms with David Friedrich Strauss, who, a little younger than he, was fond of conversing with "little Blumhardt"; to be sure, he was at that time still much closer to the latter in his views. Blumhardt later on thought that what caused Strauss to stray from his faith was his enthusiasm for the so-called seeress of Prevorst, a clairvoyant glorified by the writer Justinus Kerner. According to Blumhardt, that fascination had made Strauss's spiritual faith degenerate into a "natural" or carnal faith, which then logically merged into unbelief—this quite apart from the morbid tendencies one is liable to contract through such wanton playing around with the invisible world. Right to Strauss's death, Blumhardt retained a wistful, yearning, and not unhopeful love for him, and toward zealots that misinterpreted 2 John 10 to justify harshness toward Strauss, he would warmly assert that he would gladly welcome Strauss to his house and table whenever he might come for a visit.

Of course, what was closest to Blumhardt's heart was the gathering of Christian students—the *Stund* or meeting "hour" he mentions in his life story—an association that brought blessing to many instruments of the Lord. Here he felt at home, and from here he spun threads of brotherly fellowship, also among middle-class circles in Tübingen and the countryside around, and his labors there bore visible fruit. His numerous talks and sermons are reported to have been most gracious, attractive, and stimulating even in those days, and the same is true of his cordial, loving, and clear manner. "It would be nice if you, too, would come to our meeting," he once said to a younger fellow student, who has forever remained grateful to him. That student followed the invitation and found himself greatly blessed in the *Stund*, or meeting, especially through Blumhardt.

To conclude this account of his years at the university, reference should be made to his first literary creation. It was occasioned by a grave public scandal, which made feelings run high. An assistant minister, Joseph Brehm, was charged with murdering a child, was found guilty and sentenced to death by beheading. He was executed on July 18, 1829, at Reutlingen. The excitement among the people was great. Upon hearing that one of his fellow students was working the gruesome story up into an organ-grinder's ballad, Blumhardt, still a student, felt urged to express in a different and holy way the emotions that the heinous deed and the retribution following it stirred in a Christian heart. He wrote a flysheet entitled "Sentiments at the scaffold of the former parish assistant Joseph Brehm." The title page depicts in a primitive and most explicit way the place of execution. Then follows this poem:

At the Place of Execution

Watch in awe how yonder malefactor—
Let the sun conceal its cheering rays!—
Trudges dumbly to his execution,
Never more to show his mournful face.
Clemency has been denied this sinner;
Now he goes to meet the Judge of all,
Who with stern and evenhanded justice
Will pass sentence on his grievous fall.
This man whom the Lord had chosen
And on whom such noble gifts he poured,
That he lead his flock as their true shepherd,
Ever point and guide them heavenward;
He whom God had meant to be a model,
That in virtue should have led the way,
Did himself give in to gross temptation;
Serving blatant vice, he went astray.
Far he strayed from what he preached so loudly
In the church that he did desecrate,
Where against the path of greed and license
His dissembling lips would remonstrate.
Those he was supposed to guide to heaven
Watch him now, dishonored and abhorred,

Shuffle to the place of retribution,
That his crime receive its just reward.
Brothers, mark how human beings stumble
Once the evil gains the upper hand,
When before the passions in us rising
Our reason crumbles to the sand.
In that man about to make atonement
Greed and lust had pushed all else aside;
Urged by evil passion, he descended
To the basest crime—infanticide.
Lust, while there is time, draw back in horror
Lest into that dread abyss you slip!
Greed, make haste to break the chain accursed,
Which enfolds thee in its iron grip.
From the malefactor's blood, now drenching
Sod and sand from out the severed neck,
Can you hear the broken voice of warning?
"Change your ways!" implores the human wreck!

This, the first-fruits of Blumhardt's literary activity, a clarion call of
the conscience, less concerned with rhetorical elegance than with power
and clarity of content, already exhibits his truly popular traits of simple humility and brotherly trust in everybody. This applies also to the "Warning
and Meditation of a Wretched Man," which follows the above poem. It
mainly bids the reader take note that mere indignation at a heinous deed
is not enough, that everybody has good reason to feel on the one hand
compassion with the sinner, on the other hand fear as regards his own
person. Many times we are just barely kept from committing coarse sins
by the very same power that brought about the fall of this unfortunate
man, namely fear of losing one's honor, status, and well-being. There was
once a man who, when severely punished by an extremely strict father
in his youth, felt surge up the temptation to kill him. But when some
time later he caught sight of a gallows, he thanked God on his knees and
with tears for having mercifully protected him from ending up there. The
flysheet concludes with a short notice about the execution.

The pamphlet is suffused with the lofty hope—so typical of Blumhardt—that it might find an echo in people's hearts. Fear for all, hope for
all; abhorrence of sin coupled with deep compassion for the sinner—that
is what distinguishes here the young Blumhardt and was later to be the
mark of the mature man.

In remembrance of his student days I insert here part of a sermon he delivered in those years.

SERMON ON LUKE 10:23–35
Delivered on the Thirteenth Sunday after Trinity Sunday

In the preceding verses Jesus had expressed to his heavenly Father his joy and gratitude for the firm faith of the seventy disciples who had returned from their journey through Judea: "I praise thee, Father, Lord of heaven and earth, that you have hidden these things from the wise and learned and revealed them to babes." These words take on particular importance for us when we read in our Gospel how Jesus calls his disciples blessed—all of them poor and lowly, ignorant and unlearned. He even sets them above prophets and kings, because they had seen and heard what the latter did not see nor hear. On the other hand, we meet a Pharisee of the usual kind, who, relying on his ample and scholarly knowledge, wants to test Jesus' understanding of the Law and the Prophets, yet clearly shows that in spite of all his erudition he has completely failed to grasp aright the actual spirit of the Law. Thus we have before us both the babes and the wise, and we see how what is hidden from the wise is revealed to the babes. That leads us on to important and significant considerations. Among us, too, wisdom is often sought where there is the greatest knowledge and learning, and whoever can boast of that thinks he has done everything needful for his soul. In fact, however, what he glories in often turns out to be a stumbling block for him. It just reinforces the blindness and ignorance that he would seem to have left so far behind.

Some unlearned people, too, wish they knew more and think they would be good Christians if only they had had time and opportunity to acquire a lot of knowledge, to read many learned books and that sort of thing. Regardless of what different people may think about that, however, true wisdom comes only from above, as our Savior points out. "No one knows the Father except the Son and those to whom the Son chooses to reveal him." He likes best of all to reveal himself to those that are not puffed up by their own knowledge, do not go by human laws and doctrines, do not set their hopes on meager, vain bits of knowledge, but openly declare their ignorance and poverty and ask for the fullness and richness of grace. So this is what our Gospel teaches us concerning the wisdom of the simple and the foolishness of the wise—a humbling for some and a comfort to others.

Beloved Savior, who loves simplicity and wants everyone to put their trust in you, in your mercy help us all to become children! May we not seek our portion in the wisdom of the world; rather, open our eyes and ears to the Spirit that he may let us see your wisdom, hear your voice, and feel your grace. Then we have chosen the one thing needful, the good portion, which is nevermore to be taken away from us. Amen.

The "babes" in our Gospel—if we take that as our starting point—are the disciples, the twelve that were constantly around him as well as the seventy whom he sent before him into all the towns and villages in order to prepare the Jews for his coming. On their departure he had told them, "Go on your way; look, I am sending you like lambs into the midst of wolves." With these words he already outlines the relationship between them and the world. They were not such men as force their way in, or gain entrance by dint of cunning and smooth words; rather, he compares them to defenseless lambs, which have nothing but patience and submission to pit against the rapacity of the wolves. Outwardly they seem to stand alone, bereft of all that might enable them to make their way in the world. That is why he goes on to call them babes. A babe is a yet undeveloped child, lacking in experience and ignorant of the world and of its own circumstances, hence in every way dependent on its mother and others around it. It can do nothing by itself, constantly needs advice and support, and is helpless and unhappy when nobody takes care of it.

That, says Jesus, is the earthly situation of his people. They cannot rely on what is their own. Not because they lack what God has given to others but because they reach out with all their powers in a direction that is different from that of the world; they sense that they still lack what is true and right. Thus they transcend the world. What they can do is of no use for this world, and they seem so helpless and bereft as if nature had quite overlooked them and failed to endow them with what is needed to weather the tempests of the world. But this very helplessness, already manifesting itself as chronic uncertainty in the use of their natural powers, makes them embrace the proffered help. Joyfully they hold on to the promise that Christ, transfigured, will be with his own every day until the end of the world. Through him, they believe, they will find what they miss here. Through him their hearts are satisfied by what they had always been longing for but could not attain. Now there is harmony between the promise and humanity's innermost being. Now humanity is convinced that whatever it does and thinks is vain and empty and altogether transitory unless it comes together in him who is the source of our existence, unless we live in him whose living touch is visible throughout the world. This experience unites humanity ever more deeply and firmly with him who came visibly into the world just for this: that his people might see his glory and thus find rest and peace and firmness.

Here again, humanity may be compared to a baby that, sensing its weakness, snuggles up close to its mother and by trustingly gazing at her is filled with courage and contentment. It trembles and cries when the mother goes away, and when left alone will not be comforted, aware that its help and support are gone. So it is with a Christian for whom closeness to his Redeemer has little by little become indispensable. When in moments of sadness he loses that sense of closeness, when he no longer feels God's grace in his heart, because he is painfully aware of sin, he, too, is like a small child, totally at a loss for counsel and help. He will get no rest or peace until he once more senses the Redeemer in his heart, can again believe in his mercy and be sure of his grace.

That makes it clear to us what Jesus means with the words, "Blessed are the eyes that see what you see." He cannot have in mind here the physical perception of his person, even though the succeeding words seem to point in that direction: "Many prophets and kings wanted to see and hear what you see and hear and have neither seen nor heard it." The whole of Judea saw and heard him and perceived what he did. Jesus always singled out a small band, which he calls his own and "blessed." When he says elsewhere, "Blessed are those that do not see and yet believe," that utterance must be brought into harmony with our passage, "Blessed are they that see what you see." His own words help to guide us here. When he says, "Blessed are those that do not see and yet believe," he means that what matters is not our outward seeing but rather our believing—the inward taking hold of the incarnate Christ. Thus faith is our spiritual eye. As the physical eye is that organ through which everything that we perceive outwardly takes on form and life for us and gives us light for our whole life and all our activities, so does faith serve as the inward eye of a spiritual person. Faith takes a firm hold of that which our senses and perception merely present to us in an obscure, cloudy, and uncertain fashion; it joins us to him who is the source of all light; it brings life and serenity to our inner life by leading it back to the One who is our highest and ultimate goal. Faith makes our path safe and light, for it goes to him who came among us as a mediator and by his coming into the world firmly directed our gaze to himself as the one and only.

Thus faith, our inward eye, seeks him; to see him, to believe in him is the blessedness that distinguishes Christians from all prophets and kings. In the prophets there stirred but a faint inkling of what was to come. They yearned for such a mediator, whom they felt to be indispensable if our life was to pass from darkness into light, from emptiness to fullness, and from the perishable to the imperishable. This yearning, which by its very nature also becomes a presentiment, is their "desire to see," of which Jesus speaks in our Gospel. The reason they could not see is that humanity *seeks history*—actual reality that lets him get a firm, confident, and sure hold on all that the doubts and vicissitudes of life try to take away from him. The disciples did see him who had come; they beheld him whom the world had been longing for, and in setting eyes on him they had also opened their *inner* eye; they had seen and felt the glory in their hearts—a glory that from him is transmitted to those that are his, hence also to those that become his by opening their inner eye.

Now we may ask what it was that they inwardly saw and perceived. Jesus does not name it; he merely says, "Blessed are the eyes that see what you have seen." Previously, too, he had said only, "I thank you, Father, that you have revealed these things to babes." Hence he does not name it, nor does he *want* to name it; he just intimates that it cannot be couched in human words. He merely says to his disciples, "What goes on within you, what you feel inside, the power that you sense in all your members, which even enables you to perform miracles and cast out devils—that is what guarantees your blessedness." What he means is that it expresses an awareness that their names are written in heaven. But exactly what it is and what their seeing actually consists in—that he neither says nor does he have to say it, for their faith, their inward eye, bore witness to it.

My dear friends, that is why the faith of those belonging to him stands so firm and unshakable. No quibbling or subtle argument can reason it away, because faith—being, as it were, reason itself—is that in us which is most directly certain, and no words can adequately express it or present its full content. Indeed, the more definitely and conclusively it is clothed in words and formulas, the more do its spirit and strength fade away. That is why the person who has his eyes only on the bare words of his faith is liable to be suddenly beset by doubts, to waver and fall away until, turning away from the words and descending into the depth of his own spirit, he from there hears again the holy voice that never deceives. Then he once more takes hold of himself in his purest consciousness and his innermost being and life. Once he has turned to this, he no longer has an ear for even the most alluring doubts; he stands secure, certain of what is his, though no longer in a position to answer others that seek by apparently logical arguments to alter his conviction. He is sure of what is his, however much pressing outer circumstances may want to drive him out of it.

This then is the babes' wisdom; it does not consist in learning, in the gathering of many involved items of information, nor does it mean the ability to counter the world and its vanity with shrewd intelligence or to play one's own part in it. No, it is something that rests in our inward parts and from there lights up our whole life—all we do and leave undone. Hence it may become the property of the smallest and lowliest and lift them up above prophets and kings.

(The second part deals with the scribe's "narrow and petty" conception of the Law and Jesus' devastating reply by telling how a Jew, left in the lurch by his own compatriots [the priest and the Levite] was given help by a Samaritan.) Throughout the sermon Blumhardt regards (and treats) the text—obviously an assigned one—as demonstrating the truth of the words in Luke 10:21, which precede the text.

Second Section

4

Dürrmenz

AFTER SUCCESSFULLY PASSING HIS theological exam in the fall of 1829, the young candidate did not have to spend much time waiting idly in the market place. One of his former teachers in Schönthal, Professor G. Kern, was forced by illness to give up his post and was assigned to a parish in keeping with his merits—Dürrmenz-Mühlacker. This was the largest parish in the administrative district of Knittlingen, with more than 2500 souls. Needing an assistant, or curate (*Vikar*) immediately, he managed to get his former pupil for this post. As Blumhardt tells it, "Under his guidance I got to taste here the delights of the pastoral calling, and as I look back to this earliest time of my service to the Gospel, my recollections are all happy ones." The following account by one of Blumhardt's younger friends, Dr. Gundert, later a missionary and then director of the Calw Publishing Association, gives us an impression of what Blumhardt means by these delights. At that time Gundert attended seminary at the Maulbronn "monastery" and from there would often visit the rectory at Dürrmenz. He writes:

> Alongside the serious-minded professor, somewhat reticent because of the pressures of his earlier life, the youthful vigor and naïveté of the brand-new curate were immensely appealing. Instantly the young man won my heart. He went for walks with me and of course also told about Tübingen, the goal every seminary student longed for. Tübingen was only just behind him, yet how it was put in the shade by his present task! Even just to get out of the village

was hard for him. "I really have to pop in there for a moment; you know, she's a sick old woman who is ever so happy for just a few kindly words," and off he would go into the cottage for yet another visit, while I cooled my heels. When he came out, he apologized, "They have so many little aches and pains, you know; one just has to listen to them and not get impatient." But also when just walking along, he would have a word or two for this or that passerby; he already seemed to know all the peasants and all knew him. Sometimes he took me along into their houses and introduced me as a member of the up-and-coming generation. "And I think he'll turn out well too, God willing." All this kind of thing was completely new to me. It seemed this curate didn't need at all to search for a way to people's hearts. Without any trouble, there he was, sitting with the people right in their homes, and he soon enough managed to hit the right spot in everyone's heart.

It was all so natural and down-to-earth, so free of exaggeration that it made an unforgettable impression on me. Something of the glory of the minister's vocation dawned on me; naturally, I visited Dürrmenz as often as possible. He did not seem to be out for conversion at all; he just trusted that somehow there was a sound basis, however small, in the other person, on which one could build. It touched me that whenever he came to Maulbronn, he would visit with me too; that was always like a ray of light breaking into the monotonous and yet flighty life of the seminarian. Of course, I also used the opportunities to tell him of various things that weighed me down, and I always received excellent counsel. Usually when I came to see him, he would read to me something or other by Luther. I still recall being so gripped by a certain reading that I carried the whole heavy tome back to Maulbronn. And there were still other treasures at my disposal, for instance, a piano arrangement of the *Magic Flute*. Especially nice was Peter-and-Paul Day in 1830; there he preached in such a simple-hearted way that I thought, "That's how I am going to do it when I have to preach my first sermon." (Of course, that turned out quite differently.) Then he took me along to nearby Lomersheim to see Herr Epple, the godly schoolmaster, who had been my grandfather's assistant, and the hours we spent there were so delightful that I already felt a real part of this circle.

Otherwise we do not know very much about Blumhardt's labors in Dürrmenz. A diary he kept there tells nothing of personal experiences, with the exception of brief notes concerning texts for sermons; it only contains interesting information he had received from others and about others. In one of Wilhelm Hoffmann's letters to him there is an indication that at that time Blumhardt had in mind to write about the Reformation and Luther. The passage in question reads, "How are the Reformation and Dr. Luther coming along? I hope you are reading, doing research, and writing; you mustn't stop, or I, too, shall lose heart." It seems, however, that Blumhardt the "friend of humanity" and conscientious pastor, who enjoyed the contact with living people, got the better of Blumhardt the author.

In a remarkable way his brother Karl was instrumental in preparing the next stage in his life. Karl had come to Basel as a laborer in 1828, and after experiencing a conversion there had written an earnest letter to his brother Christoph, then a student in Tübingen, urging him, too, to find repentance and faith, having no idea that this was an utterly superfluous exhortation. Blumhardt was so happy about his brother Karl's letter that he visited him in Basel and remained there for a few days, during which time he naturally also sought out his uncle, the inspector of the Basel Mission. This contact led Inspector Blumhardt to see to it that in 1830 his nephew, "Candidate" Blumhardt, was taken on as a teacher at the Basel Mission Institute, rather to the surprise of some friends of the institute.

5

Basel

TOWARD THE END OF the eighteenth century Basel was the center of the *Christentumsgesellschaft* (Society for Christianity), with members in Germany, Switzerland, Alsace, the Netherlands, etc. Its periodical, the *Basler Sammlungen* (Basel Collections) survived the Society itself and in 1880 celebrated its hundredth anniversary. Thus Basel had become a center for Christian aspirations over a wide area, as well as a gathering point for eminent Christian personalities. These connections extended even further when the secretary of the Society for Christianity, Dr. Steinkopf, a native of Stuttgart, was called from his post in Basel to serve as pastor at the German Savoy Church in London. He at once became one of the most important elements in the various mission or Bible societies springing up just then in the British capital, and this brought about a lively contact between Christian circles in Basel and in London.

At that time the republic of Basel, that ancient city situated where Switzerland, France, and Germany meet, went through years full of turmoil and change. Even more than the actual afflictions caused by the upheavals of the Napoleonic era, it was the excitement engendered that proved a breeding ground for great ideas and resolutions among many high-minded Christian folk in Basel. Thus in 1815 the Basel Missionary Society came into being, an undertaking destined to develop in a manner quite undreamt of then. Basel, regarded as rich and pious, has for so long and so tirelessly been used as a target by all manner of shortsighted marksmen that it is only right to put in here a word in honor of the men to whom we are indebted for this outstanding missionary endeavor:

Iselin, Weiss, Pastor von Brunn, Merian-Kuder, Pastor E. Laroche, and their successors: Christ-Sarasin, Sarasin, Socin, Heussler, and others. Many a well-heeled enterprise sailing under the flag of "enlightenment" does not apply its resources with nearly as much true spirit and idealism (to avoid using the odious word "Christianity") as the Basel Mission.

Before being appointed as inspector, Gottlieb Blumhardt wrote the following about these Basel folk to a college friend who was one of the "enlightened":

> In the brotherly circle of my acquaintances here I got to know people who said little or nothing about moral perfection but strove for it all the more zealously; who never mentioned the word "duty" but put it into practice with great conscientiousness in things great and small. Urged by love, these people made extraordinary sacrifices, both seen and unseen, without appearing to do anything special. They acted nobly without being aware of it and endured the hardest sufferings with a fortitude and serenity that astounded me. Their faces radiated love and inward peace . . . Their religion was the purest and most active morality, and their whole morality the simplest, most childlike religion. I rejoiced in this happy find and tried to discover the reason for these wonderful facts. Everywhere I was told: Jesus Christ, the Crucified, the Redeemer of sinners.

An outstanding trait of this (modestly) international enterprise is the clear, courageous harmony in which from the beginning two closely related and yet very different nationalities—the Swiss and the Swabian—have worked together in guiding the Mission. On the one hand the men from Basel, endowed with business acumen, quiet energy, prudence, and (if you insist) wealth; on the other hand the Swabians—idealistic, genial, and combining sprightly wit with a solid theological foundation. They both seek and acknowledge, curb and complement one another. Thus the Basel Mission has been instrumental in bringing to Basel a permanent colony of capable theologians from Württemberg, as for example the inspectors Gottlieb Blumhardt, Wilhelm Hoffmann, Josenhans, and Schott. Among the many eminent teachers were Oehler (afterwards professor in Tübingen), Gess (later superintendent general in Posen), and others.

Above all, it was during the annual festivals of the Mission Society that Basel became a gathering point for friends of the Gospel from very widespread circles. These rallies gave thousands of people a chance to see and hear the most prominent men of faith of the day, and many a stirring moment experienced on those occasions was to remain as a lasting solemn memory in all participants. Our Blumhardt, too, would often derive great inward refreshment, also in later years, from meeting at these yearly festivals many good, sincere friends—above all from Basel, but also from among the visitors who flocked there from all points of the compass.

We have heard that the first inspector of the Basel Mission was Christoph Gottlieb Blumhardt, son of the earlier mentioned Matthäus Blumhardt and cousin of our Blumhardt's father. A special grace lay on the years he occupied this post. It was a time of inexperience, of first attempts (not always happy ones), of learning, but also the time of first love, of quiet inwardness, of spiritual wealth in the garb of outward poverty. Because of its modest dimensions, the whole extent of the work was still within the grasp of everyone involved and could be embraced with heart and mind in every detail—a great blessing for Blumhardt's inner development.

Such were the circumstances of Blumhardt's six and a half years as a teacher at the Mission Institute. In his "life story" he tells as follows about this time:

> This God-ordained call was made the more agreeable for me by my brother's simultaneous entry into the Mission Institute as a student. [This brother, Karl, was to be sent as a missionary to Abyssinia, then to India under the auspices of the Church of England mission; later on he lived in England.] I cannot find words to describe all that I saw and learned in this new school. It was for me a continuous time of blessing. Basel is a gathering place for believers from all parts of the world; here one gets accustomed to looking out with compassionate eyes over the entire world, insofar as it does not yet belong to Christ, and this made me appreciate more deeply how important is the task of spreading the Gospel. There was a close bond between my fellow workers and myself, and it is a special joy for me to see one of them here today as witness of my ordination—Karl Werner, at present rector at Effringen [later at Fellbach; biographer of Dr. Barth], my colleague and close friend during three years at Basel. Again it was at Basel, beloved in the Lord, that I first became acquainted with your previous minister, Pastor Barth. Our hearts met.

The main subject Blumhardt taught was Hebrew, which gave him an opportunity to delve into the Word of God with his students and to bring his biblical thinking more and more into a system. All his life he remained especially thankful that in those years he could lay the foundation for his later truly extraordinary ability to put thoughts into clear order and into the right form, that is, the simplest. What particularly helped him in this respect was a very difficult subject, which had been loaded on him along with various other hard ones, namely that of "useful knowledge," at that time a miscellany of physical, chemical, and mathematical information, which, it was thought, would stand missionaries in good stead.

He was well liked by his students, but he had a lively way of stirring them into active participation by firing questions at them out of turn, and this irked some of them. So at times he ran into opposition, which took the form of finding fault with this or that statement springing from Blumhardt's original way of interpreting the Bible. His was a childlike faith, but as regards the understanding of Christ's person, for instance, he emphasized so strongly the human side that he once had to answer for it to the chairman of the board, Pastor von Brunn, who otherwise loved and greatly appreciated him. This discussion actually developed into a very cordial conversation, greatly appreciated by both participants. Blumhardt's high esteem for von Brunn and his richly blessed work is shown by a poem he wrote when the latter celebrated his twenty-fifth year in office. It concludes with the following very characteristic lines:

> On that day it will be manifested:
> Where man sins, God's word will bring redress.
> Witness boldly! It is well attested
> That rich blessing rests on faithfulness.
> Come, brash unbelievers with your scoffing,
> Who our faith and hope to scorn are laughing:
> Down went hell and death at Golgotha;
> Angel choirs now sing hallelujah!

Somebody who knew him then has this to say about the general impression Blumhardt gave in those days: "A great deal of work was required of Blumhardt, yet in spite of this burden he was serene and happy. If something generally typical is to be said of him, it would be this: Fortune smiled on him in all he undertook. He managed to do easily whatever he took in hand, and he was well liked by all." Someone else reports: "When persons of some importance got to know him better and entered into serious conversation with him, they would soon shed their earlier opinion that he had obtained his teaching post mainly because he was related to the inspector; they came away impressed by his ability and genuineness."

A trait characteristic of him throughout his life—his directness—was evident even then. It was said of him: "Even when he came out with the truth in no uncertain terms, one nevertheless did not feel hurt by it and could benefit from what he had expressed in love."

With Inspector Blumhardt, his uncle, he was on familiar terms, and many families in Basel opened their doors to him—something not easily done. He had a close relationship to his fellow teachers Werner (mentioned above), Oehler (later professor in Tübingen), who had great joy in him, and Staudt (a little younger, later to become his brother-in-law and to be widely known as pastor in Korntal), who had probably been called to Basel on Blumhardt's suggestion. He was also close to Dr. de Valenti, a brilliant medical man from Saxe-Weimar, full of enthusiasm for the Gospel, who had passed his theological exam in Basel. Blumhardt did not forsake him even when de Valenti's brusqueness had alienated most of his former friends. There is still extant a little notebook from those days, in which Blumhardt had jotted down mainly stories and other bits of wisdom that the sparkling Dr. de Valenti had come up with.

The ministers of Basel and the surrounding countryside, in Switzerland but especially in Baden, would often ask Blumhardt to help them out by preaching. Later on he also spoke frequently in Sunday evening meetings in Basel and, according to reports, even then stirred the hearts of his listeners. At times he also did substitute teaching in classes of children and young people and enthralled his pupils by his lively presentation of Bible stories.

Some of his preaching excursions into the Basel countryside took place in the agitated period when the latter rebelled against its previous capital and declared its independence from it. Once when Blumhardt returned to Basel from preaching somewhere, a gentleman asked him for permission to ride with him in his carriage, and this was of course granted. It was obvious that the man kept leaning backward into the depth of the carriage, and once, when they had to stop in a village in the midst of an excited crowd of peasants, he begged Blumhardt to sit in front of him and hide him from view. This worked, and after reaching peaceful territory, the passenger gratefully revealed his identity. It was

Linder, rector of Zyfen and later assistant minister in Basel, for whose capture a reward had been offered.[1]

Another experience during a preaching trip into Baden remained deeply imprinted on his memory. A young coachman, with whom he had traveled quite a few times already, kept him waiting in a quite irresponsible way, putting him into a most embarrassing situation. When he finally turned up in the nick of time, Blumhardt upbraided him indignantly. Suddenly he noticed a strange transformation in the young man's face—an expression of consternation, disillusionment, and even something like disdain! Blumhardt's anger, though well founded, had caused him—not without reason—to fall from the high esteem in which the other had held him. This shocked Blumhardt; his heart told him at once that the coachman was right, and, as he puts it, felt ashamed "to his very marrow."

His years at Basel were punctuated by interesting episodes— journeys he undertook during vacation times, partly to his home, partly through Switzerland. He felt drawn home especially on account of his mother, who received many a tender greeting from him while at Basel—a comforting poem or a careful exposition of some Bible passage. In particular it was parts of the Sermon on the Mount that he interpreted for her, and even so early his explanation of the Beatitudes contains already some of the wonderful thoughts he expressed in later sermons on this subject (for example one he gave in Elberfeld).

For the most part he journeyed on foot, with a haversack on his back. What he experienced on the road and in inns was rich and precious, according to a friend who knew him in those days. Some of these experiences he noted down in his diary. For the most part they are conversations with people he happened to meet on the road. Always they ended on a friendly note. Blumhardt's trustful manner would cause a fellow traveler to bring out a secret grief or to tell about the best things that ever happened to him; at other times it served to soften the heart of one hostile to Christianity and leave him thoughtful, and Blumhardt would earn words of thanks. He often related how once, when asked by an innkeeper's wife about his calling, he told her about the Basel Mission, and how, throwing up her hands in amazement, she cried out, "Then

---

1. Editors' Note: Zündel is referring here to developments in the rural region surrounding Basel in 1831–1832, which occurred in the wake of the Paris July revolution of 1830. For further discussion see, Dieter Ising, *Johann Christoph Blumhardt, Life and Work, A New Biography*, 95–97.

Judgment Day will soon be here!" This biblically sound conclusion found an echo in his own heart and remained a lifelong joy for him.

It was a custom even then for the teachers as well as the students of the Mission Institute to use the vacation time for seeking out friends of the Gospel, especially in Switzerland, in order to strengthen their faith and waken their interest in mission work, through personal talks as well as meetings, or *Stunden*. On one of these trips Blumhardt once tramped all the way to Lauterbrunnen in the Bernese Oberland, where there was a small circle of believers who were occasionally visited by Moravian itinerant preachers. While he was there, two brothers by the name of Lauener from the neighboring mountain village of Wengen (close to Wengernalp) begged him to take the Gospel message up to them too. He was urged to accede to the wish of these dedicated men, all the more since they had what it takes to labor successfully for the kingdom of God up there in the mountains. So he said yes and plodded up through snow and ice, along a track a Swabian would regard as most precarious in winter, but he was richly rewarded for his exertions. The two meetings he held there remained a lifelong wonderful memory, not only for him but also for the people there. They came crowding in; he felt inspired and, to judge from his own report, spoke with special power and fire. Descendents of participants in those meetings will tell even today how at the end Blumhardt earnestly exhorted them to meet regularly in this manner. Taking the two Lauener brothers by the hand, as though exacting a solemn promise from them, he warmly committed to them the nascent *Stunde* (meeting), thus duly establishing it—a double blessing in that remote mountain village. From Basel Blumhardt sent the two Laueners a collection of sermons (by Battier, then a minister in Basel) for their use in reading aloud. The meeting at Wengen is still in existence, carefully nurtured by the Bernese Evangelical Society (*Evangelische Gesellschaft*), and with their help and that of other friends it has long since been given a chapel of its own.

Dr. Gundert, the friend who as a seminary student frequently visited Blumhardt in Dürrmenz, has this to tell about one of Blumhardt's vacation trips home. By this time Gundert was attending the University of Tübingen.

> In the meantime I had strayed far away from Blumhardt. David Friedrich Strauss, our tutor, had us all in his pocket, and the old Christianity had been left behind. Later, though, I was converted.

Now it happened in that hot July of 1834 that I was one of the first
in the seminary to come down with the summer cholera, which
was just beginning to rampage. I was lying in the sickroom, weary
and yet inwardly trusting of the outcome, whatever it might be.
Suddenly the door opened, and in came Blumhardt, gave me a
kiss and sat down at my bedside. And his heart so overflowed with
thankfulness at my finding the Lord Jesus, and with memories of
happy experiences in Basel that I could not help joining in his jubilant joy. All this, of course, without anything much coming from
me; in between I would lapse into dreamland. He, however, talked
on so cheerfully that in the end it occurred to me that somehow
the illness had actually gone away, and I *got up* so as to continue
enjoying his company in the circle of the brothers. When later on
I heard about the healings in Möttlingen, I was reminded of this
incident.

Blumhardt himself, who appears here as though enveloped by an
invisible cloud of divine blessing, was probably quite unaware of what
was happening. To be sure, he did go through something similar in his
own person. He was stricken with a serious illness, which made him
listless, sapped his mental strength, and showed itself outwardly as a
painful skin eruption. On his physician's advice he spent his vacation in
Sebastiansweiler, a sulphur spa in Württemberg. More or less restored
to health, he then returned to Basel, and things seemed to be all right.
Before long, however, the illness returned, making Blumhardt yearn for
the next vacation and renewed relief in Sebastiansweiler. A second stay
there, however, brought no real improvement. Still, he returned to his
job undaunted and trusting in God. But one morning, shortly after he
was back, with a heavy teaching schedule ahead of him, he felt the illness so strongly and was so overcome by weariness that he felt unable to
dress. He tried to pull himself together, but to no avail, and an indescrib-
able inner fear came over him. His heart trembled at the prospect of a
sick and sterile existence, and he felt that his whole life was at stake. He
fell on his knees in a corner of the room and cried to God for help. When
he rose, he could feel the illness, as it were, slip down through his body
and come out by the feet. He was completely cured!

We want to tell at greater length of something especially wonderful
Blumhardt was given during his stay at Basel.

A number of disciples had been drawn to Basel by the life stirring
there and the endeavors to bring about and nurture a great fellowship
of believers from all lands. Among them was a minister from Nassau,

an elderly, quiet, faithful cross-bearer by the name of Köllner. His auto-biography is one of the pleasant and genial memories of my childhood. We nicknamed him *Hornköllner* ("trumpet Köllner"), because of the ear trumpet that shows on the picture of the old man, who was hard of hearing. Like Zaremba and A. later on, he was one of the members per-sonally known to us children from among the great, scattered family of believers, most of whom did not know each other personally. In Basel he edited the *Basler Sammlungen* on behalf of the Society for Christianity. He was a soft-hearted, deeply inward man, who barely had one foot on the ground in practical matters. His son Karl, of similar character, was the comfort of his father, who mourned the tragic loss of two other sons. Karl had trained for a business career and had sincerely tried to recon-cile himself to this prospect, but could not endure it in the long run, finding it well-nigh impossible to be a true Christian while engaged in business.

In those years, alongside the zeal to missionize the heathen there awoke a similar zeal for mission work among the Jews. Three factors contributed to this. The one closest at hand was the Jews' presence in our midst. One might ask, "If we do not love the Jew, whom we see, how can we love the heathen, whom we do not see?" Next, feeling as one did a new love and gratitude toward the Lord Jesus, one was reminded that the Jews were his blood brothers. And there was a third consideration, then regarded as quite weighty. Since the Bible speaks of an ultimate conver-sion of the Jews as preceding the return of the Lord, it was thought that an effort to bring to fulfillment this promise might be the best way to speed up the longed-for coming of the Lord.

For this mission among the Jews Karl Köllner felt a special enthu-siasm. He wanted to be a farmer, but at the same time dedicate his life in some special way to the service of God's kingdom, and this led to his purchasing a farm with the idea of founding there an institution for the education of Jewish children. He established himself in the little village of Sitzenkirch in Baden and prepared for the reception of such children. Some did come, but not for long. Even if the parents had been willing to leave their children with him, their fellow Jews would not tolerate it; hence nothing came of this modest endeavor. This in spite of great efforts made by the Basel friends of mission to the Jews, in particular also by Pastor Barth in Möttlingen. What remained in Sitzenkirch was an idyllic, warmhearted family life, shedding a bright light into the world around, not least through manifold inconspicuous works of mercy, until Köllner later moved to Korntal, where his son-in-law Staudt was the minister. Here father Köllner was able to unfold an activity that suited his heart and mind.

In Basel Blumhardt frequently had to do substitute teaching in religion, especially with a class of girls. The girls were remarkably stirred and stimulated by his lively and colorful presentation of Bible stories. One of them attracted Blumhardt's attention by the fact that she spoke proper German, but even more by her attentiveness, understanding, and Bible knowledge. The girl was from Sitzenkirch, and her name was Doris Köllner. From the beginning she made a deep impression on Blumhardt, though at the time there was no more to it than that. Now toward the end of his stay in Basel he, together with a few companions from the Mission Institute, happened to be on a mineral-collecting expedition through the Baden countryside—probably in aid of the "useful knowledge" he was supposed to be teaching. As they strolled along the avenue of Sitzenkirch, they were observed by Köllner, recognized as members of the Mission Institute, and invited in. Mother Köllner called her three daughters in and, in line with simple, age-old custom, each one extended a welcoming hand to the guests. One handshake had an electrifying effect on Blumhardt—that of Doris Köllner.

Before very long the mineral-hunter, pursuing his search for precious gems, appeared once more at the Köllners' door, and after another brief interval father Köllner received a letter from Blumhardt, dated December 16, 1836, the contents of which may be left to our imagination.

Blumhardt waited anxiously for the reply. By ordinary human standards he could not be too certain. In spite of his winning ways in the circle of his companions and in spite of his stimulating influence on young people of both sexes as a teacher of religion, no girl would have been likely to regard "swarthy Blumhardt" (as some of the younger set dubbed him, not too respectfully) as the ideal future husband. In addition, throughout his life he retained a certain original style of courtesy and of conduct, which, wholly shaped by his own attitude and outlook, differed in many respects from the traditional and conventional. To be sure, this enhanced the clarity, truthfulness, and naturalness of his manner, but at the same time imparted to it a certain roughness of finish, like that of a Dürer woodcut compared to an etching by Raphael. However, he did receive a favorable reply, even though father Köllner found it hard to part with his daughter. On December 23, 1836, in a solemn letter full of lofty emotion he wrote, "The Lord has given our daughter the joyful conviction that she should accept your proposal as a call from him, to be followed in childlike faith and obedience." As Blumhardt told it later, he had to wait five weeks for this letter. Could it be that for some time the prospective father-in-law could not bring himself to post the already completed letter, in which he gave up his beloved daughter? Or did Blumhardt's anxious wait for the answer cause the time to expand to four times the actual length in his memory? We do not know.

God gave Blumhardt a wonderful gift in this his future wife. She was a quiet, thoughtful girl, more drawn to the realm of the ideal than to the dry realities of housekeeping, and she may well have dreamt of an idyllic life in a rural parsonage by the side of her rector husband. Yet, what renunciation of domestic quiet and of a cozy family life, what manifold self-abnegation and what grueling work and strife by day and night awaited her! And though it is not seemly to praise the beloved widow too loudly, it may not be out of place to ask how many other young women would have proved equal to the task that we shall see unfolding before us in Blumhardt's later life.

Winning a bride for himself meant that his sojourn in Basel was drawing to an end, for he was now obliged to look for a home of his own and, with this in mind, to place himself again at the disposal of the church authorities in his homeland.

We close our account of Blumhardt's activity in Basel by quoting two pieces he wrote, one an extract from a sermon and the other a poem he inscribed in a departing missionary's album.

I.

Extract from a sermon preached July 24, 1831, in St. Elisabeth's Church in Basel.

Text: Matthew 5:43–48 (Love your enemies . . .)

As in all his extant sermons from that time, so here, too, Blumhardt follows an old custom by discussing first a Bible passage other than the actual sermon text. The advantage of this is that the secondary passage casts a special light upon the text itself. In this case he begins with the words: "But to all who received him, who believed in his name, he gave power to become children of God" (John 1:12). This leads on to the theme of "love as the testimony that we are God's children: 1) it must embrace all people; 2) it must let nothing disturb it."

Prayer: Father of love, break down the barriers that still separate our hearts! By nature we are unable to love. We feel more urged to hate and hurt one another than to meet each other with peaceful and well-meaning love; we would rather pay somebody back than forgive him; we incline more to anger than to patience and forbearance. That is not your way, heavenly Father; how can we then be called your children? Therefore kindle among us the spirit of love; make us mindful of how much you have loved us poor, lost sinners, so that we may learn from you the love that shows we are your children. Amen.

The second half of the first part begins in this way:

Let us hear what Jesus says about the love that we should have. It is not love of a kind that any unscrupulous swindler or the like could have in common with us. "Therefore," Jesus adds, "be perfect even as your Father in heaven is perfect." And how does the heavenly Father show his perfection, where love is concerned? "He makes his sun rise on the evil and on the good and sends rain on the just and on the unjust." He thus reveals himself as the father of all his creatures. He wants to show fatherly love to all, whoever they be, and pour blessings on them, according to their need. No one is excluded, lest even a single individual come and say, "He has never yet shown me any kindness!" Where is there a sufferer or mourner who would know nothing of God's goodness or would deny that above him there rules, invisible, a loving Father! All people are his, and "Can a woman forget her sucking child, that she should have no compassion on the son of her womb? Though she may forget, I will not forget you," says the Lord. "See, I have engraved you on the palms of my hands." This is what the Lord said to Israel, and we who have been chosen to be Christ's brothers may regard these words as spoken to our own hearts and conclude from it that a love higher than all our own thinking encompasses all people on earth.

Such is the love of God . . . Should we then go and discriminate between people? Should we show love to one, and meet another with callous indifference and contempt or even unfeeling cruelty? O dear Christian friends, let us look deep into our hearts to see whether, side by side with a possibly great and sacrificial love to certain persons, we may not be loveless toward others. These may be people who we think are no concern of ours, strangers perhaps, or persons who don't seem to bring us any personal advantage or who may even unintentionally cause us trouble. Our daily dealings with people offer so many occasions for such lovelessness; we tend to shrug off our acts of cunning, dishonesty, or coldness toward our fellow human beings. We are not aware that by doing this we deny our divine sonship. While giving a righteous appearance in public, we try—now more, now less—by all kinds of devious ways to defraud our neighbor of his goods and honor, in order to raise ourselves up or advance our own interests. How often does an unloving, frivolous word, casually uttered, or some act apparently thoughtless but in fact callous and dishonest bring bitter tears to a neighbor's eyes! The Lord's gaze, however, penetrates into the hidden places; he, who loves *all* his children, sees also those who do *not* love them; he knows what value to put on a partisan or tax collector's love (Matt 5:46–47).

Further from the middle of the second part:

To be sure, you may reply, "How can someone possibly so abandon himself, so strip himself of his natural human rights that he just stands and looks on when surrounded by deceit and wickedness or when attacked at the point most precious to him—his honor? How can he possibly retain even a spark of love to people who show him nothing but enmity?" This is how a person will speak who makes the worst out of everything he meets with from his fellowmen, who, for example, considers everything lost when in the presence of others a fellow brother drops some barbed remark. Or when slanderous rumors against him are noised abroad, he no longer wants to believe anybody. He tends to put the most hateful interpretation on what often is merely the result of a momentary surge of temper—an interpretation such as can never spring from love dwelling in the heart. And assuming they really do take all you have and ruin your whole earthly happiness—"If God is on our side, who is against us?" Paul calls out to you: "What can separate us from the love of God—can affliction or fear or persecution?" (Rom 8:31, 35) Here, beloved friends, we have found the point that helps us clothe ourselves with a love that is not disturbed by anything—a love that overlooks every intended slight. Paul had found the Man who changed him from a persecutor to one willingly enduring persecution.

II.

"Inscribed in a missionary's album."

Since God's dear children are the pillars
That keep the world from crashing to the ground,
They must so scatter through the crumbling building
That everywhere Christ's watchmen may be found.

Although their nearness brings us joy,
We weep not when they part.
There must be sturdy pillars everywhere,
Lest falls the world apart.
To be God's children is the calling
Of all humankind, as yet engulfed in night.
May love draw all people to the throne of heaven,
Which sends into the gloom its beams of light.
Although their nearness brings us joy,
Parting, we do not grieve;
There must be witnesses in every place
Who help us to believe.
Around God's throne his children gather;
That is their meeting place, the town of love.
How we shall joy and praise our Lord and Master,
Who has already built our huts above!
Although their nearness brings us joy,
Their leaving does not smart,
For some day we shall all be there with him
And nevermore shall part.

6

Iptingen

IN BLUMHARDT'S OWN LIFE story, which up to now has supplied us with a concise sketch of every stage in his life, we read: "I stayed in Basel for six and a half years, and when at Easter 1837 I returned to my home country, I presently received a call to go to Iptingen as assistant pastor in that parish."

It was scarcely by accident that he was posted to Iptingen, a small parish of 790 souls in the administrative district of Vaihingen. Quite likely it was for a purpose that the task awaiting him there—an especially difficult one—had been assigned to him, a man of experience and an outgoing and sociable pastor. Iptingen was a center of separatism. From here the Harmonists, led by Rapp, had left and gone to North America.[1] These separatists were solid, respectable, capable people, but rigid, stern, and very sure of themselves. Because of the unbelief that had flooded the Protestant state church, they looked down on it and had wholly broken with it, to the extent that they thought it sinful even to enter a church building. Their mood is expressed in a letter in which one of them, who had come to trust in Blumhardt, poured out his heart

---

1. Editors' Note: George Rapp (1757–1847) was the most famous of the Iptingen separatists. In 1803–1804 he convinced a sizable group to immigrate to America in expectation of the imminent coming of the kingdom of God. This later resulted in the founding of New Harmony in 1814 in the Territory of Indiana. For a discussion of Rapp and New Harmony see Karl John Richard Arndt, *George Rapp's Harmony Society: 1785–1847*, rev. ed. (Rutherford, NJ: Farleigh Dickenson University Press, 1972).

to him, lamenting the poor quality of the ministers etc., and signing himself "Yours in anger."

Had these difficulties proved too much for the rector at Iptingen, in any case a man somewhat awkward by nature, or had he simply come to the end of his tether? We do not know; at any rate, Blumhardt was placed there as his unwanted assistant, with the understanding that Blumhardt was to do the parish work as he saw fit. The rector was a rather weak man. Supposedly orthodox, he was at the same time highly conservative and greatly concerned about his dignity. Because of his various idiosyncrasies, his superiors as well as his parishioners had formed a much more unfavorable opinion of him than he actually deserved. Thus he had become increasingly isolated and closed off from the rest of the world. Blumhardt felt very pleased when in the course of the summer he succeeded in getting his chief to come to a general visitation attended by the prelate (superintendent general) at Knittlingen. There sat the man who had become something of a legend among his colleagues. He was short and slight of build, with silvery locks and attired in knee breeches and silk stockings, with big silver buckles on his shoes. He wore a short, collarless frock coat buttoned from top to bottom, and all his clothes were of very coarse cloth. There he sat among his astounded fellow ministers, an object partly of awe, partly of pity, and a living, conciliatory commentary on many unpleasant misunderstandings that had arisen both through him and about him.

So, for various reasons, the parish was in a state of neglect. There was no communication between rectory and parish, nor did either side desire it in the least. There was discord among the parishioners, and the young people were running wild.

There were eight in the rector's family, all grown up. What made Blumhardt's position with respect to them particularly difficult was that they were bound to look on him as a kind of punishment. The mood awaiting him in the rectory was a very unfavorable one indeed, but something happened right at the start to break up this unhappy countercurrent. When Blumhardt arrived early in April 1837 and made his way to the rectory, the big watchdog gave full vent to his anger at this intruder, leaving Blumhardt, who was in any case scared of dogs, trembling with fear and at a loss how to reach his destination. The sight softened the heart of the rector's wife, who had been watching from the window, and moved her to pity. She came out and led him in, thus opening the door to a cordial understanding, which was to prove lasting.

In his life story Blumhardt refers briefly but with warmth to his time at Iptingen: "I cannot find words to express my feelings about the tender bond linking me to this beloved congregation." One senses immediately the difference in tone when Blumhardt speaks of his labors in Iptingen and Dürrmenz, respectively. What the name Iptingen reminds him of is not just the "sweet rewards of the minister's calling" in general, but beyond that, bonds from heart to heart of a most tender and inner kind. In Dürrmenz he had been just a beginner; besides, he had not been the pastor but only his assistant and house guest, so to speak, and this had laid on him a deeply felt obligation not to let his own personality come too much to the fore. To Iptingen, on the other hand, though again the house guest of a family, he came not as a mere helper, but as one entrusted with the pastoral responsibility itself. He had also acquired a knowledge of human nature and a store of Christian experience and understanding of the Gospel such as is rarely given to a young minister.

Unfortunately, the distinguished pen that told us about the time in Dürrmenz is silent about Blumhardt's work in Iptingen. On the other hand, we do have something like diary entries by Blumhardt himself, in letters written to his fiancée. These accounts of house calls do not, as in Dürrmenz, leave us standing outside the door, so to speak, waiting for Blumhardt to come out again, but allow us to enter with him and at times let us look deep into his heart. Here is a first glimpse of this new stage in his life. In the winter of 1837, still in Basel, he wrote to his fiancée:

> In my busy life I keep coming across all kinds of things that strike discordant notes in my soul, confuse my thoughts, and by and by bring my whole being to the boiling point. This really plagues me at times, for the old Adam so loves to stoke up the fire. The day before yesterday, for instance, I went through such a time of agitation, until finally I got fed up and opened my little Bible. My eyes fell on Psalm 131, where it says in the second verse: "I have stilled and quieted my soul. Like a weaned child is my soul, like a weaned child at its mother's breast." There I had my answer, and it put me to shame. I felt how far my thoughts had carried me away and how badly I had cut myself off from fellowship with the Lord because I had not quieted my soul. O beloved Doris, when once we are completely together, it will be easier for us to quiet one another, and that will save us from so many things. As we talk over matters that trouble us, we become calmer, more sober and surrendered and can also encourage each other to put on the gentleness of Christ. This I want to learn, and you must help me to do it. It was

by his gentleness that our Savior drew people to himself; in fact, he pointedly referred to this quality. It will also be a pastor's main tool when he has to deal with sinners. I mean, of course, not merely the *outer* gentleness but the hidden, inner tenderness in feeling and thought that would never fly into a rage.

At the same time he wrote from Basel to a friend: "Just lately a dream, forgotten by now, mightily impressed on me the need for a special cleansing from sin before entering on a new field of service. I felt reminded of Isaiah chapter 6 as well as of Spleiss's sermon on the Levitical purification from sin."

That inward gentleness proved to be his key to the Iptingers' hearts, especially the separatists. From early on, and more and more strongly and consciously as time went on, he felt a deep respect for every person, especially for those who for any reason were looked down upon. He had a gift for discovering the good kernel in a person and bringing it to the fore, and in that way he lifted up, strengthened, and ennobled many a one who had lost all self-respect. He was also anxious not to exert an oppressive effect on the other person, as though he were "more" or "better" than the other. He expresses that in a letter written later, in which he gives the following advice to a young *Vikar* (curate):

When visiting the sick, you must be really outgoing—ask about the family situation, listen to what they tell you, and talk about their work problems. Don't give yourself spiritual airs! And, please, no "official" face! Even if the spiritual does at times have to take second place—you know quite well how little I care for small talk—you will still leave a blessing behind. Above all, one should meet no one with a face that says: I know all about you—from dubious sources. It's better to be specially nice to those of whom bad things are told. Don't forget this!

Blumhardt probably had in mind to write ". . . you and your dubious deeds," that is, "all kinds of bad things told about you," but could not bring himself to say that, for in general one does not actually know but merely suspects such things, or hears them as made up and spread by dubious persons.

That was Blumhardt's attitude also toward the pietists or "separatists." When meeting them, he professed to know nothing of their attitude to the established church; he freely let the good in them impress his heart and before long came to feel a warm respect for a number of them. When he presently began to visit people in their homes, as he had done in Dürrmenz, the separatists were not left out, so they became fond of him even before giving up their separatism. One or two would turn up at a wedding or burial to listen to his sermon and were so struck that they told others. The following Sunday the separatists could be seen standing at a cautious distance from the open church doors, listening to the sermon. Each week they would come a little closer, until one Sunday Blumhardt spied them sitting in serried ranks on the front benches of the gallery, right opposite him. The sight of their earnest, attentive faces was an unutterable comfort to his heart.

As early as on May 12, 1837, he has this to say about the first timid approaches on the part of these folk:

> Iptingen has already become very dear to my heart, for I feel met by a very warm affection coming from the people, though they try not to show it. Just entering the pulpit and seeing the packed church brings tears to my eyes. In no congregation have I met with such hunger. But enough of this. Pray with me that it may come to a real breakthrough.
>
> Just one more point with respect to the separatists. Some of them have not been inside a church for thirty years and are regarded as very peculiar people. Now just the other day for the first time a pietist called on me and urged me to visit him. I promised to come the following day at one o'clock. I had hardly arrived when four of the leading separatists quietly crept into the room. "Thank God," I thought, "now I have got them!" What did I find? Lovable, upright people. I sat among them without any bickering or biting until half past four, and we got along like brothers. They were quite agreeable even as regards some of the main points, and if I stayed here, I should soon have them in my church—they said so themselves. What is holding them back at the moment is just a certain shyness, although in fact two of their women have already come to church. We shall see how things develop. I could tell more things about various others. But here again I want to be still in the Lord. I constantly beseech him to draw near to seeking souls and to strengthen me, lest through my fault somebody might have to go without something he needs and ought to receive through me.

Blumhardt's letters, used chronologically, allow us to see how it was among the *young* people of Iptingen that light first breaks through the gloom enveloping his beginning time there. On April 12, 1837, he writes to his fiancée:

For the time being, things with my work here are not yet as I would wish them to be. I am still shut in and cannot get out as I would like to. The rectory is so closed off from the congregation that I have not yet got to know one single person, even though there are many Christians here; no one invites me. I am most unhappy about this isolation, but I must not take things into my own hands and rush to break out of it. Today I took a solitary walk through the whole village, and only one old man stopped for a few moments to talk to me. As I have to consider the rector, I cannot yet break down these barriers. Here, too, I have to wait.

I work mainly with the children, and they really do need help! Chattering in school has so much become second nature to them, that when I first came in, they did not quiet down the least bit. In my first confirmation class I could not make myself heard at all; they constantly chattered and fidgeted about; they plucked at each other's clothes; those behind put their hands over the eyes of the ones in front; they fooled around with their eyes and hands and giggled so much about me that I had to look at myself to see whether something about me was making them laugh. That's how it was in the beginning. However, without being specially severe I have by now managed to have peace in my confirmation class. They are still liable to fall back into the old habits, but at the slightest sign from me they get quiet. They are really wide awake and answer questions intelligently, so that I can discuss everything to my entire satisfaction.

How gloomy the situation still was in other respects and how Blumhardt tried to find a way through shows in a letter of May 12, 1837, where he writes:

My loneliness becomes very oppressive at times, and I feel I have to watch out that no harm comes to me. Some verses of Psalm 39 were a great comfort to me the other day and gave me an important pointer: "I will be silent and not open my mouth; You will do it and do it well" (Ps 39:9). And today I read in Psalm 42: "Why are you cast down, O my soul? Why so disturbed within me?" (Ps 42:5) To be still is my task, and that also means being still in my plans and thoughts. You, dear heart, tell me of little plans you are hatching now and then; I, on the other hand, neither can nor may make plans. At times I feel I am being disciplined for doing so.

I do find myself in a peculiar situation. The Lord wants to prepare me fully for my service of conciliation. I have already been made aware how easily I could slip from this high calling to a mere search for job security. If things had just continued on an even keel, I am afraid something unclean, something mercenary would have crept in. From this the Lord in his mercy wants to protect me. Ought I not to thank him for this protection? Yes, dear Doris, join me in giving thanks to his holy name, for it is he whom I and you want to serve and to whom we want to belong. Already he lets me experience that I can contribute something to his glory. May this truly be so in the time to come, also when we can work together as a married couple! Just imagine: Some day up there on high, some who are now poor human beings, bent nearly double under their earthly burdens, might come to us and praise the Lord because of our service to them! And if it were but one single soul—should we not dare to sacrifice everything for the sake of that one? But enough of this! "We shall yet praise him for being our help and our God" (Ps 42:5).

In the following letters we see the light breaking through. Thus on May 23, 1837, he writes:

During my sermon I felt inwardly stirred; I somehow sensed I was reaching the people. In the afternoon meeting I catechized on the words "our Father in heaven" and again felt deeply moved. That was all of my Sunday's work. Standing by my window, I sighed, "If only I could really get into the hearts of my parishioners!" Then it came to me, "Just saunter through the village as though out for a walk, and maybe someone will call you in." No sooner thought than done. Slowly I strolled down the main street. Everything was quiet, but here and there a window did open, and I received a friendly greeting. A few times I stopped to chat a little, and I had the impression that people would have liked to call me in but did not quite have the courage. So I walked on almost to the end of the street. Suddenly a woman came running after me: Would I come and visit a sick relative who had a great longing to see me. I felt like replying, "I am just on my way there." Led into another street by the woman, I entered the room. It was such a joy; the sick woman was inwardly awake and told me of her long, painful illness and how the Lord had strengthened her. Once it had seemed to her that a man in white had come and reminded her of Psalm 80 and Romans, chapter 9. Although it was midnight, she at once had her boy get up and read to her those chapters, and it gave her new strength. Then some more women came in, and we had a wonderful time together. One old woman told of her sick husband, who had been a wine-bibber but was now earnestly repenting and preparing himself for death. She said he was living next door. I got the hint and went there. As I entered, the gaunt old man, who had never set eyes on me until then, called out, "There comes the *Herr Vikar*! Has God led you here?" He told me right away he was the worst of sinners and then related a dream in which a man had asked him to look up songs No. 131 and 135 in the old Württemberg hymnbook. Both these songs were completely unknown to him; they were, "Jesus, who my soul hast rescued" and "Jesus, leave me not behind." After a while a woman came in, his daughter-in-law; she talked with me quite a bit and, going out with me afterwards, asked me with tears in her eyes to have a word with her husband too, as he was carrying on with his father's former vice. To end with, I was invited into a neighboring house, where separatists lived, and I really had a good time there. That was truly a blessed day for me.

As I left the school this morning, a man invited me to his home. There I found a number of people gathered. One very old woman told of her mother, how poor she had been and how once on Christmas Eve, when all parents would prepare something special for their children, her own children found her kneeling and in tears on the kitchen floor. Frightened, they cried, "Mother, what is wrong?" "O children, tomorrow will be Christmas Day, and I cannot give you anything at all. I don't even have any bread at home; what shall I give you to eat?" "O Mother", cried the children, "don't cry! We don't need anything to eat; we will just stay in bed a bit longer; then we won't feel hungry." On entering the shed the following morning they found lying in a hay basket an uncommonly large loaf of bread. They never found out who put it there.

One more thing: One of the women in that house told how on leaving the church the day before she had said to the mayor's daughter, "Oh, if only we could keep the curate here for a longer time!" The other, however, had replied that she knew from a reliable source that I was actually applying for the next available position. Then this woman had said, "Let's all get together and pray that he will stay with us longer." So I said with a smile, "You do indeed wish me well!"

This evening I was again called to two sickbeds. You see, my dear bride, things are beginning to move. I feel greatly refreshed too and very happy in my calling. The eagerness in people is really beyond description. May the Lord give me strength, wisdom, and love to do everything well.

On May 31, 1837 he writes:

Oh, the bliss of holding out a helping hand to poor, languishing souls! When you get right in there among them, you come to understand why our Savior felt pity for the people crowding in on him. I have the same feeling when I enter the pulpit and find the whole church packed. Last Sunday, as far as I know, people had come from six neighboring villages, some of them in whole groups. Wherever I enter a house, a number of persons presently gather. In short, people are tremendously eager, and it does one's heart good to see them so receptive. Let us hope that some day you, too, will share in this deep joy, though, of course, it is not like that everywhere . . .

I am taking to heart our dear father's admonition to go about it wisely and cautiously. This is also what God's own hand constantly points me to. I am convinced that wherever I would have acted more independently, I would have gone wrong. Then I would simply have been barging in! But now I have learned how very necessary it is for people to seek me out and come to me drawn by an irresistible urge, while to begin with I just let my voice be heard loud and clear in the church, as the Lord gives it. Many people were not used to my ways, and it took them a while to adjust. If I had rushed at them, it would have left them bewildered. But now doors are opening; I have already visited twenty-one houses. However, now that the weather has turned nice, the rector, who has no inkling of all this (although I do not intentionally withhold anything from him), likes to go on walks with me. I lose a good deal of time that way, but I am discovering that it is also good for me not to overindulge the people, but rather to keep them some-what hungry. So everything has a lesson to teach me. I am holding no special meetings and have told those that keep pushing for them that hearing me twice on Sundays (at the main service and at Sunday school) has to be enough, that I find it hard to speak a third time, and that they really ought to let what they have heard sink in. Mere listening, I tell them, is not enough. Nor is it good for them to cling too much to the preacher.

From now on a concern shared by both bridegroom and bride keeps surfacing in their letters—the longing for a home of their own, meaning a parsonage. This concerned Blumhardt especially on account of his fiancée. At that time in Württemberg pastors were appointed by the king, who would make his choice from a panel of three candidates whom the consistory had selected from the applications received, giving special consideration to seniority in service. Blumhardt applied many times and, as we shall see, ended up applying for any position that was open—for a long time with no success. Doing his best to lessen the tension for his fiancée, who with this problem in mind naturally looked forward to his letters with special keenness, he made the following arrangement with her: "When by God's gracious will I am appointed, I am going to write 'Dorothea' on the envelope. As long as you read 'Doris' there, no decision has been made." Right into the early summer of 1838 we find letters beginning with, "Still 'Doris'!" In a letter of May 19, 1837, when telling her what had happened to yet another application, he concludes by saying, "Things are moving so lamely and sluggishly that it often gives me great pain; I almost feel like crying." But he continues:

> And yet I see God's finger in everything; just gazing out over my Iptingen lays all my tempestuous thoughts to rest. As the people themselves declare, something quite essential has already taken place in that the former discord has almost disappeared and the young people seem to be completely different. How this came about I cannot grasp myself, and yet it was through my feeble words that it had to happen. I had to be there; that was the Lord's will. Nor do I have the impression that my work here is finished. In short, my dear, faithful heart, here we go again—sorrow mingling with the joy! I may not write much about this, as you will surely understand; I have to hold my own feelings in check lest they break loose and disturb my work, which has first claim on my spiritual powers. Added to this are other cares that come pressing in on me. In any other place I would be better off economically than here, for how much can I possibly hope to get from my poor rector! The longer I remain here, the more this worries me, considering that it has been my custom so far to support my dear mother as well. This is another point I must not allow to get out of proportion. For the sake of the Lord I have to stay here and must not accept a position elsewhere, such as deputizing for another pastor.

The application problem, which meets us at the beginning of this letter, also earned him a wholesome lesson from his friend Barth, with whom we shall get well acquainted later on. In a letter of July 10, 1837, Blumhardt tells of yet another frustrated hope and continues as follows:

> Right afterwards, alongside some other and better posts, the parsonage at Kocherstetten was listed as vacant; so I wrote to my dear mother that though several posts had again become available, "I must not nor do I *want* to apply for these." I presently felt the word "want" lying like a heavy burden on my conscience; the letter had gone off, and I could find no rest. Later that same day, when I met W., of whom I have already told, it became more and more clear to me what a bad comrade I am—so little inclined or able to dare something in faith. I went to Barth, intending to wait and see what he would say. The first thing he said was, "Now listen, you simply

have to apply for every place that's going. You have made a start now and you must go on. By what right do you assume you are not needed there in the Hohenlohe area? They have a missionary society there that badly needs someone to put it on a sounder footing," and so on. That was the answer I needed; I felt ashamed and decided to apply. However, I still had to struggle hard for a whole day before I was completely broken and ready to let God lead me. No sooner had the letters gone off than an unutterable feeling of wellbeing came over me. Now I am so glad to be rid of the torment of making my own, always selfish, choice. From now on I am going to apply for every beginner's post as well, for I no longer want to stand in God's way, if he desires to have me at a certain place. Here I am; may God lead me just where he wants! Praise be to him—there is nothing more for *me* to do now; he, he alone, must do everything. That is the best counsel I can have; it lets me await joyfully whatever may come.

Meanwhile, the risk of his being posted to Kocherstetten unexpectedly increased. The congregation there was in a terrible state of neglect, and the consistory, which had long been wanting to send a capable minister into the Hohenlohe district, a spiritual wasteland, warmly recommended Blumhardt to the king, on the basis of the excellent testimonial he had received from his dean, regarding his accomplishments during his short stay at Iptingen. In the end, however, this anxious hope likewise came to nothing.

In a letter of July 31, 1837, he comforts his fiancée as follows:

O dear Doris, though all this is indeed something one has to learn, I do feel that I have already learned a good deal. Oh, that we might become wholly the Lord's own and some day, free from our own will, be completely given in to his. Alas, how poor and brief is a person's life! What is there to it if the eternal God does not use it to carry out his work! What are all our earthly desires and their fulfillments unless they contain what is highest of all! This thought often goes through my mind, also with respect to my future service in helping souls find the way to heaven. If we constantly have this purpose before our eyes, what a remarkable form our life is bound to take! How often we shall have to act as if we were mad (as the world is so apt to think)! How many peculiar renunciations and labors and ideas will then present themselves! And if a minister through his own guilt, whether he realizes it or not, fails to help souls into heaven, what good is then all the earthly and domestic happiness he would like to enjoy? So I say again: Oh, let us belong wholly to the Lord!

The following letter, of August 16, 1837, takes us back to the Iptingen congregation. Blumhardt writes:

Whenever I feel restless in my heart, I only have to walk through the village to regain my inner peace. Little schoolchildren come running from all sides, all wanting to shake my hand. Peeping out through windows and doors, the older folk enjoy watching them. Presently, some wagons laden with sheaves come rolling in, escorted front and back by weary reapers, who greet me with looks of radiant serenity. I must not go on, but let me tell you that in secret I have shed many a tear at the sight of these folk, who have to work so exceedingly hard, who often also have to bear this or that cross in their family lives and seem so eager to press into the kingdom of heaven. Three days ago I heard a woman who has eight children call after me. She had but recently recovered from a severe illness, but I had not visited her because I am reluctant to enter a strange house without being invited or encouraged. I stopped, and she told me loudly and urgently that she would gladly be like the Canaanite woman; could I not please visit her, too—she had such a longing to see me. O dear Doris, all unnoticed there is many a deeply seeking soul here. And now imagine the pastor's task! You will call it a blessed task, and so it is. But I can tell you that all the above has an extremely painful side too when one considers that many of the poor souls one's heart feels drawn to can so easily be again ensnared by sin, and what heavy burdens life puts upon them.

About six days ago we had a most terrifying thunderstorm here accompanied by a violent downpour lasting three hours, from eight to eleven o'clock in the evening. Down the little stream past the rectory rushed a torrent that devastated the whole street and threatened to sweep away all the houses. All the people were shut up in their houses, and nobody could do anything to help. And then the fear of totally losing the nearly ripe crops! I became aware of a burden on me such as I had never felt before. Still, we got off without too much harm. The next morning, though, everybody—men, women, and children—had to get busy and repair the road. The good folk had been in the midst of harvesting, but in spite of a threatening second thunderstorm they had to leave the crops in the field. O dear Doris, we have no idea of the inner surrender this requires. And yet, as I walked among the toiling people—how glad they were to be still alive and that it had not been worse, while the fear they had been in was still plainly visible on their faces. (In the surrounding countryside several houses had burned down.)

Such, dear Doris, are the peculiar cares laid on a minister's heart, especially when he ponders that in spite of all such earthly need many a one will not find his way to God's kingdom. And the dear children! You can't imagine how sad I often feel when I look at them. At times I have the feeling that my touch is meant to be a blessing. It is a thought that came to me just recently through an eight-year-old child who is very slow at learning. While the mother was telling me about it, I comforted and caressed the dear child. When I returned to that house a few days later, the mother told me happily that on the evening after my first visit the child, while trying to memorize a lesson by heart, had said, "Mother, I think since the *Herr Vikar* stroked my hair, it's easier for me to learn." Those words were important to me; oh, that I might always be so endowed with the Spirit that some of it could stream out according to the promise! When I look at my heart, however—oh, how very low I have to bow!

At times Blumhardt had to listen to his dear Iptingen folk express their concern that marriage might make him lose some of his zeal. His letter of August 25, 1837, furnishes an example of this. On a certain Sunday he was to preach in a neighboring congregation (at S.) and so was to leave Iptingen in charge of his rector on that occasion. At first he was unwilling, since those neighbors were in any case regular listeners of his at Iptingen, but F., the leading separatist, a good, sincere man who loved him greatly, gave him no peace. Every time he met Blumhardt, he called out, "Don't forget S.!" So he complied and noticed that F. was among the listeners. As the two went home together, F. started by saying that he must tell Blumhardt something he had long had on his heart. "You are now a good pastor; everything is fine with you, but before long the curate will become a rector. He will take a wife and start a household of his own—and what will happen then?" This was followed by a lengthy expression of concern that in one way or another a wife can so easily put her husband on a wrong track. "Thank God," F. concluded, "now I have said it. It left me no peace; I just had to come out with it." His concern escalated into outright anxiety on hearing the curate confess that he was already engaged to be married, but Blumhardt managed to calm him down by describing his engagement and his fiancée. Nonetheless he wrote to Doris:

My dear one, betrothed to me in the Lord, we must not completely ignore concerns like this one, for since our hearts are truly corrupt, one partner may indeed inflict on the other a harm that, quite unnoticed, might gradually spread like a cancer. So in this respect, too, let us rejoice with fear and trembling (Ps. 2:11). What I fear most is gradually settling into a rut, which virtually means a withdrawal of the Spirit from on high.

Otherwise I have in Iptingen learned a little of how the minister is meant to shine before his congregation. One thing in particular has earned me—although quite undeservedly—the greatest respect and been my surest way of gaining entrance into people's hearts. It is something God has let me see, and under his guidance the people, too, make me aware of the powerful effect it has when it is truly there. It should also make me strive with all the powers of my soul to become a true servant of God. What I mean is this: The impression people have of me is that I am content, no matter what I meet with, that I give myself to any task humbly, unselfishly, and self-sacrificially, that I can reconcile myself to everything and accept it without a murmur, and so forth. (They are quite aware how far removed my present position is from my former one.) Once they have formed such an opinion of me, people do not doubt that I mean what I say, and for this reason they are most receptive to everything in my sermons, even the sharpest words. Yesterday I visited an old man, very shrewd and influential, who seems to be shaken to the core. He said, "By rights one ought not to be fond of you, for you speak to us altogether too sharply, but you are right." Here I remember something I experienced on December 24 of last year in Basel [here follows the story of his annoyance at the young coachman]. These are but trifles, but how important they are for a pastor! And how little do people mostly understand what it means to let one's light shine!

On October 18, 1837, he replied as follows to his fiancée's request that he visit her:

I had the same wish and had already made plans for the journey. It did not leave me at ease, however, and I sensed only too clearly that the Lord had not yet opened the way. At times I seemed to hear an unmistakable voice, "Don't do it!" When you wrote to me, I took up the idea anew, for your sake, because I so wanted to spare you every struggle and let everything good come to you. But before long the feeling returned that it was clearly not the Lord's will. At present there is still another reason that makes it hard for me to give up my Sundays. People come in droves from other villages. My heart melts when I catch sight of them hurrying along, puffing and panting because they are often late. How sorry I would be if one day I failed to be there and the dear people were to come for nothing! Altogether, the way God keeps me here as if I were constantly about to take off and leave is to me a sign that I must not abandon my post. By their own admission, people come running the way they do because they want to make the most of it while I am still here. Quite a few times and particularly last Sunday, the rumor has gone around—from where I do not know (from a neighboring village this time)—that this would be my farewell service. So I am tied down here; I can't leave, and the words I recently preached on are reechoing in my heart: "Endure hardship as a good soldier of Jesus Christ" (2 Tim 2:3). You, too, will surely understand the situation and patiently accept everything from the Lord's hand. So let us hold out; what appears distant to us now may in the end come quickly. Let us bravely stand the test, then we shall rejoice all the more when it's over.

Then he tells of some literary work, for the most part papers on the history of Christian mission—partly independent studies, partly pieces he translated for the *Calwer Missionsblatt* (Calw Mission Journal) from the *New York Observer*, the *Boston Mission Herald*, and other papers. He continues: "I always need work of this kind, as a sideline. But I am training myself in good time to not let my actual pastoral work suffer from it—a dangerous rock that many a dear brother has not managed to steer clear of." Now comes the following description of his work as a minister:

Up to now I do literary work for only about three hours every morning. In the afternoon I make visits as I see fit, and in one house especially I enjoy the happiest and most blissful hours. I know but few houses where I could speak from the inmost depths of Christian knowledge so openly as here, yet they are just elderly peasant folk. Yesterday I heard something from them that called forth painful feelings in my heart. They told me that recently a nearby minister, about fifty of whose parishioners come to my services every Sunday, had complained in tears from the pulpit about his people forsaking him in favor of a strange preacher. You can imagine that this upsets me terribly, for I can easily put myself into that man's situation. But what can I do? I just let people come as they like; may they come, and may the Lord grant that it lead them to life. Inviting outside folk to come is something I shall never do, and quite generally I take great care that no one can accuse me of looking for followers. This reserved attitude I owe to the Lord himself, for he wants me to serve him and not my own self. I intend to pay the good pastor a visit in the near future. But don't be afraid, dear heart; here in Württemberg things simply are done differently from where you are, in Baden. Over there one lets people go where they want and even rejoices at their eagerness.

My Iptingen folk actually take it very well; far from pulling a long face over the many visitors, they not only look after them in church but even take them home for the noon meal, so that they can attend Sunday school as well.

I had to tell you this in greater detail because you, too, have done something for the folk at Iptingen by being so concerned that I remain here! If only you could be here and see it all for yourself! O my beloved Doris, often I just brim over with joy as I look at the gracious blessing bestowed on me here; how could I find it easy to depart! We'll keep it like that, and I promise you herewith not to leave for another temporary post without advising you first. I know this is what you want too. Of course, it could also happen that before I know it the Lord may fetch me away.

This is followed by the outline of a sermon on John 11:32–45 (the raising of Lazarus from the dead): "How Jesus 1) felt humankind's woe and 2) healed it." Blumhardt tells something about the first part of the sermon, based on the words, "He groaned in the spirit."

The first reason he groaned was that he pitied humanity's state of separation from God (after Mary's impatient words, "Lord, if you had been here, my brother would not have died.") Second, he groaned at the bitterness in people's lives that makes them weep so bitterly (v. 33). Third, he groaned about our corruptness and malice (v. 37), and fourth, about death, to which humankind, the image of God, has fallen prey through sin. [Blumhardt goes on to comment:] So deeply must the Savior have *felt* all this that the word "Behold, the Lamb of God, who takes away the sin of the world!" is being fulfilled right here. All this is still cause enough for us to grieve too, even though we can rejoice in our hope of redemption. There is enough left to temper this joy, and in addition there is plenty that will be laid on *our* shoulders in particular. Yes, beloved Doris, let us be very much aware of this and weep with those that weep! May the Lord sanctify our laughing and our weeping!

On November 1, 1837, there follows an account of a seventy-four year old man, who had acted most ridiculously by lying and thieving. Blumhardt also tells of various house visits and of having to give counsel regarding a person driven to insanity by excessive piety. He relates that he has again been approached about holding a regular meeting during the winter and that it should be given consideration; that he has to think of how to set about the customary evening gatherings by candlelight and of how to provide pleasant and useful entertainment on winter evenings for the

young single men—questions he would like to consider with his fiancée
and, where necessary, place before the Lord in her presence. Evidently
he did not find the rectory, still occupied by the old rector and his family,
a particularly congenial place.

> You ought to see me sitting in the living room here, pipe in mouth,
> elbows on the sofa, quiet as a mouse amid a milling crowd of eight
> big adults. If someone came along then and asked, "Now what's he
> thinking about?"—what would your guess be? You can't imagine
> how lost and forlorn I often look in that situation. Still, I don't find
> it all that trying; I am still happy, knowing that at the right time
> the Lord will change everything.

On November 6 he tells Doris about things he learned in his talks
with the people.

> I like to listen to the "wisdom of the people," so highly esteemed
> by devout Oetinger. Here is a sample. Yesterday I visited an old
> couple; they are separatists, but I can have a most lively contact
> with them. The man's countenance still bears traces of his former
> alcoholism, and we do talk a lot about that. The wife's unassum-
> ing exterior hides an exceptional intelligence. Like others, she
> expressed a concern how marriage might affect me if, as can easily
> happen, the wife pulls in the opposite direction. It nearly made
> me laugh—the way just about everybody brings that up. I only
> said that when I have left, I will give them a detailed account of
> how things are going. But then she went on to tell how it had gone
> with her and how she now had to thank God for giving her this
> husband, so unlike her in his attitude. It was just what she needed.
> "If my husband had played the same pious tune as I did, we would
> have become the world's most self-righteous people."
>
> It was strange talk, yet there is something to be learned from
> the wisdom of the common people. We two are of one and the
> same mind or, to use the woman's phrase, play the same tune.
> What do we have to guard against? Answer: Against presuming
> on it, priding ourselves on our piety, looking down on everybody
> else after the fashion of that false pietism we know so well, and
> thinking that we are the ones. Otherwise, things will go wrong.
> Thus the "wisdom of the people" has now taught us a very impor-
> tant lesson. Oh, how well the Lord guides his children!
>
> The other day I experienced a wonderful triumph. For a long
> time I had been visiting an old separatist woman and her husband,
> whose company I have come to appreciate more and more. She
> also gives evidence of deep understanding in Christ. For a long

time she did not attend my services, though she was very happy that others came. But for some weeks she has been coming, and just imagine, she has now asked to partake of the Lord's Supper next Sunday—for the first time in ages! She told me she had been hungry long enough; now she wanted to eat! I have borrowed a book from these people, which I am reading with great enjoyment and must try very hard to get hold of. It is Johann Porst's *Wachstum der Wiedergebornen* (*The Inward Growth of the Reborn*, Halle 1734) and tells how the reborn advance from one stage to the next, how from being children they become young men and fathers and are finally perfected toward blessed eternity. I have seldom been in a house with such a wealth of Christian experience.

On November 20, 1837, he has to tell his fiancée of a painful case where his pastoral care was unsuccessful. He writes:

Today I had to preach a funeral sermon for a woman who had long been ill and whom I had visited practically every day all the time I have been here. She lived in the outermost house of the village. I experienced strange things there. This good woman apparently withheld various things from me. In general she was respected, but I did hear quite a lot about her that wasn't so good. Everyone felt that she must not die without owning up to certain things. For a long time I had found her very receptive and responsive to what I had to say. A fortnight ago now, her sister-in-law told her, and afterward in her presence told me, of a murmur among the villagers to the effect that in spite of my many visits to her the sick woman could find no assurance of grace. It depressed her greatly to hear that, and I had to calm her down. From that moment I sensed a strange coldness in her, not toward me, but toward everything spiritual. It seemed to me that nothing I said found an echo in her. All who visited her came away with the same impression, namely that one could not speak with her about any inner matters.

I myself found the contact more and more difficult, and last Friday I, too, could hardly get a word out of her. I took leave sadly, and Saturday morning in bed I pondered over and over how to make a last serious attempt to reach her. I decided to tell her that I would stop coming, since nothing seemed to come of it. Otherwise the woman was actually very fond of me and had greatly appreciated my visits. Now just when I tried to speak to her in that sense, the end came. I almost felt as though I had labored in vain for half a year. Although I did have many a wonderful hour with her, toward the end all that seemed to have gone with the wind. Yet she remained fully alert for other things. I find it absolutely beyond explanation that to her last breath there came from her not a single prayer, Bible passage, or even just a sigh.

That is why today I found it especially hard to show up at the funeral meal, which I had been urged to attend. I had based my sermon on a text that I said the deceased had been very fond of *some time ago*. Psalm 130:1–4. It tells that by leading us down into the depth, God teaches us to 1) cry out to him, 2) recognize our own sins, 3) seek forgiveness, and 4) fear him. About the woman's life I could only say that *some time ago* she had shown signs of inner renewal for the kingdom of God. And that was all. O dear heart, there is something mysterious about the way we find redemption through coming to know Christ!

Otherwise I now have many friends here. As the people are all at home now, I can respond to the many requests for visits. I have a lot of wonderful experiences. Of course, only with a few is there a real *breakthrough*—with some for sure, and there is hope for others. It is clear enough to me that it is not we preachers that convert men; the Lord has to do it all.

What he writes to his fiancée on December 1, to comfort her for the long time of waiting, gives us a glimpse of the fruitfulness of his labors. He writes:

Let us stop grieving about our time of waiting and rather present it to the Lord as a joyful thank offering for the sake of my congregation here. I have already told you a lot about them, but indeed, I myself would hardly be able to form a true picture if someone else in my situation were to write me about it—that is, how important is my continued presence at Iptingen. I neither may nor can write more about this, since one is inadvertently liable to push one's self into the foreground. But you will believe me, dear heart, that I do not mean it like that. At any rate, not a day goes by that I am not appealed to by most touching demonstrations of love: "Do not leave this place yet!"

I cannot help looking at the rectory, the separatists, the many newly awakened persons, the congregation as a whole, even the atheists (there are still a few, though they hold their peace now). I also think of the children, who are given nothing at all in school and are so delighted when they see me come in, and in particular of the new confirmands. Oh, and there are still so many other concerns, especially the young people, for whom I am going to provide evening entertainment. When I look at all that, my heart is so full that it makes me forget everything, even—forgive me!—you. There is so much that still has to be set on a firm foundation before I may leave this place.

To make it easier for you, I want to tell you just one thing I experienced today. I again visited Hannes Kiefer, whose wife, formerly a separatist, has now changed altogether. Today she opened her heart to me. About twenty years ago she dreamt that she had lost a splendid golden ring (she actually never possessed one), and in the dream she felt such pressure and anxiety in her heart that she could scarcely breathe. She woke up terrified. She said the same dream had recently come back to her, and during all the long time between the two dreams it was as if she had been lying sick by the pool of Bethesda. She had had no peace, no relationship to God, and scarcely a trace of the wonderful time of grace that had once been given to her. She had also stumbled into some deep mud holes. All that time she did not attend church nor partake of the Lord's Supper, but she had been hungering for something, and nothing could still her hunger.

About eight weeks ago she had another dream in which a gentleman she knew very well and yet could not recognize came to her and gave her a beautiful ring with a heart of crystal on it. She had no sooner received the ring than the man was called away. She looked at the ring more closely and enjoyed its brilliance, but by and by the radiance faded. She thought, "What is this? The friendly gentleman cannot possibly have given me fake gold!" She examined the markings and found that it was genuine gold, but then she woke up. She kept thinking of the dream and could not put it out of her mind. It was during this time she began again to partake of the Lord's Supper. What she experienced then, she said, she could not possibly describe; the whole of heaven had once more opened before her; the blessed former time of grace had returned to her and stayed with her ever since. Suddenly she felt reminded of the dream, and at that moment it came to her that I was the man in the dream whom she had been unable to identify even though she knew him well. That, she concluded, was why she loved me so: Through God's grace I had returned to her the ring of gold, and even though my going away from Iptingen would cause its radiance to fade, it would still be hers and would remain a ring of genuine gold. I felt very touched by this account and in the end just said she ought not to forget that she had not recognized me in her dream; there was no need for her to know me—indeed, she had better forget me, for I was but a tool in the hand of God. But what do you have to say to all this, beloved Doris?

Yesterday it also became clear to me that the Lord has quite likely awakened for me a man who might later be able to take charge of a new meeting. In short: our waiting time shall be a joyful sacrifice and a sweet savor before the Lord.

In a letter of January 4, 1838, the mood is even more triumphant. We learn of a proposed journey to Basel and Sitzenkirch, including a visit to his fiancée there. Blumhardt writes:

> I know that what motivated me was not the urge to see my dear bride once again but solely the desire to gather new strength in the Lord together with you and all our loved ones, since it remains uncertain just when the Lord will unite us forever. As a matter of fact, I am reluctant to leave my present congregation. I have experienced indescribable times of grace these last days; I and the whole congregation seem to be one big family now. My sermons and meetings have left deep impressions. O my precious one, it often makes me shake all over when I consider what the Lord has accomplished in so many hearts here. I have now made arrangements for social evenings four times a week, and these, though meant in the first place for the young, are now attended by people of all ages and are listened to with rapt attention. All this will help you to understand why I have called these winter days precious ones. Only after I decided to make the journey did things open up like this, and since then I have been swept ever more deeply into the very heart of the congregation. But now I do need a rest. A little pause after such a headlong rush may in many respects also prove to be a good thing for the congregation; in any case, they will miss me only on those social evenings and on one Sunday.
>
> In general, everything has gone so much according to my liking that I can now set out on my journey in a mood of rejoicing. It is, of course, a great joy for me that all of you are so inwardly quiet and contented. As for me, the Lord has brought me to a point where a speedy appointment would almost sadden me. The people here are exceedingly attached to me; wherever I go, they voice anxiety that I might leave them. So I feel at times in a big dilemma such as anybody who has not experienced it himself can scarcely imagine. But what can I say? Thank God that it is like that! Besides, the Lord's grace is not tied to persons; it must be able to manifest itself in people's souls in all sorts of ways! And joy mingled with sadness of this kind is surely a blessed joy; I would wish that it might some day be the same in our own parish.

On his return journey from Basel to Iptingen, several evening hours spent at an inn at Kehl (on January 18, 1838) became important to him as an occasion for inner gathering. He writes:

> I did not suffer at all from the cold; the overshoes kept my feet warm the whole time. I enjoyed very precious moments of inner

quiet between 6 and 8 o'clock in the evening. There was only one other gentleman there besides me, so I was able in undisturbed quiet to imagine myself among you in your prayer gatherings. I came to see much more clearly what great things the Lord has done in and for me—in general, and specially in these last days. Yet while pondering the unfathomable love and faithfulness that the Lord thinks fit to pour out on me, I could not help casting a searching glance also into my own heart, and, O my dearest, how shamefaced I stood there again in my own sight! How much hidden malice I discovered in my heart! Most of all I had to accuse myself of hardness and lovelessness. I saw before me 1 Corinthians 13: "If I speak in the tongues of men and of angels, but have not love, I am only a noisy gong or a clanging cymbal. Love is patient and kind; it does not boast nor is it rude; it is not easily angered. Love bears all things, believes all things, hopes all things, endures all things." My dear heart, you will understand me and the increasingly lively drift of my thoughts. How I would have loved to rush to you once more and pour my whole heart out to you, just as I then poured it out to the Lord! I did, however, feel lifted up into a more joyful mood by considering how wonderfully God shields us from the many-sided deceit in our own hearts. Oh, the things we would plunge into if God's protecting hand did not tangibly watch over us! These were the thoughts I pondered in my heart during that hour, and having fellowship with the Lord made me feel greatly relieved, however low I had to bow before him.

In the same letter he writes as follows to his fiancée about engagement and marriage: "O dear heart, how pleasing is the thought that with you by my side I shall not have to figure and calculate after the world's fashion. No—in everything that befalls you will always direct me to search and probe most deeply for what is pleasing to God in it."

On January 28, 1838, after expressing his longing for his fiancée, he relates how his experiences in Iptingen comfort him:

What I can do in the meantime is be very patient and surrendered—indeed, I have to be, for no tongue can adequately describe all the Lord is doing meanwhile in the congregation here through me, wretched fellow that I am. I am once more completely immersed in my work, so much so that I am sometimes made to feel a little of the burden and heat of a day in the Lord's vineyard. You have no idea how deeply I feel again moved, even to tears, by the people's eagerness. When I look at myself and my speeches, it's often beyond me to understand where all that inner ferment comes from; at times it is just where I feel most feeble that my words have the strongest effect. It is constantly being borne in upon me that I live in what amounts to a totally new sphere and world, in which I cannot quite find my way yet. Everything becomes new to me; often all I can do in the evenings is to pace to and fro in my room in mute amazement and deep thought before settling down to sleep in the arms of the invisible yet wondrously working Lord. As I said before, I cannot possibly relate to you all that is happening, yet honor and praise with me the Lord, who grants us such a blessed time of waiting!

Some things I do have to tell you; first of all, something of how the Lord presently nourishes and refreshes my own heart. A few days ago one of the most deeply grounded believers, in whose house I have established a meeting, told me how glad she was that I had such a high regard for King David and his psalms and for the prophet Isaiah and that I quoted them so often. I took this as an exhortation from above to concern myself with Isaiah more than I have done so far, if for no other reason than that I should not let people praise me for something I am not doing. So, when I came home at 9 o'clock in the evening, I started to read the second part of Isaiah, beginning with the fortieth chapter; I spent two hours on it. The following evening I took up the next chapter and reviewed the preceding one, and in this way I have now advanced to chapter forty-five. O my dear heart, what glorious nourishment I thus receive for my soul! How refreshed and encouraged and joyful I can then lie down! I can so picture it all and make it my own as if I were the very person that the Holy One in Israel is speaking to.

But now something about my congregation. You will want to know how I was welcomed back. There did not seem to be much of a stir, but as I learned afterwards, there was anxious expectation everywhere. The good folk had been constantly thinking of me and had felt sorry for me because of the cold. During the first night several did not sleep but kept praying for me. My friends from the nearby villages, too, who so often visit me in church, had not forgotten me. The whole time I was away, I had been enfolded in their intercessions. Dear heart, don't you think that these prayers had a great effect? Everything I undertook turned out so well, down to the smallest details. That particular matter, too—you know what I mean—has been so wonderfully set right through God's grace. What a strong wall are the intercessions of believers! Some day you, too, are meant to become part of this wall, so that we can dwell safely and in peace and rejoice all the more in the invisible blessing and loving-kindness of our God.

On the same day I arrived, I held one of my evening socials, but since people were unaware of it, not many came. The following day, though, the schoolroom was so packed that several persons fainted. For the joy and edification of everybody I read out Thomas's [probably a missionary whose letter had recently arrived in Basel] letter and displayed what I had brought along. Then followed Sunday with its bitter cold. As mentioned above, a heavy sadness overcame me, because I felt so abruptly torn away from you. I felt ashamed of it later, but you will understand it. Presently, however, my heart grew more cheerful. In my evening socials, school lessons, and house visits I have met with a wonderful openness. To be sure, my absence had been felt. There had been some frolicking and jaunty singing among the young people, I was told; it also seemed that my meetings might meet with opposition. This contributed to the feeling of depression I just mentioned. In the meantime things have improved. The many sick people keep me on the run and give me constant opportunities to scatter my seeds all over the village.

I again want to set down for you briefly the story of one single day. Rejoice about it with me and get a glimpse of your own future calling, for you must become a pastor; that's settled! The Lord has given you all that you on your part will need for it. Oh, what a blessed task we have together of bringing in a harvest of dear, precious souls! At midday on Saturday I was pushed on, one might say, from one house to another until I ended up having visited thirteen houses.

One of the first persons I saw was a separatist, sick but on the way to recovery, a most sincere and childlike man, who considers me his best friend, with whom he can share the secrets of his heart. Earlier, I would not have believed such a friendship with a peasant possible. This time he was so confiding and tender that, his eyes sparkling with joy, he clasped my hand and told me he loved me so much that on seeing me enter he felt like greeting me with "God bless you, dear Christoph!" For me he is one of the most interesting and important men in the village.

Next, I visited a woman named S., who is seriously ill, but a few days ago, having been set free of a spell that had long been a heavy burden on her heart, she experienced an extraordinary day of grace. When I visited her then, it was as if she were speaking in tongues; one hymn of praise after the other issued from her lips, for example, "Throughout each year and day and hour I feel God's loving grace and power." Her face was radiant, and I could only listen quietly to her psalms and songs. When I took leave, I asked her to be prepared for a more subdued mood, which might follow. And indeed, the next day I found her with tears in her eyes and an expression of deep pain on her face; she voiced great inner fear and anxiety. I tried to encourage her and in the days following found her in the customary serenity born of faith.

After her, I called on a widow, eighty-four years of age, and, speaking words of comfort, seated myself by the stove. Young and old came crowding into the room and listened eagerly to the Gospel message.

Next I went to a poor, sick man, where no less than eight children sat about in the room. The mother was in deep distress, but the little children were extremely loving to me and said the drollest things. Three of them were sitting at the table, elbows propped up and face in hands, just looking at me the whole time. That was a heartfelt joy for me.

As I moved on, a voice from a window called me to another sick person. Again the room filled with people. When I asked the sick woman whether she had made a bond with God, she seemed frightened. I gave her directions on how to go about it and left, but not without having to fill my pockets with apples, which for months had been lying ready for me.

Then I visited a sick member of my confirmation class, a boy very zealous for the good, who took to heart with quiet warmth all I said to him. A few months ago a boy of last year's confirmation class had been buried; in my sermon I had called him fortunate since the Lord had taken him before evil could have come to his soul. Following the funeral sermon, this present boy had sat down at the table deep in thought. When his mother asked him what was the matter, he said, "Mother, I want to die too." "But why?" "Haven't you heard how fortunate it is if one can die at this age, before the time of temptation, which gets ever stronger after the fifteenth year?"

After that, I called on a convalescent—a very tall man who in the past had gone his way uncaringly but is now so inwardly awake that he can never hear enough; he even follows me when I preach in other churches. Among other things he said that sometimes tears run down his cheeks when he sees people crowd into church with such eagerness. This time he had a special concern. In the last meeting, three weeks ago, his conscience had been stirred by a sin he had committed in his youth and which left him no peace now; so he had to confess it to me. From his father, who is no longer alive, he had once stolen six measures of wheat and had sold it on a Sunday during the church service, while lying to his father that he was going to church. What burdened him especially was that it happened on a Sabbath day. I held out to him the comfort of the Gospel, and it quieted him. But in our talk I pointed out how the sin had in fact violated four divine commandments, especially the commandment, "Honor your father and your mother." That was new to him, and to my dismay he was again seized by fear and trembling; he anticipated another sleepless night until it, too, had been fought through. I cannot put into words how that touched and moved me. I could give him no further comfort though, for I recognized the healing effect these struggles have on him. (The last conversation took place only today, and as I write this, I have to think of the good man in his struggle; may Christ sprinkle him with atoning blood!)

Finally I arrived at the house of the woman whose two little daughters are alternately stricken by blindness. You will remember how one of them miraculously recovered her sight; now since my absence it's the other girl's turn again; she suffers severe pain, cannot see anything, and is also subject to peculiar struggles. She is eleven years old, of a very loving disposition, and would gladly die; she also believes that her blindness protects her from much evil. Her relatives, however, consider her bewitched and put great pressure on the mother, a devout, long-suffering widow, to have recourse to a sorcerer's craft. So the mother was now in great need and implored me for advice. I counseled her to pray fervently and forbade her to have anything to do with magic, as it is strictly forbidden in Scripture. I told her to pray that God would drive away the sinister powers and give healing through the blood of Jesus, and other similar advice.

All this and still much more on one single day! O dear heart, should we not weep to see people's suffering? O Jesus, come and look at your children's need and strengthen the weary and burdened, who without you languish in such pain and misery!

On March 16 there follows further news of rich pastoral experiences, interwoven with interesting, instructive discussions between Blumhardt and his fiancée on questions of pastoral theology.

For quite some time it has secretly troubled me a little that you should have reason to feel concerned about me. You were afraid that I might not manage to observe and respect certain limits. But now you are rid of this fear too, and who rejoices more than your happy fiancée at seeing how through the quiet guidance of our God one thing after another is set right. Let me assure you once more that I am absolutely convinced that a preacher may never deny his own standpoint and position, no matter how much he bends over backward in ministering to poor souls. That is something of which I have to become more and more assured right here at Iptingen. People need to feel there are certain forms to be observed; by

observing them they have infinitely more given to them in their
hearts than if they felt no distance at all between them and their
pastor. They want to have a minister whom they have to respect but
at the same time can approach in love and trust. Such ministers,
dear heart, we want to be to them when the time comes. May the
Lord our God let us garner a great many souls!

Oh, how good it feels to be fully assured of a complete breakthrough in a certain soul. That joy has been granted to me very
conspicuously these days. The woman of whose newly awakened
husband I told in my last letter is seriously stricken with a bilious
fever, but the weaker her body, the stronger her spirit. She quite
considers me her spiritual father. The separatists look at her and
me in amazement as they hear how, though suffering from violent
headaches, she keeps crying out for hours on end, "It is all pure
love; I cannot thank God enough for laying me low like this," and
so on. Or how she goes on reciting one hymn verse after the other,
such as: "In the Lord's bleeding wounds I glory," "The blood of my
Jesus," "Christ's precious blood and righteousness," "Thus in life
and death it be: You in me and I in You." So she goes on and on,
making her sickbed a place of rejoicing for everyone. Yesterday
one of the separatists, a man, shed many tears of pure joy as he
stood at her bedside.

O my dear heart, if the Lord is gracious, you too shall one
day get to know what it is like. It does not make the heart proud
and presumptuous but on the contrary very small, yet blissfully
happy and with a deep yearning to give praise to God. It also
shows me what a real breakthrough is like. There are so many
where something has opened up, but the tears of repentance and
of the subsequent joy in Jesus have not yet started to flow. While
I had up to now been under the impression that a lot had already
been accomplished, I am now becoming aware that things have
just barely started and that the souls in whom a true fire of the
Spirit is burning are very few.

All that is just by the way, to show you how good it feels to
know of even one soul that has been won over, how on our side
so much depends on our approaching people in the right way—
neither getting too familiar with them nor remaining too aloof. Let
us two go our way in all simplicity, without undue hesitation, just
following the beat that the Spirit of God inculcates on us ever more
insistently. At the same time we should wisely heed all we have to
say to each other in heartfelt love by way of counsel, warning, and
admonition. You shall always find me open for that, knowing as I
do that in many pertinent matters you, though the younger one,
have a finer feeling than I. So you shall never find me closed to your

wishes, admonitions, instructions, and even unspoken hints—as long as it all redounds to the glory of the Lord!

In the above I have already indicated to you how at present the Lord is leading me from one heartfelt joy to the other. You will have found traces of it in what I wrote earlier. On March 6 I experienced something special. You will recall that in my last letter I said that a headache kept me from writing more. You could not have noticed how at the same time my hand was trembling, how by and by all my strength ebbed away and a real sickness seemed to take hold of me. On Monday, March 5, it grew progressively worse, and a heavy, feverish night followed. The sweating on Tuesday had little effect, and it seemed I was going to be really and truly ill. Then on Tuesday evening I experienced a most remarkable hour. I began to read Psalm 6. O dear heart, that was such an hour of grace; it was given to me not only to pour everything out before the Lord but in the end, after earnestly struggling in prayer and not without tears, to also *obtain* a great deal from him. There was much I broke through to on that evening, for I could feel that I was being heard. It mostly concerned my service and the strength for it, as well as the impending illness, but beyond that many things pertaining to the past and the future. You will yet find out, dear heart, how gracious the Lord has been to me. That I had been heard was confirmed the following day by restoration to health, which enabled me unhesitatingly to take over again the school, the instruction, and the evening meeting. Since then I have felt more vigorous than ever. It was a special hour such as I recall on few occasions in my life. It has also had other deep-going effects on me, for I felt urged to examine myself in every respect, so that I could only stand and sigh, "Lord, help me; I am weak." The following evening I became even more joyful in spirit, when instead of going on with Psalm 7, I opened my Bible to Psalm 57:5–12 for my evening reading.

I cannot put everything on paper, but I really had to share with you some of the things that gladden my soul. What I have advanced in most is patience. I am now able to wait, and I truly rejoice in God's blessed leadings. Yes, indeed; the Lord who so graciously condescends to the feeble—how could he ever overlook the things that concern *us*! So let us look trustingly up to the Lord who will remain our confidence and joy and some day will level our path most gloriously.

On April 15 he had to tell her that once again two livings or pastorates for which he had applied had been assigned to others. He heard the news just when a crowded church gathering waited for him to hold a missionary service, yet he was able to "conduct it with a peaceful heart and unmerited power." He continues:

> It is true that later on moments of depression did try to creep in, but it only takes a day like this one to completely drive away all my sadness. There is no doubt at all that up to now I simply had to be in Iptingen. For today I have experienced a triumph of the first magnitude. It has been a day beyond my power to paint for you in all the brightness of its colors, but will surely remain forever a memorable one for me. It is Good Friday today. People came in droves from the whole surrounding countryside and crowded into the church. There were at least fifty people from the village of Heimerdingen, two hours' walk away. The church could not accommodate all the people, and I felt a flash of deep emotion as I entered the pulpit and saw everything so chock-a-block full down below. This evening a man told me that he could not hold back his tears at seeing such a throng of people. I preached about the criminals on the cross, and the Lord gave me more than usual power so that I had the feeling I could just pour it out on the people in torrents. I could not help noticing that hearts were deeply moved, and when I handed the cup to those partaking of the Lord's Supper, I became aware of much deep emotion and many tears. Actually all the separatists turned up for the Lord's Supper—something regarded here as a real miracle. They attended in so simple and childlike a way that it had a beneficial effect on all, and now they heartily and deeply rejoice at the rich blessing they have received as they say.
>
> When I preached my second sermon, things went equally well, and wherever I went this evening, I heard people say things that must lead me to believe this day to have truly been a day of grace for Iptingen. I have just come from a little gathering; at the end I sang for them, "All we that have gathered here together," etc., and I could not help beginning the concluding prayer with the words, "O Jesus, how great is thy love to us!" So much for those "stubborn separatists"! What a glorious victory!

That is followed by a further account on April 23, 1838:

> A while ago you inquired after the children in my confirmation class with such sympathetic interest that I must tell you a little more about them. Every day it has gone a bit better with them, which leads me to believe that something has really begun to move in their hearts. I could also recognize it by their increasing love to me. Once when (because of a wedding) I had to let the rector take over the class, they were ever so worried whether I would be there the following day. I had promised to be back by 10 o'clock so as to

take the class from 11–12 o'clock. On the way back I experienced remarkable things. As I walked briskly through Heimsheim, I was accosted by a man who, though unknown to me, had known me for fifteen years. I could not get around it; I had to see his wife also. Then I still had to call at another house in the same village and, for better or worse, have some coffee there. After hurrying through a long stretch of forest, at 11 o'clock and covered with mud I passed by the schoolhouse, where the children were still having their lesson. I learned afterwards that from 10 o'clock on they had been constantly peering out of the window to see if I were coming. When finally one of them spotted me, he cried, "He is coming, he is coming!" and all the children stood up and looked out toward the road. "What's the matter?" the schoolmaster asked. "The *Herr Vikar* is coming," they said. I, too, felt the quivering joy in them when I entered a little later.

The evening before yesterday I had an earnest talk with them, and when at the end I offered them my hand, all of them broke into loud sobs—first of all the one who up to then had been the least approachable. I exhorted them to seek inner quiet and pray on their knees. Today I was told how faithfully one of them had followed that advice. At the confirmation they were all quite moved, to everybody's joy and edification, and when at the afternoon Sunday school I felt in a position to ask them very simply if they would be ready to die that very day, most of them replied softly and yet firmly "Yes," looking at me with such shining eyes that I and others felt struck to the core.

But what are you going to say of the following? Today, when I visited Hannes Kiefer, his wife met me with a big smile. Holding out a sixpence, she said, "Look what a child gave me for you!" (The child in question has no parents and up to now has been raised at the expense of the village.) The woman told me that the child had come to her and said, "The *Herr Vikar* has done so much for me that I would like to show him my love. Please be so kind as to hand him this; I do not feel free enough to give it to him myself." "Really," the woman had said, "there is no need for you to do that; the *Herr Vikar* is not going to accept that from you anyway; you had better keep it for yourself." "No, I really want to do it, for the *Herr Vikar* has done such a lot for me." "But where did you get the sixpence from?" "Someone gave me a shilling today; I have spent half of it on this and that, but the *Herr Vikar* must have the rest; I really want him to," and so on. What I have in mind is to give the dear child another shilling for his sixpence. But isn't that just wonderful?

> Oh, you should look into my heart and see how it bubbles over
> with love to these dear children. I find it hard to believe that the
> seed I have sown will not come to fruition. The Lord be praised
> for the undeserved happiness I am daily allowed to enjoy, for not
> a day goes by without my hearing new things. It is with reluctance
> that I put them on paper; I would so like to tell you about them in
> person. This much is certain: the Lord is working more and more
> powerfully, even in very rough people and outside of Iptingen.
> How could all this fail to strengthen me richly during our time
> of waiting! O dear heart, you rightly call it an overflowing grace
> that we can sacrifice something to the Lord for the sake of his
> kingdom. Let us honor and praise him who manifests himself so
> gloriously in everything!

We sense with Blumhardt that the persistent failure of his applications was a leading from on high; the Lord wanted him to go on laboring at Iptingen. Nevertheless, he kept doing what he could to obtain a
firm position and with that, a hearth and home for Doris and himself.
Once he applied for a living (or benefice) dispensed by a patron, some
member of the higher nobility. However graciously he was received by
the noble lord when he called on him, it became immediately clear to
him that the position was not for him, for in a mirror he caught sight of
a lady seated in an adjoining room, who by most lively gestures lacking
nothing in explicitness, at least for Blumhardt, indicated to her husband
that this applicant was not the right man for the job. His assumption that
the living was not meant for him proved correct.

It was in a loftier way than this that the post the Lord had in mind
for him was to become his. During his stay in Basel a close friendship
had developed between him and Pastor Barth of Möttlingen, a regular
attender of the annual Basel festivals. They were bound to each other
not only by a common interest in mission but equally by something
genuine, pure, and deep they perceived in one another, as well as having
in common a streak of unusual straightforwardness. On one occasion
Blumhardt had to reassure his fiancée that the bond of friendship with
Barth could actually go on without infringing *her* rights; he also had to
allay the quiet girl's alarm at the noisy cheeriness and cordiality with
which she saw the two greet each other. Blumhardt wrote to her:

> To be cheerful in the Lord is something precious. I am always
> pleased to read in Paul's letters about the joy he wishes the faithful,
> specially often in the Epistle to the Philippians, where he mentions

it three or four times. What makes me so particularly happy with our dear Barth is that I can always come straight out with everything. Here in the rectory I am like a walled enclosure as far as my private matters are concerned, and wherever I go, I have to keep mum about my own affairs. All my wishes, hopes, and thoughts I have to keep locked away in my heart. With Barth all is openness; that is why a first meeting with him always turns into such a remarkable scene.

Dr. Barth was in the process of withdrawing from pastoral service into the private life of an author, and he as well as his Möttlingen parishioners wanted Blumhardt to be his successor. Blumhardt therefore put in his application, and we all know that it was successful. He himself expected it and accordingly told his fiancée about the sphere of activity opening up before them. "It [Möttlingen] is not all that bad, except that our dear Barth has made some things hard for his successor."

Thus in his further letters we see Blumhardt gradually preparing to take his leave, looking partly back on his previous activity, partly forward to the future, as well as taking stock of his brief stewardship at Iptingen. Hoping for an early reunion and subsequent wedding, he writes to his fiancée on June 6, 1838:

So the days of expectancy keep flowing on. They may seem long to us, but in another way they really are short, and on looking back I feel just like you: I would not wish the time behind us to have been different. Indeed, I ought to affirm that even more strongly than you, seeing what great things have taken place with me in the intervening time. This is how we, while still on a rough path and far from the longed-for goal, are often allowed to experience that God means to deal kindly with us. Now and then, as I reflect on how swiftly the past time went, I tell myself that our future, however long by human standards, will likewise slip away quickly. However, dear, faithful soul, we shall be fortunate indeed when, looking back over the past, we see something we have achieved, telling us that our days have not been in vain.

Then he tells her about an inner struggle on account of another congregation, Friolzheim, which wanted to have him.

Again I find myself cornered by my own applications; they are always the hardest thing for me. Eight days ago the nearby parish of Friolzheim I wrote to you about became available. By human considerations that would be an extremely important place for God's kingdom. It is a very neglected parish, and there is an inner hunger among the people; they come in droves to attend church here. It is also located very conveniently for the villages round about, with all their newly awakened eagerness. And the nearness to Iptingen—oh, how precious! But the parish, numbering not quite 700 souls, yields only 612 florins. That would make it one of the poorest livings and to my mind—I have to admit—almost not adequate.

I was in Dürrmenz yesterday, and some people from Friolz-heim, not finding me here, followed me there on foot. Especially one man wants to get me to Friolzheim by hook or by crook, the others having laid it upon him to do his utmost to make me apply for that parish. A fortnight ago he told me of a dream in which he had seen Barth ordain me for the ministry there. As to the remuneration, he thinks it should be rated considerably higher on account of various accidentals. I told him how it stands with Möttlingen, but he persists in his belief that I am destined for Friolzheim. You can easily imagine what a tight corner I found myself in. In the end I told him to go to Stuttgart and talk to my mother, who would be very unhappy to see me get such a poor living after so long a time of waiting. (The very poorest livings bring 600 florins.) The day after tomorrow the man will probably bring me an answer, and I am willing to act in accordance with that, even if it means offering the Lord a temporal sacrifice in that way. After all, we must be prepared to have the Lord deal with us in a strange and yet blessed way. Maybe I shall then send the application to Engelmann, with the request to either pass it on or hold it back as he thinks best.

What makes it all the harder for me to apply for such a low-paid living is that I can be almost certain to get it, which means it is *my* choice, so to speak, that is decisive. It did cause quite a commotion in Iptingen though, when those men came and asked for me. The word spread like wildfire that my stay there was about to come to an end.

I experienced touching things today. Among others, a seven-year-old child, on hearing about it at home, suddenly burst into bitter tears. The alarmed mother asked, "What's the matter with you, Catherine?" "Oh dear," said the child, "the *Herr Vikar* must not go away," and an old woman who was present replied, "May God in his mercy hear your weeping and let the *Herr Vikar* stay with us!" I, too, feel the tears welling up as I write this, especially because there is so much in this matter that pulls me in all sorts of directions. I really have to renounce *all* wishes, seeing that there is one urge, dear heart, that keeps tugging at me ever so powerfully. And yet! All these feelings of sadness—are they not at the same time pure blessings as well? And must I not cry out amid it all, "See what great things the Lord has done to me!" Indeed, I am like the heathen folk about whom I read to the people yesterday and who said, "Oh, that we might have hearts fit to glorify the Lord worthily!" Just imagine: people are now flocking to me even from across the border from Baden; at Whitsun we had some here from Durlach and beyond! I am not in a position to tell everything, but the Lord is doing great things, using me, poor worm that I am, as his instrument. Every sermon I preach makes me more aware of my unsuitability and unworthiness, and yet the Word continues to take effect.

At Dürrmenz yesterday, where I held a small meeting with some of the more prominent women, one of them made me very happy. She expressed that it must be a big temptation for me to be so raised up by the people; she could not help thinking that it must cost me a struggle. But she added that I should not take offense at her saying it. I thanked her for being so mindful of what is best for me. I had felt great love for her before, and now I had to love her all the more. However, I can say with praise to God that I remain as good as untouched by that temptation, for God has put in my way many stones to block the wheel of self-love, which is so prone to get rolling in a person's heart. May the Lord keep protecting me, for I do feel within me a tendency to pride. Your loving intercession will not be fruitless either. Another woman at the same meeting said to me, "Such lofty talk bows and humbles a man, don't you think?" See, dear heart, how the Gospel brings out the sincerity in people!

In June Blumhardt attended the mission festival in Basel and at the same time visited his fiancée in Sitzenkirch. On the way back he stopped at Schaffhausen, where he lodged at the *Rosengarten*. He tells as follows about Spleiss and other friends there (Joh. Burkhardt, Mandach in Freudenfels):

Spleiss displayed an uncommonly courageous faith and true spiritual insight; not for a long time have I so felt in my element as there, where holy matters were talked about in such a childlike and trusting way. In very few circles is the blowing of the Spirit felt so strongly; with others all too often joking, silliness, and even flippancy are liable to creep in. O dear Doris, how I long that the Spirit may truly be able to work in me, whether I am with one person or with several, so that in all my cheerfulness there may be an unmistakable element of spiritual anointing. In looking back over the past days I again had to feel ashamed; instances of foolishness and rashness have become quite a burden to me, and on looking at it closely I find that it was the intimate relationship with the Lord that was lacking. However, I am not short of courage for the future.

He writes as follows about his return to Iptingen:

> In my congregation I feel again very happy. Yesterday, on Sunday, I received great blessing, although I had trouble finding my way back into things and could not attend to everything the way I used to. I just wish I could give you a foretaste of such a Sunday where one is faced by an almost insatiable hunger. People tug at me from all sides, and I just have to let them. It was a special joy for me to hear how a newly awakened circle had tried to meet while I was away; they say they had a happy time together. What I can tell about the festival is finding such an echo that I receive here even more blessing from it than in Basel itself.
>
> The children are wonderful. When I came out of the meeting at nine o'clock last night, a dozen of them met me in the street and presented me with a lovely garland of flowers. I am fairly swimming in joy; O dear heart, and how great will be my joy when you can experience it together with me! And how great will be the joy up in heaven! There will be unending hymns of praise up there!

On July 3, 1838, he finally received notice of his appointment to the Möttlingen post. On July 27 he writes his final letter from Iptingen to his fiancée, beginning as follows:

> Yesterday I received the last letter you will write to Iptingen, and how strange it feels that this will probably also be my last letter to you from here. Little by little I am beginning to taste the bitterness of my departure from here; it is being intensified by many touching and moving experiences. Sensing as I do that many things will again be different after my departure, I have already been through some dark moments today. I have become so used to the people and have so entered into their needs that I can hardly grasp it that I am to part from them now. Often, too, there comes to me the unfaithful thought that it may well have been my finest time as a pastor; at least I scarcely dare ask God for a comparable blessing for the future. It almost makes me feel that I have been granted an extraordinary time of grace, such as God's wise intentions only rarely bestowed on people. At times there comes to me the indescribably great thought that I have already been given, if I may say so, a flock with which I may one day stand gladly before the Savior. It is only because of you that I can cherish still bolder hopes and pray, "O Lord, grant me even more and let her, the dear

companion you have given me, share in it as well!" I would have to be seriously afraid of my own nature if I were to imagine you to be just an ordinary soul—upright and good-natured, to be sure, yet not zealously burning for the Lord's cause. God has truly meant well by me, and my heart is all aflutter now whenever I may tell people who don't know you about my bride-to-be, and with such total conviction at that.

The move from Iptingen to Möttlingen took place on July 31, 1838, which happened to be Dr. Barth's birthday. Blumhardt described it to his fiancée as follows:

Last Tuesday, July 31, I really left Iptingen and moved to Möttlingen. There was much lamenting in Iptingen, and it made my taking leave very hard. The good people put me on a wagon very tastefully decorated with flower garlands, and the whole village council, including the mayor and schoolmaster, ten persons in all, escorted me to my new parish. The Möttlingen congregation was waiting for me on the high ground overlooking the village, and the children welcomed me with the song "Praise to the Lord, the Almighty, the King of Creation." After greeting them all, I was conducted in stately procession into the village itself—first the shepherd with three nicely decorated sheep, then the children, then the village council, and finally the congregation itself—very solemn and festive. We walked through the village to the song "Now Thank We All Our God." The rectory was decorated with flowers, and on entering it my eye fell on the words "God bless your entry." I presently had the congregation assemble in the church, and I spoke a few words of greeting. In the rectory my Iptingers had dinner with me, Stotz (Barth's curate), and the mayor of Möttlingen.

O my precious Doris, it was almost more than my heart could bear, and I felt totally worn out afterwards. My Iptingen folk have made no secret of their love, and even now tears come to my eyes when I recall various instances, especially the last scenes, and how the children walked with me for a quarter of an hour and then, strewing flowers on the road, stopped to say goodbye. There, under the open sky, I spoke the words of the song "I will abide in Jesus," and that was the end. God be praised for all the grace he has shown. Let it be our fervent prayer that he may look down with eyes of compassion on Iptingen and Möttlingen.

In Iptingen they had showered me with presents for our household. The single girls gave me half a dozen pretty coffee cups and saucers, as well as a fine soup tureen and half a dozen silver spoons, and another group of other persons presented me with

half a dozen large pewter plates. What touched me most was when
a woman sent me a little pewter bowl from her own store.

As regards taking leave of Iptingen itself, he writes: "O my precious one,
it was heartrending, and I am still overcome with sadness when I think
of the individuals there and of what the future will hold . . . I felt like
kissing each of them, and many I did kiss. There was a real movement of
love and sorrow. So much love as I experienced there cannot remain un-
rewarded by the Lord. Oh, how exceedingly happy I was there, in spite
of some things that were hard!" Later on he continues:

> But in Möttlingen it will also be nice for us. The love and warmth
> of the people is great, and I look forward to finding many open
> doors, though some things will be quite different. Now you, too,
> will have a part in it, and if you really give yourself to the people,
> you will soon find what fruit it brings. O my kind-hearted Doris,
> we are blessed and shall remain blessed! At this time I am being
> made especially aware of God's blessing. For everything turns out
> well; whatever I think and desire succeeds beyond all expecta-
> tions, making it often seem that I no sooner ask our loving God
> for something than it is already there. I am experiencing that in all
> manner of ways; everywhere I find the Lord's hand stretched out
> over me in blessing. Would that I could thank and praise him suf-
> ficiently! Should we then hesitate any longer and go on withhold-
> ing anything from the Lord? Surely not! Everything shall belong
> to him; everything in us and around us shall be consecrated to his
> service. This, even this shall be our firm and everlasting bond!

On August 7, 1838, this correspondence closes with the words:

> Now the pen shall rest, and we shall evermore speak quite di-
> rectly from heart to heart. May God sanctify it! He has set us an
> exercise and has taught us a good deal by it, and he will carry
> through the work thus begun. Yes, he will do it; he will let the
> bond between our hearts redound to his glory . . . With my soul
> deeply moved, my faithful hand once more sets down here a most
> heartfelt greeting to you. May you bear with a firm heart the many
> storms, struggles, and anxieties in store for us, as they alternate
> with hopes of love and joy. This is what most ardently implores for
> you your bridegroom, bound to you in eternal love,
>
> Christoph.

Blumhardt's own reports, as they have here been strung together
without further comment, tell us more eloquently than even the most

skillful biographer could how faithfully and with what rich blessing Blumhardt labored at Iptingen during the year and a quarter he spent there. When recommending him for Möttlingen, his superiors bestowed on him the following praise in simple, dignified language:

> Since his return from Basel in April of last year Blumhardt has been assigned as an assistant to the aging rector of Iptingen. He is carrying out this difficult task in an outstanding way. By his apt sermons and talks and his indefatigable care of individual souls, coupled with a modest and friendly approach to people and dignified conduct, he has reawakened the extinct church-mindedness in this congregation and assuaged the party spirit there. Iptingen was at one time the chief center of separatism. That situation has changed inasmuch as the number of separatists has been reduced to a mere twenty, and these, though avoiding the church and refusing offices, nevertheless send their children to school, obey the pertinent laws, and are not hostile to the clergy.

It was when already installed as rector in Möttlingen that Blumhardt wrote that last letter, in which he took leave of all further merely written communication with his fiancée. We have now arrived at the end of the first part of his life story, entitled "Years of Growth and Preparation." To be exact, this first part actually extends further; it should include the memorable spiritual struggle that forms the turning point of his life. We nevertheless conclude this first part with the Iptingen period in order to deal with Blumhardt's entire stay in Möttlingen in one section.

PART TWO

Möttlingen

First Section

7

Previous Rectors of Möttlingen

MÖTTLINGEN, AT AN ELEVATION of 1850 feet above sea level, is situated at the northern end of the Black Forest, northeast of Calw, its county seat, and high above the right bank of the Nagold River. As a parish it encompasses two curiously different villages—Möttlingen, where the church is located, and Unterhaugstett, a parish branch. When Blumhardt arrived at Möttlingen, the parish numbered 874 souls (Möttlingen 535, Unterhaugstett 339). Two years before he left it in 1850, there were 985 souls (Möttlingen 582, Unterhaugstett 403).

Möttlingen is part of the administrative district (*Oberamt*) of Calw. It is a compact village, similar to the Swabian *Unterland* (Lower Country) in its architecture, costumes, and customs, and sits on the *Muschelkalk* (Shell Limestone) characteristic of the *Unterland*. Unterhaugstett, on the other hand, forms part of the administrative district of Neuenbürg. It is situated on the *Buntsandstein* (Variegated Sandstone) and by its scattered layout, language, costumes, and customs belongs to the Black Forest area. For a long time, things had been considerably better, morally and ecclesiastically, in the rector's home village than in the parish branch, where a spirit of independence and opposition bordering on hostility prevailed, especially toward the rector. Blumhardt, too, was to come up against this spirit quite a bit during his first years at Möttlingen.

More remarkable, however, than these geological and geographical peculiarities of Möttlingen was the significant position it even then occupied within the (Protestant) state church of Württemberg. Its church was

91

something like a city on a hill and had long been accustomed to having visitors from far around within its walls. In 1844 there was a conference of Protestant ministers, attended by Albert Knapp, W. Hofacker, Blumhardt, and others.[1] Here the revival movement then gathering strength in Möttlingen was discussed, and Knapp remarked, "For a good hundred years now a spiritual 'artesian well' has been dug in Möttlingen."

From 1749 to 1763 Bührer was rector in Möttlingen. When already well advanced in age, his daughters would still tell how after his transfer from Möttlingen to another parish their father never wearied of praying that Möttlingen be given devout pastors. He was succeeded by Machtolf, a commanding spiritual figure, who shed a bright light far around— brilliant, original, and of great inward depth. He was the spiritual father of burgomaster Hoffmann (the founder of Korntal) and of many others. There were people, among them the father of Dr. Barth, who would walk seven hours from Stuttgart to Möttlingen in order to hear Machtolf preach. Even now his memory is alive among the people, and the reader will forgive me for telling a few of the well-authenticated stories current about him. In 1831, our Blumhardt was told the following by Machtolf's grandson Bossart, later schoolteacher in Möttlingen.

Once a down-and-out journeyman came to Machtolf, asked him for a shirt, and was given a new one. He went to an inn and had a good meal. Having no money to pay, he wanted to trade the shirt for the amount of the bill. The innkeeper examined the shirt and, discovering Machtolf's name, took it to him. Machtolf paid the bill and asked for the shirt to be returned to the journeyman. The innkeeper did so and told the man that the bill had been paid. The man inquired, "by whom?" and the reply left him stunned. Struck to the core, he became a repentant sinner and a pupil of Machtolf (the story is from the diary Blumhardt kept while he was a *Vikar*).

Machtolf treated his possessions as if they were not his at all. Whenever Hoffmann came to see him, he brought along some meat wrapped in a cloth, since Machtolf could never buy any. Many times Machtolf lent money or stood surety without having anything himself,

1. Editors' Note: Albert Knapp (1798–1864) was a colleague and friend of Blumhardt who was involved in the creation of a new hymnbook for the Lutheran church in Württemberg, which was eventually published in 1841. Wilhelm Hofacker (1805–1848) was the younger brother of the famous revivalist preacher Ludwig Hofacker (1798–1828), and a close friend of Blumhardt.

and help always came miraculously. When French troops were looting and everyone hid his valuables, he got out his silver spoons and offered them to the soldiers, saying he could well eat with tin spoons. This so dumbfounded them that they did not take any. He also offered them linen sheets for trousers, but they took nothing. Soon after, he gave those silver spoons to a poor woman to use as her pledge for a debt; after his death, though, they were returned to his heirs.

His love was actually the cause of his death. He was returning from Calw and was climbing a steep rise in the road when he came upon a handcart standing there and heard a plaintive voice from the edge of the road. It came from a man who, it is said, was actually gambling on Machtolf's kindheartedness. He lamented bitterly that he could not pull his cart (which did carry an exceedingly heavy load) any further up the hill. Machtolf set to and pushed the wagon up the steep rise, using every last ounce of his strength. He arrived home late at night, bathed in sweat, and lay down to die. It is said that after his death his preacher's coat was found to be the only one he had.

These expressions of kindheartedness imprinted themselves deeply on the grateful people's memory; however, they do give a one-sided picture. One who knew Machtolf describes him as a man full of love and of the spirit of God, whose countenance shone like that of an angel. He had a deep insight into the mysteries of the kingdom of God and longed for greater victories for it. As evidenced by the prayer hymn below, he might be compared to Simeon of old. A sense of authority shines forth from what he once told his congregation in a sermon, "When the Möttlingers come to be judged on the last day, I shall have something to say about it too." The following prayer hymn he wrote may sound strange to modern ears, but it bears witness to greatness of spirit and victorious, knightly courage. It expresses so powerfully how the Church, like the widow in the parable (Luke 18:2–8), cries out in her need, "Save me from my adversary," that we come to understand why Blumhardt valued it highly.

A Spiritual Song

Would that on earth a fire were lit
Such that none could extinguish it!
That would rejoice the Savior's heart
And would make Satan sorely smart.
A small flame is now flickering here
And has been so for many a year;

Indeed, you find its timid glow
In many a house where're you go.
A mighty wind is what we need;
O Holy Spirit, come with speed,
And where the flame is burning low,
Into the smold'ring embers blow!
O Spirit of the Lord, arise!
May thy pure breath from Paradise,
Which is with Son and Father one,
Complete the work it has begun!
Enter my heart; in it abide
And make it fit for Eastertide,
Just like Emmaus where, we know,
The Risen One himself did show.
Oh, may it burn—now there, now here,
And go on burning year by year,
That none the spreading flames could stay
Until the Lord's great judgment day.
Ye seven torches by the Throne,
That burn for Father and for Son,
Take pity on this our poor land;
Fling everywhere your blazing brand!
Then, spreading forth throughout the world,
Let, where you will, your brands be hurled,
Till by all people will be adored
The Lamb as Savior and as Lord.
Roaming relentlessly about,
Drive every evil spirit out!
To pulpits dull your fires take!
The halls of learning shake awake!
Enkindle every teacher's heart
And draw each student heavenward!
Satanic bonds burn up with flame
And our freed hearts for Christ reclaim!
Let Jesus' gospel present be
Where men prepare for ministry—
Like Obed-Edom's, a fit place
To be illumined by your grace.
Your holy incense clouds let blow
Through all the prep schools too, and so
Smoke out all evil that is there,
Leave only what is pure and fair.
Then let God's ark be placed inside,
Levites and priests be purified

And sprinkled with the sacred blood,
So will all schools be clean and good.
From there let torchbearers go forth
To set aflame from south to north
And east to west the hearts of men.
Let Satan try to quench it then!
Amen—that is, "May it come true!"
This faith be strengthened ever new!
I do have faith nor ever doubt;
I know what faith is all about.
It is not faith in God alone
(That would leave Satan on his throne);
No, faith in Christ, in his blood too,
Whereby all things can be made new.
In this faith are our hearts set free
Through Jesus' power of victory,
Which God's good spirit still today
Imparts to them that rightly pray.
Come, Holy Spirit, with your power
To fill our hearts this very hour!
Oh, what a bright and festive air
Will then both hearts and houses wear.

At the beginning of the nineteenth century Machtolf was succeeded by Gross, likewise a deeply devout man of great spiritual influence throughout Württemberg, even though there are not so many stories current about him. He came to Möttlingen after a ministry in Upper Austria, which had a rich and enduring blessing. From Gross's death in 1814 until 1824 Pastor Bach was rector in Möttlingen—a loving and gentle man but somewhat tinged with rationalism. During those years it was the schoolmaster, Machtolf's son-in-law Bossart, who kept the spiritual life of Möttlingen awake. He was a homely hunchback, but his influence was great, particularly on the children; his religious instruction meant a great deal to them. There was a time when, at a regular *Stunde* (meeting) he held in the schoolhouse, he would read the Revelation of John to the people, meeting with a lively response. To Pastor Bach's objection that such reading would only make people depressed, he retorted that it was in fact time for Revelation to be read *twice*, lest people think that this book had no place in the Bible. At Blumhardt's time it was the son of this Bossart who was the schoolmaster at Möttlingen.

In 1824 the Möttlingen parishioners went directly to the king in order to have Pastor Barth (later Dr. Barth), already well known by that time, appointed as their rector. We owe it not only to the eminence of this man, but above all to Blumhardt's lifelong deep love and extraordinary respect for him, to take a closer look at this outstanding spiritual figure.

> Never had the road to Canaan lain as desolate as of late;
> Only here and there some simple pilgrim did not hesitate.

That is how the hymn writer Spitta[2] describes the spiritual deadness around the beginning of the nineteenth century, only to thank the Lord afterward in resounding strains for changing the situation for the better. Dr. Barth was in the forefront of the chosen witnesses instrumental in reviving faith. He was a man of pure and deep piety, extraordinary gifts, a tremendous zest for work, and untiring industry. "It is my principle," he once said, "to write as much as I can [that is, for publication]." These qualities gave him a commanding position among the various vigorous witnesses to faith of that time, almost comparable to that occupied by Goethe during the *Storm and Stress* period of German literature. He set the tone of conversation in the spiritual family of believers scattered over southern Germany and Switzerland and beyond.

In his monthly youth magazine he spoke to the young people. He also cultivated a special contact with them by offering prizes for solving Bible riddles. Equally often he addressed the older generation in his Calw magazine. Every Christmas this never-aging youth would come out with a wholesome, lively story for the young. Now and then he would also entertain his readers with a bright and sparkling song, preferably about mission, or bring out a pamphlet, often anonymous, in which he cast a clear, sharp light on some subject then exercising Christian people, especially in his own country of Württemberg.

At the same time he functioned as a practically omnipresent guest speaker. He helped to start and raise to greater heights the Christian people's festival, that greatly blessed periodic event peculiar to the German Protestant church of the nineteenth century. There were few places within his far-flung sphere of activities where his commanding figure did not at least once appear in the pulpit and his words kindle a fire in listeners' hearts. Above all, he was almost indispensable at the central

2. Editors' Note: This refers to Carl Johann Philipp Spitta (1801–1859), who was a major figure in the recovery and reintroduction of Bach and the German Lutheran Chorale tradition during the first half of the nineteenth century. His hymnbook *Psalter und Harfe* enjoyed great popularity among congregations associated with the *Erweckungsbewegung* (Awakening Movement) during the 1830s and 1840s.

festival (the one in Basel), not only on account of his sparkling oratory, but even more because his purpose was so strong, his vision so broad, and his hope so confident.

Many a missionary in his lonely cabin in a heathen land could expect to be cheered now and then by a full and wide-ranging letter from Barth, who generously devoted much time and labor to that. Yet the atmosphere in Barth's home was as easygoing as if all he did was enjoy a comfortable life on his pension (which he actually did not have). An unending trickle of visitors made use of his bachelor's arsenal of dressing gowns, slippers, and tobacco pipes and enjoyed his genial, spirited, witty conversation. Not everyone was aware that he liked to hide the tumult of his inmost thoughts and feelings beneath a veneer of joviality and sparkling wit.

We have made no mention yet of Barth's main achievement, the founding and directing of the *Calwer Verlagsverein* (Calw Publishing Association), publishers of Christian writings for schools and the general public, where the threads linking writing, printing, and publishing all came together in his hands. What led to its founding was the compassion he felt for the people, as he saw on the one hand their lack of spiritual nourishment and on the other the miserable substitutes offered by the printing press. He longed and strove to provide sound, biblical, Christian reading material for the people, especially the youth. His publishing house brought out ABC-books, books on natural history and on the history of the world, the Church, and Christian missions as well as Bible commentaries. Above all, there were the *Zweimal 52 biblische Geschichten* (Twice 52 Bible Stories [one for every week of the year from both the Old and the New Testament]), which, with illustrations (initially, with varying success, by his own hand), by 1880 had gone through over 256 editions. They were meant first of all for his native Württemberg, but beyond that for all German-speaking lands as well as the mission field. This booklet has been published in 65 different languages, forty of them in Asia, Africa, America, and Polynesia.

It was in Möttlingen that Barth *became* the man he was. He arrived there with a reputation as an articulate, zealous champion of Pietism and an inspired preacher, coming straight from a "scientific journey" (awarded, Württemberg fashion, for an exam passed with highest honors), which had acquainted him with all that was most notable and significant in the religious life of Germany and Switzerland. In Möttlingen he found time to take stock of his spiritual capital and put it to use. One could suspect that this would entail neglecting his congregation, but it was not so. His ever-growing tasks did eventually compel him to install a curate and in the end were a chief reason for his quitting the pastorate. These two measures prove, however, that he was deeply conscious of his duty toward his parishioners and applied himself to it heart and soul. In fact, in his concern for them, as well as for his "wider congregation," he was almost over-zealous and over-active, not unlike that Great Elector of Brandenburg, who, it is said, wanted to extend his government into the very bedrooms of his subjects. Yet who would not be thankful for such energy, if exerted by a wise and loving hand? The people of Möttlingen owe him a great deal and remain thankful to him even today. Though his love went out to them, he was extremely strict and wanted to ban anything worldly from weddings or village feasts, for example. This had the result that the Unterhaugstett folk several times rebelled against their rector's severity—remarkably enough, every time with deplorable consequences (which, however, did not originate with their rector).

But it was preeminently to the young that Barth's love went out. To them, in all their various age groups, he gave himself wholly, above all to those preparing for confirmation. To those, as well as to the girls already confirmed, he devoted his evenings, and it was actually for them that he put together the Bible riddles he used to catch the interest of the young. In all kinds of ways he coaxed them into the Bible and urged them to think—about themselves too. He would gather the older girls, with their spinning wheels, in his rectory and among other things encouraged them to make up songs based on selected Bible passages. In this way Gottliebin Dittus, for example, about whom we shall hear more later, actually came to produce significant poetry, going far beyond ordinary versification. But it was at confirmation times that Barth's true greatness showed. What pastor, reading of his exhortations, prayers, and tears on these important occasions, has not felt put to shame by him? Later years showed in a wonderful way how the seed thus sown had taken root.

It may be that his preaching was altogether too brilliant for regular listeners and in the end had a wearing and dulling effect on some of them. And his ardent longing to see listeners "converted" by his words, may have led to an almost incurable resentment among those who felt unmistakably treated as "unconverted" in contrast to the "converted." When we bear in mind how both Barth's "converted" and "unconverted" were to come to a true conversion later on, we perceive God's wonderful leading in letting Blumhardt, the champion of *power*, follow after this champion of the *word* (in the best sense). Be that as it may—things kept getting more and more discouraging for Barth. Toward the end of 1835 he writes:

> Frivolity and indifference are clearly getting stronger every year, and preaching is no longer effective. In this congregation, once well-known for its good order and morality, I today had to discipline five men for dereliction of school duties, talk to three sixteen-year-old boys for playing cards during church, and question an adulterer—all things that used to be unheard of. I often feel discouraged, and the thought comes to me that I could be more effective at another place. For the folk at Möttlingen, who have been preached to death, it would be good if they were to go a bit hungry for a change, spiritually speaking.

At the beginning of 1836 he writes:

> Among the unconverted in my congregation the moral and religious situation has worsened considerably, while among the better elements it has not improved. Among grown-ups here I don't know of one really thorough conversion; among those I have confirmed. There are some who give me pleasure, but they are generally children of Christian parents, and their upbringing at home may have been the decisive factor, not *my* labors. The religious life has declined, coarseness has increased; all my preaching is fruitless; I try every register and mode—now minor, now major, alto today, bass tomorrow, but nothing will take. Sunday after Sunday I come away with the conviction that my congregation has been preached to death, that no stimulant is effective any more, their nerves having been dulled far too much. What is charged with inner power and spirit they gulp down as the Russians gulp vodka, showing no effect at all; they have drunk to surfeit of the sweet milk of the Gospel.

What pained him most was that the greater part of his so-called "listeners" actually *slept* in church. This was reason enough for sadness, for measured by human standards, Barth was one of the greatest preachers. However, as in the following pages our eyes are opened to the secret bonds of darkness then still fettering the whole congregation, the "converted" almost as much as the "unconverted," we come to understand how utterly hopeless was the attempt to break these bonds by means of oratorical "stimulants" and "effects."

Now while Barth's labors in Möttlingen were thus proving more and more fruitless, his more general endeavors, which were more in line with his inclinations and gifts, promised him an ever richer harvest. In the pursuit of his higher goals he had outgrown the calling to fill a local ministry, and it became clear to him that he was called to serve the cause of God's kingdom more freely and in a position of more general significance. So he withdrew into private life and settled down in Calw as director of the Calw Publishing Association, where he was in any case already functioning as a kind of employee. This found an apt, if a little cumbersome, expression in one of the curious designations Barth had nailed to the edge of his book shelf: "Mr. Calw Publishing."

He was greatly concerned to find a capable successor for Möttlingen. His eye fell on his younger friend Blumhardt, closely bound to him by a common interest in mission, and he got the Möttlingers to send a deputation to the king with the request to have Blumhardt assigned to them as their rector. We already know that this request was granted.

8

Installation, Wedding, Initial Ministry

THE DATE OF BLUMHARDT's installation (or "investiture") as rector of Möttlingen is not known to me. We are already familiar with parts of the address with which he greeted the congregation and introduced himself—I mean the excerpts from his life story, which he read out on that occasion. Here follows the remainder of that address; it begins with a reference to Blumhardt's predecessor in Möttlingen, Dr. Barth:

> It was at Basel, beloved in Christ, that I first became acquainted with your previous rector, Dr. Barth; our hearts found each other, and it has been a special joy today to have him, as well as Pastor Werner [Blumhardt's former colleague at the Basel Mission Institute] as witnesses in your midst. May the Most High give me strength to go on under his blessing with the work Pastor Barth has begun here [subsequently changed from, "the Kingdom He [the Most High] has begun here"; then follows the account of Iptingen] . . . and now, beloved in Christ, I am standing here, having been appointed your minister a few months ago. I feel deeply moved by the love you have shown and are showing me in every way, and my heart is so full of thankfulness to God that I cannot imagine a greater blessing than to be able to help many of you find salvation and to be able one day to present a great many of you to the Master Shepherd as sheep that did not get lost.
>
> Among the many mercies God has bestowed on me I still have to mention that he has given me a partner in life, Johanna Dorothea Köllner, who is in every way of the same mind as I am, and I hope that she will be happy to join me in lovingly working for the eternal wellbeing of an esteemed congregation. During the

very last weeks of my stay in Basel, through remarkable leadings I became acquainted with her in her parental home at Sitzenkirch in the upper country of Baden. Some of you may still remember her late grandfather, Pastor Köllner, who visited here several times. It makes me unspeakably happy that I may regard her as being under the venerable old man's blessing. May we both be commended to your continuing goodwill.

For years, beloved in Christ, Psalm 103 has been my favorite Bible text, which I have clung to in good and bad days. When I consider all the mercies God has showered on me from the very beginning of my life in order to prepare me for his service, how could I help crying out unceasingly:

> Praise the Lord, O my soul, and all that is within me, praise his holy name! Praise the Lord, O my soul, and forget not all his benefits, who forgives all your sins and heals all your diseases, who redeems your life from destruction and crowns you with loving-kindness and compassion.

With these words Blumhardt concludes his salutation. "Be more faithful than I and more fortunate than I" was Barth's blessing at his successor's installation. And Blumhardt's own prayer, "May the Most High arm me with his power!" was to be answered in a most memorable way.

It is interesting to compare the words with which Blumhardt concluded his life story with the account Barth gave at his own installation:

> Our trust in one another has been confirmed by the Lord of the Church, and I am fully confident that it is he who has led us together and made us conclude an everlasting covenant. The prospect of having a congregation of almost eight hundred souls entrusted to my shepherd's staff would be frightening if I could not look back on so many lovely and wonderful experiences of the Lord's faithful help and succor during the past twenty-six years; if I could not look into the merciful heart of Jesus, the Good Shepherd; if I could not look at his precious promises: "I myself shall watch over my flock and care for the weak; I am with you at all times until the world's end; the Spirit will lead you into all truth; the gates of hell shall not overcome my Church." So I stand before you today, O congregation of the Lord, fully aware of my weakness and inability, but equally aware of the nearness and strength of the Lord. All I can promise you is that trusting as I do in what he promises, his grace will not let me be unfruitful among you. Much will depend on how earnestly you pray for me that I might proclaim to you the Word of God in truth and walk among you as a burning and shining light. So may this day become for

me and you a day of blessing that we can remember in eternity
with everlasting joy!

How aptly their salutations characterize these two friends and
comrades! Beside Barth's lofty paean, reverberating with all the registers
of his bounteous mind and heart, the first impression of Blumhardt's
address is one of timidity, restraint, and almost stiffness, as for example
when he speaks of the "eternal wellbeing of an esteemed congregation"
and of commending himself and his wife to their "continuing goodwill."
He was in essence a man of deeds and, in the word's highest sense, a
simple man. He never had, nor wanted to have, two different ways of
speaking, one for use *in* the pulpit and the other *below* it. Hence his
preaching style was that of informal talk, of a high-minded conversation. Evidently, too, the very solemnity of the moment had an additional
sobering effect on him. As he on one occasion wrote to his fiancée, "I
have often found that the fuller my heart, the drier my words." In particular at this festive hour he was concerned not to lose sight of real,
everyday life, but in the very midst of it he gave voice to the holy, as
when he speaks of the "strength of the Most High," of "finding salvation,"
and of "sheep that did not get lost."

Before examining the task Blumhardt had taken on, let us look
more closely at the bond of friendship between Barth and Blumhardt,
which had been deepened all the more by Blumhardt's taking over
Barth's work.

As we already know, these men were akin to each other in their
uncommon enthusiasm for the great goals of the kingdom of God as
well as in their integrity and uprightness, but otherwise were in many
ways quite different. Barth was not only the older one, but quite apart
from the difference in age, the one more widely known. To put it in biographical terms: While we have got no further than the beginning of
the second part (of three) of this account of Blumhardt's life, in Barth's
biography (written by his friend Werner) the same events occur well
into the third (and last) volume. So it was that Blumhardt looked up to
Barth as ungrudgingly as Barth lovingly looked down at him. In their
close bond the thoroughly monarchical nature common to both was
conjugated in the active voice by Barth, in the passive by Blumhardt,
and this was taken for granted on both sides.

The birthday greeting Blumhardt wrote to Barth in 1841 (for July
31) may serve to throw more light on their relationship: "So today is

your forty-second birthday! For several days already my heart has been blessing you for this day, as best I can . . . I feel so one with you that your days are also my days. Would to God that I could be of more use to you—that is to say, not to you, but to Him to whom you belong and for whom you labor, and for whom I am to labor through you!" Similarly in a New Year's greeting the same year (December 31) Blumhardt writes: "It is my deepest wish, at times also my prayer, that I might at long last, also out of love to you, accomplish something worthwhile."

It would be hard to imagine a relationship deeper and more brotherly than theirs. On the average twice a week, but often four or five times, or even twice the same day, Blumhardt's messenger would make his way to Barth in Calw, and as we know, it was not Barth's way to leave letters unanswered.

In a way rarely met even between brothers, Blumhardt reports to his friend anything and everything, great or small, he experiences. On one occasion (before the awakening in Möttlingen) he confides to him a foreboding that he is about to be stricken by a serious illness but implores him not to make any mention of this to his (Blumhardt's) wife. Shoptalk concerning appointments and assignments, the evaluation of the various literary projects (especially periodical ones), the obtaining of sources, of printing plates and blocks, etc.—this forms, so to speak, the framework of their correspondence. On that framework are hung exact, detailed reports about conditions in Möttlingen, for example, illnesses among the parishioners, and so on. Then, too, Barth is kept well informed about even the smallest happenings in the family, and lastly, the important events of the day are frequently touched upon.

In his methodical way, Barth carefully filed and kept all of Blumhardt's letters. At his direction, after his death they went to Werner, his biographer, and after Werner's death back to Blumhardt. They virtually amount to a diary of Blumhardt's life at Möttlingen, though there are gaps in the account due to intermittent direct contacts between the two friends. Blumhardt was not able to do the same with Barth's letters. His mountainous correspondence did not allow time and space to keep all incoming letters, and since in any case the highly confidential character of most of the letters he received made their speedy destruction advisable, with him incineration largely replaced the record office. So only a small selection of Barth's letters has been preserved. Whoever reads this correspondence cannot help being moved on the one hand by the tender love expressed, on the other hand by the exquisite bluntness in their mutual exchange of home truths.

A further word may be added here as regards Blumhardt's straight-forwardness, so often spoken of: When he had something against some-body, he would lose no time in speaking to that person lovingly, quietly, and very plainly. With that the matter was finished and done with and no more to be thought of. That one could rely on. In *Täglich Brod* (April 6, 1880) he commented as follows on the word in Isaiah 53:9: "There was no deceit in his mouth": "If that can be said of a person, there is something right about him. There must be no underhandedness, no whispering behind somebody's back, else all sincerity is gone, and the lips speak differently from the heart, which means that there is deceit in your mouth or your speech or your behavior."

There was still another festive occasion ahead for Blumhardt—his wedding. On September 4, 1838, the two sisters Lotte and Doris Köllner were both led to the altar, the first one to be married to a missionary, Häberlin, the second, to Blumhardt. Mission inspector Blumhardt, our Blumhardt's kinsman and through his position close to both bride-grooms, married the two couples. Barth, thoughtful as always, sent a little greeting. It was a poem in which first the Köllner parents appear and lament the departure of their children. The two daughters reply with expressions of apology and comfort. Next, the Möttlingen parish-ioners put in a good word for Blumhardt, and a Hindu does the same for Häberlin. Then the two happy bridegrooms have their say, and at the end the "distant" friend (Barth) concludes with a benediction of his own.

Of inner significance for the newlyweds, especially in later years, was the Bible reading for that day: "Old Testament text: Light rises in the darkness for the upright; the Lord is gracious, merciful, and righteous (Ps 112:4). New Testament text: Whatever you ask in prayer, believe that you will receive it, and it will be yours (Mark 11:4)." Both these texts—the meaningful, auspicious hint given in the first and the earnest assurance of help from above of the second—would often strengthen the newlyweds in the many hard struggles and unimagined tasks of their later lives.

From this day on Pastor Blumhardt had a wife and helpmate by his side. One of the difficulties of my task is that, so as not to offend her, I may not speak too boldly of what she, her husband's faithful helper, has accomplished. Perhaps I may just say that her husband many times and in glowing terms shared with his friend Barth his joy at having a wife who so loyally stood by him in his prayers, struggles, and self-denials. And perhaps the Möttlingers should have a chance to voice their thanks for how she cared for them, both the sick and the well. I simply ask the reader from now on to always think (where it fits) "Blumhardt and his wife" whenever we hear of something Blumhardt does. The reader will then not go wrong. The Möttlingen parishioners were extremely pleased to have their rectory once more occupied by a *married* pastor.

The task Blumhardt had in Möttlingen was obviously much harder than the one at Iptingen. He faced a congregation that had learned to go to sleep while listening to one of the most brilliant preachers of the day; an air of surfeit, weariness, and discontent all around; a small circle of pietists; a group of parishioners who continued to regard Barth as all in all, and side by side with them a considerable number who felt disgruntled at the preferential treatment given the others and therefore were not so friendly disposed toward the new rector those others had specially asked for. Such was the soil Blumhardt was to till. The faithful labor of his predecessor and the promising seed he had sown were, for the moment, covered over with an impenetrable hostile crust; only later, after this crust had been removed—not without a lot of miraculous help from God—did they yield a rich harvest.

In addition, Barth himself, while intending to lighten Blumhardt's task, made it in one way considerably harder. One of the most sensitive problems in a minister's career is to find the right attitude to a congregation he has left behind and especially also to his successor. There seems to be a general agreement that the direction must simply be: "Hand it all over! Let your successor have a completely free hand, especially when you can be well assured about the spirit he works in, so that he can minister to his congregation unhindered." That being the right course, Barth has to be considered as audacious as he was original in the way he repeatedly assured the Möttlingen parishioners at his parting, "I shall remain your pastor!" It was a promise made all the weightier by his settling down in the neighboring town of Calw. Even though Barth might be justified in applying to himself a standard not applicable to others, and in having greater self-confidence, nevertheless the task of honoring this promise with the required tact and without hurting the congregation and the blessed labor of his successor was almost superhuman. What made the situation the more difficult was that by his own admission Barth had made a complete mess of his task in Möttlingen. Yet the Lord looked graciously on the *source* of Barth's intent—his deep love for the Möttlingers—and so led things that in many ways the fruit it bore was blessed after all, thanks also to Barth's nobility of spirit and purity of heart.

What contributed to the happy outcome of such a daring maxim was on the one hand the intimate friendship between the two men, on the other hand, and most of all, the way Blumhardt fully adapted himself to the situation. In whatever circumstances he found himself—small in scale or large, whether in state, church, or home—he would never "kick against the goads" when faced with wrong or awkward or maybe not exactly rational situations. Accepting everything willingly and with all due respect as from the hand of God, thus looking everywhere at the bright side of things enabled him to transform wrong situations into springs of blessing. Many an apparently hopeless entanglement brought to him as pastor would presently, as a result of his advice along these lines, find an almost effortless solution. So, too, Blumhardt entered joyfully and wholeheartedly into the situation facing him in Möttlingen. When it came to the pinch, though, he would show that he stood squarely on his own feet.

We have already heard and will hear more how faithfully he would keep Barth informed about everything going on in Möttlingen. Once, not quite happy with the way Barth put his oar in, he nevertheless wrote to him, "After all, they are *your* souls, too!" That occurred during the great struggle and at the beginning of the awakening. At that time Barth gleaned a good deal of information from various parishioners and also counseled them, while more and more avoiding talking matters over with Blumhardt. This, I believe, was the point when for the moment all the antidotes against the perils of such an incongruous two-pastor system—one of the two actually no longer living in and with the congregation—proved ineffective. Perhaps Barth would have been more unbiased in his evaluation of the new, independent paths Blumhardt was being led along if he had earlier been more aware of his friend's inner independence.

On the whole, however, this bond of friendship, with a single-minded concern for Möttlingen on both sides, was a great blessing for the village. The two ministers were held in such high regard by the parishioners that they were scarcely ever thought of as separate individuals but always as belonging together.

Let us now consider Blumhardt's beginnings in Möttlingen. It was heavy going at first. After such a brilliant proclamation of the Gospel—

now breathing poetic fire, now vigorous rhetoric—as the Möttlingen church had up to then heard, Blumhardt's preaching sounded almost too simple. People continued to slumber in church. And the few true and real listeners, the *Stunden* folk, must have felt that an indefinable something was lacking in his sermons; it was not quite the language they were used to. When we hear him speak of "fellow men" to the folk in Basel, when in front of those in Möttlingen he invokes the help of the "Most High," and so on, we already sense a stronger admixture of the ordinary, common way of thinking than these people were used to. Possibly, too, as with these expressions, Blumhardt's way of thinking, simple and concerned with simple things, made him appear to them as a not yet greatly "advanced" Christian; in short, compared to Barth, he was for a long time not esteemed very highly.

He on his part, as we can well imagine from what we know of his labor at Iptingen, loved these people very much and frequently attended their *Stunden* (meetings), which Barth had not done. But Blumhardt loved and visited the other parishioners too, ignoring the rigid division of the congregation into *Stunden* folk and others, and this attitude would again have made him suspect of not yet being very far "advanced" in his Christianity. His letters to Barth off and on contain this or that complaint about the situation in the congregation, but what continually breaks through is his way of seeing everything in the most favorable light, for the sake of fairness if nothing else. Thus on one occasion he writes to Barth:

> Thank God that at the moment I cannot say that things are *not* in good shape here. I am more content than ever, even though I am aware of all that is going on and has gone on among the young people. But who could ever make a completely clean sweep there! It is still true that Möttlingen is a Christian congregation! I meet little actual resistance, and I have to marvel at some things that I would not have expected to be so good. Well, dear brother, how about that, for a change?

Blumhardt and his wife soon made themselves at home among the families of the parish. Slowly, but all the more surely, his natural, brotherly, outgoing manner, unobtrusive yet warm, as we got to know it in Iptingen, had its effect. He took a lively interest in the village school, often substituting over longer periods for the ailing schoolmaster. He had a way of getting parents to see to their children's regular school attendance.

In his approach to the young people he generally followed fairly closely in Barth's footsteps, albeit independently and in accordance with his own individual gifts. At confirmation, he liked to hand each one confirmed, in addition to his Bible passage, a verse specially written for him, for example, this one to go with Luke 24:36:

> Your Savior, from the grave arisen,
> Is calling, "Peace be unto you!"
> He sets you free from Satan's prison
> And gives you rest and solace true.
> Take hold of his peace with conviction,
> Though rough and hard your path may be,
> Then in all trials and affliction
> You may be sure of victory.

Most effective in livening up the spiritual atmosphere was his way of reaching the young men. Barth had only been able to gather around himself the young *girls*; there seemed to be no hope of drawing the teenage boys to evening gatherings of an inner character. That is a very common situation, liable to give a somewhat feminine character to the ideal of Christian life held by ministers and their followers, which in turn serves to further alienate the men and boys.

How did Blumhardt manage to gather the young men around him? Simply by reading to them (in the schoolhouse) from the newspaper (the rector's paper quite possibly being the only one in the village) and discussing with them what he had read. There the genial and yet inwardly gathered Blumhardt was in his element. The young men came out of their shell, and a rich spiritual blessing, especially noticeable during the later awakening, flowed from these gatherings, which began and closed with a song and prayer. Everything—the spiritual, the natural, and the universally human—always merged into one for Blumhardt, and he had a way of making such talks about world events deep inner experiences. Later, during the revolutionary excitement of 1848 and the following years, these meetings (by then attended by older men too) greatly helped to quiet agitated minds.

Recurring epidemics of dysentery and typhus between 1838 and 1843 necessitated a special amount of pastoral care. Blumhardt's wife set up a regular soup kitchen in the rectory to supply those ill or endangered with suitable nourishment.

Alongside this work for and within the local congregation, opportunities for more far-reaching activities presently opened up for Blumhardt. He was, for example, appointed director of one of the two school conferences of the district. In that position he was able to put to good use the experience formerly gained as a teacher of "useful knowledge." Among the duties of this post he mentions two courses he taught in 1843, one on the teaching of German grammar in elementary schools and the other on the life of the apostle Paul.

Before long he plunged into literary work as well. Not unnaturally, the first impulse came from his zeal for mission and his lively contact with Barth. Thus he assisted him in editing the *Monatsblätter für die Missionsstunden* (Monthly Papers for Mission Meetings) and soon took over the editorship altogether. Later on, when Blumhardt had his hands more than full and his strength was taxed almost beyond endurance, the struggle to meet monthly deadlines was to require of him an almost superhuman effort. His laments about this, his pleas for leniency when copy could be got ready only at the very last moment, and his requests to be relieved of this burden would punctuate his letters to Barth with clocklike regularity every month.

Side by side with that, he continued the studies in mission history he had already begun in Iptingen. As a result the Calw Publishing Association, that is, Barth, entrusted him with the preparation of a *Handbuch für Missionsgeschichte und Missionsgeographie*[1] (Manual of Missionary History and Geography). What an undertaking it was, especially for Blumhardt, so averse to anything superficial, expecting everything to be just right, and heartily disliking words like "somewhat," "might be," or "could be." By that time, Christian mission had reached pretty well all the earth's coastlands and in places had even penetrated deep into the interior. Where, to start with, was he to find the required material for the *history* of these endeavors? The various mission societies had only just started to issue annual reports; there were very few biographies, and the accounts written by missionaries and other correspondents, though detailed and infused with wholehearted enthusiasm, were not always precise enough to answer all a historian's questions. That the main sources were written in English (partly also in French) did not bother him, but the wordiness of English reporting did, as did also the frequent difficulty of getting hold of the sources. The situation

1. Editors' Note: (Calw and Stuttgart: Calwer Verlagsverein, 1844).

was even worse when it came to geography—frequently the geography of regions no white person had ever visited, or at least inhabited, before the arrival of the missionaries. And quite often the very ablest missionaries, whose work had the most blessing, were not in the least interested in geography. The perplexity was further increased by the fact that the various European languages use the same alphabet letter to express completely different sounds. The sounds an Englishman expresses by spelling "Tanjore" and "Siam" a German would spell "Tänschur" and "Seiem." Then too, there was the problem of maps and where to find them!

The Tübingen School of Theology has clearly managed to endow many of its students with an extraordinary zest, power, and aptitude for writing. We have witnessed colossal achievements in this area particularly on the part of Swabian theologians, from both the right and the left, whether named Baur or Barth or otherwise. Blumhardt, too, was one of them. One thing he did gain from the tremendous undertaking assigned to him: It made him constantly concern himself with all peoples on earth, the poor, shepherdless human race, and this always in the name of Jesus. He was always looking for what the Lord might be intending and doing in order to bring these peoples under his shepherd's staff. So at his writing desk Blumhardt learned to stand before God as a priest on behalf of all His lost children.

At the same time another interest took hold of him. At long last efforts were afoot to replace with a better one the church hymnal imposed, to their great sorrow, on the hapless people of Württemberg by the Enlightenment. But there were dangers threatening both texts and music. As for the texts, the twin sisters Caution and Prudence seemed to have the say and to be intent on yet another watered-down product. As for the music, it was largely entrusted to musicians who were very fond of their own melodies.

Blumhardt was one of the many Württemberg clergymen who tried to confront this twofold danger, foremost among them Knapp (for the texts) and Palmer (for the music). Blumhardt took up the cudgels especially on behalf of the musical side of the proposed hymnbook. He collected the old melodies and threw himself into the study of harmony. He was enthusiastic about the rhythmic chorales and had his schoolchildren sing many of them. He also sought contact with fellow campaigners, for example, (partly through Barth) with Palmer. Above all, he loyally supported Dr. von Hauber (later Prelate von Hauber), a particularly active and successful champion of this cause. Among other things Blumhardt acquainted Dr. von Hauber with the lovely melody for "Come, thou bright and morning star," which has since become familiar to us. Blumhardt also published various smaller works. His labor for the intended goal was not without success, and he himself benefited greatly from it, for it provided a solid foundation for his delight in composing.

We know that this "new" Württemberg hymnal, in spite of various textual and musical shortcomings, turned out to be a model of its kind. It was usually the first to be consulted when soon afterwards a widespread eagerness for new church hymnals awoke. Wherever its principles of wise moderation and consideration of current linguistic taste have been unduly disregarded, the results have at times been regrettable.

Yet another task handed to Blumhardt by the Calw Publishing Association was the writing of a *Handbüchlein der Weltgeschichte für Schulen und Familien*[2] (Manual of World History for Schools and Families). While the history and geography of Christian mission had brought him into contact with all humanity in its present state, this new task put him in touch with its entire past. It was no easy assignment: an account of world history—its seventh edition was published in 1877— on 316 pages, 16 of which are taken up by the illustrations scattered throughout the text. His presentation is vivid and graphic, with such individual touches as young people are fond of. In its own way it is indisputably a masterpiece. Blumhardt starts out with the creation of 1) the earth, 2) sun, moon, and stars, 3) the realms of nature, and 4) humanity, and concludes with a chapter on mission. There are three main parts: ancient history (up to Odoacer), the Middle Ages (up to the Reformation), and modern history. The third part is divided into the periods of the Reformation, of religious wars, politics, and revolution. His Ancient History (Section VII [The Romans], Chapter 7 [Augustus—Christ]) closes with these words: "And yet God's plan for the rebirth of humanity is gradually gaining the victory, and the nations are being prepared for the day of Christ's advent in glory, until finally God will be all in all." The manual concludes (Modern History, Section V, Chapter on mission) as follows: "World history is approaching the point where in the name of Jesus every knee shall bend and every tongue confess that Jesus Christ is Lord, to the glory of God the Father. For 'the gospel of the kingdom will

---

2. Editors' Note: (Calw and Stuttgart: Calwer Verlagsverein, 1843).

be preached in the whole world as a testimony to all nations, and then the end will come' (Matt 24:14)."

Even though the modestly priced manual is readily available, I nevertheless want to quote here Blumhardt's introduction to its seventh edition (1877) to show how he spoke to young people and how he managed to present and arrange great thoughts clearly and understandably. Though the present introduction probably belongs to a later period than the one we are now concerned with, that actually fits it for a new purpose. We are now about to reach the foot of the mountain and to begin the ascent to that part of Blumhardt's life that has come to be of general significance, and his own words serve as a very fitting introduction to it. They exude his victorious confidence in, and certain hope of, a goal and conclusion of world history as holy as it will be glorious, but when they were written, that hope and confidence was already buttressed by Blumhardt's quiet awareness of being himself right in the front line of the struggle for that goal—untiring, undaunted, and not without success.

INTRODUCTION TO BLUMHARDT'S WORLD HISTORY

Dear reader, there is no need to tell you that things have not always been the way you now see them around you. Customs, religion, culture, ways of thinking, government—everything you perceive has taken a long time to become what it is, and you will understand that innumerable changes had to take place in the ages gone by for everything to assume its present form. The history of these changes humankind has undergone is called world history.

Of course, not everything humankind have ever done falls within the compass of world history, but only that which has influenced humanity as a whole. You must try to visualize the development of humankind as the gradual erection of a building. Its foundation having been laid by God's creation, one generation after the other has helped it on, of course with God always remaining in control as the master builder. But the work has proceeded in a slow and peculiar fashion. Many times one generation pulled down what another had built, and yet such wrecking in a way also pushed the construction forward. And by no means did everyone contribute to the great building, if I may put it that way, whether as bricklayers or stone cutters or anything like that. Most people, in fact, are idle onlookers, or if they do work, they only work for themselves. They are like that traveler who, when his attention was drawn to trees in blossom, replied, "What do I care for trees?" Or they restrict their activity to very narrow circles and exert no noticeable influence, either beneficial or harmful, beyond those circles. Or, to put it this way, they may slap onto the building material that will not stick but falls off again without leaving a trace. Of all such people world history has nothing to tell. Others may quietly add a stone here or there, but it remains unnoticed; hence they, too, are forgotten.

The main work in the construction of world history has been assigned to a visibly widening circle of peoples called "civilized." Each of them has its special gift for serving the whole. Among them arise individuals who add sizable blocks to the building; they are the heroes of world history. While themselves bearing the imprint of their own age, at the same time they so help it to unfold that their traces can be found even centuries later.

Of course, these heroes are not all of equal worth and importance. Some, although really not heroes, must be taken notice of as world heroes just because of their birth or position. In that sense world history is a somewhat upper-class affair, for what is lowly often gets overlooked. Others who stand at the pinnacle of world events impress us merely by their power, not by any moral dignity, or are noteworthy only for their ugly character and momentous misdeeds. There is, however, no lack of heroes one reads about with joy. Often, unfortunately, they are also bound to be heroes of warfare, for world history has to be called almost wholly a history of war; it cannot be otherwise, seeing it is after all dominated by the spirit of this world. Ever again God purifies the stifling atmosphere of the world by storms of war. Nevertheless we shall find history moving more and more toward general world peace, that is, the hour when Christ will have all his foes made a footstool for his feet. For history confirms wise Solomon's word, "The king's heart is in the hand of the Lord; he directs it like a watercourse wherever he pleases" (Prov 21:1). God's hidden finger guides everything toward the consummation of the blessed kingdom of his dear Son. The ways are frequently winding and yet straight; things often look very strange, but his lofty counsel does triumph in the end.

In this book, by the way, we cannot promise much more than stories from world history, and even in presenting those we have to restrict ourselves very much, for we must pay attention to the thread that runs through it all. What little we offer will yet be instructive. It may convince you that every person, though his name may not appear in history, can and ought to do something to help build the house of humankind. And since in the end that building is to be a temple wherein God's glory dwells, I only wish that this

> book might help you to become living stones or even pillars in
> that temple (1 Pet 2:5; Rev 3:12).

Existing letters show that Blumhardt also had a hand in the most popular production of the Calw Publishing Association, the *Jugendblätter* (Papers for Young People). For example, he contributed a lengthy article about the properties and effects of light and another about the principles of movement. He did not find that too easy and voiced complaints about the lack of resources (partly English ones) available to him for improving his own knowledge of these matters. Frequently, too, the illustrations required caused him headaches, and at times the text pretty much had to adapt itself to the pictures available.

A circumstance not to be overlooked altogether made Blumhardt's work for the Calw Publishing Association hard: Barth was the unrelenting chief editor. In some respects Blumhardt was happy to learn from his friend's writing skill, whereas Barth did perhaps not sufficiently appreciate someone else's way of working. Blumhardt submitted willingly, though not without some anguish, to the strict demands of his friend. In line with his above-mentioned principle of "writing as much as possible," Barth required that everything the Calw Publishing Association put out at that time 1) be produced fast, 2) be inexpensive, and 3) because of that, be brief. Only after insistent, well-founded pleading was Blumhardt granted an extension of the one-year deadline he had been set for completion of his *Handbüchlein der Weltgeschichte*. In the beginning Barth had stipulated that Blumhardt's account of *world* history was to be no larger than his own (Barth's) history of *Württemberg* and no more expensive than the above-mentioned *Bible Stories*—a subject matter that ensured immeasurably greater sales and correspondingly lower production costs. Here, too, in response to Blumhardt's pleading, Barth did somewhat soften his strict demand, while Blumhardt, albeit against his own conviction, yielded on other points.

Where he felt this kind of restriction most severely was with his *Handbuch für Missionsgeschichte und Missionsgeographie*, it being not an extract from material compiled by others, but in some respects itself a compilation. It was somewhat later, at the beginning of the sixties, that the chief editor's strictness hit Blumhardt hardest, when he, in any case overburdened with work, had to get out a revised third edition of this manual. With enormous diligence he collected the material, by then hugely increased, from here, there and everywhere, and arranged for it to be published in three smallish volumes. If completed as originally conceived, the work would quite likely have become an incomparably more valuable component of our scientific literature on mission than it is even in its present abridged form of only two volumes, and the price increase would have been outweighed by its enhanced value, also in the eyes of the public.

It follows from these observations that Blumhardt is not quite himself when writing for the Calw Publishing Association and that in what he wrote for it (with the exception of the periodic publications) we do not fully get to know his character as an author. But it also makes it plain that these labors helped him greatly to develop a concise and at the same time clear style.

With the exception of the *Monatsblätter* (Monthly Papers), which he edited for a longer time, it was mainly during his first five years at Möttlingen that he was engaged in these literary labors. Precisely at the times of fiercest struggle they claimed his attention the most, so that he had to make use of every minute. This almost struck him as a divine providence, since it left him no time for brooding or indulging in fantasies, had he ever been so inclined.

During his first four or so years in Möttlingen, by the way, his constitution was extremely delicate, and regularly every summer he succumbed to a fatigue that virtually did not let him take on any tasks beyond what his actual ministry required. Besides, his house began to come alive with little boys and girls, whom he gave loving care as a faithful husband and father, especially at night.

A most competent witness [his wife] gives the following account of him at that time: "Blissfully and busily he gave himself to his pastoral duties and literary tasks, somewhat as a bright schoolboy applies himself to his work."

Yet, as he himself has told, in the depth of his soul dwelt a profound melancholy, a poignant longing to be more active than seemed possible for him then for the kingdom of God, which in his eyes lay in so wretched a state.

Second Section

9

The Illness of Gottliebin Dittus

FROM WHAT WE HAVE considered so far, we would expect the further development of Blumhardt's life to be extremely fruitful and blessedly effective. One could hope for experiences similar to those in Iptingen, possibly on an even larger scale. In addition, he had prospects of serving the kingdom of God in many different ways as a writer. But the events he was about to be thrust into turned his life and work in a completely unexpected direction. The powers that often influence our lives more than we suspect were revealed to him most remarkably, but he could not expect his contemporaries to give that the notice one would wish, nor did he receive it. And yet the overarching might of the Lord, to which he clung, came close to him in a way so powerful and vivid as scarcely anybody had experienced for a long time. At the request of his ecclesiastical superiors he reported these events to them in a memorandum titled *History of Gottliebin Dittus's Illness*.[1] In his own memory they lived on as "the struggle."

Before long, through no fault of the church authorities and completely against Blumhardt's own wish, a number of partially distorted copies of the memorandum began to circulate publicly. That compelled Blumhardt, who had not even kept the original, to bring out himself a carefully edited lithographed set of 100 copies. He prefaced this "manuscript" by stating that it was not his wish to see it spread around any

---

1. Editors' Note: Johann Christoph Blumhardt, *Die Krankheitsgeschichte der Gottliebin Dittus*, ed. by Gerhard Schärfer (Göttingen: Vandenhoeck & Ruprecht, 1982).

further and asking readers to kindly bear this carefully considered wish in mind.

I, too, am going to respect that wish; in relating the history of that illness I shall touch on all the horrible manifestations of uncanny forces only as much as is necessary to demonstrate the Lord's victories over them. Going further than that in complying with Blumhardt's request would, I feel, not be justified. For one thing, it would not be right to put readers of this biography at too great a disadvantage compared to the many who are already acquainted with his report. For another, right to the end of his life, and indeed more and more as time went on, Blumhardt regarded his experiences during the struggle as so significant for the Christian Church that I feel certain he would agree to my making public now, after his death, their essential content. He himself, referring to the Lord's word, "What I whisper in your ear, proclaim from the housetops," commented that there are often times in the kingdom of God when something can only be whispered in the ear, to be followed by other days when the same things must be proclaimed from the housetops. In a sense we even owe it to Blumhardt's good name. Mere general, mysterious hints envelop the experiences he had in an apocryphal twilight; an accurate account, on the other hand, replaces the twilight with the overwhelming impression of a great reality.

As a further introduction to this part of our biography, we include here at least the gist of Blumhardt's preface to the memorandum he addressed to his ecclesiastical superiors:

> In submitting the following report to the greatly esteemed high consistory of the church, I feel urged to state that until now I have not spoken to anybody about my experiences with such boldness and candor. Even my best friends look at me askance and have put me into the unhappy position of having to keep complete silence toward them, for it is as though they felt in danger if they so much as heard about these things. At the same time, I owe them thanks for constantly trembling for me during the time of my struggle. Since by far the largest part of it has up to now remained an undisclosed secret I could have taken with me to the grave, I was completely free to select what I pleased for this report; it would have been easy for me to give an account that would not have offended any reader. That, however, I could not bring myself to do. Even though at almost every paragraph I had to ask myself with trembling if it was not rash and imprudent to tell everything just as it was, time and again an inner voice would say, "Out with it!"

So I dare to do it, and I do it in the name of Jesus, who is the victor. I considered it my responsibility to be honest and frank, especially in this matter, and not only toward the highly esteemed high consistory of the church, which has every right to expect frankness from me, but also toward my Lord Jesus, for whose cause alone I had to take up the struggle. As I speak out unreservedly for the first time, I have the understandable wish that the information given here be regarded as private, as when close friends share a secret.

There is a second request I may be permitted to make: Would the esteemed readers please read the whole report several times before forming a judgment. Meanwhile I put my trust in him who has the hearts of humanity in his power.

However the verdicts may turn out, I rest assured in the knowledge of having spoken the unvarnished truth and in the rock-like certainty that Jesus is victor.

On p. 51 of his *Vertheidigungsschrift gegen Herrn Dr. de Valenti*[2] Blumhardt makes some comments that throw further light on his report:

Since one has long since got used to stories of demonic manifestations, particularly clairvoyance, not coming to a sensible conclusion, one could, of course, say that I should have been more prudent and left out of my report whatever might be interpreted as unbounded self-conceit. But I was well aware of all this, and people should not think I was overly honest out of sheer stupidity. If I had to give an account—and that I had been asked to do—I was not going to twist the truth by presenting the case as simply one more demonic vagary or fraud, such as have so often been seen and heard in these last decades. I would have been ashamed to be regarded as one of those adventurous freaks who so often foolishly play around with happenings and appearances from the other world. I approached the matter in question in the fear of God, and if it took on a much more serious character than any similar occurrences, I had to make that clear to my superiors—to justify myself, if for no other reason. Once I put anything in writing . . . I had to write down everything, so I related openly and unreservedly how I had reasoned and acted. In this way, too, I could all the more confidently wait for the outcome; if I was wrong or in error or conceited, my superiors should know it and be in a position to judge it. For I have no wish to set up a barricade of silent obstinacy, as certain false trends and demonic spiritual cliques do

2. Editors' Note: Christoph Blumhardt, (Reutlingen: Kurtz, 1850) [*Apologia against Dr. de Valenti*].

these days, where dupes scheme all sorts of things in secret and let no one who is not yet fully one of them peer into their clandestine doings. My cause was to come to the light and was to be examined in the light, but of course only by my superiors and as if under a seal of confession. To them I would tell it but for the time being to no one else. And I kept my word too.

In Möttlingen, near the edge of the village, there stands a house of poor appearance, recognizable now just as it was then by a window shutter bearing the weather-worn inscription:

> O man, think on eternity,
> Use well the time still granted thee,
> For judgment will come speedily.

In the spring of 1840 a poor family by the name of Dittus, consisting of five brothers and sisters, moved into the ground-floor apartment of this house. There were two brothers: Andreas (at the time of his death farm manager in Bad Boll) and Johann Georg (half-blind, still living at Bad Boll, where he is known as Hans, but at that time in service outside Möttlingen), and three sisters: Katharina (still living at Bad Boll and known as *Base* ["cousin"]), Anna Maria, and finally Gottliebin, born October 13, 1815, the main figure of the following account. Their parents, especially their spiritually gifted mother, had been deeply grounded Christians, nurtured by the devout spirit of pastors Machtolf and Gross.

Gottliebin, inwardly very much awake and capable of deeper insight, had been Dr. Barth's favorite pupil. Her sharing in composing verse at his spinning socials prepared her for writing fine, spirit-filled songs later on. She on her part cherished all her life a fresh and inspiring memory of that precious man of God, Barth. (From Bad Boll Blumhardt would still write to Barth: "Nothing counts for her apart from you.") Off and on from infancy she experienced uncanny things, apparently springing from a design to make her a central figure in the magic practices rampant among the people, but in every case her strong fear of God frustrated such a design. Subsequently, she contracted various strange illnesses, on account of which she had to leave—often temporarily and finally for good—the places where she was in service and was actually well liked. Barth used his many connections to consult eminent physicians on her behalf, as a result of which she recovered fairly well from her last ailment, a kidney disease.

Inexplicably, she felt just as much attracted to Barth's successor, Blumhardt, as she felt repelled by him. At his first sermon she had to fight a desire to scratch his eyes out. On the other hand, Blumhardt could be sure of finding her wherever she had a chance of hearing an uplifting word from him, for instance, every week at the parish branch of Unterhaugstett, some distance away, even though her ailments, especially the fact that one leg was shorter than the other, made walking very difficult for her. At the same time she displayed a very marked, hangdog kind of timidity, which, as is often enough the case, seemed to mask exaggerated self-assertion and defensive closedness. She made a downright unpleasant impression on Blumhardt, and not only on him.

No sooner had the three sisters and one brother moved into their new apartment than it struck Gottliebin that she seemed to see and hear a number of uncanny things in the house. The other family members noticed it too. On the very first day, when saying grace at table, at the words "Come, Lord Jesus, be our guest, and let all thou givest in mercy be blessed," she suffered an attack and fell unconscious to the floor. In bedroom, living room, and kitchen recurring noises of banging and shuffling were heard, which often terrified the poor occupants and also upset the people living upstairs. All of them, however, were afraid to let any of it come to public notice.

Gottliebin also had peculiar things happen to her own person. At night, for instance, she would feel her hands forcibly placed one above the other; she also had visions of figures, small lights, etc. Her reports make it clear that her later states of possession had already begun then. From then on she had something repulsive and inexplicable in her behavior and a forbidding manner, which put many people off. But since nobody was greatly concerned about the poor orphan family and Gottliebin kept absolutely quiet about her experiences, it was just allowed to go on. Only little by little, and that through rumors, did Blumhardt hear about the matter, and he took no notice of it.

Gottliebin finally came to Blumhardt in his rectory in the fall of 1841, when her nightly trials and torments were getting worse and worse, but she spoke of them in such general terms that he could not make head or tail of it, nor could he say much to her that was helpful. She did of her own free will confess various things from her former life, in the hope that such a confession would deliver her from her trials.

From December 1841 until the following February she suffered from erysipelas of the face and lay dangerously ill. During her whole illness Blumhardt was not inclined to visit her often, as he was put off by her behavior. As soon as she caught sight of him, she would look to one side, nor would she answer his greeting. When he prayed, she would separate her previously folded hands; she paid no attention whatever to his words and seemed almost unconscious, though before and after his visits she was not like that. At the time Blumhardt, and others, too, regarded her as self-willed, self-righteous, and spiritually proud, and he would rather stay away than expose himself to embarrassment.

She did, however, have a faithful friend and adviser in her understanding and sympathetic physician, Dr. Späth in Möttlingen, the only one to whom she poured out everything, her spooky experiences included. He was unable to cure a strange ailment (breast bleeding), which she also confided only to him, but it vanished as soon as Blumhardt took her into his pastoral care (though he knew nothing either of the complaint or of the healing).

Not until April 1842, when the uncanny happenings had gone on for more than two years, did Blumhardt learn more details from the tormented girl's relatives, who came to him for advice. Help was badly needed, for the banging noises were becoming so obnoxious and loud that they could be heard all over the neighborhood—just as though carpenters were at work. Blumhardt was told that Gottliebin often saw the figure of a Möttlingen woman who had died two years previously; she would carry a dead child in her arms. Gottliebin said that this woman (whose name she was careful not to reveal and only divulged some time later) always stood at a certain spot before her bed; at times the woman would move toward her and say repeatedly, "I just want to find rest" or "Give me a paper; then I won't come any more" or something of the sort. Blumhardt tells:

> I was asked whether it would be all right to find out more by questioning the apparition. My advice was that Gottliebin was on no account to enter into conversation with it, all the more since there was no knowing how much self-deception might be mixed in. It was certain, I said, that one could land oneself in awful tangles and follies by becoming involved with the spirit world. Gottliebin should pray earnestly and trustingly; then the whole thing would peter out of its own accord. As one of her sisters was away in domestic service, her brother was not much at home, and it was not enough for just her other sister to be there, a woman friend of hers at my request dared to sleep with her, to help take her

mind off those things if possible. She, too, heard the banging, and at length, guided by a glimmer of light, they discovered beneath a board above the bedroom entrance half a sheet of paper with writing on it, but it was so smeared over with soot as to be undecipherable. By the side of it they found three coins (German crowns—one of them minted in 1828) and various bits of paper, likewise covered with soot.

From then on everything was quiet. "The spook business has come to an end," Blumhardt wrote to Barth. A fortnight later, though, the thumping started anew. Betrayed by a tiny flicker of flame behind the stove, more objects of a similar kind were discovered and also various powders, but an analysis by the district physician and an apothecary in Calw proved inconclusive.

Meanwhile, the banging kept getting more and more scandalous; it went on day and night but reached a peak when Gottliebin was in the room. Along with some other curious persons, Dr. Späth stayed in the apartment overnight twice, and what he experienced was worse than expected. The affair became more and more of a sensation, affecting the surrounding countryside and even drawing travelers from farther away. Then, to put an end to the scandal if possible, Blumhardt decided to take a hand in the matter himself and undertake a thorough investigation. Together with the mayor, Kraushaar, who was a carpet manufacturer and a level-headed, sober, and God-fearing man, and several village councilors—six to eight men altogether—he made secret arrangements for an inspection during the night of June 9, 1842. A relative of Gottliebin, Mose Stanger, a young married man of sound Christian insight and generally of good reputation (he was to be Blumhardt's most faithful support later on) was sent in advance, followed at about ten o'clock in the evening by the others, who posted themselves two by two in and around the house.

As soon as Blumhardt entered the house, he was met by two powerful bangs from the bedroom, followed shortly by several more. All sorts of sounds, blows, and knocks were heard, mostly in the bedroom, where Gottliebin was lying clothed on the bed. The other watchers outside and on the floor above heard it all. After a while they all gathered in the ground-floor apartment, convinced that all they heard must originate here. The tumult seemed to grow, especially when Blumhardt suggested a verse from a hymn and spoke a few words of prayer. Within three hours they heard twenty-five blows, directed at a certain spot in the bedroom. They were powerful enough to cause a chair to jump, the windows to clatter, and sand to trickle from the ceiling. People living at a distance were reminded of New Year's Eve firecrackers. At the same time there were other noises of varying degrees of loudness, as of a light drumming of finger tips or of a more or less regular tapping about. The sounds seemed to come mainly from beneath the bed, but groping for them there did not turn up anything. They tried with light and without it, but it made no difference. It was noticed, though, that the bangs in the bedroom were loudest when everybody was in the living room, and underneath the door one could always distinctly identify the spot on which they fell. They examined everything most thoroughly, without, however, finding any explanation at all. Blumhardt goes on to tell:

> Finally at about one o'clock, while we were all in the living room, Gottliebin called me to her and asked if, should she see a certain apparition, she might be permitted to identify her, for she could already hear a sound of shuffling. That I refused point blank. By that time I had *heard* more than enough and did not want to run the risk of having so many people also *see* things that could not be explained. I asked Gottliebin to get up, declared the investigation at an end and saw to it that she found accommodation somewhere else. So we left the house. Gottliebin's half-blind brother told us later that he still saw and heard various things after our departure. The remarkable thing is that just on that night the disturbance was at its height.

The next day, a Friday, there was a church service; afterwards Gottliebin went to visit her old home. Half an hour later a big crowd had gathered in front of the house, and Blumhardt was notified by messenger that Gottliebin was quite unconscious and close to death. He hurried there and found Gottliebin lying on the bed, completely rigid, the skin on her head and arms burning hot and trembling; she seemed to be suffocating. The room was crammed full of people. A doctor from a neighboring village, who happened to be in Möttlingen, had also rushed to the spot; he tried various things to revive her but went away shaking his head. Half an hour later Gottliebin came to. She confided to Blumhardt that after church she had again seen in the bedroom the figure of the woman with the dead child and had fallen to the ground unconscious.

In the afternoon the place was searched again. A number of strange objects were found that appeared to be connected with sorcery, for example, tiny bones. These Blumhardt packed up and, accompanied by the mayor, took them to the head doctor of the district, Dr. Kayser in Calw. They told him the whole story, and in due course he identified the bones as those of birds.

Blumhardt was above all concerned to quell the hubbub for good. He got a place for Gottliebin first with a woman cousin and later with her male cousin, Johann Georg Stanger, village councilor and father of the above-mentioned Mose. He was also Gottliebin's godfather and had a large family (four grown-up daughters and two sons) all of whom, being believing Christians, now felt real sympathy for Gottliebin; they also observed strictest secrecy. Besides, Blumhardt asked Gottliebin, if at all possible, not to enter her old home for the time being; in fact it was not until the middle of the following year that she moved back there. There was to be no further to-do about the matter, and so strict was he in warding off any commotion that he would not even let Gottliebin's brother, Hans, visit her. His plan was to call on her from time to time very discreetly in the company of the mayor and a few other sensible men, to see how things would go.

Blumhardt gives the following account of his concerns at that time and the measures he took:

> I had a special dread of manifestations of clairvoyance, which so often stir up an unpleasant sensation and up till now have done so little good. Since a mysterious and dangerous field was opening up before me, I could only commit the matter to the Lord in my personal prayers, asking him to preserve me and others from all the follies and aberrations one might be tempted to become involved in. When the matter took a more serious turn, we—the mayor, Mose, and I—would meet in my study for special prayers and talks, and I can truly say that that kept us all in a sober frame of mind, which alone could promise a happy ending.

Those special gatherings proved a great blessing to Blumhardt and his two friends. In his *Vertheidigungsschrift* (p. 42) he says:

> I shall never forget the fervent prayers for wisdom, strength, and help that those men sent up to God. Together we searched through the whole of Scripture, strengthening and exhorting each other not to go any further than Scripture led us. It never entered our minds to perform miracles, but it grieved us deeply to find that the devil still had so much power and that satanic nets no one was aware of were spread over humanity [this in reference to the following events]. Our heartfelt compassion went out not only to

the poor person whose misery we saw before us—no, we came before God with cries and lamentations on behalf of the millions that are turned away from God and entangled in the secret snares of magic. It was our prayer that at least in this case God would give us the victory and let Satan be trodden under our feet.

It took weeks for the uproar in the area to die down. Many strangers came and wanted to visit the house; some even wanted to spend the night in it to convince themselves that the current rumors were true. But the house was placed under the watchful custody of the village policeman, who happened to live opposite, and Blumhardt resolutely refused requests such as the one made by three Catholic priests from nearby in Baden, who wanted to spend several hours in it at night. Little by little things quieted down, and the village remained unaware of all the subsequent events, though occasionally this or that might come to somebody's notice. Blumhardt relates: "Generally speaking, throughout the long time of struggle I met with an earnest, reverent, and expectant sympathy, quiet and unspoken, from this congregation, which after all was on a higher level spiritually than many others. That made it much easier for me to hold out but at the same time rendered it impossible for me to stop without having really seen it through."

The din in the house continued; it came to an end only when the revival began, early in 1844. Yet before long, similar noises started up in Gottliebin's new dwelling. Blumhardt was told that whenever they were heard, she would presently fall into violent convulsions that kept increasing in strength and duration, so that after an attack lasting four or five hours she would barely have five minutes of rest. Once, when the convulsions were so violent that they forced the bedstead out of joint, Dr. Späth, who was present, said in tears, "Leaving a sick person in such a state—one would think there is no one in this village to care for souls in need! This certainly isn't anything natural!"

Blumhardt took this to heart and visited Gottliebin more often. He recounts: "Once, when Dr. Späth and I were with her, her whole body shook; every muscle of her head and arms was glowing hot and trembling, though otherwise rigid and stiff, and foam issued from her mouth. She had been lying in this state for several hours, and the doctor, who had never seen anything like it, seemed to be at his wits' end. Then suddenly she came to and was able to sit up and drink water. One could scarcely believe it was the same person."

Just at that time a traveling Moravian *diaspora* preacher, Weiz from Königsfeld, dropped in at the rectory. He visited the sick girl, who was known to him from earlier days, and on taking leave, he exhorted Blumhardt with uplifted finger, "Do not forget your pastoral duty!" So here was yet another challenge to care for souls in need. "What am I to do?" thought Blumhardt. "I am doing what every pastor does. What more can I do?"

Soon afterward, on a Sunday evening, Blumhardt again visited the sick girl; several of her woman friends were present. Sitting a little distance away, he silently watched the horrible convulsions. She twisted her arms and bent her whole body into a high curve, and foam issued from her mouth. Blumhardt recounts:

> After what had happened it was clear to me that something demonic was at work here. It pained me to think that no remedy or counsel was forthcoming in so horrible a matter. As I pondered this, I was gripped by a kind of wrath; it suddenly came over me, and I can only confess: It was an inspiration from above, even though I was unaware of it then. With firm steps I went up to her ["I sprang forward," he says elsewhere], grasped her cramped hands (which I should not have done, for it hurt her afterwards) in order to hold them together if possible and loudly called the unconscious girl's name into her ear, saying, "Put your hands together and pray: 'Lord Jesus, help me!' We have seen long enough what the devil does; now let us see what the Lord Jesus can do!" After a few moments she woke up, prayed those words after me, and all convulsions ceased, to the great astonishment of those present. This was the decisive moment, thrusting me with irresistible force into action for the cause. It had never occurred to me until then, and even then it was an immediate impulse that guided me. The impression of that impulse has stayed with me so strongly that later it was often my only reassurance, convincing me that what I undertook was not of my own choice or presumption. At that time I could not possibly have imagined that it would escalate so dreadfully.

As Blumhardt recognized more and more clearly later on, this was the turning point of his life. Instead of facing these sinister occurrences with an attitude of indifference or dull resignation, he dared to turn deliberately and directly to God the Most High or to Jesus, who is exalted to God's right hand, and from on high the Lord had straightway answered him with deeds.

From now on Blumhardt was a different person; he was no longer just that amiable, almost virginal figure that the friends of his younger years had known. A victorious spirit from on high had descended on him and was to remain with him. He had experienced the gracious, powerful, and purposeful intervention of the Savior, as he had read about in the Bible when he was a child. From now until his death, in fact, more and more as time went on, Blumhardt recognized how important it is for the kingdom of God—indeed, how indispensable for its ultimate victory—that for once the kingdom of darkness and its influences suffer defeat. Those spiritual enemies have managed to veil the name of God and his Son Jesus Christ from people so much that the very question of God's and Christ's existence or non-existence has become a subject of learned inquiry. If the cause of God's kingdom is to move forward, those enemies must for once be made the footstool under his feet. In the course of the struggle Blumhardt recognized more and more that it is a question of power, a matter of struggle, a task of faith. He came to see that the depth to which divine redemption does or does not penetrate into people's lives ultimately depends on how much faith and how much faithful longing there is in humanity.

We who are tracing the course of his life are likewise standing at a memorable turning point. Maybe we have become fond of the man and look for great things from such a lovable figure as he is, say, that he might go on to sow seeds of blessing, with the promise of a rich harvest. But believe it or not, such excellent persons, such excellent "great" Christians, though indeed often doing a great deal to save individual souls, sometimes accomplish very little for the great progress of God's kingdom on earth, so little that it could make one weep. Their impact fades away like the rings caused by throwing a pebble into water; the centuries roll on just as before, while the wonderful goal of a time of glory (such as foretold in the prophets) or of the return of the Lord Jesus (as promised in the New Testament) remains as distant and unattainable as ever. What we must hope and wish for is that we may experience once again the Lord Jesus himself breaking in. Surely we may say that it was heaven's wish and design that Jesus continue to intervene in response to the faith of his followers, the way he did in the days of the apostles. For many centuries such intervention has noticeably receded into the background, and yet it ought to be a chief goal of our hopes and longings. Jesus will break in anew. He alone moves things forward; he will bring them to a mighty, great, and glorious conclusion.

We are standing at a turning point. From now on in this biography the person of Blumhardt will be eclipsed, almost unnoticeably and yet unmistakably, by someone else—the Lord Jesus himself. In what follows we shall often see not so much the deeds of the man Blumhardt as deeds the Lord Jesus carried out through him. Now, after Blumhardt's death, we may be more open to this insight. Our desire not to make too much of Blumhardt is now overshadowed by a concern not to undervalue great deeds accomplished by the Lord Jesus. With childlike straightforwardness Blumhardt once put into words what he saw to be his own part in all this: "At that time the Lord Jesus stood at the door and knocked, and I opened it to him."

I would like to pursue this thought of his and cast more light on the Bible passage he was referring to: "Behold, I stand at the door and knock; if any one hears my voice and opens the door, I will come in to him" (Rev 3:20). Blumhardt did not want to rob these words of the tender meaning they are usually invested with for the needs of the individual human heart, but it did not altogether satisfy his own heart, which "hungered for deeds" (a phrase from a sermon he prepared as a seminary student). These words stand at a place of great significance; they are as it were a last call, the Lord's farewell call to his church, which is close to falling asleep (see the letters to the churches in Revelation). They occupy a place similar to the last words of the Old Testament prophet Malachi. As Blumhardt puts it: "Is this not a call of Him who wants to come again? Behold, I stand at the door; I am already in position at the door. I want to come into your human life, want to break into your "reality" with the whole power of grace given me by the Father, to prepare my full advent. I am knocking, but you are so engrossed in your goods and chattels, your political quarrels and theological wrangles that you do not hear my voice." Understanding the passage in this way, Blumhardt could thus say, "In that hour I heard his knocking, and I opened the door to him." He gave the Lord a chance to intervene himself. It is because the following reports, (parts of which are very unedifying), illustrate that tangible, powerful, and gracious breaking in of the Lord Jesus that the reader is asked to put up with them. Precisely in those circumstances the Lord's help showed itself. We now continue our account of the illness, which, far from ending, as one might have hoped, is actually just beginning in earnest.

After being given the help we heard about, the sick girl enjoyed several hours of peace. At ten o'clock in the evening Blumhardt was called again. The convulsions had returned in an exceedingly horrible way. He again bade her pray aloud, "Lord Jesus, help me!" Once more, the convulsions ceased immediately, and when new attacks wanted to come, they were frustrated in the same way, until after three hours she exclaimed, "Now I feel quite well." From then until nine o'clock the following evening she remained peaceful. When Blumhardt called on her then, accompanied by his two friends, whom he on principle took along whenever he knew her to be alone, new attacks began. The sick girl raged at him and tried to strike him, though without ever actually touching him. At the end she plunked her hands down on the bed, and it seemed as if some kind of spiritual power came streaming out through her fingertips. So it continued for some time, with breaks of perhaps three days each, until finally the convulsions petered out and Blumhardt, uttering a deeply felt "Thank God," again thought it was the end.

Concerning Gottliebin's attitude all through the time of struggle Blumhardt comments: "The remarkable thing was that the patient's spirit was actually never affected by the attacks. When she was free, she remained the same clear, sincere Christian, clinging trustingly to the Lord, and did not require the least inner help. Once the attacks, whether momentary or longer-lasting, had passed, she was once more in full possession of all her faculties and showed such good sense, circumspection, and insight into the divine as few Christians possess."

Before long, a new distress came over Gottliebin. Sounds as of tapping fingers were again heard around her; a sudden blow on the chest made her sink back, and she once more caught sight of the female figure she had seen in her old home. This time she told Blumhardt the person's name. It was that of a widow who had died two years previously, and Blumhardt well remembered how he had tried to give her inner help. She had been much given to sighing and longed for peace but did not find it. Once, when Blumhardt had quoted to her Schade's fine hymn, "Peace, the highest good of all," she asked him for it and copied it. Tormented by severe pangs of conscience on her deathbed, she confessed to Blumhardt some heavy sins, but it did not give her a great deal of peace. Blumhardt tells:

> When I got there, I heard the tapping. Gottliebin lay quietly in bed; suddenly it was as if something entered into her, and her whole body started to move. I said a few words of prayer and mentioned the name of Jesus. She straightway began to roll her eyes, pulled her hands apart and spoke in a voice immediately recognizable

as not hers—not so much by its sound as by its expression and manner of speaking. It cried, "I cannot bear that name!" We all shuddered. I had never yet heard anything like it and in my heart called on God to give me wisdom and prudence and above all to preserve me from untimely curiosity. In the end, firmly resolved to limit myself to what was absolutely necessary and to let my own feelings tell me if it went too far, I dared put a few questions, addressing them to that woman. It went somewhat like this:

"Have you no peace in the grave?"

"No."

"Why not?"

"It is the reward for my deeds."

Assuming within myself that the voice I heard belonged to that woman, I continued, "Have you not confessed everything?"

"No, I murdered two children and buried them in a field."

"And don't you know where to get help? Can you not pray?"

"I cannot pray."

"Don't you know Jesus, who can forgive sins?"

"I cannot bear hearing that name."

"Are you alone?"

"No."

"Who is with you?"

Hesitatingly, but then with a rush, the voice replied, "The most wicked of all."

In this fashion the conversation went on for a while. The speaker accused herself of sorcery, on account of which she was bound to the devil. Seven times already, she said, she had gone out of somebody but would do that no more. I asked her if I might pray for her, and this, after some hesitation, she permitted me to do. At the end I made it clear to her that she could not remain in Gottliebin's body. She appeared to be plaintively pleading but then became defiant. However, I commanded her to come out, though not in the name of Jesus (this I did not dare for a long time). The scene quickly changed: Gottliebin forcefully thumped her hands down on the bed, and with that the possession seemed to have come to an end.

We can imagine that in those days the question whether Blumhardt might, or even should, enter into at least a limited conversation with such a spirit was earnestly pondered and discussed in that circle of friends—

Blumhardt, the mayor, and Mose. Since they were always guided by the Bible in such considerations, they could not help being led to the passage starting at Luke 8:27, especially verse 30. In his *Blätter aus Bad Boll*[3] (Papers from Bad Boll) Blumhardt later (in Nos. 39–42, 1874) discussed at length and in a most interesting way, on the basis of his own experiences, Luke's story of how the possessed Geresene was healed. We owe it to him to quote here the part that serves to illuminate his approach (*Blätter aus Bad Boll*, No. 41):

> Instead of departing immediately, as was usually the case, the demons voice a request. Luke reports that what they feared more than anything was having to depart into the abyss. It is evident that Jesus does not respond harshly. Having come to redeem the living and the dead, to the widest extent then possible, he, as their future judge, cannot stand there as one insensitive to the need of the dead. Hence he shows himself approachable, so to speak, and stops to listen. He asks the unclean spirit, who represents all the others, "What is your name?" He evidently puts this question not to the possessed man, but to the spirit speaking out of him; he wants to know what name the spirit had when alive.
>
> A question like that cannot be directed to non-human beings—assuming that somebody might imagine the demons to be such. There would be no purpose in that at all. What could the name of non-human beings possibly mean, seeing that it would tell us nothing about them as persons? Therefore this question put by the Lord is the strongest evidence that many of the demons that possess human beings must be disembodied souls. But why does the Lord want to know the name? Does he perhaps want to show thereby a peaceable or even compassionate attitude, or at least an interest in the demon? At any rate, that's how it is with us. When we ask somebody for his name, it means that we do not want to treat him as just a vague, "nameless" anybody; it means that we want to show him kindness.
>
> Now one could ask whether Jesus did not know the demon's name anyhow. Indeed he did, and yet assuming—as might after all be possible—that the Lord had something favorable for the demon in mind (whatever it might be), he must have been interested in learning his name from the demon himself. It is, of course, puzzling that the demon was to reveal his name and thereby his identity in front of all those present. But could this not have had some

---

3. Editors' Note: *Blätter aus Bad Boll, für seine Freunde*, 5 vols., ed. by Paul Ernst (Göttingen: Vandenhoeck & Ruprecht, 1968–1974). [*Papers from Bad Boll*] Cited throughout as *Blätter aus Bad Boll*, issue number, and year.

further significance? So we see that there is food for much thought here and that a lot can be read between the lines, this being more obvious to someone with experience in this area.

So that spirit could have told his name but did not do so, possibly thereby showing that he was still inwardly bound or unbroken. In this way he cut himself off from whatever further consideration the Lord might have been glad to show him in front of those present, to let them see how all-embracing his redemptive urge was. The demon's answer was, "Legion, for there are many of us." This reply, though rather indefinite, was yet likely to arouse further sympathy, since it made it clear that there were many in the same need. At the same time it brings it home to us that there is something mysterious, indeed incomprehensible and horrible, about states of possession such as this one. We get a glimpse of thousands of spirits either looking outright for shelter in a human being or lying in subjection to the power of darkness, which compels them to torment the living.

It was, I think, only shortly before writing this that Blumhardt, after peculiar experiences, arrived at the above conclusion, namely that Jesus' inquiring after the name of the spirit troubling the Geresene points to the spirit's *human* origin. But at the point in Blumhardt's life where we are now standing, that is, at the *beginning* of his experiences with demons, he derived just this one lesson from the text: that there can be emergency cases where an absolute avoidance of a conversation or questioning is neither commanded nor advisable. As everybody can see who takes Blumhardt at his word, it was his very own experience—a surprising and unpleasant one—that made him realize he was dealing with the soul of a departed person. He was not one for making up hypotheses. A certain critic, theorizing that Blumhardt first constructed the above hypothesis and then made it his basis of operations, upbraided him for "the unchristian character of his hypothesis." It would have been more consistent for him to simply charge Blumhardt with giving a dishonest report. This, however, the critic did not do, for good reasons. True, Blumhardt was not one for holding obstinately to what was regarded as the received wisdom on this matter, namely that demons may stem from just about anywhere, but not from humanity—a prejudice that dogged him then just as it probably still dogs most of us today.

The above critic quotes a theologian to the effect that "Scripture distinguishes throughout between demons and the souls of the damned," but in fact Scripture tells us nothing about the *origin* of demons, and it states nowhere that these do *not* come from humanity. Since Scripture has no revelation for us about this area, there is no formal Christian doctrine respecting it either. Any interpretation is simply based on general human experience. It could be pointed out, nevertheless, that the Savior assumes that Hades, that is, the world of the unblessed dead (Matt 16:18), exerts an evil influence on people—an assumption most likely coming out of his experiences in the area of mental and emotional illness. In the light of this presupposition Blumhardt's conjecture does not seem so "unchristian." The Savior himself experienced many uncanny things of a kind not met with anywhere in the Bible before him.

The critic in question seems to think that on this subject conjecture and fantasy may be given free play and that our duty consists in just seeing to it that our ruminating and hypothesizing leads to a conclusion that is "Christian," or rather "conforms to the thinking now in vogue." The opposite is true: This area more than any other calls for thinking that is unbiased, free, and honest. Blumhardt was not the man to tell the wretched spirits facing him, "Say what you will, O soul—from my college notebooks I know for a fact that it is not you!"

Strangest of all is that this critic reproaches Blumhardt, the mission enthusiast, with putting forward "pagan" hypotheses. If Blumhardt's experiences were real, it is only to be expected that such uncanny occurrences are particularly rampant in a heathen setting. But I am actually not aware of any pagan source of antiquity that refers to this subject. The Jew Josephus, who does put forward the hypothesis in question, could well have come by it from ideas common among his own people, who showed a lively interest in this area. It might even have been indirectly suggested to him by notions that the conspicuous deeds of Jesus and his apostles had gradually caused to circulate among the people. Considerably later than Josephus, the writer Philostratus has Apollonius of Tyana describe, not a hypothesis but a factual occurrence of this kind (actual or assumed), as part of what he came across among the Brahmans in India. To my knowledge this is probably the one pertinent example from pagan antiquity. True, Horace (*Epodes*, 5) puts into the mouth of a boy who gets tortured to death for magical purposes the threat that after his death he will, by the law of *dii manes*, terrify his murderers. But such a threat evokes an image quite different from that of possession by a demon, so would not have served Josephus as a basis for his assumption.

To return to our story, a few days later Gottliebin experienced another apparent possession, but this time Blumhardt did not enter into
a conversation. Before long, it seemed as if demons by the hundreds
were coming out of her in quite definite numbers. Every time it happened the girl's face changed and assumed a new, threatening mien
toward Blumhardt. Those present, even the mayor, would receive various knocks and blows—except for Blumhardt, whom the demons by
their own admission were not permitted to touch. Off and on Gottliebin
would pull her hair, beat her breast, bump her head against the wall
and in various ways try to hurt herself, but a few simple words always
calmed her down.

Still, it seemed as if these scenes were getting more and more terrible and as if Blumhardt's influence only made the situation worse. He
relates:

> No words can describe what I endured in soul and spirit at that
> time. I felt more and more the urge to have done with the mat-
> ter. True, in every instance I could depart with inward satisfac-
> tion, knowing that the demonic power had to give way and the
> patient was again completely all right. However, the dark power
> always seemed to gain fresh strength and to be intent on getting
> me entangled in a big labyrinth, so as to hurt and ruin me and my
> pastoral work. All my friends advised me to give it up. But I had
> to think with horror of what might become of the sick person if
> I withdrew my support and of how everyone would be bound to
> consider me the cause if things turned out badly. I felt caught in a
> net; if I tried to extricate myself by simply withdrawing, I would
> endanger myself and others. And I have to say quite openly that
> I felt ashamed to give in to the devil. I felt ashamed in my own
> eyes and before my Savior, to whom I prayed so much, in whom
> I had such trust, and whose active help I actually experienced in
> so many instances. I often had to ask myself, "Who is Lord?" and
> trusting in him who is the Lord I ever again heard an inner voice
> call: Forward! It must come to a good end, though we may first
> have to go down into the deepest depth—unless it is not true that
> Jesus crushed the serpent's head.

The scenes where it seemed that demons went out of Gottliebin
increased more and more; at the same time there were other uncanny
appearances, which even amounted to physical attacks. For example,
one night when she was asleep, she felt a scorching hand grab her throat,
leaving large burns behind. By the time her aunt, who slept in the same

room, had lit a lamp, blisters had already sprung up all around the girl's neck, causing the doctor who came the next morning to shake his head in amazement. Day and night she was liable to receive knocks on her head or side, or something would trip her, whether in the street or on the stairs or elsewhere, causing sudden falls with resultant bruises or other physical harm. Finally, on June 25, 1842, on Blumhardt's return from a children's festival in Korntal, he was told that she was nearly demented. He called on her the following morning at eight o'clock, after reading, in tears and with a nearly broken heart, the memorable passage in Ecclesiasticus 2:1–8 (in the series of his daily Bible lessons):

> My son, if you aspire to be a servant of the Lord, prepare yourself for testing. Be steadfast and endure, and do not lose your head when disaster comes. Hold fast to God and do not leave him, so that your strength may ever increase. Bear every hardship that is sent you; be patient in all tribulation. For as gold is tested in the fire, those acceptable to God are tried in the furnace of tribulation. Trust the Lord and he will help you; follow a straight path and hope in him. You who fear the Lord, trust him, and you shall not miss your reward. You who fear the Lord, hope for good things from him, and you shall find lasting grace and favor. You who fear the Lord, wait for his mercy; do not turn aside lest you fall.

Strengthened by these words, he went to Gottliebin, where presently things seemed to go well. In the afternoon, however, extraordinary things began to happen. Gottliebin suffered such an attack that she lay as if dead, but then followed something that again gave the impression that demons were coming out of her, and this time in a way far beyond anything experienced previously. It felt like a victory of undreamt-of magnitude. For the next several weeks pretty well nothing happened, and Gottliebin could walk unmolested wherever she wished. "It was a time of rejoicing for me," Blumhardt says.

He had truly earned that joy. He had remained faithfully at his post like a soldier, neither advancing rashly nor retreating a single step. He had withstood in the evil day (Eph 6:13), had done everything well and had held the field. His battle was a bit like that fought by little David against the terrible Goliath. "All the men of Israel, when they saw the man, fled from him and were much afraid" (1 Sam 17:24). So it was here also; even his very best friends felt "one should have no truck with such things. There is nothing one can do about them." From Blumhardt's point of view that would have meant: The assumption that there is a

Savior must not be taken too literally. He boldly acted as if there truly is a Savior to whom all power is given in heaven and on earth; he staked everything on the assurance that Jesus Christ is still the same today, he who nearly two thousand years ago, for the sake of poor humankind and to his Father's glory, stopped the powers of darkness in their tracks. Bravely Blumhardt went forward, to "let all the earth know that there is a God in Israel" (1 Sam 17:46). And his trust was rewarded with help from on high and with glorious success. When the struggle was at its fiercest, on July 9, 1842, he wrote to Barth: "Whenever I write the name of Jesus, I feel overcome by a holy awe and by a joyous, fervent sense of gratitude that I know this "Jesus!" is mine. Only now have I really come to know what we have in him."

These words, [or rather their German equivalent] in Blumhardt's own handwriting, appear under his picture at the beginning of this book. A small spelling irregularity occurring in them, an apparent mistake seems to conflict with Blumhardt's general punctiliousness in matters of faith (mentioned when we spoke of his theological studies at the university). In the phrase "this 'Jesus!' is mine" Blumhardt puts "this" into the neuter form (*dieses*) of the accusative instead of the masculine one would normally expect (*diesen*). Now the term "my Jesus" is used very frequently in Christian literature, both poetry and prose, but occurs nowhere in the New Testament—an example of how very often our concept of Christianity as mainly devotional or edifying in character deviates from what is represented in the Bible. Blumhardt saw Jesus as too great and himself as too small to let himself speak of his relationship to him in this manner. It is different when I call *God* "my God" or "my Father"; in both cases I place myself below God or, as it were, right into him. But when I call a man "mine," for example, "my Richard," I put forward a special claim, reminiscent of private property. What Blumhardt wants to say is, "This right to turn to Jesus, to have recourse to him in every need—this is mine!" His grammatical deviation from what one would normally expect springs from his desire to make clear: What is mine is the right to turn to Jesus but not "this Jesus" himself. It expresses the holy awe he felt.

It seemed that Blumhardt's fervent longing to have finally done with the obnoxious business was fulfilled. But it was just appearance. He had taken on an enemy who constantly threw in fresh troops from the vast

deep. Wave after wave they came, "and up surged the flood spite of dip-
ping and hauling, as if one great sea for another were calling."[4] "I could
never have imagined what was to follow," Blumhardt said later.

In August 1842 Gottliebin came to him, pale and disfigured, to
tell him something she had up till now been too shy to share with him
but could keep hidden no longer. She hesitated a while, making him
feel tense and apprehensive, but then began to tell him of an ailment
that came on her every Wednesday and Friday and involved bleeding so
painful and severe it would mean the end of her unless it were stopped.
Her description of other things she experienced in connection with this
is beyond the bounds of what can be reported here; Blumhardt recognized that some of the most horrible fantasies of popular superstition
had here become actual reality. He relates:

> To begin with, I needed time to gather myself, as I sadly realized
> the ascendancy that the power of darkness had gained over hu-
> manity. My next thought was, "Now you are done for; now we are
> getting into magic and witchcraft, and what will you do against
> those?" But as I looked at the girl in her distress, I shuddered at the
> thought that such darkness should be possible, yet help be impos-
> sible. I recalled that there are people thought to have secret pow-
> ers enabling them to ward off all manner of demonic evils; I also
> thought of the sympathetic remedies people of high and low estate
> increasingly swear by. Should I possibly look around for things like
> that? That—I had long since convinced myself—would mean using
> devils to drive out devils. Then I felt reminded of a warning I had
> been given once before, when, since good advice is often hard to
> come by, I had considered affixing the name of Jesus to the house
> door of a sick person or trying something in that direction.
>
> While engaged in such thoughts I read in the morning the
> Moravian watchword (daily text) for that day. It said, "Are you so
> foolish? Having begun with the Spirit, are you now ending with
> the flesh?" (Gal 3:3). I got the hint; praise be to God, who led me
> to keep unswervingly to the pure weapons of prayer and of God's
> word. The question went through me. Could not the prayers of
> the faithful prevail against this satanic power also, whatever it be?
> What are we poor people to do if we cannot call down direct help
> from above? If Satan has a hand in it, is it right just to leave it like
> that? Can one not trample it under foot through faith in the true
> God? If Jesus came to destroy the works of the devil, ought we not
> to hold on to that, precisely in this situation? If there is magic and

---

4. Translator's Note: Quotation from the poem "The Diver" by Friedrich Schiller.

witchcraft, is it not sin to let it go on unchecked, when there is a chance to confront it in earnest? With these thoughts I struggled through to faith in the power of prayer in this matter also, where no other counsel was to be had, and I said aloud to Gottliebin, "We are going to pray, come what may; we shall dare it! There is nothing we can lose by praying, to say the least, and just about every page of Scripture tells of prayer and of its being heard. The Lord will keep his promises." So I let her go with the assurance that I would be thinking of her and asked her to keep me informed.

The very next day was the dreaded Friday. It was also the day when toward evening the first storm clouds began to form in the sky after several months of drought. For Blumhardt it was to be an unforgettable day. In addition to other horrible happenings, Gottliebin was in a veritable frenzy to take her own life. She raced madly through both rooms and clamored for a knife, which the brothers and sisters present of course would not let her have. Then, running up into the loft, she sprang on to the window sill and was already standing on the outside and ready to jump, holding on inside with just one hand, when the first lightning flash of the approaching thunderstorm struck her eye, startling and waking her. Coming to her senses, she cried, "For God's sake, I don't want that!" The moment of sanity passed; once more delirious, she got hold of a rope—she was never able to say later on where from—wound it artfully around a beam in the loft and made it into a slip knot. Just when she had nearly pushed her head through the noose, a second flash of lightning caught her eye through the window and brought her round as before. Tears streamed from her eyes the next morning when she caught sight of the rope and noose on the beam, knowing that in her right mind she could never have tied it so cunningly.

At eight o'clock the same evening Blumhardt was called. He found Gottliebin in a pool of blood, not to mention other dreadful afflictions. He said a few comforting words to her, but without much success; then, with thunder rolling outside, he began to pray earnestly. After a quarter of an hour his intercession had such a decisive effect that the attack ceased completely. Gottliebin presently came to, and Blumhardt went out for a moment while she changed her clothes. "When we came back and found her sitting on her bed, a completely different person, there was no room in us for anything but praise and thanks," he tells. "This affliction had ended for good."

There is still a memorable postscript to the dreadful scenes of that night. We let Blumhardt tell it (slightly abridged):

> Unexpectedly the patient suffered a new attack, just as on previous occasions when something demonic came over her. There were a number of incidents, but then suddenly the anger and disgust of the demons broke loose with full force. Many assertions of the following kind were heard, mostly in a howling or lamenting tone: "Now the game is up—everything has been betrayed—you ruin us completely—the whole pack is falling apart—it's all finished— there is nothing but confusion, and it's all your fault with your everlasting praying—you will yet drive us out altogether. Alas, alas, everything is lost! We are 1067, but there are also many still alive, and they ought to be warned! Oh, woe to them, they are lost! God forsworn—for aye forlorn!" The howls of the demons, flashes of lightning, the rolling thunders, and the splashing of the down-pour; the earnestness of all present, my prayers, which caused the demons to come out as described above—all this made up a scene no one can possibly picture as it really was. If, among other things, the demons cried, "Nobody could have driven us out! Only you have managed it, you with your everlasting, persistent praying," it was not altogether implausible. Scarcely anybody would have applied himself the way I did—least of all those who would accuse me of arrogant self-aggrandizement because I am honest enough to record even utterances such as that. See 1 Sam 17:28: "I know your presumption."

Though that particular affliction ceased completely, before long other manifestations of a demonic nature made their appearance. When Blumhardt poured out his need to his friend Stern, director of a seminary in Karlsruhe, Stern pointed him to the word, "This kind can come out only by prayer and fasting." Further thought led Blumhardt to see fasting as more meaningful than is generally assumed. He writes:

> Insofar as fasting is a proof for God that the object of the prayer is a true and urgent concern of the person praying, and insofar as it greatly enhances the intensity and strength of the prayer and in fact represents a continuous prayer without words, I could believe that it would prove effective, particularly since there was a special word of the Lord for the case in hand. So I tried it, without telling anybody, and it was indeed a tremendous help for me during the succeeding struggles. It enabled me to be much calmer, firmer, and more definite in my speech; I also no longer needed to be on the spot for a long time; indeed, I sensed that I could make my

influence felt without being actually there. And when I did come,
I often noticed significant results within a few moments.

Out of Blumhardt's further account of demonic manifestations
we shall include here only various instances with a bearing on religion
and morality. He tells, for example, of differences that became apparent
among the demons. Some, defiant and full of hatred toward Blumhardt,
often uttered things worth recording. They evinced a horror of the abyss,
which they now felt very near, and would say, among other things, "You
are our worst enemy, but we are your enemies too. Oh, if only we could
do what we want! Would that there were no God in heaven!" But they
still assumed full responsibility for their downfall. Especially dreadful
was the behavior of a demon who had earlier been seen by Gottliebin
in her house and who now admitted to being a perjurer. He repeatedly
exclaimed the words painted on the window shutter of that house:

> O man, think on eternity;
> Use well the time still granted thee,
> For judgment will come speedily.

Then he would fall silent, contort his face, stiffly raise up three fingers (presumably referring to the sick person's fingers), suddenly shudder,
and groan, "Hm!" There were many scenes of that kind, where Blumhardt
would gladly have welcomed more witnesses.

However, most of the demons that made themselves known between August 1842 and February 1843 or even later desperately yearned
for liberation from the bonds of Satan. They used all sorts of languages
with most peculiar articulation, most of which Blumhardt could not
relate to any European tongue. But there was Italian too (recognizable by
the sound) and French (which he understood). In some cases demons
attempted to speak German, which sounded strange and at times comical, especially when they tried to describe things for which they did not
seem to know the German term.

Now and then Blumhardt heard utterances he could not assign to
either of the two types of demons. They sounded as if coming from some
higher region. A passage that was quoted very often, for example, was
Habakkuk 2:3–4: "The prophecy will be fulfilled at the appointed time;
it will appear at the end and will not fail. Though it linger, wait for it; it
will surely come and will not delay. Behold, he that is obstinate will not
have peace in his heart, but the righteous will live by his faith." Then

again it seemed as if the same voice from on high turned to the demons as it recited a passage that Blumhardt for a long time could not identify, until he recognized it to be Jeremiah 3:25, but with the second person (you) taking the place of the first (we): "That which you relied on is now your disgrace, and what was a comfort to you, of that you must now be ashamed. For you have sinned against the Lord your God, you and your fathers, from your youth even to this day, and you have not obeyed the voice of the Lord your God." Blumhardt tells:

> For quite a while I did not grasp the meaning of these and other Bible passages, but I learned to see all of them as being meaningful and deserving of greater attention. As I listened to such declarations, sometimes occurring at the end of a struggle, I had the feeling that they came to me as a strengthening and comfort from above. Altogether, I cannot look back without feeling deeply grateful for the many times I was allowed to experience protection and help.

I will let Blumhardt himself tell of how he responded to demons that had a yearning to be set free.

> For a long time I would not listen to their talk, but often found myself in a big dilemma at seeing the tormented features, the hands raised in supplication, and the streaming tears, and at the same time heard sighs and groans of fear, despair, and entreaty that would melt a heart of stone. I struggled hard against becoming involved in any kind of an effort at redemption, because everything that happened made me first of all suspect a possible dangerous and pernicious ruse of the devil and made me fear for the sobriety of my evangelical faith. But in the end I could not help at least trying it, especially since those demons that appeared to have some hope for themselves could not be budged by either threats or exhortations.
>
> As far as I can remember, the first demon I dared it with was that woman who seemed to have been at the root of this whole affair. She again showed herself in Gottliebin and declared with a firm and decided voice that she wanted to belong to the Savior and not to the devil.[5] Then she said how much had already been

---

5. It was probably at this point that the woman asked him, "Who are you?" When he said, "A servant of the Gospel," she replied, "Yes, but a hard one." When he asked her, "Where are you?" she said, "In the chasm" (compare the statement: "Between us and you a great chasm has been fixed" in the story of the rich man and poor Lazarus, Luke 16:26)—a reply that shook Blumhardt to the core.

changed in the spirit world by these struggles but that my good fortune had been that I relied solely on the word of God and prayer. If I had tried anything else, for example, if I had resorted to the secret magical remedies in wide use among the people by which the demons thought to trap me, I would have been lost. She raised her finger to emphasize the point and ended with the words, "It's a dreadful struggle you have undertaken!" Then she urgently pleaded with me to pray for her to be completely freed from the devil's power, into which she had fallen almost unknowingly by getting involved in idolatry, sorcery, and sympathetic magic, and to be given somewhere a place of rest. I had known this woman well in her lifetime; she had then shown such a hunger for the word of God and for consolation as I scarcely found anywhere else. [Here we recall the earlier mention of her many visits to the rectory.] My heart ached for her. Glancing up to the Lord in my heart, I asked her, "But where do you want to go?"

"I should like to remain in your house," she said.

Taken aback, I said, "That cannot be."

"Could I not go into the church?" she went on.

I considered it and replied, "If you promise me not to disturb anybody and never to make yourself visible and assuming that Jesus permits it, I would have no objection."

This was a risk on my part, but I had trust that the Lord would set everything right, seeing that I did not feel guilty of presumption before him. She seemed satisfied, named the farthest corner as the place where she would be, and then seemed to come out of the patient willingly and easily. Gottliebin was not told anything of all this, but to her horror she saw the woman at the designated place in the church. Yet apart from her nobody noticed anything, and somewhat later the apparition in the church ended for good. It was actually the general case that all these things kept changing under the influence of the succeeding struggles.

It was similar with other spirits, who likewise claimed to love the Savior but were still bound to the devil through idolatry and sorcery. They, too, sought liberation and security. Only with utmost caution and earnest pleading with the Lord did I consent to what I could not refuse. My principal reply was always, "If Jesus permits it."

It became evident that there was a divine guidance in all this. For not all obtained what they asked for, and some had to depart just relying on God's free mercy. I do not wish to enlarge on this difficult point beyond saying that it did not cause any unpeace and always brought relief to the sick person. Those spirits granted a temporary place of rest must not be confused with actual ghosts or specters. The latter always appear to stand under the judgment and power of Satan, from which the former are free.

I could relate a number of things observed in the course of these experiences but would rather refrain from doing so, for it would only give offense; besides, such observations, not being founded on the Bible, do not merit further attention. There is only one very interesting case I cannot leave unmentioned. One of the spirits likewise asked to be let into the church. I answered as usual, "If Jesus permits it."

After a while he burst out crying desperately; he either called out or heard the words, "God is a judge of widows and orphans!" and declared that he was not allowed to enter the church.

I replied, "You see, it is the Lord who shows you the way, so what I say doesn't count. Go where the Lord bids you go."

He continued, "Couldn't I go into your house?"

I was startled by this request and, thinking of my wife and children, was not inclined to accede to it. But then it occurred to me it might be a challenge for me to show I would be ready for any sacrifice, so finally I said, "Well, if you disturb nobody and Jesus permits it, it would be all right." Suddenly I again heard something like a voice from a higher sphere call out of Gottliebin's mouth, "Not under any roof! God is a judge of widows and orphans!" Once more the spirit seemed to burst into tears and asked if he might at least go into my garden; that request was apparently granted. It looked as though he was guilty of having once made orphans homeless.

As regards all these experiences and his approach to them, Blumhardt refutes two possible charges. These are, first, that such experiences support the false notion of the existence of a so-called purgatory; second, that he tried to convert spirits—two unfounded but related accusations. His experiences made it clear what a terrible delusion it is to assume that the torments of the life beyond have a purifying strength. On the contrary, he had to recognize with dreadful clarity that the lost souls had no will of their own and were totally subject to the tyranny of Darkness. Hence there could be no question of converting them. On the other hand, his experiences contradicted the assumption that after death one immediately finds himself either eternally blessed or eternally damned—in other words, that there are but two places for the dead: heaven or hell.

In my opinion this very simple but also very harsh assumption is invalidated by the word of Jesus that there is no forgiveness for the sin against the Holy Spirit, either in this age or in the age to come (Matt 12:32). To enlarge on this passage: It is not a question of two localities, which the Lord sets against each other—say, "this world" and "the world beyond," with one residing in this world until death and in the other after death. Rather, over against the present world age or aeon, where the evil one has power (2 Cor 4:4; Rom 12:2; Eph 2:2), the Lord sets a future age to be brought on by him—to be sure, an age that in him, its originator, and in his kingdom already penetrates into our present aeon (Heb 6:5). Whoever dies unredeemed, falls prey to the realm of death or Hades (sometimes translated incorrectly as "hell" in Luke 16:23 and Matt 16:18), which belongs to the present aeon. Like the present aeon it will end when the future one breaks in. Hence the forgiveness the Lord speaks of in Matthew 12:32 is bound up not with the small history of an individual but with the large-scale history of the world.

The Lord allows room for the forgiveness of sins in two different aeons. First, in this present one—that is, before judgment day—a reprieve may be granted, possibly after centuries of torment. Second, there will be forgiveness of sins in the age to come—say, at the time "when God's sons will be revealed." It is noteworthy that with respect to all sins—excepting only the sin of blaspheming the Holy Spirit—the Lord speaks of forgiveness not as a possibility but as something to be definitely granted, as though he saw forgiveness merely as a question of time, perhaps in the sense that every person's life eventually reaches a boundary where he must decide whether to bow repentantly before the name of Jesus or face the abyss.

But in whatever way we interpret the above passage, which is as difficult as it is important, it does suggest two things: 1) that death does not extinguish our chances to have our sins forgiven through Christ (if one thinks, for example, of the heathen and maybe also of others not responsible for their ignorance), and 2) that the advent of the "age to come" still holds out hope of an overwhelmingly great forgiveness of sins. Closely related to this is another Bible passage, Romans 8:19–23, which from then on was of utmost importance to Blumhardt.

> The creation waits with eager longing for God's sons to be revealed, seeing that it was subjected to futility not of its own will but by the will of him who thus made it subject. Yet there is hope, for the creation will be set free from its bondage to decay into the glorious liberty of the children of God. To this day, we know, the entire creation sighs and throbs with pain; and not only the

creation, but also we ourselves, who have the first-fruits of the Spirit, groan inwardly as we long for full sonship and wait for the redemption of our bodies.

If by the Lord's intimation so much forgiveness is reserved for the last judgment, might not the yearning of all creation for "the revealing of the sons of God" be related to this? To be sure, people take the liberty—indeed, for the most part even feel obliged—to exclude from "creation" all those who died unredeemed, as if they did not form part of God's creation. Instead, they are satisfied to ascribe to, say, some worn-out and ill-treated beast of burden a poetic yearning for a day from which it is unlikely to profit. As Blumhardt often said:

> Nobody thinks of the dead, and yet there are billions of them. They live from hour to hour, and their guilt is often not so very great, if one thinks of the pagan peoples. Seen in that light, the statement that against its will this creation is subject to vanity and in bondage to corruption takes on a much deeper meaning. Through and behind it all a ruling power becomes visible, showing itself as vanity in front and as corruption from the rear. Thus the apostle's thought that the whole creation has fallen prey to this power of lying and death is as shaking as the other thought is elevating and uplifting: that through Christ's ultimate victory creation will be set free from this bondage.

It was precisely in these struggles that Blumhardt first became horribly aware how inextricably entangled the lost are with each other and with their surroundings. He also began to see why this whole forlorn multitude is consciously or unconsciously waiting with eager longing for the victory of God's children. He gained a new understanding of the following passage, which in the New Testament is often applied to the Jesus Christ: "Sit at my right hand till I make your enemies the footstool under your feet" (Ps 110:1). By his sacrificial death Jesus has gained the right and the power to redeem us and deliver us from these enemies; he tells us, "Whatsoever you will ask in my name, I will do." In his struggles Blumhardt had to recognize that in the present state of God's kingdom the question of power is all-important: who is to have power—the Savior or Darkness. It also became clear to him that in this struggle the Lord wants to conquer through the faith of his church and that only such ongoing victories will prepare the way for the Lord's coming. In his *Vertheidigungsschrift* Blumhardt says: "To be sure, there are many who imagine that one fine day the Lord will simply turn up and slay the devil, without the faithful having to be greatly concerned about it. No wonder a certain heathen expressed surprise that the Lord hadn't done it long ago."

Of course, in general people take up a quite different attitude with respect to the kingdom of darkness and its impact on the world. They are careful not to think about it, or even consider it the first duty of an enlightened mind to deny its existence. When confronted by otherwise inexplicable facts, they prefer to turn off the machinery of their intellect, so as not to have conclusions anathema to modern thinking forced on them. Much in that attitude is actually sound, and most likely Blumhardt, too, proved so fit for these struggles because he, more than others, had a healthy aversion to any inquisitive dabbling in, or musing on, these things. On the other hand, he considered it childish to shackle one's thinking when facing obtrusive facts, especially since, as a servant of the Gospel, he was duty-bound to act. Surely an officer in the field has a higher duty than declining to know anything about the enemy—his strength, his intentions, or even his very existence.

If I were to summarize in just a few words the intelligence Blumhardt gathered about the enemy's camp, I can think of no more fitting word than Luther's, "His craft and power are great, he's armed with cruel hate." Not the least of Satan's tricks is that it is simply not done, on pain of utter disgrace, to so much as mention his existence. There was one ruse, however, that Blumhardt got more and more on the track of and that more than once actually thrust involuntary martyrdom on him, and that was magic and sorcery. Simply pooh-poohing as foolishness all the phenomena in this area is really not a bad approach, but if, beset by this or that trouble, one then resorts to superstitious remedies, as if they were harmless, one courts disaster. At the very least, one ought to tell oneself, "If these things don't help, they are a laughingstock, but if they do help, there is something uncanny about them." I will let Blumhardt himself speak about this (at the same time refuting the charge that he tried to convert spirits):

> For me, it was nowhere a question of conversion, but rather a question of freeing the souls of otherwise believing—even deeply believing—persons. These had been involved in magical practices that during their lifetime they had not recognized as sins (even though an inner sense had been warning them). Because of this they had in some manner remained under the devil's sway without being aware of it. Since even with these sins they had not actually meant to turn away from God, they were in need not of conversion but merely of liberation. They could only find such liberation,

however, if somewhere on earth, in firm faith in the blood of Jesus Christ, a struggle was being waged against the power of magic.

Just the fact that no determined, earnest voice was raised anywhere against such heathen abominations made everyone feel safe. Frequently it was actually well-meaning folk that encouraged the sick and wretched to use such clandestine remedies. Though it may be hard to understand, they either regarded them as legitimate, because accompanied by prayer and calling on the name of the Most High, or at least as not harmful, because based on as yet unknown laws of nature. The wretched and tormented were ready for any kind of help and did not shrink from even the most horrible practices; unaware of what they were carrying, they would have on their persons magic scraps of paper saying among other things, "We shall see each other in hell"—at any rate papers with all kinds of superstitious figures, letters, and pentagrams, or with sacred stories and words blasphemously misused. These they would carry next to the skin by day and night or would at ungodly hours embed them in stables, trees, doorposts, and bedsteads. Nor did they recoil from rooting about in graves at night and committing abominations with dug-up bones.

But why enumerate here what could not be contained in many big tomes and what in subtle, at times scarcely discernible, form is found in all classes of society? At any rate, the result was that in spite of their faith in the redemptive work of Jesus the poor folk often remained under a spell, since they were unaware of their sin—though they could have been aware of it if they had been more awake.

There are still other sins even believing Christians openly commit, though at times with a certain inner reluctance—sins they never recognize as such and which nobody helps them to recognize either. This means that in many cases things get held up after death, for Christ is no servant of sin. Satanic involvements still remain, waiting to be dissolved in some way, for it cannot be God's purpose that such souls, which in some ways may be regarded as innocent and sincere, should simply be left in their bondage and thrust into eternal damnation. But nothing has been so heavy a burden on Christianity as the evil spell of sorcery, already referred to repeatedly, of which no one thinks nor wants to think.

I, however, have now had an opportunity to perceive that spell and to work against it, and I can believe that through a struggle such as I have waged, the possibility of being freed is opened up for many in the world beyond as well (see Matt 12:32). Of course, they would have found this liberation while still alive if they had then recognized what was amiss and cleansed themselves in the blood of Christ. It is to help men find this that I have now been given a

voice, and that is what matters to me the most. My zeal as a servant
of the Gospel urges me to see to it that every believer's faith be pure
and chaste and remain so to the end.

Let us now return to Blumhardt's struggle. Again victory and peace
had been given, ending for good and all most of the strange symptoms
mentioned above. It was like a solemn judgment pronounced on the
spirits that had tormented the sick person. A more detailed account we
may forgo here.

Now there follows the most incomprehensible of all the occurrences
in the whole history of this illness. Blumhardt prefaces his account of it
as follows: "I go on to give an honest report of what I can still remember,
firmly convinced that the Lord will hold his hand over me in this as well.
My one intention is to tell everything to the honor of him who is the
victor over all dark powers." In the course of his report he says:

> I really cannot take it amiss if somebody is mistrustful of the above
> account, for these things are way beyond anything we can think or
> grasp. It is, however, based on observations and experiences over
> nearly a whole year, for which I always had several eye witnesses—
> a practice I strictly observed, to head off evil rumors if for nothing
> else. That allows me to tell what happened freely and boldly. I am
> fully assured, on the basis of Gottliebin's character alone, that no
> trace of fraud was involved, nor could there have been.

The experiences Blumhardt relates here were of great value to him,
for they let him feel the helpful intervention of God's creative hand in a
way that exceeded anything he had previously experienced. To be exact:
For him who was led into these experiences directly and involuntarily
they truly possessed such a value. For those not so close to these events,
on the other hand, the gruesome and painful tricks of Darkness coming to light here are liable to outweigh and impair the impression of a
mighty divine help being present, because of the evident pleasure our
imagination secretly derives from such things. For this reason we find it
advisable to omit this part of Blumhardt's report. Blumhardt says: "In the
end, when these uncanny things threatened to go on and on indefinitely,
I rallied all my inner strength and besought God that he, the power who
had made everything out of nothing, might now reduce these things to
nothingness and utterly undo the devil's trickery. In this way I struggled
for several days, and the Lord who promised, 'Whatever you will ask in
my name, I will do it' kept his word—it worked!"

Yet even this apparent conclusion was once again followed by horrible manifestations of illness in Gottliebin, seeming to be deliberately
aimed at her death. On one occasion, when she had wounded herself in
an unbelievably dreadful way and the wounds, after having healed up
in an equally wonderful manner, suddenly burst open again, a woman
friend came hurrying to Blumhardt in utter dismay with the message
that every minute's delay would be perilous. "At that," as Blumhardt tells
himself, "I fell on my knees in my room and in my extremity spoke bold
words. This time—so strong had I become—I was not even going to do the
devil the honor of walking over myself. Rather, I sent a message through
this friend asking Gottliebin to get up and come to me, adding that in
faith she would be able to do it. Before long, there she was, coming up the
stairs. Nobody can possibly appreciate just how that made me feel."

I will let Blumhardt relate in his own words, in a slightly shortened
form, how during Christmas 1843 things finally came to the longed-for
conclusion (December 24–28).

> It seemed as if everything that had ever occurred before was mass-
> ing for a combined assault. Most disconcerting was that now the
> sinister workings also affected Gottliebin's half-blind brother and
> her sister Katharina, so that I had to fight a most desperate strug-
> gle with all three of them at once, the inner connection between
> the three being unmistakable. I can no longer tell the exact order
> of events; so many different things happened that I cannot pos-
> sibly recall them all, but those were days such as I hope never to
> experience again. It had come to the point where I simply had to
> risk everything, so to speak; it was a question of victory or death.
> Great as my own efforts were, by the way, I also sensed an equally
> tangible divine protection, so that I did not feel in the least weary
> or worn out, not even after forty hours of watching, fasting, and
> struggling.
>
> Gottliebin's brother was the first to be free again—so free that
> he could at once actively help in what followed. This time the
> brunt of the attack was not directed at Gottliebin, who during this
> final act, after all the preceding struggles, likewise seemed to be
> completely free, but at her sister Katharina. Up till then Katharina
> had not been affected at all; now she began to rage so furiously
> that it took a great effort to control her. She threatened to break
> me into a thousand pieces, and I could not risk coming near her.
> She made continuous attempts to tear her own body open or
> seemed slyly to look about for an opportunity of doing something
> dreadful to those holding her. At the same time she kept babbling

and rattling so horribly that thousands of spiteful tongues seemed to be combined in her. The most remarkable thing was that she remained fully conscious so that one could reason with her. When admonished sharply, she would say she could not help talking and acting like that; we should really keep a firm hold on her to prevent her doing something bad. Afterward, too, she remembered everything distinctly, even those horrible murderous attempts. This actually had such a depressing effect on her that for several days I had to concern myself specially with her, until after earnest and diligent prayer these memories gradually faded away.

Side by side with that, however, the demon within her made himself heard with equal distinctness. In this case he gave himself out to be not a departed human spirit but an eminent angel of Satan, actually the head of all magic. He asserted that his going down into the abyss would deal the power of magic the fatal blow, making her gradually bleed to death. All of a sudden, at twelve o'clock midnight, there issued from the girl's throat a howl of despair, repeated several times and lasting for about a quarter of an hour, of so shattering a force it nearly brought the house down. Something more gruesome than that could hardly be imagined. Inevitably and not without a feeling of horror, over half the inhabitants of the village were in that way made aware of the struggle. At the same time such a trembling came upon Katharina as if all her members were to be shaken loose. In the demon's voice expressions of fear and despair mingled with tremendous defiance. He demanded that God perform a sign to allow him to go to hell at least with honor, instead of meanly abdicating his role like mere ordinary sinners. Scarcely ever has such a dreadful mixture of despair, spite, defiance, and arrogance been witnessed.

Finally there came that most shattering moment, of which none but the actual eye- and ear-witnesses can have an adequate idea. At two o'clock in the morning, while the girl bent her head and the upper part of her body far backwards over her chair, the purported angel of Satan, with a voice such as one would scarcely think a human throat capable of, bellowed out the words, "Jesus is victor! Jesus is victor!" Wherever these words could be heard, their significance was grasped too; they made an indelible impression on many. The strength and power of the demon now appeared to wane with every passing minute; he grew more and more quiet, could move less and less, and finally went out altogether unnoticed, just as the light of life might go out in a dying person—but not until eight o'clock in the morning.

At this point the two-year-long struggle came to an end. Of this I was so sure and convinced that on the day following, a Sunday,

I could not help showing my triumphant joy when I preached on the Magnificat. True, there still remained various things to deal with afterward, but it was merely like clearing away the rubble of a collapsed building. As regards the half-blind brother—a modest, humble, and spiritually very discerning man, rich in faith and in the strength springing from it—there was practically nothing I still had to do. The satanic attacks aimed at him were scarcely noticed by others. Katharina for a while was still subject to occasional convulsive movements (a consequence of the extraordinary way her inner being had been attacked), but before long she, too, fully recovered, and what incidents there were with her have not come to anybody's notice, I would say.

Somewhat greater were the troubles encountered by Gottliebin during the time following, but they were more like a renewal of former attempts on the part of the dark power; they were of themselves doomed to failure and did not claim much of my attention at all. Indeed, in the midst of these rearguard skirmishes she little by little attained complete health. All her former ailments, well known to physicians, completely disappeared: the high shoulder, the short leg, stomach troubles, etc. Her health became more and more stable and over a considerable time now has remained so perfect in every respect that she may be considered a true miracle of God. Her Christian disposition, too, has increased in a most gratifying way; her quiet humility, her sincere and sensible way of speaking, coupled with decisiveness and modesty, have made her a blessed instrument of the Lord for many.

What shows the worth of her character most clearly is that I know of no other woman who can handle children with so much insight, love, patience, and consideration. For this reason, when more help is needed, it is to her most of all that I like to entrust my children. During the whole past year she has been teaching vocational skills to everyone's satisfaction. I cannot but look back with grateful wonder at the protecting power of divine providence, which allowed her to go through that otherwise very difficult time without even once having to miss a lesson. Consequently, now that a kindergarten is to be established, I have not been able to find any person more suitable than her to take this on.

We may add here a remark concerning Gottliebin's subsequent life and work, which Blumhardt, in a copy made in 1850, appended to his account of her illness. He said:

Since she became fully part of my household four years ago [1846], Gottliebin has been my wife's most faithful and sensible

support in the management of the household and the upbringing of the children. My wife has been able absolutely to entrust
and leave to her, as circumstances demanded, any housekeeping
matters, whether big or small. I leave it to others to testify to what
she means to our house and to all who pass through it. One thing
I know: that whoever gets to know her misses no opportunity to
speak of her with respect and appreciation. Especially in the treatment of mentally ill persons she has become almost indispensable
to me, since before long they develop a boundless trust in her, so
that my own contact with them requires but little time. She is, by
the way, not among us as a kind of domestic servant, for her gratitude will not allow her to accept payment for whatever she does
for us. Rather, she feels and considers herself adopted by us as one
of our own children, and the same thing is now the case with her
sister Katharina and her half-blind brother.

Later on, this brother, Hans Georg, was to be the general factotum
in the rectory, as useful in splitting wood as in watching over and han-
dling mentally ill persons, for which he had a special gift. Blumhardt
called him, even as Abraham considered Eliezer, his "majordomo." Just
how much Gottliebin meant to Blumhardt in the time to come we shall
see later.

Thus the struggle, which for a time, far from drawing to a finish,
had threatened to take on increasingly horrible dimensions, had now,
almost abruptly, ended completely and for good. One particular cross
Blumhardt had to bear has so far been merely hinted at but should now
be referred to at greater length, namely that Blumhardt found himself
more and more alone as he pursued his way through that land of gloom.
His friends as good as fled him; heaviest to bear was that even his bosom
friend Barth did not understand him. Blumhardt faithfully reported to
him from time to time and often assured Barth, who was concerned about
him, that the trouble had now really come to an end. It hurt him to see
Barth chalk up mistaken assumptions like that as grievous faults against
him. He thought it could at least have shown Barth how greatly his friend
longed to see the battle ended; then Barth might also have shared the
more deeply his (Blumhardt's) distress at seeing it flare up anew.

Barth, too, had had experiences with demonic powers, but, though
he had not been bereft of divine help, they had been of a nature he preferred not to be reminded of. Besides, while listening all too readily to
various informants with only an uncertain knowledge of the matter, he—

to Blumhardt's great sorrow and, as Barth himself confessed afterward—intentionally avoided getting precise information from Blumhardt himself. Barth was generally inclined to hold fast to an opinion or conviction once formed. He felt no need to impose them on others, but felt even less the need to change them. Also, with an eye to other friends even further removed from the scene, he took a more reserved attitude toward Blumhardt than was in keeping with the bond of friendship he otherwise had with him. Blumhardt's former humble leaning on him had accustomed him to looking on his friend as if he were under his tutelage; so he sent him advice and warnings pertaining to the events of the struggle in an almost peremptory tone.

On January 2, 1844, feeling fully certain of victory, Blumhardt wrote Barth a warm letter, from which I feel I ought to quote here some passages, with the request that the contents not be construed as discrediting Blumhardt's high-minded friend, nor as indicating a considerable tension between these friends, who actually remained inseparable throughout their lives. Theirs was a wonderfully straight and hearty relationship, both partners knowing that without detriment to their friendship they could bluntly tell each other the truth. In this letter Blumhardt, after first complaining that Barth had simply demanded obedience and been unready to enter into a discussion, goes on to say:

> You just wanted to dictate, and in a way that went right against what was called for, so that if I had followed you, I would surely have been undone. You ought to know full well that he who turns his back on the opponent he is fighting is lost. You said yourself that the enemy's aim was to ruin me. That is true, but for the sake of Jesus Christ my Savior I beg and adjure you to tell me openly: is there no power in the world other than that of the devil? Do we want to be devil-worshippers, that is, handle him with kid gloves and let him do as he likes, to keep him from rounding on us? Open your eyes, my dear brother, and tell me: Doesn't the devil seek everyone's ruin? And don't you agree that I would be in greater danger of being ruined if I withdrew into a snail shell instead of confronting the devil head-on with the Word of God? O brother, brother, you do not know the unspeakable distress weighing on poor humankind!
>
> You do not know or do not bear in mind the full, horrible extent of magical practices and alliances with the devil in the world and in Christianity. But to find out and come to know this bit by bit, to be quite certain of it and yet back out—truly, choosing to

do that would make me worse than the devil! Well, know that I dared it! I wanted to see if the devil's neck could be broken with the power of Jesus. I felt driven to do it, as you know; I wanted to see who would tire and throw up the game first—the devil or me. I dared it; I fought. My crying to God day-by-day for a whole year and a half, in the Spirit and guided by his Word, could not possibly go for nothing. Whether I was right in my belief will be made clear on that Day, and Jesus, who has been merciful to me, will vindicate me and has vindicated me.

In the same letter, Blumhardt goes on to state that the struggle helped open his eyes to the importance of mission as well as to what was great in his friend Barth. The letter also contains a reply to Barth's expressed concern that Blumhardt might harm himself in body and soul, as follows:

> You ought to see how cheerful I am, like a child, after each bout and how happy and full of gratitude I feel toward my Savior; then too, how I have learned to pray, so that there are many things I only need to ask the Savior for and I have them already. That is so noticeable, especially as regards the children, that my dear Doris, too, is just brimming over with joy. One sigh to him above, "Lord, give me strength!" is enough to restore me completely, and even after the hardest night-long struggles, I am sure nobody could tell by my face what I had been through. Go ahead and ask if anybody thought me worn-out or weakened this week, in which I stood fifteen times before my congregation [and where Blumhardt went without sleep for forty hours]. Of an overwrought condition or ruined nerves there is no question at all; of this you could easily convince yourself.

At long last we have passed the gloomy chasms through which our Blumhardt was led. Many a reader will hold it against me that I did not choose to take him across these chasms on elegant bridges of general statements. He should believe me when I say that I would have found that much more pleasant, that in my mind I would often stop before the individual parts of these gruesome stories and earnestly ask myself what I might skip and what I ought to tell. Many a reader who to begin with would have felt like turning on me for presenting him with such material might on going through it again end up with the impression: This is no light stuff, put together to tickle the reader's nerves—it is, one might say, holy ground! For Blumhardt, who experienced it, it was a deadly earnest matter; the way he conducted himself was holy, and so was his way of reporting it. The reader will also find that in order to get a faithful picture of Blumhardt's life he must gain a full impression of the battles, too, that he fought. He will also understand the necessity of setting these scenes before him individually and not painted over in any way if he is to gain such a full impression. True, they reveal to us the existence of a kingdom of darkness in a way liable to sap our courage, and if this present section had to offer nothing but evidences of that kingdom, then these pages would indeed have been better left unprinted. For, to use Blumhardt's words, a person can stand knowledge of the dark side of life only to the extent that he knows and has experienced Jesus as Redeemer. But who has not felt this Redeemer come specially close to us just in this often so gloomy section of our book?

It is true that our poor, perverted human nature may easily allow the impression of Jesus' closeness to be overshadowed by the shattering discovery that there is an invisible evil power, whose existence we had nearly forgotten. Certainly in the New Testament we hear a lot about it from the Lord himself and his apostles, but we long ago pushed it aside as rather unedifying. However, shielded as it was by being thus consigned to oblivion, this nonetheless existing kingdom grew all the stronger and when unexpectedly attacked, defended itself savagely. We would find that understandable; it would also serve to explain the scenes we have related. And yet it would leave us with the burden of simply having to acknowledge that there are situations so grim and serious that the puny strength of our faith is scarcely equal to them. That might be the effect of this account, if after passing over these cataracts the stream of Blumhardt's life had simply flowed on in the accustomed channel, irrigating meadows and turning mill-wheels or, in non-pictorial language, if his life were to go on exactly as we knew it before the great struggle. God be praised; that is not the case. This is not yet the end of the story. Only the gruesome part of it is over; its core and essence, the gracious breaking in of the Lord, goes on sublimely and powerfully in a continuous, well-nigh indefatigable manner.

The "struggle" came to an end on December 28, 1843. On January 2, 1844, Blumhardt, in the letter we quoted above, still defends himself against Barth's assertion that his (Blumhardt's) way of conducting the struggle would undermine his pastoral work in Möttlingen. Yet by January 1 the "work of grace in Möttlingen," of which Barth was to speak so highly in February 1844, was already quietly under way. Once more we can say of Blumhardt what he himself had uttered on the eve of the worst developments of the struggle, namely, that he could never have imagined what was to come. But that which came was friendly and bright; it was an experience that in his own mind pushed the events just described completely into the background; we call it the awakening.

It often pained Blumhardt that some people always wanted to hear and talk more of the struggle than of the awakening. Once when an old friend begged him to let him see the chronicle of the illness, he gave him the manuscript reluctantly, with the almost peremptory comment, "But you know: That is not Möttlingen!" To him, Möttlingen, that is, the experience that the name "Möttlingen" reminded him of, on which he built his great hopes and which to the very end of his life he considered of high significance for the Christian church, was not the struggle but the awakening.

Third Section

10

The Movement of Repentance

THOSE WHO IN SOME measure experienced the great time we are about to consider felt very definitely reminded of New Testament days, the time of John the Baptist or of the apostles. To us it seemed as if the kingdom of heaven, bent on conquering the earth, had indeed continued on right to the present day and in the same splendor as had shone forth at the time of the apostles, but that it had become covered over. Now in those days at Möttlingen the cover was lifted slightly, as it were, and through the gap there fell on us a ray from the glory of Christ's heavenly kingdom. It began with a movement of repentance, which in church circles has been called an "awakening" or revival—a term that, it is true, has been applied to various more or less unhealthy manifestations of a religious nature.

The roots of this movement of repentance reach far back into the past, as aptly expressed in the above-mentioned statement by Knapp to the effect that, spiritually speaking, for a whole century an artesian well had been tapped in Möttlingen.

First of all, the religious instruction given by Barth should be remembered, particularly his exceedingly solemn and blessed confirmation services. As people avowed during the revival, these had left a prick deeply embedded in the hearts and consciences of many of his confirmands. As we already know, the struggle itself led to a mood of solemn earnestness in the congregation, but its impact was deepest on Blumhardt himself, on his two fellow fighters, and no less on his family.

For them as well as for Gottliebin it was a serious time of repentance and sharp judgment. New insights kept coming to them from the Scriptures, and this new light was piercing and punishing. "We were being curried with an iron comb," I was told by someone closely involved in the struggle. In that circle ripened even then that utter sincerity before God and among each other that would later characterize the awakening in a way words cannot express. But the awakening itself arose "like a spring from hidden depths," totally unexpected by Blumhardt and even less deliberately provoked by him. He was by nature opposed to anything forced; his ways came out of the depths of the Spirit, which blows where it wills, but you cannot tell where it comes from nor where it goes.

A first harbinger of this springtime of peace was something he experienced in 1841–42 with his confirmands. He conducted his confirmation classes in a most matter-of-fact way, steering clear of any manufactured edification. Where he sensed such a tendency in a minister he knew he could talk to, he was apt to take up the cudgels angrily on behalf of the pupil concerned (whom he could with certainty expect to be upset and resentful). But we will let him take us along to his confirmation class and tell us himself:

> With my twenty or so confirmands (members of my class) sitting around me, I caught sight of a boy who was one of the worst in the whole school and was already regarded as a lost cause on account of the bad things he did. Suddenly I saw tears running down this boy's cheeks. I was surprised and did not know what to make of it, but after class I asked him to stay behind and inquired, "What's the matter with you? Why are you crying?" Then he told me very trustingly that he had heard a voice whisper in his ear, "Your sins are forgiven." I never expected anything like it and cannot recall any other similar experience. From then on, that boy was indeed a completely different person.[1]

On Good Friday, 1842, that is, shortly before the beginning of the "struggle," Blumhardt sensed another breath of spring. At that time, the

1. That bears a striking resemblance to Wilhelm Hoffmann's own experience while serving as a curate in Heumaden in 1829. He felt he was in a false position before God and men as an "unconverted preacher" and had long yearned for clarity and peace. While giving religious instruction to the children, he suddenly seemed to hear a voice say in his ear, "Your sins are forgiven: be of good cheer!" and presently he felt an unutterable bliss flood over him. No longer able to contain himself, he begged the teacher to go on with the instruction, rushed outside and to his room and there, for the first time after a long interval, bent his knees before the Lord to thank him.

church service in Möttlingen was still in a sad condition. True, attendance was good, and even the folk at Unterhaugstett had begun to turn up more frequently and in greater numbers in response to Blumhardt's diligence in holding Bible classes there. However, the terrible power of sleepiness Barth had complained about still held undisputed sway in the church. On that Good Friday, while still sitting in the sacristy before the service, Blumhardt was seized by deep pain at the thought of what lay before him: seeing his congregation slumber on such a holy day. He cried to God from the depth of his heart and felt he was being heard. The text he wanted to preach on—"Woman, behold, your son!" "Behold, your mother!" (John 19:26–27)—took hold of him with marvelous power; ignoring what he had previously prepared, he spoke about the suffering Savior's heartfelt love to his own in such a warm and moved way that his hearers could feel that very heartfelt love in his words. One by one the drooping heads were raised in surprise; people felt moved, began to listen, and went on listening. The sleepiness was at an end, never to return.

The actual awakening drew even closer at Christmas of the following year (1843), when the struggle ended. In the decisive night a number of people heard the cry, "Jesus is victor!" and grasped its significance. The following morning others reported hearing at the same hour horrible, mournful cries of "Into the abyss! Into the abyss!" in the air all down the valley. Everybody was shaken and stirred up. The following Sunday Blumhardt, deeply moved, preached on the Magnificat (Luke 2:46–55). It was, says Blumhardt, a sermon of triumph, with a shaking yet beneficial impact on the whole congregation.

Blumhardt related to Barth how the events of that night had affected his parishioners: "They don't talk much about it in the village; there is great amazement and trembling. One after another, they come to me and confess." The last statement probably referred, to begin with, to members of his confirmation class; it was among them that, very quietly, a movement was first felt. Even before the year ended, he received, very much in secret, letters confessing sins, first from one confirmand, then from another. More and more, a holy atmosphere came to be felt in his classes. Without telling him, the class members would also meet quietly in one or another house for prayer.

As the new year (1844) began, the movement spread to the adults. On New Year's Eve a Möttlingen man came to the rectory who until then had rarely found the way there. This man, though not exactly a downright good-for-nothing, did, in Blumhardt's words, "in many ways have a bad reputation and a nature so twisted I would have been afraid even to talk to him, for fear of being lied to." When the young folk got together on winter evenings, he would be the ringleader in gabbing and jesting. This man met Hans Georg by the rectory entrance and shame-facedly asked him if he could see the rector.

"What do you want to see the rector for?" asked the astonished Hans Georg.

"Oh, Hans," was the reply, "I am in misery! Last night I was a lost sinner in hell. I was told there the only way to get out again would be to see the rector."

Hans took him upstairs to the rector's study. Blumhardt offered him a chair, but he said, "No, *Herr Pfarrer*. I belong on the sinner's bench." Hans, noticing that the man was in bitter earnest, then left the room. As Blumhardt tells:

> Pale and trembling and not at all like himself, he asked me, "*Herr Pfarrer*, do you think I can still find forgiveness and salvation?" He assured me he had not been able to sleep for a whole week and if he could not get this burden off his chest, it would be the end of him. I had not expected this man to come to me; there-fore I remained somewhat reserved and cautious and told him straight out that I did not trust him nor would I trust him until he confessed some of his sins to show his sincerity. But I could not bring myself to let this strangely distraught man go without praying with him. Doing something I had never done before, I laid my hands on him and said a few words of blessing, which visibly comforted him.

Two days later (January 2) the man came again. On January 3 Blumhardt wrote to Barth: "Yesterday the poor sinner was back, looking so broken and distressed as he stood in the doorway that the mere sight of him made one of my maid servants weep."

I do not know how that second visit went. The man had intended to confess his sins the very first time he came, but in spite of his good will he apparently did not manage it even this second time. It was only on a later occasion that he said straight out, "*Herr Pfarrer*, now I want to confess." As Blumhardt tells:

> That is what he did and with great openness. It gave me my first insight into the many heavy sins rampant among our people. He

was still greatly burdened, and my evangelical comfort had no lasting effect. He said that to give him complete peace I would have to pronounce forgiveness in the authority of my office. I asked him to be patient until the next visit, which he made the following morning, with a heart greatly eased and comforted. He insisted on having his sins formally forgiven, and I, in any case rejoicing at the redemption of this sinner, saw no reason for not doing something I had to regard as in keeping with the office of a minister of the Gospel according to the Augsburg Confession and the catechism as well as the words of Jesus in the New Testament. I did it with the laying on of hands, and when he rose from his knees, his totally changed countenance shone with joy and gratitude.

This was the second turning point in Blumhardt's life. The first one—the response to his cry, "Lord Jesus, help!"—had led him into grim struggles and only through them to a memorable victory; this time the fruit of victory fell into his lap unexpectedly. The undreamt-of harvest he was to receive in the days following might well make him feel, on a smaller scale, as the angel of the church in Philadelphia felt long ago when hearing the Lord say (Rev 3:7–8): "These are the words of the holy one, the true one, who has the key of David, who opens and no one shall shut, who shuts and no one opens. I know your works. Behold, I have set before you an open door, which no one is able to shut."

Blumhardt more than once set this moment, so important to him, down in writing. From another such account we insert here the following passages: "I can never forget the impression that the absolution made on me and on that man; an unutterable joy radiated from his face. I felt drawn into a completely new sphere, totally unknown to me, in which holy, spiritual powers were at work. I could not yet understand it, nor did I try to, but continued to act in a similar simple and cautious way when presently other sinners came along."

Glad and happy, the "poor sinner" left the rectory and told Hans, "Now I am going to speak to my pals. They listened to my jokes, and now they are going to listen when I tell them how they can find salvation." And he kept his word. The next day he was back at the rectory, bringing along one of his cronies, who was just as remorseful as he had been himself and whom he helped find the way to the rector's study. Same procedure, same fruit! Soon another came, and so forth.

On Friday, January 26,[2] a monthly day of penitence, Blumhardt, deeply moved by these experiences, preached on the watchword or text for the day, "The right hand of the Most High changes everything" (Ps 77:11, following the Luther translation used by Blumhardt). He tells: "That was the signal for the general breakthrough, and so strong became the press of people that I was kept constantly busy from seven o'clock in the morning until eleven o'clock at night. Men of whom one would never have expected it sat in the living room for hours, silent and withdrawn as they waited their turn." Saturday, January 27, Blumhardt writes to Barth:

> Until eight o'clock in the evening yesterday people kept coming one after the other. Up to now a total of sixteen persons have made their confessions to me. With ten of them I am finished for the present, but generally I hold off with the absolution. Everybody has to come at least three times, and several who did not find peace because something still remained hidden had to come six or eight times. Many have already made appointments. One thing I would like to tell you, though hesitantly: Since last Monday, X has not drunk any brandy and, mark well, without my asking him and without his telling me, until I heard it from him and also from his wife yesterday morning. Let's rejoice, even though with trembling!

Tuesday, January 30, Blumhardt writes:

> Yesterday from eight in the morning until eleven at night there was one caller after another . . . By evening it made a total of thirty-five, all suffering severe pangs of conscience and struggling for peace with such travail and weeping that in many cases I granted absolution the very first time they came, for their hearts seemed about to burst. Others, though, have to come again. Altogether twenty-four have found peace. In F.'s house there is a gathering

2. In reporting about the revival in the journal of Württemberg churches and schools (1845) ["Mitteilung von Pfarrer (Johann Christoph) Blumhardt" *Evangelisches Kirchenblatt, zunächst für Württemberg* nos. 7, 14, 15 (1845) ["Communications from Pastor (Johann Christoph) Blumhardt"].], Blumhardt gives the "beginning of February" as the date for this sermon. However, in view of his statement that he preached on that particular "daily text" (which through the storm of events probably remained more firmly embedded in his memory than the date), we here change the date to January 26, the day to which this text was assigned in the Moravian book of daily texts for the year 1844. Also, the events that, according to Blumhardt occurred on January 27 fit in remarkably well with that assumption, making it all the more probable. On the other hand, what Blumhardt tells in the above church journal about the number of people attending his services before and after that particular sermon has been partly taken from his memories of those days in February.

every evening of newly awakened men. Otherwise, people meet at various places, especially at G.'s [a woman's], where they can all go with confidence. The billows are surging ever higher.

On February 3 he can tell his friend that as a result of the above-mentioned sermon, the total has now reached sixty-seven. With burdened hearts the callers sat side by side in the living room, waiting for their turn to enter the study. In there, even the hardest men could not help shedding bitter tears. Blumhardt's manner toward such callers was gentle and quiet, as if passive, never obtrusive, but he relentlessly insisted on the truth and rejected any excuses. As he wrote to Barth, the many unsuspected sins and abominations gave him much to sigh and pray about inwardly.

Some extracts from the letter of February 3 show that not everybody came as remorsefully as some we have described:

> When I ask some persons what makes them come, they answer that watching others become so happy and cheerful has made them wish to experience the same. To be sure, a lot is still lacking there, yet having once come, they can't escape any more. Many prayer circles have come into being, and there is nothing but godly conversation in every house. My talks on whatever subject, light-hearted and popular in their appeal, find an echo and become general topics of conversation, from which alone you may see how everything has changed. God be praised! May he help me to combine prudence and wisdom with patience and love.

The movement reached Unterhaugstett as well. Many a one who had mocked previously or had perhaps chided his wife for going turned up himself a week later, shedding bitter tears of remorse especially for his hostile attitude and confessing that he had no rest or peace by day or night.

It took a while before the attendants of the *Stunde* [prayer meeting outside the established Church]—the real pietists—showed up (though to make up for this the work of grace would afterward prove to be much more genuine and solid in them than in some of the others). In the rectory yard one evening, one of the leading men of the *Stunde* came up to Hans and said, "You know, what our rector is doing now is actually Catholic stuff!"

"You think so? He doesn't ask people to confess! But when they come and seek peace, he, as every pastor should be, is under obligation to serve them. Have you found forgiveness of sins?"

"Yes."

"Well, then let others find it too!"

Lo and behold, a few days later the man came back. He first apologized to Hans for bringing up that objection, which he said had weighed heavily on his conscience ever since. Then, like the others, he went contritely to see the rector and returned, no longer a pious person but a poor sinner, reconciled to God through grace.

Things went similarly with another outstanding member of the *Stunde*, a man highly respected, and for good reason, on account of his devout, honorable character. He, too, called at the rectory. Meeting Blumhardt on the stairs, he said to him, "*Herr Pfarrer*, I thought, that as everybody else goes to see you, I . . ."

"So you have something on your heart too?" Blumhardt asked.

"Not exactly that," was the reply.

"Well, I thought so. You are the dear, good Mr. A." Blumhardt said warmly, shook his hand and, excusing himself, bade him farewell. Early the next morning there was A., waiting to speak to the rector. He had had a terrible night, in which he had been made aware of all his sins; no longer did he come as the good and respectable Mr. A. but as one of the worst sinners. Blumhardt commented, "I thought he would come, for I had to keep praying for him ever since."

His work was constantly growing. On February 10 he writes:

> Every day I have people with me until half past eleven at night; the next morning at six somebody is already waiting, and this goes on without a letup all day long, so that I can no longer think of anything else. At Sunday school yesterday in the jam-packed schoolroom I asked to be excused from talks on account of my work for the monthly paper, but because of that I may expect all the more callers today. If this goes on . . . and yet, what am I to say to it all? It is way beyond anything I can think. By now a total of 156 persons have come, all shedding tears of repentance—if not the first time, then the second, and quite surely the third time. How I manage to come through is a puzzle also to me. Just imagine—the many different characters! And if you knew the manifold sins and abominations, which could often make me freeze with horror, you would perceive the difficulties of my situation even more than you do already . . . The gatherings, spinning evenings, and so forth, are getting so crowded I shall soon have to do some organizing . . .

That was written on Saturday; by the following Thursday the total had risen to 222. From those days we still have notes Barth wrote to another friend about the movement in Möttlingen. On February 13 he reported: "On Sunday I was in Möttlingen with Seldenschlo and met several of those newly awakened, and it was a joy to see them. True, among them are some who had long been awakened and were members of the *Stunde*, but they had in part been very sleepy and not quite single-minded, and now they have been gripped afresh by the new life. Nonetheless I see the whole thing as a miracle before my eyes." And on February 24:

> We go on for years scattering the seed; we know it is good seed and the seed merchant has not cheated us, yet nothing will come up, and people stay just the same. Still, nothing is really lost, only it takes a long time for something to sprout. Of that I now have a conspicuous example before my eyes. In Möttlingen Machtolf powerfully preached the Gospel for thirty-seven years and following him Gross for fourteen years. Through them many were converted, though only a few in the village itself. Then, after ten years when if nothing new was built, at least nothing was torn down either, I continued tilling the same old ground there for fourteen years, hoping for a harvest from at least the previously sown seed. But I was not granted that joy nor, to tell the truth, did I deserve it.
>
> Lately my successor, Blumhardt, has been laboring faithfully for another five years, during which time things seemed outwardly to get worse and worse and moral standards and the inner life kept declining, even among former *Stunden* folk. Yet now, a few weeks ago a fire was kindled that goes on spreading. One person after another has been seeking out the rector, the toughest and wildest first of all; they came along dejected and in despair, wailed and wept, confessed their sins, and found the peace of forgiveness—some quickly, some more slowly. Fearful horrors of sin committed in secret have come to light, which are most likely widespread elsewhere too. By now over 350 persons have come, from eighty-year-olds down to schoolchildren, and the conflagration has also spread to the parish branch in Haugstett, which up till now has seemed to be absolutely unreceptive. So far more than twenty persons have come from there.
>
> Last Monday, when the daughter of one of the staunchest opponents of the truth got married, some of the finest songs of our hymnbook were sung with great fervor—a resounding triumph for the Gospel. The remarkable thing is that people constantly speak of impressions they had received at the time of Machtolf, of

Gross, and of me to which they had been unfaithful for so long. In particular, the importance of our confirmations has again become clear, for nearly all admit to having had their consciences pricked then, in a way they could not forget.

On March 2 Barth reports: "In Möttlingen the triumphs of grace continue." At the beginning of March Blumhardt tells his friend the following, especially about the *fruits* of the movement:

> Imagine! Yesterday I heard that all twenty-four members of my confirmation class have been having proper daily meetings in N.'s house. They pray on their knees, with everyone taking a turn; they also sing and read a Bible chapter. M. M., the one most deeply gripped, takes the meeting and questions the others about what they have read, and everything is done in such a nice, childlike, and innocent way that one cannot listen without being deeply moved.

In those days when in the men's meeting he saw himself surrounded by so many men, both young and old, there awoke in him the longing and hope for a pouring out of the Holy Spirit. "That has to come if things are to be different with our Christianity. It simply must not continue in so wretched a state, I feel. The gifts and powers of the beginning time— oh, they ought to come back! And I believe the dear Savior is just waiting for us to ask for them."

Thus in the circle of his "boys," who had already come so close to him in the "newspaper hour," there came to him the thought that became the motto of his life: Let us pray and hope for a new outpouring of the Holy Spirit! It is characteristic of the divine protection and blessing he constantly lived under that his great experiences did not give him a feeling of wealth but rather of poverty. It kept him from falling prey to megalomania—the bloated feeling that he and those around him had more than any others. On the contrary, it made him straightway think of the others: "It must come to them too! They, like us, need even more than has now been given to us."[3]

When we try to imagine what it was like on one of these long days from six in the morning until eleven at night and consider how much of what came out cut into his heart and how much called for holy wisdom,

---

3. A certain critic has asserted that Blumhardt had expected the awakening to bear further fruits and that only his disappointment in this respect had made him feel the need for a renewed outpouring of the Holy Spirit. This is an assertion that no one who really knew Blumhardt has been able to comprehend. The above historical note alone should be enough to disprove it.

we realize that his joy in the harvest was interwoven with a great deal of toil and sweat. Nevertheless, he was able to write to Barth:

> But you have no reason to feel sorry for me, except insofar as you yourself have to pester me [with demands to have copy ready at the date due]. For unless I simply close the door, I literally have not one moment to myself. But up to now I have not been able to close the door, for people are often so tormented or under pressure that they just cannot wait. Yesterday it happened that one of those waiting got sent up before his turn, the others saying, "You are hurting so much, you had better go up first." Yesterday I also had a conference with twenty men (there will be even more today!), and everything went very well. We all came to be of one heart and soul, and again it lasted three hours. At the same time, my wife had a girls' spinning bee down below. On Monday she started a missionary spinning society for women among the tobacco twisters . . . Every day I get to hear more of the confirmations you held; even J. P. knew something.

All this took place in February, during which month Barth received twelve letters from Blumhardt. On March 2 Blumhardt reports: "My conferences have made splendid progress. On Monday thirty-one adolescent boys, Tuesday twenty-one men, Wednesday forty-six men—all together ninety-eight male persons. All of them spoke, and in such a sincere and warm way that on Wednesday I almost felt as if I were at the general conference in Basel. On Thursday thirty-three women attended, yesterday fifty, making a total of eighty-three. With them, too, things went very well." On March 9 he writes:

> The monthly is still coming today—by special delivery. Please bear in mind: yesterday morning I had personal talks and did proof-reading, so that I had trouble getting to Haugstett in time. There a prayer meeting and confirmation class; then I had talks with twenty-one grown-ups and met with twenty-six children, who asked to be blessed, so that I arrived back home at about six. Here, people were already waiting, among them K.—in short, it was half past eleven in the evening before I got to the paper. So it meant night work, but you know what happened? Apart from the fact that my own children kept me busy, at two in the morning the bell rang: Old M. lay dying. I hurried to her (who had been so happy when she had been with me the day before), and when I got there, her trembling and other symptoms quickly told me what was the matter, and she was helped at once. There they told me, by the way,

that the evening before about ten children had been in her room; they had knelt down and prayed with all their hearts, first for the king, next for the rector, and then for all men. I had scarcely got home when the bell rang again: The mayor's child was dying! I set off bravely, but this time the child was dead when I arrived . . .

Blumhardt has some touching things to tell about the way the little children, without his knowledge, would meet and pray on their knees, each taking his or her turn. We want to skip that but note that no one could have been more opposed than Blumhardt to revivals and prayer circles of an unwholesome character among children. When he was told of schoolchildren who would meet for prayer even during their free time and then drift into class late and absent-minded, he said, "I would have boxed their ears; such prayer is no prayer!" He maintained that such excesses could very well have been prevented, and to the question, "How?" he replied, "Instead of being secretly pleased about it, people ought to have felt shocked! Then such deviations could never have gained ground in the first place."

The children would also come to Blumhardt in the rectory to receive his blessing, in some cases also to confess sins, and with good reason, for it made him cry out in distress to Barth, "It looks awful among the children!" Where there had been a "brooding" atmosphere (as Blumhardt put it) among the children, the lovely sight of new life coming in greatly delighted and refreshed him. He carefully saw to it that the children, though under supervision (without being aware of it), were not exposed to observation, much less gaped at admiringly, and he found it quite in order that the above-mentioned activities came to an end soon after.

On March 13 Blumhardt writes:

> Manifold joys and struggles side by side, neither one crowding out the other. And it is good so. Yet what do you say when I tell you that it has now come to the point where even lives are in danger, threatened by the devil working through people? No matter— every day is a day of victory, for I say, the more struggles, the more victories! I am not one for giving in, so everything is bound to turn out well. St. B. for years had a grudge against you because of not getting a book for a wedding present, but he sees this now as a great sin and therefore wants to ask your forgiveness.

On March 29: "The Lord must have something great in mind. We are patiently persevering in prayer and faith. But the fact that the movement continues and even grows is an important sign that something more is coming. With childlike joy I look forward to Holy Week."

With very few exceptions (and they, too, fell into line later on), by Easter time the movement had taken hold of the entire congregation, including Unterhaugstett. During the winter it had spread to the neighboring villages too and in part farther into the Black Forest. As it was much talked about, and ridiculed as well, it became more widely known. It even made one or the other of the scoffers think, and before they knew it, they, too, would come. Once, at the burial service for some little-known person, Blumhardt was astonished to see his church full of strangers, and from then on more and more people from farther away attended his Sunday services. Already on April 6 he wrote to Barth: "The area around the church (churchyard) can no longer contain all the listeners. It shows how necessary it is for my colleagues in the ministry to open their doors too."

That was something he had very much on his heart. Gripped as he was by the needfulness and greatness of the cause, he was concerned that members of other congregations should not have to come to him. As regards his attitude and relationship to church attenders from other places, he wrote in the church journal that he found the influx of these people quite a problem, knowing that it would cause a diminished attendance in some of his colleagues' churches. He went on to say:

> But what was I to do? How was I to channel the flood? Indeed, this whole striking and unusual movement—one really must have experienced it oneself—has made me think and pray. As it is taking place within the church whose Head Shepherd we know, it could really not be seen as either folly or presumption on my part if I do not reject the thought that the Lord might possibly have a hand in such a movement. But if it was the Lord I was dealing with, it was advisable for me to take upon myself whatever labor, sweat, worry, fear, misunderstandings, and struggles it might entail, rather than let human considerations cause me to resist him. I took pains therefore not to do anything designed to draw people, and nobody can say that I flattered the visitors. At the same time, I cherished the justified hope that before long my fellow ministers would be given fuller churches than ever, while the number of people flocking here would of its own accord fall off. As a matter of fact, I could name colleagues who have even encouraged their parishioners to go to Möttlingen. Whether the many visits have borne fruit I leave for others to say; that is something I am not

answerable for. I have not sought or encouraged them, nor have I hindered them; either way I have kept my conscience clear.

I might mention that the visits of outsiders to my home, which have still not completely ceased, are even more difficult and burdensome for me. As a rule these people would come to me with something on their hearts they wanted to speak to me about; it struck and concerned me to see them before me in the very same condition and attitude as my own parishioners had been in previously. They felt burdened by certain sins they no longer wanted to carry around with them.

It put me into a very awkward situation, all the more since I soon became aware that some of my colleagues, to whom I would much rather have sent them, do not fully share my conviction about the value of private confessions, even though several of them have thanked me for referring their parishioners to them. Thus, all the advice I could give to those people was as follows: If they felt heavily burdened, they should open their hearts to a sincere and devoted friend of theirs with prayer and as in the presence of God, according to the word of the apostle James, "Confess your sins to one another." Then, I said, if they repented deeply and longed for complete inner renewal, they could be assured of forgiveness, especially if they let it be sealed by participation in the Lord's Supper. That is the line I took with persons from outside.

To be sure, occasionally a visitor would share with me this or that from his life, which might look like a confession, but I must very definitely refute any rumors that I treated such outsiders like members of my own congregation, thus encroaching on someone else's sphere of authority. There was in any case no question of an absolution. But what I cannot say emphatically enough to my esteemed colleagues is that they would do their parishioners a wonderful service by first making them aware of their old, hidden sins and then offering them a chance of ridding themselves of these through confession.

That is how Blumhardt in diary style describes the situation. We feel reminded of his statement, "The fuller my heart, the drier it seems to me are my words." If there is such joy in heaven over one sinner who repents, what an unbroken feast of joy the events just recorded must have occasioned up there! But the very greatness and solemnity of the cause calls for a simple, dry presentation.

It is hard to form a true picture of the deep earnestness with which this movement took hold of the people. Let us put ourselves into the situation of somebody living at some distance from Möttlingen who would be the first in his village to seek out Blumhardt and lay his inner need before him—how much he had to overcome in order to take this step! And after his joyful return, how much it would take for a second and third person to make up their minds, for—at least to begin with—every new instance of this kind naturally led to an outburst of mockery in the village. On the way, too, such ridicule was to be expected. If on a Saturday someone was found walking in a direction that made him out to be a "pilgrim to Möttlingen," he was liable to receive greetings such as "You, too, making for Jerusalem?" or "Have fun!" and so on.

Besides, this movement totally lacked the extravagant emotionalism that usually exerts such a powerful attraction. There was no sign here of public protestations of repentance nor of an almost boastful broadcasting of one's sins and avowal of one's own wickedness such as unfortunately often mark so-called revivals. This awakening was much too sober and earnest for that, much too deeply rooted in reality. With many it was an inner *must*; they could not do otherwise. It was just as the psalmist sings (Ps 32:1–4):

> Blessed is he whose transgressions are forgiven,
>> whose sin is covered.
> Blessed is the one to whom the Lord does not impute iniquity
>> and in whose spirit there is no guile.
> When I kept silent, my bones grew old
>> through my groaning all day long.
> For day and night thy hand was heavy upon me.

Something had struck terror into people's hearts. One felt somehow reminded of the movement in the days of John the Baptist. Also reminiscent of that movement was the earnestness and simplicity of the "fruits that befit repentance." Everywhere old enemies became reconciled, and, very specially, stolen goods were returned. A shopkeeper in Calw told me of more than one such case—among others, how at dusk one day a well-dressed man had rushed into the store, put a coin on the counter, and rushed out again. Presumably he had once paid with a coin no longer in circulation.

The restitutions of property brought Blumhardt great pain. To cite one case: A poor married couple of a Christian disposition had to pay interest on a debt, but only barely managed it. It so happened that the creditor had by mistake once signed for two annual interest payments—

the current one and the remaining one—instead of just one. They only noticed it when they got home and accepted it, so to speak, with thanks for such divine help. Years passed. Caught up in the current of the revival, the couple felt struck in their consciences, confided the matter to Blumhardt and, following his advice, confessed their misdeed to the creditor, asking for leniency and patience, since at that moment they were in no position to pay off the old debt. They, like Blumhardt, had hoped that things would not turn out too badly, but the outcome was utmost indignation and unrelenting insistence on immediate payment on the part of the creditor, and great need and distress on the part of the debtors. Sometimes, when restitution was no longer possible, Blumhardt pointed the penitent to Ephesians 4:28.

Some time later, in morning devotions at Bad Boll, when discoursing at length on his hopes for a movement encompassing all humankind, Blumhardt also spoke of the motives that drove people to repent, and to repent in this particular way. What he expressed as a hope was obviously based on what he had actually experienced. This meditation is to be found in *Täglich Brod* ("Daily Bread"), July 17–18, 1880, as follows:

> In those days ten men from the nations of every tongue
> shall take hold of the robe of a Jew, saying, "Let us go with
> you, for we have heard that God is with you" (Zech 8:23).

> A time will come when everybody will feel troubled and become aware that he does not have what he ought to have. People will feel a great need for something they do not know but henceforth regard as indispensable. Of a sudden a yearning will arise in them; they will come to feel: "How poor and weak we are, how miserable and depraved! How little comfort we have! How little certainty there is in what we think, believe, and hope!" There will come a time when they will all experience an unutterable, painful emptiness in their hearts. Then suddenly they will catch sight of some people who look cheerful, as though they had just that which the others lack, and without delay they will go up to those people and say, "We want to go with you." And they will learn from them many things: how God revealed and showed himself to them, how he has blessed them, and how definitely and clearly they know themselves to be under his protection. And then everybody will want to have that too.

> That is how conversions begin such as now and then occur among the heathen and will one day, when the time is ripe, spread through the whole world. Then those who have what is right and

true—and in whom it can be seen that they have it—will be completely inundated by a flood of people who yearn to have it too. Oh, that this time might come soon! How that would please us!

Seeking help from one another is, by the way, always a matter of importance. The present kind of piety, all genteel and self-loving, says, "I don't need anybody; I can set things right with God myself." As long as people do not need anybody, as long as they do not seek out others to find advice and to obtain from them what they lack themselves, they do not get very far. It is only when people need each other and therefore go out to each other that God's blessing is there and things go forward with them. As long as everybody just wants to quietly work out his own salvation, things are not as they should be. Therefore we want to go out to one another; each should seek to gain from the other as much as he can in spiritual matters. Indeed, when the Lord awakens in people a desire to open up to one another so as to find new strength in the Lord, then that is a time of grace.

In a letter written in 1846, Blumhardt goes more deeply into the causes of the awakening and their relationship to the struggle. In a previous letter (not available to me) the friend addressed had spoken about the impressions he himself had gained of the movement in Möttlingen. On his frequent visits there he had apparently been struck by something that could escape none but the most cursory observer. In a way that reminded him of what the first chapters of Acts (2:7, 43; 3:10; 5:11) tell of a growing *fear* that came over people, this friend had noticed that beneath the blissful peace, a sense of shock determined and governed the whole mood of the people. From that he had apparently concluded that maybe the whole awakening could be explained as the moral effect of the terrifying impact the struggle and especially the final victory had on people. To that Blumhardt replied as follows:

> Your remarks about life in Möttlingen were a joy to me, only you must not interpret the shock of which you write as a mechanical, physical fright caused by certain facts. The relationship between my struggle and the awakening is not at all an outward one. The awakening was in the fullest sense *won* by the struggle. Through battle and victory satanic powers were broken that now either cannot work at all or but very feebly. A spell that had darkened hearts and minds has been removed; people's minds, formerly dull and closed, have become responsive. But since in their benighted state people had unconcernedly committed many outrageous things, their first reaction to a living word could only be one of shock at

their own condition. In many cases they had not intended or no longer knew what they had done, but now it hits them like a ton of bricks, and they can no longer hide it from themselves or from the light. That is how you have to see it, my good friend; that is what explains the continuing shock.

An overview of the movement as a whole seems to bring out one outstanding characteristic—its *objectivity*, a distinguishing mark hard to put into words. One might say that it bore the imprint of divine origin. There was nothing fabricated in it, neither with Blumhardt nor with the people coming to him; what he, and they, did was something that simply came upon them. Blumhardt on his part had never so much as dreamt of such a movement, much less attempted to provoke anything like it.

To be sure, while still embroiled in his struggle he had been made aware that, as he put it, "Secrecy is the power of sin" and that some burdens are not lifted from a conscience until they are brought to light. Because of that, he had begun, in his hearty and brotherly way, to tell his Sunday attendance before the Lord's Supper that whoever had something on his conscience that might rob him of the blessing of the sacred meal should come to him. But that was all. True, his preaching during the time of awakening uncovered relentlessly the sins and wrongs among people both of high and low estate and cast a searching light into the innermost recesses of the human heart, but it always assumed that his listeners were in a repentant mood.[4] He once remarked: "That my sermons find open hearts is in part due to the fact that I assume all my listeners to be of like mind with me and treat them accordingly."

In a later letter to a friend he points out that this attitude did not exclude urging people very strongly to turn around. This friend was enthralled by the miracles of healing he experienced with Blumhardt and full of enthusiasm about the hope that marked Blumhardt's thinking. He wanted to urge him to be more vocal and, as he thought, more courageous in proclaiming the special luminous insights into the course of God's kingdom that he had been granted. In reply, Blumhardt pointed

---

4. This does not mean, of course, that repentance and conversion, as laid on his heart by the Lord, were not his first and last concern. As he later writes to one of his friends, "You must move more in these basic areas of salvation: repentance and faith. By this I do not want to say that you yourself shy away from them; I only want to ask you to give them more attention, work more at them inwardly, and bear them in mind when dealing with others. It is with these things that my whole cause and all our hope stands or falls."

him to the "beginning of his story," as he called it, that is, to the conversion of his congregation, as follows:

> Before it even occurred to me that I might have powers of healing, people were being led to an experience of repentance and faith. What were my guiding principles here? The same that I had known from childhood on and which, Reformation-style, I had gathered up from the Scriptures, except that I held on to them in a more inward, determined, and single-minded way than many before me. All my sermons reflected the Protestant doctrine, and I always felt that I could preach effectively and reach person's hearts only when I did it above all in the strength of the Spirit. Repentance and faith in the crucified Christ was the pivot on which everything had to hinge. Conversion and nothing but conversion was the goal toward which I had to steer, guided by the well-known teachings of our catechism. In doing that, I always put the main stress on what everybody could immediately obtain from the Savior by single-mindedly embracing repentance and faith—precisely those things the catechism has been pointing to for three hundred years as the sure fruits of faith: forgiveness of sins, peace, divine sonship, a gracious, listening Savior. I thereby followed in the footsteps of John, who prepared the way for the Lord through repentance and forgiveness of sins; I also followed the Lord himself and whatever he says, above all in the Sermon on the Mount, in which, without pointing to future eventualities, he assures us most strongly that prayers will be answered.

But Blumhardt had a real loathing for the method of attacking the "sinner's" nerves with high-powered rhetoric to get him to repent. He disapproved of "converted" persons assailing the "unconverted" with the spears and clubs of persuasion, following the motto, "Strike while the iron is hot!" It scared him to see one sinner thus thrust himself upon another sinner, bringing into play so forcefully his own supposedly admirable personality. He expected it to bear nothing but bad fruit, even though it might seem to result in real conversions. In Möttlingen he once lamented, "Would that those conversions that leave heart and behavior unchanged finally come to an end!"

Once when invited to preach in a very worldly-minded town, his host minister showed himself almost dissatisfied because Blumhardt had spoken in so kindly and loving a way. But Blumhardt replied, "Everything in the Gospel works repentance . . . Whatever flows from your own repentance works more repentance, even if it's nothing but the Gospel, but whatever is said that does not spring from your own repentance is as effective as soap bubbles against fortress walls." He worried that our present time, so rich in Christian aspirations, might bring forth a you-Christianity (in contrast to an I-Christianity), where a person would be very concerned about somebody else and that person's conversion but less so about his own. One feels reminded of the passage in Edward Young's "Night Thoughts":

> When young, indeed
> In full content we sometimes nobly rest
> Unanxious for ourselves, and only wish,
> As duteous sons, our fathers were more wise.

Thus Blumhardt carefully guarded human freedom. As we heard above, in his study he would be earnest, never pushy, but relentlessly demanding the whole truth. When asked what a person ought to confess of all that was burdening him, he would, as he once related in a ministers' conference, advise, "Tell that which you would rather not tell!" As we saw, he regarded the speaking out of forgiveness as a serious matter, but not because a sin was too great or a guilt too heavy. That did not stop him. Decisive for him was whether the other was wholehearted or kept holding something back.

Such cautious restraint he observed all the more for having himself suffered punishment when he had once acted less prudently, as we shall hear later. He increasingly felt himself to be Christ's bond servant, who, disregarding his own person, has to act solely in the name of his Lord, so that the Lord can do through him as his instrument whatever is to be done.

Here was the other *objective trait* that made itself felt: the peace that radiated from Blumhardt. It made one feel that Jesus Christ himself, acting through his servant, stretched out his peace-imparting hand to the sinner and spoke out the actual, unquestionably certain word of forgiveness, as expressed in the assurances, "Whatever you loose on earth shall be loosed in heaven" (Matt 18:18) and, "If you forgive the sins of any, they are forgiven" (John 20:23). At the time, this result was far and away the most distinctive feature of the whole movement—its main-spring, so to speak. It was just the extraordinary, striking, blissful change noticeable in people whom one had known as mere nobodies or even as black sheep that encouraged others to come too. That is why Blumhardt himself never tired of telling about it, recounting, for example, "Under my laying on of hands they felt a beneficent strength come over them, which without my knowing it had a physically healing effect as well; at any rate it changed and rejuvenated their whole appearance."

How simply and lovingly did the Savior show himself here as helper, when at last—one might perhaps say—he had found somebody who understood him better than many others and let him have more scope to rule and intervene as he saw fit! Blumhardt's way was infinitely more effective and more in keeping with the life everlasting the Savior grants than our human attempts to speak helpful words, whether threatening punishment or promising solace. We really should not be so ready to hold those on the receiving end accountable for the ineffectiveness of our counseling.

The immediate impact on the recipients of what they were being given must have been overwhelming, but what moved them even more was their subsequent perception of how deep and long-lasting the effect was. One man from Möttlingen, a robust son of nature, after he had had his turn climbing the stairs from the living room to the study and had received Blumhardt's blessing of peace, was so overcome by the crystal clearness of this peace and the certainty of forgiveness that he fell on the pastor's neck and smothered him with kisses, as Blumhardt wrote to Barth. Such redemption and liberation was in that forgiveness that people, though having to remain watchful, did not have to struggle hard to avoid their former besetting sins. Former alcoholics, for example, declared that their thirst had altogether vanished. Formerly every pub they passed had exerted a magic attraction on them, but now they felt something like loathing and disgust at the sight of those pubs.

The objective character of the revival was further evidenced by its all-embracing effect. It did not give rise to two factions—the "converted" and the "unconverted"; on the contrary, the party spirit totally disappeared. Almost without exception the movement took hold of "all God's creatures" in Blumhardt's parish.

To be sure, in a certain way that can be explained by Blumhardt's whole manner. He actually never had enemies, if one disregards those shadowy mortal foes we shall hear of in the next chapter. Factionalism and party strife did not flourish around him. His former labors, too, powerful though their impact was, had nowhere led to hatred, quarreling, or persecution, neither in Dürrmenz nor in Iptingen. All this had its root in a disposition to which he himself largely ascribed the power he wielded over his audiences. The secret of it was that he trusted each of his listeners to have the attitude he himself possessed; he had great confidence in the good will generally inherent in us sinful people. He could speak out sharply against preachers who complained about "persecution": "Don't think that it comes on you because of your piety! Your piety might have to suffer a lot more, and there isn't all that much of it. But when one of your listeners notices, 'He doesn't think much of me,' then he has a right to be angry with you."

That means that the basic preconditions for an impact on the whole congregation were there in Blumhardt, but it does not adequately explain the fact that so deep-going a movement could take hold of practically the entire parish. The whole movement—the repentance as well as the finding of peace—had the obvious appearance of being a work of God, and its all-embracing character is the clearest indication that far from being a mere appearance, it was a bright and wonderful reality and that God's mercy toward sinners was at work with special power through it all.

Yet one more sign of the movement's *objective* nature might be mentioned, even if somewhat wistfully: its long-lastingness. Wistfully, for Blumhardt had feared from the beginning, "If this movement does not become a general one and if the Spirit from on high is not poured out on us afresh, this movement, too, is going to peter out." Unfortunately that is what happened, if only partially. When you now [1883] ask the children and grandchildren of those who were awakened in 1844/45 if that wonderful time is now forgotten and no trace of it left, their eyes, radiating thankfulness, provide the answer. In 1879 the *Schwäbische Merkur* (Swabian Mercury), reporting how on May 1 crowds of people from the Black Forest had come streaming to the mission festival in Calw, commented, "They came in order to see their father Blumhardt once more." Being the children and grandchildren of those who had experienced the awakening, they knew why.

We want to insert here a report written by a man of good reputation in our circles, Adolf Christ-Sarasin, town councilor of Basel and president of the Basel Missionary Society. In 1845 he attended the above-mentioned annual mission festival in Calw, always celebrated on May 1, and from there visited Möttlingen. His report does take us into the year *following* the start of the awakening, but all the better: In the course of a year and a half or so a merely passing enthusiasm might well have flickered out.

In a letter to a friend, town councilor Christ-Sarasin described the impressions he gained on this journey, and the *Christliche Volksbote aus Basel* (Christian People's Messenger from Basel) included his journey report in its "Reminiscences of Pastor Blumhardt in Boll," which appeared in numbers 15–19, 1880. Christ-Sarasin first tells of his journey from Korntal to Calw, of the hospitality extended there to him and many others by Dr. Barth, and of other matters. He then goes on to describe the mission festival and his subsequent visit in Möttlingen, as follows:

> At one o'clock the bells called us into the big church at Calw, and we entered via the sacristy and the choir. What a sight! A church comparable in size to our St. Peter's church in Basel, but with double galleries all around and an open choir and the galleries full of people from the Württemberg countryside. The townsfolk were completely crowded out by the peasants. There was no room to sit; in pews and aisles the press of people was so great that quite literally not a stone could have fallen to the ground. Whereas in Basel we witness gatherings of believers from many "tribes," see costumes from many regions, hear all kinds of dialects spoken, and thus have before us a picture of unity in diversity, here in Calw *one* people was standing before the Lord, even in outward appearance. Costumes, features, speakers—all bore the true imprint of Württemberg. Frankly, that made a deeper impression on me than all the speeches, especially when the estimated six thousand people gathered there raised their voices to sing:

> Jesus lives!
> Your heads lift high,
> You that call upon His name,
> Him alone proclaim!

Barth's concluding words really hit the mark:

> Look around! There is still much night and darkness on earth. The extent and result of our mission work is still so small that we could scarcely enter it on a world map as large as this altar. And yet we must conquer this power of darkness. Listen! General Goodie in India had orders to take a fortress set high on a rock. He sent a regiment to carry out the order. They returned, described the difficulties of the task, and declared it impossible. "What, impossible? I have the order here in my pocket; it's got to be done!" And it was done! Something else: When Nelson fought his last battle, he gave out the watchword, "England expects every person to do his duty."

In the same way, my friends, the kingdom of God expects every one of you and of us to do his duty. Let that be our watchword!

It was five o'clock when we left the church. From the terrace in front we looked down on the great marketplace and the crowd surging over it like a living stream.

But I forgot to say that people generally regarded the appearance of Pastor Blumhardt from Möttlingen as the real center of the festival. They all wanted to see him, since through the awakening in his congregation his name has come to be in the hearts and on the lips of all. He gave the missionary report, but more than that, he gave meaning to it, for it was basically his own deep experiences, breaking forth with an astonishing power of speech, that infused and pervaded the whole. Above all it was the thought: Are we really doomed to continue in so wretched a state? Does Christian life have to stay so beggarly poor? Why do even believers, seeing a movement of awakening, comment that not much of it will last? Why this lack of faith? Should not everything become new? Yes, something new must and will be given when there is a fresh outpouring of the Spirit, and I lay it on you as a burden to pray for that. Then it will come, and we shall see great things, here among ourselves and in places far away.

After a friendly two hours at Barth's, where Pastors Mann and Zimmermann from Baden were also present, I traveled with that richly blessed man, Pastor Blumhardt, up to Möttlingen, situated about two hours from Calw in a high but fertile area.

Blumhardt has been the rector here for five years. In 1843 he went through a year of severe struggle—not with flesh and blood but with the prince and ruler of darkness. One person in particular who was grievously tormented by Satan gave him unspeakable trouble, of a kind impossible for him to relate in detail, as it went too far into mysterious, gruesome depths. The entire congregation knew about it and was seized by a certain fear mingled with awe. At the end of last year the struggle finally came to an end, and the tormented ones were given peace and freedom . . .

And then, behold, on New Year's Day there comes to the rectory a local man of bad reputation and violent character, whose neighbors live in fear of him. In tears he tells Blumhardt that the burden of his sins is getting so heavy he can no longer carry it; he must make a full confession to find rest and peace. And so he confessed his sins to the rector, specifically and at length, and the rector arrived at the firm conviction that by the laying on of hands he could give him the assurance that his sins were forgiven. And the man attained peace from God and was so full of joy that he told his friends and neighbors and wanted to help them find the same peace. (They call him the "missionary" now.)

Soon after, several came to the rector with heavy hearts, confessed their sins and found peace. Indeed, between New Year's Day and shortly after Easter all the six hundred Möttlingen folk (with the exception of ten or fifteen) and all the three hundred from the parish branch at Haugstett (with the exception of thirty or so) sought out the rector, confessed their sins, and are now joyful in the Lord. The children, too, were so gripped by the movement of the Spirit that little ones four to six years old came to the rectory in groups, not to confess but to be blessed by the rector. At times children would sit before him in rows to receive his blessing and carry it away with them. Such is the situation that the rector is confident that those remaining will also be awakened.

It was late when we drove into the village. At every house Blumhardt had reason to send up thanks to heaven. Here a serious marital quarrel had come to an end; in that house a redeemed drunkard was standing at the door; over yonder rebellious grown-up children had become obedient, and further on old enemies had mutually humbled themselves and become reconciled. From the lighted schoolhouse came the sound of lusty singing. About two hundred younger and older men had already been singing together for half an hour, while waiting for their pastor to come.

We hurried there. Very lovingly Blumhardt apologized for being late. Among other things he said:

> Look, I feel really sorry that sitting at this teacher's desk here puts me a bit above you. I would gladly sit down there among you, but it has to be like this because of the light, and so on. But even though I sit here a whole foot higher, you will still share your thoughts with me, won't you?

"Yes, we will!" came the reply from the benches.

> You see, it's necessary that we get together like this, for I can no longer see you in church, even though you are there [the church being so crowded that one has to look all over the place to find someone from Möttlingen in the attendance], and then I have to have the whole audience in mind in what I say, and sometimes I have to speak quite sharply. So it's important for me to talk with you separately. This time I want to tell first what I found out today about Möttlingen. For a hundred years you have had ministers who have proclaimed the Gospel to you.

There follows quite a bit about Bührer and Machtolf; Gross and Barth are also mentioned. Instead of "Bach," the journey report mentions a "Wagner," probably by mistake.

> Well, why has God given you Möttlingen folk such grace over such a long time, and now beyond all measure?
>
> "We don't know," said some.
>
> "Bührer's prayers" others thought.
>
> "Oh, it was free grace; we are the very least to deserve it," one voice said finally.
>
> Blumhardt's interpretation of the daily text and the prayer were quite unique. There was something fine and lofty in his whole manner, right down to the sound of his voice. It was as if his wonderful experiences reverberated in his voice. One had the feeling that people's hearts lay open before him, and that, of course, is just how it had been. I would put it like this: I felt this minister had in the highest sense a true inner relationship with his listeners.
>
> Afterwards, the schoolteacher related how things had changed with his schoolchildren, how much better and more willingly they were now learning. Godliness, he said, is of benefit in every way; it has a promise for this life as well as for the life to come.
>
> Only at a quarter after ten did we reach the rectory, and of course it was nearly midnight before we finally retired. I sat next to Blumhardt, that remarkable instrument of the Lord, who has had such a close view of God's mighty deeds, and a hand in them as well.
>
> There are many individual aspects worth mentioning. Some people's consciences were so heavily burdened by sin that at times it came to physical expression. One man had such trouble breathing and felt so constricted that when he spoke, he started to gasp with anxiety but felt relieved inwardly as well as physically when the pastor assured him, with the laying on of hands, that his sins were forgiven.
>
> A parishioner of a rough and rude type, who had long boasted that this thing would not touch him, did in the end feel a longing for redemption and told the rector, "Well, when the children start praying for their father, he can't hold out any longer. The other day I came home, and before opening the door I heard my children praying for me so urgently that I felt a heavy load descend on my heart, and now I come for help." He, too, was granted peace.
>
> When, at a meeting during the time of awakening, the pastor asked people about their prayers and if they were being answered, he was told of real miracles of grace, of being helped through day by day, and of prayers being heard—especially on the part of

children. By earnest prayer two little girls had been freed within a few days of a bad eczema, which otherwise only yields to a strict course of treatment. One of the confirmands had been afflicted with a certain bad condition by day and night, as well as in the early morning. He had prayed to be freed from it, was healed, and could take part in the whole confirmation ceremony undisturbed. When the king of Württemberg fell ill, little children would gather to intercede with special fervor for his recovery; they would kneel in a circle and in turn pray for him. In each house the married couple pray together on their knees. Since the awakening six older persons in the parish have died; it was as if they had been spared that they might still find peace, and this peace stayed with them right to the end. In each case Blumhardt closed their eyes and then sang with those present this song of praise:

> Hallelujah, let us adore
>
> Our Lord and God forevermore
>
> For all his wondrous doings!

The people have a real tender love for their rector. For the first of May they set up two small firs as "may trees" at the entrance to his humble little garden, joining them together with a boxwood garland—a little portal, more pleasant to pass through than any triumphal arch.

Early the next morning I was down in the village, greeting people and spending an hour with Stanger, father of the Stanger who died in Guinea as well as of the one who is now a student at the missionary institute in Basel. He is an elderly man, experienced and devout; therefore his impressions of the movement are quite important. This excellent man showed no trace of that "elder brother" complex mentioned in the Gospel. With tears of joy he spoke of those newly awakened; in particular, he confirmed that their walk of life had been turned upside down, that for example he now had a wonderful relationship with formerly difficult relatives. It was really true among them, he said, that "When God's grace first comes among us, it's the Lamb who guides and bears us," and he had a longing that the second part of that verse—"Later we must learn to dare and walk on our own two feet"—might also become a reality among them.

His neighbor, a blacksmith, had been an extremely rough and quarrelsome character. Before the New Year, Stanger had had an argument with him and become so angry that his conscience urged him to apologize for his outburst; he postponed it however. In the meantime, though, his neighbor was converted and at once came and apologized himself, leaving Stanger both happy and humbled.

On the morning I was with Blumhardt, he was due to hold his weekly Bible class at the parish branch called Haugstett. I went with him. Earlier, the Haugstett folk had spitefully blocked a footpath that would have shortened his way, yet now they love him like a father. The mayor, who had been especially hostile in those days, was now the first to appear in the schoolroom when the bell rang (in Württemberg every school house has a little bell). We saw people coming in from the fields with their wagons and implements to attend the Bible class, even though it was ten o'clock on a fine morning. Of the around 250 inhabitants of the village something like 150 came and filled the schoolroom. And, oh, the clear and open expressions, the brightness in so many eyes, the lovely radiance that bespeaks a new person, which met me from so many suntanned faces as well as from a number of children!

The rector was just discussing the passage where John the Baptist sends his disciples to ask the Savior, "Are you the one who was to come, or should we expect someone else?" (Matt 11:3). At that point a man entered whom he had reason to suspect of undue spiritual curiosity and a tendency to religious speculation, and Blumhardt prayed inwardly that he might be given the right word for this man. As he thought of John's question, which is usually ascribed to a wavering faith, he had the idea of seeing and interpreting it at the same time as an expression of caution. So he emphasized this aspect, without in any way discarding the other, and commented that in so important a question as whether someone was the Messiah or not, caution was well advised and that for us, too, it is the right and proper approach in spiritual matters.

"And toward whom do we have to be most cautious?" the rector went on.

"Toward ourselves," replied several of those present.

"Of course! For we have an urge to give rein to our own thoughts, to figure things out ourselves, and we have to be warned to be cautious. But while John had to *send* somebody to the Lord, we can go to him and his word ourselves."

Then Blumhardt started to speak of the people around Jesus, giving a very down-to-earth description: "Blind, lame, lepers— what a company for the Lord! How that antagonized the grand folk! But it pleases us, doesn't it, to hear that he associated with the poorest." Especially nice at the end was his interpretation of "Blessed is he who takes no offense at me" (Matt 11:6), where he described "taking offense" as something that spoils joy in various ways. "When you take offense at a path along which God is taking you, joy is gone. When you take offense at the weakness of your neighbor, joy is gone. When you take offense at something your pastor says to you, joy is gone."

While the rector conversed with a few of the people, the schoolmaster told me how since the revival the schoolchildren were more eager to learn and especially how much better the work in the fields was going. Previously, he said, there had been terrible cursing and swearing, but now everything was done peacefully and turned out well.

So we wended our way back. It was midday in Möttlingen, and people were sitting around their tables, but where somebody spied the rector coming, they all got up, the windows opened, and friendly faces beckoned from all the houses. I caught sight of a man of rather gloomy appearance standing by the roadside; he hesitated a while before greeting us. I looked at Blumhardt questioningly, and he said, "That's a stranger; I don't know him." To me it was another proof that the Möttlingen people's countenances have really changed. For a moment we also saw the person who had been so badly possessed; she appeared to be quite well.

It so happened that *Herr* Knapp, director of the consistory in Stuttgart, wanted a distant relative to learn housekeeping in Blumhardt's rectory. Since the revival had just begun, he came first himself to have a look. And this solid, sober, rationally minded man, a lawyer, was so touched by the peasants' visible love to their rector that he took part in one of their gatherings. It gave him such joy that he assured Blumhardt there was no further need for lengthy reports, for he had now seen for himself all there was to be seen.

Two more friends joined us in the rectory for dinner. Everything is very simple there, with pewter plates and spoons; there are four delightful children in the house, and a wife who shares fully in her husband's labors. And truly, the household could not help being drawn into them, what with whole rows of burdened folk often waiting to see the rector, who would speak to them individually in his study upstairs. We also saw the ancient little church and in the cemetery the graves of Machtolf and of Barth's mother. Deeply moved and joyful, I left the precious house at two in the afternoon on May 2, and at eight in the evening I was back in Korntal.

Christ-Sarasin's account serves to bring out that characteristic trait of the movement that I have called "objectivity." Blumhardt was merely the one who most intensely and closely *experienced* the great events. No one was less inclined than he to engage in a dubious "fervent struggle" for signs of revival. Whenever he really did struggle, it was because obvious needs compelled him, and in such cases he did throw himself in unreservedly. But any "spiritual" attempts to extort manifestations of the Holy Spirit through oratory or prayer made him shudder. The awakening had come upon him quite unexpectedly, and now he was being carried along by a current of great and holy happenings. He himself tells us just how much this was the case:

> What I did was not anything I had sought, made, or forced but something that came about completely of its own accord; it came my way without my asking for it, out of unmerited grace. I actually got into trouble with myself, for I, too, felt a sinner and could not imagine that God wanted to make an exception of me and take me along a different road from other folk. I found it hard to grant absolution to others, as in the name of God, for sins similar to those I myself felt guilty of and for which I had not yet received forgiveness in this way. Because I was pressed for time, for the moment I made a secret agreement with the dear Savior that he should consider me as one who had confessed his sins like every other sinner, since he knew that I was ready to do it as soon as an opportunity would present itself. Thus I was allowed to carry on with a temporarily reconciled conscience and a joyful spirit. I was in a position similar to that of Cornelius and his company, on whom the Holy Spirit fell before they were baptized but who nevertheless had to be baptized afterward (Acts 10:44–48). Before long, though, I was given the opportunity I had desired and sought (through a fellow minister).

Just because the movement had come without him—indeed, had come *upon* him, the thought that it must be of wider significance for the church and indeed for humankind took hold of him with irresistible force. The need that met him from those seeking peace was so real and imperative that he could only perceive it as common and widespread. Again, the help they received—one might say: quite independently of anything *he* had done, simply through the word he spoke as a servant of Christ—was so real and great that one could not help feeling: This is what the Lord wants to grant and give to all.

Someone other than Blumhardt, if in his position, might have found great satisfaction in declaring: "Such a thing is possible only where I am or at any rate someone like me, and there are not many of that type"; or "I am actually not surprised that such effects go out from me, for I have what it takes!" Such a one would then have set about founding a new religion and once again—for the umpteenth time since the days of the apostles—would have "established the genuine, true church of Christ," that is, he would have, to some degree, become a sectarian.

To such narrow-minded arrogance Blumhardt's whole being was opposed, which may well be one of the main reasons that it was he who was granted such great experiences. They led him on to bolder and bolder hopes for the whole world but at the same time to deeper personal humility. When the great miracles came, each one evoked in him afresh that sense of startled awe we heard about. When others, perhaps spurred by hidden vanity, wanted to extort similar answers to prayers or never wearied of recounting some instance or other where prayer had been heard, Blumhardt was apt to warn, "If you just once take it to yourself, you can expect nothing for a long time to come" or "Wanting to have it in that sense is the greatest obstacle to ever getting it."

That is also why he knew that his fellow ministers could and should have the same experiences. "It's not as if we had it; it is contained in the divine Word, which we have to pass on unembellished, and in the blessing that rests on our ministry." These are thoughts he would want to call out to all ministers even today. And how he longed for that openness in his fellow ministers in those days when the seekers for peace kept crowding in on him! Thus he wrote to Barth on April 3, 1844:

> At A. [name of a village] in the Black Forest a certain man has heard people talk of the happenings in Möttlingen, in such a way as to give him hope that A., too, might have an open door for poor sinners. B. [another village] did open the door on Palm Sunday, inviting people to come in the way I did earlier. M. has done the same; the fire is burning more brightly in N., O., and P. [all standing for names of villages], and the penitent are waiting anxiously for a chance to declare themselves. Why must Q., R., and S. [ministers] remain so hard and unwilling to respond to the great yearning among the people? All they have to do is to announce in church that whoever feels burdened should come and see them . . . Oh, things must change, for I see clearly that what has been is nothing compared to what ought to be.

The following day, April 4, he writes:

> Everywhere consciences are waiting to be unburdened. People come streaming to me from all the villages around, and how happy I would be if I could say to the heavy-laden hearts, "Go to your pastor!" I feel sorry for the people; I am not allowed to do anything and have to evasively put them off with cold official

comfort. I do think my Christian brethren could well have taken note of my communications and come to the conclusion that something might be given to them too, if they would only dare to invite the penitent in the congregation God has entrusted to their care to come and confess, if they wish to . . . People are becoming aware that I stand alone and am not being followed by my friends in a matter of such importance. Oh, the Lord knows how I feel and how my heart burns for the whole world. I don't want to reproach anybody, but I feel the need to pour out my heart to you.

A deeply moving lament! People are gripped by the movement and flock to Blumhardt, hungry for the same solace as had been granted to the Möttlingen folk, but all he can give them is "cold official comfort," as he puts it, for they are not his parishioners and he neither will nor may encroach on another pastor's sphere of authority. With and on behalf of these people he hungers for a more accommodating attitude on the ministers' part, but in vain. The harvest is ready, the reapers are there, but they have misgivings about bringing in the crop.

The cool, unsympathetic attitude of Blumhardt's colleagues had the effect that this movement, so universal and comprehensive in its whole character and direction, gradually took on the appearance of something local, special, and tied to the person of Blumhardt. That which had gripped thousands with elemental power ended up being downgraded as a "special theory of Blumhardt's." That grieved him; to him it was unquestionably a joyous, powerful, auspicious event in the life of the Protestant church; he himself had simply happened to be the one to experience it firsthand. Yet some of his theological friends almost regarded it as heresy.

What hurt him most deeply, however, was being reproached with turning back to Roman Catholicism, for he was a Protestant through and through, deeply rooted in Luther's spirit and writings. In fact, his fearful struggle had given him so deep an insight into the hidden ills of Catholicism that especially at that time he was apt to speak in a startlingly earnest way about its character. I will not quote any of those statements, because later on he was greatly concerned not to show animosity toward any of the great historic forms of Christianity, including the Roman Catholic Church.

It is no infringement of that conciliatory principle if we here remind ourselves that it was precisely the earlier brazen misuse of the two main factors of the Möttlingen movement—confession and absolution—by the Roman Church that had led to the Reformation. It cannot be blotted out from the pages of history that following an unholy and shameless confession of sins absolution was granted by way of a commercial transaction, for money. This extreme and ultimate evidence of a degenerate Christianity set the Reformation in motion. Ever since then we Protestants have been afflicted with a not unfounded irritability with respect to these two features of church life, to the degree that some words the Lord uttered with special earnestness at solemn moments bother some Protestants and make them feel uncomfortable; they push them aside as "Catholic" or prefer to "spiritualize" them. These words are:

> Truly, I say to you, whatever you bind on earth shall be bound in heaven, and whatever you loose on earth shall be loosed in heaven. (Matt 18:18)

> If you forgive the sins of any, they are forgiven. (John 20:23)

In his struggle Blumhardt had experienced something of the kingly power with which the Lord promises to work through Peter (Matt 16:19) and thus through his servants generally (Matt 18:18). If in the course of the struggle Blumhardt had come to know that power from its more warlike side, he now experienced it from a side that was truly after the Savior's own heart—peaceable and reconciling, as befits a priest. He saw how quickly and completely Jesus Christ in his redemptive power forgives any sins, even the heaviest—murder, adultery, theft, and unspeakable abominations—when they are brought to the light. In an undreamt-of way he experienced how Jesus seeks the lost and redeems sinners and how through the Lord's Word out-and-out sinners find peace in a very simple way, if they confess to another as in the presence of God that which does not let them find peace.

How are these matters dealt with usually? For the most part people whose conscience is burdened with heavy sins are unlikely to find peace at all. If unbelievers, they put on an air of defiance; if believers, they walk about moaning under the burden of a bad conscience. But then the Savior's great authority and power to act as a redeemer remains stunted; his work of seeking and saving the lost is restricted to those merely *half* lost, as it were.

But why, someone might object, confess to another person? Is it not enough to make confession to God in your own secret chamber? Let us look at the matter plainly and simply. Such a confession is like a monologue: A matter I have known all along is being told to Him who likewise has known it all along. We know quite well it is a blessed thing to consider before God all that is wrong in us, to perceive it clearly and confess it to him. But what about the secret horrors, of which there are so many on earth? Is it not part of general human experience (often met with, for example, in children or at a deathbed)—one might say, part of natural religion—that any such things must be brought to the light?[5] When I confess something to God in the presence of somebody who does not yet know it, isn't that the way to drag my secret out of the dark into the light of day? Isn't it conceivable that God expects that from me, not only because I owe it to him but because I owe it to myself, that is, to my own dignity, which he would like to restore to me in full?

This is not a call for the compulsory confession of the Roman Catholic confessional—a lot could be said about its harmfulness. Even less do I mean to advocate those supposedly pious circles where one person tells his sins to a dozen other sinners—a practice apt to either destroy one's feelings of shame or else one's sense of truthfulness. What I mean is that for somebody at the end of his tether a door is opened to a discreet brother's heart.

In spite of all the negative impressions I have received of the Roman Catholic confessional in my own pastoral experience, I cannot help feeling that it is nevertheless one of the reasons that among Catholics suicide is far less widespread than it is among Protestants. How good it would be if the ordinary person would come to think of the pastor's study as the place where, in a freer and nobler way than in the confessional, he could speak openly, sure of finding a friendly and discrete ear for everything. It would give a person the chance to choose between the pastor's study and making an end of himself by a rope or on the railway tracks. Frankly, the chase after "spirituality," freedom, and so forth has left many—poor as well as rich— languishing and scattered, like sheep without a shepherd.

A repentance as sober and dry in character as that of the Möttlingen revival resulted in a simple, open, natural, and hearty manner, evident in individuals as well as in the tone of their gatherings. In such a repentance there is nothing to feed spiritual pride. Anyone who has looked

---

5. George Eliot, that enthusiastic admirer of Spinoza, Strauss, and Feuerbach, has this to say: "An open confession seems to have the purifying influence that the hopeful lie with which we have covered our selfishness as with a false garment is swept away and the soul can once more rise to the noble height of simplicity." [Editors' note: The source of this quotation is unknown.]

at himself and his past as at something outside of himself, who has told it unreservedly to someone else and now faces it mirrored in that other person's judgment, is sure to be cured of any pious self-conceit for a long time to come. Happy as he is to have found peace through forgiveness, he naturally thinks even less highly of himself than before, as Paul writes:

> There is no distinction between those who have already been made righteous and the others, since all the righteous have sinned and fall short of the glory of God; they are justified freely by his grace, through the redemption that came by Christ Jesus. (Rom 3:22–24)

Someone with a burdened conscience, who has not brought the godlessness of his darkened heart to the light of day and has generated for himself a purely emotional peace, often needs an almost feverish degree of pious emotionalism to keep it from being extinguished.[6] But what

6. We shall presently become acquainted with Blumhardt's *theological* justification of his experiences, which in their way represented something new. But to show how he desires to bring their importance home to our *hearts* and *consciences*, we insert here one of his morning devotions, entitled "Concealing Sin," based on Psalm 32:3–5:

"When I declared not my sin, my bones wasted away through my groaning all day long. For day and night thy hand was heavy upon me. Therefore, I acknowledge my sin to thee and do not cover up my iniquity."

King David found it harder than other men to keep his conscience clear, for, not having to fear any human court of justice, he was free to do anything. But all the more did his *conscience* remind him when he had gone wrong. Fearing to give offense to the people, who looked up to him as a model, he tried to conceal heavier sins. Thus, as we know from his affair with Bathsheba, in order to conceal one bad deed, he committed a second and possibly worse one, with the result that he got horribly enmeshed in sin. He tried to keep it all secret, but the more he concealed it, the more it burned within him. Day and night, as he says, God's hand was heavy upon him. He was burdened not only by his own bad conscience but also by something that was like a judgment from above, as though God himself were putting pressure on him. Poor David! Men did not know about it, but God did. By hiding it from men he acted as if God, too, did not know it, and that increased his distress all the more. He felt a mighty pressure in all his bones; his whole inner being languished and groaned, putting his very life in jeopardy. All this because he wanted to help himself by concealing his sin.

In the end God took pity on him and helped him to confess by sending the prophet Nathan to him. Before Nathan came, David, however much oppressed by sin, was yet unwilling to stand exposed as a sinner. At bottom this is the case with all who conceal their sin and just pray against it in their hearts. But when it came to the light, David had to admit, "I have sinned against the Lord." Then how great was his fear of being a man marked for death!

about absolution? Well, nowadays that is something everybody grants to himself, some showing more and others less confidence in the result. However, many people are quite unsuccessful at that, and of them alone we have to speak. If we agree about the benefits of confession, one might think that simply having confessed would be sufficient for the penitent. Should it not give him the trust and courage needed to believe that his sins are forgiven? Assuming the penitent to be sincere and candid, generally speaking one could say a confident yes to this question. The Savior though (one might say) would regard that as too selfish and skimpy. It is not the way to act when the long-awaited lost son returns to the father's house. The Savior is not someone who demands payment and, once it is made, simply dismisses the debtor. He is a *giver*.

But there is still another aspect that makes us understand why absolution is needed. One or the other, listening to the above considerations, may have thought, "It would be better if nowadays the lost would come

---

Now in the passage before us David states that when he ceased to cover up his transgression and acknowledged his sin to the Lord, the Lord forgave the guilt of his sin. The above, however, makes it clear that in God's eyes whatever is confessed to him alone is no confession. David with his heavily burdened conscience must have entreated the Lord to forgive him. Yet he sensed that the Lord would not accept anything from him and would show him no mercy as long as his sin stayed covered up. There is nothing humbling in a man's confessing his transgression to the Lord (who in any case knows it all) as secretly as he committed it, for he can still hold his head high as an ostensibly righteous man.

So we must have a right understanding of the way David made his confession to the Lord. He had to make it to a man who came to him in the name of the Lord. In this way alone it became a confession made to the Lord. If he had not wanted to conceal his deed, he could have had a chance before to free his conscience. According to Old Testament regulations he could have made a sin offering and openly confessed his transgression to the priest. There he would have obtained forgiveness just as he did now through Nathan.

Henceforth, with his secret sin brought to the light of day, he did not shrink from having it also entered in the chronicles of the kings nor from publicly showing his repentance through psalms. In his position that was necessary, for it would have been wrong to camouflage, as it were, by a continuing silence a deed everyone had heard of.

We see how seriously God takes it when his commandments are plainly transgressed and how painful it can be for the transgressor to conceal his sin. In the New Testament, too, we read:

"If we confess our sins, he is faithful and just, and will forgive our sins and cleanse us from all unrighteousness" (1 John 1:9).

All the more so, because the blood of Christ keeps crying out, "Mercy, mercy!" Amen.

of their own accord to confess their sins instead of having to be reminded of them, but it just doesn't happen." It is indeed a rare occurrence these days and understandably so. Only the sure guarantee of finding complete forgiveness can move a person to make such a step, but then it really *will* make him do it. However much we confess our sins, we cannot assure ourselves of such a forgiveness; it goes way beyond anything we can expect. We can attain it neither as a logical conclusion of our reasoning nor as the ultimate fruit of a struggle for repentance. Sins committed are actual deeds, which cannot be undone. Any conclusion we ourselves arrive at will turn into self-justification, allowing us to retract in some way the self-condemnation that alone is fitting. The possibility of us sinners having our sins forgiven is an historic event, the inmost core of all human history up till now. It is the fruit of Jesus Christ's being sent from heaven; of his struggle on earth, his crucifixion, and resurrection. Forgiveness is a personal gift of Jesus the victor to those who come for it. That is why he does not want to grant it merely through an internal thought process but as an external historical event, taking place from heart to heart, from mouth to mouth—out there in the bright light of human goings-on. Just as he, the Word, became flesh, so he wants to speak to us not only through thoughts but in the flesh, through people.

To be sure, we do have the Lord's Supper for such an assurance of his grace, coming to us not just inwardly but as an outward event and reality. Blumhardt himself never ceased pointing to that. The question is, though, whether the Lord wants to speak a word more directly and specifically to the repentant sinner's heart, in the way we human beings converse with each other. When he told somebody, "Your sins are forgiven," he obviously was not announcing something generally valid, with no particular application to a particular case. Rather, it meant that because he said so, something was to come into being in the individual he addressed—something that up to that moment had not been there and was not to be expected. He spoke as one who in the name of the creditor cancels the debt. He spoke in a way to make even the Pharisees understand: "He forgives sins!" He spoke fully aware that he risked giving offense as one who infringes on God's own authority, and the reason he gave for doing it was that he *possessed* that authority. Instead of leaving it at the general announcement, "If you people repent and believe, your sins will be forgiven," he took the offensive by declaring, "You, yes you, your sins are forgiven!"

Did the Lord demand a confession of sins? At first glance he did not. He knew what is in us humans and did not need the other person's word to have a clear picture of him and of his sincerity. Anything formal and petty was alien to him; he was very human and natural in everything. But that a woman known all over town as a "sinner" dared to approach him; that a criminal declared, "We are receiving the due reward of our deeds"; that Zacchaeus acted as he did, and that the paralytic's undoubtedly shocked face betrayed a troubled conscience, which cried out to be set at rest instantly—surely all that is tantamount to confessions, all the more since none of those persons were able to be alone with Jesus.

"Agreed," someone might say, "but the way Jesus acted was peculiar to his divine dignity." But is that really the right understanding of the Lord's mind? We sense it to be his will that in his kingdom all communication is to be of a personal nature—from heart to heart and hand to hand, in friendly intercourse and brotherly fellowship. So he used his twelve simply as an extension of his own arm, as instruments representing him, through whom he wanted to work as if he himself were standing in their place. In his name they were to act as he acted and do what he did, and it was to be regarded as done by him. And specifically with respect to what we are considering here he spoke the weighty words, "Whatever you loose on earth shall be loosed in heaven" (Matt 18:18), and after his resurrection, "As the Father has sent me, even so I send you . . . Receive the Holy Spirit. If you forgive the sins of any, they are forgiven" (John 20:21–23).

The twelve received the "Holy Spirit" for their task. They needed it so they could judge sin in a holy and evangelical (that is, completely forgiving) way and place themselves directly under the Lord and his leading in total self-forgetfulness. They also needed the "Holy Spirit" to invest their words and actions with divine power.

Now, were the coming generations really meant to be deprived of such a personal bestowal of grace? It is easy to affirm that but not so easy to substantiate it from Holy Scripture. Blumhardt certainly saw it differently. He felt that the gracious Savior wants to have a closer, more living, and more tangible contact with our souls than is thought possible today and that therefore the general state of Christianity can, should, and must become better than it is now. In his opinion we no longer, or not yet, possess in full strength Christianity as the Savior means it to be. He also felt it to be the Lord's will that the church should unceasingly beseech him to grant what is lacking.

Similar thoughts, equally unsought and springing only from his own mighty experiences, came to Blumhardt's mind with respect to *miracles*. Before going into the question of what justification he had for such thoughts—thoughts that to his chagrin were heeded much too little—we want to let him give his reasons for his attitude to private confession and private absolution (as he calls it in contradistinction to the general confession and general absolution customary in the Lutheran Church). This is part of his *Vertheidigungsschrift* (pp. 120ff.):

> It is said that the Bible speaks very little of private confession. But consider, dear reader, how could there be much about it in the New Testament? It is certain that those who believed were baptized. What baptism signifies is shown us by the way John baptized. He baptized people on confession of their sins, to have the sins forgiven, that is, washed away. While he was in the flesh, the Lord continued that baptism through his own disciples (John 4:1–2). Would he have said, "Now a confession is no longer necessary"? Before he ascended, he commanded baptism (Matt 28:19), the effect of which he indicated by saying, "If you forgive the sins of any, they are forgiven" (John 20:23). Does one not have to say: Baptism is required for entry into God's kingdom, because that entry can take place only after cleansing from sin? But how could that cleansing take place if sins were kept hidden away? Paul knew the Corinthians and was aware of the abominations that had been rampant among them. "And such," he says, "were some of you. But you were washed" (1 Cor 6:11). In short: If the importance of baptism is biblical, so also is that of confession. Think of the thieves, murderers, adulterers, fornicators, sodomites, committers of incest, perjurers, etc., in Corinth, sinners not always easily recognizable as such because of their innocent looks—how could they have been cleansed of their sins if they had never even mentioned them? Entering God's kingdom or receiving his glorious grace required at least a confession—not a slavish, compulsory, tormenting one, but surely one that was sincere and genuine. Once grace was assured through baptism, the sins confessed were not to be committed ever again; a confessional was therefore superfluous. That is why confession was not talked about a great deal in the apostolic church; it basically belonged to the time before conversion. On occasion, though, it might again become necessary, as a number of passages seem to indicate, especially 1 John 1:9: "But if we confess our sins . . ." and Jas 5:16: "Confess your sins to one another."

As regards the first passage, some like to add "to the Lord," as though one only needed to confess to him. If that suits you, dear reader, you can have it; if not, know that the addition is not biblical. If you want to support your theory with Psalm 32:5, "I said, 'I will confess my transgressions to the Lord,'" I tell you that in the Old Testament forgiveness without confession before others was even less likely than in the New Testament, for the pardoning indulgence of God could only be obtained before the altar through a sacrifice over which the sin had to be named. That is made clear by the specific sacrifices listed for various individual sins. So when David made his confession to the Lord, he did it in the temple in the presence of the priest; it was in that way that the Lord forgave him the guilt of his sin, knowing that there was no deceit in David's spirit (Ps 32:5, 2).

Thus in the apostolic age confession and baptism, signifying forgiveness, coincided. We, on the other hand, who are baptized as little children, generally fall from our "baptismal grace" (as it is called) into one heavy sin or another—mortal sins, that is, sins which the Lord has laid a special curse on in Scripture. So now like straying sheep we must be led back to the Savior or, one might say, be turned from pagans back into Christians. How is that to be done?

Do you think all it needs is that someone suddenly says, "I believe"? Certainly not! You say that he ought to repent. He does; but when is it enough, and how is he to do it? Is he to weep for days, weeks, months, years, while keeping his guilt firmly locked in his heart? When is it enough? So we see that what is lacking is a firm, sure beginning. If we have become pagans, must we not take on ourselves that which is the essence of baptism? We confess and receive forgiveness, just as one undergoing baptism; the only difference is we are not baptized again. What can be clearer than that? And who can deny that such a new start comes as an extraordinary relief for the awakened ones? To be sure, it can be misused. One can be hypocritical, can show off one's sin, can shamelessly blurt everything out like rowdies in a pub. One could even see confession as a good work and so fall into a kind of works righteousness. But should the serpent's seed's corrupting of everything cause us to throw it all out? If only our believers would once again lay a firm foundation and learn to put it to good use with those newly awakened!

In the same *Vertheidigungsschrift*, Blumhardt goes at still greater length (pp. 126ff.) into the question of absolution, because it departs even more from our present-day views than does the confession of sins.

For this reason we quote his own words, at least insofar as they give a *biblical* foundation to his actions (omitting the reasons he adduces from the doctrines and customs of the church).

> The effect of this so-called absolution on the people receiving it was such that they impressed everyone as completely changed persons, without the slightest trace of morbid emotionalism. That was the main reason the movement kept spreading and finally encompassed both my villages. I had nothing in mind other than to act completely in the spirit of the Protestant church—not as it is now, but as it ought to be according to our written confessions of faith.
>
> My experiences with the act of absolution brought many peculiar things to my notice. As mentioned earlier, side by side with the strikingly soothing effect it had on the soul, it also occasionally made physical ailments disappear.
>
> In the case of about twelve persons, under the pressure of the moment I granted absolution too early. These persons who had more or less intentionally failed to bring out weighty wrongdoings could not testify to receiving any impression through the act of absolution. I myself presently felt a tightness in my chest and some hours later a weariness in all my members, as if suddenly all my strength had gone. I cannot describe more exactly this malaise and my general state of paralysis, which lasted for two or three days. But I recognized my fault and ever since then have remained fearful of granting absolution. I would have been glad to give it up altogether but had to regard that as a giving in to cowardice and faintheartedness, in particular since precisely the experience described made me all the more certain that there is something *real* to absolution, which I may not withhold from the souls entrusted to me, inasmuch as it is given to me for them. I had to risk it.
>
> O dear reader, there are not many who can grasp the risks I often took and had to take! Later the same summer it happened that a distant colleague who lay mortally ill was anxiously awaiting my coming. Finally I did visit him; he confessed to me and asked for absolution. I granted it to him as a favor to a friend—something completely out of place in matters concerning God—and arrived home sick in the way described above. Then I became aware what a serious matter is the authority granted by the Lord that what we loose on earth shall also be loosed in heaven.
>
> Just because this act of our ministry is the weightiest and demands the greatest loyalty—that is, if it is to have the promised validity—I began to understand why one of the most important words of our Lord has been so entirely forgotten in our church. When absolution is not granted in the right spirit, it is ineffective,

but when it has power, there is a recoil to beware of that may cause harm also to the person confessing (confessant). This accords with the Protestant doctrine of the Lord's Supper, where Luther (in opposition to Calvin) maintains that partaking of the Supper does have an effect on the repentant as well as on the unrepentant. For the unrepentant the effect is harmful and brings judgment—sickness or even death (according to Paul in 1 Cor 11:30).

What I have said bears the appearance in our time of something strikingly new, and it is only right to ask about its biblical foundation. That foundation became completely clear to me only *after* I had already given absolution to nearly every member of my congregation. My own experiences had guided me to the right understanding of Scripture. It all rests on the main passage, John 20:21–23. There we read what the risen Jesus tells his disciples: "As the Father has sent me, even so I send you." And when he had said this, he breathed on them and said to them, "Receive (the) Holy Spirit. If you forgive the sins of any, they are forgiven; if you retain the sins of any, they are retained."

When the Lord breathed on them, what else does it mean but spiritual authorization for the task he gives them? And the Holy Spirit imparted there—in the original Greek it just says "holy spirit" and not "the Holy Spirit"—what else is it but special divine power given to the disciples for carrying out their task? This power is different from the Spirit poured out at Pentecost. For the time being (one could also say) it is but a fraction of the pentecostal Spirit, one beam from the great light. Most likely the Lord imparted this power to let people see it could prove effective even if the greater gift—the Spirit of Pentecost, which encompasses all the divine powers intended for humanity—were not given. For it is above all by this power that the church of God is to be built up.

If one considers how this power is meant to work, it is clear that it is given to assure the confessant of forgiveness—direct from God, as the Reformers put it. Through this power, which comes from God, God himself speaks to the confessing person, and through the laying on of hands—probably also through simple absolution without laying on of hands (for God does not bind himself to outward acts)—this power is imparted to the confessant. That accounts for the wonderful effect, the suddenly given certainty and peace that is beyond all doubt. It accounts, too, for other beneficial effects on the penitent's nerves and on his physical and mental strength. It also accounts for the recoil experienced by a confessor endowed with that power if he uses it more loosely than faithfully; finally, it accounts for harmful effects on a confessant who is less than sincere.

Since it is a power given by God, it may not be left idle and unused either, else God will recall his gift. That makes it easy for me to understand why our church has come close to losing this remarkable power, which is so serviceable and necessary for the building up and preservation of God's church. After all, there isn't anybody now who believes in it or practices it.

Echoes of this power are still felt most strongly, it seems, in the ceremony of confirmation, especially as practiced in the church of our fatherland. It is said that in particular the actual act of being confirmed does mean a special experience for many children— something they treasure throughout their lives, even though they may go astray in many ways. Many will later on recall with tears the grace they were given at confirmation. I have experienced that right here in Möttlingen, where most of the people were confirmed by pastors Machtolf, Gross, and Barth. The younger ones always speak with special gratitude of Pastor Barth, whose confirmations left a deep impression.

Such impressions do not just relate to the instruction preced- ing confirmation, although the divine power—assuming that it is there—must have some effect there also. More than anything else they are impressions left by the last act—the actual confirma- tion, where the child receives a promise from God himself. The more clearly and definitely the confirming minister has his mind on Jesus' words of promise as he speaks, or the more actively his whole spirit (though less conscious of what takes place or should be taking place) is turned toward God's mercy seat on behalf of the child, the more strongly he will be seen to be invested with divine authority. But alas, most ministers are keener on being ef- fective orators than on standing in power from above!

While on the one hand Blumhardt's continuing experiences only served to establish his views more firmly, on the other hand he felt more and more isolated on account of them, since it seemed that they were scarcely considered worthy of attention. For that reason he went once more over the same ground when his exposition of the Gospel of Matthew in *Blätter aus Boll* (No. 3, 1876) led him to the passage in Matthew 16:19–20, where the Lord speaks of binding and loosing. In what follows I excerpt some thoughts from this very deep-going discourse.

Blumhardt points out that the mention of the "gates of hell" imme- diately before explains why "loosing" is required. "Every one who com- mits sin is a slave to sin" (John 8:34); by committing sin he has become subject to the "dominion of darkness" (Col 1:13), which holds on to him tenaciously. He cannot free himself from these bonds; he only becomes free "when the sin is truly canceled out by the blood of Christ." To be sure, those who struggle bravely will many times experience freeing through the Lord's loving-kindness; yet the way the Lord points to in our passage is easier. According to it, God's order calls for a servant or authorized agent of Christ. The loosing can only be done by Jesus personally; before him the devil gives way at once. Our text promises that the person of Jesus is represented in his servants. They appeal to the Crucified One, and no power of hell can resist the Crucified One, in whose name they have the right to loose and forgive. The gates of hell must always give way, since the prince of this world is judged (John 16:11). Thus the loosing takes place "actually without a great deal of trouble—as long as everything proceeds in the right order, on the part of both the sinner and the servant of Christ."

Some may find those words difficult and hard to stomach, especially when excerpted, which tends to make everything sound more blunt and abrupt. Yet do they not actually have the Bible on their side? Nobody is likely to think Blumhardt intended to bind and loose the church according to such and such a paragraph. For one thing, the entity administering such authority, in this case, say, the code of church law, would little fit either the solemnity of the moment or the Lord's way of thinking. For another, the legislative power thus granted to Peter would be so extended as to be meaningless. Actually, the words about loosing and binding as repeated in Matthew 18:18 clearly refer to the forgiveness of sins; that probably excludes any other meaning for the earlier passage (Matt 16:19) as well. If that is the case, it is scarcely possible to summon Scripture against Blumhardt's reasoning.

May we conclude this chapter with the discussion of a word that often came up both in what others said about Blumhardt and in what he said himself—the word "priest." It was one of his great concerns that Christians recover a feeling of priestly responsibility for their fellow human beings. At the same time, if one wants to describe fittingly the beneficent quality of his pastoral service, that word somehow comes to mind.

Yet it is a very unpopular word these days, perhaps because a truly priestly attitude and action has become such a rare thing. Evangelical freedom often seems to demand that all spiritual or religious intercourse be on a purely human level. I admonish, punish, and comfort you, and you me, just as we consider best. That procedure, though it has its justification and its blessing, also has its dangers if we do not in an earnest and childlike way ask for the presence of the Savior, who alone actually has the right and power to make such admonition, etc., fruitful and life-giving. There are many who ardently long to see church discipline reestablished, but when they take as their motto, "I tell you your sin, and you tell me mine," usually the first half—"I tell you"—proves the more popular one. That principle is a dangerous weapon in the hands of us, "who are evil" (Matt 7:11). It does not much show the mark of the redemption that is ours through Jesus Christ.

Dieterlen, a manufacturer in the Alsatian Steinthal (stony valley) and one of Blumhardt's closest friends, wrote an excellent pamphlet against the bad habit arising from the misuse of the above principle—the habit of a judgmental concern for the salvation of the other's soul. The writing, entitled *La religion pure et sans tache* (The Pure and Undefiled Religion), represents, apart from a warm praise of compassion, what might be called a sermon on Goethe's celebrated word, "One notes the purpose, and one feels displeased." In Möttlingen Dieterlen had learned a lot from Blumhardt. Every week he devoted one day to pastoral tasks, his situation permitting him to sally forth with a full purse and return with an empty one. It had not taken him long to notice that some of the sick, as soon as they caught sight of him through the window, would quickly take hold of some devotional book and open it. So he tried to break down as quickly as possible the ramparts thrown up by a fabricated piety and to find an open, natural, and brotherly contact with people. "When people I meet for the first time walk along on pious stilts, the higher they raise themselves up, the more I keep to what is mean and lowly and go on talking of their debts, their goats, and their manure, until they come down from their heights and become natural and ordinary." This is what he says in his pamphlet, noting further: "It is wrong to burst in straight away with edification. If one pounces on people with Bible reading and praying, the honest become shy, the bad laugh, and the weak play-act."

That is how he went about it. In this way he once happened to come to a poor family living several hours' walking distance away from his own village. He tells:

> I found a consumptive, dejected woman, a man who tried to drown his misery in drink, six children in rags, and a messy, disorderly household. I showed the people compassion, repeated my visits, won their confidence, and was able to speak to their souls.

One day the man told me: "You see, sir, for a long time everybody has just left us in our misery, and so we thought, 'No one bothers about us; it seems God has forsaken us'; so we let ourselves sink down lower and lower. Then you came, and came again, and we thought: 'Here is a stranger who comes in to us from the road and keeps coming. And because this stranger will not forsake us, God has not forsaken us either, and there is still hope for us.' And we found a new trust in God."

"Thus," Dieterlen continues, "we render God a service by visiting widows and orphans and working lovingly for God and with God."

I am happy to quote Dieterlen, since he was one of the first to respond with his whole heart to what he had received and experienced in his contact with Blumhardt, partly through visits in Möttlingen, partly through lively correspondence. He served the sick not only with his money and his kindly words, but he also, in a childlike, trusting way and as briefly as possible, let Blumhardt know of their suffering—"seven sick persons" or something in that style—and not in vain. His labors, which certainly also included devotional gatherings, served to awaken in many, like that drunkard just mentioned, courage to believe in a God who manifests his mercy in Jesus Christ—courage to repent and turn around.

It may seem that we have strayed from our subject. But I wanted to preface our discussion of priestly action with the portrait of a layman with priestly feeling, using his example to call to mind, more clearly and peaceably than I could have expressed it, what could be said against a certain harsher way of showing concern for a neighbor's betterment. If, without being in the position of exercising the right a special friendship bestows, you give me, however affably and subtly, the merest hint of an admonition, the old Adam in me, feeling his human rights violated, may rebel, and I am not likely to see your physician's concern about a splinter in my eye in the light you desire. Blumhardt's rule was: "Of others' sins I know nothing, no matter how much gossip I may hear about them; they are none of my business until they are brought to me along with a plea for forgiveness. I know them only in the light of redemption; my task is never to judge, but only to forgive. My Lord and Master came to save the world, not to judge it."

Here we have arrived at what he called a priestly attitude. As I said, it was his concern that we should once more learn to face sin in a true priestly way. We ought to look at others' sins in the light of redemption, with deeper trust and hope, pleading that they be forgiven and inwardly forgiving them ourselves. We ought to trust that the Savior *listens* to us as we do that and that our action can help the other to better himself.

Above all, Blumhardt longed that we, his fellow ministers, might learn to have faith that through us the Savior wants to let powers of forgiveness be poured out on the sinners in need. Then the Gospel will once more come fully into its own in a very special way. Then the Savior will let himself be experienced as the living and kindly one, who forgives sins gladly and fully, so that one can feel: Here something has *happened!* Then it will also be seen that the kingdom of God is not a matter of words but of power (1 Cor 4:20). Only then do we not stand *above* the distressed brother but *with* him as fellow partakers of forgiveness and redemption. That is why the danger that absolution might lead to a haughty awareness of one's official importance is only apparent. When we feel priestly responsibility for souls, we inwardly put ourselves beneath their feet. And we can only have such a priestly feeling toward them if we regard their sins as forgiven and if we are ever mindful of the sins we have been forgiven for.

May we ministers learn to be people to whom one can say everything that burdens the conscience, in whom one can sense the heart of a friend and brother! Let us, so to speak, listen as if we did not listen— quietly, prayerfully, aware that we are now on holy ground, that we are together first and foremost in the name of the Lord Jesus and he is now in our midst. Let us therefore curb our flood of words and our mania to admonish and exhort, and let us quietly listen in our hearts for a fitting, helpful word the Lord might give us. Oh, how much the Lord can often give us for the other person in just a few words! And how often are we suddenly made aware that we are only spectators and sharers in a great and blessed experience!

11

The Miracles

IT WAS CLEAR TO Blumhardt that the "struggle," the first great experience of his life, was of general importance for the kingdom of God. It was presently followed by a second and greater experience of no less comprehensive significance: the movement of repentance, which, even more than the struggle preceding it, came about without his foreseeing it in any way or doing anything to set it in motion. Then followed a third experience, equally wonderful and rich in promise for the progress of God's kingdom: the miracles. By the nature of things that, too, did not come about through him but came visibly from above. There is an almost unmistakable logic in the way these three great experiences of a mighty and gracious intervention from on high succeeded one another. Blumhardt felt God speaking in a way that almost bordered on revelation, that drowned out all else in him and gave him something like a prophetic certainty. To be sure, that third experience was no more separated in time from the second than the second was from the first; rather, it was an organic outgrowth of the second.

Already in the winter of 1844, when the Möttlingen folk trooped, weeping and praying, to the rectory, some of them experienced an unexpected healing of bodily ailments along with the gift of inward peace. One, for example, suffered from severe rheumatism in one thigh, which became especially violent at regular four-week intervals but so greatly hindered him also at other times that he often fell suddenly to the ground when walking. When Blumhardt laid hands on him as a sign of forgiveness, the man had a sensation of something descending from this thigh and passing out of his body. From that moment he felt free of his ailment. He did not yet believe it, however, and kept quiet about it while waiting for the four-weekly bad spell. But his rheumatism had gone for good.

Others experienced similar things, so that Blumhardt came to hear about it. To him it was a heartening sign just when his pastoral and priestly labors had landed him in a peculiar predicament. Surprisingly often the sins brought to his notice included superstitious attempts—ranging from outright sorcery to subtler sympathetic magic—to find help and healing for all sorts of hurts and illnesses. His experiences during the struggle had given Blumhardt a horror of that whole area. He had come to see clearly that every instance of actual help attained in such a way was a work of darkness, of hell, and so was something to be severely expiated, as it directly violates the authority and honor of God and in fact amounts to giving divine honor to another power. Yet when Blumhardt earnestly exhorted such people never to do that again, he would often be asked in return, "But what are we to do? The doctor lives so far away, and there is often no time, for example in case of an injury, where the bleeding must be stopped, or of severe attacks, where the doctor often arrives too late? Besides, we are too poor to call the doctor so often." What was the right counsel in such cases?

What Blumhardt learned, either through his struggle or through these recent experiences, gave him confidence to reply: "The Savior will do for you as much as the devil has done. Search your conscience whether what has befallen you might possibly be a retribution for something you have done, and pray! And if you let me know about it, I will pray with and for you." From that time on one miraculous help followed the other. In his *Vertheidigungsschrift* (p. 101) Blumhardt tells of one such occurrence, the first of its kind, which encouraged him to go forward in that direction:

> One morning a mother suddenly came rushing in, with the cry that by accident she had spilled boiling hot breakfast cereal over her three-year-old child and now did not know what to do. I hurried over and found the child, still undressed, scalded all over its body and screaming. The room filled with people. Some said so-and-so knew a spell and should be sent for straight away. That I would not have. Speaking some words of encouragement, I asked the people to pray quietly. I took the child into my arms and sighed, and it grew still. Even though covered all over with

blisters, which disappeared only several days later, the child no longer felt the least pain.

The experiences of divine help multiplied, at first within the Möttlingen congregation. The parents of a child with a severe eye disease were undecided what to do. They consulted an ophthalmologist, who declared an operation absolutely necessary. Shrinking from this prospect, they went to Calw to ask their beloved former rector Dr. Barth for his impartial advice whether they should let the child be operated on or take it to Pastor Blumhardt. Dr. Barth answered, "If you have faith that the Savior can and will heal your child, by all means go to Blumhardt. But if you do not have such faith, then don't go but accept the operation." "We do have faith," they said and went to Blumhardt. The eye improved the same day and was fully healed after three days.

Before long, the seekers for peace and salvation who flocked to Blumhardt were joined by people in need of bodily healing. The weeks following defy description. Many who were present said later: "It is my vivid impression and memory that many miracles took place, but we can no longer recall details; we have forgotten them. In those days the miracle, the experience of the actual nearness of the Lord Jesus, was the 'ordinary' and 'normal.' In other ways, too, we felt the Lord's nearness so tangibly that to us the miraculous was the natural, and we did not make a great todo about it." Nothing but praise and thanksgiving was to be heard on those Sundays, also because the whole time new people had reason to give thanks for help received. Infirmities of all kinds vanished: eye ailments, pulmonary consumption, caries, herpes, etc. What was experienced within the rector's own family was perhaps greatest of all, especially as regards Gottliebin, who a number of times was suddenly stricken either with a severe external injury, for example a leg fracture, or with some violent internal ailment. Such family experiences, however, were kept quiet, and the impression created by the miracles was in general greatly overshadowed by that of Blumhardt's preaching. Certain tender manifestations of divine loving-kindness and glory in any case do not lend themselves to publication. However, some of the miracles that took place with persons *not* belonging to Blumhardt's own family may be recounted here.

One Sunday a young man from a village an hour's walk away carried his younger brother, a dwarfish, hunchbacked, crippled boy, to Möttlingen. When they came again the following Sunday, both of them walked, though the boy was still quite deformed. A short time later he was straight and healthy. "I had something on my back; I don't know what, but now it's gone," he said.

One Saturday a youth who was preparing to enter college came to Blumhardt. His eyes were so bad that he had to be led about; at the same time they were so light-sensitive that candlelight caused him pain. In the evening Blumhardt held the usual Saturday night service, specially dear to many because of its more intimate character, and specially blessed as well. At that time, during the first years of the revival, it took place in the church. Blumhardt invited the sick young man to that service but advised him to listen from the dark sacristy, where his eyes would not be hurt by the lights. There he went, and when a light was carried through the sacristy at the end of the service, it no longer bothered him. Early the next day, a Sunday, he went for a walk, completely by himself!

I recall touching instances of illnesses such as those mentioned above (lung disease, caries, etc.) being taken away. At least one such case should be related here. One Easter time a consumptive young man came to Möttlingen from quite a distance, naively confident of finding healing during the holidays. He said that his doctor had given him up. The young man's hollow, toneless voice contrasted strangely with his brisk and often sprightly bearing. That is how I saw him on Sunday before the church service, when we young people, all about the same age, were enjoying the fresh air. After the service we met again and talked about this and that, but our friend, who had previously done most of the talking, had become quiet; the sermon had pierced his heart like an arrow of the Most High. "I have got to change; I must see the rector," he murmured to himself and asked us if and when it might be possible to see Blumhardt alone. It was as if he had forgotten about his illness. Broken and still, he walked along with us and presently made his way to Blumhardt's study. In the evening we saw him again, all cheerful and happy; he had become a different person. The inward healing given him was wonderful. "He was among us like an angel," an acquaintance of his told me later about the young man's subsequent life. He stayed with us for another day, then he traveled home and took up anew the unhealthy occupation the doctor had declared to be the cause of his illness. He was well for quite a while, sang joyfully and held his own in every way. But two years later he died; I do not know of what. I am fond of relating this case, on the one hand because the physical help given wears such a modest garb, on the other because this story gives an impression of the natural, inward way in which these things took place, far removed from magic or any craving for miracles.

After visiting many health centers, a lady who had been suffering from spinal consumption for many years and had been paralyzed for the last one and a half or two years (I think) came to Möttlingen and lodged in a farmhouse near the rectory. On Sunday she had herself carried to the churchyard so that from there she could listen to the sermon. If I remember rightly, by the time I noticed her there on August 26, 1846 (tenth Sunday after Trinity Sunday), she had already been in Möttlingen for some weeks. The subject of Blumhardt's sermon was Zacchaeus (Luke 19:1–9). He spoke of the two stages in conversion.

1. The awakening: Zacchaeus wants to reach the goal whatever the cost and will not let himself be turned aside by the first obstacle in the way. Gripped by eternity, he climbs the tree, regardless of ridicule. There he discovers that he is in fact being sought. All at once he is at the goal, overcome by the loving-kindness of the Lord, who out of love to him lays himself open to the grumbling of his own followers. Zacchaeus has been forgiven and accepted out of pure grace. There are many who get that far. They sing:

> I have been shown mercy unfounded,
> Compassion utterly unearned,
> Springing from wondrous love unbounded,
> Which my proud heart had sadly spurned.

2. The conversion: Most of those who reach that point think they have reached the goal. If they were in Zacchaeus's place, they would look down haughtily on the mutterers and pride themselves on the grace received. But to *acknowledge* the reproaches, to change, really to repent and also make restitution—that they no longer consider necessary. Now that they have been pardoned, they become great instead of small. For Zacchaeus, on the other hand, this is the point where he really gets down to work. By acknowledging that the grumblers are in the right, he makes it possible for them to acknowledge that the Savior was right in pardoning Zacchaeus. He goes to this one and that one and confesses to having cheated them (though they might not have noticed it) and so on. It is only when Zacchaeus shows this attitude and voices his intentions that the Lord says, "Today salvation has come to this house."

That was the general drift of the sermon. The sick lady had the impression that Blumhardt had preached only for her. She remained in the churchyard to listen to the following services (Sunday school and a second service) as well. After dinner the next day (Monday) she begged the rector to come to her and poured her heart out to him, without referring at all to her illness. At five o'clock in the afternoon, just when the rectory guests were setting out for a stroll, the lady's attendant came hurrying along in tears: "Don't let this shock you, sir, but she walks!" The whole company, including the rector, set out for the lady's lodging. She came walking out to meet them at the top of the stairs. All gathered in her room and knelt down to give thanks to the Lord.

It is the cases where mentally disturbed persons found healing that are remembered most vividly, due to the frequent agitated scenes. Just for this reason I want to use such material sparingly. Only one story, in which physical and inner help were intertwined, may be recounted at length.

A well-to-do woman had been thrown into a state of depression by her husband's sudden death and was plagued by suicidal tendencies. She came to Möttlingen with her mother. At first she lodged at the inn called "The Ox," but following a further suicide attempt the innkeeper understandably refused to have her any longer. Moved by compassion, Blumhardt dared to receive her into his rectory. He gave her a room near his own and provided a chambermaid as attendant, giving strict instructions not to leave the woman alone by day or night.

The sick person was not at all religious, had no stomach for Blumhardt's domestic prayer meetings, and like many of the mentally ill in those days she had an outspoken personal dislike for him. It should also be noted that not far from her room was the bedroom of several young men who had either been entrusted to Blumhardt's care or been taken in by him, partly because of nervous complaints, partly for reasons unrelated to health considerations.

One morning, while taking something up to the "young gentlemen," Hans heard a suspicious rumbling from the widow's room, and called for the chambermaid. Getting no reply, he looked for her and found her downstairs. She explained that she had said to the woman she would go down for just a moment to fetch water for washing.

"Quick, quick, there's something wrong!"

She ran up and, finding the door locked, rushed down and out into the street. From there she saw the window open and the widow hanging by her neck from the crossbar. Hans smashed the door in with an axe, and the blows awakened Blumhardt and the "young gentlemen." He took the seemingly lifeless body down; he and Blumhardt carefully loosened the scarf by which she had hanged herself and laid her on the bed.

"Rub her!" advised one of the young men, who had gained a little medical knowledge and experience from his father. This was done diligently, but without any success. In the end Blumhardt said, "She is dead, and that must not be. Let us pray!" He, his wife, Gottliebin, and Hans knelt down and prayed. Next, Blumhardt asked Hans to open the woman's mouth; when this was done, he breathed into it. She drew a few breaths, then seemed again lifeless. Later she broke into a horrible, long-drawn-out, animal-like howl.

Blumhardt had at once notified the district physician by special messenger. When the physician, with another man, drove up, he listened to the howling, examined the totally unconscious person and the terrible state of her neck, and declared that in view of these injuries the howling could be understood as an expression of pain but not as a sign of life. "As far as we are concerned, she is dead," he said and left the house, having apparently given up hope. The sick person grew still again and relapsed into a state of complete lifelessness. Hans remained by her side. It was the singing drifting over from the evening devotions that woke her. With a visibly pleased expression on her face she said, "The rector is really a dear man!" Then, turning to Hans, "You are here too, Fritz?" (Fritz was the name of her deceased husband.)

"Yes," he replied, somewhat embarrassed but trying not to upset her in any way.

"Oh," she said, "it's so good that you are back too! I had died like you; I was in hell, but the rector, the good man, has called me back, and I don't want to go there anymore."

Hans spoke to her gently, with the result that she gradually calmed down. At ten o'clock Mose and another man came to relieve Hans. That agitated her very much.

"Go away, go away! I don't want to return to hell. They want to take me back there! You will stay, Fritz, won't you?"

So they went again, and Hans remained, but for a long time she continued to be agitated about the men who she thought had wanted to take her back. Finally Hans decided on a little ruse.

"Dear wife," he said, "don't you think it would be better for you to be quiet now and try to get a little sleep?"

"Yes, thank you, Fritz; you might be right," she replied and before long sank into wholesome slumber. She woke again at five the next morning. "Are you there, Mr. Hans?"

"Yes."

"How odd that I took you for my husband before!"

Now Hans began to rebuke her mildly, saying, "Do you know what you have done? How could you do such a thing!"

"Yes, I know it quite well; it was my greed. When my husband was alive, we put aside a thousand florins every year, and I could not get over it that that had come to an end. I kept thinking, 'If only the girl would go out for a moment!' and all night long something said to me, 'See that scarf? You can hang yourself with that.' But I shall not do it again; I know now where suicides end up. I was in hell, and I don't want to go there again. Oh, the rector is a good man!"

Before long she was completely well in body, soul, and spirit. Three months later she remarried and remained a diligent attendant at the Möttlingen church.

As mentioned above, I want to be brief as regards such cures of mentally ill persons, even though there were many and very conspicuous cases of that kind. A lot of such people came of their own accord, and there was often a strange conflict between their sick will (and correspondingly deranged or contrary actions) and the firm resolve of their spirit to find healing. This may have strengthened Blumhardt's belief that the German term *Geisteskrank* (spiritually or mentally ill) misses the mark. "A person's spirit in the biblical sense—that in him which is holy and of God—is immortal, and what cannot die cannot be ill either."

On one occasion a man came into the rectory courtyard turning somersaults right up to the rectory door; he had come on his own, all the way from Calw, in this unusual way. He, too, found healing.

In his military service the young, well-to-do, intelligent son of a farmer had fallen into the hands of a hard drill sergeant, who disliked him from the start and for whom he could do nothing right. The angrier the instructor became, the more dense the recruit, and vice versa, as unfortunately is often the case. This cycle ended with the young man's going out of his mind and being reduced to repeating endlessly, "hm, hm, hm, one, two, three," in three-eights measure. In this state he presented himself to the rector and told him his need in just those words, "Hm, hm, hm, one, two, three, hm, hm, hm, one, two, three." There was a shaking eloquence in that language. He arrived on a Saturday and took part in the usual evening service from the sacristy. Then he attended the Sunday services and, occupying himself by splitting wood, stayed in Möttlingen for the week in order to experience there yet another Sunday. On that second Sunday he recovered completely.

The sacristy usually contained an odd assortment of people; epileptics and mentally disturbed persons were often gathered there in varying numbers. Blumhardt was very large-hearted toward the sick; on the other hand he expected much more than is usually demanded from the healthy as regards their attitude to the sick. "Even just for your own sakes—don't be shocked by whatever happens or make too much of it! Instead, *pray* for the sick when you see that someone is having an attack." And for the sake of the sick themselves, he would not permit their infirmities to be blown up by expressions of shock or exaggerated pity on the part of the healthy, since that might dishearten the sufferers. Even the actual meeting hall of the church was not completely closed to the mentally ill; the congregation was to perceive itself as an *ecclesia militans*, a fighting church, and was to help by intercession. When exciting disturbances did occur now and then, Blumhardt would feel sufficiently vindicated by the fact that similar disturbances of church services are also reported in the Gospels. Once when a man got up in the middle of the sermon and began to recite blasphemous doggerel, Blumhardt had the congregation sing a hymn stanza, whereupon the man quieted down. Another time an epileptic collapsed with severe convulsions and lay as dead. The people nearby wanted to pick him up, but Blumhardt told them to leave him and continued to preach. The man gradually came to, got up and was well. Still another time a sick man who had not been allowed into the church shouted to Blumhardt from outside, "Just carry on like this, and you will yet get the whole world." All these people were healed.

Blumhardt took considerable personal risks in this area. Many a disturbed person, in a fit of frenzy, felt driven to vent his anger on the rector. One time, luckily enough, a burly fellow sitting in the sacristy next to the pulpit steps could not keep his designs to himself. "I'm going to throw that little man right out of the pulpit," he muttered as he got up. However, he was quickly calmed down by Blumhardt's "major-domo" Hans, who wielded a remarkable authority over such people.

I still want to report two such cases on the strength of Blumhardt's own information. They are related in the sense that in both of them the illness had been caused by a false spirituality and exaggerated so-called piety. While still in the nursery, a certain boy had begun half playfully to preach to his brothers and sisters. The parents listened admiringly, which served to egg him on. He did it more and more earnestly and solemnly; in the end he even turned on his parents and preached repentance to them. They dissolved into tears. Other people, too, became attentive and flocked to hear him, and the presumed little prophet became more and more something of a sensation. All of a sudden a strange nervous or mental malady put an end to the prophetic glory. If I remember rightly, he became dumb (though I am not sure)—at any rate quite deranged. The physicians, unable to help, advised the parents to take the boy to Blumhardt. When Blumhardt learned of what had gone on and the boy was brought to him, he thundered at him, "What is the fifth commandment?" When no answer was forthcoming, he repeated the question imperatively, until the boy with an effort managed to stammer correctly, "Honor your father and your mother." Then Blumhardt rebuked him most indignantly, particularly for daring to preach repentance to his parents but also for his preaching generally. He added, "If God wants repentance preached to your parents, he certainly won't use you to do it." The boy recovered quickly.

The other case is as follows. One day—I don't remember if it was Sunday evening or Monday morning—a woman came to Blumhardt's study with the question, "Tell me what you think of visions and revelations? Yesterday (or today) in Sunday school I noticed that you completely mistrust them and think nothing of them. There you are mistaken and wrong." Then she told him she had been sick most of her life and unable to work; so during the last one or two years God had favored her with a wonderful substitute to console her. She said she felt almost constantly surrounded by a bright light; in this light she at times saw Jesus and heard him speak either to her or to God the Father; now and then she would also hear the Father reply to the Son. What she could tell of the content of these conversations had a strange aura of spirituality about it. Blumhardt then remembered hearing about this person; he also recalled that she was regarded as an uncommonly gifted seeress by certain people whom one would have credited with some judgment concerning these things. As he tells it: "I thought, I have to say a clear word here." Bluntly he replied,

"That's all from the devil!" In utmost indignation she stormed out of the room. But a day or so later she came back in tears to thank him for healing her. True, when she left him, she had felt very angry and hurt, she said, but from that moment the light and all the rest were gone, and she had no longer seen or heard anything special. Not only that, but it had become clear to her that all this had been sickness and evil deceit and that she was now well. With deep shame she acknowledged having been cured of unbounded spiritual pride and brought down to simple humility.

In telling about the miracles we have plucked them out of the context of life as a whole and presented them bunched closely together. Reported in that way, however, they do not convey the lovely, almost intimate impression of the Lord's nearness, as kindly as it was holy, that they gave when they blossomed like flowers on the field of everyday life. To regain that impression, we must imagine ourselves transported into the midst of the Möttlingen congregation, where people very simply brought all their health needs to the Lord in a repentant and believing spirit and just as quietly and simply experienced his help time and again. This was of course most striking where it concerned innocent children. The type of convulsions, usually coupled with fainting, that frequently afflicts children almost regularly disappeared at once after a brief prayer for help.

There was no question of forcing anything through. In February 1846, writing to a colleague who had fully entered into Blumhardt's way of thinking, Blumhardt shared what he experienced with various ailments of his own:

> You have to accept it when your own ailments do not go away quite so quickly. I, too, have been troubled by this or that and am still not free of it all; I just have to wait it out. Thus, all through last summer I had a cough and a sore throat, as well as such trouble with my shoulder joint that I could hardly use my arm, and more things like that. I had to put up with it in the hope it would eventually go, and now it is gone. Healing cannot be forced by prayer; we just have to go on hoping that once an ailment is commended to the Lord, it will not stay with us all our life.

I will venture to cite yet another example of this simple way of committing everything to the Lord. Although we townsfolk may be inclined to smile at it, I hope to be understood all the better by farmers. I refer to the need caused by disease among domestic animals. Livestock is the basis of a countryman's wealth to such a degree that we find it understandable when pagan peoples, even highly civilized ones, pay divine honors to the cow. Once, when a girl herding cows was asked why a cow has four feet and we humans only two, I heard her reply, "Because we are only human beings." It is well known too that in many a rural household the cow's sickness is (unfortunately) regarded as a much more serious event than the illness of the wife or of a child. Against this general background, I will now let Blumhardt tell how this need was dealt with in Möttlingen. He writes:

> According to the catechism, cattle are part of the daily bread. We pray for bread in the Lord's Prayer, so why should we not also be allowed to pray for the cattle to be preserved? To us it may seem strange, but not to the peasant, for whom unfortunately a calf is often of greater value than a child. In short, here they simply pray, and the beasts improve almost at once. The people kneel down in a corner of the stable and say the Lord's Prayer, and that's all. If there is sin, of course it has to be faced squarely. But I can cite many, many instances to prove that help is being received in this way; it also shows that it is right to pray for it.
>
> Often, too, the cattle are tormented by demons (cf. the Gerasene demons); people are liable to ascribe this to witches. You must see to it that witchcraft does not gain a footing among the people. Against the demons the Lord's Prayer is of help (though not always), if the people stand right otherwise. When people from farther away come to me with complaints, they usually find that things have improved by the time they arrive back home. That is why it is often good for the likes of us to get involved.[1]

And what did the authorities have to say to these extraordinary happenings? Admittedly, Blumhardt had become a considerable problem for the church authorities. There were quite a few clerics and physicians who felt their rights were being infringed. Besides, before 1848 the higher levels of government in the various German states displayed a marked dislike of any kind of "Pietism"; they looked down almost with suspicion on any living expressions of Christianity.

---

1. I do not want to withhold this information on how the Möttlingen folk acted when faced by calamities (often rather odd ones) of this kind, because it shows in what a simple and matter-of-fact way they lived their faith. But anyone itching to imitate this procedure in somewhat similar cases ought to remember that it was through the earnest judgment of repentance that these people had been brought to the reality of peace and thereby to a special divine protection. Stories could be told of such unwarranted attempts, whose bad outcome is suggestive of the account in Acts 19:14–16.

The difficulties were eased in two ways: for the authorities by Blumhardt's tact, and for Blumhardt by various kindly dispensations. Blumhardt had a keen sense of our obligations toward governmental authority. Though he could hold his position valiantly when the need arose, he also tried very conscientiously to see things from the viewpoint of the authorities. His sincere respect for them made him more than ready to let himself be taught by them where possible. However much it was urged on him by various hotheads, he guarded against misusing in his own favor, in a high-handed, fanatical way, the word, "One must obey God more than men." Such an attitude benefited him by reducing the danger of serious conflicts. From the very beginning it gained him the benevolent trust of his clerical superiors, while the various kindly dispensations mentioned above helped to strengthen this trust further.

It so happened, for example, that the ranking member of the Stuttgart consistory, Director Knapp, arranged for a distant female relative of his to get a training in home economics in Blumhardt's house. Official considerations may have suggested that to him as an opportunity to look personally into what was going on in the Möttlingen rectory. The consistory had heard quite enough of the "struggle" as well as of the revival and its peculiarities to desire to have first-hand information about these matters. Anyway, on Easter Monday 1844 Knapp himself brought the girl to the rectory to begin her training. He was just the right man for Blumhardt—a lawyer "firm, sober, and reasonable" (as town counselor Christ-Sarasin heard him described). Blumhardt writes:

> I at once brought up the main subject and told him of experiences with satanic powers. He shuddered. When I said, "I really can't put such things in writing, can I?" replied, "No, you can't." In this way I have got out of having to submit a written account to the consistory, I think. [As we know, this hope did not materialize.] More: Knapp watched the people crowd in, including those coming from farther away; he saw how I had to rush off time and again and had barely a quarter of an hour to be with him undisturbed. It gave me a chance to speak of my work and of the shortcomings of the church in this respect. He hemmed and hawed at first, for he naturally shies away from all popery and the Roman Catholic type of absolution. But he noticed my results, and guess what happened: Quite on his own he offered to go with me to the brothers' conference [men's meeting]. There I spoke in his presence, the Möttlingers gave a testimony, and in short,

Knapp was satisfied and took leave in a way that assured me of his support. It is the Lord's doing.

The peasants' love of Blumhardt is what seems to have impressed Knapp particularly. Actually, such a personal inspection was highly necessary for an evaluation of Blumhardt's experiences. Especially the meetings, so frequent and well attended, were liable to give an unwholesome impression. From a distance they could hardly be imagined other than as half-feverish goings-on, degenerating into idle chatter. If anybody detested that, it was Blumhardt. "When spiritual things are carried on without the Spirit, it is bad," he once remarked with reference to activities of that kind. It simply had to be *seen* how with all their solemnity of spirit his meetings were of a most natural, hearty, healthy, and sober character. One could say they were thoroughly congenial to the ordinary person.

A little later—just when, I could not discover—another visit took place, which helped to clear the air for Blumhardt at the very highest government level. It may even have stood him in good stead later on, when the question of acquiring Bad Boll came up. One Sunday morning two gentlemen came walking up from Märklingen, one of them obviously in attendance on the other, and took up lodging in the inn called "The Ox." The "other" gentleman attended the church service and just managed to secure a seat next to the organ—not the best location, since the organist was hard of hearing and made astonishing demands not only on his poor instrument but also on the listeners' ears. The gentleman attended the afternoon service as well. In between he kept a diligent vigil, either in the rectory garden, where one could watch the peasants come flocking in; in the rectory courtyard, right among these people; or in the churchyard behind the rectory. He had been recognized already during the morning service by a recruit who had just come from Stuttgart on furlough. He said to Hans, "You know that gentleman up there next to the organ?" "No." "That's the king!" After the service, up in the study, Hans, pointing through the window at the gentleman promenading outside, told Blumhardt that according to the recruit that was the king. Blumhardt looked at the gentleman and said, "He might be right that it is the king." Nothing further happened, not only because of the press of people around Blumhardt but even more because the gentleman himself apparently wished to remain incognito. In the evening a stately carriage drove up and took the two gentlemen to Weilderstadt.

Was it in fact the king? Nothing more has ever been heard about it, but this episode is in keeping with the character of the then reigning king of Württemberg. He liked to go about incognito and mix with the people. On a street in Stuttgart Gottliebin once asked an unknown gentleman for directions to a certain store; he went with her to show the way, and it was only from the astounded shop assistants that she learned of her guide's identity.

So much about events that served to shield the extraordinary life that had taken shape around Blumhardt from at least the more severe forms of governmental censure. To be sure, he did have obstacles put in his way. In January 1844 the ministry forbade him to "transfer healings into the pastoral area instead of directing people to the medical profession." Blumhardt's answer to this was a twelve-page document, which ended: "I shall no longer lay my hands on any stranger nor let any person stay here over the weekend. In short, I shall not undertake more with anybody other than to let him tell me of his ailment, maybe give him some advice and then let him go. But then if healings continue—for God will not let his hand be tied—and people go on flocking here, I want to protest in advance against being reproached with disobedience."

The remaining content, said to be "of a serious nature," is unfortunately not known to me. In May of the same year, so as to meet the embarrassed consistory halfway, he went a considerable step further. In a letter dated June 18, 1846, he tells a friend the following:

> As for the rest, I can say that things are going forward, in spite of an outward hitch. That is to say that about four weeks ago I stopped people from telling me their ailments; they have to be satisfied with attending the church service. And since [a gap in the letter] I don't let myself be seen at all by strangers. All this because I would otherwise risk everything. I am doing it voluntarily, but as though acting the cowherd of Ulm [probably someone who forestalled being fired by resigning himself]. In spite of it all, quite a bit is happening in the church, though there is less faith and the stream of sick people has fallen off considerably. The consistory feels in a very embarrassing situation . . . [etc.]

What Blumhardt tells here so simply and not without humor was actually a heartrending experience, and it grieved him deeply. In these depressing circumstances it was uplifting and moving to hear him announce from the pulpit that he had promised no longer to allow outside people into the rectory. "You sick ones, just come into the church, lay your sufferings before the Savior, and listen carefully to the sermon. You are assured of my intercession and that of the congregation. There is really no need for me to know your ailments."

There was greatness in the way he thought and spoke, but putting it into practice was painful. Time and again new people came who had not heard the announcement. Very much against his will, the "major-domo" Hans became a Cerberus, relentlessly turning away the folk who came crowding in. I still have before my inner eye the scene on one of the following Sundays: From the living room we could see the peasants that had come for help standing, pretty well in serried ranks, outside the rectory. Blumhardt, his eyes filled with tears, lamented, "Oh, the poor people! You gentlemen—officers, students, merchants—you are all right; no one stops you, but the poor folk are not allowed in; they just get pushed about."

Once—I believe it was on that Sunday—I saw a peasant who had apparently managed to slip through come up the stairs. Blumhardt ordered him back.

"Oh, *Herr Pfarrer*," was the reply, "there is nothing wrong with me now; I just wanted to say thanks."

"Well, that's nice."

"Yes, *Herr Pfarrer*, I had something wrong with me, a whole lot. There was . . ."

"Well, I don't want to know what it was. So you did have something wrong with you?"

"Yes, *Herr Pfarrer*, and I did just as you said; I went to the service and listened carefully, and now I'm all right."

But the influx of seekers for help may have continued for yet another reason than simple ignorance of Blumhardt's prohibition. As far as his duty allowed, Hans was actually quite a soft-hearted Cerberus. Was he required to close his ears to the people's needs? And the next time he found himself in the rector's study, would not his mouth overflow with what filled his heart? Should a healing be given, that channel for people's complaints to reach Blumhardt's ears was sufficiently complicated to be safe from an accusation of illegality.

Of course, a certain amount of friction between the clerical authorities and Blumhardt was unavoidable. On one side was the consistory, under pressure from physicians, clergymen, and journalists, and on the other was Blumhardt, facing a tide of misery. They could hardly arrive at a common view of the novel situation facing them. There is now an acknowledged division of labor, which entrusts our body to the physicians' keeping while letting clergymen attend to purely spiritual concerns. For a time this seemed to be so much the consistory's ideal that it frowned on any evidence that religion had an influence on physical recovery, especially when such influence was recurring and eye-catching, and regarded it as an almost willful disturbance of that harmonious division of responsibilities. Therefore, Blumhardt was informed, the task of religion was simply to console and to stress the blessing of suffering and the value of patience. But when this advice developed into a demand that Blumhardt should simply turn all suppliants not only away from his own person but also away from any hope of receiving direct help from the Lord and that he should explicitly direct them to medical practitioners, Blumhardt no longer felt able to obey, especially since only those sick came to him whose infirmities had baffled all the skill of physicians. On the one hand he had recourse to the views of Holy Scripture, which harmonized with his experiences and procedures, on the other to his civic freedom, which entitled him, like any citizen, to let his counseling be guided by his convictions. He declared that no minister had ever been asked to comply with such a demand. Indeed, the request of the consistory that he forbid visiting strangers (excepting his personal friends) to stay in Möttlingen overnight was a remarkable demand made on a rector—putting it to him that he *could* do it, *wished* to do it, and, more than that, *must* do it.

By the nature of things, Blumhardt's compliance with such decrees was of a very elastic kind. Still, he wanted to obey the principle that the established order should not be disturbed, and he did it too. Therefore it pained him doubly when he was once, in the presence of two colleagues called as witnesses, given a reprimand "on account of disobedience" by the deanery on behalf of the consistory.

Here mention should be made of two friendly experiences belonging to that time of ever increasing restrictions—the first period (from January until May), a stricter second period, and finally the later time of strictest observance. The first account comes from Blumhardt himself (*Vertheidigungsschrift*, p. 103ff.).

One Saturday or Sunday in the spring of 1846 a candidate of medicine by the name of Steinkopf came from Stuttgart to Möttlingen with the avowed intention of examining the healings and unearthing the true facts. Purposely avoiding the rectory, he took up lodgings in the "Ox" inn. After the Sunday morning service, a few young men from various countries were sitting together in the summer house (the gable of which had been decorated by Barth's skilful hand with a colored painting show-ing Jesus and the two disciples walking to Emmaus). They were joined by this young man, who was in a state of great excitement, for, he said, among the people leaving the church he had just discovered a former patient of the Tübingen clinic, a woman whom they had discharged as incurable. When he greeted her with, "Well, Magdalena, are you here too?" she had replied, "Yes, of course; I got cured here!" And to all appearances she was indeed well. When asked how, she had answered that in December 1845 (at a time when Blumhardt could still work unhindered) she had seen the rector two or three times after church, had complained of her ailment, and had told him how it was going (there was no laying on of hands in her case); in this way she had been healed. Faithful to his inten-tions, Steinkopf pursued the matter further. He had Magdalena come with him to the rectory, introduced himself to the rector, and openly declared the purpose of his coming to Möttlingen. He asked for a room and examined the patient with Blumhardt's permission (or even at his request). His findings were set down in the following document, which he made out for Blumhardt (*Vertheidigungsschrift* p. 104). It reads:

> In March 1844 Maria Magdalena Rapp from Enzthal near Wildbad, now thirty-five years of age, was accepted into the medical clinic at Tübingen, as she suffered from pemphigus. She was treated with various remedies, but the blisters, though often disappearing for a few days, would always break out fresh in different parts of the body. The application of arsenic caused the blisters to vanish completely, and for some days the patient was fully free of them.
>
> But in the winter of 1844 serious vomiting of blood, bloody stools, and stomach pains set in. From then on, doubtless in con-sequence of a chronic stomach inflammation, the patient could not take any kind of warm food. The spells of blood-vomiting recurred regularly every 3–5 weeks. As a result the patient came several times very close to death. The pemphigus reappeared with all its earlier persistence.
>
> She was discharged in July 1845 in a condition that was completely hopeless, according to the judgment of all physi-cians observing her. As a last resort she tried the mineral baths at Wildbad for some weeks, but without the least success. Her condition remained unchanged until December, when she went

to Möttlingen to seek help from Pastor Blumhardt. After her first visit she already felt much better. After she had seen the pastor once or twice more, all symptoms vanished completely in the course of three months. In May 1846 the undersigned found the patient in Möttlingen, where she attended church. To his great surprise, she was fully restored to health.

A detailed history of her illness is to be found in the Tübingen clinic. After so protracted and totally unsuccessful a treatment she had to be considered completely incurable.

The truth of the above is attested by

K. Steinkopf, med. cand.
Möttlingen, May 24, 1846

The other episode took place in May 1846. One Saturday a woman arrived with a convulsively clenched hand (I was told that her finger nails had actually grown into the palm). She had been treated without success in Tübingen. She wanted to enter the rectory but was turned away. However, in the manner we know of, Blumhardt did hear of her infirmity. She attended the Saturday evening service. The following morning she marched triumphantly across the rectory yard and went up to the major-domo, "But now I *must* see the rector!"

"I know, dear lady, but it's just not possible."

"Why not?" she retorted, stretching out to him her hand—open, flat, and completely cured. Her hand had opened the day before during evening devotions, she told him. Unfortunately, in her triumphant mood she went also to Tübingen to show her hand—not very tactfully, it is to be expected—to those who had treated her there. Of course she did not meet with a friendly reception and was regarded as an impostor. Blumhardt, soothing her indignation, advised her to "Go home, be still, and first turn over a new leaf yourself."[2]

---

2. This case had various unpleasant consequences for Blumhardt. For one thing, the woman was considered a "sinner" (she had several illegitimate children), a circumstance that by itself made the cure offensive to some; for another, she caused not a little embarrassment to Blumhardt because of the boastful and in part highly fanciful talkativeness, with which she advertised her experiences. It was a fact, for example, that Blumhardt, stretching out his hand to greet her, had taken hold of her sick hand with a special expression of sympathy and blessing. But as embellished in her colorful description it took on an appearance that could easily be construed as a breach of promise on Blumhardt's part. Besides, the fact that in the course of her rhetorical exploits, and quite likely because of these, the healing came to a full stop naturally provided valuable material for critical misgivings.

Such a standstill or even reversal of healing did indeed occur at times. Blumhardt was pained by it, but it did not surprise him, for he was accustomed to regard the divine help received as no more than crumbs and possibly as promises of a better time to come. Sometimes, though, a relapse seemed to be connected, as for example in this case, with an ungodly and unspiritual acceptance of the help received (say, treating it as if it were Blumhardt's doing and not the Lord's). This once caused Blumhardt to remark that it was questionable if the healing of the nine unthankful lepers had been a lasting one.

At the time when his friend Dieterlen was more and more swamped by a flood of sick people asking him to get Blumhardt to intercede for them, Blumhardt wrote to him as follows, both with reference to the above problem and to what was so remarkable in our present case—the unexpectedly speedy help given to a seemingly unworthy person:

> When some persons who had been sick and found healing suffer a relapse, that probably is to lead them inwardly deeper. With the influx of sick persons constantly increasing, one or another among them may well come with a more outward approach. The Lord does what is up to him, but in turn he also *demands* something.
>
> What about people who are bad? My experience is that the Savior pays little attention to that when such people come. It surprises me how many times the worst are given the most, and often much more quickly than others. Why? When they come, it means more than the coming of others; they are more humble and broken. Then the angels rejoice, and they are given something special. Oh, the loving-kindness of the Lord! And all that free of charge and totally undeserved—out of pure grace!

Some miracles of that kind continued to take place; at least they served to put to rest the talk of Blumhardt's possessing "magnetic powers." However, from now on the influx of people dropped off considerably, since a personal talk with Blumhardt, now denied, had naturally been to them the greatest and finest in "all of Möttlingen." The words of comfort, admonition, rebuke, and forgiveness he spoke to a person were imbued with a power such as only he that experienced it can know. Humanity's need for priestly and pastoral care, which slumbers unrecognized in thousands of hearts, had powerfully wakened everywhere. Now this need found that the only place where understanding and satisfaction could be found was closed to it. That was hard; for anyone who had once obtained benefits from this source desired again and again to garner more of them for his constantly changing circumstances and new relationships, as well as for his children, friends, foes, relatives, etc.

The sufferers, too, found it very hard that henceforth this door was closed to them. True, to a believing heart the same help was still available, as was experienced by a good many who attended the service, simply following the instructions Blumhardt had given from the pulpit. Nevertheless, there was so much a burdened heart missed, now that the natural inner sharing between the sufferer and the comforter, so strengthening and uplifting, had been forbidden. Along with the prospect of help, the grieving had found here also what they could not find just anywhere: wholehearted love, full truth, and strong, wholesome comfort. No wonder that what was still open to them—that impersonal and deficient system of communication—did not satisfy people in the long run, and so Möttlingen lost for them its main attraction. Times became ever more quiet, also because the following year (1847) was one of scarcity and the next one (1848) full of political turmoil. Blumhardt's direct contact with people outside his congregation dropped off; its place was taken by an ever growing pastoral task with people from the so-called upper classes. In this way there gradually grew up in his own household a small congregation consisting of guests of various kinds in need of help.

Let us, too, enter the rectory and learn of four memorable personal experiences Blumhardt had in the summer of 1844. It is suitable to include them in this chapter, since they are also of a more or less miraculous character.

To begin with, there is the scene connected with his song of triumph, "Jesus is victorious King," a scene that remained an uplifting memory for him and his companions throughout their lives. On a certain apostle's day Blumhardt had gone with some other Möttlingen folk to take part in a mission festival in the neighboring village of Ostelsheim. Afterward, in the company of the Ostelsheim rector and two men from Möttlingen, he walked back to his own village. He was ahead of the others, immersed in thoughts of his great experiences, maybe also of various instances where his own life was preserved (as we shall hear later). Quietly he composed the following stanza, which he at once shared with his companions:

Jesus is victorious King,
Who o'er all his foes has conquered.
Jesus, soon the world will fall
At his feet, by love overpowered.

> Jesus, stooping from his throne,
> Comes and takes to himself his own.

Later, in Bad Boll, he altered [approximately indicated in the present English rendering] the content of the two last verses of this stanza, which remained precious to him throughout his life:

> Jesus leads us with his might
> From the darkness to radiant light.

Having meanwhile arrived at a lovely spot named *Kirchplatz* (church square), they sang the stanza to the well-known tune of "Holy God, we praise thy name." All at once it felt as though hundreds of voices in the nearby woods joined in jubilantly and so powerfully that at least the one of the two Möttlingen men who is still alive today stopped singing, so overawed was he. Blumhardt, on the other hand (he tells), went on singing lustily. When on arriving home he greeted his family, Gottliebin, equally moved, recited to him the very same stanza he had just composed and sung!

Then there are three instances of divine preservation, all striking in varying degrees, when hostile attempts were made on Blumhardt's life. In general, Blumhardt scarcely ever had real enemies, but, hard to believe though it is, his courageous witness and action against the devious ways of superstition seems to have earned him the deadly enmity of a small number. In short, it came to light at that time that there were hidden enemies who secretly plotted to take his life. For a time the authorities even had his house guarded by nightly patrols.

In July 1844 things were particularly bad. Every night sounds as of men's footsteps were heard along the corridors of the house, even though in the evening each nook and cranny of the rectory was carefully searched and the entrances were bolted. The inhabitants got used to it, since the harassment did not go any further. For this reason, too, they paid no special notice when one night they heard various noises from the adjoining barn. Just at that time, Blumhardt had a visit from his mother; a carriage had been ordered for her departure early next morning. The coachman, arriving in good time, noticed smoke coming out of the barn door. A teenage boarder in the rectory (called "the English girl" in the village, because her mother was English) heard the commotion, hurried to the spot, sized up the situation, and ran into the village, crying "Fire!" Presently the rectory yard filled with young and old villagers and a motley array of water containers. With great presence of mind the innkeeper of "The Ox" took charge of this fire brigade. He gave orders to put out at once any flames that might break out when he opened the barn door. Skillfully he forced the door open, and a mountain of straw came in sight. Flames started to flare up from it but were immediately extinguished. Embedded in the straw were four to six packs of matches, some charred, others intact. Pockets of various flammable materials were found scattered throughout the barn, among them dozens of packs of matches, some of them still intact. One of these arson devices was especially ingenious. Long bean poles had been placed in a tub, with their tips pointing precisely to the floor of Blumhardt's bedroom; they had been charred to a height of one and a half feet. When the hubbub (which, by the way, had left Blumhardt unruffled) was over, he read, deeply moved, the text for the day: "No weapon that is fashioned against you shall prosper" (Isaiah 54:17).

In the same month, on Blumhardt's birthday, the riddle of those nightly disturbances was solved. The one causing them must at times have been directly over Blumhardt's room. Once, when he made his presence felt all too audibly, Blumhardt (who, by the way, prayed for him a good deal) shouted up to him, "Jesus is victor." The following morning, Blumhardt's birthday, there stuck out from under a board by the rear entrance door the following letter, scribbled in pencil on a scrap of paper.

July 16, 1844

Dear friends,

I am leaving your house at four in the morning, but not as the man I was when I came in. I came as a murderer with murderous thoughts, until I heard the shout, "Jesus is victor." Yes, Jesus is victor, and now my conscience has woken. I spent this night in despair among the roof timbers. To be sure, your efforts have been in vain, for the devil has thwarted you. And unless the blood of Christ cries out mightily even today, all that is left for me to do is to take the knife I wanted to pierce your heart with and turn it against my own breast. God's flaming eye has seen me; he has thrust a prick into my heart—not half . . . I am getting what my deeds deserve. I served the devil faithfully, and now hell is his reward for me. Something went right through me when I heard the name of the Most High called out so often. It made me so tame that I would readily come and stand before you. But . . . be so kind and intercede for me with the heavenly Father.

I thank you for your faithfulness. Think of me for Jesus' sake.

Your enemy

The place of the signature was taken by two lines of scattered letters, the one on the left apparently indicating the name and the one on
the right the place of residence. In his Bible class that evening Blumhardt
read out the letter, thus passing on the poor man's plea for intercession.
It was a man from a nearby village.

Yet another instance of divine preservation has already been brought
to public notice. One afternoon Blumhardt went to Unterhaugstett for
Bible classes and catechization. His wife had been made nervous by the
attempts on her husband's life and sent Hans to meet him, so that he
would not have to come home by himself in the dark. Blumhardt was not
pleased about it; he said his wife must have forgotten that there was a full
moon. But her precaution had not been for nothing, for presently two
men appeared at the edge of the woods. At first Blumhardt took them for
peasants working late in their fields and then, seeing their rifles gleam
in the light of the moon, for hunters. The men took aim at Blumhardt,
but on hearing him exclaim "Jesus is victor" they lowered their rifles.
Once more, in the middle of the wood, someone took aim at Blumhardt
from the edge of the road; they could hear him cock the gun. Hans was
about to tackle and grab him, but Blumhardt restrained him and prayed
for the poor persecutor. Coming out of the woods, they again saw rifles
pointed at them, this time from the meadow. Hans, by now in high spirits, shouted, "Go ahead! Pull the trigger; it won't go off," and presently
the gunmen peacefully went their way. They were evidently strangers,
come from a distance. Right from the first attack Blumhardt and Hans
had been singing hymns ("With God for me, I fear not what 'gainst me
is arrayed; I need but call upon him, and they will flee, dismayed," and
"Jesus Christ as king is ruling"). This was something Blumhardt often
did in moments of danger, remembering Psalm 18:3: "I will praise and
call upon the Lord; thus I am delivered from my enemies."

One last story should be included, more for the sake of him who
told it, a man remembered lovingly by all who knew him: Wilhelm
Hofacker of blessed memory. In the summer he sometimes came to Bad
Liebenzell, and from there he liked to visit the church and rectory in
Möttlingen. He happened to be in Liebenzell in June 1845 and was there
visited by Blumhardt. Just at that time Blumhardt's wife was suffering

from recurring attacks of illness that almost proved fatal. Blumhardt wrote to Barth about this visit as follows:

> After quite a good night my wife got up feeling well. I went off happily to Haugstett and from there to Liebenzell to see Hofacker, arriving there at two. No sooner had I got there than my chaise drove up and I was called home on account of my wife. Shortly before twelve, just after a rest on her bed, she had suffered an attack similar to the one eight days ago. That was bad news, for there was a lot I wanted to talk over with Hofacker. It upset his own plans too, so that he could think of nothing better than to ride home with me. I arrived here already at three and again found my wife so close to death that all I could think of for the moment was to breathe into her mouth. All this time I had dear Hofacker right by my side. The faithful brother was so loving to me that while we talked, I more than once could not help falling on his neck in tears, so grateful was I that after waiting anxiously for three years I had finally found someone with whom I could talk, who wanted to understand me and actually did.

The same richly blessed preacher (Hofacker) tells of the following experience in Möttlingen:

> I once attended the main Sunday service in Möttlingen. It was in the summer, just before harvest. I was seated in front, right below the pulpit in one of the pews reserved for honored guests. The church was crammed full, and the churchyard outside was also crowded with listeners. During the opening prayer the sky got darker and darker and more menacing; there was thunder, and the clouds had the particular hue that forebodes hail. All of a sudden Blumhardt calmly departed from the fixed track of the liturgy with the words, "Loving God, if you want to punish us for our sins and undo the blessing of our harvest, we do not dare to plead with you against that. But please be kind enough to let us still hear your word undisturbed." Then he went on with the liturgy. I felt like hiding under the pew at such audacity, but, lo and behold, it suddenly became light, and in a few minutes there was a blue sky and bright sunshine.

We shall see later on that things did not always turn out like that for Blumhardt, but like a child he was never afraid of getting a negative response to a request.

A good deal could be said about such experiences, which struck us present-day people as miraculous but were so much in keeping with the apostolic age. We shall return to them but for the moment would rather cast an eye on Blumhardt's own attitude to these demonstrations of divine help. He had arrived at a remarkably intimate fellowship with God and recognized ever more clearly and simply that everything that happens, including evil, stems from God. He learned to turn directly to him in a childlike, respectful, contrite, and trusting way. He also learned to see with reverence the footsteps of God even in what usually is considered almost profane, since it belongs to the realm of nature. Ever more clearly he perceived it to be the Christian's duty to look at everything with the eyes of faith and to approach it all accordingly. "Faith has pulled me through again," he would remark in those days, when victory had been his, either in a need of his own or in someone else's predicament that had been thrust upon him. In self-defense, he expressed such thoughts also in his letters to Barth. Here are some scattered extracts:

> My theory about illness is biblical. It took root in me through reading the Bible from childhood on, which I did more than anyone else. Later on I was given repeated intimations of its truth, and these were strengthened and raised to certainty in me by the experiences you know of. The supreme maxim is: Everything comes from God. If I had time, I would so guide you through the Bible that you would not be able to produce even one text in support of your system and that of others as against ten of mine.
>
> To have faith is our duty; everything that does not spring from faith is sin. Let's assume that someone recognizes God is afflicting him with such and such an evil for such and such a reason. He becomes aware that it is his duty to have faith but is too lazy to pray in faith. It is laziness that stops a man believing; a man would rather walk ten hours than search his conscience and earnestly bend his knees. In such a case unbelief is sin, for it is connected with a bad conscience. When I sharpen the people's consciences, it is done through the power of the Word. God's Word is a power, and when it awakens something in the conscience, there is nothing forced or fabricated or artificial there. You actually know me too well to suspect anything like that from me.
>
> It does not say anywhere that one ought to seek God's help in a roundabout or zigzagging way.

As we can well understand, Blumhardt was in those days very bold and confident of victory. The struggles people's distress involved him in were now of a peaceful nature and invested with priestly splendor; they were like so many journeys of discovery into the land of God's mercy, and ever-new glorious vistas opened up before him. His word to the effect that people have become too lazy to bend their knees earnestly before God possibly sums up all his experiences from the beginning of the "struggle" to the days of miracles; that is, if we invert the sentence and for a change turn our eyes to those Christians who *renounce* such laziness. God lives, and he that holds to him must also be prepared to *live*, that is, to be active in faith, to go forward intent on victory. This was Blumhardt's stand: living for others day and night, ever straining forward, always borne up by the nearness of the Lord. Avoiding mention of persons still alive, we can at least put on record that Blumhardt's co-fighter Gottliebin, too, gave herself heroically in faith, love, and hope so that the Lord's cause might go forward from victory to victory.

Blumhardt completely failed to understand one objection raised at times by otherwise devout people to the confident joy with which he pleaded for physical ills to be taken away. The objection was that this violated the duty of patience and resignation. Two errors are at the root of this objection. One is that asking for something means putting pressure on God. Do we not rather tie God's hands by *not* asking? He might be inclined to help us if we implore him earnestly enough; if we fail to do so, it is *we*, so to speak, who prevent his coming to our aid. Asking God for something does not yet imply exerting pressure on him. A true prayer must be prepared from the outset for a possible negative response. Blumhardt once said, "This calls for patience and faith on the part of the saints [Rev 14:12]; faith expects everything, patience nothing."

He detested the kind of prayer that would put pressure on God and also warned very seriously against the long, fervent, passionate type of prayer popular in some circles:

> I have learned sufficiently how little good comes from that, and I like to say so to those willing to listen. Is such praying still a prayer in the Spirit? Is it not rather based on the assumption that by sheer fervent praying something can be wrested from the Lord? Yet the Lord says: "In praying do not heap up empty phrases as the gentiles do, for they think that they will be heard for their many words" [Matt 6:7]. As long as the words of Jesus are accorded any importance at all, we should take this word, too, in its full meaning and not fly in the face of it. Also the "little children" [Matt 11:25] whom the advocates of this type of prayer might claim as their authority are brief and simply say what their wish is.

Hence Blumhardt's way of praying was as simple as can be. At the same time though he could say, "I have often noticed that something not attained by asking for it once or twice will yet be given when prayed for a third or fourth or yet more times." Still, in this respect he often let himself be guided by the apostle Paul's example—"three times" (2 Cor 12:8)—and then assumed it was not the Lord's will to respond to that particular request.

The second error behind the above-mentioned objection is the notion that a truly devout and exemplary patience would not wish at all to be freed from suffering. Scarcely anybody respected as highly as Blumhardt did the true patience of souls that quietly endured suffering for years. But when he came up against a patience that was said to forbid praying for help, he would look closely to see if it really was patience. "It is much easier," he once said, "to slip into a kind of submission to God's will than to draw the bolts that hold up God's help." And he once wrote to a sick woman: "One should beware of showing off one's patience. Such frippery will be burned up. Everyone should at least consider: It could be that what is demanded of me is faith, and if I go on ignoring that, I might make myself guilty!"

In his *Vertheidigungsschrift* he chastised the kind of patience that will only bear but not ask, in a way that showed his anger with all un-genuine pious talk. He says:

> Among us a virtue is made of necessity. If someone has an incurable ailment or infirmity, it is said to be the will of God, and one has to resign oneself to it, since in the end everything works out for humanity's benefit and is also intended that way. Evil, it is said, is the greatest good fortune, and one must be thankful for it. It is even wrong to drive it away by prayer, for that would be resisting the will of God. However, while engaged in such supposedly pious thoughts (which I, by the way, do not actually reject), one still does all one can to get rid of the ailment or pain. The "patience" that refuses to pray for deliverance from adversity out of fear that it might displease God will try everything, even the most bizarre things. It runs from one doctor to another, avidly looks out for likely new remedies, and is ready to travel any distance when it hears of someone or something that might promise help. At times it actually stoops to frankly sinful ways, even following instructions to do what is shameful and indecent; it lets persons and names be inscribed into sorcerers' books, giving as a flimsy excuse that in need one simply has to

try everything. This is the patience that pretends so piously that it submits to God's will and does not want to ask for anything against his will, a patience that has attained a height rarely attempted by any other virtue, for it finds nothing too difficult, too heavy, too hard, too painful, too weird and adventurous (at times even too shameless and sinful) provided it helps. But by no means from God, for that would be impatience!

The poor, misguided people—will they never recognize the delusion in which they live? I don't want to reproach anybody but merely ask: The omnipresent, evident sense of desperation in the face of ailments and infirmities that humanity's nature cannot possibly put up with because they disturb its harmony—does it not prove that help would be more necessary and profitable than such a hopeless whining and straining and chasing after all manner of remedies, always coupled with lying to God about being patient?

Suffering is said to give birth to the inner person. I don't want to deny it, but it is also a common experience that people afflicted with chronic illnesses get ever more contrary, headstrong, self-willed, grumpy, and impatient as time goes by and are more and more unmerciful and cranky to their attendants and nurses. Does that count for nothing? It shows that things are not as they should be and that some other way should have been found, otherwise things would surely be different.

To be sure, there are also cases where the sick get more amenable and amiable and gentler, where everything goes as well as can be expected under the circumstances, for it is never right to make a rule. Yet it is as clear as daylight that at present men lack something they ought to have in thousands of cases: the direct intervention of the Lord, who purchased us with his blood. When that intervention takes place, it is a miracle to be sure, but a necessary miracle, without which we cannot exist nor find joy in our faith. Incidentally, such a miracle must also serve to make the works of God manifest, as in the case of the man born blind (John 9:3).

As we see, it is not only anger at people's lying manner of speech that permeates this vehement outburst. It also expresses compassion for people's need and even more, a lofty courage born of the unwavering confidence that the relationship to God opened to us through the death of Jesus Christ will once more come into its own.

In his *Vertheidigungsschrift* (p. 63) Blumhardt tells in his inimitably simple way how he gradually reached that height of faith and rich store of wonderful experiences. He speaks there of his treatment of the mentally ill. Even though he very often suspected demonic influences in such illnesses, there was nothing disheartening or even humiliating in the way he referred to them, for he became aware how often high-minded and noble souls were actually affected more than others. Just this fact made him confident that the Lord would send help, that is, grant a freeing, if asked for it.

Dr. de Valenti had demanded that Blumhardt leave the treatment of such mentally ill persons to physicians and restrict his activity to pastoral care, that is, to "instruction, rebuke, and comfort." In reply Blumhardt pointed out that before anything else it must be possible to make an impact on a person's spirit.

> As regards those three things—instruction, rebuke, and comfort—they can be used least of all. As a rule, the application of such spiritual pressure only serves to excite the sick, the agitation often increasing to a veritable frenzy. For this reason, when asked for advice it is precisely these three approaches that I will not allow relatives to use. In my own ministry, too, I only use them very cautiously and with such great moderation that even in the sermons I ask these unfortunate ones to attend I say nothing with special reference to them. Something must come from above, as the Lord clearly indicates. Unless that is given, there can be no help or only an apparent help, which does more harm than good.
>
> But how can we receive this gift from above? Indeed, the gates of heaven, which at one time stood open, seem now to be closed. There is a lot of praying going on, but how little it actually achieves! How often people come and say almost despairingly that in spite of all their praying nothing will change. One thing is lacking.
>
> According to the whole economy of the New Testament, as it shines through in all my scriptural references, God wants to offer his gifts by way of brotherly help; he wants to do it through instruments. It is not by dreams or visions or special revelations that the Gospel is to be made known to those that do not yet know it; rather, it is to be proclaimed by servants of God, who are ambassadors for Christ [2 Cor 5:20]. By the same token, according to Christ's original plan, these messengers were also to be bearers of heavenly gifts and powers for the church. For this reason the apostles were equally equipped with both—the gifts of preaching *and* of healing.
>
> But present-day Christianity knows absolutely nothing of this any more. Hence all the despair in face of so much misery, and the devious ways that so many take. Hence, too, the plight medical

science finds itself in. It is called upon to replace by its skills what the bearers of the Gospel ought to provide for the church but have long since forfeited and up to the present have made no effort to reclaim. In this situation, medical science is to be acclaimed for having on its part worked and labored infinitely more faithfully than the bearers of the Gospel, and this in spite of the unbelief it professes as a body, some individual physicians excepted. Especially in the case of the mentally ill, the Gospel bearers as a rule cut a pathetic figure alongside the faithful diligence and care of the physicians. Though they may mouth excellent words of comfort, at bottom all that the bearers of the Gospel know is, "May God counsel you!" [Jas 2:16] Yet at the beginning the servants of the Gospel were meant to be endowed with actual divine power. O poor Christianity, which has thus spurned Christ and the power he obtained for us through his blood!

But is there no longer hope of a change? In my struggle with powers of possession I dared once again to do more than a pastor is accustomed to do. I prayed in accordance with Christ's guideline, "This kind does not go out except by prayer and fasting" [Matt 17:21; Mark 9:29], and with my eye on James's word, "But when he asks, he must believe and not doubt, because he who doubts is like a wave of the sea, blown and tossed by the wind" [Jas 1:6]. I put no trust in myself and my strength; I did not credit myself with more gifts than any other pastor has. But the fact is that I approached the matter as a servant of the Gospel, who does have a certain right to ask for something.

I soon came to see, though, that the doors of heaven were nevertheless not really open to me. Many times I felt like giving up in discouragement. But the sight of the sick ones, who could see no prospect of help anywhere, gave me no peace. I thought of the Lord's word, "Ask, and it will be given to you; seek, and you will find; knock, and the door will be opened to you," and of the repeated promise, "For everyone who asks receives; he who seeks finds; and to him who knocks, the door will be opened" [Luke 11:9–10]. I thought further: If through unfaithfulness, unbelief, disobedience, negligence, and indolence the church of Christ and its servants have lost what is indispensable for the driving out of demons, Jesus might have been thinking of just such poor, lean times of famine when he spoke the parable in Luke 11:5–8:

Which of you who has a friend will go to him at *midnight* and say to him, "Friend, lend me three loaves; for a friend of mine has arrived on a journey, and I have nothing to set before him"; and he will answer from within, "Do not bother me; the door is now shut, and my children are with me in bed; I cannot get up and give you anything"? I tell you, though he will not get up and give him anything because he is his friend, yet because of his importunity he will rise and give him whatever he needs.

So I, too, had the feeling that at this midnight hour, when everything is shrouded in darkness, I, God's friend, was not worthy to obtain anything from him for a member of my congregation; still I could not bear to leave such a member uncared for. So in line with the parable I kept knocking. Some, including Dr. de Valenti, feel that amounted to tempting God and was impudent, spiritually presumptuous, fanatical, etc. So it was, if you insist, but I could not leave my guest unprovided for.

The parable of the widow and the unjust judge [Luke 18:1–8] became no less important to me. I felt that the church was the widow, and I, as a servant of the church, had the right to represent her before the judge against her adversary. I had to be patient, as for a long time the Lord was unwilling. Yet all I wanted was those three loaves, that is, whatever I needed for my guest just then. My story proves that in the end the Lord did accede to my, the impertinent beggar's, request; he did help. Was it wrong of me to so importune him? Somehow the scriptural passages I quoted should be susceptible to practical application. Could any situation be imagined where it would be more necessary to apply them? If I am considered presumptuous nonetheless, you might as well erase a good half of the Scriptures. What good are they if they may not be used and applied? Let someone else do that; I will not!

But what was the result of my entreaties? The above-mentioned unwilling friend did not say, "Just go away; I myself will bring your guest what he needs; I don't need you for that." Rather, he gave the three loaves to his friend to use them for the guest at his discretion. It stands to reason that there was something left over then, for the guest would be unlikely to consume all three loaves at once.

By that I want to say and admit that the Lord did indeed confer power on me, even the power that, in accordance with God's order and through the brotherly ministrations of his servants, can bring help, especially in cases of possession. I was given this power in order to free a member of my congregation who was severely tormented by the devil and was entrusted to my charge. I used the three loaves and had something left over. Still, the supply was small, and new guests arrived, who came all the more eagerly as they became aware that I have the heart and will to care for their needs and also take the trouble to approach my slumbering friend for further handouts at inappropriate hours. Each time I received what was needed, with something to spare. How could I help it if now the wretched and tormented came running to me! Was I to become hard and say, "Why do you always come to *my* house? There are so many other houses in town, big and roomy ones; go there!" But they replied, "Good sir, we cannot go there. We have been there already, but they told us regretfully that they could not feed us and could not be troubled to get what was needed from a friend. *You* should go and see to it that we get enough to eat, for we are suffering much hunger and pain." What was I to do? What they said was only too true, and their distress touched my heart. Though it troubled me greatly, I went again and again to get the three loaves. I was given them many times and much more quickly than in the beginning and with more left over, so that I no longer have to run so often for just that amount. Of course, this bread is not to everybody's taste, or whatever may be the reason; in other words, it does happen now and then that someone leaves my house hungry and unfed.

Here Blumhardt reproaches the bearers of the Gospel for showing no signs of wanting to recover the gifts of apostolic times for the benefit of the sick. He was deeply convinced that what he was given came to him simply in his capacity as a servant of the Gospel and that one of the things the Lord had in mind thereby was to give new courage to *all* servants of the Gospel. On the other hand, he felt he had to warn against that one-sided, self-willed, unspiritual insistence on having one's prayers answered that is often rooted in spiritual ambition. Probably his main immediate concern was to dampen the euphoria that lets one say in the name of one's office and church: "I am rich and fully satisfied and do not need a thing" (Rev 3:17). At the same time he wanted to enlist those ready to pray with him for the coming of a better time.

Let us conclude this chapter with a sermon Blumhardt gave on Jesus as the healer and forgiver of sins. To be sure, it was not delivered in Möttlingen but in Bad Boll, at the very beginning of Blumhardt's work there. Also, because of the different composition of the audience, it does not quite sound like his sermons in Möttlingen. But it summarizes in a vivid, concise way the thoughts that came to Blumhardt from the experiences related in this and the previous chapter. We feel all the more justified in committing this little offence against the chronological order because there are scarcely any existing transcripts of the sermons he delivered in Möttlingen.

SERMON DELIVERED IN BAD BOLL ON THE NINETEENTH
SUNDAY AFTER TRINITY SUNDAY, 1852

Text: Matthew 9:1–8

Beloved in Jesus Christ, we have before us a remarkable and in many respects instructive passage. It shows us Jesus as a healer and as a remitter of sins. Nothing can give us greater comfort than a Savior who does these two things. If we look at ourselves, we must confess that we are poor sinners and need nothing so much as forgiveness; if we look at the state we are in, we are well aware how many burdens we have to carry in body and soul and how many afflictions we can expect daily. What do we need more in this situation than a Savior who takes away all those burdens and frees us from all those infirmities? So this Gospel message is always of special concern to us. Whoever feels burdened in his heart or conscience must be eager to hear of Jesus the remitter of sins. Whoever moans under the weight of some torment is bound to have a great yearning to hear more of Jesus the helper and healer after hearing this Gospel story.

We want to reach out to both these seekers for help and, applying the story we have read to our own situation, we want to speak 1) of Jesus, the remitter of sins and 2) of Jesus, the helper and healer. May he himself give us his blessing for this! We now want to come to him and imagine him to be present among us. We all want to stand before him as people in need of forgiveness and healing. May his grace grant us what we need and are ready for.

Let us first speak of Jesus as a remitter of sins. For that we must take a closer look at our story. In the Gospels of Mark and Luke it is told in greater detail, namely that the paralytic was carried on a mat by four men. Since a crowd had gathered in front of the house where the Savior was, they could not get inside with the sick man, so they climbed up the stairs by the side of the house and on to the roof. In the Orient the roofs are flat and one can walk on them. Up onto this roof they carry the paralytic on his mat. The roof is covered with stone slabs and tiles. They take off the slabs and make a big hole in the roof just above the room where the Lord and a lot of people are gathered. They lower the paralytic through the hole and set him down directly in front of the Savior. Those up above are keen to see what is going to happen, and those down below think their various thoughts. There are, among others, some proud, self-satisfied Pharisees, who shake their heads, thinking, "Whatever is getting into these people? That's really the limit what they are doing now!" They do not have much compassion for the poor, suffering man, so tormented that he did not know what else to do. But it is not to the Pharisees that his friends wanted to take him; they think, "You can pull faces as much as you like, as long as the Lord Jesus looks at him with kindness."

The one who must have felt strangest of all was the paralytic, who found himself so suddenly transported into a different atmosphere. It must have been a specially holy atmosphere, since the Lord was there; everybody could sense that something divine went forth from him. Maybe a deep inner pain seized the sick man; we cannot help thinking that at that moment such fear came over him as made him forget all his physical suffering. In the depth of his heart it dawned on him that he was a poor sinner, unworthy of being in the Lord's presence, and that it would go badly with him for daring to come into the presence of the all-highest Majesty. The poor man must have started to tremble and shake, and in the end he may have thought, "If I could only get out of here!"

Something like this, we must imagine, went on in him. Perhaps, more than that, it was brought home to him that he was not just a sinner in general terms; certain main sins may have risen up before his inner eye, heavy sins with which he had grieved his God up till then. Now these sins loomed up so vividly before his soul that someone like Jesus could practically read them in his face, as though he had just confessed all his misdeeds in so many words. At any rate, what must have specially shown in his whole demeanor was sincerity. Maybe he also spoke out various things that are not recorded. Anyway, he must have faced the Lord as an honest, sincere sinner; that much we can glean from the Lord's consoling words. In place of any reference to healing, we hear him say, contrary to all expectations, "Take heart, my son, your sins are forgiven."

Possibly, what had gone through the sick man's mind was: "If only I could get rid of my sins!" Maybe he secretly wished that this holy Jesus would above all else forgive his sins if he could. And the Lord ever so quickly reached out to meet that secret, unspoken wish of his. To take him out of his fear he said, "Take heart, my son, your sins are forgiven." With these words the Savior announced that he forgave sins. To be sure, they were words that the Pharisees present took in bad part. The Lord perceived their thoughts, as he had earlier perceived the sins of the paralytic; he saw their thoughts and rebuked them. Instead of justifying himself with a lot of words, he *did* something to make plain to everybody that he had power to forgive sins.

Thus the Savior presents himself as a remitter of sins, and the whole story teaches us that we have to see him as a remitter of sins above all else. Everything else we may request of him is of lesser importance. In fact everything else he may give us has no value if forgiveness of sins is not implicitly a part of it. For instance, if someone wanted to get well in body without at the same time or earlier receiving forgiveness of sins, he is not given much, even if he does get well. Perhaps it does him more harm than good because he has lost his warning bell, because just that which was to remind him of his sins has been taken away. Thus many pray contrary to their own best interests if all they ask for is to get well; they pray contrary to what is good for them if they do not first, and along with it, ask to have their hearts and consciences purified. It would certainly do all of us the greatest harm if we were simply to be freed of all our afflictions, without anything changing within us. Hence this story teaches us that whenever we request anything, we must first ask to have our sins forgiven.

We know that illnesses make us seek out the Savior more quickly than anything else. It has already been pointed out in this context that when facing the trials and sufferings of illness we must first of all attend to the inner person. But there still are many other requests we like to bring to the Savior: We may desire his blessing for this or that vocation or for some enterprise we undertake, and we implore the Lord in heaven to bless it. When doing that, we must first carefully consider if our request can be granted. It cannot be if we do not first get rid of whatever drives away the blessing. Many a time a person burdened with heavy sins will ask for a blessing. You dear one, ask first that your sins be forgiven, else no blessing will come.

Let us assume that someone enters into a relationship of some kind, for instance the most common one, marriage. Oh, how many prayers requesting the Lord's blessing on it are sent up by those concerned. But what is the first thing both partners have to do? Earlier on they committed ever so many sins, transgressed God's commandments so often. Will not all these debts have to be written off and wiped out? That is why all entreaties for blessing must pass through repentance.

Or somebody may want to open a new business. His previous one did not turn out well, so now he pleads: "Lord, give thy blessing this time!" But consider: Do you not have a spell lying on you from your former business? Did you not cheat, lie, steal—all to turn a profit in this or that way? And now you are asking for a blessing before those old sins have been forgiven. It has to go through repentance! Before anything else, you must repent for

your former life; only then can the Lord bestow his blessing on
you, provided that you henceforth live in true fear of him. When
we want God to bless something, repentance must come first.

Let us, for instance, think of our children. There things can
happen to make us feel in a special way urged to ask the Lord for
his blessing. You dear one, you must first obtain forgiveness for
where you went wrong, for where you acted against the Lord's
will. You must recognize it, must repent for it, and be forgiven
for it. Only then can the Lord in heaven draw near and show you
his loving-kindness. O you dear ones, in most of our prayers repentance is forgotten. We are always ready to request something,
but what kind of a person are you who request it? Is it because
so few pray in a humble and repentant way that so few prayers
are answered?

That is the first and most important lesson our text has for us;
if we learn it, we have learned what is most precious of all. Today,
when we want to plead for a new blessing on the church, we are
in a special way reminded of this, for this is the day when kermis
[annual fair held on the dedication day of the local church] celebrations are going on everywhere. True, many a one has in his
heart the wish that something better would be in store; however,
everyone who prays must start by beseeching the Lord to forgive
first the heavy sins that are being committed on this day. Indeed,
if the curse resting on our Christianity is not taken away first, if
the spell is not broken, nothing new and great can arise among
God's people, and things will just go on in the old, wretched way.
All our supplications must pass through repentance. Every time
we cast ourselves down before the Lord, we must first repent as
poor sinners. Then the Lord will show us kindness and will hear
and answer our plea.

Something more ought to be said about Jesus as a remitter
of sins. Up till then only priests could forgive sins. For each sin
a sacrifice had to be offered, and as a result of this sacrifice the
repentant sinner could obtain forgiveness. But something was
lacking in such forgiveness; it was not really an inward forgiveness but more just an outward one, in which God, at least for
the time being and for this life, let a sinner's sins go unpunished.
Everyone was still left feeling that God in heaven had not completely canceled the sin.

And now Jesus steps forward and says, "I have power to forgive sins." He says it in a way that makes it clear: This is not just
an outward forgiveness but an inner one, for it can be seen what
comfort it gives to the paralytic, who had been tormented by his
sins. So here is somebody who from now on truly remits sins and

who carries this power within himself as a gift he can impart to the sinner. He stands visibly before the sinner and gives to him as one gives alms to a beggar. Even so Jesus personally grants remission of sins. There is no need for the sinner to handle the matter by and in himself, thinking: I think and hope that God will forgive me; I really have reason to believe that my sins are forgiven. This means that in the end it is left to him to decide and inwardly persuade himself that he is forgiven. Not so. On the contrary, it is given from without through the Lord Jesus, so that from the moment someone hears such a word of forgiveness, he can take it for granted: Now it's finished; now my sins *are* forgiven. I need no longer worry about it and doubt if it is really true; I can simply accept and believe what the Lord says.

Just consider what a very special thing it is that has begun here. There stands the Lord, a true man and acting like a man, and says: "I have authority from my Father to remit sins, and those whose sins I remit are forgiven." That is something great, glorious, and incalculable. Of course, one of you may say, "But if Jesus remits sins, it grieves me that he is not here and therefore has no forgiveness for me. If he were here, that would at once take all my doubts away; how quickly it would end the struggle in my soul! But now, struggle as I may, I cannot hear the word of forgiveness; I am not sure, not certain. I go over it again and again and doubt if my Savior has really forgiven such a sinner as I am. Oh, what a comfort it would be if he stood bodily before me and said, 'Take heart, my son; your sins are forgiven.' But alas, he is not here."

Indeed, things should not be as they are, and that brings to mind something of importance. What the Lord does really ought to continue in just the same way! Everything he does as a human being he does in a human way, and it shall be done in a human way until the end of days. He forgave sins as one authorized by the Father, and what he wanted to see established in the world is just this: that authorized people should impart the remission of sins. His word to the disciples comes to mind here, "As my Father has sent me, so I send you." Thus his disciples could speak just as the Lord did himself; as decisively as he did himself they could say to repentant sinners, "Take heart; your sins are forgiven." And what is to shake our conviction that things ought to have gone on in the same manner? That this gift and power should have remained in force for those standing in the service of the Gospel and called to proclaim it? That they, too, should have authority to forgive sins?

The remarkable thing is that the better ones among the people crowding around the Savior in our story seemed to regard this gift not as transitory but as something permanent, something destined to remain among them. At the end we read, "When the people saw it, they were amazed, and they glorified God, who had given such authority to men." The way they saw it, this power was not to remain restricted to the one standing before them but would henceforth be given also to others so that this supreme solace would never again disappear from the earth but would continue as long as there were sinful hearts longing for forgiveness.

Hence we may be allowed to plead with the Lord that he would draw near to his people once more, so that there would be servants of the Gospel with the same freedom as he had himself. Not only should the Gospel be proclaimed, but something should be *imparted*, as the Lord said, "If you forgive the sins of any, they are forgiven" [John 20:23], and "Whatever you loose on earth shall be loosed in heaven" [Matt 16:19; 18:18]. Oh, it is really beyond conception how important it is that this power of forgiveness be exercised once again among Christians and pagans. The loss of it is the reason that everywhere things are not as they should be and that prayer is so bereft of strength. The many promises connected with prayer ("Ask, and you will be given," etc.) remain unfulfilled because the power to forgive is not exercised. Without forgiveness the second thing—the hearing and granting of our prayers—cannot but be weak and skimpy, far short of the full measure clearly promised in Scripture. Thus, in big things as well as small, people must again learn to come to Jesus as the one who forgives sins. If only there were repentance, making people humble themselves through and through! Then more and more is bound to be given, until at last it comes to the greatest of all, namely forgiveness leading to complete peace of heart through his mercy.

Let us briefly consider the second point: Jesus as a helper and healer. The Pharisees standing around him doubt his authority to remit sins; they even consider him a blasphemer for going that far. But Jesus says to them, "Why do you think such evil of me in your hearts? Which is easier, to say, 'Your sins are forgiven,' or to say, 'Rise and walk'? When I say the first, you doubt; but when I say the second, how then can you doubt the first? I can prove to you that I have authority to forgive. If I now say to this man, 'Get up!' and he gets to his feet hale and hearty, picks up the mat on which they carried him here, and walks home—does that not prove to you that I can remit sins?" He does not wait for the Pharisees to reply—let them think what they want!—but that paralytic has to be given proof that truth has been spoken and he has not simply been fobbed off with cold comfort of the kind one is liable to get now and then. Therefore, "Get up and walk!" The man feels new life in all his members; all sickness is gone;

his limbs, formerly gouty and crippled, start to move; he is given new strength and gets to his feet; in short, he is well. In this way he was given the comforting proof that his sins were remitted, and the Pharisees could see by this miracle that Jesus really had authority to forgive sins, since a mere word of his could restore one so painfully infirm.

It is something unspeakably great that the dear Savior could prove so powerfully the efficacy of his forgiveness. Even if he had announced everywhere, "I am here to remit the sins of the contrite," who would have believed him if he had not proved it in some tangible way? How many would have risen up to tell him, "You are nothing but a windbag that tells people stories but cannot prove what he says." But now he gives actual proof, and everybody who hears his word, as that paralytic did, feels at the same time the loving-kindness of God stream back into his whole being.

For what else is such an illness but the wrath of the Almighty; what else are all the torments of our time but signs of God's displeasure—a displeasure not specifically with the afflicted individual but of a kind that hovers above humanity generally. If one sees how hundreds and thousands of people pray and yet nothing happens, one cannot help concluding: Here is a divine displeasure that lies above the people as a whole. At that time, too, believing Israelites would pray, for they had been given the assurance, "I am the Lord, your healer" [Exodus 15:26], yet nothing would happen. But now somebody comes and says, "You are forgiven" and "Rise and walk!" Was one not bound to think, "Now the curse is gone! Here is a man who can break the spell, can take away all that has been saddest among us—who can remit sins"? Oh, it is surely a great fault that this power to speak so as to make sick persons well has vanished from among his people; it indicates that there is an evil spell over them all.

To be sure, there are still a number of points to be made clear. Many times people will rise up here or there and ask us to believe that they have the gift of healing—a phenomenon that will come more and more to the fore. However, it is only outer ailments they want to take away; they do not simultaneously declare that they have power to remit sins. But, you dear ones, without that it will not work; without forgiveness it is not the right thing, not what the Lord has ordained. Where it is done without the power of forgiveness making itself felt at the same time, it is not done rightly, for the one is to be nothing else but the proof of the other.

That is why I return once more to this point: If we desire happiness and blessing and health but want to obtain it without conversion, we are on the wrong track. The goal will be reached only through conversion, through a canceling of the debt. For this reason, where the gift of healing is present in some form, it will make no progress without a general movement of repentance among the people. Never will a divine gift of such a kind make itself felt unless it is preceded by repentance, where there is a cry of "Lord, take away the curse under which we moan!" The Savior is not interested in playing a game of making people ill and making them well again. If you are laid low, repent! That is what you must seek.

Of course, what you would like is simply to get well, but what are you going to do with your health if you do not consider beforehand who you are, in order that as a healthy person you may one day find your way into heaven? Oh, how many afflictions could be cleared up if more attention were given to the *inner* side! If the Lord Jesus is a helper and healer, that applies only to the soul. Whoever forgets that and prefers to seek help for the body had better look out whether the Lord feels inclined to grant him such a grace. In all he does it is your *soul* that the Lord is after. If you let him have your soul, you will also experience many kindnesses in outward things. Once the sin is forgiven, healing follows on its own. The paralytic in the Gospel story had no need to say, "Now heal my body too!" The Lord did it of his own accord. Once he has forgiven you, you can take it for granted that he will cure you as well.

Let us see to it that our souls are safe and that we are cleansed by Jesus' blood; then everything else will come right too. But if we have to doubt our forgiveness, we have a lean time. May the Lord put everything on a different, a more biblical foundation among his people! Things will not move forward unless he brings about something new. We want to pray but at the same time wait patiently for him to break forth once again as a remitter of sin and as a helper and healer. It will surely come to pass if we wait for it in patience and faith. Amen.

12

Blumhardt's Message and Expectant Hopes

W E HAVE DEALT SEPARATELY with the two wonderful phenomena of those great days—the movement of repentance and the miracles. Both of them represented a direct intervention of the Lord Jesus and revealed his personal nearness in a clear and matter-of-course way, which cannot be adequately reflected in a mere account. Blumhardt's own person quietly receded into the background. He and his house were simply the focus of what was experienced, and naturally he was the one most gripped by it.

Struggle, awakening, miracles—what an uninterrupted, consistent, holy train of events! Blumhardt and his friends had struggled with the hidden powers of darkness, which burst forth ever more horribly; they had wept over that undreamt-of distress, that satanic trick played upon humanity, and they had ever again experienced the victorious, kingly intervention of the Lord Jesus himself. Then immediately after the final, conclusive victory they saw an unheard-of redemptive mercy take hold of thousands of people. They felt Jesus Christ manifest himself anew as he had been in his days on earth and had made himself felt also at the time of the apostles. The miracles were like an outward confirmation of the peace of forgiveness that had come over the sinners. They assured them that they had not fallen prey to a deception or illusion and that what their hearts told them was really true: The living Jesus had taken them into his loving care.

But the link between these two phenomena was not at all an unfeeling sequence of promise and confirmation but was of a much more friendly and intimate character. One could sense something of the joy in heaven over one sinner that repents; the miracles were like the father's welcoming kiss for the returning prodigal son. In an overwhelmingly blissful way one was made aware that this interrelationship was a matter of course. These peace-bringing powers, these miracles, were like radiations of the glory and loving-kindness of Jesus Christ, the risen and living One. Even today, to be sure, every believer is made aware that Jesus is alive, but here in Möttlingen the recognition was brought home to men's hearts with truly overwhelming clarity.

In the church services, too, the nearness of the Lord could be sensed in an indescribably simple and powerful way. I cannot very well put down here how the peasants themselves described their experiences, since their down-to-earth way of viewing and expressing them might give rise to misunderstandings. The people's eagerness to listen was as untiring as Blumhardt's flow of words was inexhaustible. Every weekend there were four services: first the Saturday evening devotions, then on Sunday the main service, Sunday school, and Bible class (with a sermon based on a shorter, more freely chosen text than in the main service). These gatherings were like a dialogue with the people, who in between the services would find their way to Blumhardt's study; they were inwardly related in an original, unsophisticated way.

Blumhardt had always been simple and straightforward in manner. His preaching had failed to create much of a stir just because he did not have a gift for high-flown grandiloquence. In the pulpit his speech remained simple and sober, and more so when he was in a moved and solemn mood. But now this great thing had burst into his life. His experience of men's sin, which grew week by week and moved his heart deeply, but still more his awesome experience of Christ, and the bond it created between him and his hearers—all this furnished him with plentiful material and imparted a heavenly inspiration to his words.

In a certain sense his sermons were about penitence. He emphasized the seriousness of sin and, in line with his own experiences, pursued sin with the piercing light of the Word into hiding places where with ordinary preachers it could feel safe. Nevertheless, the term "penitential sermon" would scarcely do justice to Blumhardt's way. Then, as later on, the subject and content of his sermons was Jesus Christ. Early in his life his need and gift for seeing everything clearly, almost tangibly, had enabled him to form from the Gospels a more living, distinct, and real picture of the Lord Jesus than many others had. How much more was that the case now! Those scenes from the Lord's story—the various miracles of healing and his driving out of demons—were brought to life for him through experiencing the same deeds of the same Lord. How powerful was the impact when he spoke of them in his church in the very midst of similar experiences!

Regardless of whether we preachers are firm or uncertain in our faith, we adroitly apply those miracles to the present circumstances of Christianity in a "spiritual" sense and speak of "spiritual liberations," etc. In a way, we are justified in doing that; however, it does leave us with a lingering wistfulness, with an unpleasant feeling. We sense that the sacred text is being handled and manipulated in a manner that the *secular* word—say, the language of business, law, or scholarship—would indignantly object to. No businessman or lawyer would put up for long with talk of "spiritual" dollars, inheritances, lumber, or whatever. In our own field we preachers may and must do it, because any physical help a person receives comes from a spiritual source and serves spiritual ends. But it was not like that in Möttlingen; there the Bible stories left quite a different impression, for one experienced in such a living and real way that Christ is the same yesterday as well as today and in all eternity.

Blumhardt's preaching was based on his experiences and hopes. With him these two always went hand in hand. Just as a keen business-man will straightway plow his earnings back into the business or a minor victory will spur a general to pursue the war all the more vigor-ously, so each experience made Blumhardt look forward to the future. "Experience generates hope" was his motto. What urged him on in this direction was his worldwide, all-encompassing vision. From childhood on he had retained a feeling of confident hope for all people, even though the circles in which he moved were characterized more by a feeling of al-most hopeless pity for all outsiders. His sense of hope was strengthened even more, first during his time of struggle, when he became acquainted with destructive powers that affect all people almost without exception, but still more during the time of awakening.

To be sure, he was made aware of the power and curse of sin, which, also in the case of his Möttlingen folk, lay like a pall over everybody, in-cluding the so-called believers. Even more, however, he came to know an overwhelming grace that was earnestly concerned for the sins of all the world to be put under forgiveness. The more sins were brought to him in his study, the more he saw people's unforgiven sins lower like grim thunderclouds of wrath over humankind. But he also saw something else, which made all of that fade into the background. His firm, universal hope actually stemmed less from the considerations just mentioned than from his own experience of the Lord Jesus. He had come to know him not only as the Risen One, who lives as Lord and Victor, but irrefutably as the one who wants to come and whose coming is heralded by powers of grace, redemption, and conciliation rushing like flood waters before it. "I am coming!" was the cry that came to him from the mercies he saw bestowed on the sinners and the sick. In the Möttlingen church the very air seemed to echo that cry.

As we know, Blumhardt was mistaken time and again as to the nearness of the goal. Some day it will be said, I think, that he was a bit like Columbus, who would never have discovered America if he had not been mistaken about the remoteness of that continent—that is, if he had known how far away it really is. Or one could say Blumhardt was like a mountaineer that deceives himself again and again as to the closeness of the goal. But of all who have not given up hope that the Lord will come none saw as earnestly and soberly as he did the obstacles blocking the approach of this event.

To be sure, Blumhardt did not share the widespread, dismal view that sees all things coming to an end with the return of Christ. As many imagine it, general decay and deterioration, apostasy, and the victory of unbelief and evil will increase more and more, both in degree and extent; the small flock of believers will go on shrinking until finally, when everything points to the extinction of Christianity, the Lord will come— I don't know whether in wrath or out of necessity or for both reasons. He will garner his meager harvest and hand the great mass of men over to the devil or hell. As Blumhardt describes such a view:

> People think, probably correctly, that our time is the end time, but what they mean by it is that God has now done all there is to be done to convert men and that all to be expected from now on is judgments. Wrath and nothing but wrath is approaching, they say, since God does not care to do any more for those that until now have proved unruly. What this leads up to is that God will have regard only for the few that still believe. All the others he will let go to hell, not caring to still do anything extraordinary out of love for them. Those few, it is thought, will then be allowed to enjoy all the benefits of the saints' inheritance in the

light. There is no mercy, no weeping and sighing over the lost ones, no love that would still hope, or plead with God, for them. It is regarded as foolishness and wild-eyed enthusiasm to believe that God might once more stretch out loving arms to save the lost before the day of wrath is upon us. According to that, the day of wrath is here before it is due!

On another occasion he writes, "Do not believe that the Savior is going to come as the great wrecker!"

Let us grant Blumhardt his anger. In him lived something of the compassion of Christ: it would have made his hair stand on end had he been asked to believe for even a moment anything so dismal. After all, he knew something of the love of Christ that surpasses all understanding (Eph 3:19) as well as of his power, and he sensed that Christ wants to come as victor, as a merciful victor, as redeemer. On the other hand, as said earlier, Blumhardt's assessment of the task the Lord Jesus Christ still has before him was more serious and sober than anybody else's. The delay in his coming he saw as stemming from Christ's determination to let human history come to an end in a blissful and kindly manner. According to the apostle Peter it is that determination that postpones the Lord's return. "The Lord does not wish that any should perish, but that all should come to repentance" (2 Pet 3:9).

In his struggle Blumhardt had been given an inkling of what is meant when we read that Jesus shall reign until God has put all his enemies, including the last one, death, under his feet (1 Cor 15:25–26). Blumhardt saw humankind entangled in snares of spiritual resistance, fettered by bonds of wickedness, enveloped in a lying fog, and it was more than just an inkling when behind all this he discerned personal powers of great cunning and steely determination. It had become clear to him what is actually entailed in the work of redemption, for which the Lord Jesus had obtained the necessary authority and power only through his coming, death, and resurrection. Redemption means that those enemies are put under his feet. But that requires that men should believe in him and be willing. They act in his name; he acts through them. For that a holy faith is needed.

When we hear the Lord's command, especially to his servants, to pray in his name, the simplest interpretation is that things should go on in the very same style in which he established his kingdom and that heavenly powers of grace are to be victorious—visibly victorious, not merely in the so-called "spiritual" sphere. I say "so-called" because in all that is invisible one is free to imagine spiritual processes. The latter may consist, say, in successes one thinks one has achieved (successes said to be invisible because they are spiritual in nature). Another example of such imagined spiritual processes is sensing a divine participation in one's own work. Thoughts of this kind, which are apt to wear a garment of great humility and gratitude, are nonetheless very prone to self-deception.

It could perhaps be argued that Jesus' word, "Blessed are those who do not see and yet believe" (John 20:25), refers to such contentment with a purely spiritual blessing. However, Peter did not say to that lame man, "Even though you see that you are still lame, have faith in the helpful nearness of the Lord Jesus whom you do not see, and remain lame!" Rather, he cleaved to the Lord he did not see as though he saw him and healed the lame man.

It sounds good to ascribe human achievements of a spiritual nature to God, "The Lord has done it." Yet there is always the possibility that he did not do it. What Christ did through the apostles was so clearly, simply, and unmistakably *his* doing that no special insight was needed to perceive it. It could be, however, that because our sense of the task of true faith has been lulled to sleep, the Lord, who will only act through the faith of his own, is deprived of almost every opportunity to act powerfully and graciously upon the human race. What if for this as well as other reasons his enemies (1 Cor 15:25; Heb 10:13) had regained power?

It is often stated that an empire can only be sustained by the principles and forces that brought it into being. What if it were the same with the kingdom of Christ? In his celebrated book, Johann Arndt attempted to present true Christianity to his generation.[1] He did it by describing the true Christian. That, however, is but one side of Christianity. Christianity does not restrict itself to the state of an individual soul; it is a work, a plan for the redemption of the *world!* What is essential to true Christianity is first of all the true Christ, Jesus Christ as he is and as he wants to give himself to us. My impression is that there and then in Möttlingen the Jesus showed us a page in *his* book of true Christianity,

---

1. Editors' Note: Zündel is here referring to the work of Johann Arndt (1555–1621), *Vier Bücher vom wahren Christentum* (1609) [*True Christianity*] which had an enormous influence among Christians of all confessions during the seventeenth and eighteenth centuries and is widely regarded as a touchstone for the reforming work of Philipp Jakob Spener (1635–1705), a key figure in the formation of early German Pietism.

telling us, "This is who I was, am, and will be. I have not changed, but you, not excepting the believers, have arbitrarily changed the conception of my person and work."

Blumhardt's experiences gave him fresh insight into the present situation of the kingdom of God, its need as well as its wonderful prospects. He expressed this insight in the following terms: Christianity has lost the spirit of Pentecost, which God had intended for it (cf. p. 17). The pouring out of the Holy Spirit, which in the end is to be extended to "all flesh" (Joel 2:28), was fatefully broken off. To be sure, the Holy Spirit did not at a certain point somehow withdraw from the church of Christ; rather, he was not imparted to the generations following the apostolic one in the measure and manner of a personal indwelling. We still have him to the extent that we need him for our spiritual life but not in the way he was indwelling in the early Christians.[2]

One can dispute that statement by affecting the highest possible regard for oneself and the lowest possible for the apostles, so reducing the difference between then and now. Or one can accept the statement, with the comment that that is quite in order, since in God's plan the Spirit's personal indwelling had been a special dispensation for the apostolic age. But the Holy Spirit of those times was merciful—merciful to the

---

2. Blumhardt's feeling that in Christendom something higher had been given, which ought not to have receded, does not mean that he depreciated what we still have. For instance, he once wrote to a friend:

> I have the impression that you overly downgrade certain basic scriptural doctrines, because they are admittedly being presented in a clumsy manner. I mean the doctrines regarding grace and its reception through faith. You might also fare better in your struggles if you kept your eye more firmly fixed on him who went to the cross because of men's lust, if you more quickly took refuge in grace, and if you were more repentant instead of merely feeling unhappy. If I may put it like this, you tend to leave the solid ground the Gospel has prepared for us and instead hover above it with nothing to hold on to. Though we indeed lack much, there is still a good deal left—enough to enable honest souls to fight their way through. Where would I be? Where would you be? Where would so many be that have been renewed in spite of things being as they are? Bear in mind that also in our present state of spiritual penury we *can* become new creatures, who in all weakness can at least feel sure of their Savior. Anyhow, this I have to avow: Through the Gospel we can even now have ever so much that is glorious, refreshing, and blissful. With so many riches spread out before us, as compared to the world, I would be ungrateful to my Savior if I told people that we just have to put up with the wretchedness of our condition. But we must be ready to give ourselves. When we fight and are in earnest, we will not be left empty-handed. And the mere hope of something still better will then give us peace and joy.

many incurably sick in body and soul, merciful even to the unbelievers, who do not believe if they do not see. And we can say that Blumhardt, too, was merciful and could not join in the adroit mental acrobatics that make it possible to vault nimbly over the horrible misery on earth. His great maxim, "We Christians should ask unitedly for a new outpouring of the Holy Spirit," was a cry of need, giving vent to men's distress, as he saw it crowding into his study.

Already at the time of his struggle and ever since, two of Jesus' parables had encouraged Blumhardt to cherish such thoughts, wishes, and hopes and to push on toward their realization, even though all by himself. We have seen above how he looked at one of these parables, that of importuning a friend at midnight. The other was the parable of the unjust judge and the widow (Luke 18:1–8). Blumhardt interpreted this text as follows (though I make use here of a sermon delivered in Bad Boll, the same thoughts already occupied him in Möttlingen).

This parable, Blumhardt says, refers to the last time, the time before the Lord's return, for at the end the Lord appends to it the question whether the Son of Man, when he comes, will find faith on earth—the faith required for doing what he asks us to do in this parable. Hence at that time the church of Christ will be like a widow. The Lord has distanced himself from her, because she no longer puts much confidence in him or because she has otherwise been unfaithful to him; in this sense she is a widow. The adversary, taking advantage of this, proceeds to rob her impudently, harasses, and oppresses her, as is evident today. In his time Jesus came to the rescue of those in distress, but now there is no such succor. The "judge in a certain city" (Luke 18:2) is God. He has to be compared to an "unjust" judge to indicate that the widow is without any legal protection, for the widow can no longer claim any legal rights. God sent his son, delivered him to be crucified, raised him up, and even poured out the Holy Spirit, and yet the fruit of all that turned out to be that the church of Christ fell away and that things now are the way they are. It is surely unreasonable to assume that God will once more take pity on the widow. And that, the parable seems to indicate, will be the general opinion in the final time of tribulation. "Do you think that when the Son of man comes, he will find faith on earth?" (Luke 18:8). Blumhardt says:

> Faith in one's own salvation is not what is meant here; that is
> something the Lord will still find. But what about the faith that

by doing what he advises us here to do—to imitate the widow—
something will still be accomplished? If a person does try and in
the teeth of the great and universal ruin still dares to plead—not
for himself alone but on behalf of the widow, of humankind—
"Save me from my adversary!" he is liable to be pitied by just about
everybody as half crazy, as the widow in the parable may also
have experienced [and as dear Blumhardt himself experienced to
some extent]. "What? Our 'normal,' visibly 'God-ordained' times
ought to change? And the hopeless idea of really obtaining something great from God by pleading with him! What on earth are
you thinking?" Nevertheless, the widow goes on begging. There
may well be but very few of the "elect" (verse 7) that dare to stand
up for the widow in the sense meant here by the Lord, who are so
unhappy about the state of things that it will not let them sleep,
who have but the one thought, "Save us from our adversary!" But
though these be very few and though it seem ever so unlikely—
they will attain it!

Let us add to that what Blumhardt once said about this parable in
a morning devotion in Bad Boll. After describing the widow's way of
pleading, he continued:

With many people supplication is but a cry of need or mere words
rather than true faith. We can express a lot in prayer, but all too
easily it turns into mere talk and sighs and does not spring from
a firm, immovable faith. So when it comes to presenting a determined front to the adversary, there is more fear of him than faith
in the power of Jesus. Particularly in our present time there is a
tendency to think that on the whole there is not much hope left
for apostate humanity. That is why we do not intercede in firm
faith for those oppressed and ruined by the adversary; in fact, we
have just about given up the whole lot as irretrievably lost. But if
there is no trust that he who came to save the lost will yet retrieve
what is already in the wolf's jaws, then there is no faith in the Lord
Jesus, however much we may boast of having such faith. Faith in
the power of the redemptive blood, which can prove victorious
even in those who have strayed farthest away, has in fact ceased.
There are at most just a few still considered recoverable, while
the masses are written off as lost. Bearing in mind this mood, in
particular among the believers, one begins to understand why
Jesus expresses a fear that in the end there might be no faith at
all left on earth. Whoever cannot believe in a great redemption
to be wrought by the Lord before he returns for judgment has, I
would say, no faith at all in the sense that Jesus meant it. What is

one to think of a Savior who, though firmly determined to save sinners (1 Tim 1:15), cannot rescue the vast majority of them from the adversary's grip? Nevertheless, he can yet do it, as our text tells us, if there remain even a few—just one widow, as it were—who believe in it. As Jonathan said, when, alone except for his armor-bearer, he dared to attack the Philistines: "Nothing can hinder the Lord from saving, whether by many or by few" (1 Sam 14:6). Then the impotent prayers of the other—otherwise well-meaning—believers will also come into their own, since the Lord will let the redemption they desired but did not believe in take place anyhow. Oh, how gloriously the Lord will yet bring his cause to completion! Amen.

In my whole account of the revival time I have related my impressions of those days in a direct, unabridged form, hoping that that would be the best way of doing justice to my task. Equally directly and therefore in quick, informal succession I have presented the expectant, hopeful thoughts then blossoming forth. However, these thoughts are so great and far-reaching and in many cases also so new that further discussion of them may be appropriate here. It did hurt Blumhardt deeply that his attitude of expectancy met with so little approval and that apart from his own no other voice independently represented the same thoughts, which were often contradicted but never refuted.[3] Hence I would like to enlarge on them and establish them on a broader foundation. In the interest of my task, though feeling free to make my own contributions, I shall mainly use the thoughts of Blumhardt.

The twofold experience of repentance and the miracles awakened the thought that at the time of Christ and the apostles Christianity must have been somewhat like this, though of course on a scale much greater and more glorious. Further, if such Christianity were to return, it would have the power to extend to far larger circles than we are used to in present-day Christendom. Without any human agency, as though wrought by an invisible power, a shock came on the Möttlingen folk— shock at the deep earnestness of eternity and the exactness and justice of God's judgment. On the other hand it came to light more clearly that the crucified Jesus wants to save all sinners, what saves us is not our poor

---

3. In answer to his cry for help, one voice did speak up in a fine and dignified manner, that of H. Ph. Schnabel, a Protestant minister, in his thorough biblical and ecclesiological study, *Die Kirche und der Paraklet (der andere Tröster)* (Gotha: Schlößmann, 1880) [The Church and the Paraclete (the other Comforter)]. It was published just at the time of Blumhardt's death.

piety and repentance but Jesus Christ alone; instead of forgiveness being found through piety, the way lies through repentance and forgiveness to peace and godliness. The simplicity and power of forgiveness awakened in the hearts of precisely the toughest sinners is an inkling of God's extraordinary mercy, which surpasses all our thinking. They were made aware that in the way opening up before them God for the sake of Jesus gladly and immediately forgives every transgression, however heavy.

There is a widespread complaint that people no longer feel a need to repent. That is not true. More than one might think, a lot of unbelief or even scorn and derision is concealed despair. People have no idea and but rarely are told that for the sake of Jesus God will show them love beyond anything they can imagine, as soon as they sincerely turn to him. In Christendom a veil has fallen on us and hides from us that loving-kindness of the Lord, that simple, deep meaning of redemption. No human rhetoric is able to lift this covering from us; God himself must do it.

Just as it was with the relief of moral distress, so, too, in the case of emotional and physical needs and their removal through miracles, a similar trend toward the general and universal became apparent in Möttlingen. In response to the uniform way this misery engulfs both the "just and the unjust," the Lord showed a visible readiness to also help comprehensively, heedless of petty distinctions. One could almost say that he showed the same generosity that shines forth so conspicuously from the miracles he wrought in his days on earth.

Blumhardt regarded each individual case as a reflection of the general distress; he saw in one sufferer all those afflicted similarly, and he felt for them all. When, for instance, he would meet an individual epileptic, with his mind's eye he saw before him the scourge of epilepsy in general. Hence it was against that whole scourge that he would pray and also expected the patient and his family to pray. Of course that did not mean that all those so afflicted would suddenly and without knowing why be healed; it rather expressed a hope that the Lord would once more give his church power over this scourge and that entreaty against it might at least find an open door again. In that sense Blumhardt later wrote as follows from Bad Boll to a woman who had recovered: "You ask, 'How am I to give thanks?' I will tell you and also say how you can best think of Boll. As often as you see wretchedness, misery, or sin, you must think that through God's grace something better must come from above, that the Lord ought to be implored to show his mercy anew and help where help is still possible. Think of that and do it. In that way you thank the Lord and think of Boll."

Such praying was more like praying "in spirit and truth" (John 4:23–24) than just pleading—out of love to the person concerned—for an individual exception to be made, which is like praying for one little house to have summer in the middle of winter. It was after the mind of him who "makes his sun rise on the evil and on the good" (Matt 5:45) and helps to explain the greater success of such entreaties.

To be sure, such praying was based on a worldview different from that held today not only by unbelievers but also by some of the believers, but it hardly differed from that of the Bible. Because of his experiences during the struggle, Blumhardt perceived, more distinctly than our ears can hear, the active involvement of the enemy in many such sufferings, as Peter expresses it very simply in Acts 10:38. That involvement had become all the stronger for being able to proceed undisturbed, since practically nobody still dared to confront it in the name of Jesus.

Today, of course, we have arrived at a more cozy conception of things. We find everything in the great web of events in excellent order and have learned only too well to trace evil in each individual case back to God's wise educational purposes. That view indeed presents one side of the truth correctly, since God as supreme authority does ever again guide everything according to his purposes. Not in vain does individual piety (and religious poetry in general) make great efforts to let us see all hardships befalling us in as favorable a light as possible. Yet that labor does perhaps fall short in one respect, namely that everyone thinks only of himself. If we look at the whole, the appearance of purposefulness gives way to the impression that all these ailments afflict the righteous and the unrighteous without distinction. That sheds a bright light on Blumhardt's conception of things and shows its validity alongside the view just referred to, not only because it obviously makes sense but also because it agrees with the Bible.

To be sure, in the New Testament one reads a lot about suffering through persecution, which a Christian must be prepared to bear, but there is little or no glorification of any and all suffering, say, in the form of sickness or even emotional disturbance. It is the Bible's all-encompassing view of things that makes it so pleasing and appealing and gives additional clarity, credibility, and greatness to all Christian thinking. Just the fact that Blumhardt, like Jesus and the apostles, saw the influence of hostile spiritual powers behind all wrongs gave a corresponding universal thrust to his hope for victory. He confidently expected help for the many as well as help in all areas of misery. It benefits many, and not only the individual immediately concerned when yet another enemy is made the footstool of Jesus. It may even benefit these enemies themselves, for as Blumhardt commented at a later time, "It is a good thing even to be the Lord's footstool—of course only for those who willingly bow down."

This naturally holds true most of all in the moral area. Blumhardt felt people's whole moral depravity weigh heavily on him, and he often cried out with Jeremiah, "Oh, that my eyes were a fountain of tears, that I might weep day and night for the slain of my people!" (Jer 9:1). But he also suggested that in many things God might not be too hard on the present children of the world, because they are so terribly fooled and enslaved by darkness.

He had also learned to take it more for granted that the Lord earnestly and reliably wanted and still wants to work redemptively in all areas of our need: in the realm of the spirit (sin) as well as in that of the soul (emotional disturbances) and of the body (physical illness). Perhaps it may be permitted to cite here a Gospel passage that, though well known, may not always be read with an unbiased mind. It shows that the Lord took to heart the physical and emotional needs of all men in general and that he had it in mind to begin a campaign against those needs. The passage (Matt 9:35—10:1) reads:

> And Jesus went through all the towns and villages, teaching in their synagogues, preaching the gospel of the Kingdom, and healing every disease and sickness. When he saw the crowds, he had compassion on them, because they languished and were scattered, like sheep without a shepherd. Then he said to his disciples, "The harvest is plentiful but the workers are few. Ask the Lord of the harvest therefore to send out workers into his harvest field." And he called his twelve disciples to him and gave them authority over unclean spirits, to cast them out and to heal every kind of disease and sickness.

It should be pointed out that "preaching the gospel of the kingdom" could be rendered closer to the original Greek, "He announced to them the glad news of the kingdom." Thus, what is meant here is not preaching as we understand it today. The whole passage seems to suggest that when speaking of the harvest, the Lord has in mind the entire human misery—

not least the most visible aspect—as something ready to be garnered and stored. It hardly gives the impression that he would one day find it quite in order for the Father to send out workers that are not equipped with the authority mentioned in the last verse of our quotation.

It is argued, though, that miracles were necessary then to demonstrate the truth of Christianity but are no longer necessary today. To be sure, the inexhaustible fountain of the certainty of faith is still bubbling in the Christian church, but it is also true that millions in our church are "languishing and scattered, like sheep without a shepherd." God has to deal with a people that since time immemorial has had on the whole a purely literary knowledge of the God of revelation. Therefore, God may well take a more merciful view than we do when confronted by people who have had no godly childhood impressions. Such people are apt to approach the basic record of revelation critically and to probe the value of its testimony with a certain degree of independence. If we ask what criteria they use, one of these will turn out to be that they regard the way things happen on earth (as they themselves experience it and have learned it from their fathers) as the law that must have always governed earthly events. What makes it so hard for some to believe in the miracles related in the Bible is less their miraculous character in itself than that they no longer *occur*. The miracles ascribed to Jesus flow from him in such a matter-of-course way and fit in so harmoniously with his whole being that something in them is apt to win everybody's heart and mind—if only they would still happen today. When the apostle wrote (Heb 13:8) that "Jesus Christ is the same yesterday and today and forever," the Lord, through the hands of his servants, was still doing "today" what he had done in his days on earth. But how is it with "today" when it refers to our present time?

Blumhardt did not simply yearn for miracle workers to appear. People working miracles without God, curing the sick without proclaiming repentance and the good news—that would not be from God. On the contrary, it would be the worst that could befall the church of Christ. Blumhardt longed for something to be given to the church as a whole; he sensed that the higher spiritual gifts have remained with us in but a very stunted form, just as those gifts whose presence or absence fairly leaps to the eye have been lost to us.

He felt somewhat like Gideon, who in reply to the angel's greeting "The Lord is with you, mighty warrior" said: "But sir, if the Lord is with us, why has all this happened to us? Where are all his wonders that our fathers told us about?" (Judg 6:13). Or he felt with Psalm 77:4–11:

> You kept my eyes from closing;
>   I was too troubled to speak.
>
> 5 I thought about the former days,
>   the years of long ago;
>
> 6 I remembered my songs in the night.
>   My heart mused and my spirit inquired:
>
> 7 "Will the Lord reject forever?
>   Will he never show his favor again?
>
> 8 Has his unfailing love vanished forever?
>   Has his promise failed for all time?
>
> 9 Has God forgotten to be merciful?
>   Has he in anger withheld his compassion?"
>   *Selah*
>
> 10 Then I thought, "To this I will appeal:
>   the years of the right hand of the Most High."
>
> 11 I will remember the deeds of the LORD;
>   yes, I will remember your miracles of long ago.

Or he might feel with Psalm 103:9: "The Lord will not always chide, nor will he keep his anger forever." Those psalmists, too, thought of the whole and not only of themselves; they reckoned in centuries, not only in years.

I recall the following characteristic expression of Blumhardt's yearning. On his birthday—I think in 1846, still at the peak of the revival movement—some long-term lodgers in his house that already knew a little Hebrew, decorated the door of his study with the greeting *Shalom aleychem* (Peace be with you). He looked at it wistfully and said, "You should rather have written, *Mih jitthen* (Who will give!) That, rendered literally, is the beginning of the last verse in Psalms 14 and 53, usually translated: "Oh, that deliverance for Israel would come out of Zion and the Lord turn away the captivity of his people! Then would Israel rejoice and Jacob be glad." Blumhardt was and remained the poor man who pleads with God on behalf of the whole. How people could console themselves by saying, "Thank God, I have it!" or "We have it!" and even mean it boastfully, he could never understand.

It was with old Simeon (Luke 2:22–35), one of his favorite Bible figures, that he identified most. In Simeon's time, before the Savior's appearance, eschatological studies flourished among the Pharisees, but their end result was only the vision of a great crusher of nations and left the heart without real hope. Simeon, on the other hand, was waiting for a "salvation God had prepared for all peoples, a light for revelation to the gentiles" (Luke 2:31–32), therefore his heart beat with longing. He was aware that there are but few that still plead with God on behalf of the whole human race and ponder in their hearts God's great and gracious intentions for the good of men. He had to be afraid that in the end all waiting and praying for that might peter out completely. That is why he did not want to die, did not want to leave his post until he could feel reassured about the Lord's coming.

I insert here two excerpts from a lovely portrait Blumhardt sketched of Simeon in a meditation on the above text (Luke 2:22–40).[4] First the beginning (which also gives us an impression of Blumhardt's descriptive gift):

> Here the Gospel introduces us to some more dear, friendly persons, whose very names are enough to touch our hearts. There is Simeon. Nobody knows where he comes from; he is simply known as Simeon and is referred to as "a man." He was no gentleman, nor was he a person of high repute, except insofar as his devoutness may have gained him a reputation among honest, sincere folk. Then there comes a woman; her name is Anna, the daughter of Phanuel of the tribe of Asher, and she was of a great age. We are not told how old Simeon was, but Anna was eighty-four—such a good old granny as made people flock to her wherever she was. When people came to the temple, they would all want to see and visit with Anna, and she would cheer and refresh them all, especially those looking for the consolation of Israel. So it was with Simeon too. All that thirsted and yearned for redemption and grieved at the Savior's long delay flocked round either Simeon or Anna. In this way our loving God constantly provides honest souls with someone to have recourse to. They can always find persons to comfort and uphold them, if these persons are simple and pure like Simeon and Anna. I can just imagine how people no sooner came up the temple steps than they looked about and asked, "Where is he? Where is she?" and hastened to them.

4. From *Predigt-Blätter aus Bad Boll, enthaltend nachgeschriebene Predigten und Vorträge von Pfarrer (Johann Christoph) Blumhardt*, 1880. [*Sermon Papers from Bad Boll*] Cited throughout as *Predigt-Blätter*.

Many must have shared the outlook of these two, because they also shared the same hope. And look, dear people, so it is still today. Wherever somebody is waiting for redemption, is serious about it, and lives in it with his whole heart, he is bound to have around him a circle of people, though maybe only a few, who are always happy to be together and cannot bear being separate, for out there in the wide world one stands so completely alone.

And the following description of Simeon:

It is not known how old Simeon was, but he must have been pretty old, because death had already come close to him. He had thought, "My last hour may be near, but can I actually die? No, no, no, I cannot! I cannot die! Before I die, I must have seen something; I must be sure that He is there, that He is coming! I want it to be quite certain that it's really starting, that redemption is at hand. Of that I must be quite sure; I simply cannot leave before that. O thou God of Abraham, Isaac, and Jacob, thou wilt surely not do this to me, that I have to close my eyes before catching sight of it?" Maybe death was already trying to drag him away, but: "No," Simeon protested, "you can take me as soon as I have seen it—but not before!" That is how he forced it through and was inwardly assured by the Holy Spirit that he should not see death before he had seen the Lord's Christ. That was the answer to his entreaty. To stop his worrying about death, God finally promised him: "You shall not die, you shall not see death before you have seen the Savior. Death you can always see, but first you shall see the Savior." Oh, how this one assurance may have been enough to make the old man young, to make him shout for joy! How he must have told his people: "Listen, listen, I am not to die until I have seen Him!" You can just imagine what joy that caused and what new courage it gave to many. And of course the spirit of the Lord was in him, so that there was much he had to say about the promises. He knew how to interpret the prophets and inwardly refreshed many men, women, and children, as he pointed them to a final time of blessing that the promises said was bound to come.

Thus, thought Blumhardt, we ought to yearn in joyous hope for holy times to come, where God will once again draw nearer, with his actual return as the glorious ultimate goal. To begin with, the state of God's kingdom on earth should hark back to the time of the apostles, when it could still be perceived in a visible, living way as the kingdom of *heaven*. A very tangible illustration was brought to his mind one day when the train in which he was travelling was left standing because the engine had been detached in order to fetch more carriages and add them to the train in front of the others. When the engine had come back and resumed pulling the train, he said to himself: "This is how it is with us; the carriages are the church; the engine represents the gracious powers of the kingdom of heaven, still active at the time of the apostles. The engine has become detached from the carriages; we are left sitting and have to wait for it to return; then things will go forward again." Later more about this "forward."

If people dared to follow Blumhardt in his hopes, they would be more likely to agree with him that there is great need for such a return of the "days of old," the "years of long ago" (Ps 77:5). It was his own experiences that stimulated and encouraged him to cherish such hopes, but beyond that he also relied firmly and strongly on what God had promised through the prophets of the old covenant. His own experiences during the "struggle" had deeply engraved on his heart that these promises were truly God's word; the significance of that fact had been brought home to him. Of greatest importance to him, of course, was the promise Peter referred to on the day of the pouring out of the Holy Spirit—an event he called the fulfillment of that earlier promise. It is the passage Joel 2:28–32, quoted by Peter in Acts 2:16–21.

Blumhardt discussed this passage as fully as its great value (in the eyes of all to whom this prophecy, as a divine utterance, is of importance) deserves.[5] The following is Blumhardt's complete exposition.

> The outpouring of the Holy Spirit, as told in Acts, caused many Jews to say that the apostles that spoke in other tongues were filled with new wine. Then Peter stepped forward and replied that it was not so and could not be so, because it was only the third hour of the day (that is, nine o'clock in the morning). Then he quoted Joel's prophecy, which he said was now being fulfilled. He cited Joel's words accurately and completely, for which reason I insert them here, as recorded in Acts:
>
> > But this is what was spoken by the prophet Joel: And in the last days it shall be, God declares, that I will pour out my spirit upon all flesh, and your sons and your daughters shall prophesy, and your young men shall see visions, and your old men shall dream dreams; yea, and on my menservants and my maidservants in those days I will pour out

5. *Blätter aus Bad Boll*, Nos. 29–31, 1875.

my spirit, and they shall prophesy. And I will show wonders in the heaven above and signs on the earth beneath,
blood and fire and vapor of smoke. The sun shall be turned
into darkness and the moon into blood before the day of
the Lord comes, the great and manifest day. And it shall be
that whoever calls on the name of the Lord shall be saved.

Thus spoke Peter, quoting Joel. Now some people give special
emphasis to the beginning of Peter's speech, where he says, "This
is what was spoken." "This is" makes it clear, they say, that the
prophecy is now fulfilled and that no other or further fulfillment
is to be expected as regards the outpouring of the Holy Spirit. But
let us take a closer look at the passage and see whether the prophecy was really fulfilled completely at that time. We note especially
that God wants to pour out his spirit on *all flesh*. Did that actually
take place at that time? It is clear that Peter, with his "This is,"
only wanted to say that the prophecy was then beginning to be
fulfilled and would go on being fulfilled until it extends to all
flesh. As Joel puts it, the gift God wanted to give was to continue
until the great and manifest day of judgment. That this is his
meaning is indicated by the concluding words, "And it shall be
that whoever calls on the name of the Lord shall be saved." The
Holy Spirit is given and is to come upon all flesh precisely so that
in the end all flesh may be in a position or have the opportunity
to beseech the Lord for exemption from his judgment.

Now, assuming the gift of the Holy Spirit to be no longer
there (at least not in the fullness God has in mind when he speaks
of an "outpouring,") even while there are still 800–1000 million
non-Christians on earth, is Joel's prophecy still to be regarded as
fulfilled once and for all? In making such a promise, could God
have had in mind only a beginning and not an ongoing process?
Or could it be that God did not really mean his word "all flesh"
seriously? He would then be like certain exegetes that consign
many more people to hell than to heaven, because they have no
stomach for a more general redemption than their system permits. Let them see how they can square their dictum that a mere
few will be saved with the words of Scripture.

We should take note that Peter quotes the passage from Joel
in full, including all the elements that could not possibly find
such a sudden fulfillment. How could all at once the Jews' sons
and daughters have prophesied, their young men seen visions,
their old men dreamed dreams, their menservants and maidser-
vants prophesied? These things only occurred very sparingly in
the Christian churches. Wonders in the heaven above and signs
on the earth below, blood and fire and vapor of smoke—none of

these were seen, nor did it come to pass that the sun was turned into darkness and the moon into blood. And yet Joel does here tick off one by one all that is to happen in the last days, in such a way that it obviously belongs together and occurs in quick succession. Hence, not everything contained in the prophecy was fulfilled—including what it foretells about the Spirit being poured out on all flesh.

In any case, how can we assume that Peter wanted to say more than that the prophecy was now beginning to be fulfilled! He certainly did not want to state that the beginning was already the end. Now some may still insist that that comparatively small beginning, which later waned and finally petered out altogether, was the fulfillment and nothing more can be expected. If so, one may justifiably ask if being content with such an inadequate fulfillment really gives the promise in question its full due.

In the foregoing I have said so much that it may seem superfluous to add more, but I am concerned to deal with the subject exhaustively. Ever since it dawned on me how much we need a new outpouring of the Holy Spirit, I have heard that very prophecy of Joel cited time and again as proof that nothing more is to be expected. In any case, I am told, Scripture says nothing anywhere of a second outpouring of the Holy Spirit.

In connection with this last point, I want to deal with the following objection. It is said that according to Peter at least the pouring out of the Spirit has already taken place, even though the signs forecast in the prophecy refer to the end time. I have heard it said that once poured out, the Spirit has remained and goes on spreading of its own accord to all believers (who therefore have the Spirit). I have been told it is not surprising that the Spirit is not so conspicuously in evidence as at the beginning, for it was only then that its effects had to be so extraordinary. Once the Spirit is poured out and there is no promise of a second outpouring, the Spirit must be assumed to be there.

Such reasoning simply ignores innumerable biblical statements concerning the Holy Spirit. How else could it be imagined that anyone has—with the exception of the extraordinary powers—exactly what the apostles and early Christians had! If we do not allow the Lord to foretell through Joel anything in the way of divine powers beyond what we still have we actually cross out the whole prophecy. Then we can not only do without its extraordinary powers—we can do without the Holy Spirit altogether! Then we simply carry on in our natural spirit the way we are doing now, with maybe a little whiff from up there now and then, but not as though the downpour from above that Joel speaks of were needed or had been promised. What good is the whole prophecy if also the less extraordinary manifestations—what is said about prophecy, visions, and dreams—are to remain completely absent!

Is it really so that we have God's spirit? The Holy Spirit is supposed to be one, yet how many thousands of spirits, all priding themselves on being spirits of truth, rule in Christendom! Who then has the Holy Spirit? The churches? But which of them? The dissenters? But which? The separatists? But which of the innumerable shades among them, all at loggerheads with each other? I cannot understand how one can say that the Holy Spirit is there, without being able to tell where it is. Where is the spirit of truth that leads into all truth? To be sure, a lot is known about the spirit of contention and wanting to be in the right, where someone thinks that he has the spirit of truth and others do not have it. But where is the other, the Comforter, the personal representative of God and Christ, who is to remain with those that have Christ? Where is the Spirit of whom the Savior says, "It is not you who speak, but the spirit of your Father speaking through you"? (Matt 10:20) Where is the spirit of gentleness and humility of whom the Savior speaks to his disciples, "Do you not know the spirit whose children you are?" Where is it? Who has it? Or are the quoted sayings of the Lord mere phrases or turns of speech, which actually are to be understood in some other way than they sound? And yet believers are supposed to be able to say, "We have the Spirit, and when we don't have it, we have it nonetheless, for the prophecy is fulfilled."

However, when I look at what we have, I cannot help sighing deeply, "O Lord Jesus, is that the promised Spirit for whose sake thou didst hang on a tree, having become a curse for us?" (Gal 3:13–14) The prophecy is after all meant for all flesh. Yet where is the Spirit that penetrates nation after nation as swiftly as at the time of the apostles and places them at Jesus' feet? And when we open our mouth to proclaim the Gospel here at home, where is the Spirit that shakes many so deeply that they cry out, "Brethren, what shall we do to be saved?" There are people that, in complete ignorance of the Holy Spirit's nature, are apt to call pretty well anything an outpouring of the Holy Spirit, even though there is not the least sign of what was witnessed in the apostolic time.

We have to bear in mind that the Holy Spirit must be recognizable, tangible, even visible, as something coming personally from God. It is to be there as fire, at least with the fiery glow visible at apostolic times. It is to be there as power, which is destined to drive out the forces of darkness, to help the wretchedly disfigured human race rise up to something better, to restrain all evil, and to blaze a trail for the Word in all people's hearts, even the most corrupt. For the Spirit is to convict the world (John 16:8). That is how the Spirit was present at one time but is no longer. It may be startling that something that was once so emphatically there should be there no more, but if that is a fact, we can try to determine how it came about that the Spirit, after being there, withdrew again.

In his first sermon Peter tells the Jews to repent and be baptized in the name of Jesus Christ for the forgiveness of their sins so as to receive the gift of the Holy Spirit (Acts 2:38). "For the promise is to you and to your children," Peter says, "and to all that are far off, every one whom the Lord our God calls to him" (Acts 2:39). Understandably enough, these Jews expected that what they witnessed in the apostles would also show in their own persons, once they were baptized. So it happened and indeed went on happening; everyone could see that something, whatever it was (I speak of a fire glow, similar to what had fallen on the apostles) came upon those baptized. It could therefore be determined definitely who had received the Holy Spirit and who not. But can we perceive anything at all, be it ever so faint, that distinguishes a baptized child from one not baptized?

Before long, however, already in apostolic times, there was a change. It happened first in Samaria, where the Holy Spirit failed to fall on any of those baptized there. Only when Peter and John came from Jerusalem and laid hands on them did they receive the Spirit, which shows that the Spirit should actually have been imparted already at baptism (Acts 8:14–17). But if even then the Holy Spirit delayed coming in individual cases, how much more must it have been the case subsequently, and without the lack being made up through laying on of hands. So here we already witness, with no indication of the reason, a decrease in the imparting of the Holy Spirit, and it had an influence on the inner situation of the churches. When John in his epistle speaks of some believers (or church members) that were born of God, and of others that were not born of God, one can infer from this that the Holy Spirit had at baptism descended on the first but not on the others, who were then more liable to go astray. That is why John says of those who had already assumed the character of anti-Christians:

> They went out from us, but they were not of us; for if they had been of us, they would have continued with us; but they went out that it might be plain that they all are not of us (1 John 2:19).

And when John adds, "But you have been anointed by the Holy One, and you know everything" (1 John 2:20), it becomes plain that those others had not really been part of the church because they had not received the Holy Spirit, although they could surely have done better nevertheless.

Thus Joel's prophecy began even then to be fulfilled somewhat more feebly in those baptized, and such fulfillment became still weaker and rarer as time went on. Finally, after the time of the apostles (as we have reason to believe), the Holy Spirit no longer came visibly down at baptism, and it evidently has remained that way right until now. Peter surely had the right to say, "This is what was spoken by the prophet Joel" (Acts 2:16), but it is equally sure that the fulfillment soon lessened and finally ceased before it extended to "all flesh." Along with the personal spirit of God, his extraordinary powers, still so mightily at work in Corinth, came to an end. Since that time we lack not only the person but also the powers of the Spirit, even the explicitly named powers of prophecy, visions, and dreams. Yet both, the personal impact and the powers, ought to be in evidence if the Holy Spirit is still to be poured out upon all flesh—something quite unimaginable as things are now. No mission is able to impart the Holy Spirit to the heathen, as Peter did in Samaria.

Now, if anybody wants to close his eyes and think that it's all there and that it is our own fault if we don't have it, we have to let him talk. But he should kindly allow me to think differently in the face of the utter dejection engulfing many people (especially believing Christians), the corruption rampant everywhere, the enormous ignorance and disunity among Christians, and the over-all impotence of the word and sacraments, not to mention the unbelief, which is spreading ever more strongly and widely. The lack of powers from on high is very distressing to me; I find solace only in clinging to the prophetic promise, and my heart burns with longing for its fulfillment.

It is a fact that "all flesh" has never received the Holy Spirit, nor can it expect to ever receive the Spirit if it remains as it is. And yet, the promise is there. Now, is God going to leave things as they have turned out to be? Will he shrug his shoulders (if I may be forgiven such an indelicate expression) and say, "Well, this is how things are. I leave it at that, whether what I have said is completely fulfilled or not"? I for my part cannot possibly go along with that. I have too high a regard for the word that issues from God's mouth to think like that. I say: A time must come for Joel's prophecy to be fulfilled afresh! And then it must come in such a way that the gift of the Holy Spirit comes swiftly on all flesh. Then also all the other signs to come that are spoken of in the prophecy will become reality. God does not want anyone to be lost; he will try everything to make all generations on earth acknowledge his name, so that they may escape judgment. Then that part of Joel's prophecy not quoted by Peter will also be fulfilled: "In Mount Zion and in Jerusalem [words pointing to a fulfillment here on earth] shall be deliverance, as the Lord has said, and in the remnant whom the Lord will call" (Joel 2:32).

I am going still further. According to Joel, "It shall come to pass in the last days, says the Lord." Now we know that in all their forecasts concerning the end time the prophets on the one hand totally disregard the length of time the fulfillment takes and always let beginning and end merge into one. On the other hand, though, they keep their eyes above all else riveted on the actual end. It can be maintained that all the prophecies we are accustomed to relate, and rightly so, to Christ were not completely fulfilled by his coming in the flesh. There is a lot more in these prophecies than became reality at the time of Christ. They picture processes set in motion by Christ that were to be completely fulfilled only later. The beginning of a prophecy must always be distinguished from its complete fulfillment.

The following passage may make this clear. We all know Isaiah chapter 40, starting with the words, "Comfort, comfort my people." That very beginning points to a fulfillment much greater than the one given with Christ. Next follows the voice in the wilderness, which John the Baptist related to himself. He was right, but here, too, more is promised than actually happened; thus we, again rightly, must be prepared for further voices in the wilderness. However great was the glory radiating from Jesus before and after his time on earth, the goal of the promise remained unattained: "For the glory of the Lord shall be revealed, and all flesh shall see together that the mouth of the Lord speaks" (Isa 40:5). To that end the way of the Lord is now to be prepared properly and successfully and "in the wilderness a highway is to be made straight for our God" (Isa 40:3).

So it is also with Joel's prophecy. Though it began to be fulfilled with the apostles, its real and complete fulfillment still lies in the future. The "last days" may well have begun with Christ. Who could have thought at that time that they would stretch to eighteen hundred years! But the end time proper is only now, before the return of the Lord, "before the great and terrible day of the Lord comes" (Joel 2:31). Complete fulfillment is something we still have to expect, and it is precisely Joel's prophecy that clearly foretells a renewed outpouring of the Holy Spirit. The promise had a preliminary fulfillment to begin with; it is due to be fulfilled properly, fully, and adequately before the end, for "it shall come to pass that all who call upon the name of the Lord shall be delivered" (Joel 2:32) applies especially to the end time.

This also answers an objection I often meet with, namely that the Scripture does not speak anywhere of a renewed or second outpouring of the Holy Spirit. I always find this objection strange. How can there be thought of a renewal if nothing has been said of a fading out? If the promise, taken at its full value, has remained unfulfilled, all that is required is to believe that its complete fulfillment is yet to come. It might also be said that it was not at all in God's plan to let the great redemption be delayed so long. If there is a desolate interim—probably due to the guilt of Christendom, which ought to have been more faithful—we obviously must hark back to the first time, for without that we cannot imagine a consummation of God's kingdom.

Finally we must bear in mind that the Holy Spirit did not depart from Christianity altogether. Throughout its history and right until now it has affected many—some more strongly and some less, especially, for instance, at the time of the Reformation. Without these often significant influences and workings of the Spirit, which also imparted faith and trust to individual souls, we would scarcely have the Gospel left anymore. But to see the true outpoured Spirit in what little is left is and remains a misconception of the gift itself as described in Scripture. Meanwhile, whatever is still left—it would be more if we were more open to the workings of the Spirit—is for us a thread that can lead us more easily than we may think to a recovery of the whole. Accordingly, it would, if you like, not be a question of an actual second outpouring but merely of a strengthening of the first one, so as to bring it back to its original state, to an imparting of the personal Holy Spirit, who should come to us anew. I am bound to believe that that is to take place, because I may not delete Joel's prophecies or reduce them to nearly nothing by pretending that the realities of our own time represent their fulfillment.

But the pouring out of the Holy Spirit was not the be-all and end-all of Blumhardt's hopes; rather, he saw that prospect more as simply the clearest, fullest, and briefest expression of the message he wanted to cry out into his time, as a task for men's hopes and prayers. He set his hopes on everything promised in the prophets, hence on a wondrously beautiful time of grace as foretold by them, above all by Isaiah (especially in chapters 40–66) but also by Ezekiel, Hosea, Micah, Habakkuk, Zechariah, etc., who never tire of telling how glorious things will be "at that time." As we all know, their prophecies have almost more to say of that wonderful time than of the Messiah, who brings it about.

If I may here render Blumhardt's thoughts freely, there are three ways of weakening one's joy in these promises.

First, one can twist the interpretation of much that is foretold in an attempt to persuade oneself that it has already been fulfilled. What was promised there, it is said, was no more than what we actually have in this era of the new covenant, that is, in our present time, however poor it may be in things divine. I bypass here the forced character of such interpretations; I simply want to point out how Blumhardt's thinking opposed the despondent mood that no longer expects great things from the living and merciful God and leads one to dampen and quench the word of promise.

When Moses asked God, "What is your name?" as though to say, "How do you differ from other gods?" God replied, "My name is 'I am who I shall be.'" God's approach to the human race is not marked by decrease, weakening, and aging but by increase: "I will do more good to you than ever before" (Ezek 36:11). He wants us to see him as one who manifests himself ever more gloriously and lovingly. By sending his own Son, how splendidly God fulfilled the promises he had given to the forefathers—far beyond anything they could have imagined! This is his nature; it is not fewer manifestations of power and mercy we may expect of him but rather more and more as time goes on.

Second, in the opinion of some people the larger part and the finest of the prophetic promises apply only to the Jews of today. When Jacob or Israel are addressed, it is said to refer to them: Zion and Jerusalem always mean that particular hill in Palestine and the town at its feet. Now we can certainly expect the Lord to show one day that his promises indeed apply to the Jews. The very fact that these continue to exist as a nation, while all the nations that were once their contemporaries, such as the Phoenicians, Egyptians, etc. have long since disappeared, argues that God still has great and wonderful things in mind for them. "As you have been a byword of cursing among the nations, so you shall be a blessing" (Zech 8:13), "I will take out of your flesh the heart of stone" etc. (Ezek 36:26), and various similar prophecies will be fulfilled mainly in them, and that will indeed mean a great step forward in the kingdom of God. Yet it cannot be the case that descent from circumcised fathers should count more before God than descent from baptized ones and that those Jews who have remained stiff-necked should in the end have their obstinacy rewarded by preferential treatment. However, especially in the beginning days of Christianity thousands and thousands of Jews entered the family of Christ's church, and gradually others, too—maybe more than one would think—have made us more kin to Abraham in the flesh (as well as in the spirit). With this thought Blumhardt lifted himself above a too petty and narrow understanding of the prophetic promise. But he naturally had still other and more weighty reasons: "Jesus is Abraham's offspring and is the vine; we are his branches and thus Abraham's offspring." That is but a variation of Paul's word, "If you [gentile Christians] are Christ's, then you are Abraham's offspring, heirs according to the promise" (Gal 3:29).

In a fine, important passage of the same letter (Gal 4:22–31)—a passage unfortunately little heeded and understood due to various misadventures—the apostle Paul shows how seriously he takes the point in question. Perhaps I may be permitted to throw a little light on this passage.

The most devastating misfortune that befell it is well known: Some copyist smuggled Hagar into verse 25. This verse originally read, "For Mount Sinai is in Arabia and corresponds to Jerusalem (seeing that this Jerusalem is in slavery with her children)." According to Paul, the vaunted law of the Jews brings about slavery, such as Hagar's; it was given from Mount Sinai, a mountain situated in a foreign country. Now present-day Jerusalem (i.e. at Paul's time) is akin to Sinai and Hagar, for she is in slavery (under the law). Therefore she always has children (Gen 16:11), but they are brought forth in a forced, artificial way, just as Ishmael's birth represented a forced effort to take hold of a divine promise. But such an unnatural offspring of Abraham, the product of a human attempt to force the fulfillment of the promise (Genesis 16), is only a constant embarrassment for God's kingdom. In the end there can be nothing but, "Out with him!" The true Jerusalem, on the other hand, has to wait for the promise to be fulfilled; she is free, and all she has to do is to believe. For this reason, it is true, she remains infertile for a long time, like Sarah, but to her applies the word, "Sing, O barren one who did not bear" (Isa 54:1).

Paul's statement (Gal 4:24) that one can glean more from the story of Hagar and Ishmael than mere historical facts does not spring from some "arbitrary rabbinical sophistry," which conceited self-confidence often wants to see in him just here. Rather, the direction of his thinking actually links him with modern thinking with its perception and grasp of the laws of growth and development. Just as we moderns see how the structure of the future oak tree is already hinted at, implied, and grounded in the composition of the acorn, Paul sees how both the wonderful divine experiences and the human waywardness of the people of God in his own time reflect or repeat corresponding experiences and crises in the family of the forefather Abraham. To wait in faith for the Lord and his promises was and still is the path marked out for Abraham's family, the people of God and faith, from their very beginning. In the newly born church of Jesus Paul could see a miraculous child of promise, comparable to Isaac; on the other hand the waywardness that gave life to Ishmael and the slave's presumption characteristic of him reappeared in the conceit with which the Jews of Paul's time basked in their legalistic piety. By that poor surrogate of their own making they considered themselves compensated for all that remained unfulfilled—unfulfilled at first in fact and then merely supposedly. Of all generations our own should be least inclined to willfully disregard that lesson of history.

So this is the apostle's final conclusion: "You gentile Christians are the children that God, through Isaiah (Isa 54:1ff.) promised to desolate Jerusalem. You are Isaac, and the unbaptized Jews are Ishmael." "Therefore," he says, "they torment and persecute me and the gentile Christians just as Ishmael once persecuted Isaac" (Gal 4:29). What a great, simple, and clear way of showing that God's family, God's people, are defined by the Spirit, by their holding fast to the principle of faith that Abraham clung to! And how is it to be reconciled with Paul's words if in direct opposition to him one excludes from the promise those whom Paul calls Abraham's offspring and Jerusalem people, and will admit only those whom he excludes? If, as Paul states pointblank, the Christians of apostolic times were children of that Jerusalem of which the prophecy speaks, then that Jerusalem is independent of geography. In a sense, every center or starting point of a divine revelation through the Holy Spirit is then the Jerusalem or Zion of the promise.

Now if this is so, how great is the promise we have! The beginning of chapter 40 in Isaiah is then meant also for our poor Christian church: "Comfort, comfort my people, says your God. Speak tenderly to her, for her iniquity is pardoned." And likewise also all the glorious promises in the second part of Isaiah, as well as those from other prophets—how all nations will yet come to her, so that her rooms will prove too small (Isa 54:2–3), etc. From chapter 54 of Isaiah, which Paul refers to, I still want to mention here verses 4–8: "The reproach of your widowhood you will remember no more," etc. Does that not call to mind the parable of the widow and the unjust judge? Does it not tell us that what is said in that parable applies most of all to the widowhood of our poor Christian church? In short, once we believe the apostle Paul's statement that we are the bearers of those promises, it is to us that that unutterably great and wonderful time of grace is promised and announced—as a transition period to everlasting glory.

The certainty that the comfort granted the prophets as they faced the then decay of Israel is also addressed to, and meant for, us, let Blumhardt, whose heart ached at the distress of his time, likewise draw comfort from the prophetic message. In a Sunday afternoon service in Möttlingen he used the concluding words of the prophet Micah to set forth powerfully the hopes we may cherish:

> 18 Who is a God like you,
> who pardons sin and forgives the transgression
> of the remnant of his inheritance?
> You do not stay angry forever
> but delight to show mercy.
>
> 19 You will again have compassion on us;
> you will tread our sins underfoot
> and hurl all our iniquities into the depths of the sea.
>
> 20 You will be true to Jacob,
> and show mercy to Abraham,
> as you pledged on oath to our fathers
> in days long ago.
>
> (Micah 7:18–20)

"To the remnant who still cry on behalf of the widow, 'Save me from my adversary!' he will grant that in the end the sins of *all* can be cast into the depths of the sea. Hearing of what will be given 'to Jacob' and 'to Abraham', we may add, 'And to your son Jesus Christ'—which is even more." That, in essence, was Blumhardt's exposition of the text.

Now comes the third objection. It is presented by what I call the millennium, or eschatology. What God has promised indicates loving-kindness and mercy on a vast scale, but we humans find it very hard to let our hearts be touched, so that they become warm and beat faster. That is why we prefer to push all the true promises of God as far away from us as possible, that is, all the immense kindliness he still wants to show, and everything by which he wants to reveal himself as the living one, the supreme ruler, yet at the same time the merciful one. There is a chasm that prevents us from looking beyond the present familiar pattern of events, where there is no trace of any action of God, nor of the ascendancy of his kingdom, such as we find related in the Bible. That chasm is the return of Christ. Whatever great manifestations of divine power and mercy we may still hope for we like to assign to the land on the far side of the chasm. There we visualize some kind of millennial kingdom, which we liberally endow with everything glorious. All that remains on the near side is the sad dregs or leftovers of prophecy, that which represents a menace rather than a promise or, more accurately, is a forecast of all sorts of wickedness yet to be committed by men.

Thus the way to the wonderful object of our hopes, the return of our Lord Jesus Christ, is barred to us by all kinds of impending fearsome unfoldings of evil: apostasy, the anti-Christ, the ultimate tribulation. And we think we know almost down to every detail just how it will all come about. It makes us shudder and think secretly, "If only I am spared this!" But let us beware of such an outlook. It is a mistake to want to know everything so exactly; that is not the Spirit speaking but the natural human mind, which has no ear for the Spirit of God. That's how it was with the Pharisees; they were expert eschatologists and knew it all to a T, but none of what they expected came about, or it came about quite differently. Indeed, it turned out so differently that, blinded by their sophisticated learning, they stood totally unaware amidst the most wonderful divine happenings. And of all the enemies of God's kingdom they fancied to be approaching, they themselves were about the only ones that materialized. With their contemporary Simeon it was just the other way round; he had read the promises with his heart and in the Spirit. He didn't know nearly as much as the Pharisees; he only knew one thing, the salvation and light of the nations, and that quickened his pulse. The Lord came in a way so totally different from what the Pharisees (in strict accordance with the words of the promise, as they supposed) had imagined it. How much simpler yet much greater was his actual coming, how much more human and more divine, how much less as judge and more as savior! Let us take that to heart!

Blumhardt fought shy of such speculations about the future, which satisfied only man's intellect or, maybe still more, only his curiosity and imagination. The prophets were concerned with the future only to the extent that they hungered and thirsted for comfort, and it was because their quest sprang from such hunger and thirst that they were granted disclosures. That, Blumhardt felt, should also be *our* approach to inquiring about what is to come. What ought to concern us is that which has something to give to a man's heart and to the indwelling Holy Spirit.[6]

Once when two people had an argument about whether Blumhardt visualized the anti-Christ before or after the onset of the hoped-for time of grace, he replied to their question, "Well, our most immediate need is not the anti-Christ." When or how the anti-Christ might come was of little concern to him; what did concern him about the future were such matters as he could and did make objects of his prayer and expectation. He was firmly convinced that the "final tribulation" (the time of persecution preceding the ultimate victory) would not turn out as fearsomely as many imagine. It was a heartfelt need of his that made him assume that: He saw that for many people the bliss of seeing the Lord and his day draw near was soured by such horrible prospects, which pretty well took away all the joy of expectancy.

As we know, the main passage quoted for the horrors in the end-time tribulation is Matt 24:21: "For then there will be great tribulation, such as has not been from the beginning of the world until now, no, and never will be." To those who want to conclude from this that a tribulation of unsurpassed severity will precede the Lord's coming, Blumhardt replies as follows:

---

6. To exemplify Blumhardt's opposition to a probing of Bible texts out of mere curiosity, I quote here from a letter he wrote in reply to a question concerning the significance of the new temple described by Ezekiel (chapters 40–47).

> Ezekiel? To what end do we need light on this subject? We have sufficient light to notice where the text is not evangelical in character, hence cannot be taken literally. It is a mystery, meant to trip up meddlesome fellows who, snubbing the Gospel, pounce on something like that and thereby are liable to deny Christ. For the Bible, as for other things, one must have a norm. That norm is Christ, as he is presented by the apostles. Wherever in Scripture I cannot make that norm fit, that passage is not for me until I *can* make it fit. In the meantime, I just have to let the text stand and must wait for light to be shed on it. In the end it will be given. But does it do any harm if there is this or that in the Bible that will only be understood when the right hour comes? Why should I want to extract its meaning forcibly before that time? So it is with Revelation too. There are many things I do not understand, but then must I need an explanation and therefore make one up before the right time? We should wait till that time comes and not let it bother us. When it does come, we shall be glad that it says what it says.

1. The final sentence implies that the tribulation referred to here may yet be followed by others less severe.

2. That means that the reference here is not to a final tribulation or to something taking place immediately before the end but rather to the tribulation connected with the destruction of Jerusalem.

3. That again means that if, as indeed seems likely, a final tribulation is yet to be expected, it will not be as severe as the one this verse foretells.

There was still another powerful reason why Blumhardt argued against the tribulation theory:

> From the perspective of the New Testament prophecies these past eighteen hundred years are as nothing or at most something quite small. Yet imagine all the tribulations that were compressed into that brief span of eighteen centuries—what a huge pile of wars, plagues, famines, and persecution that makes! Think of the streams of shed blood, think of a famine such as the recent one in China that devoured between seven and nine million people, the plague in the Middle Ages, the fagots of the Inquisition—does that not seem to be enough? Could it not be our compensation for the long, long wait that in the end things will not be quite as bad as had been imagined?

As we know, in Matthew 24 the destruction of Jerusalem appears at first glance to be seen as nearly simultaneous with the return of the Lord. Closer inspection, however, shows that a distinction is after all made between these two events. The distinction becomes evident in the concluding sentence of verse 21, which sees world history continuing even after the destruction of Jerusalem. Still, these two great points in time—the judgment visited on the Jews and the return of the Lord—are seen so much together that it is hard to separate the thoughts referring to the one event from those referring to the other. Blumhardt's own way out of the difficulty provided him at the same time with an answer to an objection frequently raised against his view of today's situation in the kingdom of God.

The objection was that the New Testament does not foretell the decline of Christianity Blumhardt assumed had taken place, nor the revival he hoped for. Of course, this is a problem not only for Blumhardt but for the Protestant church generally, which likewise perceives a serious decline in the centuries from apostolic times to the Reformation and then a considerable revival during the latter. The difference is, however, that a revival as glorious as Blumhardt hoped for may only be expected on the basis of a *promise*. In the previous pages we have watched him elucidate the promise on which he set his hopes. But how does he reconcile it with the Bible's silence about the ensuing interval of seventeen hundred years?

The Lord is no soothsayer. He does not want merely to foretell future happenings, which will then unroll mechanically according to the forecast. When individual events that are neither promises nor threats are foretold, they are indispensable hints or warnings of imminent dangers. Given the way humanity behaves, it is unfortunately more likely for threatened chastisements to come to pass than for promises to find fulfillment. God's promises are not automatically fulfilled; their fulfillment depends on our behavior and is always more or less contingent on our free will—whether or not we really *want* what has been promised.

Now everything the Lord says concerning his return suggests the view that whatever his servants still have to do on earth before then could be accomplished within one extended human life span (Matt 24:34). In the parable of the laborers in the vineyard, for instance, those starting work in the morning (the apostles) are pictured as still active in the evening, when work is completed. Apparently, the Lord at least considered it possible that things might go that fast, and here we should bear in mind that with the infinite resources at God's command even the greatest difficulties could have been overcome—see Isaiah 60:22: "I am the Lord; in its time I will do this swiftly." On the other hand, Jesus might well have had a premonition of the coming delay, though he might still have hoped that at any rate the main push toward final victory would be accomplished within a man's life span. After all, he, too, had no certain knowledge of what was to come, as we gather from Mark 13:32: "But of that day or that hour no one knows, not even the angels in heaven, nor the Son, but only the Father." To head off feelings of discouragement at a delay, in several parables the Lord expressed a hunch that there might still be considerable delays. Yet he could not by many ifs and buts weaken the impression that quick progress was possible, nor did he want to. The Lord had no compelling reason to dishearten his servants by definitely forecasting a slowing down. The concept of "within one generation" (Matt 24:34) may yet be of significance for the time when the final developments will take place.

God did not want to have a "but" mixed in with his promise, namely: "*But* you will mess it all up again; with your unfaithfulness and laziness you will again spoil it and slow it down." That would be beneath God's dignity as well as harmful to people; it would excuse their conduct, so to speak, or might even provoke it. As a general principle, those times of human history in which through the people's own fault "nothing happens"—that is, when God's great work comes to a halt—do not exist for the prophetic eye; it looks beyond or right through them as if through mere nothings.

But, it might be objected, if that is the case, what about the Reformation? No one felt more keenly than Blumhardt that the Reformation was not one of those nothings. More and more clearly as time went on, he saw God's finger in it. Though the movement had again ground to a halt, it was to him the beginning of the great revival. But only the beginning, for he felt the Reformation was still a long way from regaining all that Christendom had lost in its deep decay.

These thoughts found an expression, as remarkable as it was unexpected to Blumhardt himself, in a sermon he delivered in Möttlingen on the subject of Peter's second haul of fish (that is, after the Lord's resurrection). As we know, the disciples had fished all night and caught nothing. In the morning Jesus, standing unrecognized on the shore, counseled them, "Cast the net on the right side of the boat, and you will find some." So they cast it and were not able to haul it in because of the quantity of fish. "And Simon hauled the net ashore, full of large fish, a hundred and fifty-three of them; and although there were so many, the net was not torn" (John 21:11).

On the Sunday when this was the prescribed text for the sermon, there was an even greater press of visitors than usual, so Blumhardt had pretty well no preparation time, which in any case he was always very short of. The church bells were already ringing, when he opened his book of pericopes and found this text. At first he was completely at a loss how to approach it. At the very last moment the following train of thought came to him, which he voiced.

Two things strike us in this passage. In the first place, there is the visibly emphasized connection between this second haul of fish and the earlier one (Luke 5:1–9), both as regards what is similar and what is dissimilar. Next, there are noticeable hints that the episode related here is actually a symbolic prophecy, particularly as regards the (otherwise completely irrelevant) number of fish. In the case of the first haul, too, the Lord's word, "From now on you will catch men" (Luke 5:10) points to a symbolic, prophetic meaning of the event.

Could it be that these two hauls of fish foreshadow the two great periods of the church of Jesus, the first and the last? The first haul would then mean the ingathering of souls at the time of the apostles, beginning at Pentecost. Before that, in Old Testament times, it was nighttime, so to speak, and the fishing was just by line and hook. Then at Pentecost Peter heard the call, "Put out into the deep and let down your nets for a catch!" At that time and throughout apostolic times so many fish were caught that the net—the teaching or doctrine—started to break. It tore and got holes, allowing fish to go back and forth and the distinction between within and without to get blurred, making it possible for redeemed persons to be without and for some of those within the net to be unredeemed. The church was going to seed; it was night again (the Middle Ages), and fishing was once more just by line and hook, with little success. At Reformation time the net, meaning the doctrine, was mended. A good deal did take place, but a decisive victory over sin, a real return to God on a large scale did not come about, nor did the mercies of the apostolic time come back. Many things remained in darkness, and in some respects night descended once more. Yet the Lord will manifest himself anew, and the word will go forth: "Cast the net on the right side of the boat!" There will be another big haul, and this time for good, for "although there were so many, the net was not torn" (John 21:11). The number of fish is counted, for in the last time things may well be so hard "as to lead astray, if possible, even the elect" (Matt 24:24). But then it will no longer be possible.

The allegorical character of this sermon makes it unique among Blumhardt's sermons, for his whole nature was otherwise thoroughly opposed to allegorical interpretation. Probably he indulged in it here because both Scripture and experience had already given him clarity and certainty about the basic ideas he voiced.

That the Reformation was a blessing surely came to full and wholehearted expression in this sermon, but in my memory (my sole source for it) that recedes into the background before the new thoughts Blumhardt outlined so vigorously and which have remained more deeply engraved in my memory. Thus the above summary may show a bluntness that did not mark the sermon itself. For balance I feel obliged to insert here a special sermon Blumhardt delivered on the occasion of a later anniversary of the Reformation, from *Predigt-Blätter aus Bad Boll*. I give it in full, as it resisted all attempts to select excerpts.

THE LORD IS COMING

Sermon on 2 Peter 3:9, delivered at a Reformation festival.

TEXT: The Lord is not slow in keeping his promise as some understand slowness but is patient with us, not wanting anyone to perish, but everyone to come to repentance.

You may be surprised, beloved, at my coming upon such a passage today. We must remember, however, that when Luther took his stand, he was convinced that the Lord was about to come; he saw his own work as a preparation for the Lord's taking the field against the anti-Christ. His writings are full of this; words of his have even been collected and published in a special booklet to show that Luther is also to be respected and esteemed as a prophet, who could speak in a very stimulating and deep going way of the future, of approaching judgments, and of the final coming of the Lord according to the promise. Hence none of you should think it peculiar that at a Reformation festival in our time just this aspect of Luther's thought should be given prominence. There is good reason for looking with him also at the last things.

When God let the new light shine forth, it was not his main purpose to have a more appropriate Christian outlook, religion, or denomination arise just then, by which one was to live henceforth. Rather, it was to be a preparation in deed and truth for the Lord's advent. And if I may add something more, it is that to me the Reformation three hundred fifty years ago has never been anything other than a model of a spiritual renewal that must extend through the entire world, beginning with the rising of God's light and glory upon all nations on earth and leading to their awakening to a new, divine life.

When considering the Reformation it is a mistake to think of it merely as the establishment of Protestantism—the Evangelicals, Lutherans, Reformed, or whatever. What the Lord had in mind with the Reformation was much greater and more far-reaching. For a long time it was held that all the redemptive purposes of God were bound to be realized only in and among the Protestants, as if no other peoples and churches even existed. Protestants saw themselves as a new Israel, but it was an Israel that dreamed egotistically and self-lovingly only of herself. That was not at all right. Such thoughts, if they are still harbored here and there even today, are not what we ought to think according to the Lord's mind and will.

The Lord is coming! That was already implied in the theses or propositions that Luther nailed to the church door in Wittenberg. The Lord is coming as he has promised. And when we recall everything that took place from the time of the Reformation until today, it should all cry out to us, "The Lord is coming." The promise remains firm, even if its fulfillment is delayed; for there did come another slowdown. At that time a vigorous knocking was heard throughout Christendom, letting all hearts know, "The Lord is near." But it quieted down again. It was the midnight hour, and the watchmen cried, "The bridegroom comes." However, when the bridegroom tarried, people went to sleep again. What was being expected at that time was once again put off, and for nearly two centuries people forgot altogether about the Lord's coming. It was only a century ago that things livened up once more in our fatherland, yet there still are large districts, Protestant ones too, where the promise of the Lord's coming and faith in it remain dormant. There has been something of an awakening among us, but not enough. True, the Lord's coming is being discussed, but always as though it were something to be talked about at length but never to be realized. That is also largely the situation in our Protestant lands. But we want to let the thought of the Lord's coming be awakened in us, and today we want to speak of three things: (1) How it began with the Reformation; (2) How since then it has again slowed down; and (3) How it will finally be consummated.

(1) The promised coming of the Lord began with the Reformation; the Reformation prepared it and set it in motion. That is a sublime thought, which must not be left unheeded when remembering God's great work at that time.

First of all, the fetters that held everything in humankind and Christendom bound and shackled had to be loosened. People's spirits had to be set free so that they could stir and move. Under the influence of the Holy Spirit men were given freedom to develop and mature inwardly and so get ready for the great things to be expected with the Lord's advent. While up to then everything had been bound and fettered and even gagged, as can be demonstrated from history, that had to change now. The fetters had to be struck off and the confinement of spirits come to an end.

It took place with a mighty jolt. At the news of Luther's theses a feeling of liberation pervaded all lands and especially the whole of Germany. A wonderful sense of freedom was also felt later on, when on June 25, 1530, the Augsburg Confession was read out freely and publicly in the teeth of the prevailing ideas of that time, which kept minds and hearts darkened and in subjection. Souls had to be set free for the Lord, that they might be bound, not by human flesh, but by him through his Spirit. People had to enter into inner community with Jesus himself; everything obstructing that had to be removed. Much has been done in this direction, but much has also been left. Yet everyone has praise for that aspect of the Reformation that allowed people to breathe more freely and to meet the Lord without constraint.

A second factor that at that time prepared the way for the Lord's coming was the new perception and revelation then given through the Word of God. People everywhere no longer quite knew what Christianity was all about; they were not supposed to know. That there was such a thing as a Bible was hardly known; what was in it was known even less. Thus God's will to redeem humankind, his great plan of salvation for all generations of the earth, was all covered over, as was also the full significance of Jesus' first coming. What was the purpose of his coming, his sojourn on earth, his miracles? It was no longer known. What was the meaning of his death on the cross? True, it was being pondered a good deal; many pictorial representations were made of it, but at bottom no one rightly understood any more what its purpose was. What was the meaning of his resurrection? It was a fine story, which one enjoyed, but its significance for humankind was no longer known. His ascension, his enthronement at God's right hand, his return—all this was so wrapped in darkness that the whole Savior, as he is revealed to us, seemed not to be there at all. What was said about Jesus offered nothing to the heart nor gave any hope for life here and beyond, except that people mechanically—one might say: superstitiously—expected some things they had heard about to happen.

Now the Reformation brought Jesus back. He had been there in the creed, but he was to be once more brought close to people's hearts. The Reformation was to show Jesus again as he is; it was to show afresh that his gospel brings light and salvation. His miracles, as we find them recounted in the Gospel, were to demonstrate that he is there for us in all our need. His death on the cross was to show how Jesus defeated the powers of darkness and canceled our debt. The splendor of his resurrection and ascension, his enthronement at God's right hand, and the certain hope of his return—all these the Reformation revived for us. Without it, they would all have remained dead and buried under debris. At the same time it prepared the ground for his coming, for if he is to come, one has to know who it is that comes in the clouds of heaven. Thus the Reformation brought Jesus back into the light of day so that we can have him, trust in him, and also with great longing wait for him until he comes.

Yet a third factor paved the way for the Lord's coming at the time of the Reformation: It was once more brought home to the people how Jesus and his salvation can, and quite surely will be, gained. Previously people had wanted to obtain the goodwill of God and of the Lord Jesus in a mechanical sort of way through practicing an outward works-holiness; they relied on that as an infallible means. For instance, salvation could be purchased for money; or it was believed that by making various sacrifices or denying oneself this or that one was doing more than enough and could be fully assured of a God and a Savior and of heaven. I don't have to go into all that, for you know it.

Then Luther arose and thousands with him, who stated clearly that only faith in Jesus Christ and his salvation can open the way to heaven and divine glory. The whole person was to find his way back to childlike faith and trust in God and Christ; the whole person was to be immersed in the revelations of Jesus Christ, just as they are given, and let light come into his heart. Our hearts were to be illumined through learning to trust, ask, and hope, and through obeying God's good commandments. We were to let ourselves be taught by the Spirit and receive light from God's word for our conduct—our everyday living, our suffering, and dying. We were to receive solace and uplift amid life's adversities and its besetting storms, and we were to be taught how to remain true to faith, so as to attain the heavenly things. In short, the Reformation spread light all around, so that we might prepare ourselves for the Lord's coming, fill our lamps with oil, light them, and go to meet the approaching bridegroom.

Thus, however we may look at the Reformation, every individual aspect we see lets us avow, "This points to the Lord's coming." That is why I called the revival of the Christian church during the early years of the Reformation a model and already a beginning of that which must still take place before the Lord comes, so that he can come.

But of course a good deal of darkness has come in again since. True, we Protestants are no longer enslaved the way we were in former times, but we are enslaved in other ways—by abuses aplenty, by wrong ideas, by false teachers and prophets, by secret and public alliances of all kinds, which individuals have entered into and sold themselves to, with the result that they clamor for license instead of freedom. We must become free, free in and for the Lord!

The Scripture—true, it is there, but who reads it? Who knows it? And who knows Jesus? Oh, how the Lord Jesus has again been covered up! How he gets put in his place! People will not have it that he came from God and from heaven; they will not let him amount to anything and simply dismiss him as somebody who at one time was very much talked about and who got the world excited, but whose day is now over. There are thousands who take this stand. Others talk a lot about him but will not let him come close to them, will not enter into real community with him. If one inquires how many have entered into community with Jesus, the answer is saddening. There are but very few. It makes one wish that things might again be as they were in Reformation times.

Still, we can at least *have* all this; we can read it and ponder it unafraid, and once the spirit of God comes down to us anew, how much could be given quite quickly, because the Reformation paved the way for his coming. We *can* have a life of faith; no one is barred from it. Here too it only needs the Spirit to descend on us for thousands to be made ready for the advent of the Lord.

(2) Now we have already been brought to the second point to be considered, that is, how since the Reformation the Lord's advent has again been delayed.

The delay is there, and it is understandable. If the Lord wanted to come and had come quickly, where are the people whom he could take to himself? He does not want anyone to be lost but wants everyone to find repentance, to turn around and live. His procrastinating is nothing but a sign showing that he is patient with us and has not yet given up the hope that in the end he can come in such a way that his coming will bring salvation also for persons as yet hardened and defiant. Oh, they are all still too far away from him for him to come and have joy in them at his coming. It can truly sadden us not to see any adequate readiness, either among us or others, for the Lord's coming. And yet we must thank God that he holds back, for it would go badly otherwise. If the last trumpet were to sound now, what would things look like among humanity?

In the main, however, the delay has taken place and become necessary because the brightly burning light of the Reformation has become closely confined. Whatever areas turned Protestant then have remained so, unless outward force brought about a change later on. It didn't go any further. Everything has been hemmed in most tightly. Even in so-called Protestant territories the true Protestants in villages and towns are shut in on themselves and remain so. Closed doors everywhere! The evangelical light cannot penetrate them nor can it shine out.

Side by side with this seclusion there is something even sadder: the mutual exclusion. There is much in Protestantism that wants to exclude the other, the Roman Catholicism, but it should not be so; it does not belong to the essence of the Reformation and of what it brought. There is little feeling for the Roman church. There is relentless arguing and quarreling with its members and hierarchy about all kinds of things, in secret and in public. There is a dividing wall, which also the Protestant church is making no efforts to penetrate with its light. Cheerfully one leaves everything as it is, as though hatred and enmity between the churches were naturally part of it all. To let one's light shine forth so that the others, too, might be won—that occurs to nobody. But light must come also into this dark area, though the separation between here and there run ever so deep.

There is also separation between the Protestants themselves. Some adopt a certain form, with which they close themselves off and remain by themselves; others take another form and equally keep to themselves. True integration where each is there for all and all for each does not exist. Luther had it. He sent messengers as far as Constantinople and was always keen to bring about a great unity among all Christians. Nothing was so contrary to his mind as the thought of a separation or split. But with us it is different. Look at our church people—how they shut themselves off and keep entirely to their own group, not caring at all about the others but only about those bearing the same name as they. But that is no getting ready for the Lord, no preparation for the moment when the trumpet from heaven will sound forth above them all, "He is coming, he is coming!"

The disruption among Christians does not admit of the Lord's coming; it delays it. The slowdown comes about because, as our text says, the Lord is patient with us; he does not want anyone to be lost but wants everyone to repent. But who is the "everyone" that is to repent and the "anyone" not to be lost? Lutherans are wont to think of their church and of no one apart from them; the Reformed apply the "everyone" to themselves and to nobody else. I should like to ask, "To what degree does the Protestant church feel for the other [Roman Catholic] church and hope that there, too, everyone might come to repentance?"

There is bound to be a delay until the light we have, given to us through grace, breaks through as light and not as something to be argued about, until it pierces as a uniting light all the separations and divisions among the Protestants, and then penetrates all Roman Catholic countries as well. I say explicitly that *light* must pervade it all—not an outward confession—that they may all turn around and look toward the day of Jesus Christ.

The Reformation has given us Protestants a great calling, to which, however, we have hardly remained true. We should have become a light throughout the world, just as it was once said of Abraham that he and his seed were to become a blessing for all generations on earth. With that light in our hands, we Protestants ought to be the light of the world, and we could truly be that, for we have the wherewithal for it, as we heard at the beginning. We should carry the light of the world everywhere for the conversion of the nations, which are all in one way or another shrouded in darkness. However, given our present condition, millions of men remain unenlightened and unconverted. They know nothing of Jesus apart from the name, know nothing of the possibility of being graciously accepted by a Savior that is to come. Why don't they know it? Because we make no effort to let them know and to show them the light. Though here and there one or the other may find the light for himself, the masses remain in darkness, and oh, how dark it is! Wherever we look, we see unconverted people, indulging the lusts of the flesh, and sunk in idolatry. The light given to us has not been effective nor could it be, for we have not placed it on the candlestick. That is why the coming of the Lord is deferred.

How it hurts me to hear that, after Protestant churches have been built here and there in the diaspora, the preachers appointed for them turn out to be practically atheists, at least in some cases. Of course, I don't want to say by this that no one is doing his duty; many do it conscientiously, at least to the best of their lights. But generally speaking, nobody is actually terribly concerned to shine forth into the darkness and lighten it. And the shining forth should not take the form of untimely and obnoxious conversion attempts nor of propaganda but should be done in such a way that the others can bear it and that all who seek the light can easily find it. What splendid work the Reformation did in some German provinces! Yet if one looks now, the people there have become anything but a light; on the contrary, the darkness has actually made inroads into them.

O light, where are you? Under the bushel! Pretty well every Protestant society and church is a bushel; there is light underneath but not outside it. And whoever seeks light must also get down under the bushel, or else he doesn't get any. But God doesn't want anyone to get lost, hence the Lord will not come while our light is locked away. As long as the light granted three hundred and fifty years ago does not shine in all Christian churches and beyond them everywhere in the world, the Lord will not come, however much we wait for him. If they are all far away from him and unrepentant, how can he come? No abyss would be big enough to receive all the impenitent in the world. That is why he procrastinates and why there has been this slowdown since the Reformation.

(3) In the end, though, it *will* be accomplished! In the end Christ's return, as it was set in motion at the time of the Reformation, will be consummated in spite of the delay; it will become an accomplished fact. What am I to say about this third point we meant to consider? I have to say something that few will want to hear. Here I stand again, full of that which stirs my soul and which I can never cease talking about. In short, what I have in mind is a harking back to what was given and took place at the Reformation time. What I hope and wish is no different from what was hoped for, wished for, and wanted by the Reformers; it is nothing but the longed-for light (longed-for especially by Luther), which must come through the Word of God in the strength of the Spirit. People take it amiss that I say such a thing. But who can explain the Reformation without assuming a stream from on high? Who can otherwise explain that within four weeks, at a time still without railways, telegraph, and newspapers, Luther's theses kindled a fire throughout Europe? A fire flood came down from above, a wind of God's Spirit, which carried the fire into all towns and villages and made the flames leap high. If not interpreted in this way, it remains an unexplainable phenomenon.

If no more were to be given than a repetition of that stream of fire, what a great thing that alone would be! And why should we not be allowed to wish that such a stream might come anew and be even stronger? If the Lord's advent is not to be reduced to a mere nothing, it must come about that what the Reformation set in motion but which later ground to a halt starts moving afresh. That can take place only through the stream from on high pouring forth afresh and, joining forces with the earlier stream from Reformation times, setting it, too, in motion again. This is what I desire and what I shall testify to as long as I live. My last breath shall contain the prayer: "Lord, send forth your stream of spirit and grace to revitalize the whole world! Wherever there is a human being to be looked upon with compassion, let thine eye fall on him with a true Savior's gaze, which will assure him of salvation." To this I hold. I shall struggle and cry to the Lord until all nations on earth have this light and turn to repentance, lest they be lost.

You dear ones, let this be our concern today. Learn to pray with me that such a stream will flow again, and even more fully and extensively, through the whole world, until things are such that the Lord can say, "I am coming!" And when he does come, how wonderful that will be, for grace and mercy will go before him. Therefore rejoice in his coming! Amen.[7]

Blumhardt always saw the coming of Christ as the ultimate object of his hopes. The time of grace he hoped for was to precede it like a breath of spring (Luke 21:29–31). Christ's return alone would complete his victory and his redemptive work and would still the groaning of creation (Rom 8:22).

Blumhardt's inner attitude to the great event differed from that of some Christians. In his eyes it was the outcome of a fierce struggle in heaven and on earth. With that attitude he was more firmly rooted in apostolic Christianity than we are if, though subscribing to the doctrine of the Lord's return, we face with utmost equanimity the question whether it is to take place now or some thousands of years hence; also if it leaves us quite unconcerned that during all this time most men walk the broad way that leads to destruction and only a few find the way to life (Matt 7:13). For him Christianity, that is, the great work of redemption, was not complete until the last victory (which is one with the Lord's return) has been gained. In a similar sense Peter speaks of "times of refreshing" when God will send Jesus anew (Acts 3:19–20).

I think the reason for our facing the return of Christ largely with more equanimity (not to say indifference) than Blumhardt did is that in

---

7. The principles of the Reformation, especially as set down in Luther's basic writings, were actually much more apt to lead to organic growth (in particular to an increased familiarity with the recently "rediscovered" Bible) than they were likely to enthuse people for, or commit them to, an awkward standstill. The reader will sense a spirit truly imbued with the principles of the Reformation also in the following informal assessment that Blumhardt confided to a friend:

> As regards the spirit of the Reformation, we need *more* than what it represented—not something different but more. Through no fault of their own, the ideas of the Reformation suffer from a certain poverty, inasmuch as they in no way exhaust the full content of Scripture. That is why a hanging on to the symbols (creedal statements) of the Reformation and an unwillingness to go beyond what these point to only does harm in our day. Pretty well all Reformation dogmas lack comprehensiveness; some are not fixed at all, for instance, the ministry of the keys. The symbols are, so to speak, completely silent about the Lord's coming and are not conducive to an attitude of expectancy, and yet we actually ought to be "like men waiting for their master" (Luke 12:35). Then, too, the symbols everywhere confuse his coming with death; in short, I could still cite much else, not in the sense of remonstrating with the Reformers but to show that, if we want to go by the word of Scripture, we have to teach and practice much more than they give us.

many cases we think too much of our own selves or at least of individual people. Also, many of us see Christianity too much as a divine institution concerned only with the individual and not as a great struggle for a tremendous, vast restoration of divine glory in all its fullness.

Hence, strangely enough, for us the place that should be occupied by the Lord's return is largely taken over by what Scripture calls the last enemy to be conquered: death. Where Peter says of our salvation that it is "ready to be revealed in the last time" (1 Pet 1:5), we put "our death" in place of "salvation." Where in the same chapter he assures us, "You will receive the goal of your faith, the salvation of your souls, when Jesus Christ is revealed" (1 Pet 1:7, 9), we translate it "when we die." Where Paul writes, "We are saved, but in hope" (Rom 8:24), we set our hope on death, forgetting that just before, Paul has stated, "We ourselves who have the first fruits of the Spirit, wait with eager longing for the revealing of the sons of God" (Rom 8:23, 19). Well, not quite like this. He actually says, "for our adoption as sons," but it is only on that great day that he expects that, as is shown by the following sentence, "We wait for the redemption of our bodies," that is, for the resurrection. Some may even take the "redemption of our bodies" to mean our death. Poor decaying body, what a horrible redemption that would be for you! While death, the reaper, still keeps mowing us down like grass, we sing (supposedly with Paul), "Where, O Death, is your sting?" (1 Cor 15:55). Yet what does Paul actually say? When the last enemy, death, will be conquered (1 Cor 15:26), when at the sound of the last trumpet the dead will be raised, when this perishable will clothe itself with the imperishable (1 Cor 15:52–53), then will be the time to ask, "Where, O Death, is your sting?" Where the Lord says, "Let your loins be girded and keep your lamps burning like men waiting for their master to return" (Luke 12:35), we put "waiting for death" instead.

I am putting it crassly to make the point clear. Though there is, to be sure, a good deal of Christian truth in all this, such artful rendering is dangerous. One can indulge in fantasies about how wonderful things will be on the other side of death, but . . . ? Here is a field where a merely presumed faith and all manner of self-deception can flourish freely with no fear of disillusionment—in *this* world! But what about the hereafter? At times, death may well have been treated too playfully; it has even been glorified as almost a savior.

To be sure, today death still remains for us the divide between seedtime and harvest, between struggle and victory. That is a remnant of truth left in the consciousness of all higher religions. But whereas those religions offer to a dying person a guarantee of blessedness that is illusory, Christianity can offer one that is certain. For every individual that guarantee is linked with what is the innermost content of all human history—with God's redemptive work from the very beginning. It is linked with the redemptive work of Jesus Christ, whose victory, grounded in his expiatory death and resurrection, will only be completed by his return. A person's salvation before that ultimate victory is nonetheless bound up with it, and so it should also be in the faith of a dying person. The Savior brings about redemption by nothing less than a removal of the prince (John 16:11) and god (2 Cor 4:4) of this present age and world order, thus initiating a new age, the kingdom of God and of heaven. As we know, when the New Testament speaks of "this world," it is not meant in a spatial sense—say, opposed to an "upper world"—as if the Lord only wanted to help some get from this world into the upper one. Rather, he wants to put an *end* to this world and bring in a new and different era, the age of God.

That is how the apostles thought. Paul writes, "The night is nearly over; the day is close at hand" (Rom 13:12). It is unfortunate that Luther took the liberty to translate it as, "The night is over; the day is here." Did he perhaps think that the Reformation had brought on the full light of day? At any rate he was mistaken, for the day Paul has in mind is the day of the Lord. We children of the day are still walking in the night, even though amid the darkness we can walk in the light. Yet our time is still nighttime, and we long for day to break.

The great struggle of God's kingdom for final victory moved Blumhardt deeply all his life. Already in the days of his great experiences he felt pained by the honor accorded to death and by the petty conception of Christianity as, so to speak, the private matter of each individual. The Lord had pleaded with his Father on behalf of his own "that they might all be one" (John 17:22)—not only united but *one*, and this is how it should be. Everyone should feel one with the church of the Lord—not isolated as an individual. And the church of the Lord does not have her mind on dying but on conquering; hers shall be the throne now occupied by death, as Paul writes, "If Death reigned . . . how much more will those who receive God's abundant provision of grace and of the gift of righteousness reign in life through Jesus Christ" (Rom 5:17).

When reading such passages, some will almost mechanically add the thought "after death." And, of course, Paul would readily agree to such an addition, but only on condition that we should not imagine we had exhausted the full content of his thought or even so much as grasped its real meaning. If we came to reign only through the good offices of death, that would properly elevate death to a position of honor and dignity. A child once put his finger on that conception, which is pretty general among us, by brilliantly reasoning that God must at one time have died—how else could he be in heaven!

But it is actually contrary to the Gospel to accept death so passively as an integral part of the heavenly kingdom. As far as humankind is concerned, Paul does not regard death as a law of nature, something ordained by the Creator, but as something that originated within human history and that humanity brought on itself. That is why it can also be overcome by a process within human history. As Paul says: "For since death came through a man [that is, through a man's guilt], the resurrection from death comes also through a man [that is, through a man's doing]" (1 Cor 15:21). To be sure, when Paul speaks of the coming in of death, he has in mind Adam, and when he speaks of the overthrow of death, he speaks of Christ. Still, it is a pity that by his overly free rendering of the text Luther blurred the apostle's thought.

What Paul says is that it is part of our human task and now that God has given us the true human in his Son, it is also within our power to free ourselves from the dominion of death, to which we recklessly submitted in the person of its first parent. This view assigns humankind a high dignity, a victor's task, and in Jesus Christ a lofty victor's right, which we are not always aware of. The Lord himself must have felt very deeply that one part of his task consisted in setting humankind free from its imprisonment by death. His miracles, too, whether performed by him or in his strength by his servants, were a campaign against the last enemy—death. Jesus declared war on death, and that was also one of the causes of his own death, "so that by his death he might destroy him who holds the power of death, that is, the devil" (Heb 2:14).

Such is the gist of Blumhardt's thoughts. He felt it to be the task of Christ's church to have her eyes fixed expectantly on the final victory, full of hope but also earnestly praying and fighting. I did not find it easy to elucidate these views as they deserve, but everybody that knows how Blumhardt's life and the life of his household was one constant, earnest struggle to bring that victory closer will understand it was a task I had to do. It does not trouble me that I had to adopt a somewhat didactic tone at times, for we owe it to the dignity of Holy Scripture that we expend a little sweat of the brow on studying it. And more important than the question of what edifying things can be said or thought about this or that text is the other question: What does Scripture actually say?

Something I do regret is that in order to be both brief and clear I have been somewhat brusque in my presentation. As I tried to show, all the truths here faulted on account of their one-sidedness may fall short of exhausting the depth of Christian thinking; however, set in the right context, they are and remain holy, precious, comforting truths. How all these matters were seen in Blumhardt's own house is reflected better in a poem Gottliebin Dittus wrote for the consecration of the new burial ground in Bad Boll on August 13, 1863. I am happy to insert it here since it is so free from whatever one-sidedness my presentation may unintentionally suffer from. It takes its cue from the account of the raising of Lazarus (John 11:1–44).

How my whole being quakes and shudders
As on this fallow ground I stand,
Where my frail tent and those of others
Who part in pain from this beloved land
Will come to rest at God's right hour,
Since here on earth Death still wields power.
How I can see the sisters weeping
For Lazarus, their brother dear!
So wept his friends, to see Death keeping
Their loved one's corpse in prison drear.
But he, the Lord, with eyes overflowing,
Felt holy anger in him growing.
At this place, too, just dedicated,
How many bitter tears will flow,
When one by one, as we are fated,
Our coffins through this gateway go.
The dead are silent, but the living
Must bear the burden of their grieving.
But hark! The Lord, grim Death defying,
Declares, "Your brother, he shall live!"
O Martha, hope! With trust undying
Await what great things God will give.
Though anxiously your hands still wringing,
To that bold word I see you clinging.

"On that day, yes, it will be given,"
Martha replies despondently.
Yet, to her heart, with anguish riven,
How welcome Jesus' word must be.
For all who now in death lie bound—
O blessed hope!—the trump will sound!
A solace to me too? Most surely
It is, hence patiently I wait,
By my Redeemer held securely,
Who for my guilt did expiate.
Yes, though I rest for many a year,
He from my grave will call me here!
He speaks, "I am the resurrection
And life." O Lord of life and light,
Thou endest our vile subjection
To Death and lead'st us out of night.
Though my poor shell must pass this portal,
It will yet rise to life immortal.
Yet will my heart not leave off quaking;
I look at Martha pensively.
Can she behold the far-off breaking
Of the great day she longs to see?
Poor soul, how very far away
Seems what you fain would glimpse today!
When they will lay my poor frame mortal
Into the darkness of my tomb,
Waits there no solace at that portal
To set me free from fear and gloom?
O Jesus, whom my heart desires,
Thy loving gaze fresh hope inspires.
"He that believes in me shall live
Although he die," thou dost proclaim.
What welcome cheer these bold words give,
Which promise us that longed-for aim!
They will becalm my anxious heart
When once my soul and body part.
No need for me in fear to tarry
Till the dread trump sounds from the sky!
When my poor body they will bury,
Will not my soul have soared on high?
For me the Lord died and ascended,
That I may live when life is ended.
Yet do men's woes call forth my pity,
For Death among them still holds sway.

They writhe distraught in dreary city
Till Death cuts short their fleeting day.
As their unhappy state I ponder,
In fields of grief my thoughts must wander.
But hear yet more the Lord's own story:
"He who believes and lives in me"—
Who lives, I think, when breaks in glory
The awesome day of destiny—
"Those living then shall. Death defying,
Inherit lasting life undying!"
How these words on my mind are flashing!
What wondrous things God has in store!
The gates of hell will come down crashing,
And death and tombs will be no more.
O soul, with glad anticipation
Await the day of consummation!
The dead will all be resurrected,
And those alive will never die.
To earthly pain no more subjected,
God's children raise a joyous cry.
All those who for his rule have striven
The Lord will take with him to heaven.
My heart revives, but truly merry,
O Jesus, it cannot yet be.
That man ends in a cemetery
Fills me with grief and misery.
Oh, may soon strike the blessed hour
When Death shall lose its fearsome power!
Thou, too, stoodst by a graveside, weeping,
And holy wrath arose in thee;
In thy great love thou hadst been keeping
An open ear for misery.
Thy heart first bled at mankind's suff'ring,
Then bled to death as holy off'ring.
Must not we also feel aggrieved,
Here standing on this somber ground,
That no relief can be perceived
To the affliction all around?
Hear us, O Jesus, our Salvation!
And rise with conqu'ror's indignation!
When wilt thou end our anxious waiting?
Take pity on us, hero strong!
See how in anguish unabating
The world has groaned and suffered long!

Rise up, the evil host to scatter,
Their every sword and spear to shatter!
When, by that gloomy graveside standing,
Thou didst call, "Lazarus, come out!"
Death set him free at thy commanding,
And perfect joy reigned all about.
So let thy word of liberation
Free from its chains the whole creation.

To conclude my presentation of Blumhardt's expectant, hopeful outlook (one could say: of Blumhardt's theology) I may perhaps be permitted to discuss one more point. When it comes down to it, the center of any theology, or teaching about God, is its perception of him. Blumhardt's thoughts, so full of hope and expectancy, may have struck us as great and far-reaching, and along with that also as clear and set in a grandiose context, yet they strike us as too bold, even though we may have little to say against their biblical foundation. Perhaps we do not sufficiently think of God as God, that is, in a way that is simple and childlike enough.

The seventeen centuries bare of miracles have left their mark on the thinking of Christ's church. If Jesus was right, our "Christian" world history has been consigning one generation after the other for the most part to perdition. This can hardly be seen as particularly wonderful and God-ordained. And yet we are in danger of half unconsciously making that state of affairs into a second canon, which we use to adjust and correct the thoughts of the true canon, Holy Scripture. We are in danger of believing God to be in many ways tied to the present state of things. Although we say that he allows it freely, of his own accord, we yet consider him bound by the great ground rules, foremost among which is that man dies, and just about also that he dies in unbelief. Things can go so far that the question might well be put to us: Do you really believe in the Son of God? Or do you think that God, especially after sending his Son, is so restricted or is willing to so restrict himself that all he wants to do henceforth is to fill the framework provided by the "iron law of necessity" with spiritual influence and solace and otherwise with fair promises for the hereafter? Do you believe that God created the world and sent his Son into it only to save a small bunch of lucky people? To be sure, it is to the little flock that he wants to give the kingdom (Luke 12:32)—that is, not salvation only but the *kingdom* and *dominion*, and this dominion will again be used to save the lost. Should it not be possible even today for the right hand of the Most High to change everything?

This may entitle me to touch on yet another train of thought, which came to Blumhardt from Scripture and his own experience. At one point Isaiah voices the hope that God will take away the "veil that shrouds all peoples" (Isa 25:7). That passage is what Paul has in mind when he says that God discarded (or stripped himself of) the "cosmic powers and authorities" (Col 2:15), those powers of darkness that had shrouded and concealed him from the nations. The veils or shrouds were like more or less ugly masks; some saw God as a bloodthirsty Moloch, others as serene Zeus, etc. But have not these veils in part returned? Do we simply believe in God the Creator of heaven and earth, in God the Father of our Lord Jesus Christ? Do we believe that, as the Lutheran catechism teaches, he is "gracious, merciful, patient, and full of loving-kindness" and that he has all power and freedom to demonstrate this his attitude to the whole human race in the full measure of his promise? Not the last of his mercies will be to remove one day all the veils that hide from us his majesty and love.

Viewing Blumhardt's great experiences as an organic whole, we shall, for one thing, come to understand the boldness of his hopes. For another, we shall perhaps sense that those experiences of his are ours too—a lofty divine challenge to us that we should take courage to hope and plead for the whole world.

I want to conclude this chapter, which is followed by a selection of Blumhardt's comments on the same subject, with a prophetic word that still reechoes in me from those wonderful Möttlingen days: "He will again have compassion on us; he will tread our iniquities under foot and will cast all our sins into the depths of the sea" (Mic 7:19).

13

Expectancy as Expressed in Blumhardt's Writings

OUR SELECTION STARTS WITH four questions Blumhardt put to some friends who (in conversation with others) had tried to undermine the biblical foundation of his thinking. Then follows a section from his essay on angels (now out of print), which sheds further light on matters we discussed above: his conceptions of God, God's nature and way of revealing himself. Next a lecture (slightly abridged, on the inner readiness of a Christian), given by Blumhardt on November 25, 1870, in the deaconesses' motherhouse in Karlsruhe. There he stresses the important position hope in the Lord should have in a Christian's whole attitude. Then follow two Saturday evening meditations on passages from Isaiah: 1) The feast for all peoples (Isa 25:6–9), on the lifting of the veil, and 2) the great flood of the Spirit (Isa 44:1–5), on the hoped-for pouring out of the Holy Spirit. Next, a talk on the lack of faith in the end time and finally a devotional talk on Jesus' joy as joy in a redemption of vast proportions.[1]

I. Blumhardt's Questions to His Friends

I ask you without bias either for or against, and I hope you will answer in a similar fashion too.

(1) What justification is there for assuming so decidedly that the original outpouring of the Spirit was something extraordinary, a gift bestowed only on the apostles of the beginning time? All the arguments reason puts forward could equally well be advanced,

---

1. Both talks are from *Blätter aus Bad Boll.*

either completely or in important respects, in favor of a *continuing* endowment with the Spirit.

(2) What justification is there for asserting so definitely that John 14:12 refers only to the apostles and excludes from the "greater works" any miracles?

(3) What justification is there for concluding from the qualitative difference between the apostolic and the post-apostolic age that such a comedown had to take place and was therefore pleasing to God? Coming as unexpected as it did, was it not rather a punishment?

(4) What justification is there for asserting so definitely that the power (I do not speak of it as "authority") to forgive sins was granted only to the apostles? And what justification is there for stating that the church is acting rightly in doing things differently than the Lord wished? Prove it by scriptural passages or by inferences from Scripture!

II. On Divine Manifestations.

(First section of Blumhardt's essay, "About Angels, According to Holy Scripture, With Special Reference to the Angel Appearing to Zechariah")[2]

> Text: Then an angel of the Lord appeared to him, standing at the right side of the altar of incense. And when Zechariah saw him, he was startled and was gripped with fear. But the angel said to him, "Do not be afraid, Zechariah, your prayer has been heard, and your wife Elizabeth will bear you a son, and you shall call his name John." (Luke 1:11–13)

Beloved in Christ, the fallen world is to receive help from on high. God himself wants to draw near to his children and offer them his helping hand. Many people ask, "But can that really be so?" And because they consider it unthinkable, without more ado they relegate stories of this kind to the mists of a fairy tale world, which, they assert, have somehow come to envelop all sacred history, including that of the Gospels. According to such people, the only conception of God to be countenanced by reason is one in which he remains forever concealed, unseen and unheard, manifesting neither his nature nor his person—assuming that he is conceived of as a personal God at all. They say that only the laws he has implanted in the world can and should constitute a true revelation of God to humanity. They might accept in addition some kind of divine rulership wrapped in deepest obscurity.

---

2. Editors' Note: *Über die Lehre von den Engeln* (Stuttgart: 1865) [*Concerning the Doctrine of Angels*].

They think God is much too great and exalted, much too holy and unfathomable to draw personally near to us humans.

To such a conception of God and his rule over the world we can, to begin with, only say that it takes God far away from us and tears him completely out of our hearts. Should the great, holy, unfathomable God have no way at all of drawing near to us? After placing human beings on earth to be brought up there, should God be unable to manifest himself without detriment to his own dignity and majesty? If so, God would be as good as non-existent! That is what it actually comes down to with those doubters. However, we humans need God, and, being needed, God gives himself to us as need requires.

You dear ones, let us imagine a number of children just above the age of tenderest babyhood and helplessness, whose parents put them in a splendidly appointed garden, to live in a house equipped with all niceties in regard to food, clothing, and pleasure. (That was actually the way humankind was originally put into the world, though to be sure he did *not* have everything so freely available to him in the beginning.) What would we think of parents who after preparing all that for their children would then leave the children completely to themselves and withdraw from any personal contact with them, in the way animals deal with their young after a very short time? What would we think of such parents if they would not even let other persons mind, help, and guide the children in their stead? How such children would be deprived emotionally! As time went on, how little joy and what painful longing the children would feel if, though surrounded by plenty, there was nothing to make them aware of their parents' love and affection aside from the outward things they saw around them! If in addition these children were to get into bad ways and come to serious harm through disregard of the directions and prohibitions they are given, if they were to ruin themselves in body and soul (particularly through the influence of stealthy enemies that are after them), what would we think of parents that completely refused to come to the rescue?

To be sure, such a comparison may strike doubters as childish, but that is only because, for one thing, they see our human existence as it now is as too remote from God. They think so in spite of the fact that we bear within us enough traces of our original godlikeness to enable us to understand when we are said to be created in the image of God and to have within us a breath and spirit akin to God's.

For another thing, these doubters view God as having no trace of heart or feeling in his relationship to those created in his image. Yet the very fact that God puts us into the world in a more helpless state to begin with than other creatures could be considered proof that he has reserved to himself the right to draw near to us personally. What is dormant in humankind was not to develop in the mechanical way of animal instincts; rather, it was to unfold, in a process involving thought and struggle, with an autonomy that under guidance blossoms into self-awareness. We experience often enough how persons growing up without any kind of guidance end up horribly brutalized, the degree depending on how much of the required help they have missed. How that helps to make us understand what Scripture relates of humankind's childhood: how God goes to meet the first man and woman in the primeval garden, cautions and disciplines them, how he still faces personally even the fratricide of Cain, and all the other things we find written there. Reading such stories with an open and unbiased mind, one will feel no resistance or opposition at all stirring in one's heart, for our sense that such communication between God and us is necessary in order to preserve the inward fellowship between both brooks no objection.

You dear ones, it is not hard to visualize a process by which a contact that occurred often and almost regularly to begin with, grew more and more rare as time went on. God cannot be expected to just throw himself at a people that rejects him. One could further conjecture that after memories of how God had once manifested himself among us humans had been passed on from one generation to another, succeeding generations would simply feel satisfied with the *memories,* with the consequence that direct manifestations of God became restricted to the most necessary. But as long as we still want to preserve a childlike attachment to God, can we possibly conceive of all divine manifestations as having petered out soon after those early days? Can we possibly admit that therefore all such manifestations as we continually read about in Scripture must without more ado be relegated to the world of fairy tales, that they have to be seen as childish or even as made up in a spirit of deceit and superstition? One could not possibly conceive of divine manifestations ceasing completely, especially when the time came for steps to be taken to save the human race from its irresistibly advancing ruin.[3] Therefore we can read everything reported in Holy Scripture with great inner freedom and assurance, including the story concerning the parents of John the Baptist.

The necessity of God's manifesting himself in some way is borne in upon men's hearts as an absolute requirement if man is to

---

3. Translator's Note: Blumhardt is referring to the angelic appearances preceding the births of Jesus and of John the Baptist.

be assured of his true salvation. That is why a time may yet come when divine manifestations are necessary once again, if only to shame and render harmless those who make bold to dismiss such things with contempt. As the great work of redemption draws to a conclusion, the struggle, far from abating, will become so fierce that the success of everything achieved so far will be called into question. It is written: "If the Lord had not shortened these days of tribulation, no human being would be saved" (Mark 13:20).

Hence let no one take away our childlike faith in those venerable accounts, so pure and noble in character, including the stories that preface the great message of salvation. Let us rather rejoice that we may visualize God as a father that looks after us and knows how to draw near to his frightened children where necessary and helpful to salvation. Consider well, you dear ones, what does a person have that neither can, nor wants to, believe that?

II. A CHRISTIAN'S INWARD READINESS

(Advent Meditation)

PRAYER: Lord Jesus, merciful Savior, who comes into the world to save sinners and therefore will come again to lead to yourself the living and the dead that are yours, in order to give them, after they have gone through much affliction, eternal peace and full salvation with you, be with us in this evening hour. Let our souls be lastingly uplifted through considering your Word. We look up to you for instruction and for comfort and encouragement as each of us needs it. Help us to choose the way leading to you or to hold to it and go forward on it, as we run our course down here. Let us be more and more so minded that when you, as promised, will return from heaven, we will be ready to welcome you with joy. Be gracious to us, Lord, and impart good things to us out of the fullness of your mercy. Give to us as we have need, as you have promised to your children who ask of you. Amen.

The day before yesterday we celebrated Advent, the first Sunday in the church year. In this context, let me speak to you concerning the following Scripture: "Let your loins be girded and your lamps burning, and be like those who are waiting for their master" (Luke 12:35).

May the Lord give us grace as we consider these words. May he build us up inwardly and above all help us to be more ready for his coming.

Beloved in Christ Jesus, Advent reminds us of the coming of the Savior, Jesus Christ, for whom the believing Israelites had been waiting for thousands of years. Advent reminds us that those who waited for the Lord in the earliest times did not wait in vain. That which they had believed in for thousands of years did come in the end, and those that had failed to experience it throughout all that long time and thus had died without seeing their hope fulfilled will also have gained their reward by his coming into the world (when it eventually took place). One day, after the consummation of all things in heaven, we shall see that more clearly than we presently can down here. He who came departed again and ascended to his father on high, yet with the promise that he would return and take to himself those who are his and that he would complete the redemption that for the time being he, too, had merely been able to *announce*. So we are once again asked to wait. We wait as those others waited before Christ came. We expect him who will return, and according to the Lord's words we have read, we are meant to wait for him.

Our church has placed the Advent Sundays at the beginning of the church year for the purpose of reminding us pointedly, every year anew, to wait for the Lord. Most people are inclined to skip this and pay but little heed to it in their hearts. And yet, judging from the many times that both the Lord and the apostles refer to it in Scripture, it must be a point of extraordinary importance.

The expectation of the Lord has weakened in Christendom because for nearly two thousand years so many have waited for it in vain. At least, that is the way it is being put. To be sure, the Lord has not come yet. But those who waited for him without seeming to gain anything from it will one day experience how the Lord will requite them for their expectancy, even when they are no longer down here. In any case, no upcoming generation is in a position to assume that the Lord will not come during its life span. On the contrary, his return is possible at any time, and I scarcely need to make clear to you dear ones how especially in our days we have good reason to remind ourselves of the Lord's injunctions to expect him.

Beloved, at Advent time we are well advised to think of Jesus' return and in particular of what he requires of us as we approach the day of his coming: what our attitude must be if that day is to be for us a day of salvation. May the words we have read tell us what belongs to a Christian's readiness for the Lord's return. The Lord is telling us three things. He says first: "Let your loins be girded," next, "Let your lamps be burning," and last, "Be like those waiting for their master." Let me speak to you more in detail about these three points. They tell us a lot, more than many of us might think when reading or hearing them.

The first thing the Lord says with respect to his return is: "Let your loins be girded." What does that mean?

When someone wanted to undertake a journey, especially in antiquity, the last thing he did before actually setting out was to gird his loins. That was because of the style of clothing the ancients wore. So when the Lord says, "Let your loins be girded; stand with your loins girded!" what he means is: "Make sure that you have seen to everything and have all your affairs in order, so that I can simply come and pick you up—just as those that have already girded themselves are ready for a journey." If somebody about to make a journey still has something to see to, something to arrange for the time of his absence, unfinished business to deal with, or has on his heart certain concerns he feels he must attend to before leaving—as long as he is still occupied with such matters, he cannot set out; not feeling ready for the journey, he does not gird his loins. Consider how detrimental the delay can be to him—to be thus held back!

Beloved ones, you can already see what the Lord wants to say to us with this metaphor. He wants us to be ready to leave at all times, so that we can go forth unhindered to meet the Lord when he comes. Just as we are often challenged to be ready to die, so the Lord warns us here to be ready when he comes to leave behind all we have been involved in. We should not have a great deal of unfinished business, which would then cause us problems; as much as possible we should set everything right with everybody, lest things we have missed rise up to disturb us when the cry rings out: "The Lord is coming." We should not be in a situation where we then have to say with trembling, "I still have to do this and that; there are so many obligations I still have to fulfill; I am still burdened by so many sins and trespasses that accuse me and take away my courage in the presence of the Lord." That must not be; rather, we must be done with all such things, if it is to go well with us. Mindful that time is short, we must not start a lot of things we will not be able to finish, for it will take us away from what is most important. We ought not to be sluggish or slow in seeing to what is most necessary, so that we can be unworried, calm, and peaceful. We should not fritter away our time with frivolous and worldly concerns, which only serve to estrange us from the divine for which we ought to prepare ourselves. We should be intent on bringing every matter to completion, thereby showing that our highest goal is to meet the Lord.

Above all, that means that our hearts may not hold on to anything that lessens our love to the Lord, that we must have taken leave of everything, as though it had but little value. Having left it all behind, we are as one standing with our loins girded when the Lord comes. If our heart is still bound to something, it disturbs our relationship to the Lord and takes away some of our joy in him, so there is not much to our readiness. The tie keeps holding us back and prevents us from making headway. If we are not free from the things of this world, we are liable to clutch at them frantically, be it vain mirth and pleasure, money and possessions, or glory and honor, or maybe, too, nobler things, like arts and sciences, which still, however, belong to this world. As long as we are still grieved and saddened by the loss of what we have to leave and have not put it behind us, we cannot yet gird ourselves; we are not ready. To many of us the Lord may yet come like a thief at night, as he himself says many times.

When this occurs, many of us will lament: "Look at all the things I could still do, and now I have to die!" I once knew a highly skilled physician, a friend of mine and a dear, kind-hearted man. He felt his end approaching, and it grieved him very much. "Alas," he lamented, "now I have learned so much and put so much effort into it, have gathered so much experience, have such a good position, and could still do so many things. Now, still young in years, I have to depart." That he had to leave behind his knowledge and expertise, all of it of noble character and contributing to humanity's well-being, and go hence—it was almost more than he could cope with. It was moving to listen to him, but true readiness for death was given to him only when he had let go of everything. Only then did he find complete peace.

On the other hand, there are many people for whom it actually becomes easier to get ready when they see their end draw near. I experienced that some years ago with a lady from the upper classes who died in my house. She was still young, unusually gifted and cultured and of an especially refined spirit. In addition she was an art connoisseur of the first rank and a pianist who could sweep an audience off its feet—all this in spite of a frail body. She said herself that she came into my house only to die. No sooner was she there than her affectionate father, wanting to provide her still with entertainment, had a piano taken to her room—an instrument she used to play with an astounding agility. The piano in place, the sick lady tottered to it and began to play—a chorale! Everything else was forgotten and had lost its attraction for her. A chorale such as "My life is only Jesus" was now her one and all; everything else had gone. I shall never forget the impression that made on the grieving father, who for the sake of his talented daughter had spared no expense. To be sure, already in her good days and alongside her other interests she had turned to the Savior in her heart. But what readiness, beloved ones! She died only three days later, to go where the deepest of all harmonies are heard.

To be sure, in this world we are not required to let go of everything while we live and circumstances do not make it necessary. But there is an *inward* letting go that can take place even when we must *outwardly* still hold on—even with interest and zeal. That occurs when our hearts, fully aware of something higher, take up such an attitude to everything that we can let go of it all at any moment, as we saw in the case of that lady. Even when we are vigorously and strenuously occupied in many ways, whether practicing our profession or just earning our living, we must not get so attached to it all that our hearts will hang on to it when the hour comes to leave it behind. We can say of somebody that he has his loins girded, meaning that he is ready to depart, if his position is such that he can easily be called away from everything, though he may seem to be wholly engrossed in it.

When people who know the Lord face death, death itself often seems to help the person to let go of everything, including parents and children, relatives and friends. It is as though the Lord himself were at hand to get his people into the right attitude of readiness.

Things may be harder if circumstances force a person still in the full vigor of life to make up his mind in advance to part from everything inwardly while waiting for the Lord's call to surrender it also outwardly, in whatever way required. Yet the Lord wants us to take his return so seriously that, not knowing either the day or the hour, we nevertheless stand with our loins girded, as men that have cut loose from everything. Even before the Lord comes, we may have occasion to surrender everything for his sake: father and mother, brothers and sisters, house and property, wife and children, home and fatherland. Anyone holding on to this or that and therefore unable to gird himself as one ready to be called away at any time is liable to discover that he is one of those of whom the Lord says: "He that loves his life will lose it" (John 12:25).

As for today, it seems as if the Lord wants us to prepare to be truly ready for his return. So many are right now losing everything through this great and devouring war.[4] There is much we do not even care to look at because we have to surrender it—much that we thought we could never bear parting from. Along with sacrifices of all kinds we in our German land must hand over fine and

---

4. Editors Note: This meditation was delivered on November 25, 1870. This was during the second stage of the Franco-Prussian war (i.e., after the capture of Napoleon Bonaparte III and the establishment of the Third Republic) in which the war had expanded across much of France and had led to the siege of Paris.

beloved sons, brothers, fathers, friends, and husbands. Over there beyond the Rhine River even more is demanded; at many places they are losing, along with their sons, also goods and chattels and everything they have—even, as many think, their homeland. It is in the first place for the fatherland that all the sacrifices are being made; for its sake one has to stand with loins girded. What helps us feel better about it is that we may trust that many of those who went out have been made ready for death and are not held back inwardly by anything troubling them.

However, our times are likely to get still worse, and in the end it may become necessary for the sake of the Lord to let go of everything and thus stand with one's loins girded. How serious those times will be, whenever they come, and how perilous if we do not stand with loins girded as people ready to leave everything behind! When it comes to the point of letting go of everything for the sake of confessing the Lord—and such trials are bound to come toward the end—how can we come through unscathed if we still cling to something we cannot give up or let go of? If we are still caught up in this or that—how liable we are to be unfaithful to the Savior, cowardly in our confession, and soft in tribulation! All is lost for whoever is found unready when the Lord comes. The Lord is interested only in those that have girded their loins and are truly ready to let go of everything if only they may welcome him, their deepest longing.

Let us now consider the second point in our text: "And let your lamps be burning."

The lamps should burn! The picture makes us think of someone who keeps a lamp burning at night to scare away thieves that might want to break in, and to be ready for unforeseen happenings. We also need light so as not to be duped by the enemy, who can most easily mislead us where there is no light. A person bereft of the higher light easily gets caught up in false ideas, views, or trends, while believing himself on the right track. In reality he gets lured into extremely dangerous ways, which are liable to corrupt his whole attitude and his relation to the Savior. In those last times it will be most necessary to keep one's eyes open so as to perceive quickly where the Lord is and where he is not, also what is in the Spirit and what is not. In the end God will afflict the unrighteous with "a strong delusion, to make them believe what is false, so that all may be brought to judgment who do not believe the truth but have pleasure in unrighteousness" (2 Thess 2:11–12). Then too, "false prophets will arise . . . so as to lead astray, if possible, even the elect" (Matt 24:24). To prevent the latter from happening, we must keep our lamps burning. Our own generation especially has in many ways become estranged from the true light. Oh, that the Lord would help it through his Holy Spirit to regain greater clarity, so that it may perceive in everything what is right and may not become entangled in dangerous errors!

It also seems to me that by exhorting us to keep our lamps burning the Lord is hinting that he is ready to give us light, particularly with a view to the serious times to come—a light we are to tend faithfully and must not allow to go out through disloyalty, negligence, and other proofs of worldly-mindedness. After all, the only lamps we can let burn are those we *have* and which the Lord gives us. What I want to say is that we may yet expect light-imparting times of grace.

We can discover still more in Jesus' exhortation to "let our lamps be burning," for we are always entitled to interpret metaphors in various ways. The light, being ever within our reach through the Gospel, shall burn in us; we ourselves are to be light, and a burning and shining light at that. In the Sermon on the Mount the Lord says to his disciples: "You are the light of the world" (Matt 5:14), and he adds: "Let your light so shine before men that they may see your good works and give glory to your Father who is in heaven" (Matt 5:16). That should be so always, but it will be especially needful in the last days. It is they that the Lord has in mind when he warns in our passage: "Let your lamps be burning." We truly ought to take that to heart in our time! There are so few Christians in whom the light is fully visible. It is the light we can receive through knowing Jesus Christ, through faith in him, the Savior of the world, who became man, died for our sins, rose from the dead, and has been proclaimed to us as Lord over all. This light can be imparted when the points of faith urged on us by the Gospel are not just recited mechanically but are allowed to light up the soul, so that it shines and beams. The more deeply a Christian lays hold of and appropriates all that pertains to the Lord Jesus, the more light-filled his whole being is or ought to be. Yet so many people have not even been reached by the rays of the Gospel, let alone penetrated. And how weakly and feebly it gleams even in the few that do let it in! Let us consider how hard it will be to come safely through the trials awaiting us in the last days if one is not really familiar with the light of the Gospel and therefore neither joins the ranks of those confessing it nor gives evidence of its wholesome influence on one's own person and behavior. How will it go with such people when the Lord comes? Hence the Lord's earnest warning, "Let your lamps be burning!"

Beloved, you want to be God's children. Let me ask you: Are you really burning lamps? Lamps to make people with no lamps stop and stare in astonishment? Lamps bright enough to make others, too, see the way? Lamps that contrast with the darkness and blackness in which we find the great majority and in many cases even people confessing to belief in Jesus? Are you lamps that burn in the way indicated by the Lord? Some will scarcely muster the courage to answer yes to this question, and many are simply not able to answer, for to ask somebody to let his lamp burn who does not have one is expecting too much of him. And yet, all who do not know Jesus and do not accept with a glowing heart that which has been said about him and by him are without a lamp. They do not have one, so we cannot say to them, "Let your lamp be burning."

But you that are gathered here do, I think, believe in the Savior and his word; you do not resist that which is proclaimed to you about the good Savior, Jesus Christ. You should therefore have a lamp in you. But my question is: Do you let it burn? Does it shine in you and out from you? There is a kind of hand lantern with a little door in front. When the door is open, the light within shines out, but if it is closed, the flame, though it is there, sheds no light. So what kind of lamps are we? Do we keep our light covered so that it cannot shine? Or do we let it burn freely and openly, so that we can see our way and others around us also benefit from this lamp of ours?

O you dear ones, what shall I say to you to bring it about that the light in you is not placed under a bushel (as the Lord puts it) but set on a lampstand, so that everybody can see it and your lamp may truly shed light? To begin with, it demands that one confesses freely to what one has in Christ, according to the proverb, "Where the heart is full, the lips overflow." We must be able to declare and avow for the comfort and encouragement of others what a treasure we have in the Gospel. Instead of being secretive about it, as if it were a clandestine matter, we must be able to witness in a childlike, open, joyful, free, and loving way to what kind of person we are through the Gospel, and to the solace it offers for time and eternity, of which the expectation of Christ's return is a part. In the end time one will, as at the time of the apostles, have to confess one's faith when summoned before authorities hostile to Christ, also if it means risking goods and chattels or even life and limb. The one who can and does do all this lets his lamp burn, and by the light of that lamp untold numbers of people are apt to be stimulated, encouraged, stirred to imitation, and helped to find salvation in their hearts—the loveliest fruit of having the Gospel. Blessed is he whom the Lord finds awake. But if all this is lacking in us who want to be the Lord's, how is it going to be with us when the Lord comes in his sublime glory?

The Lord's injunction, "Let your lamps be burning" requires us to stand as lights in the world in an even fuller sense. I want to take the above quoted words of Jesus to his disciples, "You are the light of the world" as the starting point for what I am going to say. These words remind me of what I discussed with you once before this year, when in an evening talk I expounded to you the Beatitudes. These, standing at the beginning of the Sermon on the Mount (Matthew 5–7), name the Christian attitudes and virtues that should form the basic character of the disciples and for the sake of which the disciples are called blessed. And when immediately afterward the Lord declares, "You are the light of the world," it makes it clear that it is through the attitudes and virtues listed that the disciples become and are such a light.

If the disciples are to keep their lamps burning, precisely these attitudes and virtues must be the light in which they have to stand. The one the Lord calls blessed and who stands as a light in this world is not someone raising himself up in any way (though he might plead his righteousness or even piety and faith), nor is it anybody that is selfish, hard, ruthless, or contentious. On the contrary, those called blessed are the poor in spirit, whose attitudes and mind-sets he describes in detail. The poor in spirit are also those that mourn and therefore are gentle; they hunger and thirst for righteousness and therefore are merciful; they are pure in heart and therefore also peacemakers. The disciples are to shine as a light by showing these qualities; it is then that they "let their lamps burn," as our text puts it.

There are ever so many lamps lit in the Beatitudes, and they should all be burning in us. I can almost see before me the seven-armed candlestick that stood in the Lord's temple in Jerusalem: spiritual poverty—one; mourning and gentleness—two and three; hunger and thirst for righteousness, combined with mercy—four and five; finally purity of heart and peaceableness—six and seven. What a wonderful array of lights on one candlestick! What a lovely sight even when just the three most conspicuous ones—gentleness, mercy, and peaceableness—are lit, in particular when they burn so brightly that everybody perceives them and is affected by them.

Should such a light remain a thing unfamiliar to disciples of Jesus? Do they not hold to a Gospel that makes righteous also the godless and sinners, that leads from damnation to salvation, from hell to heaven? Should not such a Gospel kindle in them a light that burns with sheer longing for righteousness, with sheer love and kindness to fellow creatures? Having received grace, mercy, and salvation, should they not, as blessed—and blessed undeservedly, out of pure grace—shine and beam in the world like the sun?

They really should be able to. How ill it befits them if in this respect they resemble a closed lantern, which, though alight within, casts no beam outside.

The Lord lets us know how tremendously important and necessary it is for his disciples to let their lamps be burning brightly, particularly in the last time preceding his return. There will otherwise be such black darkness and confusion in the world that simple folk who cannot make a go of it without having others to lean on will no longer know what to do amidst the ever increasing gloom and distress—unless they catch sight of children of light, whose goodwill and kindness they can hold on to. But if then precisely those that have light shroud themselves in sheer black darkness through hardness, harshness, severity, contentiousness, and loveless exclusiveness, if they so lock away what light they have that one cannot possibly find the way in their company—of what use are they to the Lord? And when he finally comes, what will he have to say to such disciples who have hidden their talent in the ground, who, instead of shining as a light, have walked about robed in darkness?

What I am saying here agrees completely with the words of the apostle: "Let your gentleness be manifest to all; the Lord is near" (Phil 4:5). Let us practice becoming ever more gentle toward everybody, also toward strays and sinners and even unbelievers, so that they may all perceive a light in us, in contrast to the gloom, darkness, repulsiveness, and superciliousness generally met with. That is how we shine as lights, how we become men who, as the Lord says, let their lamps burn and so stand ready for the day of his return.

Let us now turn to the third exhortation in our text: "And be like those waiting for their master to return."

One or the other might say that having your loins girded and your lamps burning shows plainly enough that you are people waiting for their master. However, not all that are ready to follow the Lord's call and not all that have their lamps burning really do wait for the return of the Lord. We know—do we not?—we must be ready also for death, and to have one's lamp burning is a Christian's general duty. Hence it is possible for us to do both these things without actually waiting for Christ's coming. Yet the Lord's will for us is that we should *expect* him; this is what he tells us quite explicitly. Above all, we must really *believe* in his return, must bear it on our hearts as a matter of importance and as necessary for the consummation of his kingdom. We must not allow the belief in Christ's return, as he announced it to us when he parted from the earth and his apostles, to be just an indifferent article of faith for us. If we want to really be waiting for our master's return, we must at least be able to think of it, speak of it, and testify to it; we must have a real feeling for it, must let a yearning for it spring up within us. This we must do in full opposition to the present general attitude in Christianity, which almost without exception observes a strange silence, an unbelieving silence, as though secretly not really reckoning with a return of Christ.

Over against this, the Lord declares in words that apply to whatever time we live in: "Be like those waiting for their master!" Sublime thoughts are going through the Lord's mind. His coming is to end all the distress in the world and check every sorrow; humankind is to be redeemed from all evil and from the evil one, from Satan. Should that not move our hearts and make us yearn for it? And if it is right and good, can it be right for us to remain indifferent to the return of Jesus, thinking in our hearts: "If he comes, fine; if not, that's all right too. Enough for us to live in such a way that we come to a blessed end." Of course, dear ones, do see to it that your end is blessed. But Jesus wants more. It is not just my and your redemption he has in mind—he wants to redeem the whole world, wants to put a complete end to the evil ruling there. He wants to *liberate* the whole world, walking as it does in sheer godlessness; where one unhappy generation succeeds the other; where ever anew a generation goes down in a welter of pain, distress, tribulation, and unending woe, only to make room for another, which is bound to suffer the same fate. This being so, should the expectation of a total change be a matter of indifference to us? Do we want the conditions, as we know and see them around us, to go on *ad infinitum*? Will not the whole dismal business—the way we all carry on with each other—have to come to a stop at some point? Everyone in whom there is still a spark of love for his neighbor or a sense of what Christ sacrificed when he atoned for the whole world should ardently desire the great Savior and Redeemer to complete his work. Yet how else can that come about than by his descending from heaven as a Lord who will change everything at one blow?

If we consider this aright, it surely ought to be our desire to have Jesus come down from heaven into this wicked world and do away with all the evil, whose strength and might he, Jesus Christ, experienced on his own person. That alone ought to awaken in us the wish that things in the world might not forever be such that the most righteous of all men is liable to be abused and rejected with horrible cruelty, not only by individuals but by the masses. Indeed, you dear ones, we ought to be people that wait with profound longing for the Lord to come and render true and complete help—not only to the living but also to the dead. How greatly the latter yearn for this is hidden from our sight, but we can have an inkling of it if we bear in mind how their perfection, as we know, is actually bound up with their *resurrection*, which should likewise have its beginning with the advent of Christ.

Some people, of course—just to mention this in conclusion—do not quite see why it should be so important for a Christian to expect the Lord in the way indicated, as long as nothing else is wanting in his Christian conduct. But this is just the point: His entire Christian attitude will be different, according as he does or does not cherish the hope in question. It cannot be otherwise than that this hope accords preeminently with the mind of Christ the Savior, who carries all his brothers and sisters, the whole of humanity, compassionately on his heart and for its sake is ready to sacrifice everything, even his life. That mind comes to life also in us when the return of Jesus, necessary to complete the redemption of all creation, becomes important to us.

And how is it with our praying, our fulfilling of Jesus' command to "pray always and never give up" (Luke 18:1)? What is it that we should bear on our hearts with such ceaseless, burning zeal and pray that it might finally be given? Is it not, once again, the redemption of all creation from its groaning? Let us look at the model prayer the Lord taught us to pray. It begins with the words: "Hallowed be your name, your kingdom come, your will be done on earth as it is in heaven," and it ends: "Deliver us from evil" (Matt 6:9–13). Can we pray a true "Our Father" if we do not have our mind on the return of Jesus, which will mean the *completion* of the kingdom of God? We see, too, how it is in *answer to our prayer* that everything must be given; so how can it be given if, not considering it important, no one prays for it? Finally, our whole readiness for the Lord, or for death, suffers when we consider Christ's return remote. Conversely, if his return is a lively concern of ours, it spurs us powerfully to show more patience, sobriety, faithfulness, and prudence, as well as more love and peaceableness, during the time of waiting.

A lot more could still be said to point out to Christians the importance of becoming people who wait for their master. Let us obey the Lord and daily pay heed to his call "Watch!" lest we unwittingly turn into people who, failing in expectancy and thus lacking true readiness, are in danger of losing everything when the Lord actually does appear in his glory.

Let us therefore be mindful of Jesus' exhortation to wait for him. Let us believe in his return, which holds out such solace. Let us talk about it, and may our hearts derive fresh strength from the promise that all the sinful goings on, all the abominations committed on earth, will come to an end completely, that one day the whole might and malice of darkness will be destroyed and everything in heaven and on earth and under the earth will become one in pure joy and unity. That is what our eyes ought to be set on. If our mind is firmly fixed on it, we are like men waiting for their master, as the Lord requires of us.

O beloved, if my few feeble words have succeeded in making you desire to be henceforth like men waiting for their master with loins girded and lamps burning, I give thanks to the Lord for it. Oh, how badly everything needs to change!

Just to mention one thing: Let's assume that peace is restored. Is that going to make the world better? It will still be the same old misery. Malice and sin in every form, grief and tribulation, despair in the hearts of thousands—it will all remain unchanged. To be sure, peace is better than war, and in that sense may the Lord grant us the peace for which we pray so longingly. But it will not mean that we then have everything. We will have true peace only when Jesus will manifest himself in his glory and will lead the whole creation he has purchased with his blood out of sin into the glorious freedom of the children of God (Rom 8:21).

May the Lord give grace that when he looks down at his descent from heaven, we may be among those who straightway meet his eye, standing with loins girded and lamps burning, like men waiting for their master. Would that he might say to us then, "It is to you, to you that I bring comfort. I can see: You are ready; your lamps burn; you are waiting. Come, rise up to me, as you have been promised" (1 Thess 4:17). "Yes," we cry out to him, "come, Lord Jesus! Put an end to all the misery on earth!" Amen.

CONCLUDING PRAYER: Merciful Lord, we have pondered your word to the best of our understanding. By comparing it with everything else we hear from your mouth, with all that Scripture sets clearly before us, we shall surely be able to catch your meaning. Grant that what we have heard and learned may bear fruit in us. We would indeed stand with our loins girded and our lamps burning when you come, so that it can be seen that we are expectant people. Free us, O Lord, of everything that would stand in the way of such readiness. We want to wait for you, shining with humility, gentleness, mercy, and peaceableness, as well as with patience in persecution and tribulation—shining before you and before each other. Help us to find that, O Lord! We want to believe and cleave to your promise that you will come in the end and deliver the entire world from all evil. Help us to stand firm in patience and faith, in love and hope, that you may recognize us when you come and receive us into your glory. Oh, help us come to this! Amen.

IV. The Feast for All Peoples and Its Effects.

(Saturday Evening Meditation)

Text: On this mountain the Lord of hosts will make for all peoples a feast of rich fare, a banquet of pure wine, of fat things full of marrow, of well-matured wine strained clear. On this mountain he will take away the covering that is cast over all peoples, the veil that is spread over all nations, for he will swallow up death forever. And the Lord God will wipe away the tears from all faces; he will remove the disgrace of his people from all the earth, for the Lord has spoken. On that day they will say: "Lo, this is our God for whom we wait, and he will save us. This is the Lord for whom we wait; let us rejoice and exult in his deliverance." (Isa 25:6–9)

These words of the prophet Isaiah refer to the coming consummation of God's kingdom on earth. They are not presented as spoken by the mouth of the Lord but rather as the prophet's own prayerful and instructive utterances. He started the chapter with words of prayer: "O Lord, you are my God. I exalt you; I praise your name, for you do marvelous things" (Isa 25:1) and goes on praying for another four verses. He turns in prayer to the God who would ordinarily put his word into the prophet's mouth. His heart is so full of all that he was usually called upon to proclaim that his praying lips overflow with hymns of praise and thanksgiving for what the Lord has in mind for his people and all nations on earth.

Then, from verse 6 on, he speaks as one teaching and instructing. As said before, he does not speak as one into whose mouth the Lord has put his word; we are not told as usual: "Thus says the Lord: I will," etc.—rather, we hear the prophet's own words. As he starts to speak, he refers to God in the third person: "On this mountain the Lord of hosts will make for all peoples a feast of rich fare," etc. That lets us see how with the prophets the entire person has become permeated by the divine concerns, regarding which God has put so many messages directly into their mouths. That is why even passages such as these should still be regarded as utterances that the *Lord* has put, if not into the prophet's mouth, at any rate into his heart. They are not words of a man that reasons and calculates but of one filled with the spirit of God. Hence he utters the full truth and in such a way that, though it is seemingly he that speaks, one is nevertheless left with the impression that the

Lord is the speaker. Hence our passage ends with, "For the Lord has spoken" (Isa 25:8).

Now it is clear that this prophecy has not yet been fulfilled; it is *awaiting* fulfillment. To make the meaning clear and adapt it to the thinking of people living in his time and in succeeding centuries, the prophet has to use the Mount Zion as the basis for his hopeful thoughts and prophecies. But there is no need to assume that it is on that mountain in Palestine that what he foretells will one day take place. The land is now in ruins; Mount Zion is almost wholly worn away, and the people are scattered outside the Promised Land. Now the prophecy will be fulfilled wherever the God of Israel is a vital concern among men and wherever this God has his people. To be sure, through Jesus Christ's suffering and death in Jerusalem an important part of the prophecy has indeed been fulfilled right in that place, namely the actual preparation of the good that is in store for all peoples. Spiritually speaking, it is to Zion and Jerusalem that all peoples must go for salvation, for there it has been achieved for all, and from there it goes forth. But now it may be had wherever the Gospel is proclaimed purely and clearly, for the Savior wants to go with his own "even unto the end of the world" (Matt 28:20), that is, to the ends of the earth, and wherever he is, there is salvation, there is Zion, there is Jerusalem.

Now what are we being promised?

(1) "The Lord of hosts will make for all peoples a feast of rich fare, a banquet of pure wine, of fat things full of marrow, of well-matured wine strained clear."

That is the first point. It tells us metaphorically of the pure spiritual food the God of Israel will one day offer to all peoples on earth—pure, strong food, marrow being considered the most strengthening of foods and matured wine on the lees the purest drink. In a certain sense the Savior has already fulfilled this. As noted above, during his time here on earth he prepared the food: He gave the bread, that is, himself; he gave the meat, again himself, and the true wine, his blood. That is why he declares: "I am the true bread, which came down from heaven; . . . he who eats me will live for ever" (John 6:51, 58) and, "He who eats my flesh and drinks my blood has eternal life" (John 6:54). In this way he prepares the feast that is to refresh and strengthen all. It is to be shared by *all* peoples on earth; it is prepared for *all*; as time goes on, *all* are to partake of it. The whole earth shall become a paradise, a holy land, where all souls will be given the same spiritual food. Grown by the Savior in the Promised Land, this food is to be distributed over the whole earth until all men have it; over all the earth a table will be spread for all peoples. That will be the great quickening and strengthening of souls promised to all peoples; it takes place where the Gospel is preached. Since it is still not proclaimed everywhere and not all peoples as yet share in the feast, the prophecy has not yet come to a truly large-scale fulfillment.

It is a fact that the Gospel has to be accompanied by a special divine power, the Holy Spirit. The Holy Spirit is what makes the Gospel truly enjoyable; through the Holy Spirit, which illuminates the Gospel in men's hearts, all peoples on earth are to be revitalized, so that, having received new life from God, they are given joy in their hearts. That is why other prophets express in non-metaphorical language the same message that Isaiah conveys here through the picture of a great feast of nations. Joel, for instance, hears the Lord promise: "I will pour out my spirit on all flesh" (Joel 2:28). That is the Lord's intent and purpose. How happy it makes us that the Father in heaven bears such a plan in his heart—not only to set in motion but also to bring to completion when the time comes.

(2) When that takes place, the following will happen as well: "On this mountain he will take away the cover that is cast over all peoples, the veil spread over all nations." Here again it is obvious: The earthly Mount Zion is not where all peoples are, and all peoples are not where the earthly Mount Zion is. But it is on that mountain that the cover and veil begins to be removed from the peoples, and it was Jesus Christ who began it. At that time something was cleared away, though not from *all* peoples, but it must still be removed from *all* nations throughout the world. This something Isaiah calls the "cover" cast over all peoples and the "veil" spread over all nations.

Up to now this cover and veil is still in place almost everywhere, and we are painfully aware of the shroud enveloping us, too. We are still not living in a divine, wholesome, and pure air. Elsewhere, too, Scripture speaks of evil spirits that rule in the atmosphere and are still around even the children of God, for which reason these have to struggle against them. Truly we are involved in a dark cloud cover; there is still a lot of sinister power in and around us. We have much more of a spiritual shroud over and about us than we are aware of. How powerless we are in every way; how little light is there in our spirits and how little freedom in our hearts! How much pressure our souls have to endure! Our thoughts are often so befogged that we cannot grasp even the simplest things. There are people that simply cannot be reached, so boarded up, covered over, veiled, and shrouded are they.

Such conditions are all demonic covers and shrouds, cast by the dark power's cunning over all of us, even in Christendom. True, in the early days these had been removed among the believers, but later on, side by side with faith, a cover came to be spread even over believing Christians. What is finest and noblest is now under a shroud, inasmuch as it is unable to rise up in strength. Oh, if you only knew how much is still covered over in and among men and how much has still to be cleared away before the path to Jesus' mercy is opened up for them. The merit of Jesus Christ and reconciliation through his blood simply remain inaccessible for many people; grace and forgiveness of sins are veiled to them. When they have it proclaimed to them, they fall into despair and think they cannot possibly accept any of it. There simply *is* something like a cover and shroud. That is why there is a lot we cannot understand, and even when we do understand the outer words, we still cannot possess and enjoy their meaning.

But now look at what is promised: Every demonic covering is to be torn off. One day there will be such a tremendous trumpet blast of grace that all the devils have to flee, unable to endure it, and we will be free! Just as the sick and possessed were set free at the time of Jesus, one day the peoples on this earth will be liberated from their demonic cover and veil. To be sure, we are not able to grasp how that will happen, and even if I could tell you this or that, you would still not understand it. But ponder the matter itself, just this one thing: What a mercy it will be throughout the world of nations when one day all people will be delivered from demonic influences. That will take place thanks to the delicious food Jesus will serve. How precious is the nourishment we have in Jesus and in everything we hear about and from him! And when, to complete it all, every cover will be gone, so that the full value of this food can be perceived and it can all be tasted and partaken of—what joy that will be!

(3) The removal of the cover and veil from the peoples will bring about a third result: "He will swallow up death for ever." All these coverings are offshoots of death; they make us dead and insensitive to everything divine. Once these covers go, death, too, will go. Up till now, death has swallowed up everything, but in the end death itself will be swallowed up for good. And what has once been swallowed is no longer there; it is dead. Thus, one day death will be done away with—whether in this age or not for a long time to come is not for me to determine.

But even in this present world God may well grant us a foretaste of how it will be when death is gone. People regard the existence of death as a process of nature. That is why it must be shown: No, death has no place here! That is why the prophecy is so worded that everything, including the abolition of death, is presented as still taking place in this age, or at least as beginning in it. If there is still a parting from the earth after that, it will no longer be death but more like a being carried off, surrounded by sheer peace and life.

(4) Once all covers and all death are gone, pain and suffering, too, will be gone—all those many torments and illnesses. And when all pain, all sorrow, and all death agonies are gone, what has happened then? Then tears, too, will be gone. That is why we read as a fourth point:

> The Lord God will wipe away the tears from all faces and will remove the disgrace of his people from all the earth. The Lord has spoken. On that day people will say, "See, this is our God for whom we wait; he will help us. This is the Lord for whom we wait. Let us rejoice and exult in his deliverance." (Isa 25:8–9)

In brief, it will all end up in a great exultation of deliverance, where everybody will joyously point to the One who brought it about, saying, "See, that is our God; he alone has brought us to this point. Without him all our yearning and waiting for deliverance from tears and from the disgrace of sin and death would have been in vain, and the pall and shroud of darkness spread over us all would never have been removed." That is what they will say at that time; they will rejoice and exult in the deliverance he has wrought.

To be sure, we rejoice even now as we recognize the Lord Jesus aright, yet how much sorrow has remained along with the joy! But once we have joy without sorrow—how glorious that will be! We may expectantly wait for it, for "He will help us!" Indeed, the Lord has said it; he will do it too. Amen.

V. The Great Floodtide of the Spirit

(Saturday Evening Meditation)

> Text: But now listen, O Jacob my servant and Israel, whom I have chosen. Thus says the Lord who made you, who formed you and from the womb has helped you: Fear not, O Jacob my servant and you devout one, whom I have chosen. For I will pour water on the thirsty land and streams on the dry ground; I will pour out my spirit on your offspring and my blessing on your descendants, so that they will spring up like grass in a meadow, like willows by flowing streams. This one will say, "I am the

Lord's"; another will call himself by the name of Jacob. Still another will write on his hand "The Lord's" and will be called by the name Israel (Isa 44:1–5).

It is to Jacob or Israel that the Lord here speaks, that is, to the people stemming from Jacob, also called Israel. To them the Lord speaks. This is not just a turn of speech, there really is in Israel a God who speaks, even if he only speaks through angels as representatives of his person or through prophets filled with his spirit. They speak just as though it were the Lord himself; their own person quite recedes into the background. That is a wonderful thing, not to be found anywhere else in the whole history of the world, that God deigns to speak to a people. He cannot do that without at the same time having an eye on *all* peoples on earth, of whom the people of Israel is but a small fraction.

This people is to be the servant of the Lord; it is to be used for his purposes and is to render services to all peoples on earth. When God says of this servant, "I have made and formed you; I have chosen you," he refers, to begin with, to the actual people of Israel. However, since the coming of the Lord Jesus every believer in him belongs to this people of Israel, for he that loves the Son is loved by the Father. The Father abides with him, and all the wonderful and glorious things prophesied for Israel he may apply to himself. So we, too, want to consider ourselves addressed. We are chosen like Jacob, made and formed like Israel, and consecrated to the Lord through baptism from earliest childhood on, as Israel was through circumcision.

What does the Lord want to say to us? We would so like to hear his voice and put this or that question to him. We would all like to ask, "What does he say?" Everything heard elsewhere, all that is heard here on earth from men, is altogether unsatisfactory. But when we hear, "The Lord speaks!" a voice in us should say, "Why, that's what I want to hear!" Now what is it he says?

(1) "Fear not, my servant Jacob and you devout one, whom I have chosen."

Truly, the people confessing the Savior find themselves in great fear and tribulation, just like Israel long ago. Everybody wants to turn against those that are the Lord's. The world goes its own way and, at best, just bypasses the people of God. Many times, however, it also scorns and reviles them, seeks to harm them in any way possible, and may even threaten their lives. In other respects, too, much distress is abroad, and yet whoever wants to be the Lord's should also be his servant, that is, he should do something for those further away. Only in that way can we be his servants. But when we try it—look at the hindrances and dangers we meet! The murderer from the beginning is on the spot and wants to sabotage everything! For centuries Christianity has just sat brooding, and what is the outcome? The outcome is that no single day goes by free of fear. If a person sets out to accomplish something, fear is his bread of tears. Tackling a problem means risking everything. All too many perils and afflictions rise up all around as soon as one stops making concessions to the enemy. And when it comes to cherishing the hope that the Lord will yet assert his rule over all peoples, that's enough to frighten us out of our wits. "But how? Who is to do it? Is there anything at all to build on?" Such are the responses. Utter ruin is all that people can see before them. They look up to heaven and would like to ask for counsel: "What are we to do? Everything is going to pieces; nothing endures." That just about describes the lot of those that are the Lord's. We get up in fear and in fear go to bed. Any person of deeper feeling lives in constant worry that sooner or later everything will be lost.

That is the inner state the Lord has in mind when he says to Israel, "Fear not, my servant Jacob and you devout one (that is, beloved one) whom I have chosen." When things are in such a state that one sees nothing one can hold on to—no matter! Things will change presently; presently the Lord will intervene. Let's not be scared as if all were lost or give way to despondency and despair as if death and the end of everything were in sight. No! Fear not, O Jacob my servant! Why? Because he, the Lord, wants to do something. And when we perceive that he wants to do something, our fear is gone. While we think we have to do it, fear and worry rob us of our sleep. But when we know that he takes it in hand and that his people, his servants, need be no more than sod carriers on the job, all worry is gone.

(2) What does God have in mind? Listen: "I will pour water on the thirsty land and streams on the dry ground; I will pour out my spirit on your offspring and my blessing on your descendants." There you have it. When everything has turned parched and arid so that nothing more can be hoped for and all life seems to have perished, when all things languish and faint away, then heaven will drop refreshing rain and water will come—first in drops and then more and more, until it pours down onto the parched ground.

Hearing and reading this makes one feel like jumping up and asking: "What is this? God wants to send something down from above? We are to receive something from on high?" Then we take heart again. Here in the world no help is to be had; everything gets completely parched and dry. But if something is to come from above, that is another story.

Just what God has in mind when he says, "I will pour water on the thirsty land and streams on the dry ground," quickening the fainting and softening the dried-up hearts, we read in the following verse: "I will pour out my Spirit on your offspring and my blessing on your descendants." Hence what he means is the Spirit of God, who is to come down. Israel did not yet have the Spirit, nor is it promised to him for that moment, but it will come upon his offspring, his descendants. In other words, "Be patient! You will not experience it, but your descendants will, and then you, too, will benefit from it."

You see, that is what I, too, am hoping for; it is what all of us must trust in. There is no other way to quench our thirst, to revive what is parched and arid than through God's pouring out his Spirit. To be sure, there are many in this day and age who no longer want to believe that. Why? Because it is something out of the ordinary, not fitting into the usual pattern of this world. It is so new, so extraordinary that one cannot find anything to compare it to in this world. Just imagine a recurrence of what happened to the apostles at that first Pentecost, compare that to our ordinary manner of living and thinking and feeling, and you will have to admit that all this is as nothing in comparison with what is to come about through the Spirit. That is why it strikes most people as something too big altogether. But I can't help that; I can't make it any smaller, or think of it as any smaller than it is. Maybe if it were less great, people would believe it more easily, but I really can't make what is great smaller than it is. Like a flood the Spirit will come upon the offspring, the descendants, of Israel, hence also on the Christian descendants, on us. Let us confidently expect that.

Indeed, a small part of it was already fulfilled in the time of the apostles. But because—for reasons we cannot go into right now—the endowment with the Spirit has once more receded into the background, so that it no longer is as it once was, does that mean it should not be given afresh? Indeed, if it was then given on a limited scale, must it not now be fulfilled on a large one? In that first outpouring of the Spirit we had proof that God keeps his word. But now we need a new outpouring. We are dehydrated people; the thirst is almost killing us, and it is entirely too awful how people go to rack and ruin both inwardly and outwardly. And since we need it again, God will also give it again. We have the promise: Fear not, Jacob! Your God knows what is needed. He only has to send the great divine gift, the Holy Spirit, who comes from God and gives men a new, divine nature. Then everything will be different.

(3) Now follows a description of the effects wrought by the Spirit when it is poured onto the parched and thirsty ground like a stream of life from on high. Again, the metaphor first: They, the descendants of Israel, "will spring up like grass in a meadow, like willows by flowing streams." That means that there will be an immeasurably great change everywhere as soon as God sends forth his Spirit and new life springs up among men of childlike faith. In non-pictorial language that is expressed as follows: "This person will say, 'I am the Lord's'; another will call himself by the name of Jacob. Still another will write on his hand 'The Lord's' and will be called by the name Israel." Thus, everywhere children of Israel will arise, springing up like grass out of the ground, until a great Israel emerges from the people of the earth. The human race will be so renewed into something divine that we cannot but marvel how quickly and extensively the Spirit takes effect among the people. From all sides they will come running and say, "I, too, want to be the Lord's; I, too, want to belong to Jacob's people and be called by the name 'Israel.'" Nobody wants to be left behind and be excluded from the blessings that flow from God to his people. And then God's servants will be authorized to tell them, "Yes, you, too, shall be the Lord's and shall belong to the Israel of God. You shall have what the others have; just come along!" Oh, what a wonderful time it will be when the people that are now caught up in all manner of follies and wrongs will be filled with the one thought of how they can find their way into the realm of divine mercies and blessings and be called by the name "Israel" and "Jacob."

Oh, might it begin soon! And should it not be possible in our poor, arid time? Oh, may we, prepared as we are for great things by the Father in heaven, implore God to let the new time break in, to tarry no longer but come to quicken and revive all that seems doomed to death. Let us take heart! May this word from God's mouth give us fresh courage to await, in confidence and joy, the great hour to come! Praised be his name! Amen.

VI. About the Lack of Faith in the End Time.

(Morning devotion)

Text: However, when the Son of Man comes, do you think that he will find faith on the earth? (Luke 18:8)

It is a serious and striking word that the Lord speaks here. A good deal of thought has been given to it, and yet it continues to puzzle us, also in connection with the end time. There is probably more unbelief in our age than in any past period. At the same time, though, there is a great and—it almost seems—ever growing number of believers (as we have reason to call them). And when it comes to the crunch, a good many people do rally around the Savior's banner. So, if our time is to be considered the final one, the one in which the prophecies will be fulfilled to the very last, it is hard to understand the Savior's word that at the end time, before the Son of Man comes, there will be practically no faith left on earth. Let us try to say something about this.

Just previously the Lord had been speaking of the widow that stands before God as a representative of the faithful and keeps pestering the judge (who at first is unwilling to listen to her) with the request, "Save me from my adversary!" That widow has the courage to face the unrighteous judge and to bring her request forward again and again, even though she meets with constant refusals. I do not think there will be many like her here on earth at the time when the end draws near. To be sure, immediately after (Luke 18:9), the Lord speaks of his chosen ones that cry to him day and night, and he declares that God will save them, and that though he may defer his help for a while, he will in the end vindicate them speedily. That would indicate that there are many who cry and plead. Nevertheless, if the Lord says at the end, "When the Son of Man comes, do you think he will find faith?" that makes it clear that the one widow's crying and pleading somehow differs from that of the many elect. With a lot of people, prayer is more a cry of need or mere lip service than an utterance of true faith. We can express a lot in prayer, but all too easily it turns into mere talk and lament, which in no way spring from a firm, unshakable faith. And when it comes to taking up a decisive attitude against the adversary, we are more apt to show fear of him than faith in the power of Jesus.

Especially in our own time there is a tendency to believe that on the whole there is not much more to be expected from apostate humanity. That is why one does not plead in firm faith for those oppressed and corrupted by the adversary and has just about given up on the whole lot as irretrievably lost. We may boast of our faith in Jesus, but there is no such faith if we doubt that he who came to save the lost can rescue also what is already in the wolf's jaws. Faith in the power of the redeeming blood, which can prove victorious even with those utterly lost, has just about dried up. Some few may still be considered redeemable, but the masses are regarded as beyond hope. If we are mindful of that mood, especially among believers, we understand a little why Jesus voices a fear that in the end faith might be completely extinguished on earth. Whoever cannot believe in a great redemption still to be wrought by the Lord before his return for judgment, has, I would say, no faith at all, as Jesus understands it. It is hard to grasp how someone can be deemed a savior who, though firmly resolved to save sinners (1 Tim 1:18), is yet unable to tear the great majority of them out of the adversary's clutches.

However, as our text indicates, the Lord will yet carry it through, as long as in the end even just a few—maybe hardly more than one widow—believe in him. As Jonathan said when he dared go out against the Philistines alone, accompanied only by his armor-bearer, "It is not hard for the Lord to save, whether by many or by few" (1 Sam 14:6). Then the impotent prayers of the otherwise well-meaning elect will also come into their own, for the Lord will bring about the redemption they desired but did not believe in. Oh, how gloriously the Lord will yet bring his cause to completion! Amen.

VII. The Joy of Jesus

(Morning Devotion)

Text: "I have told you this so that my joy may remain in you and that your joy may be complete" (John 15:11).

The Savior is with his disciples for the last time. That being the case, they could all have been shedding tears. Yet he declares, "I have told you this so that my joy may remain in you." What he is saying is that they, too, are to be given the joy that he has and that goes out from him. He rejoices because he is now in a position to redeem the whole world and to free all creation from its distress and because he is certain that in the end things will be as his love wants them to be. He says, "This joy I give to you, and you, too, should be glad that you may help to reap what others have sown" (John 4:37–38).

To be sure, we do not yet have complete joy. On the contrary, we have to make a real effort to feel joyful. When we do rejoice, we do so more in hope of the redemption held out to us and vouched for by the Crucified and Risen One. Otherwise it could be considered strange for anybody to break into hymns of joy, especially at present, amid so much sorrow of one's own and so much need on the part of others and amid the powerful, insidious attacks of Darkness. Indeed, it is often hard to imagine how one day joy will break in. Then, too, we have to say, "Until *all* rejoice, I cannot rejoice"—unless we rejoice while simultaneously thinking, "The others will also have their turn." Still, we cannot help grieving that it has not yet come to that. While we are aware of the many folk sunk in sorrow and misery or even lost in the deep abysses of the beyond, because redemption has not yet reached them, we cannot feel perfect joy. But once redemption is complete and concluded, joy, too, will be complete, as our text says.

Hence there is something strange about Christians that continuously sing hymns of joy and can never be happy enough about being one of the elect. They do not think with heartfelt sympathy of the many millions that, far from being happy, are sunk in deepest distress and misery because they do not have, or know of, a Savior. It is not right for me to want always to have sweet sensations of joy and to be drenched in happiness at the thought of having a Savior, for then I think too much of myself and of nothing but myself. Genuine joy means rejoicing that he is *the* Savior of *all* people. Once the universal awakening comes, the finer and nobler kind of joy will break forth. By then, too, the world's redemption may have advanced to the point where we can assume that things can and will *remain* as they then are. Oh, that will be a joy without compare; it will have a kind of completeness even down here.

Let us recognize, though, that it is *joy* that God the Father and his Son have in mind, and that means a complete joy, henceforth untroubled by anything. That is something we want to tell ourselves every day anew. Then the joy of our Lord, our joy-imparting Savior, will remain with us amid all hardships and never leave us. And being joyful in hope as he is himself, we shall attain our happy goal. Amen.

14

Worship Services and Christian Fellowship

IN THE LAST FOUR chapters we tried to distinguish, as much as possible, the various forms in which the great, new manifestations made their appearance: first their root, the movement of repentance; next, one of the fruits, the miracles. Finally, we witnessed the spiritual life sprouting from both of these—the way in which divine thoughts, old or forgotten, were brought back into awareness with new power and were seen in a new light. It still remains for us to consider the outer frame of this great picture, that is, the forms of the worship services and of the wider Christian fellowship, in which this newly awakened life pulsed. We begin with the natural center of this life in Möttlingen: the church and the worship services.

As in Old Testament times, so in Möttlingen, Sundays actually began the evening before. Every Saturday evening Blumhardt held an informal Bible class, something he had begun when he first came to Möttlingen and which remained his favorite worship service right to his end. These evening devotions were originally held in the schoolhouse and had to be transferred to the church during the early days of the movement. They were held there for quite a time, until the ecclesiastical authorities forbade this and obliged Blumhardt to move the meeting back to the schoolroom, which of course was then crowded far beyond capacity.

Naturally, the center of all worship services was the main service on Sunday morning. When already in the summer of 1844 the number of people became so great that the church could hold barely half of them, Blumhardt persuaded his Möttlingers to adopt a noble resolution: They gave up their seats in church for this service in exchange for Blumhardt's promise to hold after Sunday school yet a third service, in which they were to have first claim on the seats in church. Thus, during the main service the church was filled with strangers, while the villagers, seated on chairs brought from home and in rainy weather armed with umbrellas, took up position in the yard outside the church, which before long was trodden firm and hard like an oriental threshing floor. The children's service or Sunday school was, of course, also overcrowded with adult listeners. After a short interval came the third meeting, that additional service the parishioners had been promised. These now trooped into their church and left the courtyard, complete with chairs and umbrellas, to the strangers. Actually, the two preceding services had caused the air in the church to become so stuffy that the outsiders' portion was much the better one.

Blumhardt's voice had to reach the listeners' ears through the open church windows and often had to pierce a solid wall of unfurled umbrellas. This extraordinary effort caused his voice to acquire a fortissimo volume, which in later times would often be considered unpleasant, particularly when out of proportion to the locality, but also because his voice later on lacked the melodiousness to go with such volume. At that time, however, it had a full, trombone-like sound, which had a wonderfully moving effect and was later sadly missed by all who had heard him earlier on.

As mentioned earlier, due to Blumhardt's inner, pastoral relationship to practically every one of his listeners, his preaching had a holy intimacy about it. It was, to use a fine post-apostolic term for a sermon, a homily or "discourse"—in fact, a fatherly discourse with his large family. Thoughts would float up to him just as much as they flowed down from him to his audience. In every weekend cycle (from Saturday evening through the third service on Sunday) an unstructured, organic progress could be observed. Frequently, the concluding sermon at the day's end provided an answer to the questions the morning sermon had raised in people's hearts. The main sermon was, of course, based on the Bible text appointed to be used on that particular Sunday, whereas the text for the concluding sermon was chosen freely, generally from the Old Testament.

As is well known, Blumhardt was a public speaker of the first rank, yet he never stooped to affect the common person's way of thinking nor did he, with the conceit of the educated, supply him with cheap, supposedly "popular" merchandise. On the contrary, he had a high regard for the people's way of thinking and thought and felt with them. When the Lord asked his disciples "Who do people say the Son of Man is?" (Matt 16:13), the answers they brought back to him (as they had heard them from the people) were strange but bold and in their own way great. Blumhardt, commenting on these examples of popular speculation, remarked, "The wheels never stop turning in people's heads." Is that not true? Is not the one who is educated much more imprisoned in certain fashionable stereotypes, and is not the common person freer in his thinking, in many cases also more inward and more receptive for enduring, changeless ideas?

Blumhardt benefited from the fact that as a teacher and writer he had been through a strict school, where he had learned both to think and to give expression to his thoughts. His sermons contained two or three interrelated, pithy thoughts, expressed briefly and succinctly, which, however, he was fond of reiterating and highlighting over and over in ever-new variations. He never wearied of doing that, nor did he weary his listeners. At the end of the sermon he would usually sum up these thoughts in words such as, "Mark this now: first . . . second . . . third . . . ."

So much about the outer form of his preaching. The spirit pervading it is of course hard to describe, nor is it evident in the sermons quoted above, since none of those we have quoted verbatim belong to the early days of the revival. What Blumhardt himself tells (as we shall hear further on) of a sermon he preached on Ezekiel 34 gives us a particular impression of the deep earnestness and sincerity of his preaching.

One occurrence exemplifying his cordial, free, and engaging ways ought to be related here: For quite a while Blumhardt regularly had among his listeners spies, whom he knew quite well. Among them were reporters from a certain radical newspaper, who would frequently turn up, hoping to pick up and carry home in their notebook this or that sensational tidbit for the benefit of their paper. Once it happened that in the middle of his sermon, when the train of thought lent itself to it, Blumhardt turned directly to these persons, saying with the overwhelming warmth characteristic of him, "I know quite well that you are here, and why, but don't think you can for long join us with impunity in listening to the word of grace! In the end it will turn you around too! You must believe what you hear and wake up to the fact that the Lord loves and seeks you too."

We cannot leave our account of those church services without mentioning the powerful singing that was part of them. We Swiss often miss in German churches the four-part singing we are used to, though on the other hand we must admit that it detracts somewhat from the popularity of a church hymn, that is, the chance of its also being sung *outside* of church. For example, our Swiss soldiers could hardly be expected to sing "Now thank we all our God" as the Prussians did after the battle of Leuthen,[1] since our men would only remember their own bass part in every hymn. Still, to us Swiss something seems to be lacking in the unison singing we hear in German Protestant churches. And yet, when it rises up from moved hearts in a church full to overflowing, such unison singing, too, has a mightily uplifting and moving effect. And here in Möttlingen, the singing of thousands crowded together in a narrow space, coming straight from the heart and imbued with reverence and faith, left an unforgettable impression. When at home in later years we sang, or listened to, one of the chorales we had once joined in at Möttlingen, we could not help feeling transported back to Blumhardt's services. This applied in particular to the concluding service, where the local parishioners filled the church and the choice of songs was not wholly restricted to the hymn book. Here, songs like "Jesus Christ as king is ruling"[2] or "Jesus is victorious king" sounded forth like holy paeans of struggle and victory. They gave one a feeling of what is meant in Psalm 22, where the psalmist says to God, "Thou inhabitest the praises of Israel" (Ps 22:3).

It is not hard to understand that in Möttlingen people would quite naturally visit the pastor in his study after the church service. This study was in a sense an organic part of the church. Blumhardt advised other ministers to remain in the sacristy after the church service, in order to give people a chance to see them; he himself used his study for this purpose. There he made himself available to people from Saturday until Monday noon, the whole time both before and after the services, with the exception of mealtimes and a short siesta following the afternoon service.

1. Editors Note: The Battle of Leuthen was fought on December 5, 1787. In this battle, the Prussian army, led by Frederick the Great defeated a much larger Austrian force and secured Prussian influence over and rule of the region of Silesia.

2. It is worth noting that in stanza 6 of this song Blumhardt changed the concluding line from "Life he giveth after death" to "Life he gives instead of death."

He was sought out by a constant stream of visitors. They would crowd into his study in groups of twenty or thirty and stand around him in a circle, while Blumhardt, in his dressing-gown (without a necktie, as somebody related in astonishment), his little briefcase in hand, walked from one to the other. With a simplicity that puts "educated" folk to shame, each person stated briefly what pained him. Often it would be a concern that in our opinion would require a private and confidential talk of at least a quarter of an hour. Blumhardt would reply briefly, sometimes consoling, at other times reproving unceremoniously and for everybody to hear. Occasionally he would lay his hands on someone, especially children, and speak a word of blessing. Now and then he would jot down a name. When all had had their turn, the room would empty, only to be filled with a new group straight away.

As simple as his method was, it is even now hard to grasp how Blumhardt managed to cope with the hundreds of persons that arrived every weekend in search of inner or physical help. We should also bear in mind the effort required to preach to these crowds once on Saturday and three times on Sunday. Along with all that, Blumhardt still found time for the numerous persons of education and culture who preferred to voice their requests privately, as well as for people whose troubles were not fit for the ears of others.

Strenuous as they were, these hours of counseling nevertheless had in many ways an uplifting, quickening, and invigorating effect on Blumhardt. They were holy and blessed hours, in which the Lord's hand was at work. The Lord manifested his nearness through manifold instances of help given to visitors' bodies, souls, and minds. Blumhardt felt inwardly strengthened by his contact with these people and their simple fear of God; their clear, childlike faith; and their humble, broken, and repentant attitude.

Let us go with these people as they leave Blumhardt's study and look around in Möttlingen on such a Sunday. Let us observe life there as it went on *outside* the church—the inner life of ordinary folk.

In a small way those Sundays in Möttlingen must have been a bit like festival days in the Jerusalem of old. Many outsiders came already on Saturday, partly in the hope of a better chance to see the pastor than on the Sunday, partly drawn by the desire to attend the Saturday evening meeting with its holy intimacy. Though having to endure many a mocking word on the way, they nevertheless reached the blessed village full of joy. Then early on Sunday morning people would come streaming in from all directions. On Good Friday 1845 the count showed that visitors had come from 176 villages. At times the young people of Möttlingen made it their task to count the people as they departed, and once, on a Whitsun festival, the number reached two thousand.

Yet where had all these people, most of whom had quite likely taken part in the whole festive weekend, spent the night? In Württemberg this was indeed a more difficult problem than in sunny Jerusalem. Well, the Möttlingen folk proved incredibly hospitable and the visitors were content with little. The men slept in the hay, and the women were bedded down on the floors of the dwelling houses. Many of the men would also camp out in the wood on the neighboring hill named *Köpfle* ("little head"), on one occasion no fewer than two hundred fifty.

The food problem was solved very simply. The visitors claimed to need next to nothing but did do their part in providing the hospitable villagers with what was required. All this was attended by a marvelous blessing, not just figuratively but literally. A Möttlingen host might just about manage to make room for fourteen guests around his table and to provide food for about that many but would still feel uneasy as to whether there would really be enough for fourteen. Yet lo and behold: Having eaten their fill, the fourteen leave the table and make room for another fourteen, and these yet again for a further fourteen, and still food was left over. The village policeman did a brisk trade in cups of coffee—at one (or was it two?) farthing a cup.

Still simpler were conditions in the airy night quarters up on the hill. "Man does not live by bread alone!" someone once exclaimed there, full of happy enthusiasm. And it was true: People rejoiced in a blissful fellowship in the Lord's name. From the houses the adults' voices were heard raised in song, and the streets reechoed with the singing of children and young folk.

The center and focus of life in this extended family was the rectory or parsonage. The peasant visitors Blumhardt left in the care of the village folk, but whoever had the looks of a townsman had to stay in the rectory. Blumhardt made special arrangements to have *young* people of that sort sought out and brought in, for he never liked to see such folk roam about unsupervised. But he also gladly accepted it when such visiting students were content to sleep on the living-room floor of the village pub, for not only was every nook and corner in the rectory used to provide dormitory accommodations for ladies and gentlemen, sick people etc., but also any available rooms in the mayor's house and other houses of the village were drawn upon for such guests, not to mention the "Ox," the village inn, whose bedrooms might often have marveled at the strange ways in which the most various persons met in them.

As soon as the visiting students mentioned above got up in the morning from the living-room floor of the pub, they were expected to appear for breakfast at the rectory. In fact, they were expected to regard the rectory as their home throughout the day, but most definitely at mealtimes, failing which they might not be allowed ever to set foot in it again. The house rules at the rectory were similar to those in Bad Boll later on, but there was not the slightest flavor here of life in a hotel or inn. Breakfast, with Sunday cake expertly baked by *Frau* Blumhardt, was followed by morning devotions, consisting of a song, the reading (rarely a discussion) of the Bible text for the day, and kneeling prayer.[3] The latter custom alone is suggestive of the inward, gathered, and consecrated character of life in the Möttlingen rectory, such as could scarcely be imagined in the much larger circle at Bad Boll. The midday meal was extremely simple, partly because of the church service yet to follow. At least at the upper end of the table, guests were carefully placed according to rank. There appeared massive bowls with the invariable noodle soup, as well as large quantities of potato salad. Finally there came a platter with meat, which was passed from the upper to the lower end until somewhere in the middle of the table any further passing became purposeless, as the platter was empty. Yet how we enjoyed the inexhaustible "bowl"!

If something like an open table was kept even at the midday meal, at supper the doors to the dining room were opened still wider for all comers, frequently up to seventy persons. There Blumhardt, having

3. In a letter to one of the guests of those days, Blumhardt accounts as follows for this praying on one's knees:

> Our kneeling prayer was something new to you. Among us here in Württemberg, too, it is not the generally accepted way, but with me it has become customary since the revival in my congregation. We did not take it up in a legalistic sense but because we felt that a humble posture before God befits prayer, and kneeling is after all thoroughly in keeping with Scripture. If one day every knee will have to bow before the Lord (Phil 2:10), then, I thought, we had better do it in good time. By the way, I only do it in the circle of my household, and when I sense that a certain person finds it difficult, I leave it. On the other hand, precisely this domestic kneeling prayer has already had great effects and left deep impressions. That kneeling in and by itself enhances the value of prayer, I do not believe.

completed his church services for the day and in between listened to
hundreds of people, could relax and sit happily in the motley circle
around him. He would then maybe tell of fresh miracles of healing he
had learned about that day in his study from people who had gratefully
told him of their recovery. For example, a mother had jubilantly shown
him her child, completely cured of the caries that had disfigured it when
she brought it to Blumhardt a week earlier—or other cases of that kind.
Or Blumhardt would discuss questions either occasioned by the day's
sermons or brought up freely by one of those present. Such informal
conversations often proved even more fruitful and illuminating than
sermons. Blumhardt once pointed out that when the Lord commanded
his disciples to preach or proclaim the Gospel, he was thinking neither
of sermons nor pulpits but of ordinary converse, where the lips overflow
with what the heart is full of. "Professing the Lord from the pulpit is
often not a great, courageous achievement, nor does it have a big effect. A listener is apt to think it is simply the accepted way of talking
from a pulpit. What is much more important, goes much deeper, and
finds more faith is the word uttered informally in the course of ordinary
social intercourse."

To Blumhardt himself such conversations were an ever-bubbling
wellspring of new and original thoughts, while his interlocutors found it
enlivening just because of this fresh originality. He was always the same:
holy and natural in the pulpit, natural and holy out of the pulpit, with the
term "holy" to be understood in the simple, biblical way.

For the present we will leave the rectory (which we shall get to
know better in the next chapter) and turn our attention to Blumhardt's
pastoral work in his Möttlingen parish. Since his labors in this field remained hidden from the eyes of outsiders, we have to rely on his own
reports, which follow here. In the Württemberg journal for churches and
schools he reports:

> In the meantime my labors and concerns with respect to the con-
> gregation had greatly increased, for I, too, was not free from the
> worry voiced by outsiders, namely that the fire might die down
> just as quickly as it had flared up. I now saw it as my task to spare
> no effort to lead my people to deeper understanding and to keep
> their hearts and wills open and free. Among other things I did
> that through evening meetings held twice weekly, first in my
> house, then in the large schoolroom, and finally, when the press
> of people became too great altogether, in the church.

Along with that, three times during the summer I held so-called conferences, each a series of eight consecutive meetings, to assure that all members could participate. The meetings lasted three hours each and were under a special blessing for the further-ance of Christian conduct in daily life. Here my main concern was to let love and a peaceable, conciliatory attitude become firmly established in the families and thus to let Christian fellowship grow in them through joint prayer, singing, and conversation. It became customary for married couples to pray together daily on their knees, either by themselves or with other family members, including children and servants, a habit that more than anything else kept a Christian spirit alive and active.

At these conferences I also gave advice regarding the weekly meetings, which I hoped would remain very flexible in form. For this reason they were not always held in the same house but in each house in turn. As far as possible every member was to be drawn into the conversation, in the hope that everyone's partici-pation in discussing, pondering, and digesting the subject would lead to a more active sharing as well as to a warmer relationship between individuals.

In addition to this, of course, I had a lot to do privately, what with counseling, settling disputes, straightening things out, issu-ing warnings, and watching out for possible emotional excesses. The safest way of combating the latter, I thought, was by fighting with might and main against self-love and spiritual pride. That was not hard, for I found people's hearts so open and so full of love and affection to me that I could speak to them very freely and be most frank and sharp with them without having to be afraid of giving offense. Rather, I received warm thanks for it.

In the branch parish in Unterhaugstett, too, there was a lot to do. Evening visits, whether in private houses or (later) in the school, were greatly welcomed, but apart from that, the attendance from there at worship services in the mother parish in Möttlingen, especially the evening services, was frequent and numerous. Often people would walk over even in bad weather.

When we compare this account with Adolf Christ's description,[4] it shows us how close Blumhardt had grown to his parishioners. Indeed, the relationship between him and his congregation reminds one of the messages to the various churches in Revelation. There the bond between a church and its shepherd is seen as so indissoluble that the term "angel of the church" is applied indiscriminately both to the church and to its

4. See *infra*, pp. 180–86.

shepherd. Similarly, when Blumhardt was forbidden to let sick persons enter his house, he would deliberately refer them to the intercession of his congregation (that is, the believers gathered for worship) just as much as to his own prayers. This intimate connection with his congregation shows even more clearly in the following account, also taken from the Württemberg journal for churches and schools. Blumhardt wrote:

> Something more remains to be reported about the progress of the religious movement in Möttlingen up to the present. During the summer, under the pressure of the many outward cares and concerns (for my parish is one of the poorest in the land) the initial zeal, which became manifest in the spring of last year, slackened somewhat, even though the daily meetings never ceased completely. In fact, many found it refreshing that after the day's toil and sweat they could still enjoy an hour of brotherly fellowship. In late summer I began to feel troubled by the increasing lassitude, lukewarmness, and indifference I noticed. I therefore went back to a very serious tone in my talks, especially when facing just my own congregation.
>
> At the same time I was made aware of various shortcomings in people's hearts. Though these shortcomings are generally not much heeded, they are actually of real significance if there are to be no gaps in a person's Christianity. I was always allowed to discover these failings first in myself. Even though earlier on, following an inner urge, I had chosen from among my colleagues a father confessor for myself, to whom I opened my heart unreservedly, I nonetheless was again brought low by ever so many previous omissions, follies, and slips, whose seriousness I had not seen so clearly till then. From that point on I have been marching in step with my parishioners. What I came to see as a failing in myself I shared with them, and the effect was that before long there arose a new movement toward humility and repentance.
>
> In particular the special days of prayer and repentance in the church year—days on which many would also fast—became memorable in this respect. On one of these days the lot directed me to the thirty-fourth chapter of Ezekiel, and when speaking about it I could not do otherwise (considering how I had been and acted in the past) than admit to being one of those shepherds that feed themselves rather than their sheep (even though outwardly it might have seemed to others that the opposite was the case), and in such a way that many of the sheep fell prey to wild beasts. I spoke simply and calmly, in a tone expressing my firm conviction that it had been so with me. Since my parishioners

were aware (as they might well be by now) that I never exaggerate when I speak, this confession impressed them deeply and was a cause for them to search their hearts thoroughly once more, with the result that many again felt urged to seek me out. Thus we were shown much grace throughout the winter a time when we were not disturbed by outsiders—and the Christmas holidays and later on Holy Week brought us special blessings.

All parishioners—only a very few kept somewhat aloof— were divided into eleven groups of twenty-five to thirty persons each. Throughout the winter these groups met daily in more or less full numbers, mainly for consecutive reading, interspersed with brief discussions, of the Holy Scriptures. The women and girls would bring their spinning gear for this. There were three meetings of a similar character in Haugstett, where I went almost regularly every Monday evening. Every Tuesday and Thursday evening I would read the Scriptures in the Möttlingen schoolroom with the men, both old and young, and make a few simple comments. That was greatly appreciated. We managed to read all of the five books of Moses. On Wednesdays all married women, and on Fridays all the single girls, gathered for a missionary spinning bee, to which I gave an hour of my time. On Saturdays I held a meeting for women and girls in the schoolhouse. We kept to this schedule throughout the winter, and almost every week things that people had experienced in their lives and hearts led us to discuss some special subject, which drove us to penitent prayer.[5]

All this still left a lot to be desired, both on my part and on that of my congregation, and I feel sure that no matter how firmly and deeply the work is now being established, if it goes on in its customary way, it is bound to peter out again sooner or later. This recognition has made me more and more familiar with the

---

5. As against these efforts Blumhardt made to nurture the spiritual life of his congregation, I should like to comment briefly on the judgment of a reviewer in the *Allgemeine Evangelisch-Lutherische Kirchenzeitung* (General Evangelical-Lutheran Church Journal), 1881, Nr. 3. He writes that Blumhardt ought to have reestablished private confession as an institution, since the Lord had, as it were, dropped it into his lap unasked. Then, thinks the reviewer, Blumhardt would have established something enduring—a lasting *form*. That, however, he could not do. It was not his intention at all to reform creatively the order of the established church. To be a willing helper in the Lord's work was all he wanted, and he altogether regarded such forms as of doubtful value, since they can serve so easily to give and maintain the *appearance* of godliness. His study was constantly open for all his parishioners' concerns, including the confession of sins. But if anything would have hurt him deeply, it would have been the recognition that relapses were becoming so frequent and general as to turn confessing them into a *rule*. And nothing would have been further from him than to acknowledge such a morbid state as normal by institutionalizing it.

thought that Christianity lacks the special pentecostal Spirit of the first church and that without this Spirit nothing of lasting value can be accomplished.[6]

To these accounts I add a few others—either from the year 1845 or from the following years—which cast some further light on Blumhardt's attitude to his congregation and his view of it. They testify further to the lasting and also outwardly visible fruits the revival movement bore. These reports are confidential in character but do not contain anything the publication of which could conceivably cause harm. That is why I take the liberty of including at least fragments of them with the sparse material I am able to offer the reader about this area—Blumhardt's labors in his congregation since the revival.

The first report, dated 1845, tells about the general moral and religious situation in the congregation:

> In a special report I submitted the previous summer to the esteemed church authorities, I described in detail the big changes that have taken place in the parish since January 1844. The main features of it I recently published in the Lutheran church paper, and what I write here is in reference to that account. Due to the above-mentioned changes the present religious situation of the congregation is highly gratifying, as the great majority of the parishioners have remained faithful to the inspiration received at that time. The change shows in people's whole way of thinking and acting, and in both villages the character of the inhabitants has become open, hearty, confiding, and responsive to everything good. The church services are attended very diligently and with all signs of deep interest. Public nuisances, already rare before, are non-existent, and in the branch parish in Haugstett both the so-called *Morgensuppen*[7] and the wedding dances have been

6. With respect to Blumhardt's supposed "hope syllogism," the above-mentioned reviewer is of the opinion that only the failure (real or assumed) of the hoped-for fruits of the Möttlingen revival to materialize made Blumhardt conclude that nowadays we lack altogether the Holy Spirit in the measure it was there in the early Christian church. Yet here we see Blumhardt's reasoning proceed in just about the opposite direction. He has received what he had not found anywhere else, and it gives him an inkling of something still vastly greater, which by rights belongs to the church but has got lost. But he does not delude himself into thinking that he could keep even this small grace as a special privilege, so to speak, granted to him and his circle, unless there is at the same time a large-scale change for the better.

7. Editors' Note: *Morgensuppen* refers to a notorious practice not unique to Möttlingen, in which young people gathered in the morning to consume beer and wine to the

abolished, something Möttlingen had done long before. Since the awakening there has been no known case of unchastity, and to this day the young people have all participated actively in the movement. The zeal for prayer that has arisen everywhere is especially gratifying. When in danger of weakening here or there in a family, it always returns with fresh vigor, nurtured as it is by visible answers to prayer, particularly in the case of illnesses. Marital quarrels do not occur, and the pastor's efforts to promote marital chastity, as is pleasing to God, seem to be blessed with success. On every hand one has an impression of warm love between marriage partners. They have generally accustomed themselves to praying together on their knees.

In the following report Blumhardt tells how the Möttlingen folk found inner upbuilding also apart from the actual church services:

> There was formerly in Möttlingen a separate conventicle numbering about thirty members. Before long these shared in the movement and merged with the other parishioners, so that at present there is really no private meeting in the former sense. Since people do feel the need for daily mutual strengthening, even if just briefly, they have been divided into groups for this purpose, amounting to eleven meetings all told. These differ from the usual type of conventicle in that they have no overseers and are held in turn in the various houses. When they meet, people discuss and go over what the pastor has spoken about in church, read sections of Scripture, or tell of their daily experiences. All this is done so freely and informally that every member can have his say. Each one also tries now and then to say a prayer straight from the heart. It is gratifying, too, that there is no noticeable pietistic tinge and that everything generally remains firmly on the ground of the church, with no self-importance creeping in. That is why these meetings actually serve to strengthen yet more the bond between minister and congregation.

In 1847 Blumhardt gives a somewhat similar account of the general moral and religious situation in his parish. He reports that on the whole the congregation had remained the same; that some individuals with whom one would have wished this or that to have been a little different had nevertheless not lost their love for the cause and, showing humility and love, had ever again found the way back. There were many signs, he

---

point of drunkenness. According to the parish report, Blumhardt was able to put a stop to this practice in 1841.

says, that among most of the parishioners, especially in Möttlingen, inner genuineness and good sense in Christian matters were on the increase.

Concerning separate meetings he remarked at that time:

> We have no separatists here, nor, I would say, are there any so-called pietists left, if one means by that a certain peculiar religious attitude that is often characteristic of them. There are also no such conventicles as would meet in certain definite houses and have appointed leaders. Instead, most parishioners—at least in Möttlingen, not so many in Haugstett—come together almost every evening in smaller groups, as circumstances permit. Men, women, young men, and girls gather separately and are, in part, subdivided into smaller groups. Meeting in turn now in this house, now in that, they strengthen and encourage each other in free and natural converse. Frequently they also collect the children together and have them read and answer questions about what they have read. Equally informal and mostly catechetic in nature have been the rector's meetings in the schoolhouse, held separately and by turns with the male and female members of the congregation; they have been attended with visible interest. The whole congregation is filled with a sober, Christian spirit, and there is no sign of religious excesses.

A similar report dating from the last period of Blumhardt's time in Möttlingen is shorter.[8] His account of the general situation is a little more muted; the special meetings are described more briefly but otherwise just as above, with this one addition: "Though there is no lack of men who take a lead in speaking, these cannot properly be considered leaders or overseers. Conversation is always quite free and natural and centers on a Bible passage or a recent talk or sermon."

How much these simple reports have to say to us! Just as the dry figures at the bottom of his final computation tell a merchant of past days filled with strenuous work and past nights without sleep, as well as of manifold hopes and worries regarding the future, so, too, this simple description of Christian village life gives us much to consider. It takes our thoughts back into the past as well as forward into the future. We see before us an active, spirit-moved, Christian life. Its one pole is the home and family, earnestly striving to have Christ in the center; the other is the church, in which all, including the youth, take an active part, and that is

8. Editors Note: The Blumhardt family moved from the Möttlingen parish in 1852. This probably refers to the period after 1848 during which the revival had run its course but before the move to Bad Boll.

how things go on for years on end. It is easy to say this, but it says a great deal. Precisely the simplicity and naturalness that meets us at every turn is something so ideal that it makes us wish it would come to be like that everywhere.

And would this miniature model of a Christian society endure? We know what Blumhardt thought about that. If this lovely picture was to be no more than a kind of spiritual "sight" to be admired, it had but little value and no meaning for Blumhardt; he did not expect it to continue for long in such an exceptional condition. To him it would have seemed as if one village wanted to have spring while it was winter in the land all around. He saw Möttlingen, as it was then, as an outpost thrown out into the present by the future, a vanguard, which can hardly hold its position for any length of time unless the main body of the army is brought up, that is, unless there is a general bursting forth of something similar and greater. That is why his hope, fired as it was by worldwide misery and distress, especially in the spiritual area, was also fed by another concern: As housefather of his extended Möttlingen family he kept hoping that its spiritual food supply would not run out before there was a change for the better in the situation generally.

On every hand we see Blumhardt driven to long, pray, struggle, and hope for the world as a whole. In that way he grew, under a visible divine dispensation, into a calling oriented toward just that—all-encompassing redemption. For a time he had vainly hoped that the movement whose center he was would soon acquire general significance. In a certain way that hope now began to be fulfilled at least in his own person. He came to be a pastor and counselor for thousands of people from all points of the compass and all strata of society—partly through correspondence, partly as the housefather of an ever-growing family of guests, who passed through his house in an unending stream.

How he grew into this vocation we shall consider in the following section, which will also include whatever is still to be related about his remaining time in Möttlingen. Thus we conclude our account of those great days in Blumhardt's life—days that, as mentioned above, often made him and others feel that for a while a veil was being lifted, letting the amazed onlookers see: That is how it should and could be; that is how it is to be! Hope for it! Pray for it!

Fourth Section

15

Blumhardt as a Private Person

As we come to consider Blumhardt in his more general calling as a pastor and counselor, we have to leave the strictly biographical path of chronological reporting. Instead, we must content ourselves with piecing together a picture of that side of his work from all kinds of scattered instances of his pastoral activity. The reader will find that understandable. Anyone who has experienced pastoral care will, as a rule, not be keen to see their self brought into prominence at some point in their counselor's life story, as an example of their pastoral procedure, so to speak. That is why we have so little detailed knowledge of Blumhardt's extraordinarily fruitful labors in this area. For Blumhardt possessed to a high degree the prerequisite of a true pastor and a counselor's discretion concerning the secrets confided to him, and it often grieved him deeply to find that quality missing in other ministers. "As soon as I am back in ordinary social intercourse, I no longer know anything of what has been confided to me as a counselor." That was his rule, a rule without which a true pastoral relationship is indeed impracticable and unthinkable. For this reason, what few individual instances of Blumhardt's care for souls are known to us can only be related with great caution and a blurring of temporal, local, and personal particulars. Yet within these limitations we must dare do it, lest our portrait of Blumhardt turn out all too hazy and indistinct.

Blumhardt's special calling to care for souls grew out of the way his personality had been prepared for it; it grew out of what he had come to be under the impact of his own experiences. I will therefore try to draw him as the human being he was, as well as showing him as one who, being what he was, came to be a helper for others, one who cared for their souls. Naturally, there will be some overlapping between these two aspects. Not being able to come up with a more fitting term, I grouped them together under the heading "Private Person."

Blumhardt as a human being: Anyone reading the second part of this biography is liable to share the experience of just about all who heard of Blumhardt in those days but had not yet met him personally. They imagined him to be an awfully solemn, terrifyingly earnest, at any rate imposing individual. Some even pictured him as a grim exorcist engaged in all kinds of mysterious doings. How amazed they all were when they actually met Blumhardt! A modest, lively, friendly man—one could not imagine anybody more simple and natural. "That is Blumhardt?" many a one would ask himself in happy surprise and feel a weight being lifted off his chest. The engaging reality of Blumhardt's person would make the observer see also all he had heard about the man and his great experiences bathed in the friendlier light of a pleasing reality. Many people would come away with the impression that "things may after all be as Blumhardt thinks, and if so, this is a good and gracious time also for me."

In Bad Boll, too, later on this impression he gave would win the hearts of many who thought they had long ago broken with Christianity as an antiquated and outworn cause. Yet here in Blumhardt they met a true man, a completely whole man; they found that all he did and said gushed forth in an original, free, and spontaneous way. There was nothing manufactured, unfree, or ungenuine in him. He was always inwardly gathered, always borne up by a sense of the Lord's nearness. False piety, sanctimonious sighs, and hypocrisy were foreign to him. "What's Mrs. L. coming to me for?" he once asked confidentially. "She is much too pious for me; she just wants me to join her in acting sanctimonious, and that I can't do."

I said that he conquered people's hearts, as the saying goes, but of course it was not he that conquered, but another, higher one conquered through him. Or rather, it could be said that Blumhardt's heart was conquered by whoever came to him. Anyone whom Blumhardt had once seen and talked to, particularly if there had been a heart-to-heart contact, was loved by him so earnestly, faithfully, and persistently that it defies description. "If you want to draw a picture of Blumhardt, please show most of all his love. Of all there was in him that was the greatest!" That is what more than one person told me, and I hope that as our story goes on, the reader will receive many impressions of that love, which was not "in word or speech but in deed and in truth" (1 John 3:18).

What maybe surprised people most in Blumhardt in those Möttlingen days was his irrepressible cheerfulness and along with it such a naturalness and humanness as is not always found combined with, in particular, sincere piety. Let us try to get at the roots of that distinctive manner of his, which was not the least of the reasons people were struck by something in him that was new and unexpected.

In large measure this naturalness sprang from the special character of the movement of repentance he had experienced. The uncompromising insistence on truth so characteristic of it undid all spiritual pretense and false appearance as the sun drives away the night. With many persons an overly pious and "spiritual" disposition would immediately give way to a simpler manner if it had to pass through the fire of truth; this might even hold good for whole groups of people. In Blumhardt, peace was an enduring fact rather than a matter of mood; this, too, would have had something to do with his strikingly natural demeanor.

To an equal extent his naturalness was rooted in that second phenomenon of the revival time, the miracles, in the sense that these, too, relentlessly excluded any spiritual exaltation and called forth every day anew a deep sense of spiritual poverty and dependence. When a person has no wish to receive anything at all from God or only makes requests whose fulfillment (or non-fulfillment) he can interpret as he pleases, he has no trouble soaring to lofty heights of self-assurance and need not fear to have his comfortable delusion shattered by some fact. It was different with Blumhardt. He took it upon himself to plead for suffering people to be delivered from this or that very tangible distress, and anyone in a position of having to beseech God daily like that will always remain poor. He "suffers torment all day long and is punished every morning" (Ps 73:14). Such a situation lets us feel a holy need to be humble and modest in our expressions of piety, but at the same time it imparts a natural cheerfulness, for it is well known that no one is as merry and carefree as the poor.

Yet another invisible root of Blumhardt's sprightly and joyful disposition might be mentioned: gratitude for the blessings that flowed out from him and returned to him like an invisible stream from all around, as well as the uplifting, ever clearer sense of the presence of a powerful, kindly Redeemer, our Savior Jesus Christ.

Blumhardt's joyfulness had such a refreshing effect because he felt joy in every person he met. Unhesitatingly he took everyone for a Christian. The Lord's redemptive work had come powerfully to the fore in those years, and his loving-kindness toward everyone made itself felt through Blumhardt. "We are all redeemed"—that was the cause of Blumhardt's joy. It was the overwhelming awareness that a strong, mighty grace is ceaselessly at work on us all and that our salvation rests on this grace and not on our achievements. I would like to show by an example how in this sense Blumhardt made it easy for everyone to be a Christian, how out of his own deeply founded conviction he comforted and heartened precisely the despondent and those unhappy with themselves. Our sample is taken from one of his morning devotions headed, "God's Children, on Galatians 3:26: 'You are all children of God through faith in Christ Jesus.'"[1] He says:

> It is striking how often Paul says something concerning everybody, where we might think he ought to apply it only in a limited sense as not really applicable to everybody. There were among the Galatians believers of all kinds, including persons to whom he had to say, "Having begun with the Spirit, are you now ending with the flesh?" (Gal 3:3) He also found it necessary to tell the Galatians very seriously that, since God is not mocked, they ought not to sow to their own flesh but to the Spirit [Gal 6:7–8]. But even though there were all kinds of things among them that would make us shake our heads and think to ourselves that divine sonship wasn't really all that clear in every one of them, Paul says nevertheless, "You are all children of God through faith in Christ Jesus." To be sure, in this way he also suggests to them that being God's children enables them on the one hand to make good through repentance wrongs of the past, on the other to guard against such things in the future. Take note, however, of the power and relevance of a faith that is not merely intellectual but a real trust of the heart in Christ Jesus—in Christ, the Lord who came from God and was anointed with the Spirit of God as a man, and in Jesus, the redeemer from all sin. Only such faith, which has overwhelming power, makes man certain of his divine sonship.
>
> Many Protestant Christians actually make divine sonship dependent on something other than faith in Christ Jesus. They

1. *Blätter aus Bad Boll*, No. 20, 1873.

concentrate exclusively on moral improvement, deliverance from wrong and impure thoughts and feelings, and on the state of sanctification they may have achieved. And because they cannot get rid of their failings, they will never consider themselves children of God. Such people should let themselves be told who Christ Jesus is, and that all one needs do is cleave to him in childlike trust, for he is able to make children of God out of weak and (for the time being) still sinful people, as long as they have a childlike trust in him. Indeed, he already accepts and treats them as children, nor will he straightway consider their sonship invalidated when they make mistakes—even serious ones at times (look at the Galatians!). Dear Christian, do hold on to the Savior who is there for sinners, for weak, failing people such as you, and who in the end will lead through and beyond all failings, as long as faith is not misused as a pillow to rest on. Nor will true Christian faith ever turn into a pillow for anybody; it has too much life and vigor for us to go on sinning while pleading faith. Faith can become a pillow for resting on only if faith is an intellectual matter and not a real trust of the heart, yet giving the soothing sense of having Jesus. Let us make it very clear to ourselves, and remain firm in the belief that God's mercy in Jesus Christ is very great toward all that cast themselves on it wholly and utterly surrender to it. Amen.

Blumhardt's naturalness led him to a conception of the human condition that was often extraordinarily large-hearted and broad-minded. He himself once emphasized the spiritual relevance of such naturalness by saying, "we humans must be converted twice: once from the sinful natural (that is, fleshly) self to the spiritual person and then again from the spiritual person to a holy and godly natural one." That means that when someone is converted, his first obligation is to attend properly to his natural duties, to see his natural relationships bathed in a divine light and to discharge his natural duties as a son, husband, father, etc.—rather than falsely take upon himself supposedly spiritual duties.

For instance, there was a young man of a rather pious disposition, who felt drawn to Möttlingen. He plaintively confided to Blumhardt that he was afraid of the task awaiting him in his parental home, where he was due to return soon after being away for a time. The reason he gave was that his parents had not experienced a real conversion. "What are you saying there?" Blumhardt thundered at him. "That's not the way to think and speak of one's parents! You go home and love your father and mother and brothers and sisters! That's all you have to do!"

Normally Blumhardt's hospitality was unbounded, but his aversion to a false spirituality was apt to make him cold-shoulder in a way that would take others by surprise—visitors he suspected of trying to profit by their piety. One festive season, for example, a man came to Möttlingen from central Germany who traveled about holding religious meetings. He found time to make up to a young guest, whom he told how much he had already been persecuted for the sake of the Gospel and how often he had even been thrown into prison. The young man was startled, his respect for the man mingling with misgivings, but the other went on talking in an ever more "spiritual" way, revealing this or that to show the wondrous heights of piety a man could and should attain. The man also said that he had a book that would turn every thought into a sin, thus showing how a man sins at every moment. God be praised, thought the young guest, that such a patient has found his way here where he can find healing. To the stranger's question if it might be possible to stay here for a while, he confidently replied, relying on Blumhardt's large heart, "Oh, certainly, certainly!" At the other's request, he took him to Blumhardt's study. The man greeted Blumhardt with unusual humility, told him that his way had led him to Möttlingen, that he had spent the Sunday here and in due course also intended to visit Dr. Barth. "Oh," said Blumhardt, "that's not far at all; you can easily get there before nightfall," and since the man's politeness had not allowed him to give any hint of his wish to stay on, Blumhardt had bid him good-bye and godspeed, before he knew what was happening. Surprised, the young guest asked Blumhardt why he had seen the man off so curtly, adding that his conversation with the man had made it evident that a longer stay in Möttlingen would have benefited him greatly. Blumhardt replied, "You think so? There is nothing one can do with such people. He only wanted to pry into my supposed secret art of driving out devils and working miracles."

In the same way as Blumhardt stood up for respect for one's parents, he also rose to the defense of children against their parents. Among his replies to readers' questions in *Blätter aus Bad Boll* there was, for example, an advice he gave to a married couple on how to deal with their grown-up children, and this counsel must have benefited a good many readers. In particular, however, he stood up for the younger children, who, so to speak, are handed over defenseless to us older folk. I feel urged to offer here two examples of such advice. In the first case he takes up the cudgels for adopted children, in the second for parents' own very young children. It was very much his concern that children are not need-lessly and uselessly disturbed in their free, inner development and that adults might find a better understanding for them. He said, for example, "It is not right to ask a child to say—as a kind of accomplishment, so to speak—something he is not thinking at that moment. If children do not obey such commands, it is a matter of self-will not on the children's but on the grown-ups' part."

People almost took it amiss that he was against starting too early and being too strict with making a child offer his right hand in greet-ing. As we know, a child will offer his hand gladly and heartily, but it is mostly the left hand that he has available, since his right hand is holding a toy or a piece of bread or the like. Thus he offers his left hand because that comes from his heart and stretches out the right one because he has been broken to it. It was Blumhardt's surely not unfounded concern to protect the unfolding of a child's heart as long as possible from such breaking in.

Blumhardt's love to children and respect for them earned him in turn their love in rich measure. None was happier in his presence than children, and with his bold maxim, "For the children, freedom; for the adults, love to children!" he obtained good results. A little boy from the ranks of the higher nobility, suffering from an extreme nervous break-down, recovered completely through being with him. The healing was the result of a wonderful divine blessing, but the sweet air of freedom was surely a contributory factor. How this little fellow, so harassed and hemmed in by rules and forms, benefited from being allowed to take hold of a sausage with his own hands and to sink his very own teeth into it!

We insert here the two examples mentioned, followed in turn by two fragments from unpublished letters.

(1) On Taking in Children

Whoever adopts children must accept them with all their in-gratitude; otherwise it will not go well. To take in children and expect thanks is unnatural and not right. As a rule, it will go badly. Children never show special thanks to those who feed and clothe them, apart from showing love the way children do. They take it quite for granted that we don't let them go hungry or na-ked, also that we don't do just the minimum for them if they see that we could do a little more. That is theirs by rights, whoever cares for them.

Many who adopt children, however, think that such children should acknowledge and feel awed at the compassion of these people who really owe them nothing—if that is true at all. You simpletons! That is just what they do not feel, so do not demand it of them. Love them without expecting thanks, even if they cause you a lot of trouble; you have to accept them along with their naughtiness. They will feel that, and they will love you for it, but without words.

Often foster children are given what they need, but without love, and they are made to feel that even in words. It hurts them deeply and can even give rise to hate in their hearts. I have known of two different girls who were prepared to do anything rather than put up with any more false generosity from their foster parents. Foster children do not want to have fewer privileges than the children they live with; they have a sharp eye, and if they see differences, it hurts them terribly. Why is that? They are simply children, and they do not see why one child should have more than another.

So if you want to adopt children, consider whether they would not be more unhappy with you than they would otherwise be, even under miserable conditions. If you do adopt them, adopt them fully so that they feel they can be really children with you and can simply make any childlike demand of you and indulge in any childlike ways. If not, you will receive no thanks either from them or from our dear Father in heaven.

(2) About Children's Education

Question: From a letter:

When my children have been naughty and disobedient, I make it a rule to get them to ask their father's forgiveness. My experience is that some of them find that very easy and soon do it quite on their own, but for the others it costs an inner struggle and often great strictness before they can be persuaded to do it.

Answer:

This rule of yours with your children is quite unsuitable and wrong. You could completely ruin them with this rigid, moralistic treatment. More often than not so-called naughtiness and disobedience in children is quite unpremeditated; they have no sense of doing something wrong and therefore cannot understand why such a fuss is made about it. Adults so easily call something naughty and disobedient when it is not. Children are often ordered about capriciously, hastily, or excessively, so that they can hardly take in what is expected of them. After all, they are also beings to be respected. It is not at all right to make a big crime out of everything and demand that even the father, who had not been present, should be asked for forgiveness. It stands to reason that things will not go well then. Look what else it leads to: many reproaches, then sternness, then scolding. The children become more and more confused, and it may end with great severity and harsh punishment.

Dear mothers, that is not the way. It will destroy all that is childlike and unselfconscious in the children and take away what is most endearing in them. A good rule as to what may be expected of little children is that if they do not respond well to a certain demand, it should be dropped as not yet suited to the child's stage of development.

(3) To a Young Girl Who Was Taking Care of Other People's Children

With all my heart I wish you the Lord's blessing on the task you have been given. I will gladly intercede with the Savior for you and the children that everything may go well. By the way, in such a situation it is important not to make too much of the task. Otherwise one is liable to make things hard for oneself and the children by asserting authority needlessly, bossing the children, and getting rattled. What more is needed than simply to be with the children, love them, play and talk with them, without seeing the task as something great and special? If you do these things I have mentioned, to which in any case various small services are attached, it will be quite enough. The worst thing for children is being corrected and ordered about. Your one task is to serve and love.

(4) To a Young Mother

One thing I would advise you that is very important! Small children are hindered most in the right development of their souls by being hugged and played with too much, being torn out of their own thoughts, passed from one person to another, and denied the rest that is needed for a healthy development at this tender age. Remember that!

From early childhood let us pass on to that field of education so notorious for its abundance of thorns and thistles—sometimes called the "awkward age" or "terrible teens." Blumhardt found the right way, in particular also with boys whose hearts were filled with bitterness and confusion, maybe due to an enforced pious upbringing. One such boy claimed that he had had to put up with too much religious instruction. On the whole he felt very happy in the free atmosphere of Blumhardt's house, but he was still inclined to play all kinds of tricks. One day a maid came storming into Blumhardt's room: "*Herr Pfarrer* now he went and stole the eggs from the hen house and put this hymnbook there instead!" Another maid came with similar stories. What did Blumhardt do? He said, "The rascal hiding in the boy's heart is also hiding in yours. And behind your anger, aren't you really enjoying it too? We must overcome the boy's mischievousness in our own hearts! You [to the first maid] just put the hymnbook back in the henhouse, and [to the other maid], too, put things back as you found them! And let's simply ignore these things." For quite a while the boy waited, in suspense and not without a certain impish glee for the blowup he was sure would follow. When he realized that nobody was taking any notice, he gave up his nonsense. The hymnbook was probably ruined. But a boy is surely worth a hymnbook.

With young men Blumhardt proceeded similarly. One of these had already turned consciously against the Christian faith and had been put with Blumhardt against his own will. He kept trying to talk with him about biblical matters, in a critical spirit, of course. Blumhardt avoided that and preferred to talk about anything else. Then the youth tried him with all kinds of mad pranks, but Blumhardt took no notice. The temperature in the young man's breast rose ever higher, and his escapades grew worse and worse until of a sudden the hard crust broke. He went to see Blumhardt in his study and poured out his heart to him. There he learned, among other things, how earnestly and powerfully Blumhardt had been watching over him in prayer, thus visibly guarding him against more serious aberrations.

Let us accompany Blumhardt the educator into some further areas. To be sure, it will take us partly into the field of pastoral care, but this is a freedom we have reserved. Many times, pastoral care takes on an educational character; besides (an especially exhilarating part of it) it can often free a person from the fetters of a wrong upbringing. It is of the special nature of Blumhardt's pastoral care—the recovery of freedom and a return to natural ways—that we want to speak, with special reference to some wrong tendencies among the women of his day.

There were several cases of young ladies who, due to over-concern with matters "spiritual," had for years not dared to eat their fill and in that simple way had managed to contract all kinds of nervous ailments.

Here the first symptom of inner healing was that they felt hungry and began to eat, just like other mortals. And this inconspicuous turnabout was linked with a great inner freeing.

One such case was especially gratifying. A deeply devout lady and mother of very dear children had suffered a nervous breakdown, partly caused by such excessive spirituality. She was in a very weakened condition and totally bedridden—not in pain, but unable to function out of bed. In her state of lonely idleness her mind went into ever queerer flights of fancy, so that she finally came to regard all eating as base, not to say sinful, and she wanted to renounce it completely. Even the most urgent pleading of her family simply bounced off the presumed holiness of her resolve. Finally Blumhardt, called to her bedside, declared imperatively, "The first commandment in the Bible is, 'Eat!'" (Genesis 2:16) and ordered her to take food. She did. Then he told her that he would call on her at a certain hour the following day and expected her to be dressed and ready to receive him at the door of her room. This she also did, and presently, after Blumhardt had been away for a day, on his return she met and greeted him at the entrance to her house, exactly as he had asked her to do.

We know of quite a few such persons, both men and women, who were intent on dying. Blumhardt remonstrated with them, now kindly, now severely, but always appealing to the person's conscience—"You must want to live!" Many a time after a successful recovery he would exclaim triumphantly, "She wanted to die!" It should also be said that he felt misgivings when someone seemed only too happy to die, as well as when he listened to accounts of how wonderful someone's death had been. He was afraid that under the influence of the "murderer from the beginning" a kind of self-deception might be involved in such cases, leading to hallucinations from which there might be a terrible awakening after death.

As we observe Blumhardt's very natural approach to people's individual and social condition, we are struck by such broadmindedness as would almost take some people's breath away. It did not spring from frivolity or superficiality but rather from the fact that his experiences had let him look deeply into men's hearts. He often found something genuine in souls where one would not have expected it. On the other hand, he discovered much that was ungenuine where there had seemed to be pure gold. The following letter to a young girl about an important life question gives an impression of his judgment in one particular area:

It is not always right for a girl to insist that a prospective husband should already be a believer. What is not yet there may still be given; in fact, with most men it is only given in and through marriage. The main qualities to be considered are companionableness, modesty, a quiet manner that shows consideration of others, and a high regard—or at least no actual disregard—for the church. It is only out-and-out unbelief, bordering on atheism, that one has to shy away from. Further to be considered are an upright conduct, a good reputation, diligence—in short, every civic virtue and everything not raising a fear that it might be hard to get along with such a man. Many times any of these qualities may well be lacking in so-called believers, whereas they may be there in others whom one would still consider part of the world. Many a girl has already fared ill with her so-called pious husband. What else is to be considered here you can bring to mind yourself. May the Lord guide you aright through his spirit!

Many a reader would also wish to learn about Blumhardt's attitude to worldly amusements like dancing, games, theater, etc., which were at one time subjects of lively discussion between early pietists and representatives of orthodoxy. Finding the right attitude to these matters—what a struggle it means for young people, and how many difficulties it causes for their parents and educators! Blumhardt writes about them as follows to a younger theologian employed as tutor:

I do not find it easy to give an answer, because with us here conditions are so different. What are considered worldly amusements in one land are not necessarily so in another. Where they do not meet with much opposition, it is easier to take part in them guilelessly and innocently than in places where people more or less feel and know that these things are at least very questionable. That is why here with us those keen on dancing can be expected to be persons of a sensual nature, whereas at other places that is not always the case, because there dancing and such things are accepted as customary. The same goes for games and the theater. This at any rate makes one thing clear, namely that wherever such amusements are accepted parts of social custom you are much more liable than where this is not so to be labeled a hardliner or rigorist if you simply call those things sinful. By doing that you are liable to offend and even hurt the people there, for they do not intend to sin.

I think that quite generally in contact with people of the world one should never pillory the enjoyment of the *adiaphora* or border-line amusements as sin. That term is always too strong; it is admissible only with persons that have already been led deeper and therefore deny their better self by indulging in those things. One must not be so quick to make every little thing a matter of conscience. Even though the abstaining from such pleasures may in and by itself be more pleasing to the Lord, in many cases the abstemious person with his harsh attitude may well be the greater sinner.

The question whether to go along with the world without actively joining in is a separate one. I think it would not be right for you to simply abstain from something your employers would wish you to take part in. In your job you will have to be obedient and submissive and since you are in a position of dependency, you have to put up with quite a lot. Hence you will be obedient and go to the ball where the whole family, including the children, whose tutor you are, is going. There you cannot excuse yourself, without, in a sense, pretending to be your own boss. When they all, including the children, go to the theater, you may not downright refuse to go along, for you must go for the sake of the children for whom you are employed. Thus, as a tutor you may go anywhere, especially when it is part of your job. Many times, too, your employers may wish to have you with them; they may expect from you certain services and favors, for example, to escort a lady. That is then part of your job, for your employers want to get something out of you and would not be very happy with a stiff character that keeps asking, "Shall I? Can I? May I?" In all such cases one should follow 1 Corinthians 7:31, "Those who use the things of this world should be careful not to abuse them."

The third question is: May I join in with the dancing and playing? That brings back to me my own youth, and I have to admit it did not suit my conscience, even when I was still a student. I felt flattened out and inwardly bruised. But I had no objection to playing checkers or chess or other such games, if in moderation. Playing cards never agreed with me, though I would not simply rule it out for you in your situation. Following the above principle, you may at times have to give in so as not to offend. Dancing, however—that I could never have done. I was too shy to come into such close contact with a lady or to let her touch me; that was enough to put me off. So when it comes to that, I think you ought to be mindful of your vocation, which is a serious one, you being a candidate for the ministry. I think you might say that you do not feel comfortable doing it, and would they please excuse you. In an intimate family circle it might still go—just in fun, so to speak, and with whoever can do it. Actually, once it gets known that one doesn't dance, one is left in peace—as long as one doesn't put on a stoical face but remains friendly and loving. If one lets one's inner, spiritual approach be apparent in every situation, one can always find a way through, provided one does not get hard and rigid about it. That is what I think, so enough about this subject.

In a paper he read to the Württemberg synod, Blumhardt once highlighted in a very pleasing way various Christian and human features in the life of the people. He expressed himself in favor of preserving the "apostles' days" and other minor church holidays still being observed in Württemberg. In essence, the paper reads as follows:

> The mover of this resolution speaks of fourteen such holidays, in part dedicated to apostles, in part to Mary. The apostles' days, of which we celebrate a total of only ten, include St. Stephen's Day and St. John's Day, with its question, "Do you love me?" These two are also the second and third day of Christmas. How can anybody think that these days leave our people cold and should henceforth be treated more like workdays than holidays? Our people could not grasp that at all! And how much would be taken away from our children if their Christmas joys, so long awaited, would be over so quickly! True, there is quite a string of holidays just then, especially when a Sunday gets added to them. But then, too, what a high regard we should have for the joys of family life, which then grow and increase correspondingly. It is an opportunity for family members to gather from all around, often from far away, and to enjoy a happy time together. And the special meaning of these days is apt to cast on them a peculiar holy glow, and that is really the case in many instances. It is an occasion for the individual members, otherwise separated from one another and often groaning under life's burdens, to bring together their joys as well as their sorrows and share them. And how they can mutually strengthen each other for their further pilgrimage! At no other time in the year does the human heart have such an opportunity. To be sure, there are many who complain every year about the accumulation of holidays. Their special grievance is that on these days the poor, the workers, earn nothing. Let us take note, however, that such complaints in the main do not come from the poor and the workers themselves but from others, who dislike being without their services.
>
> If we think of the other apostles' days, those dedicated to Matthias, Philip and James, Peter and Paul, James the elder brother, Bartholomew, Matthew, Simon and Jude, Andrew, and Thomas— we come to a total of nine days. They remind us of men of importance, and with some of them a good many Christian memories

are connected, which exert their quiet influence on men's hearts. Besides, they can all be as meaningful, on a more limited scale, for families and for the human heart as the Christmas days are, especially when coming right next to a Sunday. Let us beware of offending the feelings of a good many people! An individual is not only a worker; she is also a Christian and a human being. That is why God ordained a number of other holidays in Israel besides the Sabbath; he even commanded them to be observed. Here I will just mention the new moon festivals, which occurred every month and along with the worship services also gave the people an opportunity to rejoice and be merry.

It is asserted in favor of the abolition of these holidays that their church services are poorly attended. To begin with, it has to be said that that is actually not true. From but few congregations does one hear well-founded complaints about church attendance being so low that it is not worth the trouble to deliver a sermon. On the contrary, church attendance is generally quite satisfactory on holidays, as is attested by the petitions received.

But if attendance is less than on Sundays, it has very natural reasons. For one thing, if we except the feast of Epiphany (where attendance everywhere seems to equal that on high festival days), these days occupy a position midway between workdays and Sundays. In the second place, people make use of these days for purposes they don't like to use Sundays for. They will visit friends and relatives near and far or attend religious or other gatherings. It is also a fact that in recent times it has become customary for employers, whoever they may be, to demand more services on holidays from the working class, thus making it harder for many of its members to attend church. And people not going to church in general do so even less on these holidays. That explains the lower attendance on those days. On the other hand, the congregation is often noticeably more attentive then (as is also attested by the petitions), because those that do come really wish to receive something for the inner person. That is why precisely these church services may often have a particularly stimulating effect on people's hearts and souls.

Now there are three objections frequently raised against these holidays—objections that also the mover of this resolution refers to as being voiced by others. In the first place it is said that people—to put it bluntly—just use these days to gratify their flesh, especially with drinking bouts in public houses. That a lot of sin is committed on these days cannot be denied, but that it is more than on Sundays will be hard to prove. For that matter, Sundays do have an even higher incidence of murders.

There are still other things to be said. The actual days of worst abuse—though this, too, does not apply everywhere—are not the holidays in general but Easter Monday and Whitsun Monday, and yet nobody is suggesting doing away with them. Some of the holidays are definitely almost free of offenses; in the case of others disorderly behavior is more noticeable in the vicinity of the bigger towns than out in the country. There are many more villages and towns up and down the country than one might think where misdemeanors are really not all that frequent.

Then, too, certain persons are inclined to call pretty well everything a nuisance, including, for example, occasions when people come together in a garden to enjoy being with each other, when they gather in intimate circles of friends and relatives, frequently with singing or listening to music. Is there anybody who would roundly condemn such activities? Who dares censure all those who amidst the manifold toils and sorrows of life also wish to have a little joy now and then, just as the Israelites had at their festivals? Does it not have an uplifting and enriching influence as long as the general attitude is good? Are these not occasions where the heart, man's inner being, can come into its own? Let us imagine all such joys taken away—how totally desolate that would leave men's life!

To be sure, the others, the wrong-minded ones, are always there as well. They, too, move in their own circles, and it is of course a pity that they spoil things for the better folk, till at length they find themselves alone and come to a bad or even very bad end. But is it right to condemn the whole thing—lock, stock, and barrel, because of them?

Finally, and this might not be unimportant, there are cases where working people are left with only those hours at their disposal that present them with temptations. They are no longer given free time for themselves and their own needs, to be used sensibly. Freed from their yoke only at a late hour, they turn boisterous and at times kick over the traces, so that they are almost unfit for work the next day, a complaint heard now and then. Yet where lies the guilt? It is similar on Sundays. If, as would be right, people were allowed to have the entire Sunday from Saturday evening on, the situation with "blue Mondays" would be quite different from what it usually is. Indeed, everything could be so much better in many ways if there were a general feeling that workingmen and day laborers and others in a dependent position should as far as possible be granted a full and reasonable period of rest.

As regards the second objection to holidays, the mover of the bill gives an imagined department of political economy the chance to voice it:

Consider the damage these holidays, this flagrant case of privileged idleness, inflict on the national prosperity, on the thousands and thousands of workingmen! The loss goes into the millions in terms of wages left unearned. Instead, as a result of this Swabian custom in our beloved Württemberg these millions are being squandered. Just consider rationally the advantages enjoyed year after year by our competitors in the neighboring states to the right and left who are unhampered by these holidays. Anyone not closing his eyes to just this one fact will quickly reach the conclusion that it is an injustice inflicted on precisely those fellow citizens—a great number of them—who do most for the general welfare of the people. We completely misjudge the spirit of the time if we delay for another moment laying the axe to the root of this rotten tree.

This is the charge supposedly coming from a school of political economy. Serious though it sounds, it has not persuaded the mover of the bill himself to raise the axe and swing it at the tree. He subsequently turns out to be the warmest advocate of the holidays in question and does not regard the time "sacrificed" for them as lost—for the schools! As an experienced teacher he testifies that the loss of time caused by the holidays is actually no loss as far as the schools are concerned. His testimony is important and should be taken to heart. He says:

No one qualified to judge has yet had reason to maintain that in our Württemberg, so abounding in holidays, the achievement level in the schools is lower than in the neighboring land, Baden, with its dearth of holidays. No institution has to be more economical in the use of time than our seminaries, leading up as they do to an exam of the strictest kind. Please believe a seminary teacher of many years' experience that we, too, would in no way regard it as a gain if there were to be lessons on holidays in future.

And we add: If from early on our young people can have holidays where they are free and temporarily relieved of their usual work load, with a chance to move about and occupy themselves in all kinds of ways, they can gain a great deal for their outlook on life and the unfolding of their mind. That means a gain for the whole cultural development of our people. True, such a gain cannot be calculated in figures but surely must not be overlooked when those millions would shock us that our country is said to be losing in terms of money due to the holidays.

It is the workers, they allege, that are losing these millions. Yet it is obviously not the workers that do the calculating here, and indeed, to the best of our knowledge, one never hears them calculate in this way. Four weeks ago your speaker took the opportunity to ask the gathered ministers and parish councils of the diocese of Brackenheim if, since it had never come to his ears, they had ever heard workers complain about their serious loss of wages due to the holidays. He put this question slowly and repeatedly, and in the course of the discussion it was time and again answered in the negative. The situation may be a little different in proper manufacturing towns. But the complaints cannot amount to very much, else one would be aware of them, and your speaker has a lot of contact with the people and with the lowly among them.

Our people still believe that there is a blessing not to be calculated in figures, because it is indeed incalculable. If the days that cannot be dropped under any circumstances are deducted, the holidays in question come to a mere ten. It is really hard to believe that those few days are the reason our Württemberg is lagging far behind the neighboring lands in its economic development and industry—an assertion actually still to be proved. Let us not try, by brandishing these big figures, to tear a genuine piece of Württemberg out of our people's heart, as would be the case if the holidays were abolished.

We want to mention yet a third objection to the holidays, which the mover of the bill once again, it seems, puts in the mouth of some professor, this time of theology and ethics. He is assumed to say:

> Furthermore, I detect a Jewish and rabbinical leftover in the way you cling to your holidays. You see in these days a sort of fence or a kind of lightning conductor, for the Sundays. That is nothing but a rabbinical device of the great synagogue, which said: Since human beings are by nature inclined to violate the holy law of God, the Ten Commandments, and since every such transgression is deserving of death, we must erect a fence of less serious prohibitions, which, if transgressed in a case of need, exact a less severe punishment. But I agree [continues that fictitious professor] with what somebody with a deep knowledge of the human heart has said: just as I cannot keep a child from committing big thefts by my closing an eye to smaller dishonesties on his part, the desecration of the Sunday cannot be prevented by allowing people to indulge in wild orgies on the holidays. And if perhaps in

times gone by the holidays did form such a fence for the Sunday, they certainly do so no longer now. At present in most areas Sundays, and in some social strata the great feast days as well, are misused for amusements and merry-making just as much as the holidays. In truth it is just the overabundance of holidays that is co-responsible for the desecration of the Sunday.

Thus the purported professor, who with strange sophistry twists what is usually brought up in favor of preserving the holidays into an argument against them. But how audacious and most unjust is already the assumption that our people quite generally do not know what else to do with the holidays than to "spend them indulging in wild orgies." That is not the case; all observation, even the most painstaking, merely establishes that though there are some common people in our land, too, who misbehave, the attitudes and customs of by far the great majority of our people are quite different.

What makes one inclined to call the holidays a fence around the Sundays is an awareness of certain needs felt by many people. These needs are not really low; at times they are actually noble. They arise from human nature and our emotions and should not be rejected or downright repressed. And yet, their satisfaction is unfitting for a Sunday, since it would disturb the holiness of that day. Dancing, for example, is not in keeping with the hallowing of the Sunday, for which reason we do not permit it here on Sundays. Yet how can it possibly be considered totally unacceptable and the whole people be forbidden to dance? Just because that is not possible, we notice that wherever our holidays are not observed, dancing is invading the Sundays. It is to prevent this happening also among us here and to preserve Sunday as a holy day that we like to speak up on behalf of the holidays. Having their place midway between Sundays and workdays, they are better suited for dancing parties (where people can't do without them) than Sundays. In this way they are a fence around the Sunday.

There are still many other such things that are acceptable elements in the life of the people but would spoil a Sunday if engaged in then. I am thinking of men's choir festivals, gym meets, fire brigade practices, and gatherings of all kinds, where various social classes, trades, and parties such as are part and parcel of a people's life engage in social intercourse. All these things are not at all wrong in themselves; they have a right to exist, and their existence may at times be of great value for the direction and unfolding of our people's whole life, yet what lover of a tranquil Sunday would wish them shifted to Sundays? But if such events are held on holidays and these are thus seen as a "fence around Sunday," how can one call it a "Jewish-rabbinical leftover"?

Since our holidays are halfway days of rest from everyday work, they are also used for fairs. It could easily happen that these fairs end up being transferred to Sundays, as has actually long been the case in Bavaria and elsewhere. Then, too, religious associations of all kinds like to use holidays for their meetings. I think of mission festivals and institutional celebrations, which are truly festivals of inestimable value for the inner life of Christian people and yet are not so suited for Sundays, even just on account of the traveling it entails for visitors from farther away.

Then, too, we must take into consideration the more autonomous expressions of religious life (such as are not found anywhere else) among the people here in Württemberg. What a lovely picture it is to see the roads crowded with people on their way to places where they want to gather for brotherly upbuilding and sharing! They can be recognized from afar by their red and blue umbrellas. Are they to give that up? Or should it all be transferred to Sundays? It would deeply grieve many of our people if it were suddenly made known: There are to be no more holidays now!

In the foregoing we have already touched on other considerations, for example, how the holidays generally lend themselves to friendly visits with acquaintances and relatives, which in a peculiar way contribute to the genial character of our Württemberg life and are now made still easier by the improved means of traveling. Should this henceforth take place on Sundays? Should people ride in trains instead of going to church? It is quite saddening to see even now how all those things our people used to do on holidays are now frequently done on Sundays; people go off in all directions and no longer care about being inwardly nourished and built up in church. Where does it come from? It is the consequence of starting to do away with the holidays, which, sad to say, has in fact already largely taken place. Nonetheless, there are still countless numbers of people who hold fast to the good old custom, go to church on Sundays and use the holidays for other things.

This paper shows that Blumhardt had a very high and favorable opinion of Christianity's quiet working among the people. One or the other might be tempted to think: What he says may indeed hold true for his blessed land of Württemberg but not everywhere else. Blumhardt would have agreed with him as to the blessing resting on Württemberg but would have stood by his confident assessment also as applied to other countries, though perhaps in a more restricted way. He once wrote, "In other lands, too, I could not but form a higher opinion of the hidden Christian outlook of the common man than do others who are wont to judge more severely in such matters."

Actually, Blumhardt's participation in the synod of the Württemberg Protestant church carries us forward to a much later period of his life, the time of his ministry in Bad Boll. But since we are concerned to present a true picture of Blumhardt rather than a chronological account of his life, it may be right to deal with this side of his work in the present context, where it helps to throw light on his character as a private individual. The people twice elected Blumhardt as a lay member of the synod (for the districts of Crailsheim and Geislingen), just because they had confidence in his sound and (in a holy sense) liberal judgment. Although he did not speak much at the synod, his influence there was great, particularly because when a vote was taken by name, because of his age he was among the first to cast his vote.

As the above paper shows, he could make a brave and effective stand in favor of good, old-established customs. On the other hand, he was surprisingly cool—pleasing some and displeasing others—toward any attempts made by persons that actually shared with him the same foundation of faith, to promote piety artificially by legislative measures. As a likeminded church dignitary says of him, he was an inwardly composed man, who had his center of gravity in himself. And it may be added that it was very much on his heart that the sacred duty of the legislator—unbiased justice and equity—and the basic law of the Lord—love—should not take second place to party loyalty. Indeed, where he had the feeling that zealous emphasis on sacredness of purpose led to a less than scrupulous attitude as regarded means, he was apt to flare up in anger. It was his urgent concern not to antagonize the Lord, from whom he still expected great deeds for the salvation of all. In the journal of the Württemberg Lutheran church a correspondent wrote as follows about Blumhardt's contributions at the synod: "One had the impression that steering a whole body along guidelines laid down by the church was not his special gift. His loving optimism and joyous hopefulness amid all the misery was excellent for pastoral care, but in the administration of the church it allied him with the liberals. He simply had no feeling for church policy."

To be sure, many a one among the liberals might well have felt enlivened and refreshed by such a living Christianity, which breathed and inspired love and trust. One has the feeling, too, that precisely the kind of Christianity expressed in the above church paper was bound to meet with understanding and sympathy in wider circles.

Blumhardt saw the many novel features of today's society very much in the same light as he did the life of the common people. Such an assessment was apt to lead others to suspect him of being almost morbidly unguarded in his opinions. It did not disturb him, for example, to hear of the growing number of mixed Christian-Jewish marriages. He welcomed them as a significant element in the Christianization of the Jews that is inconspicuously going on. Once he even defended a certain well-publicized marriage between an unbaptized Japanese and a Christian woman, as well as the clergyman who had married them. He had heard, he said, that that Japanese was quite a good fellow, and hadn't the couple sung at the wedding, "Jesus, still lead on"? Compared with the obstacles the kingdom of God had to face and which he was fully aware of, such things were of small account to him. With such broadmindedness and his clear vision, which perceived everything very simply, he had an outstandingly beneficial and freeing influence on many people and cleared away a good deal of narrowness and prejudice.

Scarcely anybody will dispute this with regard to a reply he gave in *Blätter aus Bad Boll* to the question if it is really, as some say, a lack of trust in God to insure one's movable property with a fire insurance company. Blumhardt's reply is so characteristic of the way he perceived everywhere the Christian spirit still grandly governing—the quiet supremacy of the Lord—that I insert it here. He writes in 1876:

> I can never quite grasp what objections there can be to the usual orderly and honestly set-up insurance companies, which are properly regulated and supervised by the state, especially when it concerns insurance of the kind referred to in the question. What I find particularly startling is that taking out insurance is called a lack of trust in God. God tells us time and again that our fellow brothers should help us, or that his help should be channeled through their hands. He does not supply our earthly needs directly from heaven; rather, they should be met through the goodwill and help of our fellow men. Now when men agree among themselves how to go about providing help of the right kind in special needs, who is to get up and argue that what they do is contrary to trust in

God? We are asked to make sacrifices where there is a need, and if these are made beforehand so that the need can be met when it arises, what is wrong with that?

We should feed the hungry, give drink to the thirsty, and clothe the naked. How can one individual do that all the time? Now if all together share in doing what is to be done, should that not be seen as obeying the command to love instead of as an act opposed to faith? What good is faith and trust in God if it amounts to a lessening of love? Could I not put in my contribution with a quiet prayer that it might be of benefit, if not to myself then to others? If I believe that misfortune will not strike me—and many are conceited enough to assume that God will spare them—should I then say, "It won't hit me; so I don't give anything"? By no means. We must all feel concerned when somebody has lost everything—say, through fire or hail. See how God once helped Job to his feet again through his brothers' laying the foundation for a new fortune, which was then blessed by God (Job 42:11). Now, prompted by feelings of sympathy, insurance companies have been set up, mostly under state supervision. If we keep aloof from them, thinking that we must trust *God* to restore what he takes away (though it is through *people* that he does it!), that actually turns faith in quite a wrong direction, for what keeps us from chipping in is in fact trust that *people* are going to help us, or so it seems. In this way, faith in God imperceptibly turns into trust in men. Experience shows how deceptive that is.

Those who will have nothing to do with insurance are actually unmerciful and hard toward their fellow men. They load impossible burdens on them when it comes to the point of helping someone struck by misfortune—precisely because it is not God directly but *people* who have to supply money, clothes, and other things. Or would a man go so far as to downright defy God, as if saying, "If God took it from me, he ought to restore it to me too," as though God were under obligation to let it rain straight down from heaven? Yet we know what pressure the thousand-fold distress all around puts especially on philanthropists, who are expected to help everywhere yet cannot possibly do so. Why should these men have to shoulder the heavy financial burdens that persons struck by misfortune but uninsured (who therefore could have helped themselves in another way) are bound to lay upon them?

Let us consider how much each private person would have to contribute in order to provide even the most necessary assistance to somebody reduced to beggary by fire or hail. Even though many would gladly give quite a lot, they simply cannot afford it. In particular those that counsel against insurance ought to ask themselves if they are ready to give to someone thus stricken even so much as the amount of the premium the latter had been unwilling to pay. And let us consider how small is the circle of people from whom those struck by calamity can expect to receive assistance, whereas the insurance companies can easily obtain the funds needed from their much larger circle of members. Frequently, the exhortation to trust in God does not amount to anything more than telling the one in distress, "Go in peace; keep warm and well fed," but not giving him what his body needs, as James points out (Jas 2:16).

As things are, it can even be a duty to take out insurance, since only the participation of many can make a company viable. I know from my younger years that for a long time companies insuring against hail could not flourish, because too few farmers participated. Avarice certainly played a part there under the cover of trust in God. Their trust in God consisted in thinking, "I trust that God will spare me, that's why I pay no premiums." Now assuming that you are spared but your neighbor suffers harm, are you ready to let him have even as much as you ought to have paid in by way of premiums? Thus, all this trust in God turns out to be nothing but secret avarice. Therefore do your part where you are asked to join in—not for your own sake, if I may say so, but for the sake of others, who in the end will be grateful to you for contributing to a fine gift they receive. What a shock it is to hear that this or that uninsured person has suffered a misfortune, for one scarcely knows what to advise in such a case.

As regards big calamities that befall individuals, we must see them generally as having come upon us all. For we cannot say that the stricken individuals have deserved more than anyone else to be afflicted so severely—almost beyond measure. Rather, so that all may take notice, they have been hit by what is liable to strike *everybody*, as the Savior speaks, "Unless you repent, you will all likewise perish" (Luke 13:3, 5). In particular, the total ruin striking them ought to remind us of the total ruin through judgment that the godless have facing them unless they repent. If the ones struck by calamity are to be a warning example for us all, should we not compensate them for the loss sustained? When we advise against insurance, we shift the burden onto the afflicted individuals and treat them as the only guilty ones, whereas in reality they are, so to speak, martyrs on behalf of all and as such maybe much less guilty than some others. So if all together make advance provision that the persons fated to suffer the shock (on the others' behalf!) shall not have to bear the damage alone, what is so objectionable about that? He that disdains to insure what he has often does so with the self-assurance of a righteous man who is not about to be struck by misfortune; he that takes out insurance fears for himself as for a sinner the wrath he may well deserve. Which of the two chooses the better way? Therefore, where love and sympathy work together for the benefit of persons grievously hit, you should not step back and declare, "I will not join in; my conscience does not allow it."

I know well that insurance can also lead to serious sin. There I can only say, "Keep clear of everything that is against your conscience." Especially where so-called life insurance is concerned, one is liable to come to grief, often acting in a way that does violate trust in God. But it is not possible to make rules. Whoever stands in the fear of the Lord has within himself a warning voice he ought to heed.[2]

There was also a great mildness in Blumhardt's broadminded attitude. When people complained to him that feeling sleepy in church was a need to them, he would likely tell them, if strenuous work or sleeplessness or sickness was the cause: "Have a little snooze then! It will do you good, and afterward you can really be attentive. Don't stay away from church because of that!" Of course, he also said: "Some people sleep because they are quite satisfied with what they have and are. They know everything, and if they hear anything new, it only annoys them. They are not ready for a new burst of life. What is one to say in a case like that? One just lets them sleep." In a similar way he spoke of another need, that of distracting thoughts arising during prayer: "This hangs together with the whole way our thinking works, where everything is in flux the whole time and the most diverse elements rub shoulders. It doesn't mean a thing, as long as the intruding thoughts are not wicked ones. It can even prove a blessing the Lord bestows on the sincerely praying person by reminding him of this or that matter he ought not to forget."

A gentle broadmindedness also informed Blumhardt's view of Sunday work. I enclose here an excerpt from what he wrote about that subject:

When people talk of Sunday work going on here or there and the question comes up whether such work is forbidden or not, an important point for me is whether or not it is customary in that area and whether or not the doing of it interferes with the awareness that it is Sunday, both on the part of those who do it and of those

2. *Blätter aus Bad Boll*, No. 10, 1876.

who see it. I gladly leave uncensured whatever is customary and does not really disturb Sunday and the devotion proper to it, even if I do not like it very much. To me it seems presumptuous to campaign against something that is generally accepted and not otherwise sinful.

Strict legalism is not good in any case and does not accord with our evangelical freedom. The words of Paul should not go unheeded where he says, "Therefore let no one pass judgment on you in questions of food and drink or with regard to a festival or a new moon or a Sabbath" (Col 2:16). The apostle is evidently thinking of the narrow-minded way some Christians kept these days, unjustifiably claiming that this or that was against the conscience. There must have been instances of such narrow-mindedness also about the Sabbath, but Paul says we should not let anyone judge us with regard to such things. It is not the festivals or holidays themselves that the apostle opposes, especially not the Sabbath, which the prophets in several places clearly regard as part also of the *new* covenant. What he does speak out against is rigid legalism, where one says to the other, "This and this you may not do, else you sin against the divine commandment to keep the Sabbath." And when the Lord Jesus says, "The Son of Man is lord of the Sabbath," in the first place he probably wanted to stand up for his disciples against the Pharisees as regards their plucking heads of grain. At the same time, though, he clearly indicated that in the heavenly kingdom he was founding there would be freedoms not allowed under the law to which Israel was subject. However, it was not his intention to do away with the Sabbath, as many misinterpret it. We may take it that Jesus here spoke out against the extremes that zealots are now and then inclined to go to.

Quite generally, there is much in human life that is strange; there is much to sigh about, also as regards Sunday, and the effect can only be to make us mild and lenient. I want to mention just one thing. Once, when I was rector in Möttlingen at the time of the great revival, a servant-maid came to me from Kentheim, half an hour's walk from the district town, Calw. She had been inwardly awakened, and things were no longer all the same to her. She was in domestic service with a baker who daily, and particularly on Sundays, sent freshly baked goods to Calw for sale. The girl had to carry them there on her head. Once she had to do it on Good Friday as well, and it troubled her conscience. It seemed to her a sin to be engaged in such a workaday task on the day of the Savior's passing. Deeply disturbed, she asked me if she must not, for the sake of the Lord, give up a job that required her to desecrate

Good Friday as well as Sundays. The girl was sincere and free from affected piety. The Crucified One had simply become too dear to her, and her conscience had been awakened. Now what was I to say about such work on Good Friday? I pondered it and finally replied what I shall set down here in detail:

> When you have gone into service, you are in fact not quite your own master. You have an obligation to your employer. Now the apostle says that those who serve should remem- ber they render service to God and not to men (Eph 6:7).

I told her she should see this unavoidable Sunday work in that light and that she did not sin if she did obediently and dutifully what she was asked to do. If there was sin in it, the responsibility was not hers, and if she did what she had to do with forbearance and not with sighing, it would mitigate the responsibility. Quitting the job?

> Don't think you will have it better elsewhere! You are liable to have so many things to do on Sundays and holidays that it might look as if these didn't exist for you. After all, you can still go to church, and if now and then you can't, you just have to put up with it and observe the Sunday in quiet and in spirit. I therefore advise you to stay and to do it for the sake of the Lord as a service of love. When you walk along the lovely valley path from Kentheim to Calw with your baked goods on your head, you are really at liberty out there. In your heart you can think of the Savior, who was crucified for you and who on the day of his death had to bear on his head not just baked goods but the crown of thorns, as well as his cross. Do it in that sense, then your Savior will be with you, and your Good Friday will surely be richly blessed.

The girl was greatly reassured and satisfied. But you see, that is how one has to counsel in such cases. Or should I have spoken differently? I actually could not help pitying the poor girl, and yet there are so many who have it much worse, and on Sundays too. I also had to think of her employers. They have to make a living by baking, and the people in Calw want to have freshly baked goods, most of all on Sundays and holidays. So what can you do there? But is the Sunday really being disturbed by a business activity of this kind? When someone who is tied down in this way lifts his eyes up to the Lord, he can always have blessed Sundays. But you who are free, do not unduly burden those dependent on you.

Their sighs will bring you no blessing. Above all, however: Let us not judge or reason harshly and rigidly![3]

Such were Blumhardt's guidelines also when it came to questions of a more general nature concerning both state and church. It was, of course, not very often that questions relating to the *State* were brought to him. In this respect we can only emphasize that he strove almost enthusiastically to understand, appreciate, and defend measures taken by the state or government. But it was more than just enthusiasm; it sprang from the depth of his heart. When Paul says, "There is no authority except from God, and those authorities that exist have been established by God" (Rom 13:1), Blumhardt had a deeper respect for the word "God" than many others and was afraid of coming into conflict with it. Thus he once publicly defended the synod for not facing the authorities with a demand to "terminate the running of all special trains and goods trains on Sundays," as had been urged.[4] He suggested it would be better to reawaken the conscience of the public by preaching, Sunday schools, and private conversation, and in this way give people a fresh appreciation for the Sunday. The government should not always be made out to be the culprit, often due to inadequate knowledge on the part of the critics. Blumhardt pointed out that the government simply arranges such matters to suit the needs and wishes of the public. "I do not like the sort of language frequently used (more recently coming from Christian quarters too) to criticize the state, now in this matter, now in another. Such a tendency, also on the part of persons of education and standing, to find fault undermines respect for the state."

Naturally, it was questions concerning the church that were brought to him more frequently. Here, too, we notice in him the same simple, broadminded approach. When a certain pastor had misgivings about solemnizing the marriage of previously divorced persons, Blumhardt declared: "The previous history of such persons is of no concern to you as a minister; it is a matter for the secular authorities to deal with. The situation is that these people are getting married. For this they do in any case need God's blessing, and that is what you give them—all the more so if they ask for it." The last remark refers to the recently introduced regulation to the effect that couples were no longer *required* to obtain the blessing of the church for their marriage. After what we heard earlier, it

3. *Blätter aus Bad Boll*, No. 42, 1875.
4. *Stuttgarter Landbote* (Stuttgart Country Messenger), No. 16, 1869.

will come as no surprise that Blumhardt actually welcomed this lifting of the burden of a "compulsory blessing" from both clergy and laity. Amid the turmoil caused in some church circles by the introduction of the civil wedding, he was able to impart greater clarity, freedom, and firmness to numerous consciences, both of clergymen and laymen. He did this in particular by pointing on the one hand to the high *outward* juridical value of governmental authority as compared to the legally insignificant standing of the clerical office and on the other hand to the supremely high *inner* value of the church and its spiritual authority.

This may also be the place to insert a written and in many ways characteristic statement of Blumhardt's on our attitude to the Jews. It is in reply to misgivings voiced about present methods of mission work among the Jews:

> As regards mission among the Jews, it cannot be done any other way. I know its shortcomings as I know those of mission among the heathen, but at present I do not know of any way to improve either the one or the other. You say that it is a matter to be taken up by the whole believing church of Christ. You are right, but how will you accomplish this? What is believing Christendom doing for those around it? How does a believing Christian act toward his servants, his tailor, shoemaker, at the market, in business, etc.? Does he in every way so conduct himself that he may possibly convert those he meets? That he may give offense to no one? Now if in fact this is far from being the case in ordinary life among *ourselves*, how will a believing Christian behave toward a chaffering Jew? O brother, believing Christendom has to become different itself before it can convert Jews! You can systematize things as much as you like, but you are reckoning without the host! I am convinced that there will be no large-scale conversion of Jews until they once more have an opportunity to see the power of Christ manifest itself among Christians, also in the form of signs and wonders. In the meantime I consider it very important to treat them really as brothers and to let them recognize the brother in you, inasmuch as we believe with them in the God of Abraham, through whose seed all peoples on earth are to be blessed [Gen 12:3]. In this way I have found an opening with many Jews. Anything further must then come by itself or with merely some assistance on our part.

We have been observing Blumhardt's natural, human ways from the small circle of family life to the widest circles of state and church. I have deliberately presented that aspect already at *this* stage of our biography, so as to complement in good time the other and quite different impressions we receive of him. Having thus become generally acquainted with him as a private individual, we want to accompany him once more to the specific setting of Möttlingen and take a look at his own house, meeting him there principally as a pastor and counselor.

We have already seen how it was in his rectory on Sundays. How Blumhardt managed to cope with the mountainous work load pressing on him between Saturday and Monday was beyond the grasp especially of those people in the neighborhood that remained somewhat cool toward the movement. So legend tried to explain it in the queerest ways imaginable. We have seen how during the week he gave time and energy liberally to his Möttlingen parish. In those days he used whatever spare time was left to tutor the "young gentlemen" lodging with him (of whom we heard in the chapter about miracles) and later his own children as well. Beyond that, however, a new field of activity began more and more to demand his energies.

As already noted, his house gradually filled with long-term guests who under his roof sought refuge from all manner of ailments. In the main they were persons suffering from nervous complaints, most of all epilepsy. It was touching to see how simply and courageously Blumhardt dealt with this strange malady, against which he incessantly pleaded for divine help. In his house he did not want much to be made of the attacks peculiar to this illness, mainly for the sake of the afflicted person himself (for whom bystanders' supposedly sympathetic dismay at his misfortune is most harmful) but also for the sake of the Lord's honor. When one of these patients suffered an attack, say, at breakfast, all those present knew what to do: They remained quiet and inwardly interceded for the sufferer; as a rule such an attack passed quickly and easily, and there are even now in 1881 people who gratefully remember the miraculous and lasting healing they received in those days. When a certain lady complained that her sensitive nerves were badly affected by such an attack, Blumhardt ordered her as a discipline to pay an immediate visit to the patient concerned.

Still, these house guests did not actually require a great deal of time, but there opened up before him another area where he could put his experiences to use in a quite new, unusual, and fruitful way—the field of correspondence. It is interesting to watch this work grow, as it is reflected in his letters to Barth. In the beginning, for example, he found

it important to let Barth know how every mail brought him two letters of this type, then four, then ten, etc., not omitting to tell him at the
same time how deeply he felt moved by the contents of these letters.
Distress (at both high and low levels of society) sharpens our senses;
much more than wellbeing and comfortable circumstances it makes for
sensitive eyes and ears. Thus remarkably soon, sufferers at distant places
became aware of this wonderful man. Many a person who had heard just
a little—and maybe even this little bit in a garbled form—of the happenings in Möttlingen was suddenly and almost miraculously overcome by
the feeling: That is where you must turn! Presently there formed around
Blumhardt an invisible, far-flung congregation of people that regarded
him as their spiritual father: like weak vines climbed upward by attach-
ing their tendrils to the strong stem of his faith and love.

Probably only those who actually experienced it can have a real idea
of the love with which Blumhardt embraced also persons he only corresponded with and whose face he never saw. Through the many decades,
right until 1880, there were many hundreds of families of the educated
classes and thousands of families of just ordinary folk whose concerns,
with all their ins and outs, moved his heart. Indeed, they so moved it that
he continuously brought them before God in true priestly manner, with
the result that probably all these families could tell of manifold blessings
and of wonderful help received. Not without reason they ascribe their
benign experiences largely to Blumhardt's intercession. Their letters of
thanks (quite a number of which still exist) tell, for example, of a boy's
successful passing of an exam; or of a child being given, after years of
waiting, to some married couple, be it of the aristocracy or of the poorer
classes; or of many cures of illnesses, and so on.

This correspondence naturally helped to swell more and more
the ranks of those who desired to stay for a longer time in Blumhardt's
house. He refused many such requests because he did not consider a
stay necessary for obtaining divine help. Nevertheless, that still left a lot
of cases where a stay in his house would clearly be a real help or where
a refusal, not being absolutely necessary, would have been unkind. In
these cases Blumhardt went to the utmost limit in giving up all his own
comfort and carefully using every space in the house for those in need
of help. More than once he gave up his own study for persons needing a
heated bedroom, and did his work, however awkward and difficult this
was, in the living room crowded with children.

Since in the next part of our book we shall come to know Blumhardt as a pastor and counselor, I limit myself here to these brief sketches. However, to give the reader as vivid a picture as possible of the Möttlingen rectory household, I would like to let a witness speak who had a chance to look closely and with a more practiced eye into what went on in those endearing rooms. The writer tells of her coming to Möttlingen and her extended stay there:

> I had actually been sick from childhood on. When I was nineteen, a serious nervous illness (convulsions) broke out, probably as a result of outward circumstances. Everything possible was done to find a cure. My fatherly friend E. had great sympathy for me and showed me much love. He tried in every way to help me up, but it was all in vain. All medical aid was of no avail either. At that time a newspaper article directed our attention to Blumhardt's most remarkable work at Möttlingen. E. went to Möttlingen, recognized very quickly who he was dealing with, was at once won for the cause, and came to me with the message: "I have found a man who already has helped many sick persons through prayer. If you have trust, I will take you to him." I was ready and we traveled.
>
> When we stopped at a small town to obtain a wagon and went to a little inn to have something to eat, who would be sitting there? *Herr Pfarrer* Blumhardt just returning from a journey. Together we rode to Möttlingen. At the entrance to the village the wagon stopped, and we caught sight of the whole family, who had come out to greet the returning father. What a moving welcome, especially from his wife—so deep and warm! Two persons were meeting who bore tremendous burdens, which they could scarcely manage alone. The children, too, were happy.
>
> Now we approached the rectory. Various sick people were there, among them a girl suffering terribly from epilepsy. Actually everything made me feel at home, only the epileptic filled me with fear and terror. I even thought I might have to share the same room with her, and that made me quite unhappy. Otherwise I found everything very attractive. To be sure, it was with an anxious heart that I first entered the study, thinking there would be a long talk, and how my heart became light when the interview was over so quickly, in that simple manner everybody is familiar with. Gottliebin could not understand at all why I would not start unpacking, since she had given me a dresser for my use. Timidly I told her that I did not yet know if I would stay longer. I noticed she could not fathom that at all. In the living room I suffered an attack of spasms, but it began quite mildly and was soon over,

which struck me as remarkable. Still, I could not get rid of my anxiety with respect to the epileptic girl. I told that to the *Herr Pfarrer* and also that I felt homesick, as I had now been away from home for a whole year. "Well, why don't you go home then? You can get better just as well at home." And that's how it went. I cheerfully returned home; there were still light fainting fits, but there was no question anymore of violent attacks of spasms such as I had had before. But since there were still some rough spots in my emotional life, I corresponded with Pastor Blumhardt, and the problems disappeared one after the other.

Feeling deeply attached to Möttlingen, E. and I decided to go there for Easter. A lady and a young girl wanted to come along, and so we went. We arrived and entered the dear, familiar living room with the fine, grey sofa and the long table. We felt as if we were in Abraham's bosom and happy, so happy—all through my life I had had no inkling that a person can really be happy! The epileptic girl was gone. We were soon familiar with everything and felt so much at home as one would hardly feel in one's own parents' house.

Suddenly the cry went up. "The Turks are coming! The Turks are coming!" "Who are they?" Gottliebin informed us that they were four former pupils of the pastor. Now begins a great hustle and bustle in the house, for there are always lots of visitors over Easter. The barn gets cleaned up and beds are put in there, very neat and orderly, and that's for the "Turks." We had to help sew the linen sheets to the bed covers, as was then generally the custom in Möttlingen. It was so much fun to sew and lay it all out—there is something wonderful about a happy heart such as you have been given quite unawares in Möttlingen! And now they have arrived; they come pounding up the stairs and are welcomed ever so warmly—oh, how wonderful it all was! I think the table was so long it extended right through all the rooms.

I should have said something about the morning devotions too. Everybody had a Bible in front of him, even the domestic staff, if I remember rightly. All had to take turns reading a verse, including Blumhardt's own sons. One of them still read feebly and timidly, another bravely and briskly, as his whole nature was—red-cheeked, sun-tanned, solid. The youngest one, quite little and still on his mother's breast, caused Gottliebin a lot of work by day and night.

There was also Mariele, a young, petite, and very assiduous girl, who could not stand it at all if somebody took a teaspoon different from the one she had provided for him. Her fussiness often made us smile and irked us a little too, in the way young ladies such as we were are prone to react.

In the morning we had to wash and dry the cups. I remember how much I liked at breakfast to see the cups of the whole table lined up, always two by two, in a long, long row, with the *Herr Pfarrer's* cup at the head. Then, when the big milk jugs and coffee pots had been brought in, *Frau Pfarrer* would fill all the cups herself and pass each to the person it was intended for. She always managed to let the thick skin of the milk plop neatly into the dear housefather's cup, and we found that very touching and amusing.

Yet with all that, one would nevertheless feel in a serious mood, and E. commented more than once that after the devotions and worship services here no further inner exertion was required; one simply felt inwardly carried along and constantly near to God. I myself have never been one for religious reflection, and at least from the Möttlingen time on (it had not been so before) my nature was simply to accept things. But even for more deeply thinking persons such as E. and our traveling companions the Möttlingen experience left nothing to be desired. I still remember how we felt in the church there on Good Friday and how the words flowing from the *Herr Pfarrer's* lips went straight to the heart in a living and powerful way. We sang "I have now found the ground I trust in, to which my anchor firmly holds," and I can still hear how mightily the words "Thy mercy, Lord; Thy mercy, Lord" resounded through the small Möttlingen church. They have kept re-echoing right to the present day.

We very much loved Gottliebin, who often told such remarkable things. As to *Frau Pfarrer*, my impression was that at that time as well as later in Bad Boll she was in delicate health and not very robust. I kept noticing how in the midst of a prayer meeting, all absorbed in devotion, she would often heave a deep sigh. One became aware of the great load being carried in the Möttlingen rectory, yet amidst it all there was this guilelessness of the dear *Herr Pfarrer*!

More than once, too, somebody would seat himself at the piano in Möttlingen—oh, everything in Möttlingen was nice, even the big stoneware water pitcher on the table (if I remember rightly) and the large bowl with scrambled egg. But once, when a guest of very high station was expected, how it amazed us when a beautiful water jug of crystal glass appeared on the table. And the bed linen in the fine guest room was of such snowy whiteness that it filled us with great respect, even though everything in the house was very simple.

They had a washday while we were there, and the drying was no small matter, for there was no drying-loft, and everything had to be dried outside. "What if it rains?" I asked the dear *Frau Pfarrer*, with whom I was chatting about it. "Oh, the Savior always sends us good weather; he knows that we cannot do it any other way." As the entire rectory right up to the roof had been converted into dwelling space, a remarkable number of people could often be accommodated in that little house. I also saw Hansjörg Dittus at work in the house, as well as Katharina Dittus in the kitchen and elsewhere.

But then we had to think of traveling back, and so we did. Yet what a remarkable change had taken place with B., a person formerly so turned in on herself, so unfree and fearful! She was just full of joy and life. All who had known her from childhood on were amazed. When a doctor was consulted about it, he declared, "It's not the cold water treatment that did it!" And so it has remained. Although the vicissitudes of life put stones—and rocks, too—into the way of this young woman and mother, she has to say over and over again: "God be praised that there is a place such as Möttlingen and Bad Boll! Thanks be to them all from the bottom of my heart!"

We want to remember yet another kind of work Blumhardt did in his Möttlingen study—his writing. Passing over those literary endeavors mentioned earlier, some of which went on throughout his Möttlingen period, we want to tell here only of the new insights that his actual experiences there caused him to write about.

Two of these papers have already served us as sources for our narrative: his report of Gottliebin Dittus's illness, written for his ecclesiastical superiors, and his account of the subsequent revival movement, published in the journal of the Württemberg Protestant church. In the latter article, besides what we have already quoted, he particularly addressed two great evils afflicting people's lives in all social strata, the gravity of which the movement of repentance had made him aware of—magic and immorality within marriage. He discussed the latter issue so earnestly and severely that an opposition paper, thinking it had finally stumbled on what it had long been looking for, simply printed lengthy passages from that part of the article, with the remark that any further comment was superfluous. That was indeed the case, for this one statement by Blumhardt, which thus found a wide circulation, spoke powerfully to many hearts and drew a considerable number of new listeners to the Möttlingen church. Blumhardt concluded his account with the song by Machtolf inserted at the beginning of the second part of our narrative.

Another undertaking very dear to him consisted in putting into singable verse the psalms of David as well as individual passages from the prophet Isaiah, especially from chapters 40–66. Characteristically, it was a practical need that made him do it: He just loved singing and did not like Christians to sit together without expressing their feelings in song. He said, "A Christian who cannot with all his heart join in singing hymns of praise has something lacking in him." He considered the church's hymns adequate for church services but not fully satisfactory for singing at home. He found that there was much too much in them about the "I" and about the relationship between God and the Lord Jesus and "me." Then, too, it saddened and almost pained him that a great number of the finest hymns conclude with thoughts of death and dying. Filled with the spirit of the Bible from childhood on and newly immersed in it through his more recent experiences, he could not go along with that unbiblical way of feeling and thinking. We already know his basic position on this point: The Church of Christ, is not waiting for death but for the Lord's return and victory over death, and at the end of every hymn of supplication there ought to ring out the cry the whole Bible concludes with, "Yes, come. Lord Jesus!"

This feeling and temper Blumhardt found especially in the Psalms and the Prophets and therefore also the same confident hope of victory. He set himself the task of simply putting the text into meter and rhyme, without adding or subtracting anything—an undertaking that of course could succeed only if elegance of diction was not the main consideration. These songs based on the Psalms and Prophets show a mastery of the language but wear a very simple garment. When Blumhardt showed them to the hymn writer Albert Knapp, the frequently rather forced rhymes gave his former fellow fighter for a good hymnal something of a toothache. It is only by actually singing them that one comes to appreciate the worth of these songs. Listening to the pure, clear Bible tone put into song, one feels transported back across the centuries to the days when holy events took place, when God's people still felt they were a "people" and not a "small flock."

It is typical of Blumhardt that in these songs based on psalms and prophecies he was greatly concerned to avoid anything that might offend the sensibilities of Jewish people, so that these, too, might find edification in them. This was in tune with his desire mentioned above that in any contact with Jews the emphasis should first be on what is rooted in the faith we have in common with them. Many a pearl from our hymn poetry would also appeal to a devout Jew, especially songs from the group that speaks of comfort and trust, as for example: "Commit thou all thy griefs and ways into his hands," "If thou but suffer God to guide thee," "What'er our God ordains is right," but also others, such as Luther's paraphrase of Psalm 130 ("Out of the depths I cry to thee"), etc.

All these hymns make use of the meters that our most popular church melodies are based on. But in his own restatements of psalms and prophecies Blumhardt's powerfully moved heart could not be long satisfied with these church tunes. For verse that had sprung from the very depth of his heart he composed melodies of his own, for example the shaking minor tune for the prophet Isaiah's yearning prayer, "Oh, that thou wouldest rend the heavens, that from on high thou wouldest come" (Isaiah 64:1), or again a lovely melody for his rendering of Isaiah 40:1–11, which may follow here as one example of the poetic translation work Blumhardt did in those years.

GOD'S COMFORT FOR HIS PEOPLE

Tune: *Womit soll ich dich wohl loben*
"Comfort, comfort my dear children,
My own people," says your God.
"Lo, I come to save the sinners
Who were smitten by my rod.
Speak to them in accents tender!
For their evil, good I render.
Let Jerusalem take heart
And her sorrow now depart.
"You, my people, have been given
Double measure for your sin.
You had turned your back on heaven
Through the vice you wallowed in.
Now, once more by me befriended,
You shall see your bondage ended,
And what evil you did do
I have long forgiven you.
"In the waste land witness bearing,
Let your voice ring through the land,
That my people be preparing,
For my coming is at hand.
Through your hills let roads be driven,
Where may ride the King of heaven,
Bearing high, that strife may cease,
The bright banner of his peace.

"Valleys are to be uplifted
And all mountains be brought low,
Rocks and boulders must be shifted,
All unevenness must go.
Tell all men the wondrous story
That our God, the Lord of glory,
Is to come in all men's sight
And reveal his sovereign might."
By whose mouth were these words spoken?
By the Lord God's! While, alas,
Man's own words are but a token
That all flesh is like the grass.
Truly, all our human powers
Are like grass and meadow flowers.
Flowers fade, grass wilts away,
But God's word endures for ay.
From the mountain summit crying,
Zion, lift with might your voice:
"Judah's cities, cease your sighing!
Gather courage and rejoice!"
Bonds and chains no more now dreading,
Send the gladsome tidings spreading:
"Ended is your need and fear,
For behold, your God is near!"
He, whose arm rules all with power,
Lo, he comes, your mighty Lord!
He will make the wicked cower,
Give the just their due reward.
He as shepherd will be feeding
All his sheep and, gently leading,
Will protect his flock from harm,
Bear the weak lambs in his arm.

It was only at the request of the authorities that Blumhardt had written his, "Account of Gottliebin Dittus's Illness." Later, and indirectly because of that account, he saw himself obliged to compose against his will yet another paper, his *Vertheidigungsschrift* a more detailed presentation of his experiences and views. Dr. de Valenti, known to us from Blumhardt's Basel period, had meanwhile settled in Bern. Here he devoted himself to the care of emotionally ill persons, work for which he might have seemed qualified by his double medical and theological training. The extremely combative nature of his Christianity had long since isolated him and had caused most of the then leading men in Christian circles to feel embarrassed by him. Nevertheless, his unrelenting activity on behalf of the Gospel had still retained for him a number of adherents, who admired his keen intellect and courageous language. For these he published a magazine entitled *Licht und Recht* ("Light and Right"), the names given in Luther's Bible translation to the Urim and Thummim in the breastplate of the high priest of Israel.

Dr. de Valenti had offered to the Calw Publishing Association a brochure entitled *Ehestandsbüchlein* ("Booklet on Matrimony"), which contained some things that deeply grieved Blumhardt (who, as we know, was very strict on this point). As a member of the Association, Blumhardt felt constrained to speak out against accepting the brochure for publication. That led to a break between Blumhardt and de Valenti, as Blumhardt was soon to find out. De Valenti addressed a memorial to the consistory of the Württemberg Protestant church, warning it against Blumhardt's wrongheaded activities and urging them to take steps against him. For a long time Blumhardt remained unaware of it, as the memorial had simply been shelved, but in 1847 he received the following note from August Heinrich Mayer, journeyman clothmaker in Calw:

> Reverend Sir:
>
> At the request of Dr. de Valenti in Bern I herewith submit to you the following questions, which the doctor asks you to answer and address to me, as I shall post a letter to him in the near future. In this expectation I remain
>
> Your obedient servant, August Heinrich Mayer, clothier

As regards Dr. de Valenti's enclosed note, I quote its beginning and end in full, but shorten the questions themselves:

> To be submitted to Pastor Blumhardt in Möttlingen for his answer:
>
> - What do you think of the wrath of God? [According to de Valenti, wrath is part of God's nature.]
> - What do you think of the sinlessness of Jesus?
> - How do you see the justification of a sinner?
> - And how the sinner's sanctification?
> - What do you think of Hades [the place of the dead]?
> - And what of the restitution of all things?
> - What sins, in particular of present-day believers, are to be punished especially strictly and vigorously?

Through the agency of August Mayer, the undersigned expects a
clear and unequivocal answer to these questions, bearing in mind
1 Peter 3:15–16.

Dr. de Valenti

When these questions remained unanswered for several weeks,
August Mayer, on behalf of de Valenti, demanded a reply "between now
and four to six weeks," failing which Blumhardt would have to blame
himself for any further steps Dr. de Valenti might take. Thereupon
Blumhardt sent August Mayer the message that he was convinced his
old friend Dr. de Valenti would surely write directly to him if he was
interested in getting information from him. In reply to "Blumhardt's polite rudeness," as de Valenti put it, the latter threatened to treat him as a
shady and therefore false prophet and magnetic charlatan, if he did not
let him have the answer demanded "between now and four weeks." We
will skip the further correspondence.

It was Blumhardt's definite impression that good-natured compliance would do his friend no good, and he stuck to his gentle but firm
refusal, telling the clothier that he was ready to reply directly if his old
friend would ask him directly. The consequence was that de Valenti, who
in some obscure way had obtained a copy of Blumhardt's confidential
account of Gottliebin Dittus's illness, published it in his magazine *Licht
und Recht* and discussed it in a most spiteful way. That was the reason for
Blumhardt's *Vertheidigungsschrift* in which he demolished de Valenti's
flimsy charges. The passages we have quoted from this paper give an
impression of its general tone.

Its effect on de Valenti was tragic: He recognized that he was in the
wrong, yet not completely. He tried to compose a sort of retraction, but
with a number of provisos, and therefore could not produce anything.
Unfortunately, he neglected to do the nearest and most obvious thing,
which Blumhardt urged him in a warm and brotherly way to do, that is,
to visit him and get a firsthand impression of the matter he had presumed
so audaciously to judge. Increasingly, darkness enveloped his spirit.

He had earlier on felt drawn to investigate morbid aberrations in
the sphere of religion. Once he had written a paper on Francesco Spiera,
a preacher of the Gospel at the time of the Reformation, who, afraid of a
fiery death at the stake, had recanted and later died in the firm conviction
that he had committed the sin against the Holy Spirit. De Valenti held
that Spiera had judged rightly, and now a similar temptation took hold

of him. As far as I know, it did not leave him completely until shortly before his own death, when, under the faithful care of a younger pastor who was himself indebted to de Valenti for blessed inner help in earlier years, he was said to have found peace and consolation.

Henceforth he was friendly and very humble toward Blumhardt. When Blumhardt attended the mission festival in Basel, where de Valenti also happened to be, he visited de Valenti, hoping to be of some service to him in his present disconsolate condition. He returned from this visit deeply moved by the reconciliation with his former opponent but also quite shaken by the state he found him in. Then, at the annual festival of the Beuggen institution, the usual conclusion of the Basel festival, de Valenti in his turn sought out his old friend Blumhardt. Blumhardt had to deliver a supplementary address to a small overflow crowd, for whom there was no room in the large main meeting. There de Valenti went to see him and hear him speak, and afterward they greeted each other most warmly and completely reconciled. After so serious a dissension, it was touching to see the two men walk arm in arm. Unfortunately, Dr. de Valenti never brought himself to accept Blumhardt's insistent and repeated invitation to visit him in Bad Boll.

As Blumhardt would surely have wished himself, I have given but a very brief and scanty account of the initially so unhappy experiences of that time, even though a more circumstantial report would have shown him in a still more favorable light than the present short one. When de Valenti threatened him with making public his report of Gottliebin's illness, Blumhardt saw it as yet another divine signal to go forward courageously. That was confirmed in the sense that the *Vertheidigungsschrift* he was compelled to write brought much blessing to many a heart.

That brings us to the end of this chapter, whose contents in many ways hark back to the time of the great awakening. We still have to consider the last part of Blumhardt's life in Möttlingen—the time of transition.

16

The Time of Transition

BLUMHARDT EARNESTLY TRIED TO give his parish the character of a model congregation and to keep it so. He aimed very high, and what he saw actualized in the congregation came only in part up to his wishes and hopes. He also concerned himself with its economic needs. When during the period of scarcity in 1847 the "royal central committee of the Württemberg charity association" urgently appealed for the setting-up of local charity societies, Blumhardt immediately founded one in Möttlingen.[1] To begin with, it loaned people tow for spinning, as well as seed grain, but later on devoted itself exclusively to easing the purchase of cattle, thus protecting people from falling into the hands of usurers. That is why the society was later called a "cattle loan bank" or simply "cow bank." The articles of association of this "credit union" phrased in a rather original way, are very practical but presuppose a Christian disposition among the members. Therefore in 1875 Blumhardt, commenting on a recent revision of the articles of association, observed, "The fact that this society has been able to carry on at all, considering how it works, is proof to me that the spiritual uplift given to the congregation at that time through the grace of God has not yet completely vanished."

1. Editors Note: In 1846–1847, much of Europe suffered from food shortages due to a series of bad grain and potato (this was the period of the Irish Potato Famine) harvests in 1845–1846, which led to large-scale immigration to the United States. These food shortages, which ended in the fall of 1847, were compounded by a financial crisis which began in late 1847 in London and then later spread to the continent. This confluence of events was the social and political background of the revolutions that began in Paris in February 1848 and spread across continental Europe.

This society or credit union is ready to provide every reasonably trustworthy inhabitant of Möttlingen at his request with a cow for his use. Any calves this cow produces are then sold by the society, and the money realized is credited to the user's account as an installment payment toward the cow's purchase price plus a slight interest charge. When the combined amounts thus credited to the user equal the cost of the cow plus interest, the cow is his. The society is overseen by a committee of seven members under the guidance of a president, who has the decisive voice in all matters. Blumhardt remained the president right to his death.

This credit union has had a most beneficial effect and helped quite a bit to raise the general level of prosperity in Möttlingen. Blumhardt was glad to receive contributions for this pet enterprise of his, and by 1875 they had increased to 1300 *gulden*. Once, when a *Herr* Socin in Basel sent him a donation of "only" 360 *gulden*, as the total amount of a collection he had organized for the purpose, Blumhardt wrote to Barth that on receiving this gift, "I almost jumped right through the ceiling for sheer joy!" (This at a time when Blumhardt's physical stature was still very different from what it was later in Bad Boll.)

In other ways, too, Blumhardt cared warmly and actively for his congregation during those years of famine. A time of severe affliction had come upon the whole country, and the general distress seems to have been quite a factor in keeping more distant country folk from flocking to Möttlingen to the extent they had done earlier. The famine year 1847 was followed by the agitated year of revolution, 1848, which likewise had a paralyzing effect on the spiritual life of the people. It was precisely then that Blumhardt's far-reaching influence on the people made itself felt in a surprising way. The neighboring land, Baden, was in a topsy-turvy condition;[2] "they are all in a state of intoxication over there," it was said, and to some towns that could actually be applied in a more literal sense. People there had counted on vigorous applause and a great influx from Württemberg. But the part of Württemberg bordering on Baden,

2. Blumhardt himself was an eyewitness to that. On one occasion, when traveling through Baden in a hired carriage and putting up briefly at an inn, he barely managed, by a hurried departure, to save the carriage from being seized by the rapacious hands of the insurgents. On a journey to Elberfeld, too, he experienced at first hand the unsettled conditions. He happened to be traveling on the Rhine River in a boat filled with insurgents; it was dark, and when he looked out of the cabin window, the ship was fired at from the shore—probably, due to a misunderstanding, also by insurgents.

especially the Black Forest, where in any case the people are of a more placid disposition than their Baden neighbors, had also been strongly influenced by the movement in Möttlingen and resisted the prevailing agitation. We shall scarcely go wrong in assuming that this influence was at least one of the reasons that the area remained quiet. This supposition becomes the more plausible when we consider the ensuing elections for the national parliament.

During these times of political unrest, in Möttlingen the "newspaper meetings" came once more into their own and had their effect on the neighborhood. While in the *Bruderkonferenzen* ("brothers' meetings") spiritual questions were talked about, in the news gatherings civic matters were the topics, with the difference that here the Möttlingers made their own voice heard more freely than in the "conference" meetings. Their complaints and wishes were expressed and brought to the attention of the authorities, who at that time were most ready to listen. However, their wishes could not be complied with, for these mostly concerned the harsh forest laws and other such features of the modern state. (In fact, these latter found even more favor with the exponents of the new liberal tendencies than with the rulers of the past.) It took quite an effort to calm the people down.

Blumhardt enjoyed a good, truly fatherly reputation among the people of the Black Forest; they were confident that he had a heart and understanding for people's needs. That trust in Blumhardt was expressed memorably when the elections for the general German parliament in Frankfurt were proclaimed. The Black Forest folk rushed to put Blumhardt's name forward. The other candidate, a "well-meaning" man whom he felt obliged to endorse in place of himself, could not be trusted to know and appreciate the needs of the common people, and that made it all the harder for Blumhardt to squash his own candidacy. Even though he did his utmost to keep from being elected, he just barely escaped this. What was his chief reason for being so apprehensive of such a mandate? It was not the loss of time involved but—most characteristic—the oath that a representative would have to swear! "After all, an oath is an oath," he wrote to Barth.

However, the honor thus accorded to him was but a paltry comfort for Blumhardt. To be sure, it never worried him that those revolutionary aspirations might conceivably achieve their objectives, nor did he take such a dim view as others did at the time of the spiritual conditions among the people, as though there would be a general falling away from faith. Increasingly and in all classes of society, he had noticed telltale signs of life, indications of a great spiritual need. Yet on the whole he felt oppressed by the stillness that followed his great experiences and threatened to descend upon the religious life of the people. He was often overcome by an unutterable sadness, which also showed in his Möttlingen sermons of that time. He would ask his congregation whether they had really repented fully in the days of the revival, whether perhaps whole clusters of sins had been left unrevealed and a germ of disease been thus placed into the very cradle of the revival. Feelings of this kind made it easier for him to accustom himself little by little to the thought of leaving Möttlingen.

In and by itself it is usual for (Protestant) ministers in Württemberg to apply for another pastorate after ten to fifteen years at the same parish—in general a custom benefiting both the ministers and the congregations. The situation in Möttlingen was not of a kind to make Blumhardt feel obliged to disregard the custom. The spirit ruling there continued to be a good one, yet he saw no sign of the *progress* he had hoped and longed for. Besides, in some people's minds there did stir something of the revolutionary spirit of those days, even though merely with respect to local conditions in Möttlingen.

On the other hand, Blumhardt had been growing more and more into a new and more general calling, which began to crowd his local ministry. Above all, there was the influx of people desiring to spend some time under his roof, and this made him wish more and more for at least a bigger parsonage. And quite generally there may have stirred in him the hope that from a vantage point better suited for a more far-reaching activity he might take a more active hand in the affairs of the kingdom of God. It weighed heavily upon him that things were going from bad to worse, yet so little was being done.

He received various offers; in particular one from Barmen attracted him greatly. He was also invited to work as an itinerant preacher at Cologne. Besides, an important parish in his native land, Kornwestheim, very much desired to have him as its rector. A couple of traveling journeymen had inadvertently been acting on his behalf there by enthusiastically telling in a public house of their friendly reception in the Möttlingen rectory, how they had first been given some money and afterward, at their request, food as well. The Kornwestheim folk had asked the king of Württemberg to intercede for them and had been given some hope. Now when Barmen, which was very eager to have him, requested a definite reply, Blumhardt went directly to the king to ask his opinion. He acquainted him with the work he was engaged in and what further hopes he cherished for the church. The king was very friendly, but gave only short, if sympathetic, replies and did not go into anything in detail; nor did he respond in any way when Blumhardt made a passing reference to Kornwestheim. The king ended by saying, "Write to Barmen that it is your king's wish that you go on serving your native country." That word was to be of importance for Blumhardt in the time to come.

He thereupon turned down the offer from Barmen. As regards Kornwestheim, it went on looming on the horizon as but a distant possibility. For one thing, this outstanding benefice was coveted by men who had a right to be considered; for another, some persons of influence and authority in church affairs were reluctant to entrust it to somebody as unpredictable as Blumhardt. The rumors about the behind-the-scenes struggle for this benefice touched his heart. One day he met a fellow applicant for Kornwestheim, L., and when L. stretched out his hand for a brotherly handshake, the thought flashed through Blumhardt's mind, "Now, is this man about to suffer disappointment because of me? No, God will work it out differently!" Soon after he learned that L. had been awarded the post, and he felt at peace and of good cheer.

> God wants to go other ways with me, where nobody need envy me or feel hurt because of me ... But where the way will lead the Lord has to show. In the meantime I still have to go on serving the Möttlingen folk, who are so poor, so beggarly poor, and I may still be of some use to them during the coming year of hunger.

In spite of offers and requests from here and there Blumhardt had not applied for any other post, because he felt he had pledged himself to the Kornwestheimers. Soon, though, another parish, Fellbach, requested him to apply for the pastorate there. But this, too, was an above-average benefice and in great demand, and on hearing that somebody close to him, who was also a friend of Barth's, wished to obtain it, Blumhardt withdrew immediately.

In the meantime he had got fully used to the idea of a change and, confident of moving soon into a more roomy residence, had begun to build up a stock of bedding. He already had accumulated a considerable supply when burglars broke in one night and stole the lot. Blumhardt, whose life had been protected so wonderfully and so often from attempts made on it by those who hated in him the servant of Christ, was not to be exempted from those wretched signs of the times that have nothing to do with the Gospel.

What was to become of him? He once told about the thoughts that occupied him at that time:

> The visits I receive from persons afflicted in all kinds of ways and the requests from so many to spend some time under my pastoral care became ever more numerous. I finally had to resolve to devote myself wholly to the vocation that had fallen to me without my doing anything about it and which I could not sidestep without resisting the Lord. Since this would no longer go together with my Möttlingen ministry, which was very demanding too, I had to decide to give Möttlingen up.

Quite a few people are still not convinced that Blumhardt's choosing of such a vocation was really the way God had in mind for him. Perhaps if they had had to share his grief when so often—and it *did* happen often—he had to turn away persons in most desperate situations who pleaded with him to take them in, these doubters would find it easier to understand him. When, for example, a newspaper prematurely announced that Blumhardt's negotiations (to be related presently) for the purchase of Bad Boll had come to a successful conclusion, Blumhardt, to his deep embarrassment, immediately received notice of prospective arrivals from Holland, Nassau, France, and Tyrol. And when those negotiations did go forward and gave promise of a favorable outcome, how the joy that he could at least give some hope to applicants came to expression in his replies! How happy he felt at the prospect of having "plenty of space for sufferers, *queis nulla spes* (for whom there is no other hope)"!

Thus he quietly cast about for some larger facility obtainable at a modest price and suitable for the setting up of a much larger household, which would also accommodate guests that requested his pastoral care. Various possibilities were being considered—here an old castle, there a closed-down factory—and more than once the two in charge of Blumhardt's household, his wife and Gottliebin, were sent out to inspect them. Yet nothing really suitable came into view. In Göppingen, for example, he had a look at the so-called *Christophsbad* (Christoph's Spa), which was up for sale, only to learn that he was too late, the spa having been sold to a Dr. Landerer for use as a mental hospital.

While still in Göppingen, he paid a visit to Dean Osiander, who directed Blumhardt's attention to the spa called Bad Boll, about two walking hours away from Göppingen, calling it the most suitable property for Blumhardt's purposes. However, Blumhardt was so far from even considering this much talked-about spa that, although so close to it, he did not even bother to go there but traveled home with his wife. A little later, though, he did want to take a closer look at it and did so in the company of his father-in-law, Köllner. The sight of the imposing building only served to increase the reluctance of the two men, yet Blumhardt declared, "It is true, I have no courage, but I leave it all in God's will. If we take over this house, my wife and Gottliebin will have to bear the main burden. If they muster enough courage, I want to regard it as the will of God and take steps to acquire the property."

A few days later he sent his wife, accompanied by Gottliebin, to have a look at Bad Boll. These two inspected everything from the attic down to the cellar. Their courage grew as they proceeded, especially on discovering the large stock of furniture and beds, which would make it possible to take in guests immediately. When in the end they stood on the raised orchestra section of what was then the dining and ballroom and looked at the beautiful, spacious hall in front of them, it occurred to them what a fine chapel that would make right in the center of the house. As though gripped by something from on high, they shook hands and said as with one voice, "We mustn't let this one get away—don't you think?" They returned to Möttlingen with their minds made up that the house was well suited for the purpose intended and that the two of them would dare to shoulder the burden of looking after it.

Bad Boll, an old sulphur spa restored in a grand style in 1823 by the Württemberg government, was a large, palatial building two hundred feet wide in front, with two side wings, standing in nicely landscaped grounds. It had been a headache for the government for quite a while. In spite of all efforts it failed to attract many patients, and the income was far from covering the expenses. The state finance department tired of making up the chronic deficit by constant subsidies, and the government finally decided to find another use for the building. They first planned to adapt it for use as an orphanage and again and again came back to that idea, but what stood in the way was the same obstacle that also deterred would-be buyers: the lack of drinking water. Consequently, the house, plus grounds and accompanying buildings, had been up for sale but, as we have seen, with little success. Thus the asking price was reduced more and more, until it descended to a level that allowed Blumhardt, who had no funds whatever at his disposal, to regard purchasing the place as not completely outside the realm of possibility.

Now let us return to the Möttlingen rectory. Blumhardt listened to the two women's opinion. Gottliebin, true to her valiant character, spoke out most resolutely in favor of acquiring Bad Boll, and Blumhardt decided to take steps in that direction.

Quite apart from the problem of money, the difficulties were considerable. Because of the great things he had experienced, Blumhardt's name evoked in part uneasiness, in part unfavorable prejudices. In particular B., the official who handled the sale of the spa, was opposed to Pietism and, as he himself confessed later, had a special dislike of Blumhardt as a prominent leader among the believers. Nevertheless, one after the other the difficulties were resolved. One day Blumhardt presented himself in the office of the above functionary to announce formally his desire to purchase the place. The business formalities were quickly dealt with. Blumhardt was about to take his leave, but B., captivated by Blumhardt's joyful, natural ways, kept engaging him in conversation about this and that until a full half hour had passed. When Blumhardt had gone, B. went to see his wife and told her, beaming with joy, "Today I experienced the happiest half hour of my life. Do you know who was with me?" She could not guess it of course, and his mention of the name "Blumhardt" left her thunderstruck. From now on B. was a close and true friend of Blumhardt; he liked to spend what few hours of leisure he had at Bad Boll and valiantly took Blumhardt's side against powerful opponents, even in front of the king.

Of course, when it became known that Blumhardt intended to buy Bad Boll, quite a few tempests blew up. The same papers that had earlier spewed poison on the whole movement in Möttlingen were horrified at the disgrace that such a transaction would inflict on the country. The medical society (*Medizinal-Kollegium*) of Württemberg was worried, partly lest the healing spa should be forever lost to the public, partly also lest Blumhardt should set up a "lunatic asylum" without any medical control. It therefore urged the government to require Blumhardt to keep the spa open for public use, and to employ a physician to supervise the mentally ill. It based its misgivings especially on the probability that the spa would in any case pass into other hands before very long.

Blumhardt readily promised to give all possible attention to the first concern. The second demand he rejected most firmly, declaring that it had never entered his head to establish a mental hospital.

But also these difficulties, which for a time grew to such proportions as to appear insuperable, were cleared away. In April 1852 Blumhardt could travel to Stuttgart to sign the contract of sale. To his friend Barth he at once sent the laconic report, "Bad Boll is mine; purchase price 25,000 *gulden*." The down payment had been set at 8,000 *gulden*. His friend Chevalier in Stuttgart stood surety for the rest on his behalf, thus showing lofty courage and trust and obviously less pessimism as to the permanence of the undertaking than the medical society, whose misgivings actually do not appear so unfounded by ordinary human standards. How was Blumhardt, who at that time had only 400 *gulden* to his name, to meet the down payment of 8,000 *gulden*? For the present, he cheerfully returned home, where he shared the news of his good fortune with his faithful Alsatian friend Dieterlen, who happened to visit him at the time and who earlier on had indeed promised him substantial help in case of a serious need of this kind. "How much must you put down?" Dieterlen asked him. "8,000 *gulden*." "That's just the amount I put aside a while ago [he enjoyed a good income] to be used at some time for a larger charitable purpose, and you can have it."

Many of us will even now feel grateful to Dieterlen, now no longer among us, for this truly purposeful use of that sum.

Let us look back on what had thus been achieved! Blumhardt had acquired one large building, plus a number of subsidiary ones, of a size and usefulness for his needs that surpassed his boldest wishes and hopes. The ballroom needed only some application of Christian art and skill to be transformed into a fitting place for religious worship. Also, as we know already, the house was amply supplied with furniture and bedding, thus luckily replacing the stocks that had been stolen earlier. But more important than all this was the circumstance that for good reason had agitated the press so much, namely, that the party selling the property to Blumhardt for the universally known purpose was none other than the royal Württemberg government.

The government itself made this building over to the well-known rector of Möttlingen with his strange experiences but at the same time achievements that were obvious to every right-thinking person. He was to continue there on a larger scale the work he had started in a small way in the Möttlingen rectory. Knowing these circumstances, we are better able to appreciate how great were the difficulties besetting this transaction. Doubtless, too, the facts that the king had requested Blumhardt to continue serving his native land and that the sale of Bad Boll was more immediately subject to the monarch's influence than the assignment of ecclesiastical benefices contributed materially to the ultimate favorable outcome.

During the summer of 1852 Blumhardt's goods and chattels were bit by bit moved to Bad Boll; before long the family, too, left the house in Möttlingen. Not unlike the captain of a sinking ship, Blumhardt alone remained behind in the rectory. Finally, on July 31—the same day on which he had begun his tenure in Möttlingen—he, too, left his beloved parish, which was to remain a sacred memory for him, to begin a new activity as pastor in Bad Boll.

To conclude this section, I quote from a Whitsun sermon of Blumhardt's, which in his mind was at the same time a farewell sermon.

FAREWELL SERMON, WHITSUN 1852

SUBJECT: On the gift of the Holy Spirit: 1) what it was given for, 2) who may experience its influence, and 3) how it can be given anew in full measure.

TEXT: John 14:15–21.

The section we quote from this sermon forms the second half of its first part and the first half of the second part, as follows:

The Holy Spirit substitutes for the Lord Jesus in two ways: as a teacher and preacher, and as a comforter.

He is the spirit of truth; as such he preaches in the heart, especially by reminding one of what Jesus said, by renewing it in the heart and illuminating it more and more. Thus, a believing Christian carries, or should carry, the teacher in himself, so that he does not constantly feel in need of a preacher to tell him everything and explain it in all detail. No longer shall a person stop being instructed because the same teacher and instructor is no longer there. The instruction goes on, in fact all the more effectively, for it no longer just reverberates in the outward ear but issues from within. As a result, one's spirit and mind are lifted up, and a person sees everything much more clearly than if, at the prompting of the outer word, he had to spend time pondering what the words he has heard want to tell him. With this teacher one receives inward sights; one *sees* that which otherwise is merely heard and thought, and one grasps it to the very depths, even if now and then words are lacking. Thus the Holy Spirit is meant to be a teacher who opens everything up to the believers. All they have to do is to be inwardly gathered, place themselves into their Savior's presence, and put their questions to him; then they will presently be given clear insight.

You dear ones, I think this knowledge can also be a comfort to us now, where I have to say to you, "You will presently hear my voice no more." But is that the end of everything? Was hearing my voice really what mattered? I never wanted that; rather, you were to hear the voice of Jesus through me! Now that you will hear my voice no more, does that mean that my words have left no echo at all in you, that they no longer prompt you to ask questions to which the Holy Spirit can give you an answer? Is the Holy Spirit to leave just because the previous teacher leaves? When I think of it, I cannot put it any differently, and you, too, have to admit that whenever my words found an echo among you, it was not because of the words themselves. The words were commonly uttered in weakness and many times came out awkwardly and liable to be misunderstood, as did happen now and then.

In short, if the word here proclaimed found a response in people's souls, I do not ascribe it to my word but to the Spirit that bears the word, according to the promise. It was not the word but the Spirit of the Lord Jesus through the word. The important thing was not the word but what the Lord promises through the word. And when now this outward word falls silent, shall the Spirit that spoke through the word speak to you no more? Will he that until now has been the actual and proper teacher go away because a weak man goes away? That cannot be. Every one of you can cherish a joyful confidence in his heart that the Spirit that was at work here will not go away just because a weak person goes away. Therefore take courage, do not lose heart, and rejoice that you at least felt the Spirit of God at work. Remain joyful and convinced that the Spirit, having once begun, will go on working! As long as we keep yearning, begging, seeking, and knocking, the Spirit will go on teaching and will make this or that still clearer.

Outer words will often serve as a pillow to rest on; they may keep people from pondering and digesting them; they may cause them to feel satisfied as long as their ears hear the words and their lips can repeat them. Then it is certainly better if they hear no more but have to bring what they heard earlier out of the closet they had chucked it into, because they did not consider it important. When they hear it no more, they will think, "I had better look at it again and see what it is." In that way, through the working of the Holy Spirit, the word once proclaimed is apt to be all the more effective when the actual sound of it has long since died away.

Therefore may the Lord Jesus leave a substitute with you! You have no need to be taught by anybody, nor does one have to say to the other, "Come, I want to teach you." All of them, from the least to the greatest, will know the Lord (Heb 8:11) and will be able to help themselves through the working of the Holy Spirit and will always have the required instruction to hand.

But the Holy Spirit is not only a substitute for the word of instruction but also for the *comfort* that the personal Jesus imparted. Wherever Jesus was, there was blessing; that is true. When someone grieving saw him, he felt comforted; his grief departed. When someone tormented or tempted came into his presence, his burden fell off. There was no one sick or possessed who was not set free in the presence of Jesus; it was a wonderful comfort to find a present help in every affliction. This was something glorious, which in the days of our Savior was experienced by everyone who came close to him.

But then it was ordained that he should leave and go away. "Who will now give comfort and help?" the disciples might have asked, for they did not trust themselves to do anything at all. They could heal the sick only while he was with them. "But since we can no longer ask him and seek his advice, who will now console, heal, free the possessed, cheer the grieving, and give comfort and relief to those sorely tempted? Now the old misery will start all over again." This is what they could have thought and said. But Jesus says, "No, not so! Someone else will come; you will be given something else—not only a spirit of truth and instruction but also a comforter and helper. Thus, if anyone has experienced kindness until now, it will go on."

And indeed, sacred history tells us that the disciples were given all power and authority to do what Jesus had done. The Holy Spirit was to instruct them how and whom to help in body and soul, whom to forgive and whom not. The Holy Spirit was to show them inwardly the road they were to take for the salvation and comfort of many, indeed, of all who suffered. Thus, the Redeemer, the Comforter, the helping, strengthening, saving Jesus did not go away but remained with them in the person of the Holy Spirit, who substitutes for the Lord Jesus.

Now, you dear ones, as we look at our present situation, I have already heard one or the other of you say (to speak quite openly), "Oh, how will things go when you are no longer here? What are we to do? Up till now you have often given us help;

we only needed to come, and things changed for the better effortlessly and in manifold ways. We found much comfort and help. But what is to become of us now? Are we to be left without comfort and help? Will it again be as before, when we ran to the leaky wells and found no water in them?"

O you dear ones, are you in earnest with these laments? Should it be so that when the instrument goes, the cause itself goes with it? Who was it that comforted, helped, brought relief to the sick? Who—this may indeed be testified—did now and then do great things in one or the other? Was it I? Was I the cause of it? "No, indeed," you will all say; "all you did was believe in the word; it was the *Lord* who did it; the Lord's hand did it all—not you." And now that I leave, will it simply be all over? Will the Lord leave with me? Will the Spirit leave, in whom we put our faith and through whom this or that was indeed given easily and effortlessly? Is this beloved congregation to remain orphaned? Shall it henceforth receive no comfort for its concerns, just because one poor human being goes away? Is your prayer to remain ineffective from now on and God's Spirit not to be able to replace perfectly what you have had so far?

O dear souls, I would indeed feel afraid if the Lord's hand were not at work wherever the power of his Spirit had once been experienced. Beloved, have faith! Whatever you have received from the Lord Jesus by way of comfort and help through the hand of his servant must all remain with you if you let it dwell within you; on that you can rely in faith. May the fellowship of the Holy Spirit be with you!

So all you have to do is see to it that, as before, in all your concerns your teacher and minister is included in the fellowship of your prayers. And if, disregarding the human person, you put your trust entirely in the *Lord*, it will be just as if a servant of the Lord stretched out his hand and laid it on you, as if he comforted and strengthened you. Thus none will come short. You will not miss me, except as love, so deeply rooted among us, will claim its due, but in all that matters most you will miss nothing. Indeed, there things may become ever more wonderful, because you will have to get going yourselves! You yourselves will have to struggle harder, and there is nothing wrong with that. In that way you will also learn to call on the Lord Jesus *on your own* and, jointly with all believers, take hold of the power of the Holy Spirit and draw it to yourselves.

This is how it should go, you dear ones. For this purpose the gift of the Holy Spirit was promised, namely that the disciples and after them all believers in Jesus should have a substitute for his person in word and deed. Initially everything depended solely on the Lord's person, but now it should no longer be so. Rather, everything should depend on the wind of the Spirit blowing in every heart.

But if it did not depend on the Lord's own presence, how much less does it depend on that of a poor servant! The Spirit *can* remain! I am telling you—and I believe I can tell you in the name of the Lord Jesus: Everything *can* continue among you in the way it has so far. But do you believe that it can be so, or are you mistrustful?

Let me go on. Our text tells us something more about that point of who can experience the influence of the gifts of the Holy Spirit. May you take it to heart.

To be sure, it cannot be taken for granted that things will just go on as before or that they will go on in every individual. That is a matter of course. After all, we are no mere machines; things must in some measure depend on what we *want* and *do*. Therefore hear it, grasp it, and take it to heart! If you do take it to heart, things are bound to go on without any change—even better than you had it before. Just listen to these Gospel words: "If you love me, keep my commandments, and"—an important word, this "and," which we ought to ponder with care; it means as much as "then"— "then, if things are like that with you, I will ask the Father, and he shall send you another comforter, so that you can do without me." Further down it speaks of "He that has my commandments . . ." Now I do think you have them; I am sure of it. Nothing has been withheld from you, and you can't hold anything against me on that account, even though I do feel my guilt as a useless servant. I think each one among you knows very clearly what the Lord has commanded in the New Testament. Hence you do have his commandments. Now listen: "He that has my commandments and keeps them, he it is that loves me. And he that loves me will be loved by my Father, and I shall love him and reveal myself to him."

So the question is, Who experiences the influence of the Holy Spirit? Now you already know the answer. I deliberately do not ask, Who will *receive* the gift of the Holy Spirit? Then, instead of comforting you, I would in effect put you off till some far distant time when the Lord will again pour out the gift of the Holy Spirit as he did in the beginning. What I do mean is, Who experiences whatever can at present be attained of the Holy Spirit's working? Although we feel poor and the Spirit of God no longer works as fully as he did in the beginning, he nevertheless is still active and manifests himself. We would have been finished and done for long ago if no influence of the Holy Spirit were to be felt anymore.

Who then may experience the effects of the Holy Spirit at least to the extent the present state of things allows? The Lord says: "To him that loves me I shall reveal myself." If someone experiences the influence of the Holy Spirit in himself, it is as if the Lord Jesus revealed himself to him; it is the same thing. So I might also have asked, To whom will the Lord Jesus reveal himself? Answer: To him who loves Him.

I repeat: Among you everything must continue without change or interruption, for in the Holy Spirit you have a substitute for everything, for the word as well as the comfort. It will continue like this if you keep on loving the Lord Jesus. If you become estranged from him, he will indeed cease to manifest himself to you. If you run away from him and no longer care about him or fight for him, the seed here scattered will flourish less and less. More and more of it will get eaten by caterpillars; the influence of the Holy Spirit will get ever weaker, and then it may well happen that everything peters out.

But I do not think that will happen. Today's meeting and the previous one, coming at a time where it is not easy to make sacrifices, show me that the dear Savior has many souls among us here who are really intent on loving him. And you do feel drawn to him in your hearts. Yes, I have had reason to rejoice, even though in this last time I have often thought, "Oh, is it all going to peter out? The longing is gone, the zeal is gone, child-likeness and brotherliness are gone. Shall the Lord's work come to nothing?" On the other hand, I have been raised up again in these last weeks and have been given an assurance that— praise to God! —he does have a sizable people among us and that there are many who must never get lost, who belong to the Lord Jesus and whom he will not allow to be snatched out of his hand. This is my impression, and I thank the Lord for his unmerited kindness, which eases my leave-taking from here.

This is how the sermon concludes (extract):

The Holy Spirit can be given to us anew in full measure when, through the working of God's Spirit as it now takes place, the world is put to death in believers' hearts, when there really is as much faith as God desires. Oh, I ask all of you to make it your urgent concern to get the world out of your system. You know what grace you can attain in that way. Keep at it; in the end the souls left out may be but very few! Dear, beloved congregation, if eight years ago you had taken greater pains to put off the world and had continued to put if off more and more—oh, things might well be quite different now! But never mind! Pull yourselves together and go to war against the spirit of the world, so that the Spirit of Jesus may blow through you and bring forth something new to the praise and glory of his wonderful name. Amen.

Johann Christoph Blumhardt (1802–1880).

Doris Blumhardt née Köllner (1816–1886).

Print of the Village of Möttlingen before 1860.

Gottliebin Brodersen née Dittus (1815–1872).

The Sanctuary of the Parish Church at Möttlingen.

The Kurhaus in Bad Boll.

From left to right: Doris Blumhardt née Köllner (1816–1886), Gottliebin Brodersen née Dittus (1815–1872), and Christoph Friedrich Blumhardt (1842–1919).

PART THREE

Bad Boll

17

Bad Boll

WHEN WE PORTRAY BLUMHARDT in the following pages as the pastor of Bad Boll, biographical matter will go more into the background, for to all of us that knew him, he and his house had, so to speak, no history. For us, Bad Boll was simply there as a lovely, comforting fact, always remaining the same. It was like seeing and greeting from some lookout a certain wonderful mountain that always loomed at the same point on the horizon. Bad Boll owes its existence to a sulphur spring. By the middle of the sixteenth century it was already being used by sick people in the neighborhood for both drinking and bathing. At the order of Duke Frederic I the spring was enclosed and a stately well room erected. This ruler called the spa a "miracle spring" and took a lively interest in his creation. That is shown by the interesting spa regulations written under his influence. Here are some of them:

> At five o'clock in the morning the bell rings, calling each guest of the spa to say his prayers with due reverence.
> When the bell rings at eight o'clock in the evening, every guest is to conduct himself in a quiet and orderly manner, in accordance with his station.
> If his condition allows it, no one may, without valid reason, miss the church service held every second Saturday between twelve and one o'clock in the afternoon.

Any person blaspheming the name of God or naming the devil without reason must put a fine of one batz[1] into the box.

Anyone swearing by the devil or commending himself to him shall pay a fine of no less than four batz.

Frivolous language, disparaging gossip, and offensive songs are forbidden on pain of a fine of half a gulden, obscene gestures or advances toward honest women and maidens on pain of a fine of one gulden.

Anybody found tipsy or drunk in the spa shall pay half a gulden the first time. Challenges to fight are completely forbidden in the spa, and peace shall be strictly and securely maintained.

All spa guests without exception are to refrain from unnecessary disputing on matters of religion, from grumbling at the bathing procedure or the spa attendants, and also from splashing water.

During the Thirty Years War the bathhouse fell into decay, and even at that time Bad Boll became a source of embarrassment for the government. Finally, in 1822, at the urging of one of his ministers, King William made the spa one of his pet concerns. It is to him that the present main building is due. We will add only a little to its description in the previous chapter. The section of the building containing the ballroom stands out tastefully in the center of the front. Even then there rose by the side of the main building a modest structure called the *Gnadenbau* (charity building), as it accommodated, free of charge, patients unable to pay. The pleasant grounds with the pump room in the back of them came into existence at the same time—in part, it is said, through the labor of young men who in that way had to make amends for committing offenses against decency.

We already know that even that impressive creation did not win the favor of the public and that this was why it finally passed into Blumhardt's hands.

What exactly did Blumhardt have in mind with this spa? To him that was actually not the first question. He was firmly convinced that the Lord had given him this place, so convinced in fact that he never dared to look at it as his property but instead saw it as a holy talent entrusted to him by the Lord. He looked forward in solemn expectation to what the Lord might have in mind with Bad Boll and what tasks were waiting

---

1. Translator's Note: A *batz* was a small base silver coin, formerly found in parts of Germany and Switzerland.

there for his servant Blumhardt. To be sure, what he had to do there in the short run was clear to him, as we know. Had it not been, the authorities would have obliged him to get clear about it. In 1853 a government department did ask him to give an account of his work, which by that time he could do all the better on the basis of one year's experience. Part of the account follows here:

> In 1844, while serving as a minister in the parish of Möttlingen, I experienced things that attracted wide attention. Many souls were in a particular way stimulated and uplifted . . . gradually, troubled and suffering persons of every kind came flocking to me in search of comfort, relief, and help through my encouragement, preaching, and prayerful sympathy. Most of these persons parted from me awakened to a new trust in God and in the scriptural promises that prayer will be answered. To say the least, they were comforted and inwardly strengthened. Some whose previous efforts to find healing for their tormenting ailments had all been in vain did find real help. With such visible effects in front of me, I could not in good conscience just turn away such seekers for help. I could not withhold from them that which I, purely and simply as a pastor, offered to them and which alone I wanted to offer. So I let them come. For nearly ten years now there has been a constantly increasing influx of people, even from far away, which may well be seen as proof that my ability to help the sick was not just a product of their imagination. The large majority just came for a passing visit. Now and then, depending on circumstances, some stayed for days and weeks, either with me or nearby, but that is no different from the way physicians, too, try here or there to find a suitable rectory out in the country where certain patients can stay for a while.
>
> My modest country rectory in Möttlingen was much too small to accommodate all those suffering from certain afflictions who sought me out and for whom a stay with me offered some promise. My conscience reassures me that it was solely this predicament I was in and the compassion I felt particularly for a specific class of afflicted people who turned to me especially often that made me wish I could open for them a place of refuge suiting their condition and in that way provide healing (*sit venia verbo*[2]) for them. So when Bad Boll came on the market a year ago, it was these considerations that prompted me to purchase it, at the advice and encouragement of many friends and acquaintances. Since my aims and methods had long been public knowledge, how could it possibly occur to me that I might thus do something illegal?

2. Translator's Note: "If I may use this word."

I also have to refute most decidedly the charge alleging that I receive and treat other mentally ill persons. It was never my intention to take in real cases of mental illness, for the purpose of curing them. However, the outer appearance of a person gives no sure clue to whether or not he suffers from this or that specific mental illness; even the most expert physicians dare to pronounce an opinion or judgment only after extended observation. The people seeking my help are burdened souls that do not have the strength to free themselves or to find comfort, either from within or without. It is only at their own request that I take them in. For these, apart from the peace and tranquility surrounding them here, the very lovely scenery my house is fortunately located in, and the invigorating influence of the air here, the only remedy I use is that mentioned before: an awakening of trust in God and confident prayer to him.

It cannot be denied that there are hundreds, or even thousands, of such unhappy people everywhere and that, if they are not to suffer a tremendous injustice, they should never be thought of as mentally ill persons. Consider, for example, the great number of so-called hypochondriacs. There is also general agreement that for such persons a removal from accustomed surroundings and occupations and lodging at a place of the kind just described holds out the one possibility of a cure. As I said earlier, I keep such sufferers with me only after first observing them in my house for some days and convincing myself that they do not suffer from actual mental illness in the pathological and psychological sense. This shows that the charge against me has no basis at all. Surely no physician, not even the bitterest among my opponents, will maintain that such a short—or even a longer—stay in my house, with no medical treatment of any kind administered by me, could have a negative or harmful effect—one that positively hampers what is good—on such a sufferer.

I never intended to meddle in any way with medical science. I hope I gave most conclusive proof of that by various public declarations as well as by my public conduct, visible to everyone. In response to last year's well-known attack on me by a number of physicians I at once declared my intention to make the spa as such open to the public the following year (the present year of 1853) and to keep my house open for ordinary, decent persons coming simply because of the spa. This year I did the same thing by means of a public notice early in the spring. Indeed, even the most biased observer of the guests in my house (close to a hundred in number) would find it extremely hard to discover any who are truly mentally ill. Instead, he could convince himself that both the sick and the healthy—the healthy including also young people full of joy in life as well as men of high standing politically, morally, and intellectually—move about freely, talk together, and interrelate in a pleasant and mutually refreshing way. By observing the conversation closely he might be able to detect here and there a burdened and troubled soul, but no sign of mental illness.

By opening my house to the public as an institution (and that only in the sense described above, which in every way agrees with the facts) I merely exercise an undeniable right. I follow the urging of my heart, which cannot remain indifferent to the manifold needs of our present generation; I fulfill a high and sacred duty, a divine command, and I meet the demands that, according to the convictions I have formed from Holy Scripture, can be made on a minister of the Gospel. In fact, far from wanting to oppose the medical profession, I am actually doing highly beneficial spadework for any medical treatment that might still be needed and requested.

Just at the time this demand for an accounting was hovering over Blumhardt's head, his new friend Bardili[3] paid a visit to Bad Boll. Bardili seized the opportunity as an impartial observer to take up the cudgels for Blumhardt, using the full weight of confidence and repute he enjoyed in high places. He gave an excellent circumstantial witness to Blumhardt's work, to its success as well as to its thoroughly wholesome character. Semi-officially (so to speak) Bardili challenged Blumhardt to state just what power it was that Blumhardt expected to be of benefit to his guests. Blumhardt replied:

I am a pastor and nothing more; I bear witness to what the Bible says and never go beyond that in what I teach. The Gospel is not just a word but a power. That I believe in it and cleave to it, in particular that I credit the promises of Holy Scripture with more reality than others do, that I hold carefully to the whole Bible and not merely to fractions of it—that is what gives my teaching, comforting, encouraging, and reproving the effect that is being testified to.

To introduce his vigorous defense, Bardili gave the following reasons for his visit to Bad Boll:

The gathering of many people of both high and low estate; the pervasive peace and tranquility; the general atmosphere of an

3. Editors Note: von Bardili served as the Superintendent of Construction in Stuttgart and oversaw the sale of Bad Boll to Blumhardt.

unpretentious family life, heightened by the unaffected and relaxed mingling of all classes; the quiet, inward, tolerant, unpietistic attitude felt in most persons; in addition the free, open, genial, cheerful bearing of Pastor Blumhardt, the owner of Bad Boll, richly gifted as he is with faith and trust in God and far removed from sectarianism—all this made me decide to spend my two weeks of vacation here in Boll.

In these two reports we already see two different perceptions of the term "Bad Boll" standing side by side. For himself Bardili hoped to receive there spiritual refreshment and new vigor as noble as it was beneficial. Indeed, Bad Boll came to enjoy an increasingly good reputation as a "spiritual" spa and health resort. It was considered a very well conceived and timely undertaking, so much so that in due course more such health resorts ministering to "spiritual needs" were established and proved successful. Spiritually speaking, in Bad Boll one walked in the shade of trees that had their roots in those serious struggles in Möttlingen; its fresh and invigorating spiritual air was an outcome of historic events. In the great Möttlingen days the whole atmosphere around Blumhardt had been purified and cleansed of any poisonous and dark elements; that was what everyone could sense, even if he was not able to spell it out clearly.

Blumhardt was in no way displeased to have such guests that looked for rest and recovery come to him, and he embraced them all with the arms of his heart. There were often very interesting persons among them, and converse with them brought refreshment also to him, enriching his heart and widening his horizon. It is true that, particularly in the beginning, some did come just for the fun of it or to escape boredom, and there were young men who simply wanted to take advantage of Blumhardt's well-known hospitality to such people. Yet of these, too, many a one did get caught in the snares of Blumhardt's intercession and would later be brought back by deeper needs.

Still, it was not for such seekers for a rest cure that Blumhardt had taken on the burden of Bad Boll. What he longed for was to have human need, distress, and misery, as well as the anguish of guilt and sin, brought to him and *left* with him. And that came to him in plenty—as "that Day will make clear."

But perhaps even that was not yet the innermost and final thought in Blumhardt's conception of Bad Boll. In some ways he felt like Abraham, for from Möttlingen, the spiritual home where he had struck such deep roots, he had moved with the goods and chattels of his hopes to an unknown land. He had come as a man of hope, and in Bad Boll, too—indeed more and more as time went on—he saw every divine help he experienced on behalf of others as a gift and power imparted in advance of what was yet to come. In his eyes, one—and not the least—of Bad Boll's missions was to be a focus for the expectation of God's kingdom. This expectation was not lame and inactive with him as it was with that lazy man of whom Solomon says, "The sluggard's craving will be the death of him, because his hands refuse to work" (Prov 21:25). On the contrary, it was his inmost longing that the battles still facing the kingdom of God—not battles with opponents of flesh and blood but with that power he had taken the field against in Möttlingen—go forward to victory. One might say that this spirit of hope was the pulse governing the life in Bad Boll; it animated the small band that had moved from Möttlingen to Bad Boll. And that points us to the one and only *historic* element in Bad Boll—its *inner* history, that is, the developments within the small circle consisting of Blumhardt and those of like mind that stood by him.

18

Bad Boll's Inner Circle

Two families moved together from Möttlingen to Bad Boll—the Blumhardts and the Dittuses. The Dittuses could be said to represent the Möttlingen parish. Gottliebin's elder brother, Andreas, had been a village councilor in Möttlingen. He was an upright man that could be trusted with much. To begin with he looked after the house and the gradually growing domestic and agricultural departments of Bad Boll. Gottliebin's other brother, Hans Jörg, was also used to good advantage there, as was her sister Katharina. The link between the two families was Gottliebin, who was regarded as being fully Blumhardt's daughter and a member of his family.

Henceforth these two families closely bound together by experiences as serious as they were wonderful and by holy memories and hopes, formed the hidden core in the varied and constantly changing population of Bad Boll. Next to Blumhardt, but keeping very much in the background, Gottliebin was just about the most important element. Blumhardt left behind an account of her life in manuscript form. He says there:

> As regards outer activity, she so became the heart and soul of everything that it is not too much to say that every arrangement and plan made was fully and solely hers. Nothing either big or small escaped Gottliebin's careful eye, and her inner gifts, too, contributed significantly to the blessing resting on the house. To be sure, not everybody understood her or was at ease with her, for she had (if I may say so) a natural dislike of certain spirits, as though

her nerves, which had remained sensitive to such influences, were unfavorably affected by them. For that reason she could assume a forbidding manner to such people. But whoever found the right approach to her could benefit greatly from contact with her and would retain for her a special love and appreciation. She was of great help to us by evaluating quickly and accurately the state of mentally ill or disturbed persons, especially as to whether we could have hopes for them or not—one of the most difficult parts of our task. Besides, she was able to give clear and definite advice in physical problems; in particular, her counsel and services were outstandingly successful in cases of bodily injuries to children and others. Thus, she was of great help to us in every respect, and because of that we could never regard her otherwise than as a special gift of the Lord. We never had the courage to think or say we might have earned that by what had been done with her, for what the Lord gave us was altogether too great; hence we could accept it only as unmerited grace.

Of what Gottliebin accomplished during the later period of serious illness and of the gap left by her death, Blumhardt has this to say:

She had a special knack of seeing an inner significance in all outer activities, however small; to her any work she did was always a kind of service to God. That enabled her to be strong during illness and to be active again as soon as she felt better. We are ever so indebted to her also in that respect, since we often keep going simply by trying to think as she would. Even in the days of her illness she was to us like a Joseph, of whom we read, "From the time he put him in charge of his household and of all that he owned, the Lord blessed the household of the Egyptian because of Joseph, and the Lord's blessing was on everything he had, both in the house and in the field" (Gen 39:5).

As regards the services Gottliebin rendered to his wife in particular, Blumhardt relates: "My wife did everything together with Gottliebin. She did not dare undertake anything without talking it over with her and getting a direction from her, for everything she said and put her hand to carried with it something like a commendation from on high. It never led astray and afterward turned out to be the best and only right course, even if at the time it was hard to understand and seemed almost enigmatic." To begin with, it was therefore mainly Blumhardt, his wife, and Gottliebin that, bound together in the Lord, held fast to the memories of the great Möttlingen days and strove to keep the spirit that had been

at work there alive also in Bad Boll. A stranger crossing the threshold
of the great house could scarcely have had an inkling of the wonderful, invisible bonds of intercession enveloping him at once. Gottliebin
welcomed the Blumhardts to Bad Boll with a blessing in verse. It was a
lovely expression of the spirit in which they applied themselves together
to their still unfamiliar calling at the new place:

> God bless you! May he let his spirit rest,
> Beloved ones, on you.
> And may his promises, in which you trust,
> In your own life come true.
> May he now prosper your endeavor
> And show the way in all things ever.
> God bless you!
>
> God bless you who the old home left behind
> A new life here to dare,
> For which you had to break with settled mind
> The bonds that held you there.
> Yet, while beloved souls there losing,
> New fields of work you here are choosing.
> God bless you!
>
> God bless you who in coming here forswear
> A life of ease and rest,
> Who boldly go to shoulder loads of care
> That leave the flesh distressed.
> Yet, while your selves no longer matter,
> To others quick'ning love you scatter.
> God bless you!
>
> God bless you! May he let Bad Boll for you
> A holy Canaan be.
> And may he ease your pain of parting too
> And set from sorrow free.
> May precious fruits your faith be showing—
> Bad Boll with milk and honey flowing.
> God bless you!
>
> God bless you! May his angels go with you
> Into this new-won place!
> God bless you! May he every day anew
> Let shine on you his face
> And, gazing kindly down from heaven,
> Let strength divine to you be given.
> God bless you!

God bless you! May he make it known to all
That his word still holds true
And they who follow faithfully his call
Will find ever anew
That Jesus listens to their crying
And turns to joy their tears and sighing.
God bless you!

God bless you! May the Savior show his might
To set the captives free.
He, whom the world does scorn and slight,
May grant you victory
And let your pleading bring salvation
From sickness, pain, and depravation.
God bless you!

God bless you! May he soon let come the day
When faith has its reward,
When throngs will to Mount Zion wend their way
To meet their gracious Lord
And foil with resolute resistance
The devil's onslaughts and persistence.
God bless you!

God bless you! May he e'er encourage you
When darkest seems the night.
May he bless you and everything you do,
Till you behold the light
For which your hearts have long been yearning,
Though blind the world and undiscerning.
God bless you!

The small inner circle received an unexpected addition from one of the very first guests to come. In the autumn of 1852 Theodor Brodersen, a young man from Schleswig-Holstein, arrived at Bad Boll, walking with two crutches. The following summer, almost fully healed, he returned to his homeland to look for a sphere of activity there. Since he had a sizable fortune at his disposal, he had reason to hope this would not be difficult. But already by the summer of 1854 he was back in Bad Boll, his search having proved fruitless. Like those laborers in the parable, he stood idly in the market place, ready "to serve the Lord with all I have and am" and waiting to learn if and how the Lord would use him. Meanwhile, Blumhardt had long had his eye on him, thinking that he might be the man to take over the outward management of the spa, but in his usual manner had kept the thought to himself and waited for the Lord to make his will known. The longer Brodersen stayed at Bad Boll, the less he could bear the thought of living elsewhere, so before long the ideas of both men came together. Thus Brodersen became Blumhardt's support in the outer administration and even in many ways his helper and representative in inner matters as well, until Blumhardt's sons took that over. Many friends of Bad Boll still remember gratefully the loving letters he wrote in Blumhardt's name, maybe even more the equally loving visits he made on his journeys, and his warm, encouraging talks.

When Brodersen joined the administrative staff of Bad Boll, his new office brought him into many contacts with guests, both male and female. Discretion required that he marry, but where would he find a partner that, as would be necessary, was in complete agreement with the spirit of the house and willing to take on herself all the great efforts and self-denials to be expected? Various suggestions were made by competent persons but did not meet with his agreement; then suddenly there came to his mind, remarkably enough, the thought of Gottliebin Dittus. Was it not as if the whole purpose of the house were embodied in her? His proposal came as a shock to her and as an almost greater shock to Blumhardt—but before long, with everybody's agreement, the idea became a fact. Gottliebin expressed what was moving in her heart in the following poem she wrote for her bridegroom for their wedding day (January 9, 1855). The poem sheds a bright light on Gottliebin's life and on the bond uniting her with the Blumhardt family:

> To you my hand and heart I've given,
> And God himself has sealed our bond.
> Let us, two pilgrims bound for heaven,
> Walk through this life to life beyond.
> Oh, my poor heart cannot but wonder
> At how the Savior, ever new,
> Stayed by my side through every blunder
> And in the end led me to you.
> For years I struggled, wept, lamented,
> A helpless, poor, and ailing maid;
> Death would come close but then relented,
> And the dark angel's hand was stayed.
> With dread I many times saw looming
> The stern gates of eternity,
> But God did keep this flower blooming;
> For you he kept it—yours to be!

How with the fiend I oft contended,
Who would have dragged me down to hell!
But by the Lord's strong arm defended,
I was helped up whene'er I fell.
Two faithful friends to me were given,
A second pair of parents true,
Who filled the breach by Satan riven;
Out of their faith my vict'ry grew.
In their house I did find a haven—
Poor me, from fire plucked a brand!
But more yet I have now been given:
The Lord moved you to seek my hand!
When I consider all this rightly,
Will joy, will grief now touch my life?
How could my sun shine still more brightly?
Why would I need to be your wife?
If after such things I had hankered
As does the world, it would be sin.
My little ship lay safely anchored;
On earth naught else I sought to win.
I saw my life as consecrated,
And errant cravings all had ceased;
I stood with those men dedicated
To God's great cause, from self released.
Then, under heavy burdens reeling
And seeking help, you came from far.
To you, too, did the Lord give healing;
Like me, a miracle you are.
"Here, where my chains fell," you decided,
"This is where I will pitch my tent!"
So we both, by our parents guided,
On showing love to them were bent.
You loved the two as I did love them
And felt the call to lend a hand.
When threat'ning storm clouds loomed above them,
We rallied round their fighting band.
We sensed the urge in one another
To join their faithful company;
So our hearts were knit together,
And I loved you, and you loved me.
Thus is our marriage bond embedded
In holy love, which faith imparts.
For such a fighting faith were headed
The first strong urges of our hearts.

And was not this our common yearning
That we might serve our parents' dream
To see Christ's fire, brightly burning,
Light up all earth with radiant beam?
Yes, holy be our love forever,
My dearest Heinrich Theodor,
And nothing shall us from him sever,
Who brightly lights our path before.
Let us love him and his work solely,
From which our love springs ever new;
Then I shall be "Gottliebin" wholly
And you my faithful "Titus" true.[1]

Three fine sons were born to this marriage. Blumhardt was greatly concerned that this branch of his family, although tied to him by no bonds of blood, be assured of a home and citizenship in his family and in Bad Boll. That desire, as well as the need for more living space, led to the erection of the tastefully designed new building on the west side of the spa. It was called *das Morgenland* (the Orient), because the rooms were given oriental names (Bethlehem, Bashan, etc.). Blumhardt wanted that house to remain the special property of the Brodersen-Dittus branch.

It was not always easy for that circle to remain in control of the spiritual atmosphere in the house. The numerous domestic staff were often a more difficult problem than the throng of guests, who after all were drawn there by serious inner need. Blumhardt had taken several of the staff into his service out of pity, and he found it hard to dismiss employees. There was a time when things really began to look bad among the staff, which put Blumhardt in a very difficult position. One after another cases of hidden immorality and similar things came to his attention. He said to himself and those around him, "*We* must repent!" Days of earnest self-examination followed, waking a new zeal for prayer and joint Bible study in Blumhardt's family. What happened? Before long one after another of the erring ones quietly found their way to Blumhardt's study to confess their sins, and a movement like the one we know of in Möttlingen went through the staff.

1. Translator's Note: "Gottliebin" means "she who loves God"; Titus was Paul's "partner and fellow worker" (2 Cor 8:23).

Outwardly, too, things were sometimes difficult in those days, as we learn from the report of a friend of Blumhardt's, one of his co-fighters in the struggle for a good new hymnal:

> "It goes!" he wrote me several times, when he tried to adapt an old tune from Freilinghausen to some hymn. This "It goes" seems to have become for him a general expression of confidence. Once when I visited him in Boll later on (it was at the time of the Crimean War, and he kept receiving letters and requests for intercession from France and Russia), he had no firewood and no money to buy it with. But not long after he let me know that "it went" all right—and quite soon, too.

How faithful a fellow fighter Blumhardt had in his wife at such times of need is told by their son, Pastor Christoph Blumhardt:

> It is hard to describe how oppressive the conditions were that had to be struggled through to make the house in Bad Boll feel in even a small way like a purified, Christian home. A friend has written to me . . . that he once met my mother standing in the corridor by the linen chest, writhing like a worm and crying so that her streaming tears wet the flagstones. All she could say was, "I can only cry for the Savior to look on our need and not deal with us as we deserve." That friend writes that she would often sob out in tears words like that.

In the time following, a burden of a different kind pressed in on the inner circle: disorders and illnesses that afflicted Gottliebin Brodersen more and more as time went on and frequently to an unheard-of degree. It often seemed that there was no ailment she did not have to experience. Some years Blumhardt's energy was consumed almost entirely by just these struggles; hence it was not quite without reason that his strength was said to have diminished, for he did seem to be somewhat hampered, at least in what he could undertake away from Bad Boll. The struggle intensified until it ended with the death of his beloved fellow fighter—a profoundly shattering event that at the same time had a wonderfully uplifting effect on him.

Although she was very close to death, Gottliebin urged Blumhardt to hold his regular Bible study in Stuttgart. He left in the hope of finding her still alive on his return. His son Christoph, who by that time was already his father's helper in the service, took the father's place with the dying woman. For quite a while she still wished and hoped to experience

Blumhardt's return. Finally Christoph said to her, "We want to be also ready for you to die without seeing Papa again. How do we know but that it might actually be easier for Papa if you die before he returns?" He prayed a few such words, to which she softly replied "Amen." A few moments later she passed away.

Meanwhile, Blumhardt had experienced a restless night in Stuttgart. When he got off the train in Göppingen, he saw his family waiting for him with the sad news. With a loud voice he called out to them the text (or watchword) for that day: "I sweep away your offenses like a cloud and your sins like the morning mist" (Isa 44:22).

When we hear Blumhardt tell of the last sufferings and death of his fellow fighter, it makes us appreciate the whole weight and significance of this event for him:

> The blessed departed retained great—indescribably great—strength of soul, especially while enduring the successive stages of her last illness, which lasted two years. There were still many instances of answered prayer. She might be weak unto death one day, while the very next day she would take on quite big work tasks, for instance, in the laundry, paying no heed to objections. A whole series of ailments, each of which alone might have caused death, were conquered by the prayer of faith and earnest, persistent entreaty. In all this we must give praise to the Lord's kindly, redemptive mercy, which again and again let that precious life stay with us a while longer.
>
> Once when I was on a journey, I was informed by telegram that she had been in a cold sweat for hours and was already far away. When I arrived back, she looked up feebly; new life came into her eyes, and in a moved voice she said, "Now it's getting serious, Papa!" But these words had already given me courage to pray, to believe, to hope. And true help did come. She sank into a gentle sleep, and when she woke, the doctor was simply amazed. An ailment not greatly heeded before, which in this instance appeared to prove fatal, was now completely overcome . . .
>
> The main trouble, however, kept growing worse. Once when she was again in extremities, she cried, like a dying person struggling for breath, "I won't die, I won't die!" My children were all standing by her bed, including a son who had come from a distance. This time help came so quickly and conspicuously that Gottliebin herself urged us to give public thanks to the Lord in the devotional meeting just about to start. However, it was again only a dangerous complication that had been overcome; the main

disease advanced relentlessly. To us, who were grieved at that, she said, "Don't say that the Lord does not hear prayer!" and pointed to the many ills that had all vanished. But she herself cut off any hope we might cherish of the Lord's freeing her from the main illness, which was bound to lead to death. When we wanted to entreat the Lord earnestly about that, she would not let us. That it was the Lord's will, we had to accept as certain, but how deeply it bowed me down inwardly, after experiencing so often the Lord's power over so many ills afflicting her! The friends reading these words will surely feel that with me.

I freely admit that I was not worthy of her life's being saved— perhaps also because the experiences already given had not been sufficiently heeded and used for the glory of God. In many quarters the first sequence of events (the struggle and the awakening) had been eyed with mistrust. One really couldn't speak anywhere of those matters without being looked at askance. Indeed, we ourselves had to live our faith in a downright clandestine way; we had to hush up those great events and all the Lord's doings and generally had to stand alone. That has had a paralyzing effect also on us, and as a result the Lord has derived but little gain from it all. However, I take all the guilt on myself and remain most confident that the Lord's arm has lost nothing of its power. To be sure, his hour is still to come.

To begin with, her home-going has been to us an urge to face whatever comes with a deeper and more resolute earnestness; it has left its mark on every member of my household. It deeply grieved and concerned the departed one that my children were slow in growing into the special spirit of the house, for she feared it would mean the collapse of my house and of a work of God; she could almost see it happening before her eyes. But through her death her wishes have been granted, for from that point on— actually in such a way that she herself could recognize it as she lay dying—the new spirit she looked forward to for the Lord's sake has broken through in them all. It still has to grow, but at any rate it has begun to work in all. Since then we have often asked ourselves: Did she have to die—that is, did she have to become a sacrifice on our behalf so that this might come about? However it may be, we bow low before it. All we want is to stand ready so the Lord can use us for anything, just as he pleases.

Two things strike us in what Blumhardt says here of Gottliebin Brodersen: for one thing the extraordinary esteem in which he held her but in addition the deep humility of his heart. Such humility was actually the basic attitude in that small circle. Gottliebin in particular felt, with an almost anxious intensity, that whoever wants to be of any use for the kingdom of God must let his own self become as nothing. Yet she had an equally strong sense of the duty to be something.

Let us tarry for a moment by the grave of this fighter whose life story was linked with Blumhardt's in so holy, earnest, and intimate a way and exerted such a powerfully decisive influence on his. One feels tempted to ask if Blumhardt would have become what he did if his faith had not been tested—through the struggles and sufferings of that other heroic soul—in the crucible of his own "struggle." It is not for us to raise such a question, but whoever recognizes that a blessing of far-reaching significance resulted from Blumhardt's experiences will see the hand of Providence in the memorable way these two fighting souls were assigned to each other.

To be sure, for many a reader, maybe even for some who got to know her in Bad Boll, the person of Gottliebin may still remain a problem, an enigma, for she did carry her treasure in an earthen vessel. In Bad Boll she dressed like a lady, as befitted her new station, and people that had known her in the homely garb she had worn in Möttlingen might well feel reminded of David wearing the armor of Saul. To be sure, it would quickly become apparent that her whole being was pervaded by the Spirit. Like invisible warmth, a tender attentiveness to and sympathy for every kind of suffering and distress radiated from her somewhat rough shell. It was impressive too, for example, how even during the last days before her death, when she was plagued by recurrent vomiting, she summoned her last fading strength to satisfy her uncompromising need for cleanliness—so successfully it was hard to grasp.

But she did have a rough shell, as the saying goes. From her poverty-stricken childhood she had retained a certain uncouthness, which also showed in her features and build. In some respects that was actually quite a fitting garment for her personality. She was anything but what we think of as "amiable" or "gracious" or "pleasant" and are wont to like and cultivate in one another. For that, she had been through too hard a school of life. In her own mind she viewed people as if they had already died, that is, according to the state they would now be in if they had died. That is why rank, position, and the like were as good as nonexistent for her and why her discernment could be vexing, since her eyes radiated rather bluntly her disgust at any hidden corruptness. But it was the indelible impression of all who knew her better that in her heart dwelt nothing but goodness and self-sacrifice and that her uncultivated behavior toward others concealed an earnest, fervent, and compassionate love such as one would unfortunately have difficulty finding elsewhere. Her innermost being was wholly dominated by one thought: Forward to victory for God's kingdom! It was clear to her with compelling matter-of-factness that Blumhardt's great experiences were the start of a struggle that must end with the Lord's full victory and a total surrender of the power of darkness. For that goal she would have sacrificed anything with a warrior's ruthlessness.

The history of Gottliebin's life was—to a rare and almost unheard-of extent—a story of suffering but also of victory. "Overcoming" was the special stamp of her Christianity. In greater detail than would have been fitting for a wider circle of readers Blumhardt relates in the above-mentioned manuscript how the torments of her Möttlingen struggle came upon her because of her very sensitive conscience and deep fear of God. She resisted every enticement to accept seemingly good things (such as a lot of money) that unholy powers offered her. Most likely, if she had given in on that point and accepted such offers, all her sufferings would at any time have come to an immediate end.

Still, although she was ready to suffer, she had nothing of that morbid zest for suffering that regards one's personal perfection as the one great purpose. Equally far from her was any desire to use her suffering to make herself important. She felt she suffered for the Lord and his kingdom, and everything endured for him, whether by herself or by others, she saw as something to be taken for granted and made little of.

We cannot, of course, relate in detail how that soldier-like ruggedness of manner, diametrically opposed to all empty talk, sentimentality, and mutual commiseration, did in fact do a lot of good to those exposed to it. A gentleman of noble birth once told me in tears of the victorious breakthrough that Gottliebin's blunt exhortations—in fact, commands—had effected at a decisive hour in his life. So it is not surprising that she had a dislike bordering on loathing of any intentional outward show of piety. She rather tended to that incivility that Goethe in reference to himself called "hypocrisy in reverse": an artificial coldness that made her appear a puzzle to many. But that was only appearance and did not flow from her extremely simple, natural, free, and truthful nature. For instance, due to lack of time she usually came to the breakfast table just before the start of morning devotions and had her breakfast while listening attentively to Blumhardt's exposition of the Bible. To a friend who was put off by that Blumhardt wrote: "Our devotions have the character of family talks; there should be no stiffness. Many knit . . . Was not the disciples' plucking of ears on the Sabbath even a lot more offensive, by the standards of that time? I cannot take this up with Frau Gottliebin Brodersen, since it would amount to banishing her from the table for not having sufficient time to get her work done."

As we can gather from what Blumhardt says, Gottliebin's death was a remarkable turning point, the signal for an upswing. From the end of the forties, but especially since his move to Bad Boll, Blumhardt had been continually led down into the depths. He felt it as a privation that he no longer had a congregation of his own, but, more than that, in the eyes of the public that fact had changed him from a servant of the Gospel to a "miracle doctor." Those who sought him out believing him to be just that caused him a good deal of trouble. What was he to do with them? It was only natural that as a rule nothing happened with such persons; indeed, one could say that that was indispensable for the purity of the cause or was even a sign of it. It was in the main from such people that the rumor of Blumhardt's fading strength went out, which in turn had the beneficial effect of reducing the influx of such wrong-headed persons. But being misunderstood by the wider public depressed him less than the fact that he found so little of an echo and response among those of like mind and belief. He felt more and more lonely and increasingly weighed down by the distressing evidence that darkness was able to extend its power, unchecked and unbroken, over the whole of mankind. In November 1862, after the death of Dr. Barth, which shook him deeply, he wrote: "Farewell then, all you dear ones! Oh, if you only knew all that goes on in my soul! So many struggles! So much sadness! Often, when my thoughts go winging over the earth, which is now familiar to us in every detail, horror grips me. My heart is laced so tight, it is ready to burst. Then I thank God again that I am like that, for we ought to put on sackcloth. Oh, if only more were doing it!"

And a decade later (May 1873) he writes: "But I stand alone, all alone! No one understands me and my experiences. How can humanity be so blind as not to perceive the devil's claws and might! Everywhere I have to keep still as a mouse, and I do: Through stillness the breakthrough must come!"

Almost the only friend who fully understood him and agreed with him was the manufacturer Dieterlen in Rothau, Alsace, already known to us. He had not only experienced the life in the Möttlingen rectory but had also seen the wonderful ways Blumhardt's intercession had brought rich blessing to his (Dieterlen's) people in Rothau. It depressed him all the more that the great significance of Blumhardt should remain so unknown, should be so hushed up by his contemporaries. In his youthful impetuosity he felt that Blumhardt himself was partly to blame for that. He thought Blumhardt should be more active and vocal in bringing to a wider public the special message entrusted to him, that his published sermons expressed too many generally accepted ideas, that they were too one-sidedly good-natured, and so on.

Here are some excerpts from Blumhardt's replies to Dieterlen. They show how Blumhardt felt obliged to let the new that he was given strike root in the old, to let the new grow out of the old. In one letter he writes:

> In all my sermons I only want to explain the text, to make it come alive. Hence, right through they offer nothing but a rephrasing of the text, of what the Lord did and said. What the text suggests to me, I talk about; what it does not, remains unsaid and is saved up for another text. Look at the three sermons in question to see if there is anything in them beyond what the text yields. If there is not, be patient and wait for more sermons on other texts to come along.
>
> If you call my sermons merely good-natured, you do them a grave injustice. They don't fulminate, that is true, but there is something very earnest in them and much that is stimulating and new.
>
> You are too full of certain ideas that stir you up and that you rashly assume to stir others too. Many persons that you think are in a struggle are not actually ready for conversion. They do not *want* to change, even though they could; we have evidence enough to prove it. Thus what should be repentance in them turns into discontent and even grumbling. In such cases the conscience must first be sharpened. It won't do for me to console them by telling them that for the present things can't be different with them than they are. No! They have to apply themselves more. O brother, think it over! There are of course many "beautiful souls"[2]—that is, they could become beautiful souls but are not yet, because they do not let the simplest teachings on repentance and faith work and gain strength in them. How am I to get them to do it? I have to face them with the imparted and written word of God just as it stands and must show them what it gives and what it demands. I must plead with them to be reconciled to God. And I must speak

2. Translator's Note: A phrase coined by Goethe.

to them in a kindly, good-natured way, because that penetrates most deeply into the heart. With my most genial talks I unsettle people most. I well remember what a powerful movement my sermon No. 1 set off in Möttlingen when I gave it.

What is lacking in other preachers is that they do not rouse people's consciences. Do you find that in my sermons? Is there anything false in them, anything apt to lull to sleep?

There are people who always want only to have questions answered. What need is there for a lot of questions? Let a one do what they know. Let him read and ponder the Scriptures. Let him start placing himself before God's countenance. Let him test himself and his self-centered works. Let him find out that at bottom he is still a real child of the world, that it is only through the fear in his heart that he shows his Christianity.

Do not forget, by the way, all the divine grace and help that justification through faith, brought to light anew by the Reformation, makes accessible to all of us.

You think I am in no hurry. You are right. You expect too much of me if you think that my cries will make all the difference now. A crier must know that his cry is really heard, or else it is nothing but sounding brass. He must be certain that it finds open ears. Without the Holy Spirit one cannot hear. No one knows better than I how little I am heard. What I really want passes people by completely; all they pick up are a few snippets from along the fringe. I have been watching what people in fact take in from what I set before them, and I have noticed that they take in nothing apart from what I am actually offering in my sermons now. True, even a good deal of what I say in them, though it is read by thousands, is not *heard*. Yet, a teacher should not face his hearers with more than they can take in. That is why the Lord was so reserved in what he said—there were no open ears. Those that ask so many questions are the ones least able to hear; please believe me.

Now what is the good of setting oneself up against the whole present state of things? How many souls would I hurt and cause to close up instead of opening? By raising my voice against false trends, sects, and parties, how many plants would I break off? I am certain that with my quiet, gentle, good-natured manner I have already won over many who were hostile to me and whom I would have antagonized for good if I spoke differently.

Another time he writes:

I need not tell you that it is a divine cause I am engaged in. You also know that this is clearly evident to whoever is willing to see it and who himself seeks the Lord—indeed that it has manifested itself in a wonderful way. But I also ask you to consider that I live in daily fear whether what I do is pleasing to this holy God. I am aware that slipping away from *God's* thoughts and intentions into my own strivings and doings could ruin everything for me. Moses, too, when already called, was still in danger of being struck down by the Lord. So I constantly have to be careful how to proceed, how to think and act in a way that I have nothing to reproach myself for and that I do not hold up the advance of his cause. The thought that it is *God's* cause often makes me tremble.

These last years, too, I had to wonder now and then if there wasn't something amiss, since things have become so quiet. And when I was here and there reproached with having, like Samson, let my hair be cut, it caused me, too, to retreat into quietness, although I soon discovered that I am not meant to be a Samson. Again, some think that I am too accommodating and that, being what I am, I should keep at a distance from others. Perhaps that point carries some weight with you too. But I have come to the opposite conclusion and must honor God also in others. I feel I may not forsake the support I have rested on since childhood— the inner fellowship with believers, even if these are found wanting. I may not throw over the old props in order to set up new ones made by Blumhardt. It is a struggle for me, right down to the smallest matters, to keep on the right track, for as I know and have experienced, the enemy wants to tempt me in various ways to go ahead and map out my own direction. It is the Lord I am dealing with, who is holy and does not want any to be lost.

I must ever again return to the beginning of my story—not to the healings (for secrecy and stillness was what befitted them) but to the conversion of my congregation. There people were being led to faith through repentance, before it even occurred to me that I might have healing powers. And what were the principles guiding me then? None other than those I had learned from childhood on and which in true Reformation manner I had myself garnered from Scripture. All my sermons reflected, as they still do, Protestant doctrine, and I always felt that my preaching was effective and touched my hearers' hearts when I did it above all in the power of the Spirit. Repentance and faith in Christ the Crucified were the pivot on which everything had to turn. Conversion—nothing but the conversion of people—was the goal I had to steer toward, using as levers the generally known teachings of our catechism. I have always laid the main stress on that which anybody can immediately be given by the Savior if he singlemindedly takes hold of repentance and faith; I have pointed out vigorously that he can receive what the catechism has pointed to for three hundred years as the sure fruits of faith: forgiveness of sins; peace; sonship of God; a gracious, listening Savior. In that way I followed in the footsteps of John, who prepared the way for the Lord through repentance and forgiveness of sins, and in the footsteps of the Lord himself with what he stands for in all he says, particularly in the Sermon on the Mount. In that sermon the Lord promises most emphatically that prayer will be answered; he makes no allowance for qualifications; that is, he gives no indication that that assurance might possibly have a more restricted application later on.

I often ask myself if perhaps my calling has changed. Many have judged me by mere secondary happenings (the healings), and I have gradually ceased to be regarded as one who preaches first and foremost repentance and faith and nothing but that, so as to prepare the way for the Lord. However, I see more clearly every day that I could not hinder the cause of God more than by letting go of this first priority of mine. Every day I experience anew—and in these days have also thought and spoken quite a bit about it—how many Christians, here and there also such as hold to me, actually still have an unconverted heart. They are really more concerned with themselves and are far from submitting their own ideas, inclinations, and predilections to the Lord. But be that as it may, my calling is a Johannine one, to put it like that, and whoever does not see me from that angle does not understand or support me. What also keeps pointing me in this direction is the success of my preaching, for many continue to turn around and become servants of the Lord. The more I strike conversion chords in what I say, the better people like it and the deeper I can go with them. And where healings occur, they very often make people turn to the Lord, just as that was meant to be the fruit of Christ's miracles too.

When looking at prophecy, one must consider what has to *precede* the pouring out of the Spirit, according to both Ezekiel 36 and Joel. The last words in Malachi also belong here.

Of course, when I look at the conversions taking place, I see how much is still lacking. But it frightens me to think how things might be held up if conversion is no longer viewed as the center point. The Lord will not grant anything, nor will he reveal himself in the way I wish and hope if the work on men's hearts does not come first and last. I notice more and more that the Lord's revelations have already started and are in evidence here and there, very quietly and in secret, and that hearts are being made ready by repentance. Yet in spite of all their seeking and striving for manifestations of the Spirit and of grace, many miss the goal because

their hearts are not turned to the Lord in a completely pure way.
I am afraid that where that is so, many are bound to find themselves locked out in the end, because the paths will diverge more
and more. There are two kinds of virgins. Both wait for the Lord,
some with oil (a converted heart), the others without oil (without
a converted heart).

Dieterlen seems to have found some of Blumhardt's printed sermons too hard, partly because they spoke too sharply to the conscience
and partly because Blumhardt emphasized in them the general truth
that prayers are heard and answered, even though he knew from his
own deeper experiences that that was actually not the case at present.
Blumhardt replied:

> What do I say that is different from my Bible texts? What I say
> is aimed at the conversion of people's hearts. You think I say too
> much, make great promises that remain unfulfilled, or whatever
> you mean. In your opinion I should qualify what I say by explain-
> ing that for the time being much of what the Lord promises and
> what he wants to be to us does not apply fully. You think that by
> not doing that I slip into the tone of other preachers and offend
> people. Yet what entitles me to so qualify the words of the Lord?
> I am well aware that I once did say to you something like that in
> confidence, particularly as regards the miracles, but I stressed that
> one may not say that openly because it would not be understood.
> Now you demand I should tell people quite publicly that until
> the Lord once again draws closer to us, the great promises must
> *not* be thought to apply to us as they did when they were given.
> But why should I do that? "So that people don't give up praying
> altogether." As if they had more trust in prayer when I say that it
> actually doesn't quite work out as yet! Or: "so that people don't
> keep thinking that they are not praying rightly." Here is the rub.
>   O brother, it simply is a fact that in innumerable cases people
> are not as they should be, even though I cannot tell them where
> the lack is. Now to you it seems rather hard and wrong to chal-
> lenge people's consciences. But you know I don't even do that; I
> get around it by pointing to a hidden will of the Lord, to which
> we must submit. However, it is asking altogether too much of me
> if you expect me to keep folk from deepening their hearts and
> lives by declaring it a rule—without any justification from Holy
> Scripture—that prayers are not heard and answered. It offends
> against the very first requirement: repentance and faith. What is
> more, I receive daily evidence that the Lord does answer prayer.
> Each post brings me such evidence. So how can I say of the dear

Savior that he acts in a strange way, giving here and withholding there? What is more obvious than to assume that where people are left empty-handed, something is amiss with *them*?

That is just the trouble: So many consider themselves complete and satisfactory but are not so before the Lord. With what they have received they could and should advance further than they have done. But to make them aware of it they must be confronted with the biblical truth, for it is not right to tell them to their faces where they are lacking. To make them see it, recourse must be had to the Scripture just as it stands. Whoever takes away even one iota will be called the smallest in the kingdom of heaven.

Then he continues:

So it is also with other things. You speak of people that feel a need to hear from us something quite different from what they find in those sermons. There I don't understand you at all. I really meet a lot of people but have not come across any of the kind of which you say there are many. What all people want (if they do want anything) is simply to be helped on inwardly. And it happens again and again that they are helped forward best by my putting before them the ordinary Gospel in my own understandable way, while other things scarcely register with them. Now if you find it different, can you take it amiss if I suspect that you are too quick in putting yourself and your ideas into the souls of others, so that you think you hear from others what actually comes from you? And that you do not speak with those persons enough of those pillars of the Gospel: repentance and faith? With your people in W. you do it the right way, but whether with others I question.

I, on the other hand, run into trouble with all those people who skip the first stages of spiritual life and feel dissatisfied by what the "ordinary" Bible message can give them. And yet I constantly receive evidence of how infinitely much the "ordinary" still gives to people. Everywhere people are being converted, without me. In all parts of Germany the ordinary Bible word brings forth children of God. When thus gripped and made aware of the deep sinfulness of their hearts, they come to me in their troubles. Then it is easy for me to offer them what they inwardly need. That shows me that the Lord does indeed supply all that is required. All that remains for us to do is to ask that the Lord bring it about that more and more people seek what is needful. We can assure them boldly that they will never come away empty-handed if they follow the true way, the way of the heart. But there is nothing at all I can do with people who have not thoroughly examined their hearts first. With them I only have trouble, since I continually have to defend,

justify, and excuse myself at great length, without achieving anything except that they perhaps come to appreciate me. However,
my purpose is not to be esteemed by people but rather to convert
them through my ministry.

In the following, Blumhardt pleads with Dieterlen to have a high
regard for the jewel of the Protestant church: justification through faith,
and not to underestimate, in a false broadmindedness, the shortcomings
of Catholicism. He continues:

You see, dear friend, why I feel disturbed. What concerns me is
a vital question, which affects my whole work. I am accountable
for everything to a Lord who is very particular. He surely does
not like it that the church, which under the guidance of his spirit
has enabled his Gospel to survive till now, is not properly appreciated. It would displease him even if it were only a question of
keeping the hearts of thousands, indeed of *all* Christians, open to
me. These hearts will be closed to me if I offend their convictions,
even if it only *seems* I am doing that. Before the Lord I have to see
myself as one whose field is Christendom, and I have to show him
my gratitude by honoring and cultivating that field.

May the Lord grant us clarity and a humble sobriety! The parable tells us: "For a long time he would not" (Matt 21:29). Why?
There is a reason for it. Brother, it takes an effort to pry the doors
open!

These outpourings of his heart in letters tell better than any description Blumhardt's inner attitude in that period of stillness and apparent
decline. He stands before us firm, solid, free from sanguine optimism but
undaunted, conscious of the goal, the task, the responsibility but also of
ultimate assured success. The spiritual upsurge that followed Gottliebin
Brodersen's death—at any rate in Blumhardt's own family circle, to begin with—owed something also to the fact that at about the same time
Blumhardt's children, in particular the two sons who had chosen to
become ministers, returned to the parental home or its neighborhood.
From now on they took a place in the front line.

In the education of his children Blumhardt had gone his own ways.
We are already acquainted with his courageous, not to say audacious,
leniency toward young people. We also understand well that since his
great experiences in Möttlingen the deepest wish of his heart was that
his children would grow up under the influence of the spirit ruling in
his house. He took great pains to protect them from the influence of the

world, and that entailed considerable sacrifices, both for himself and for his sons. He had them educated at home, either by himself or by a tutor, till they entered the upper *Gymnasium*.[3] For him, overburdened as he was in any case, it was a task requiring every last bit of his strength and what spare time he had, but in some respects it was a sacrifice also for his sons, since such tutoring could not achieve a level equal to public education and made it much harder for them to pass the entrance exam.

Blumhardt found original ways of introducing his sons to the various areas of general education. He was well versed in all of them and gave to every subject matter the characteristic imprint of his mind. He was certainly an agreeable teacher, all the more so since with him the principle of freedom and voluntariness had absolute validity. On the other hand, it was a great drawback for his pupils that time and again their father-teacher was prevented from giving them lessons or was called away from them. Yet the chief goal of this bold plan of education was attained: His sons did also become his children in the Spirit and remained so; thus in the end the daring venture proved wonderfully justified.

From being tutored at home his three sons—Karl, Christoph, and Theophil—went on to the upper *Gymnasium* at Stuttgart, where they found an ideal home with the von Heider family. Various other families of friends, too, such as the Chevaliers and Engelmanns, in some measure replaced for them the parental home. Nonetheless, the whole time his sons were at school away from home, Blumhardt kept an anxious watch over them. His letters to his sons reveal a most remarkable spirit of freedom and broadmindedness toward youthful ways, combined with an anxious, strict earnestness about the real dangers that the spirit of the world has for young souls.

Once, when Blumhardt visited his sons in Stuttgart, he did not find them at home and was told there in rather a shocked manner that they had gone to the circus, more or less on their own. "To the circus?" Blumhardt said, "then I'll go there too." He did, and managed to find a seat just above where his sons were sitting. Completely unsuspecting, the boys were watching the horse riding stunts when they suddenly heard their father's friendly voice from behind: "Christoph, I am here too!"

From the upper *Gymnasium*, Christoph and Theophil, who wanted to study theology, went on to Tübingen University and in 1866 passed their exam together. Christoph was posted to Spöck (a name more widely

3. Translator's Note: German secondary school preparing students for the university.

known through Henhöfer's work there) as curate to the venerable rector, Pastor Peter. It was due to Peter's fatherly and encouraging ways that Christoph did not give up the clerical profession, to which he felt unequal. From Spöck he came, again as curate, to Dürnau near Boll. There he remained for two years and through frequent visits grew more and more into the work of his father. In 1869 he moved to Bad Boll to stand by his father's side, helping and serving.

Theophil first went to Gruibingen (near Reutlingen), then as house guest of an Alsatian family to Nice (France). This connection soon led to his being posted as curate and acting rector to the little town of Barr in Alsace. In the fall of 1869 he, too, came to Dürnau, where in 1870 he was appointed military chaplain. In that capacity he accompanied the German troops to the gates of Paris. After serving as acting rector in three parishes (Gruibingen, Kaiserbach, and Jesingen), he returned to his father's house in 1872. There he first helped out with teaching and later supported his father in his literary work. At the same time he served the Württemberg church as acting rector or in other capacities, now here, now there in the district, leaving behind everywhere marks of rich blessing.

Second Section

19

The Housefather

A VISITOR ARRIVING AT BAD Boll discovered at once a peculiarity of the lifestyle there, that is, that almost no notice was taken of his arrival. That was a foretaste of the general tone of the house: with the exception of mealtimes and religious services, the host left the guests completely to themselves. There was warmth, love, and joy toward the newcomer but none of the people-grabbing officiousness that marks commercialized hospitality. On the other hand, Blumhardt carefully saw to it that no one absented himself from mealtimes and devotions needlessly.

The colorful assemblage of guests in Bad Boll, in particular the many weak and sick but also the numerous members of the upper classes, caused breakfast to be served no earlier than eight o'clock. If that induced someone to sleep in, he would be wakened at seven o'clock by the sound of singing coming from the morning devotions of the domestic staff. These devotions were led first by Blumhardt, then by Theodor Brodersen, and later by either Christoph or Theophil, Blumhardt's two minister sons.

Soon afterward, Blumhardt's big family would gather in a large room for family devotions. Here, first consideration was given to the children—twenty-four of Blumhardt's own grandchildren as well as other children that had become part of the family. This is where Blumhardt felt really at home. I think he looked upon these children as his "household troops" or "elite corps," whom he could credit with a simple, pure trust in the Lord and in what he wants to bring. Blumhardt prayed with them as a child among children, not as one stooping to their level but straight from his own heart. Those prayers, born as they were of childlike trust, were therefore specially brief and simple.

When parents and children were gathered, Blumhardt came in, took a seat, rang for silence with his little bell, and said a prayer. Then those gathered would sing *"Der Herr segne uns"* ("O Lord, bless us"). At the last notes the little toddlers present would begin to stir. No sooner had the song ended than they went pattering up to their grandfather. The mothers would follow, carrying their babies, and then came the older children. Blumhardt put his hand on each child, saying, "May the Lord bless you, dear Maria" or something like that. Of course, when a child was sick or had a birthday or was otherwise in a special situation, he would say a few words in addition to that short blessing. The meeting ended with another song, either "Lord Jesus, I live to thee" or "Hosanna." Even the tiniest tots joined lustily in singing these songs (all composed by Blumhardt himself), without being the least disturbance.

In the meantime the bell had rung for breakfast. On entering the dining room, Blumhardt would find his household already gathered there. To start the breakfast, he would say a prayer such as "Father, bless the food before us." After breakfast the Moravian book of daily texts was opened. First, mention was made of any that had their birthday noted in it as falling on this day, then of those friends to whom the day had been specially allotted. It was a custom that on each New Year's Eve a lot was drawn for everyone listed for this as a friend of Bad Boll, mainly so that on a certain day of the year Boll might be specially reminded of that friend and he of Boll.

After the midday meal a psalm was read out (often taken from Blumhardt's "Songs from the Psalms"[1]), and a prayer of thanksgiving was either spoken or was sung by the children. The evening meal was followed by a reading, in running sequence, from Holy Scripture, which would then be discussed at varying length by Blumhardt. Both the morning and evening devotions were accompanied by singing, mostly from Blumhardt's "Songs from the Psalms and Prophets."[2]

1. Editors' Note: Johann Christoph Blumhardt, *Psalmlieder oder die Psalmen, in singbare Lieder umgesetzt,* 2nd enl. ed. (Reutlingen: Kurtz, 1864) [*Psalm Hymns, or the Psalms Transposed to Singable Tunes*].

2. Editors' Note: Johann Christoph Blumhardt, *Prophetenlieder nach Jesaja, nebst ausgewählten Psalmliedern, nach dem biblischen Texte bearbeitet* (Reutlingen: Kurtz, 1850)

What many remember best are the conversations that took place after breakfast, after the midday meal (while enjoying a cigar), and above all in the evenings. Blumhardt often longed for genuine questions to be brought up; such questions helped him by lighting up the mysteries of God's kingdom from ever new angles. Many times these talks reached deeply into the heart and conscience. What shining lights they kindled! It was such conversations about matters of the heart and conscience and the great concerns of the kingdom of God that Blumhardt liked best, but beyond that he was interested in all things human and discovered in everything a direct relationship to that kingdom.

He found it specially pleasing and stimulating when he could dispute with men of distinctive character and eminent position, not least with such as had until then been critical of Christianity. Perhaps it was he that gained most from such exchanges, for he had the virtue and gift of perceiving what was most sensible in what the other said and of drawing that out. He never wanted to advise and instruct except as one learning himself; that was what made such talks so extraordinarily stimulating and fruitful.

Of course, in those things where divine certainty had come to him he was not open to "enlightenment" designed to shatter those convictions. The more firmly, clearly, and viscerally these views lived in him, indeed, the more he felt practically alone in holding some of them and was constantly obliged to be on the defensive, the harder he found it to be open even to right ideas if they were new to him and he suspected them of contradicting his own views. That, however, was a side of him that very rarely came to expression. Wherever he recognized competence, he was only too glad to let himself be instructed about anything touching on men's life and activity. Of course, he would at once relate these things to the Lord and his kingdom, thus doing what alone is appropriate to that kingdom's reality and significance.

Yet alongside that broadminded attitude one could sense in him a gathered, steely energy. Inwardly he held firmly to the Lord. If he noticed, for instance, that some dialogue close by was in danger of becoming irritated and getting out of hand, he would intervene with all his accustomed heartiness and tell those involved (using *du*, the familiar, intimate form of address in German, even though they might be gentlemen of

---

[*Hymns of the Prophet According to Isaiah, with Selected Psalm Hymns, Treated According to the Biblical Text*].

high social standing): "This has no place at my table! Now you be quiet! And you too!"

That brings to mind a peculiarity in Blumhardt's way of speaking, namely that the so-called *pluralis majestatis*, *Sie* (the formal, polite form of address in German) hardly ever rose to his lips. A certain count once commented, "I think if a king came to Boll, he could expect to be 'thou-ed' within three days." That might have put it a bit strongly, for when addressing ladies of a high social position, Blumhardt did manage to say *Sie*, but in general the count was right. Even though the use of *du* was quite unselfconscious and instinctive with Blumhardt, it did have deeper reasons. Regardless of who it was that crossed his threshold, Blumhardt would take up that guest's cause before God in so priestly a way that from then on he saw him (or her) only in the light in which that person stood before God.

On the one hand, his brotherly heart felt the need to break through the barrier of that strange falsehood peculiar to our time (i.e. using *Sie* in polite secular conversation and *du* in religious language), on the other hand such a breakthrough could (though he was not conscious of it) be regarded as his duty as housefather of Bad Boll. Men are not to be approached in two different ways—a solemn, religious one in church (where no minister will address his hearers with *Sie*) and a secular one at table (where *Sie* is considered proper). Blumhardt's use of the *du*, which, as said before, was in no way conscious or deliberate, contributed to the impression once described by a visiting theologian as feeling transported back across the centuries into Bible days. For many unmarried women, for example, who felt half-orphaned in our cold world, it may well have been a first quickening experience when Blumhardt in his fatherly way greeted them with *du*: it would waken in them a long-missed feeling of being at home. And how that *du* helped clear away unnaturalness and stiff formality!

There was another aspect of Blumhardt's converse with people that was much talked about—his conduct toward persons of the upper classes. It is well known that members of the higher and highest aristocracy were tied to Blumhardt by bonds of intimacy and gratitude. This he owed to his pastoral gifts, but, of course, indispensable to such pastoral contact was a holy, sober approach to class differences. One could feel that his *du* did not spring from fanatical narrow-mindedness or hypocritical envy. At times he acknowledged the higher social station in a way that certain middle-class guests, misinterpreting it, were apt to hold against him. When it came down to it, though, Blumhardt saw even in persons of exalted rank only the human being, the brother who, like anybody else, needed redemption and received it.

During the Möttlingen time, he was once accompanied on a train journey by a certain dean, who had long felt misgivings that his friend was in danger of being corrupted by the reverence in which he was held by members of the upper classes. When they left the train at a certain station, a duchess came hurrying toward Blumhardt to greet him. He returned the greeting warmly and respectfully when he suddenly spied, standing on one side and behind her, an old, dear friend and brother in simple peasant garb. With an apology to the duchess, he rushed to him, and the noble lady waited patiently for the two friends to express their affection to each other. That ended the dean's worry.

Another time, a certain "royal highness," indirectly well known to Blumhardt, learned that he was on the same train with her and on arrival at the destination sent a gentleman-in-waiting in search of him. Blumhardt came with his traveling-bag, bowed and greeted her, wishing her the Lord's blessing, but then excused himself saying that he had to see to his luggage (he was quite nervous on journeys) and took his leave. The most telling examples of his hearty approach also to persons of exalted rank are unsuited for publication, precisely on account of the prominence of the names concerned.[3]

---

3. More light is shed on Blumhardt's approach to the higher social position of some of his guests by a letter he wrote from Möttlingen to a friend. In that letter he comments on the (moderate) luxury that had entered his house through the extended stay there of a lady of high rank:

> I should like to say something about the luxury that has come into our house for the sake of the princely person in residence there. First of all, I must note that I have not paid for it out of my own money, inasmuch as I have no money to start with. If I am nevertheless in a position to purchase such things, and that without falling short in generosity and charity, I see it as a sign from above that I may and must do it. It would be my greatest sin to use the calling God has placed me in to lay up capital for myself. I am not allowed to grow rich, but *I must be suitably set up* for all kinds of people so that I can give service for eternal life to them all. I am not looking for luxury, you know that, but I have to guard against a stubborn unwillingness to go *beyond the bare ordinary* even though God nudges me in that direction. So when, quite unsolicited, a princess comes to me, it is my duty (which I actually owe to any person) to ask myself: What can I and must I do—given that I *can* do it—for the good of the princess?

The brochure *Krankheit und Heilung*[4] (Sickness and Healing) contains such a colorful description of life in Bad Boll and Blumhardt's ways that we quote the following excerpt. It tells how the narrator and a seriously sick lady he accompanied arrived in Boll.

Finally our long-awaited goal lay before us. Behind ornamental gardens laid out in the English style beckoned a stately mansion with two wings, recently built in modern style and painted a friendly yellow with green jalousies. It is set against the wooded slope of the *Rauhe Alb*. Before we had much time for reflective thought, we were already rounding the little park, where we could see a number of ladies and gentlemen either sitting or strolling about. We drove into the courtyard between the building and the park, and I jumped down from the driver's seat to find out at which of the many doors we were to pull up—at the portico of the main entrance or at one of the side doors. Various silken gowns rustled across the courtyard but none of the wearers took any notice of us. "Oh, how genteel!" Auguste sighed in anguish. However, some compassionate soul that took pity on our plight shouted down from a window of the main story, "The entrance is over there to the right." The driver pulled up there, and I went inside.

At first I couldn't see anybody, but then a noble lady came, and I asked her if it were possible to see Pastor Blumhardt. "That I couldn't tell you" was the reply. I entered the dining room and put the same question to several women I found in there. A pleasant, gentle voice said to a child, "Go tell *Papa!*" That was the dear *Frau Pfarrer* Blumhardt. I told her straight away whom I was bringing. "Oh, her room isn't ready yet; I thought it was tomorrow she would be coming!"

I do not know what God has further in mind for me. Often the task seems more than I can manage, and it frightens me sometimes, but I have to follow as I am led, or I am disobedient. In our days nothing is needed more than men willing to be of both low and high estate at the same time. I have already worked a good deal among the upper classes and shall still have to do so a lot. I must be just as accessible to them as to the lower classes; both are headed for the same heaven. However, by sticking doggedly to a *low* standard I do not attract people, to say the least—instead I put them off. There is nothing I fear more than having it held against me on the day of judgment that I so put off somebody through rigidity or obstinacy and proud lowliness that he could not come close to me. By the way, at least half the cost of that furniture was paid by another party, and more would have been paid had I agreed.

4. Editors' Note: A. von Harless, *Krankheit und Heilung: Eine Lebensskizze* (Brandenburg : Wiesike, 1863).

While she came outside with me, I explained that it was important for Auguste to be taken at once to where she could lie down. Meanwhile Auguste got more and more impatient in her carriage and shouted, "For God's sake get me out of here! I can't stand it any longer." Blumhardt appeared himself and quickly arranged for her to be taken to a sofa in the family's living room for the time being. Two men carried her there in an armchair. Blumhardt came for a moment and explained that he would be busy until four o'clock. He spoke a few friendly words to Auguste, telling her not to worry; everything would soon be ready. Then he excused himself.

We were now quite alone in the room. Auguste was terribly exhausted and agitated and cried. She asked us to leave her alone, so I went out into the park. There I met *Vikar* (curate) Sp., who had followed me out, and straightway got into a nice contact with him—an amiable, devout, intelligent Swabian. As we strolled in the park, he introduced me to several persons. I plied him with a lot of questions, and soon it was four o'clock, the communal coffee time. The signal is a little bell; it brings the house guests streaming into the dining room from all directions. In the meantime Auguste had been taken to her room, which was on the ground floor in the opposite wing. In the dining room are two long tables, each accommodating from sixty to seventy persons.

Next follows a description (similar to the one given earlier) of the breakfast and the morning devotions.

The Bible reading is followed by a song, which Blumhardt reads out line by line. Far from being a forced, boring sing-song, the singing is strangely moving, with peculiar melodies quite different from the ordinary hymn style. There follows a brief prayer of thanksgiving. If told like that, it reeks of pietism and has a conventicular flavor, but let me assure you that there is no trace of unhealthy religiosity in anything Blumhardt does. A fresh, joyful spirit blows through this house, giving a vivid impression of what the peace of God is all about, the peace that surpasses all understanding. That wind of the Spirit pervades everything, both practical and spiritual, significant or insignificant. It is an atmosphere that affects the soul as free mountain air affects the body. In a wonderful way a bond of peace enfolds the whole large household, making one family out of a strange conglomerate of most varied personalities.

Several nationalities meet daily in the dining room. During my stay the following countries were represented here: Norway,

Holland, Denmark, France, Switzerland, Prussia, Saxony, Russia, Baden, Bavaria, and Württemberg. The non-Germans all spoke or at least understood German. All levels of society were represented, from the highest to the lowest, at times even persons of princely rank. A peasant, for example, was seated at a table just a short distance behind a lady from the Russian imperial court. Any false separation of men through lying etiquette, egoism, and pride is done away with here, whereas all true distinctions and limits, rooted in nature, are observed with a tact so fine, free, and natural that the general tone of this house would have to be called a masterpiece from a social point of view alone. But of course it is something much higher, namely the organic outgrowth of a Christianity grasped in all its depth with full evangelical freedom and allowed to penetrate the practical life. One's heart unfolds and exults in this house, where Christianity has visibly become flesh in a way not easily found anywhere else. Here the dividing wall everywhere else separating the sacred from the profane has fallen. And yet the sacred has not been dragged down into the profane nor has the naturally human been deprived of its rights. Everything holy has become truly human, and everything human has been transfigured. It's all quite unconstrained and so natural that while in the midst of it, one thinks it really could not be otherwise, and one cannot understand why it is not like that in all other Christian homes.

A small but characteristic incident comes to my mind. One evening there was a woman at supper with her little four-year-old daughter. She was sitting near Blumhardt; the child was just behind a pillar. Following the meal Blumhardt had the Bible brought to him, and we were waiting for the evening reading to begin. Suddenly, while everything was quiet, Blumhardt's voice was heard: "Peek-a-boo! Peek-a-boo!" In that way he had fun with the child for a little while. Then he broke off, saying, "So, now be nice and quiet, like a good little girl. We left off at the second half of the second chapter of the Letter to the Ephesians." He then proceeded to read. And I am certain that like me, no one felt in the least disturbed or put off by such childlikeness.

The evening reading is always followed by a simple, wonderfully clear and deep exposition. After that, Blumhardt asks if anyone has something to add; he may also put direct questions to one or the other. He speaks without any pathos, in a conversational tone, at times rising to moving earnestness but never sermonizing in any way. He does not possess what is usually called an imposing personality but rather a most glorious and amiable informality. He is totally unassuming, does not talk of extraordinary things, and

is constantly full of humor and at times earthy jokes. He is an enemy of pious talk, and it does not flourish around him. Simplicity,
freedom, and down-to-earth, world-embracing love are the basic
traits of his character.

His wife is the happiest union of a Mary and a Martha I have
ever met: Mary by nature and upbringing and a Martha by long
practice, if I may say so—that is, through practicing self-denying
love. When we arrived, her youngest child, not half a year old yet,
lay hopelessly ill. Blumhardt himself no longer dared to hope, but
anyone not aware of it would have noticed nothing either in him
or in his wife. They showed the same serene equanimity as on
the following morning, when the child unexpectedly improved.
With others that might be thought unnatural, but I have seen
with admiration what a noble and great thing it is when a heart
has become firm through grace.

For most, the morning devotions were the high point in the communal life of the large guest family. Of all the ways in which Blumhardt
was active as a "servant of the Word," his reflections on the Bible have
been engraved on the memory of those present as his finest and most
remarkable service. Here he was in his true element, that of free, natural conversation. He came unprepared. If he had nothing to say, he said
nothing. It was against his grain to produce an edifying meditation by
dint of drudgery. But it was rare for him to have nothing to say.

Two sources fruitfully influenced his mind: the Bible and people.
The Bible was to him like a great park whose every nook and corner he
had explored over and over again from childhood on. There was not a
single section in it he did not know well; there were but few that did not
bring back to him some especially holy memory. It was a thrill for him
when on opening the Bible his eye fell on a passage that unexpectedly
took him back to some well-loved scene but let him look at it from a
new angle.

And what about *men* as a source of inspiration? What I think and
am about to say here may well be regarded as exaggerated by some,
but not by any who really *knew* Blumhardt. When he appeared at the
breakfast table on a given day, he had most likely become more closely
acquainted with this or that guest the day before in his study. During the
night he might well have prayed for him fervently, and now he would
longingly search the guest's countenance for any sign of success. Before
starting to read, he would have interceded inwardly for everyone present.

His thoughts would have already taken him far afield as he glanced at the names of friends specially connected with that day, either because it was their birthday or because the day had been "allotted" to them. With all that in mind, hungering and thirsting on behalf of many, he sat and faced the word of the Bible. That is why time and again even the most familiar Bible passages shone out to him in a new light, the light of that day's crying need. How did he manage to be so bright, cheerful, and genial, particularly at breakfast, in the face of all that? It was because he knew well that his entreaties did not go unheard, that the Lord was constantly near and held out rich, gracious, victorious blessing.

We are greatly indebted to Blumhardt's son Theophil for taking down these morning devotions. For three years running[5] he has gathered them into annual collections, designed for daily family reading and inner uplift. He published them under the title *Täglich Brod aus Bad Boll*. The 1878 issue, an initial volume selected from Bible expositions over many years, contains perhaps the most striking examples of Blumhardt's manner of speaking at these morning devotions. It is therefore mostly from that issue that the following examples are taken. Naturally, it is not easy to pick out and choose items from an already carefully chosen selection; the volume abounds in pieces just like the few we include here. Some of Blumhardt's sayings may at first put us off; they may hurt us or, if we do not understand them straight away, may leave us cool, but often it is precisely those that afterwards strike one as most instructive and quickening. Let us first look at a sample of his pithy *diction*, reminiscent of proverbs.

On Hosea 14:2:

> Forgive all our sins, and receive us graciously, and we will sacrifice to thee the bull calves of our lips.

> The sacrificed bull calves represented the sacrificer's self-surrender to God unto death. Thus the bull calves of our lips are our free confession of the grace of God in Christ Jesus, even though at the risk of our lives. But there are also persons that keep their bull calves penned up; that is, they do not come out openly with their confession, being afraid that it might get them into trouble.

Now some samples demonstrating the *content* of the devotions. On Matthew 5:3:

---

5. Editors' Note: From 1877 to 1880.

> Blessed are the poor in spirit.

What matters is being poor. Possession of temporal and earthly goods is completely out. If you have them, act as if you did not; if you don't have any, so much the better. Then you come closer to feeling poor. Rich folk find it terribly hard to feel poor. You can see straight away when a man *has* something. The awareness "I have something" gives him an ungodly air. It gives him an ungodly, anti-godly character, as if all the angels had been scared away from him. Thus, the poorer we feel, the more certain we can be of the kingdom of heaven.

On Genesis 32:10:

> I am unworthy of all the kindness and faithfulness thou hast shown to thy servant.

Jacob feels inwardly humbled and deeply moved by all the kindness and faithfulness God has shown him. "Why all this to me and not rather to someone else?" Others, when boasting of God's kindness, often think by themselves, "No wonder, really; after all I am better than others." But they all get their ears boxed because they think so highly of themselves. That attitude is truly unworthy of God's kindness. Considering oneself worthy of everything good is enough to make a man unworthy of God's kindness and faithfulness. People are often down on Jacob for having lied to his father and cheated his brother of his inheritance. Indeed, they even take it amiss that the Lord God shows so much kindness to this rascal, as they put it. But with the word in our text Jacob lets us look into his heart, which is humbled by its sin. Thus, though he runs away from home as one driven out, the following night he beholds the ladder to heaven and on his return, the angels of God. His awareness of being unworthy makes him a favorite with God. We often have so much that we think gives us some status in God's eyes. Away with it! Be like Jacob and drop your self-love, then you will be God's beloved.

On Genesis 1:1:

> In the beginning God created the heavens and the earth.

What does that imply? The heavens and the earth are his and remain his. Whatever lives in heaven and on earth, all belongs to him who created it. He cannot cast away like shards anything he has created, thinking, "I will make a new one." What once lived or lives now he cannot let perish, thinking only, "Well, that's gone now"; rather, it stays with him. Having been so kind as to call the world into being, he cannot simply discard it, especially not that which has his spirit, that is, the beings endowed with reason. That is why God will not cast away heaven and earth but make it new. The first word of the Bible makes the last one come true: "Behold, I make all things new" (Rev 21:5). Its very first word contains all we hope for. The Creator God cannot but be concerned about what he created. Hence, already that first word calls for a God that saves; it tells us that we are in good hands, since God is the creator of the whole world.

On John 16:24:

> Ask, and you will receive, that your joy may be full.

Believing and asking, prayer and faith—that is something we must never forget. When we no longer believe and ask in faith, things don't go right. Then the wagon stops, so to speak, and in the end rolls backwards. The wagon should go uphill, but when there is no faith and prayer to push it, it not only stops but by and by will roll back—toward the abyss. Believing and asking is what moves it forward; if we keep doing that, we get farther and ever farther, and in the end our joy will be complete. We would always like to have joy, but often we just want it to drop into our lap. That does not work. Whoever wants to have joy, above all perfect, eternal, heavenly joy, must make a daily effort to climb upward, slowly but surely, by prayer and faith. The higher he climbs, the more wonderful and perfect everything gets; the more freely he can breathe, the greater are the splendors that open up before him, and in the end he reaches the summit, where his joy is complete. Yet the peak of joy will only be reached when not merely your and my redemption but the redemption of *all* is achieved, as far as that is ever possible. That will be the joy supreme, which we shall one day, through our prayer and faith, be allowed to receive from our Savior's hand.

On Matthew 6:21:

> For where your treasure is, there will your heart be also.

When we consider something a treasure, we give our heart to it. Oh, how little a man often values his heart, how easily he gives it away, what a low regard he has for it! It is really terrible. He flings it into the nearest mud puddle, locks it into the money box, or lets go of it in some other way. That is why every sin is such an abomination, such a desecration of our own self; it means throwing the best we have, our heart, into the gutter. David often refers to his heart as his "honor," thus showing how he values his heart, that is, his own person, his inner self. May the Lord grant that we learn to value ourselves and esteem what God has given us, so that we may become autonomous personal beings that refuse to hand their hearts over to, or let them be captured by, anything.

Actually, we ourselves should be a treasure for God and keep our hearts free for him alone. Many times, however, man almost seems to tell God, "Go away! What do I need you for? I give my heart to something else!" When you do that, evil days will come upon you, and you will pay heavily for what you so lightly cast away. Oh, what would become of us if it were not for God's mercy, which even pursues disloyal children!

On Psalm 85:1:

> Lord, thou didst show favor to thy land; thou didst bring back captive Jacob.

In later times that happy experience again and again kindled a hope that the Lord would do it anew. It is the basis also for my hope. When I reflect how everything is captive and bound, I cannot help looking toward a redemption from captivity and bondage to be sent by God. We must always trust God to do again what he has done before. God does not want what he has done to be forgotten. Having done such great things two or three thousand years ago, he cannot possibly say, "Once and never again!" Rather, to refurbish what happened once and give it renewed significance in all men's eyes, he will do such deeds again. The Savior, too, having worked miracles and let himself be crucified for it—how can we expect him to do nothing more, as though he were afraid they would crucify him again? On the contrary, Scripture everywhere directs us to expect him to do wondrous deeds until redemption is fully completed. If we would only read more zealously and take to heart the words of the prophets, through which after all God himself speaks, we would soon note that the miracles of the new covenant, beginning with the coming of the Lord, are by no means all we can expect. He will yet manifest himself anew with great power and glory before and during the time leading up to his visible return.

On Revelation 1:16:

> Out of his mouth went a sharp, two-edged sword.

This is the sword that separates genuineness from ungenuineness, true faith from apparent faith; it cuts and strips away from a man what is hypocritical, what makes him look as though he were something, until nothing is left but nakedness and shame. If the Christian skin were stripped off some Christians, it would leave them plain devils. In their Christian skin they really look like somebody, but when that is gone, then what do they look like? When the Lord takes his sword and cuts and strips away from a man all the hypocritical trimmings of self that are around him like a false, alien skin, the man stands there so vile and ugly the very angels would turn their backs on him. Oh, if the Lord would only take a hand and start right now to use his sword! People will not change, will not humble themselves nor long for salvation until the Lord himself uncovers the shame and nothingness that is theirs, ripping away the whole glitter and sparkle of their pretence. And he will do it. His loving counsel for humanity's redemption must be carried through, though it may mean that many people will yet have to go through many judgments. His mercy will be victorious. Once the false adornments are stripped from man by the sword of the Spirit, the Lord can put on him the garments of his salvation and ornaments of his righteousness.

On Hosea 14:4:

> I will heal their waywardness; I will love them freely. Then
> my anger shall turn away from them.

Looking after the backsliders with tears in his eyes, so to speak, the Lord thinks, "I am going to get them back" (in other words, "I will heal their waywardness") and, "I will love them freely"—namely when they return. We will grasp the intent of our God and Savior best when we visualize him as one who is merciful toward the wayward or backsliders, who wants to cure their wicked defiance. He will try a thousand times to heal before he condemns; he will exert all his strength to bring them back. If punishment will not work, he will try lenience, softness, patience, and stillness—with his eye continually on them. In the end he may quite likely still use powerfully shattering and shaking measures (in a good or bad sense), but always with the intent of curing the backsliders. That is God's counsel. That is also the sense in which we have to understand the gospel of Jesus Christ. We have no gospel if we simply consider the backsliders lost. What is the gospel there for? To bring the backsliders home! Thus, before hell opens its gates, heaven will open up, and God will display his wonderful power as in Egypt to draw wayward humankind back to himself. At the same time he will do his part also in secret—through a renewed working of the Holy Spirit—to make people turn away from their apostasy. Then he will say to them, "Come, dear children, let me love you."

On Revelation 1: 14:

> His eyes are like a flame of fire.

His eyes, which are like flames of fire, see everything. Dear children, big and small, when you are about to do something evil, just imagine the Savior standing before you with flaming eyes! You will then leave it, I think. When you are good, his eyes are full of loving-kindness, but when you feel like doing something bad, they are eyes of fire. No, if it's like that, we had better not do it but rather avoid all evil, lest his flaming eyes fall on us and pierce us. And when the day of judgment comes, there will be many to whom his fiery eyes will speak a serious language.

On Psalm 25:16:

> Turn thou to me and be gracious to me, for I am lonely and afflicted.

Many people may speak words such as these but not in the faith that it will be so, that the Savior will actually turn to them and be gracious to them. Instead, such a word makes them even sadder than they already are. Such fools we are! We say, "Turn thou to me" and afterward cry twice as much as before, and "Be gracious to me" and then cry three times as much. What we ought to pray for is that a gentle breath of grace would waft over us. But many just pray wildly, and the more they pray the more depressed they get. So much has become just a habit, a matter of words and emotions but not of faith. When we read a passage like that, faith should pull us out of loneliness and affliction. When faith is lacking, a divine word that is read but not believed is apt to plunge us still more deeply into misery. Of course, it is not the divine word that does it but our lack of faith. Oh, that we might learn to have faith and pray in faith!

On Psalm 34:8:

> Oh, taste and see that the Lord is kind! Blessed is the man that trusts in him.

What is so hard about our time is that the Lord is indeed always kind but there is an unkind being that constantly thwarts him and us. That is something terrible—that an unkind being so obstructs and thwarts the paths of our kindly God. It is the pain of earthly existence that we apparently have more to do with the unkind one than with the one that is kind. So wicked is the unkind one that where he notices that things are well with us, he gives us a kick to put a stop to our well-being. These are the struggles we have to face if the unkind one is to be got out of the way and we are to taste and see none but our kindly God. The unkind one can often make us lose the kindly God and all trust in him; indeed, many times what the unkind one does is attributed to God, and with some people that leads to terrible blasphemy. It is most ill-considered to take God and the evil power ruling in the world as one and the same, but the main thing is not to lose trust in our kindly God, even if it is many times almost impossible to hear him. Whatever obstacles may often seem to block the way, making a man just about lose all trust—only he that does trust in God will experience, taste, and see that to the trusting man God is all in all.

On Jeremiah 23:5, 6:

> "Behold, the days are coming," says the Lord, "when I will raise to David a righteous branch, and he shall reign as king and govern wisely, and shall execute justice and righteousness on earth. . . . And this is the name by which he will be called: 'The Lord who is our righteousness.'"

So "the days are coming," even if they are not yet here. The branch—the Savior Jesus Christ—has grown, but he is not yet everywhere manifest as king. In that first time after his ascension he did show himself as the one seated at God's right hand, as king. But afterward he again became of low estate on earth. In general, people have pretended to let him be king, but in fact they have ruled on earth themselves. They got used to following their own will and whims and paid no attention to the Savior. That self-government has also increased mightily in spiritual matters. In our days, too, the Savior does not actually function as a king, neither in the church nor elsewhere. People do as they see fit, and that's supposed to be the king's way, but it is not. Hence the time is yet to come when he that was born a king and became one will manifest his kingship on earth. It says: "He shall govern wisely and shall execute justice and righteousness on earth. . . . And this shall be his name: 'The Lord who is our righteousness.'" Yes, those days will come!

May we still expect on earth something like the prospect held out to us here? Let *us* give this word the honor due to it. Let us wait for the King; let us expect him, now seated on his Father's throne, to yet manifest himself as king in the world, until "to him every knee shall bow and every tongue swear, 'In the Lord are my righteousness and strength'" (Isa 45:23–24). In so doing, they will call him, just as it says here, "Lord, who is our righteousness," since without him their cause would come to nothing.

Passages such as this one are important to me because they refer to the end time—the time people usually just connect with the black king, the terrible one, the anti-Christ. Now Scripture does say that there are enemies and adversaries and also an anti-Christ, but it does not speak of an anti-Christ that is just about *omnipotent*. On the other hand, numerous passages refer to a king that will bring peace to the whole world, so that it is the *good* that will culminate toward the end. Otherwise people always talk of a culmination of the *bad*. Well, that is what experience teaches us. But the Scripture says also that toward the end the *good* will reach its climax, so that not the good but the bad will be defeated. The Lord will yet be master of the earth before he returns, for when he comes, we must already be in a position to call him the "Lord who is our righteousness."

On John 13:8:

> If I do not wash you, you have no part in me.

Peter would not allow the Savior to wash his feet. The Lord said to him, "If you do not let me wash your feet, you have no part in me," that is, "you remain dirty, and I cannot use you." Unless he has cleansed us, he cannot use us. He has no use for unwashed people. Those that still bear the character of sinners, that do not desire or seek forgiveness but want to be righteous in their own strength, without him, are as yet no good to the Lord. He cannot do anything with them nor can he help them; they have no part in him. It is remarkable how many times the Savior, in spite of all his love, cannot help people or do anything for them, however great their misery, *if they do not ask him*. The fact is that such a request is already a kind of reconciliation. When a man is unwilling to ask, he is and remains unreconciled. Then God simply lets things take their course with him, nor does he restrict the devil from wreaking havoc with him. That is why the Savior helped all that *asked* him. Their entreaty reconciled them to him. So few people bear in mind that our loving God *accepts* the simple requests of sinners. It is his way of telling them that he lets grace come to them also as regards their sins. So, if the Lord cannot wash us, he cannot give us anything either. That means: Unless he brings about a reconciliation that allows us to be called righteous and clean because of him, he cannot do much with us, because things do not yet run according to the divine rules. Therefore, let us allow him to wash us really clean from our sins.

Psalm 19:7:

The law of the Lord is changeless, quickening the soul.

The law of the Lord has the effect of forming and educating people and giving them sense—for one thing because his law is good, for another because it is changeless, that is, it does not alter, at one time demanding this and another time something else or the opposite. Thus it is beyond blame and benefits anybody holding to it as to a good friend that never counsels what is evil. All who do not bear the law in their hearts are foolish. "The law of the Lord makes the foolish wise." It does great harm when man lets himself be guided by his own wisdom and cleverness instead of by the Lord's law. In the end, such a one will fall into the pit in spite of all his cleverness.

Therefore, too, it is all wrong when people want to have only faith and grace preached to them but not the law. The law is absolutely necessary to develop spiritual understanding and gain wisdom for life. That is why it says here that the law quickens the soul. That holds true also when one is redeemed through grace. Does anything do us more good than reading the sound admonitions given by the Savior and the apostles? And what are they but the law of God? To be sure, the wrath of the law falls on any that transgress and despise it, but it quickens them that love it.

Psalm 25:3:

No one who waits for thee is put to shame.

Who then is put to shame? He that does not wait. And who is wiser, he that waits or he that does not wait? Is it wise or unwise to wait for the Lord and the revelation of his glory? "You are hoping too much," people say. But I say it is quite impossible to wait too much for the Lord or to hope for too much from him. He who does not wait much for him nor expect a lot from him is a fool that does not know the Lord at all. If a man sets any limits to his expectancy, he does not have the right understanding, especially if he sees how boundless are the promises. If the promises were limited, it could be said that the things the expectant man waits for are not God's intent. But if they *are* the intent of God, the wiser and godlier one is he that waits for him.

For the time being everything is in the devil's power and subject to him. Yet Scripture tells us that the Lord came to destroy the works of the devil (1 John 3:8). So the expectant man says, "Away with the devil!" Is he saying too much? Scripture clearly declares and proclaims that the devil must go. So we wait for the Lord and are not overdoing it when we yearn for the coming of him that will free and redeem all the bound and enslaved from the power of darkness. Either all Christianity amounts to nothing or our faith and prayer must win the day. What does it matter if for the time being people call us fools? No one who waits for the Lord is put to shame!

On Lamentations 3:58:

> O Lord, plead thou the case for my soul and redeem my life.

That actually means: "Do thou, Lord, act as my soul's advocate in court! It is facing a heavy charge, and my life is in danger. The judge casts a stern eye on me, and I am afraid. My soul is done for, and I am at my wit's end." To be sure, at that time Jeremiah was accused wrongly by his people, but how is it with us who stand accused before God? Well, we all have now an advocate, and his name is Jesus Christ. When it looks bad for us in court, he pleads for us and says, "I have set it right, I have paid the penalty; let him go free." That is the advocate we must choose; without him no one will come through. He is an advocate that always wins the case if a man entrusts it completely to him. But if somebody wants to conduct his own defense in court, brings up excuses, claims to be in the right, and presents himself as a good fellow, and in this way expects a lenient sentence, the great advocate cannot plead for him, for he would then have to engage in artful lies, as other lawyers often do, in order to back up the assertions of his client. But that the Savior will not do; on the contrary, in that case he has to declare, "No, things are not as he says. I cannot take on his case." That is why we must drop all self-righteousness and rely wholly on his blood, by which he atoned for our sins. The following word then applies:

> Who will bring a charge against God's elect? Here is God who justifies. Who is to condemn? Here is Christ who died, yes, who was raised from the dead, who is at the right hand of God and intercedes for us. (Rom 8:33–34)

On Revelation 21:6:

> To the thirsty I will give from the fountain of living water without payment.

A lot of people come to me and urge me to pray for them to make headway in their Christianity—become purer, more perfect, and so on. With many, though, the opinion behind it is that in order to be accepted by the dear Savior one must pile up a good stock of positive items. One wants to scrape together as much as possible to hand to him in exchange for the water that he gives. One wants to be able to reach down into a big sack with lots of goodies, so as to recompense him for his water. Yet here it says that he gives it without payment! That means that exaggerated piousness doesn't help a bit; we get the living water for nothing. All the Lord wants is a repentant heart. There is no question of payment when God is gracious to us. The Pharisee in the temple wanted to reimburse him with good works. The tax collector had nothing to pay with, and yet he was the one that went home a sinner made righteous, whereas the other got nothing. Yes, dear one, you can have sufficient water right now to keep you from getting parched; it will be adequate, even if it is often barely enough. But how will it be when the Savior's righteousness comes flowing in streams! How happy we shall be then if we have waited humbly, patiently, and faithfully.

Finally (in 1866) on Matthew 7:15–16:

> Beware of false prophets, who come to you in sheep's cloth-
> ing but inwardly are ravenous wolves. You will know them
> by their fruits.

There are people that take the sheep's clothing for the fruits. Where do you find any sectarian or queer dissenter that is not so gentle and amiable in his manner as to make the very angels bow down before him? His fruit, however, is the confusion he creates everywhere in spite of his sheep's clothing. Such people have no regard for the harm they cause among honest, simple folk, yet when they are told so, they come at once with Bible passages such as: "The Lord has said, 'I have not come to bring peace but the sword.'" There are babblers no one can get through to, and stupid people that believe everything. I have many heavy forebodings; the final time may well show how hard it is to distinguish truth from falsehood.

20

The Spiritual Guide and Counselor

B LUMHARDT'S PASTORAL WORK MAINLY took place in three areas—in his study with those who came to see him there, in the rooms of the guests of his house, and in letters.

On the day of the Lord it will be revealed how much misery, need, and guilt of all kinds came to him via these three channels, and how much help, light, deliverance, forgiveness, and blessing flowed back from the Lord through him. At Blumhardt's funeral a speaker pointed to the study, visible to the gathered mourners, and spoke of all the need and guilt that had been brought and *left* there, and there was an immediate response in the tears shed by listeners of both high and low estate, who felt reminded of their own experiences in that room.

Blumhardt once found himself in a circle where many were basking in the bliss of supposed perfection, easily obtained by a certain newly discovered method. As if apologizing for not being able to join in all that bliss, he confessed, "I am *buried* in distress on behalf of others, more than any of you are." So it was. His longing for the promised new time was no mere hobby but sprang from an insight into the crying need of humankind—in individuals as well as in the mass—such as has rarely been given to a man. But he not only longed for the new time—he hoped and fought for it! He did not just wait with an empty pocket or purse, if I may put it like that; no, he *had* something that enabled him to infuse help and solace into all the misery. With increasing clarity Blumhardt saw that his victorious battles against darkness had secured for him a right to confront its power on behalf of others; they had given him a license to free other men from sinister influences through priestly intercession and blessing. In that sense his pastoral work was to him an unbroken continuation of the struggle he had waged in Möttlingen.

The Lord had endowed him with a blessed gift for others. Not the gift of healing—that would mean making both too much and too little of that gift. Too much because, compared to apostolic times and also to the enormity of the need, the miraculous help he rendered was still of very limited extent. Too little because his gift was far from being so one-sided. Apart from healing, many received and experienced through his blessing clarity in personal problems, right understanding and blessing for their vocation, strength for carrying heavy responsibilities, as well as a tangible easing of difficult outer circumstances.

Naturally, such blessing also came through the *advice* he gave, since it is fitting for a divine gift to be of a spiritual and not mechanical nature. But how did it come about that his advice was so full of light, that it would so unerringly hit the nail on the head? How did he always manage to find the most obvious and natural answer—an answer no one had been able to find and which, just for that reason, was so strikingly surprising and refreshing? Simply because it was not *his* advice! He was afraid of the strong human penchant, in others as well as in himself, for offering advice; instead, he always stood with a listening heart before the Lord, waiting to be given light and direction for the case in question. He considered the following passage extremely important, especially for a pastoral relationship: "Where two or three [in our case: one being the other's spiritual guide and counselor] are gathered in my name, I am in the midst of them."

That is why he did not really like to see people leave Bad Boll without a personal talk. He felt sorry for them and, particularly in the case of timid persons, could not always resist inviting them most cordially to see him in his study. He had regular daily hours set aside for that. Once, for example, a certain deeply religious lady spent a longer time in Bad Boll. She had tried in vain at twelve other spas to find healing for her ailment, a general physical exhaustion. Even a five minutes' walk was too much for her. She had come with the definite understanding that she was in Boll strictly for her *inner* needs. Although Blumhardt's sermons had already helped her toward a simpler and more childlike way of thinking, some kind of fear still kept her away from his room. One day Blumhardt, meeting her on the stairs, said to her, "It would be so nice if we could get to know each other a bit better." So she dared enter the study, where she was received in the well-known cordial manner. She spoke but little of her ailments, however, and on leaving received a blessing from Blumhardt. The very next day she was able to walk for more than an hour. "The Lord's mercy will help you further," said Blumhardt, himself elated by this change, and so it did; after a little while she was well.

Many persons that imagined the stay in Blumhardt's study to be of an awfully solemn nature came away thoroughly undeceived, some pleasantly, others unpleasantly. A young lady plagued by emotional and nervous complaints liked being at Bad Boll. However, she was kept from visiting the study by the unfortunate way others made so much of it in conversation and spoke so importantly of their either having been there or intending to go. There were indeed persons that pestered Blumhardt needlessly and uselessly. At any rate, the young lady avoided the study. But one day, after an agonizingly difficult night, she decided to see Blumhardt, naturally with a heart full to overflowing. There was so much she wanted to share with him. But she had scarcely started to describe her sufferings when Blumhardt broke in saying, "Dear child, I have no time now. May the Savior bless you and take these things away!" She left the study feeling put out, hurt, and almost exasperated by this treatment, so lacking in "solemnity"; however, the "things" were gone!

Such disgruntled feelings were not infrequent. In this case it was hardly the young lady's true self that was angry but rather the something in her that had to yield so suddenly. Actually, in cases like that Blumhardt was deliberately brief, briefest of all when dealing with truly emotionally ill persons—cases that so tempt us to sermonize. "A glass of turbid water does not become clear by stirring it but by letting it settle." Just because he knew that only divine power could help here, he was most sparing in the use of a "moral" approach or influence.

It was similar with Auguste, the patient of whom the brochure *Krankheit und Heilung*[1] tells. She suffered from most violent emotional and nervous disturbances and came to Boll only after eminent clergymen such as Löhe had vainly exhausted on her, orally or in writing, all their resources of scriptural and personal experience. After a particularly bad night Blumhardt was called to her room. After listening to a full report, he just said, "Well, the Savior will set everything right; I will pray for you earnestly." Although the patient and her female companion

---

1. Editors' Note: See *infra*, pp. 439–42.

thought it most unlikely that such exceedingly simple words could be of any use, Auguste's emotional troubles had gone for good!

Some people were pleasantly surprised in Blumhardt's study. That is what happened to two teenage boys, true Württembergers, who paid a weekend visit to Bad Boll with its open door for students. Here they learnt that the Lord's Supper was to be celebrated the following day. What were they to do? As good, recently confirmed church members they did not want to be shirkers, but Lutheran usage demands a personal application and request, and that meant going to the study. With beating hearts they dared it and made their request to Blumhardt. "O you dear boys!" he replied, putting one arm around each of them, and with that he let them go.

How cheerful and happy people looked on leaving the study! Especially joyful were those who, confronted by difficult situations (whether real or imagined), all at once found themselves set right, and oh, ever so simply. In place of the superhuman obligations they had imagined, they now saw before them an encouraging, natural, and therefore easy task. The reason was that they now had a clear perception of the Lord's true will, instead of what they had *assumed* to be his will. Many times it is only when man turns away from *human* precepts (whether his own or others') and comes to perceive *God's* will, which is so simple, that he recognizes: "The precepts of the Lord are right, rejoicing the heart" (Ps 19:8).

Let us accompany Blumhardt from his study to the rooms of his patients. That is where his steps would lead him day and night, and there were times when it left him with little or no sleep. "I find the going hard," he once wrote; "I always feel drowsy and tired, because I can neither sleep nor rest." And another time: "I often think I am the most burdened man on earth, and at times I find it a bit hard." If Blumhardt had a weak spot, it was that his soft heart and good nature would not let him refuse a request. That meant that he accepted patients and allowed them to remain even when he did not expect the stay in his house to bear much fruit. He was too compassionate to refuse their urgent entreaties. Hence he often had in his house for long, long periods patients whose illness appeared to serve no other purpose than to wear him out uselessly and make fun of him, as it were. That was particularly so after the death of Gottliebin Brodersen. Gottliebin had the gift of discerning (as mentioned earlier by Blumhardt) whether a certain person could be helped or not and would also move resolutely for non-acceptance with an almost military decisiveness if there seemed to be no prospect of a cure.

The ailments that found their way to Bad Boll—not only illnesses with no prospect of cure but also those where in the end help was given— brought with them much that was trying and disquieting. At one time, for instance, a man subject to depressions had his room directly above Blumhardt's study. One morning just before two o'clock, while Blumhardt was still, as usual, engaged in correspondence, he heard from above, but from the outside, a strange whining and moaning. Sensing trouble, he rushed upstairs into the man's room, found both bed and room empty, the window open, and the man hanging outside, his fingers just barely clutching the window ledge. What could Blumhardt do? The man was heavy, which made it all the worse, and his strength was about to give out. "In the name of Jesus!" Blumhardt cried with commanding voice, seized the man by his arms, and with one tremendous heave lifted him right into the room. He had been light as a feather, Blumhardt told afterward.

We will let Blumhardt himself tell of an experience that without any visible miraculous help nevertheless represented a great victory of grace in the face of seemingly insuperable obstacles (in *Blätter aus Bad Boll*, No. 26, 1873):

> On the farm I used to run in Boll I once employed as a milker a Roman Catholic man from Switzerland. He was a lay brother, had received an Italian doctor's degree, and was thus deeply and consciously rooted in Catholicism. Toward the end he had been the schoolmaster at home, but since his zeal for the school set the people against him, he lost interest in it and, as it turned out, ended up being my milker. I let him do his work unmolested, and he faithfully carried out his task.
>
> At first he only rarely attended our services, nor did he want to have anything to do with me, a heretical parson, even though he was secretly fond of me. When he was sick and I visited him, he would turn his back on me, probably thinking it would hurt his salvation if he became defiled through my presence. He certainly would not let me pray with him. Otherwise my household got along well with him, and he very much liked the children's meetings as well as the morning and evening devotions for the employees; it touched him to hear my wife hold them.
>
> Eventually he contracted an incurable illness, ileus,[2] and he had to suffer very much. But he did not like me to visit him. I asked

2. Editors Note: This refers to a bowel obstruction that can lead to severe vomiting.

him if I should call a Catholic priest, and he said yes. The priest came and did with him according to the practice of his church.

Before long, his situation became critical, and it often seemed as if the end was near. Each time I hurried to him, but for quite a while he did not want me. But one day, just when I got ready to leave him and, with an inward sigh, made for the door, he cried out, "*Herr Pfarrer*, you must not go!" I stopped and asked, "May I pray?" "Yes," he said. Preferring to be cautious, I prayed very briefly, "Lord Jesus, receive him through grace as thy child!" He became very quiet and stared into the corner, as if he saw or heard something. Finally he cried, "Through grace! Through grace! I hear it! Through grace! Is it possible for a wicked man like me to be saved?" A shattering prayer of repentance followed these words. Then we sang, "Through grace I am to find salvation." He joined in with a strong voice and wanted to sing more and still more. I recited the words of several songs, verse by verse. When I came to the hymn, "I have been shown abundant mercy" and the words, "Now I rejoice that this is mine and glorify the grace divine," he raised himself up, put both arms around me convulsively, and cried, "*Herr Pfarrer*, you are a wonderful man!"

All my employees as well as some of the guests gathered around the dying man's bed, and all declared afterward that they had never seen anybody die in such a fine, evangelical way. All his peculiarities had dropped off quite by themselves, and only what was truly evangelical was still of any value to his soul—all this without a single word to that effect from me. Time and again he began to sing, "Through grace," but since he lacked further words, I had to add some more. In this way originated, as though from the dying man's lips, the stanza:

> Through grace I am to find salvation,
> Through grace does Jesus call me his.
> Through grace I leave this earthly station,
> Through grace I rise to heaven's bliss.
> Through grace I found from sin release,
> Through grace I shall depart in peace.

Shortly after he died—it was on February 15, 1857—his Catholic father came from Switzerland and at first did not want to join with us in prayer. But in the end that came about by itself, as he saw our attitude. For the funeral I called the Catholic priest. I told him how the man had approached his end, how he had wanted to be saved through grace. "Isn't that," I asked, "what you believe in your church, too?" "Yes, we do," he replied in a friendly and satisfied manner. Side by side, clad in our respective vestments, the two of us accompanied the coffin to the grave. He did according to the rites of his church, and I could say a prayer after him. The word "through grace" had brought us together.

Many other things that Blumhardt experienced in his patients' rooms cannot be related. The shaking and shattering element in them was in many ways reminiscent of the struggles in Möttlingen, but in Bad Boll the *uplifting* aspect generally came more to the fore and in a much more lofty and peaceful way. In his last years, grown old, it was as if he often lacked the physical strength to keep all these great matters that filled his heart locked away inside. At times he would say with shining eyes and very confidentially, "If I could only tell, you would say, 'It's a wonderful time!'" Such awareness that his work was not in vain was truly his reward, his food, his strength, as he went about visiting his patients by day and night.

Sadly, he would never leave his study except as his calling required. The families of his children, too, would only be visited when his inner help was needed. His pastoral duties, he felt, tied him to his house. To a woman acquaintance living at some distance, who would have wished to still see him as she lay dying, he wrote, "I would so like to visit you, but it would require days, and those I am not free to give away. I regard my time as sacred, for it belongs to the distressed."

A large part of his time, usually from nine o'clock, the hour when he rose from his evening talks, until two o'clock in the morning, was given to correspondence. He really *read* the letters—usually from six to fifteen per day; he read them with love and also patience when they were difficult to read or longwinded. With a red pencil he marked what was essential, underlining words (such as "lung," "brother-in-law," etc.) that served to bring to mind the entire content of the letter. He read them as in the presence of the Lord, inwardly commending to him at once and in a very simple way the requests they contained. With that, *his* part was done. And how many times help, great and wonderful help, was given at places far away, just as soon as he had read the letter concerned! When in the course of his work one or the other whose distress or need he had on his heart happened to come to mind, he regarded it as a hint to think of him before the Lord, and he did so inwardly without interrupting his work.

A lot could be told of such help given as a result of correspondence. Two examples may be mentioned here. An emotionally sick man wrote to Blumhardt from a mental hospital in America. He quickly recovered and could be discharged from the hospital. In true American fashion he used the papers to publicize what he had done as well as the successful outcome and counseled his fellow sufferers to follow his example. At greater length we want to relate another experience, which moved Blumhardt deeply. The result of it was that in the area where it took place he became involved in a pastoral correspondence activity that was ever more richly blessed as time went on.

From a little town in northeastern Germany, hitherto completely unknown to him, he received a letter containing a heart-rending cry for help. A boy of about ten years had contracted a horrible ailment endemic in that area, the so-called *Weichselzopf* (Vistula braid). This is a degeneration of the head skin beginning in the hair and its roots, which produces strange malformations of the skin and may in the end even lead to idiocy. The mother (or aunt?) of the boy concerned had in some way heard of Blumhardt and urgently implored him for advice and intercession. Blumhardt's soothing reply, assuring her of his heartfelt sympathy and prayer, was answered by another letter in a more confident mood, which, however, was not at all to Blumhardt's liking. It said: "*Herr Pfarrer*, we have now good hopes that the boy will recover. We have been advised to contact a man living at some distance from here who it is said can in some secret way do something against this disease. He has given us every hope that the boy will get better but says we should on no account cut or even comb his hair, for with his method of cure that would unfailingly result in the boy's death." Blumhardt felt once again called to speak his mind: "It's either-or! You cannot ask both the Savior and the devil for help. Go at once and cut the boy's hair; the Savior will help that no harm will come to him. If you don't do it, I wash my hands of this matter." The mother (or aunt), shaken and ashamed, resolved to follow Blumhardt's advice and talked it over with the boy. All her relatives and friends urged her not to do what they felt bordered on crime; they also tried to scare the boy. She, however, spoke to him kindly and found him very responsive. She promised him a fine new cap once his hair was nicely combed and cut and he was better, and both felt confident of the Savior's help. She took him on her knee and went to work with comb and scissors. The boy said trustingly, "The Savior will help," and then exclaimed with happy surprise, "Yes, yes, he is helping now! He is really helping!" Within a short time he was well and went around greeting everybody with his new cap and a radiant smile.

When Blumhardt received news of this victory, he read it out at a mealtime in Bad Boll, and scarcely an eye was left dry. As mentioned before, this wonderful experience of the Lord's help was only the beginning of an endless series of similar experiences in that district, for from then on that lady became something of an agent for Bad Boll on behalf of sufferers.

The best and most numerous instances of the Lord's immediate help were experienced where the request came in the form of a telegram. Blumhardt stated that himself and explained it by saying that the humble, brave confession contained in such a near-public request was appreciated up in heaven. In 1879 about fifteen hundred telegrams were received (business and family telegrams included). Since the telegraphic method was only used in emergencies, partly for the reason just mentioned, that lets us draw conclusions as to the number of *letters* received, which was certainly much higher. We relate just a few instances of such help.

A little girl had broken her leg in a very bad way. Worst of all was the terrible pain she felt, and evidenced, at the slightest touch. Just at the time when the telegram arrived in Bad Boll, the doctor came and began the long and, as he said himself, in this case specially painful work of setting the broken leg. But the girl felt *no* pain. Before long the leg had healed.

A young lady who had some contact with Bad Boll was subject to violent attacks of sickness lasting three to four days. Once, when she had just committed herself to the rendering of certain important services, she suffered such an attack the very day before she was to start. Every conceivable remedy was tried unsuccessfully, and the physician was at his wits' end, so she decided to send a telegram to Bad Boll. However, neither her relatives nor even the servant maid were willing to dispatch such a telegram. So she hoped that the Savior would listen to her own prayer and implored him in the most childlike and trusting way, but in vain. The pain increased from hour to hour, until the following morning the servant, aghast at the lady's distress, offered of her own accord to go and send the telegram. At the time it reached Bad Boll (as reported later), the worst pain faded, and she quietly dropped off to sleep. Two hours later everything was gone, and for a very long time at that—whether for good is not known to me.

A case where a baby mortally sick almost from birth on quickly recovered when a telegram was sent should also be mentioned here, at the explicit request of the child's mother.

Naturally, it was not only with his intercession that Blumhardt served those who wrote to him. In some cases the answer to be given exercised his mind for days, since he wished to reply in a satisfying and exhaustive way. He did not shrink from giving this or that correspondent a piece of his mind, but most of his answers, like the language he used in the study, were effective through their tremendous gentleness and liberating comfort. Understandably, only a few of his letters are available to us, mostly from persons now deceased. We include here a selection, first some comforting letters to a young woman friend about to die and then similar letters to different persons.

From a number of letters to the sick girl, whose life was hanging on a thread, I quote here the most important sections, numbering the letters consecutively:

1. There is a struggle between life and death going on in you. When you feel life stirring within you, you also feel pleasure. But that has nothing to say. Any moment God gives you, you are allowed to savor with pleasure. When things take a different turn, you should look upward. But in the case of such a long-lasting illness it is really a grace when at times the heart feels joy and hope. Accept it in a childlike way. When you do feel better, however, don't let feelings of discontent about the past rise up in you, else you spoil your joy.

   It is quite wrong to conclude that you would be better off now if you had been more careful with yourself two years ago. For a young person like you, you did not overdo it. That you did not reach the goal is an indication that the roots lay deeper, so deep that even if you had taken it ever so easy, you would still have become what you are. Besides, a man does not want to take it easy; rather, he wants to work and work. And you enjoyed your work, too, at that time. Therefore, don't let the thought that you overdid it trouble you. Doing nothing is more apt even than work to make you sick, once you have the germ in your constitution. So take heart, and don't let it vex you, but say to yourself that what is has been willed by God; it is not due to other circumstances.

2. O my child, you must really submit to God's way. What are we poor folk to do once he has made up his mind? We do know that his heart is full of love and has wonderful things in store for those that patiently trust in him right to the end. And thank him very much for setting your soul right and making it sober. It would be so bad if you were still as you used to be and now had to face such a future. You are after all a rescued lamb; you know him and he

knows you. That is why you can joyfully face whatever may come. Your way goes heavenward, toward the Savior, and you deserve to be envied more than many others in this sad world, however well they may be. For the present and in the days ahead, make the best possible use of your inheritance in heaven; don't allow yourself to become gloomy and sad but be cheerful in the Lord, who loves you in all eternity.

3. In everything that happens the heart must become patient and find comfort in hope. Don't let the enemy nourish thoughts and feelings that are sinister, ungodly, and unloving! He is always out to lure men's hearts into his dominion. That is why he makes us so touchy and irritable as you, too, experience. But with you it has also been due to physical weakness. When you feel pain, force yourself to speak and act kindly; that's your best way to become free.

4. Make it your concern that the Savior might soon take pity on languishing humanity, whether you will experience it or not, and that he might have even more work for the likes of us. Be such a poor human being as does not forget about the Lord's coming but with sighs of pity implores him to let everything become quite different soon. If you can find that attitude, you have still a wonderful task, and your sighs will not be lost; indeed, they will help you to be more serviceable over yonder for the work that those who have finished their course here are still engaged in. And they do have work to do! Well, now I have really said something, I think. It will be all right, though. May the Lord be your comfort and strength, and may the spirit of God teach you to sigh with longing, as it pleases him.

5. How I wish I could send you attendants from heaven! Actually, they are with you, but their task is not to take off you all that is hard to bear and to chase away all pain. Tell yourself that all that still has to be. Once you have gone home, you will see that everything had to go as it went—just like that. So pull yourself together! Find patience and surrender, and get ever smaller inwardly until you are no more than a poor sinner that in herself has not the slightest claim to mercy. Oh, how you will then come to value and love the Savior! That is the best and most blessed way to die. Through the mercy of God it leaves nothing to be still cleared up and set right over there. Now you have much in hand that you will no longer have when you have gone home. Make sure that it is all dealt with; that is then pure gain for eternity.

6. Postscript: I have just received a second letter from your dear father. It gives me a feeling that your hour might soon be here. Now we ask the dear Savior to show you mercy and shorten your sufferings. The Lord will be close to you. Oh, how wonderful you will feel! I have no words to express it. All the more may God's spirit speak to you; may he let you savor a fragrant breeze from the heavenly home. O happy you! With you all is well. There by the Savior we shall see each other again. Oh, how often I, too, would wish to have done with my struggle! But the Lord sees to it that his own may have joy everlasting. Halleluiah!

7. Now you are worrying that you might still have a hard struggle. You worry too much, my dear child. In the first place, now, right at the end, you still have to learn to look no further than one day at a time like a little child, who only thinks of what it needs at the moment and does not worry. So you, too, must become completely a child. That is what the Savior wants, for he can use only children.

Secondly, consider well what my last letter said. Become as nothing, become just a sinner, and seek and want only grace. That completely wipes out anything that might still be held against you. But if there is nothing more against you in the account book, you certainly do not have to fear a further painful struggle. Only what a man still clings to as his own causes him trouble. If you have completely immersed yourself in grace, there will be an easy passing over to joy, when the hour comes. Now I pray for you that without fail anything wrong, however small, might be revealed to you. That will cause you no more pain now but can only do you good. Then you can say to your Savior, as you did so often in the last years, "Oh, how dumb I have been, but how loving are you!" Now I leave everything to the quiet rulership of the Holy Spirit, who can speak better than I. But believe me, what the Lord has in mind for you is a triumphant journey to heaven. Therefore hold out patiently and faithfully to the end.

Regarding a woman about to die Blumhardt wrote:

As to her mood, you need have no fear, for blessed are the sorrowful. It is the most blessed way to die. Pleasing to God is the one who always wants to be low and lie in the dust. Of course, the Lord might still deliver her. But his will be done! Be of good cheer; the Lord will not forsake you.

To a seriously ill woman:

> Even though I did not write at once, I have nonetheless thought of you faithfully. The Lord will yet deliver you from this tribulation. Have confidence in him, and although, as you say, you deserve *not* to be delivered by him, yet, as a repentant and believing soul you *are* deserving of the Lord's mercy. Stop looking for anything particular that might still be hidden (some guilt perhaps?). Now and then the Lord still wants to shock and shake us, so as to make our hearts more childlike toward him.

To a woman who had recovered from emotional illness:

> I understand you and your letter, but you do not understand what goes on within you. I wish you would put all the past out of your mind. While you keep staring at it, you will get confused. There was always a jumble in you, a struggle between the good person and the bad one. The bad person got herself mixed up with everything the good one thought and did. So your good person, too, turned into a caricature of what she should have been. Your attachment to me, for instance, was a pure one, but the bad person in you wanted it to be impure.
>
> In everything you shared with me I have all along deducted, as well as added, a lot, and I think I have always hit it just about right. When I comforted you and spoke to you about grace, that was not a shot in the dark. I knew what was still troubling your soul, but I addressed the good person in you and wanted to help her get free.
>
> Light and darkness were always fighting within you. Often darkness had the upper hand, though without your being fully accountable, even if you now think that you were. The light did always break through after all. At one and the same moment you would lie and not lie, dissemble and not dissemble, curse and not curse. But it was the *light* in you that the Lord always had his eye on—your *not* lying, *not* dissembling, *not* cursing.
>
> What is at work in you now is but an insidious attempt to annul what the good person in you has been struggling for. Therefore turn courageously away from the tangled past and just let it be! Start afresh! Resist the convulsive urges to bring up the past, and hold on to the Savior in a childlike way—like a poor, helpless child that in everything seeks grace and wants nothing but grace. Your Savior will give it to you if you start now to be simple. You must praise him for rescuing you victoriously, in spite of all the confusion the enemy enmeshed you in. That you must believe and hold fast.

I do not think you have to die yet. You must now go on living, must serve the Savior and your family and others in just as sober and childlike a way as you formerly went about befuddled and confused. The Lord did not forsake you, nor does he now, and remains your Redeemer in eternity.

To a pair of sisters:

How are you? And how is dear B.? I hope that you feel how the Savior is Lord and no one else and that you will overcome in all your trials and not yield to the evil one in any way. I pray for you a good deal and know, too, that the dear Savior lets you sense it. What kind of a face does B. show? Does she get among the people? Does she walk or run or jump? One or more of this, I hope, will be true. Of course, now and then she is liable to have hours of gloom. But these, too, must be, so that we learn to pull ourselves together, take heart, and come earnestly before the throne of grace, which is actually accessible at all times, if only men would not be so dumb as to draw back from it.

To a sick woman greatly attached to Blumhardt:

I am sorry that you are so tormented by homesickness for Boll, and I ask the Savior very earnestly to free you from it. I think there is still something to be fought through there, for these feelings impede your spiritual growth. There is in it something like a creaturely love; the Lord, however, wants to be loved alone and with the whole heart. I can well understand that you feel a little forlorn as regards the state of your soul and that you think you ought to have more given to you, according as it is fitting. But it does go a little too far. You must train your heart to look more contentedly and confidently to no one but the Savior, in whom alone is all salvation. Think of yourself as having, through me, joined a large circle of fighters for the Savior. Therefore let go of me and look to him alone, otherwise things get on a wrong track. Such emotional ties can be a great hindrance and may give trouble even in the life beyond, if they are not completely purified through the Spirit of God and find their center in him alone, so that the heart truly cleaves to him and not to any creature.

So you can truly remain my daughter, and that you shall be, and when one day I can present my children to the Savior and say to him, "Here I am and the children you have given me," you, too, will be among them. But remain valiant, brave, and steadfast, and bear in mind that it is a question of having to let go of everything, just as dying persons have to, as though already placed into a quite new situation. As things are now, the natural and creaturely still makes itself felt in you, but it must be overcome, until your soul can say exultantly, "Thou alone, my Savior, in time and eternity!"

As regards a sick child:

I used these last days to go through the pile of letters received, too numerous to count, and there I came upon your dear letter of November ?—unopened! I don't know how it happened. I can only think that it got mislaid before being opened. I feel very sorry about that, but it explains to you the reason for the delay.

Your description of the child's illness has touched my heart. How can I resist a child's entreaty? I love to pray for children, for we have the Lord's word asking us to bring them to him. I experience many and great things especially with children. To be sure, it looks at times as if they were chosen to be among the martyrs of humankind, for many seem to be born only to suffer. That, however, has a special significance for the kingdom of God. As a rule, such children are lovable, surrendered, and serene? They love the Savior and gladly trust in him. There is nothing more uplifting than seeing such a child.

I do not know how it is with the dear little girl you tell about, who likewise so loves the Savior. Perhaps she will yet be allowed to get better or recover, but it seems to me that the illness is already too deeply rooted. Meanwhile, we will keep turning to the Lord. He is sure to respond in some way, if only by making his kindly nearness felt. I would just advise you against letting every available medical skill and resource be exhausted on the poor child. I hesitate to say much about that, but it is certain that with such inexplicable illnesses the simplest treatment is always the best. Greet the dear child (and her parents) from me and tell her that a faraway friend is praying for her and that through his prayer many children have been helped. He asks her to be patient and go on loving the Savior, even if she has to suffer a little longer, and he sends her these two little verses for a keepsake.

A counseling letter:

I have read your letter to Gottliebin and want now to reply to it. Most of what you confess I had known long ago; I have already prayed a great deal for you because of it and also hope that the Lord has forgiven you, unless pride, which does not really want grace, stands in the way. Your peculiarly proud manner harms you greatly. It is also the reason you got so entangled in that which M. represents. As to that involvement, guard against one thing, that is, against letting your conscience be bound. Since you know that M. expects those taking the Lord's Supper with him to stop celebrating it elsewhere, you had better stay away. Binding comes from below; freeing through the Spirit comes from above. Otherwise, being with M. does not matter, as long as your heart and mind remain free.

Again, it is your pride that you will not let anything be given to you. So I ask you to prove that you really want to have done with your pride, that is, that you come and make use of what can help you with your physical ailment. May the Lord deliver your soul from all that troubles and corrupts you; may he help you through and make you straight and genuine. The Lord will do it!

To a woman patient that had returned home from Boll:

I would not have expected to get a letter from you, but it has made me very happy, especially that your inner state is rather good. Actually I expected that, for I felt that strength had come upon you. What I told you so emphatically has turned out to be true, namely, that you would not feel the distance from here as much as you had thought. The Savior is with you with special grace because you need it, and you will experience that not for nothing have you been brought out of so many foolish things and have really found the Savior. Try hard to grasp and hold on to what comes to you in the Spirit, and guard against sinking into depression. You have no cause for that, as you will find out one day. Here we think of you a lot and also speak of you daily. There was lively talk about you at table just today, and the prayers of many hearts rise up for you. So be of good cheer! Your Savior will not forsake you.

To the same person:

You are a diligent correspondent. I am glad to hear that you are tolerably well and that I counseled or comforted you well. So the dear Savior is with you and even makes you stronger than you often were here. You see, he is now doubly with you; I also send him to you quite often! Accustom yourself to think of him as nearby, and do this always with a joyful heart, for he loves you and means well with you. From various indications I see that he supports and upholds you. He will go on doing so, for he is faithful.

About some unhealthy religious traits:

I cannot spare the time for a journey such as you desire, nor do I think that it would lead to anything. Your father has always wanted to make a confession here, just because that was talked about as the thing to do, but when it came to the point, he didn't know of anything. Please do not put any more pressure on him in that direction, because it only makes him more confused. He simply is feeble-minded, almost childish, and the best remedy for that is patience and yieldedness on the part of the family.

Sympathetic magic is of the devil. When a certain woman says, "But Christ and the apostles also did miracles," I cannot understand that it does not occur to you how in that way she wickedly puts herself on the same level as Christ and the apostles and that she therefore should be shunned. The sorcerers in N. I know well. When I visited there recently, I was asked a good deal about them, but I convinced each questioner that it was satanic business. Assuming that such persons speak the truth in one area, is it therefore divine? And supposing they do help in some way, is that from God? And if it isn't from God, will it do good or harm? The Word bids us ask, seek, knock, but not hang little pads or suchlike charms around our necks. Paul says, "My children, flee from idolatry!" (1 Cor 10:14)

On patience and faith:

I could not reply so quickly to your dear letter of November 27, and even now I am so inundated with letters that I shall hardly be able to give an exhaustive answer to all the questions you pile up. Nor is it necessary to explain everything so fully. When light falls into our darkness, everything gets presently lit up, so that an honest soul is bound to find out on its own what there is to be found, provided that the matter as a whole is of the truth.

When somebody has to be regarded as bound by Satan on account of his ailment, that does not preclude his being at the same time a child of grace. The woman bound by Satan for eighteen years was yet called a daughter of Abraham (Luke 13: 16), and she was no dearer to the Lord for being set free. A shadow would have fallen on her only if she had not believed when she ought to have, but because she believed, this *faith* made her dearer to the Lord, just as Abraham's *faith* (that he would still become a great people) was reckoned to him as righteousness (Jas 2:23). Job was afflicted with loathsome sores (Job 1:7)—by whom? "He is in your power; only spare his life" the Lord had told Satan (Job 1:6). For all that Satan did to him, Job remained as before a man well pleasing to the Lord, but he had to remain steadfast and firm in *faith*. Paul was buffeted by Satan (2 Cor 12:7)—how, we do not really know, but in our time his illness would have a name. He asked to be freed because he felt bound, but he had to let grace be sufficient for him (2 Cor 12:8–9). That already takes care of a good many of your questions.

In times when the Lord strikes us we must show patience; whoever dies in that patience with Satan possibly being the beating tool—will all the more triumphantly enter into glory. But whether *all* sufferings are a work of Satan is not for us to brood over. In all suffering we must remain faithful to the Lord; nothing more is needed. Along with patience, though, the Lord also demands faith. If Satan can be driven away through *faith*—whether it's the body or the soul he is allowed to torment—is something gained by it or not? If yes, is it not the sufferer's duty then to show faith as well as patience? And if he does not believe or simply regards faith as superfluous as long as patience is there, will he not bear a certain guilt in spite of his patience? What matters here, of course, is whether one is entitled or required or even obliged to believe. In this respect, times and circumstances differ. But at times every sufferer may be required to *believe*, for the Lord's glory and to weaken Satan.

A most essential part of faith is to recognize what it is that still gives Satan a claim to us, so that we may first set that right or fight it. There was no accusation against Job; it was Satan's confident assumption that when made to suffer, Job would be shown up as lacking in faith that gave him power to try it. But when Job stood the test, the devil had to give way, and Job recovered. When it comes to us, we may indeed have charges facing us—some more against us as individuals, others of a general nature and implicating the whole human race. So we must uncover what is wrong, turn completely away from it, and plead in faith for the affliction to go away. If we have got to the bottom of the trouble, what stops us from believing that now the rod of punishment will be taken away too? If all of us were to plead, fight, and believe in that way, would it not mean a completely new turn for the cause of God's kingdom? It is, of course, clear that an individual person cannot bring that about, but faith should really come back into vogue just as much as patience. "Here is the patience and the faith of the saints," says Revelation (Rev 13:10).

That makes it clear that sin and Satan's power on earth are not overcome by patience alone but by patience *and* faith. It is customary to cite the word, "The Lord disciplines him whom he loves" (Heb 12:6) quite inappropriately, as if God wanted to give his dear children a good hiding without any provocation, just because it's good for them. Is that what a father or mother do? God only disciplines his dear children when there is a need for it, that is, when they deserve it. So we must understand the passage in this way: The Lord does not leave unpunished those he loves when the loved one does wrong. Those children that are not his, he simply lets go on in their sins. From that it follows that a beloved child should know why it gets beaten and that when it becomes aware of its faults and leaves them, it is also comforted. So the dear child is ever again brought back to faith. Since it is a beloved child, it must be able to expect love from its Father in every way.

But why should we only want to suffer and not to believe? When we look closely at what lies behind it, we find that a man often just wants to suffer, or would rather suffer than repent. Without recognizing one's sin and turning away from it one cannot believe.

Concerning a woman suffering from depressions:

As regards your wife, I would first advise you to do as little as possible with her. The less strenuously you attempt to quiet her, the sooner she will be quiet. In particular, it is harmful to encourage, console, exhort, and instruct her persistently. Agitation and anxiety of any kind should be avoided, and not too many persons should be allowed to visit her. In moments of excitement show calm and patience; that will cause the excitement to die down of its own accord. Nor is it good to pray with her as regards her condition. If that counsel is observed carefully, the suicidal thoughts will not take firm root, whereas otherwise her illness could work itself into a frenzy. When members of the family become aware of a change in mood, they should not let the mother feel they have perceived it and in any case should not let it affect them deeply and make them look sad, since that will only have a contrary effect on her. I ask you to pay close attention to that. She simply is mentally disturbed, and what she does and says in such a state must not be taken as expressions of her real personality. Otherwise I cannot tell you anything particular you ought to do. Leave any special efforts, such as fervent prayers or even fasting; it might lead to a worsening of her condition.

With respect to a clairvoyant girl:

In reply to your esteemed letter, I declare it to be my firm conviction, based on Holy Scripture, that one may not nurture any kind of magnetic sleep or clairvoyance. The reason is that it leads on to soothsaying and questioning of the dead, which are strictly forbidden, hence the dark power always has a hand in it. Therefore my advice as regards the girl is simply to pay no attention to what she says in her trance, to be still as soon as she starts talking, and to put no questions whatever. No strangers should have access to her, in particular no curious or inquisitive persons. Do not tell the girl what she has said but act as though nothing had happened. Apart from that, the parents should ask God to take this affliction from their child, and I shall join my entreaty to theirs. You will see that within a short time everything will cease. Otherwise her condition might well develop into clairvoyance, which could only be regarded as a great misfortune for the child. I have experienced how in the way described a girl was completely set free in less than two weeks after being a big sensation for years, especially in France.

In 1875, against the importunate and presumptuous ways of a peculiar religious direction then very active:

It is surely incorrect to say that you are only half given over and dedicated to the Savior. You have the Savior as truly as he can be had at all. You do not need anything else; that other thing would only make you lose something, for it turns all that has been until now upside down. It is not scriptural; hence, not being in Scripture, it wants to be a new revelation. In brief: It is not to the Lord that those others are dedicated but to men and men's petty inventions. "Do not become slaves of men!" (1 Cor 7:23). By pressuring their fellow men into joining them those others enslave them. In early Christian times non-believers were not pounced on so tyrannically, though there would have been more sense to it then. In spiritual matters it is sin to let oneself be coerced. It is to freedom that we are called, not to enslavement contrary to our own feelings. What does it matter if all forsake you or if in the end you have to let them all go their own way? Those people are nothing but captive decoys. Stay away from them altogether—all the more when they apply such pressure! As long as the Lord remains your portion! Nor can you any longer exert influence on those people, for they are lords and masters to such a degree that they will accept nothing. Sever all fellowship with such pious folk as still want something else beside the Savior! But do not argue! Refuse to talk about it and ask to be left in peace. If that doesn't work, keep to yourself and wait for the time when the Lord himself will speak, accompanied by great signs, which will not fail to come.

Against superstition:

> I regard as sin anything for which Friday is specially selected—
> not only because of superstitiously picking a certain day but also
> because it means misusing the death of Jesus.
>
> I have read quite a few books like the one by N. Any deliberate
> communication with the dead is forbidden and brings misfortune.
> When something true does go hand in hand with lies, it does not
> yet prove that man has a right to that sort of thing. People's deny-
> ing that the devil is involved just shows clearly that they them-
> selves do not care to be caught trafficking with the devil.

To a mystic:

> I have read your letter with great sympathy, and as far as I am
> concerned I would gladly help with word and deed. But I must
> leave it to the Lord too; ultimately he is the one that knows how
> to make the best also of a needy situation. I cannot, by the way,
> refrain from sharing with you in a brotherly way the thoughts
> that your letter has brought to me. I find in your Christianity
> much that is exaggerated and is not so taught in the Bible. You
> should be simpler and more childlike and not cherish so many
> lofty thoughts, which do you no good and will in the end take
> away the blessing. The Bible says nowhere that one should go out
> of oneself through daily prayer. Who prays like that prays falsely.
> The Bible says nothing of imperishable gold, of tincture, of im-
> perfect metal, and the like.[3] That is too high flown and makes for
> spiritual pride, which the Lord cannot abide. Such Christianity
> cannot expect any blessing; on the contrary, it calls for many
> tribulations to restore soberness. That you are in despair and
> even wish you had never been born shows me that things are not
> right with you. These are not the ways of one believing in a Savior
> that will in the end deliver from all evil. I implore you to take
> my words to heart and hold to the simple Christian teaching.
> Then you will soon find that the Lord is not far from you and will
> gladly deliver you from your need.

To a young lady who found it hard that so few fruits of her awakening
were as yet outwardly visible:

> You must not go looking, on the basis of your own feelings, for
> a really tangible change in yourself, else whatever change there

---

3. Editors' Note: Probably a reference to the teachings of Jakob Böhme (1575–1624),
who writes that prayer is "a going out of himself, so that a man gives himself to God
with all his powers" in his work *The Way to Christ* (Ramsey, NJ: Paulist, 1978). The term
tincture also occurs in many places in that work.

is becomes unchildlike, forced, almost Pharisaical, and is more likely to put others off. You were not exactly more annoying and offensive than others even before, so you may just as well carry on. Only you have to drop more and more all that is annoying or offensive, such as there is in everybody—self-love, obstinacy, contrariness, selfishness, touchiness, envy, and any other objectionable traits—all things that you as someone who feels poor may gladly put aside. People will not say right away, "My, how she has changed!" It isn't all that conspicuous. But you yourself will soon notice that people are happier to have contact with you, that they like your company and feel something beneficial flowing from you to them, without your intending it. There is no need for you to think a lot about it; the main thing is that it makes others happy. All who are not downright opposed to what is of God will be aware of the difference between what is and what was, without giving much thought to what it implies for you. So just carry on. Your sense of your own nothingness makes you a light wherever you go, whereas self-important persons carry sheer darkness with them.

21

Answered Prayer

A REASONABLY FULL ACCOUNT of the blessings that flowed from Blumhardt's intercession would in itself fill a small volume. For that reason and because more ought to be said about the significance of his praying for others, this chapter is meant to supplement the preceding one.

A good deal has been said for and against Blumhardt's way of interceding for others. Some people have even thought they could use him as a model to show that consulting a physician is almost sinful and should be avoided. But that was not his way. He had as much experience with people's illnesses as many a medical practitioner, and it led him to an increasingly high regard for capable physicians. In many cases they would reciprocate with at least appreciation and trust.[1]

To be sure, Blumhardt was quite apprehensive about the use of poisons, and the argument that such things, too, are divine gifts did not find much of an echo in him. In his view, they bear the same message as the fruit in Paradise: "Do not eat of it, lest you die." "They are indeed gifts of God for some purpose," he said; "but is everything to be eaten?" Still, he

---

1. In a letter Blumhardt writes as follows about rigid avoidance of medical help:

The rejection of medical help, especially of surgery, is completely wrong. It is a mistake to set up such extremist principles, which actually degrade prayer to a mere special method of curing illness. (Divine) healing powers are simply lacking in our time, so why not make use of the help men can render each other with the experience they have gained? Rejection of such help springs from self-will and lovelessness and from an impudence that simply wants to exact everything from God, whether he is willing or not.

was less afraid of remedies that act in a purely mechanical way than of those whose effectiveness is unexplainable and mysterious and requires belief in them or which are even being accorded a quasi-religious veneration. If no help came from the Lord in a case of need, he regarded the most common remedies as the most legitimate ones.

Of course, he did look very much to the Lord for help, but never in the sense that he expected every ill to depart and every longed-for help to be given provided one had the right faith. Such attempted coercion horrified him, and he disliked being credited with an ability to "heal through prayer." In time that phrase evolved into the almost blasphemous term "prayer-healing institution"—almost as if one only had to discover a certain kind of prayer in order to get one's hand on the Lord, as it were, and have him at one's disposal.

Prayer by itself can do nothing; the Lord alone is able to help, and he helps at his own discretion. In cases where such coercive prayer was seemingly answered, Blumhardt definitely suspected that it was not the Lord who had his hand in it. Many of his own prayers remained unanswered, and he was not surprised. As regards divine help for others, he did not expect to receive more than a certain modest measure—not until the expected great turn of ages. There are times when the Savior seems to be saying, "As long as you down there persist in your sin, hardheartedness, and lack of faith, you just have to keep on being blind and lame; it doesn't matter all that much. Go on weeping; we in heaven weep too." Blumhardt's comment on the parable of the talents in Matthew 25 shows how humbly he thought of what he was meanwhile allowed to experience: "I think if today one of us had only *one* talent, as so many did at the time of the apostles, we would surely not be lazy and bury it in the ground."

Some people have found it hard to accept that the Lord should listen to one particular man's intercession more than to that of others— especially their own—and also that God seems pleased to be approached through such an intermediary. James 5:14 gives a legitimate explanation: "Is any among you sick? Let him call for the elders of the church, and let them pray over him." James sees it to be the Lord's will that miraculous help be regarded not as a privilege granted to the individual receiving it but rather as a mercy shown to the entire *church*, to be entered into the logbook of the church's experiences.

We can well understand the reason for such a view. If I receive a miraculous response to a prayer uttered in need, I am liable to fall into spiritual pride, self-righteousness, and self-satisfaction. While ordinary folk are often plain healthy and remain so, there are certain persons that ail most of the time but find themselves restored to health in some supposedly miraculous way about once a year. They are liable to work themselves up into a morbid religious solitude, where they hear and see pretty well nothing but themselves. "Humble yourselves under the mighty hand of God" (1 Pet 5:6) can at times mean: "Do it by humbling yourself under a brother, as if in the presence of God." As we learned earlier, Blumhardt saw clearly that in such matters the Lord desires more togetherness and sharing, especially a closer contact with the servants of the Gospel, than some people may think.

Some wanted to explain the special fruitfulness of Blumhardt's intercession by pointing to the last words of that passage from James ("The heartfelt prayer of a righteous man works very powerfully" [Jas 5:16]), asserting that his intercession was more effective because of his greater piety. Blumhardt very earnestly rejected that view as completely false. He himself was more inclined to see the fruitfulness of his praying as a special calling given to him on behalf of the church—a calling that had gradually come to him through his unceasing concern for people in need of help and through his experiences in the course of the "struggle."

James continues, "Elijah was a man just like us" (Jas 5:17), as if to say, "What's keeping us from being men like Elijah, or at least from having such men among us?" That could sadden us. James is indeed right: It was surely not the purpose of Jesus Christ's coming, dying, and rising again that we should subsequently have a poorer, cooler, and more distant relationship to God than did the people of God under the Old Covenant and that there should now be *no* men through whom the Lord can manifest himself the way he did in Bible times. This train of thought takes us back to Blumhardt's characteristic hopes. One might say that he was himself a little of what he hoped for, a forerunner of another, better time that will once more be in tune with the Bible. "He was an apostolic man." Many, theologians not excluded, could find no more fitting description of Blumhardt's character than that. One theologian remarked of him: "One felt transported back across the centuries into biblical times." Such a characterization, taken soberly and modestly, largely explains the special position among his contemporaries that his great experiences gave him. Blumhardt discussed the above passage from the Epistle of

James in a letter. In it he sheds light on his own view of the special gift he had been granted:

> When we hear James refer to Elijah, we should bear in mind that Elijah had a special calling for the work he was to do; it could not have been James's intention to say that every believer can do what Elijah did. Something more is needed. That something was in Elijah, as we know. In apostolic times, too, it was not automatically in every Christian but depended on a personal calling and gift. One therefore has to be very careful not to read too much into such passages, for one is liable to be led astray by appealing to them. If someone wanted to investigate whether everything the Lord does through me is tied to my person or whether it can be copied, I would have to admit that something quite personal, which not everybody can have in just the same manner, has indeed been given to me as a result of my struggles. But I am convinced that it must become more widespread and that we may generally ask for the original powers to be fully restored. For the time being, what happens through me does no more than prove that we are justified in pleading for such a renewal.
>
> But until the heavens open up, so to speak, that renewal will not take place. It is quite wrong to think that all that has to be done to get back what the apostolic time had is to believe. No, those powers have in truth been withdrawn and can but slowly be won back. Christianity's faithlessness and apostasy over more than a thousand years has entailed the Lord's disfavor as well as an upsurge of satanic powers. That is why we cannot simply start afresh; when we try, we presently come up against an unbroken wall. You can see how I differ from the Irvingites (or Catholic Apostolic Church), who overlook the status quo of Christianity and want to have everything back (or think they have it). The first thing needed is a new conversion of Christendom, but of a more complete nature than what one can observe here and there on a small scale. If it is to come about, we must struggle more earnestly, preach more biblically, and pray more urgently. Once there is a large-scale pouring out of a repentant spirit, such as I experienced in a small way with my congregation (where then straightway the first traces of spiritual gifts made themselves felt), one thing leads to another, until there is a true return of apostolic times. Side by side with that, of course, the antichrist is going to rise up.

Let us insert here yet another letter, this one to Dieterlen, in which Blumhardt takes a stand against one-sided pushing for miraculous help in individual cases at the present time:

I understand you quite well. But you will still find quite a bit in the sermons. Only, I can never quite operate the way you want me to; I have to go easy. For the time being I must set forth what Christ wants. I must present the gospel according to Scripture and may not give too free a rein to reflections on what is *not* scriptural.

I have to think of the Lord's own way of preaching. He had in front of him despairing people, who had even less spiritual nourishment offered to them than we have. Yet he said, "Blessed are the poor in spirit; blessed are they that mourn, they that here weep and sigh." For the moment he could not give them anything to relieve their plight, nor did he point them to things they might receive in *this* life; rather, he directed their hopes to the life beyond. We must not expect too much for this present world. The apostles, too, sighed and yearned for the redemption of their bodies, and Paul had to pommel and subdue his (1 Cor 9:27). The struggle goes on; it may become easier but will not cease. What we receive are divine powers to prove that there is a Savior. The tempted ones are indeed destined to overcome, but their inner need must *aid* in the struggle, must help to overthrow Satan. We remain in the fire until *all* becomes light and the victory is complete.

True, the influence of darkness is greater than before, for Satan is enraged. Spirits have been sent out to torment, to stir up, and to incite to sin, and we must be tested if in spite of all suffering we shall yet overcome and let the Lord have the glory. Inwardly we must be like Job and guard against sulking, to which the devil wants to incite us. If that sets in, things are really bad. You mention the mocking question, "Where is now your God?" Truly, that's how it was from the very beginning, throughout the days of old, with David and the prophets, with Jesus and the apostles. We cannot expect anything else than that we, too, must pass through trials where there is a temptation to ask, "Where is now your God?" This is the struggle that demands resistance to the point of shedding one's blood (Heb 12:4). I think I don't have to write more. Only this: Amid all the trials there is yet victory upon victory—with you too. It is through the weak that the Lord carries out his work.

You raise the question of a general awakening of all, even the most corrupt and perverted—among Protestants, Catholics, Jews, Turks, among high and low, in situations where the mere sight of all the corruption and perversion almost makes one relinquish any further praying and hoping. A short while ago I was given this certainty: One day will bring in the whole harvest! You may not have a grand enough conception of the miracle to come, but come it must. Only, we cannot force it. One can use up a lot of ammunition for nothing. The Lord will do it himself; he just wants us to be faithful and patient.

Let us go back again to the great things Blumhardt experienced. In Bad Boll the miracles were not as conspicuous as in Möttlingen. Those that had the biggest share in them were the country folk, who every week, in smaller or larger numbers and almost unnoticed by the guests, sought out Blumhardt's study. Almost as many miracles, however, were given as a result of correspondence. It was visibly the Lord's will that the miracles were not to be publicized. Apart from many other reasons, one in particular makes that understandable: some of those who looked up to Blumhardt with grateful reverence felt urged to propagandize him and his views in ways that were clumsy, importunate, inflated, or even separatist. Still, some of the many responses to his praying should be related here.

First an experience with one of those house patients that generally made the biggest demands on Blumhardt and his circle. Many guests of Bad Boll would remember a friendly boy named Johannes. Acting as Blumhardt's "armor-bearer," he had the honored task of bringing him the Bible for morning devotions. Some may have sensed a special note of kindliness, springing from deep gratitude to God, in the way Blumhardt summoned "Johannes!" This boy had come to Bad Boll in the following way.

One day a tightly closed chaise pulled up in front of the big house, and a father and mother alighted, leaving behind in the chaise a rug under which something fairly large appeared to stir. Lifting the rug brought into view a ten-year-old boy. He was completely naked, as he would not tolerate any clothes, and in a constant state of rage, hurling abuse at everybody. The titles he bestowed on Blumhardt and his son Christoph are not fit to print; he also behaved in so bestial a way that decency forbids description. Nevertheless there was something in him that gave cause for hope.

He was shut up in a big empty room on the ground floor with nothing in it but a bed with a straw pallet and mattress. There his loving mother waited on him, constantly exposed to his insults. Once, for example, she emerged from this room green all over. A journeyman painter, engaged in painting the jalousies, had unfortunately left in the stove of that room a pot of green paint, which no one had noticed. But Johannes put this material to use: While his mother had her back turned, he put the pot upside down on her head.

Christoph Blumhardt, who had already begun to assist his father (Theophil was still away), often stayed with the boy for long times. He had to stand in the farthest corner, constantly facing the sick boy, in order to be somewhat safe from his tricks. If Christoph turned his back for even a moment, quick as a wink Johannes would be up on his shoulders and grab hold of his hair. In the beginning, the elder Blumhardt, too, would come to visit the boy, until one day Johannes kicked him hard in the groin, causing him considerable pain for quite a time. Blumhardt took it as a hint to stop exposing himself to humiliations of that sort and left the personal treatment to Christoph. What father and son Blumhardt heard from the boy's lips in that room is beyond description; it was reminiscent of the worst scenes of the Möttlingen struggle. Christoph visited Johannes twice a day, but the visits continued to be difficult. Once, for instance, Johannes tried to pry a brick loose from the wall and threatened to hurl it at Christoph's head. Christoph's standard reply to the spirits raging in the boy was, "Mercy must and will conquer!" The demons usually retorted, "But the boy is done for!" There seemed to be no immediate prospect of a favorable conclusion, when quite unexpectedly a peculiar circumstance promised to bring some light into the darkness.

A son of Theodor and Gottliebin Brodersen, of the same age as Johannes, often played outside the sick boy's room and would chat with him through the window. Noticing that, Christoph asked him to show Johannes all possible kindness, for instance, to bring him fruit. The boy did; he brought Johannes plums and the like. Johannes took them, strung them on a thread he had probably obtained from the mattress, and made them into garlands. That was a promising beginning.

As directed by Christoph, the young friend then told Johannes he would not bring him anything else as long as he remained naked; he should at least put on pants. Johannes complied, and gradually the garments he agreed to put on increased in number, until he was decently dressed. As a reward he was allowed to go for walks with his young friend. But Johannes insulted all passers-by in the worst manner possible, in particular the gardener and his son. Finally, provoked beyond endurance, the gardener's son hit Johannes over the head with a stick, so that he fell down unconscious.

A capable surgeon, who had been called, declared the boy's skull to be split beyond recovery, and also a specialist summoned at once from a distance gave the boy only a few more hours to live. He was lying unconscious, and both Blumhardts, father and son, went to him. When the father came close to him, Johannes still made a vain effort to spit at him.

For two hours the two Blumhardts sat quietly by the poor lad, then the father left. Soon after, as Christoph bent over the boy, he heard Johannes say softly, but with a totally changed natural voice, "I would like some water." Christoph gave it to him; then, convinced that the boy's life had been saved, he rushed up to his father with the news, "Johannes is well!" And so it was. He still had a terrible headache for several hours, but under the tender care of Christoph, who was jubilant past description, he recovered fully the next day. Blumhardt father happened to be away just then. When he returned the day after, he saw among the throng of children welcoming him outside the boy Johannes, who greeted him with a friendly, "*Grüß Gott* [God bless you], *Herr Pfarrer!*" Before long the "*Herr Pfarrer*" gave way to "*Großpapa*" (grandpa), as the Bad Boll guests of that time remember well.

On his journeys Blumhardt was almost constantly surrounded by people pleading for help. Here is an example of how such help was experienced. A factory worker living about an hour's walk from Elberfeld was afflicted with an ugly skin eruption; according to his description it was a kind of leprosy. When every prospect of medical help had vanished, he was told that a well-known pastor had come to Elberfeld for the festival and that through his intercession many people had already been delivered from very serious illnesses. The man, who otherwise did not think much of "pious gentlemen," resolved to seek the pastor out.

He met him just when Blumhardt was putting on his preacher's gown to set off for a church where he was to preach. The man's affliction was one of those that had long burdened Blumhardt's heart; at any rate he quickly perceived what was troubling the man. The latter had scarcely begun to unfold his tale of woe when Blumhardt said, "My dear friend, I have no time right now, but I can quite see that you are a poor chap. Now just attend the service and listen carefully, and may the Savior help you!" The man scarcely managed to conceal his anger at seeing himself so curtly dealt with. "So that's the compassionate Blumhardt for you; that's what those pious folk are like! Now I am expected to go to church!" So he grumbled in his heart, but yet he decided to attend the service "for no good reason," just hoping that in his sermon Blumhardt might say something addressed to him. The man was unaware of the extent to which Blumhardt did so, for he preached on the text: "Ask, and you will receive." Blumhardt's words worked in the man's heart, but he remained disgruntled: "He doesn't speak at all about me or for me!" After the service, half moved, half angry, he turned his back on the church and the town and set off for home. "Those pious people and their compassion!" he fumed, but at the same time the words of the sermon kept reechoing in his heart.

Presently, while his mind was filled with these discordant thoughts, he became aware of a strange sensation in his skin. It started from a number of points, kept spreading, and got stronger and stronger. "Could that possibly be the healing?" Full of anticipation he hurried home, asked for a light, closeted himself in his bedroom, and there beheld in amazement that the disease was beginning to heal. I heard indirectly from the man himself that it was "the actual healing," whereas Blumhardt spoke of a healing process lasting two weeks. In brief, the man kept his hope to himself until he was quite certain of the result, but then he hurried to Elberfeld and through acquaintances passed on to Blumhardt the tidings of victory.

Here is just one instance of what an average guest in Bad Boll itself might experience. The quoted letter, *written* by a person who had been almost blind, is itself the finest testimony to the healing that had come to her. She writes:

> Even as a quite young girl I was afflicted with a severe eye disease. At the advice of famous oculists I was subjected to courses of treatment so drastic that after a few months they made me sick for many, many years; indeed I was hardly able to live. Only very slowly did I recover from the effects of the medicines used; but as soon as my general health improved about thirteen years ago, a frightening loss of sight began to develop. After a long struggle I decided to consult once again an oculist, the celebrated Professor Gräfe. He at once waved aside any prospect of recovery, giving me just a dim hope that further deterioration might be halted if I completely gave up any occupations such as reading, writing, or even knitting. I was advised to agree to a long-lasting stay out in the country.
>
> Then arose in me the thought of Boll and the longing to go there. In 1868 I had heard Pastor Blumhardt preach, and while I was still able to read I had acquainted myself with his writings. Without having more detailed or precise information on his great calling, I felt greatly drawn to him. I sensed that only in Boll would I find what could help me in my sad and often very dejected state.

God wonderfully and unexpectedly opened a way. I could come and stay for half a year. My eyes did not get better, but neither did they worsen, and I was given strength to carry my affliction.

Two years later I came to Boll again, still in much the same state, unable to make myself useful or occupy myself in any way. I often poured out to the dear pastor the need that weighed heavily on my heart. One day he asked me whether my family would not actually like me to obtain medical advice once again. I had to answer yes to that but added that I was resolved not to do it, since the treatment had such a devastating effect on me. "No, you shouldn't be like that," said the *Herr Pfarrer*, "you just like it too much here with us and are afraid of being sent to any old spa. That is why you shy away from the doctors. But it doesn't let me have a good conscience toward your father. To me your eyes look as if something could possibly be done for them; an operation might still accomplish something. So next week let's go to Stuttgart, where I know a well-known oculist that is also a good friend; I want him to give your eyes another checkup." No sooner said than done. We traveled to Stuttgart, and I shall never forget how the dear *Herr Pfarrer*, seated in an armchair, earnest and thoughtful, followed the examination with liveliest interest. The oculist's verdict was: "Nothing to be done; drugs would only speed up the loss of sight. The optic nerves are worn out; the muscles and mucous membranes are so weak they barely function. It's a marvel that there is still so much sight left. Only absolute rest may somehow still maintain the present condition." This agreed in every detail with what Professor Gräfe had said, except that the professor apparently regarded the illness as the beginning of amaurosis.[2]

On the train back, the *Herr Pfarrer* asked, "Are you sad, my child?" "Oh, no," I replied, "I already knew all that. I was just afraid the doctor would still want to attempt an operation." "Well," he said, "I think you know that where men can do nothing, the Savior enters in with *his* help. Now you are completely one of us, and we want to hold out in faith and hope for healing from him, even here where nothing more can be expected."

Since that day nine years have passed. I have not gone blind. I am still extremely shortsighted, but my eyes have been marvelously strengthened. I feel no pain; the very troublesome sensitivity to light has gone, and with the aid of glasses I can keep busy all day long with no trouble, for instance with writing and any womanly occupations, and can live just like other folk. Whenever the condition worsened, I would complain to the dear pastor, personally

---

2. Editors Note: Amaurosis refers to the beginning stages of the loss of sight.

or in writing, and before long help would again come. Indeed, the Savior has done great things for me through the beloved *Herr Pfarrer*, and I rejoice in it.

Let us also listen to a clergyman's grateful testimony to what he had been given in Boll. After expressing thanks for many spiritual blessings received from Blumhardt, he continues:

> What particularly moves my heart at this time is what the Lord has specially done for me, doubtless through my connection with the blessed deceased Blumhardt, through his prayer and blessing. I can never forget his words when he laid his hands on me once as I was leaving, "May Jesus Jehovah give you back your sight!"
>
> A few days ago I was once again with my eye doctor, who had operated on me, a student of Gräfe and a highly skilled surgeon. He is always greatly interested when he has a chance of examining me with his ophthalmoscope. "Completely healthy, both eyes!" (He had himself operated on one of them.) Time and again he assured me that what had happened here was utterly puzzling and unbelievable. A crack had opened in the lens—actually the only way of facilitating the reabsorption of its content, but according to him a process that ordinarily does not take place by itself. "Even if I could imagine that the contents had been reabsorbed—what happened to the capsule? It is completely inexplicable. If I had not seen it myself, I would not believe it, and if I tell others, they will not believe me," he said.

22

The Preacher

SINCE WE ALREADY KNOW Blumhardt as a preacher from the Möttlin-gen days, here in Bad Boll let us accompany him first to the children's service (Sunday school). Watching grandfather Blumhardt in action at the children's services (which were attended also by the younger ones among the housemaids) had a charm of its own. Here, since he could leave religious instruction, especially the memorizing part, to the well-managed in-house school, he found it all the easier to apply his gentle educational principles to the full. Fear, anxiety, and the like were absolutely kept away from the children, and he had a very free and lively way of drawing them into active participation through reading and answering questions. Following the prayer, two pairs of children would stand opposite each other on either side of the altar, where they recited to each other, as in a dialogue, Bible passages that Blumhardt was sure they already knew by heart. Blumhardt's way of discussing points of Christian doctrine with the children in an exhaustive, lucid, and practical way aroused great interest among both clergymen and lay folk. He was always lively, never facetious; always objective, never dry; always imposing in a fatherly way, yet never overawing.

On Sundays and Thursdays he preached in the stately room used for religious services (later equipped with an organ), where he also held the Saturday evening devotions so dear to his heart. In place of a description we give here a brief excerpt from such a Saturday evening service and preceding that a sermon he preached to the gathered household circle some time during the winter. That winter sermon is still more intimate in character than his summer sermons and therefore provides us with an even more faithful picture of him. It is taken from a somewhat imperfect transcript, which I have edited just slightly, as I did not want to spoil the general impression of freshness and genuineness.

SERMON ON LUKE 11:14–28

That is something one could say again and again in our time too: "Blessed are those that hear the word of God and keep it." The woman in our story meant well; she had received an impression of the Lord Jesus and thought, "That is a true man; his mother is indeed fortunate. Such a son's mother must be called blessed."

Nevertheless, receiving good impressions is not what is decisive. When I hear something, the question is: Do I hear it just for the moment or for a longer time? When I retain it, it's for a longer time. But when I hear it and an hour later ask, "What was it? What did he talk about? It's all gone!"—what then? So it is with hundreds of people: Whatever they have heard, it's all gone. There is ever so much one hears from childhood on, but what one actually retains would fit into a nut shell—at least with many.

Now and then it also happens that one hears, but with a shake of the head: "No, those things are not for us!" That may be many persons' reaction to today's gospel. Countless people just shut their eyes when one starts telling, "He was casting out a demon." They don't want to see or hear any more. They have had enough. When they hear those words, "Now he was casting out a demon" (Luke 11:14), they think, "Nonsense! Away with it!" And then comes still more—about the devil and demons and Beelzebub. People don't want to hear that sort of thing.

Alas, in that way people cannot hear their own misery either! Because they do not hear the Savior, they do not hear their misery. If they believed in their misery, they would find it easier to believe also in their Savior. The misery consists in this, that natural man is sold to the ruling authority of darkness, which has uncounted wretched, close-hidden beings in its power. And look: The distress climaxes in what our text tells us right at the beginning. I mean when a demon enters into a man so that it is no longer the man that speaks but rather the demon speaks out of him—what a violation that is of the poor man's dignity! How he is misused! And that occurs in countless shades and gradations. It doesn't go that far with all men, but they are certainly all attacked or influenced by such invisible powers. What misery!

Now when one reflects who these demons are, one is apt to conclude they are beings that belong in hell forever. Don't think that! They are deceased persons that also desire life and salvation but are still under the devil's power. He makes them as wicked as possible. There is such an abyss of misery and all manner of evil as one could scarcely imagine. And that's why the Savior's word is so wonderful: "If I cast out demons by the finger of God, then the kingdom of God is coming upon you" (Luke 11:20). That is the other climax or high point—that of *help*.

Now if we are not aware of men's wretchedness, we are not aware either that the Savior is at hand with the kingdom of God, which means the end of the devil's kingdom. When the devil loses his power, his kingdom comes to an end, and God's kingdom appears, but that is something people do not grasp. Instead, they ask for signs, signs (Luke 11:16)! O you simpletons! Is it no sign when a man is freed and redeemed from all dark powers? Is there a greater sign to see and hear than darkness losing its kingdom and the merciful, gracious One getting the upper hand? And it will yet come to that! Further: If in these days we are made aware of once more having power over the invisible prince of the world, then there is reason to think: It will come soon, for God is beginning to take up his rulership.

It can be said that almost since the time of the apostles men have no longer known how to cast out demons, except those that did it in the name of the devil, which only makes things worse. As the Savior puts it, "If I cast out demons by Beelzebub, by whom do your sons cast them out? [Luke 11:19]. By whom do your sons, that is, your own Jewish magicians [there were such] cast out demons?" They are the kind that do it by the power of the devil, which only serves to thicken the darkness. It is sheer profit for the devil when men have recourse to superstition and attack the demons after the devil's own fashion. It simply amounts to promoting superstition.

From apostolic times right up to the present the realm of darkness has been helped forward in this way. There were so-called exorcists, who wanted to cast out devils by magic; they were allowed in everywhere to ply their trade, and it has continued to the present. Later on, many Catholic priests, too, were such exorcists, but they did it exactly as the devil wanted it. Right up to the present day false treatments and methods, which involve devilish powers and serve only to shore up the realm of darkness, are in use. On the one hand it might seem that darkness has gone for good, but on the other hand everything has been done to restore it to power, and nowadays it is so much all around us that it is no longer even noticed.

Nevertheless, it has now become evident that there is divine help available for persons sick, possessed, and assailed by darkness. We can point to many examples of such help to show that God's finger is again active. Indeed, God's finger is again doing something! For people that want to have eyes to see and ears to hear there are no greater signs than these. More than anything else they justify a hope that we may experience great developments and see the ground being prepared for the kingdom of God. That is if one is alert to it. With the finger of God it is once more possible to accomplish something against darkness, and one can't help thinking, "Now watch out!" For eighteen hundred years people have been advancing the kingdom of darkness, have constantly helped it on, and I know of no single instance in church history where this particular area of human misery was satisfactorily attended to. Many things did happen, but nothing so pure and unadulterated as to let one say: God's finger has done something. And now that is just what has recently become widely visible: God's finger is again doing something! Only, one cannot yet say that because people will not believe it.

But I remember how it was back in May 1842. It was at nine or ten o'clock in the evening, and I had witnessed all sorts of things for several days. I stood looking on while a certain person was attacked by Darkness and tormented from head to foot. I stood by the stove in the little room, and my heart was heavy, for I had had to be in attendance there for several days already, and things got more and more horrible. Suddenly, as I stood there, I felt something come over me. I could feel it quite clearly and knew it was not something wrong. I said, "I have seen long enough what the devil does; now I want to see what the Lord Jesus can do." I looked up to the Savior and prayed, and in a twinkling everything was gone!

That was the first time God's finger again did something. From that time on I have often been through things that made me say, "The finger of God has done that." To be sure, on that occasion the relief granted was just for a short while, but God's finger helped me through every day, and after a year and a quarter, with the help of God's finger, I was given such a breakthrough that the devil himself had to concede, "Jesus is victor!"

So you see, I have experienced the finger of God in action against the invisible powers and authorities of darkness. When I firmly declare, "The time is here," when I am firmly convinced that we will not have to wait much longer, I have the Savior's word to back me up, "If I cast out demons by the finger of God, then the kingdom of God is coming upon you." It's starting now. If it continues—and it will continue—then God's kingdom will arrive.

In these recent times, our main ground for hope has been that when the Savior provides help against the invisible powers, the kingdom of God is about to come.

But we have to ponder these things rightly. The sayings of Jesus are important; we can hardly grasp all that is contained in the words before us here—all they have to say to us from beginning to end. Every sentence opens up something new to the attentive mind. But of paramount importance is always this: a Savior who drives away the powers of darkness! The Lord is a Savior that can cope with everybody; he comes as a strong, armed man. As the stronger one he comes upon the heavily armed prince of darkness and overpowers him. He takes from him his armor, that is, the souls with whom he wreaks havoc in creation, in the world, and on whom he used to rely. The Savior is at hand; he is always at hand to help us—he, the stronger one!

At that time I dared to take on the strong one: "I have now seen what the devil does, but isn't there one stronger than he?" Sure enough, it took barely two minutes, and the person attacked was completely free. It took just the one thought—"Now I want to see what Jesus can do"—and it was all gone! That was where God's finger showed itself. I recognized I now had a handle on the devil, and it's gone on right to the present day. It doesn't take much—a prayer and God's finger; then a lot can happen. I could tell a great deal about how the Savior manifests his finger ever anew.

Here Blumhardt gives several examples of divine help granted to others that he experienced in Möttlingen and Boll, including the story of the boy Johannes.

When I write a letter to far-off America, as I often do, they, too, will experience something of God's finger. There is not much to catch the eye, but it is something done by God's finger. You know, when once the finger of God starts working, it can and will go on! One just has to go along in faith with the finger of God. When the Lord takes a hand himself, it is a sign that he is about to rise up! So we want to go on quietly thinking of this: When something takes place anywhere that shows God's finger is again accomplishing something against the invisible powers, let us take notice. The finger may be active for only a moment, for Darkness will not give way at once, but it does make us think, "Aha! Now he is getting what is coming to him!" So we want to *believe* in the finger of God!

At present we have with us a mother—I may be permitted to say this—with her daughter, who is deaf and badly tormented by dark spirits. Let us look at our text. It says, "He cast out a demon that was dumb, and when the demon had gone out, the dumb man spoke" (Luke 11:14). In a similar way the devil is now tormenting this poor girl. So now you may all join me in praying that God's finger will help to deliver the poor girl from her torment and that nothing will be left to worry and be anxious about. In a case like that there is good reason to pray. Lord, Lord, may thy finger prove itself so that help is given! Truly, once multitudes come to believe and God's finger is really trusted to do something—dear people, then things can really happen!

Anyhow, so many people come every day who need the finger of God to work on them, and God be praised and thanked that his finger is becoming active again through our Savior Jesus Christ. Who knows how soon the power of darkness will collapse and God's finger indeed, not only his finger but his arm—will rule and govern and subject everything to him and work mightily in creation. Amen.

From an evening meditation on Psalm 62:6–8 we give the following section, which deals with verse 7, beginning with "With God is my salvation" (from *Predigt-Blätter* 1879, p. 5):

Salvation is the goal of everything. Our God in heaven, with our exalted brother, Jesus Christ, the crucified, risen, and exalted Savior, at his right hand, has nothing else in mind than to provide salvation. It should not be so that we just barely manage to squeeze through. No, "your salvation is with God!" Everything will culminate in a great redemption, not only for you but for the whole of creation. Precisely the darkest paths we are at times led along are our road to heaven. Oh, let us not forget that our God in heaven, who has sent us his Son, has nothing but thoughts of salvation for his expectant children.

You dear ones, whoever you are and whatever oppresses, disquiets, and burdens you, do not forget that you have a God in heaven in whom you may trust, a God in heaven who throughout each day and hour of your life ponders your salvation—how he might lead you to it safely and also that it might be lovely and invigorating in every way. The God we have over us is a God of salvation. And if you are in deep need through sin, have a burdened conscience, feel weak, and are just a poor sinner—dear child, should God's thoughts of salvation therefore not be valid for you? You are the object of his concern precisely because he wants to help you get out of all your sins, weaknesses, and follies.

Such are the thoughts of your God right through everything. He wants to provide a deliverance for you that will take you from salvation to salvation, so that all eternity will not be long enough for you to thank your God sufficiently for all he does with wondrous loving-kindness to let his salvation become your salvation. Just to know all that—oh, how quickening and comforting it is amid the sheer ruin all around us! It means that his salvation is already beginning to be realized in you if amid all the sorrows of this time you can find comfort in setting your hope on the God of salvation, who will lead everything to a glorious conclusion.

23

Journeys

OF GREAT IMPORTANCE FOR Blumhardt's general calling were his journeys. There is plenty of material for a report on them, but it would take years to collect it all. That is why I will give only a general and not a chronological account of that side of his activity. His travel commitments had their origin mainly in the time of the Möttlingen revival. The attention it had caused, as well as the public response to his addresses at conferences and rallies, and on the other hand the constantly increasing number of people that had come to know him personally or through correspondence committed him more and more to undertake journeys.

His journeys may be divided into one-time or at any rate irregular visits and those of regular recurrence. As regards journeys *outside* Germany, he once traveled to Paris, where in the company of the Monods he enjoyed inwardly quickening hours, which remained cherished memories for him. Once he went to Amsterdam and many times to Switzerland, where he visited Bern and Lausanne once, Zurich, Schaffhausen, and Winterthur several times. In these towns he had old friends and was always very welcome.

In Germany itself, it was particularly the annual church rally (*Kirchentag*) that led him frequently into new areas. As regards the larger German towns, I know that he once visited Berlin, Nuremberg, Frankfurt, and Altenburg (church rally), as well as Karlsruhe, where in an earlier chapter we met him in the deaconesses' motherhouse. As to Nuremberg, he remembered with much warmth a sermon he preached at a Christian folk festival in the neighborhood. Because a natural rock had to serve him as a pulpit, he used to refer to that sermon (which appears to have been a very inspiring one) as the "rock sermon."

In Frankfurt a friend once lured him into a neat trap. He invited Blumhardt to a hotel for a certain evening hour, telling him he wanted to bring together a number of friends that wished to become acquainted with Blumhardt. When Blumhardt took a look at the gathered friends, he discovered them to be nearly all medical practitioners. They proceeded to cross-examine him concerning his experiences with illnesses, and the evening is said to have been most interesting and satisfying for all participants.

With some regularity, though not every year, he attended the great mission festivals in Basel and Elberfeld, as well as a number of smaller mission festivals. According to one old missionary, Blumhardt preached at hundreds of such festivals. Naturally, his own places, Möttlingen and Bad Boll, would almost unfailingly be sought out by missionaries; here they all found inward refreshment and a fatherly home.

Two events that Blumhardt would mark in his calendar as occasions to be attended without exception were the children's festival in Korntal and the May mission festival in Calw. While at the Calw festival, during the last years he always visited his old Möttlingen congregation.

To him, these opportunities to bear public witness to what filled his heart were most important and welcome. He was greatly concerned that on these occasions his listeners might receive a true heavenly gift. The fact was that he could not always rid himself of a wistful feeling that the flocking together of even huge crowds often produced but meager results. He said, "When I saw those great gatherings of people, I often asked myself, 'And how will it be afterward?'" Corresponding to that earnest concern and intercession for all the people he found himself among was the often electrifying and energizing power of his words, about which many that listened to Blumhardt's addresses never tire of telling.

For a long time he paid monthly visits to the towns of Stuttgart (where he also once attended a church rally), Esslingen, and for a time Ludwigsburg. Taking turns with others, he conducted a weekly evening meeting in each of these towns, where a circle of listeners he grew more and more familiar with gathered around him.

How am I to describe Blumhardt on his travels? Things were similar wherever he found himself. To his host's household, right to every last member, child, and servant,[1] Blumhardt's outgoing, warm, endearing manner and the peace flowing from him remained unforgettable. For this pleasure, however, the host had to pay. His hallways and staircases suffered considerably from the press of supplicants; in the evenings and maybe already during the morning devotions he had to put up with quite a number of unaccustomed guests.

Blumhardt felt right in his element in every such throng where the misery so close to his heart rushed in on him. And how he enjoyed meeting new people that desired to learn and receive something from him! Once he wrote to his wife: "I am sharing a room with a dear *Vikar*, a splendid fellow, who would not let me go to sleep nor let me sleep my fill, so many questions did he have." Every spare moment in such towns was used as much as possible for visits all over the place. The preparation time for his sermons usually coincided with the time he spent in bed. Two examples may suffice to give an impression of such days—one a day in Esslingen as reported by an eye witness, a friend of Blumhardt; the other a day spent in Calw as I personally remember it.

Let us first go with Blumhardt to the mission festival in Calw, in May 1878.

> When he alighted from the train on the eve of the festival, small groups of people in need of help were already waiting for him; there and then at the station he at once conversed with them as he would do in his study. As he made his way toward town, short of breath as he was it was almost a respite for him to be repeatedly stopped by further supplicants. Pretty well worn-out, he reached the hospitable house of Dr. Gundert, where loving friendship and physical refreshment awaited him. As the evening advanced, many more people called to see him; still, compared to what lay before him the following day, he had a quiet time. Next morning, a flood of country people, especially from the Black Forest, came pouring into town. Already quite early their waves washed at the house where Blumhardt lodged. As reported in the *Schwäbische Merkur* (Swabian Mercury), the Black Forest folk had come to greet Blumhardt, their spiritual father, once more.
>
> There was a church service the morning of the following day—an "apostle's day," according to the tradition of the Württemberg Protestant church. Blumhardt preached on the Samaritan woman (John 4), laying special stress on Jesus' word to her, "It is I." He

---

1. To a manservant he once gave a booklet with the dedication, "The servant to the servant."

spoke of the distress of our own time, with its contradictory views in matters of religion, and declared that even the attitude of believers was in danger of being watered down and of paling to a mere "view." He pointed to the crying need of these days, which the Lord will be sure to satisfy, for with a call of "it is I," he will one day bring our generation back to a living knowledge of the true facts. That, of course, is no more than a snippet from the sermon. We saw a dense crowd of young men with tears in their eyes; they understood Blumhardt even better than we.

The afternoon was given over to the mission festival; the concluding address and prayer were again Blumhardt's. As in the morning, he had to work his way through all those that still wanted to greet him and talk to him in the street. During his address dark and ever darker clouds kept moving up, and when it came to the final prayer, one had to reckon with an imminent outburst of the wrath of the elements in the form of a calamitous storm. Soberly, humbly, but courageously Blumhardt prayed that it might be turned away, but in vain. It got darker and darker; finally the storm broke, and the gathering dissolved in the downpour of a cloudburst. What went on in Blumhardt's heart during such an experience would give us an even better idea of the continuous inward struggle he stood in.

The Nagold River was in spate, carrying with it all kinds of booty; its rapacity even endangered the carriage standing ready to take Blumhardt to Möttlingen. The *Steig* (the steep road leading up to Möttlingen), too, had become a torrent, which spread devastation in the town of Calw. For a while the Nagold River split the festival crowd into two camps, one on either bank, until gradually the bridges were again fit to be crossed.

After a few sociable hours spent with mission friends, we— Blumhardt, Pastor Bunz, and I—traveled by carriage up the *Steig*. The flood water still rushing down the road (though the volume was much less), the deep holes and gullies it had gouged, the gathering dark, a coachman who had completely lost his head—all this made the journey almost perilous. When we finally reached the plateau, Blumhardt raised his voice in a hymn of praise: "Praise the Lord, O my soul." Singing, we rode into the gathering night toward Möttlingen, on a badly damaged, unsafe road and in pouring rain. In Möttlingen we were welcomed by the teacher, at the head of the schoolchildren. The lighted windows in the village and the contours of people's heads in them showed us how eagerly we had been awaited.

Scarcely arrived at the rectory and having shed the wettest of his garments, Blumhardt inquired of the local minister, "Are the lights on in church?" "No, *Herr Pfarrer*, I thought you would first eat a bit." "Not at all; on with the lights!" Well, until that was done, we did have time to eat something. Then straightway into the crowded church for a brief, powerful sermon breathing earthy warmth and brotherliness. The living Lord Jesus Christ was so palpably assumed to be near us as I thought I had never experienced before.

Back in the rectory, Blumhardt asked, "Now, Bunz, where are the people?" "Oh, those, *Herr Pfarrer*. I have asked them to come tomorrow! I thought you would be too tired now." "O . . ." (here Blumhardt employed one of those Swabian titles of honor that he dispensed liberally to persons close to him), "don't you know me? I am never tired!" He obviously had to swallow a slight annoyance. Still, the evening spent in a small circle turned out to be a rich and fruitful one. Next morning was another church service, in which he again treated his Möttlingers like a loyal family in a way so comforting and at the same time so strict as cannot possibly be described.

Herr Mögling, a missionary, tells as follows about Blumhardt's visits to Esslingen:

For almost ten years, from 1869 on, we in Esslingen have had the joy of seeing Blumhardt here on the third Thursday of every month. Usually, a number of people suffering either in body or soul and seeking comfort and help waited at dear *Herr* Viel's house for Blumhardt's arrival by the five o'clock train from Göppingen. There might be thirty, forty, or fifty such persons; for each he had an open ear and heart, vigorous intercession, and a hearty and— where needed—robust admonition. Many, and I say this as a sober and conscientious witness, owe him their physical and emotional well-being. *Herr* Viel's home was often crowded with people, some of whom had walked hours to bring to Blumhardt their requests, which he listened to with untiring patience.

Then, after a slight repast, off he went to the meeting house, mostly filled to capacity, to give one of his simple, hearty biblical talks. Full of deep insight, these talks always offered something new from the rich treasure of knowledge he had gathered in his lifelong intimate association with the Word of God. There was something special to his exposition of Scripture: one was given fresh, gushing spring water, not water pumped up from a well. What he could share was not something he had learned and prepared laboriously but a live experience, springing directly from the heart. Mostly, the way he spoke was just like the way in which for a number of years he communicated his thoughts in print in *Blätter aus Bad Boll*. An older clergyman and good theologian that visited Bad Boll several times told me about Blumhardt's sermons: "He always offered something fresh; his thoughts were often as surprising as they were natural. As a theologian, too, I learned something from him every time."

At eight o'clock, when his talk in the meeting room ended, usually some people, townsfolk or strangers, stayed behind, waiting for a word of encouragement, consolation, sympathy, or blessing. After attending to such stragglers, he went with us to where he was to spend the night, the familiar home of the dear *Herr Stadtpfarrer* Kraus, the town minister, where a few of those that had listened to him in the meeting house would still gather around him. He was pleased then if this or that question gave him an opportunity to say more about points he had touched on in his address; he liked to answer objections and above all to give a lively presentation and justification of his great hopes for a soon-to-come, extraordinary manifestation of the Lord's mercy.

He felt deeply the misery weighing on humankind and the overpowering influence of the realm of darkness upon our world of sin, and he yearned more and more for a coming time of refreshment and quickening. There was something overwhelming in his love; in every person he could see something good and of God. To condemn anyone was deeply offensive to him; his heartfelt wish was that all might be helped. He believed that that was God's purpose, as clearly expressed in Scripture (for instance in 1 Tim 2:4), and that this loving will of God would surely be fulfilled. He was too certain of his cause to brook any objections, nor were we inclined to argue with the precious man of God. So it went on until we others took our leave at ten o'clock. The following morning we often learned that the dear guest had still been up till eleven or later, engaged in light or serious talk. On Friday morning, after breakfast and family prayers, he would for many years pay a half-hour visit to Miss F. H., to bring spiritual comfort to this dear sick friend, who was confined to her room and chair right until her blessed end.

I would like to add just a little to that report. On the days Blumhardt lodged there, the house of the retired town minister, Kraus, reminded one of the Möttlingen rectory. Frequently every available room, including the study, was converted into sleeping quarters. The hospitality of that house, combined with *Herr* Viel's ready helpfulness contributed a lot to making Blumhardt's visits in Esslingen dear and precious to him as well as fruitful to others.

His regular visits to old friends that lay sick, whether in Esslingen or elsewhere, have remained an especially wonderful memory for all that accompanied him on one of these errands. There was such a heartfelt intimacy in his manner as might but rarely be found in a brother seeing his sister again after a long time. One of his peculiarities was that the daily text (or watchword) he had discoursed on at morning prayers in his host's house would also be used by him on subsequent visits during the day; he would look at it from ever new angles.

As time went on, Blumhardt's increasing age and weight forced him to reduce his journeys more and more and finally to restrict his activities almost completely to Bad Boll. The spare time this and the active help of his sons gave him, he used for literary work, which we will discuss at the end of this section.

24

The Author

IN CHAPTER SEVEN WE made mention of Blumhardt's most exacting literary task in Boll: the third edition of his handbook of missionary history and geography. Thanks to the great missionary advances since the forties, it was a huge task, but to him it was a sweet burden. With holy joy he traced where the Savior of the world had been at work all over the globe. His research and data-gathering left him with an overall impression so great it fairly overwhelmed him. After the conclusion of his struggle in Möttlingen he had told various missionary friends that such a victory would make itself felt even in the mission field. Practical experience there has in no way contradicted him, for since the forties great revolutions have taken place in the whole area of mission; our generation has seen a new age dawn in China, India, Africa (Madagascar), and America.

The handbook was a venture Blumhardt had undertaken on behalf of the Protestant church. The remainder of his writings bore witness to what was moving in his own heart. They were addressed partly to the limited circle of his acquaintants, partly to the wider one of the Protestant church.

It was for that wider circle that a collection of fifteen Advent sermons, published in 1864, was meant.[1] It actually represents a series of

1. Editors' Note: Johann Christoph Blumhardt, *Fünfzehn Predigten über die drei ersten Advents-Evangelien, zur Beförderung christlicher Erkenntnis* (Stuttgart, 1864) [*Fifteen Sermons on the First Three Advent Gospel Readings, for the Promotion of Christian Knowledge*].

careful theological treatises, which at times appear a little ill at ease in their garb of sermons. They discuss thoroughly and as exhaustively as possible important points of Christian doctrine, especially the final judgment, the ultimate fate of the unredeemed, and the hope for a new time of grace.

The fate of the unredeemed takes up the larger part of the first half of this collection. From every angle Blumhardt discusses the view held by some that in the end everybody will be saved, that is, the hypothesis of the final restoration of all things. If true, that doctrine would indeed take the heaviest load of grief off Blumhardt's heart, yet he shows over and over again that it takes too lightly the holiness and justice of God on the one hand, and the seriousness of sin on the other, and that it finds no justification in Scripture itself. His final conclusion is: "To the lost, Scripture indeed shows more the *hope*lessness than the *end*lessness of their situation, but it does not behoove us to deny the latter all the less since this would at once invalidate the former as well."

The second half of this writing centers on the heroic figure of John the Baptist, whom Blumhardt contemplates with great love through the relevant Advent texts, in such a way as to gain ever new light on what we may still hope for. In these biblical treatises the reasoning is conducted as though with magnifying glass in hand. The arguments are weighed so meticulously they often lack the quality of easy readability that has nowadays become almost a necessity for us. That style is equally characteristic of all the other Bible expositions (still to be mentioned) from Blumhardt's pen; however, if we are truly concerned to obtain satisfying insights, we may end up really liking it.

For the smaller circle of his acquaintances he brought out (in 1865) a collection of morning devotions.[2] Encouraged by the acclaim they found, he published for a wider circle in 1868 a number of devotions for family worship—a most substantial booklet, with an appendix that discusses a variety of important points, for instance, the command to honor the Sabbath, spiritualism, and others.

We pass over the various lectures Blumhardt delivered on his journeys and published at the request of his listeners, and turn to his last and best-known literary output, that is, the *Blätter aus Bad Boll*, which

2. Editors' Note: *Sammlung von Morgenandachten nach Losungen und Lehrtexten der Brüdergemeine, gehalten zu Bad Boll* (Bad Boll: 1865) [*Collection of Morning Meditations on the Old Testament Texts Drawn by Lot and Appropriate New Testament Texts of the Moravian Brethren, given in Bad Boll*].

from July 1, 1873, to July 1, 1877, appeared every Saturday and were on principle edited by him alone. Their main content is a continuous exposition of the Gospel of Matthew, excepting the account of the Lord's suffering and resurrection. They, too, exhibit the peculiar style discussed above, but in view of the richness of his own great experiences they deserve attention on two grounds. For one thing, in order to gain these experiences, he had been obliged to delve more earnestly into the Gospels than others did; for another, these very experiences supplied him with additional light on the Gospels.

Not a few readers may have preferred to look beyond that first part of the weekly paper to the second, devotional part, where Blumhardt speaks in a relaxed conversational tone and yet in a profoundly moving and uplifting way. Or they might have jumped directly to the third section, where all kinds of questions from readers were given thought-provoking answers. Or finally to section four, which, in small print and headed "Miscellaneous," always offered something of interest.

We already became acquainted with these "Papers" in an earlier chapter. In his later years, with so many other claims on his time, it often meant a superhuman effort for Blumhardt to get this paper ready every week. Having come to the end of chapter 25 in his interpretation of the Gospel of Matthew and seeing no particular need for an exposition of the account of the passion, he regarded the task he had set himself as completed. He went on to expound various points in the Gospel of Luke but then discontinued the publication of these papers, chiefly because it seemed to him that he had now said all he had felt the need to express and that he neither could nor would labor just to satisfy the demand for regular Christian edification.

Yet, such a demand did exist. The publication of this weekly, which came to us as such a welcome messenger every Sunday, had awakened it particularly among Blumhardt's friends. Hence, immediately after its discontinuance that demand was addressed very audibly to Boll. It was then that Theophil Blumhardt stepped into the breach with his treasure of the father's transcribed devotions. As we heard earlier, from then on until 1881 he published in annual installments a small volume entitled *Täglich Brod aus Bad Boll.* This series gives a much more faithful picture of Blumhardt's spoken devotions than his own publications (discussed above), for he himself would never have dared to use his unabashed conversational tone in his writings. The charming naturalness of these devotions is due to their remaining unedited by Blumhardt. Right to his death, however, he continued to supply monthly sermons and meditations composed by himself to the *Evangelische Sonntagsblatt* (Protestant Sunday Paper) in Stuttgart.

We now come to another literary activity of Blumhardt's, one we already met with at the revival time: his work in the area of poetry and music. Blumhardt saw poetry as of great importance for the Christian church; he almost considered it the duty of a useful servant of God to accomplish something in that area too. He considered it an indication that the author's mind is turned lovingly and unhurriedly toward the thoughts of God; he felt need would drive a man to do so. He expected ministers of the gospel to possess spirit and did not think it truly Christian to restrict the hymning of God's praise in so tedious a way to what is in print or known by heart. To him, the challenge, "Sing to the Lord a new song," had above all the deep meaning that we long for new deeds of the Lord, which would then also call for new songs. But not only that—it also meant for him that praising the Lord should not always consist in just warming up old songs, and that especially one's own inner experiences should call for praising God in one's own new way. Thus it was to him a matter of honor before God, as well as a heartfelt need, to adorn the great stations in the life of the church and particularly in the history of his own house with manifold flowers of the Spirit. Many people have cherished delightful memories of such festive occasions—a christening, wedding, or the like—in Blumhardt's household.

Still, poetry in today's sense of the term was not one of his gifts. His sober mind, oriented as it was toward truth and reality, was unable to evoke the "elevated" moods of that actually nonexistent world poetry transports us into. Also, amid the sweat of his labors and the gun smoke of his battles he had completely lost any feeling for the high demands we place on elegance of diction. Besides, his own vocabulary was that of the people—or better, that of informal conversation. He thought in the language of the people; that made his speech concise and telling but rendered his verse somewhat dry and sober. However, he did in the end achieve rare mastery in the art of forcing the language into rhyme and rhythm without in the least obscuring the train of thought.

The field he tilled in this his own fashion was the same as in Möttlingen. He continued to provide biblical singing material for his household, making use of texts from the Gospel of John, the Pauline Epistles,

Revelation, and other parts of the New Testament. Now and then he would also compose a song for a celebration or about mission or the like.

We include here just three examples. The first represents the third part of an unprinted poem (in three parts), composed in the autumn of 1879 on the parable of the ten virgins: 1. The parable in general; 2. the foolish virgins; 3. the bride and the virgins. This third part links up with the general exposition of the parable in the first part and describes in particular the bride and the virgins, as follows:

The Bridegroom does not name his Bride,
Nor can a name be given.
The Bride he loves—his joy and pride—
Means all those bent for heaven.
So Abraham and all his stem,
To whom the Lord descended,
Into one whole are blended.
That his dear Bride, his church, he win,
And see her multiplying,
Christ had to answer for men's sin,
Redeem them through his *dying*.
Then was to soar as conqueror
Up to the throne of heaven—
Henceforth for all be *living*.
From heaven's throne by eager search
'Mongst people of every nation
He gathers in his bridal Church
And worldwide congregation.
For her he fights until he smites
All foes with kingly power
And makes the Darkness cower.
Yet has the Lord a staunch helpmeet,
A small, self-giving nation,
Which serves him wholly till complete
His task of expiation.
He as a guide walks by their side
Until from Satan's prison
Humankind through him has risen.
When dawns at last the longed-for day
Of all his foes' undoing,
The Bridegroom will without delay
Seek her whom he is wooing.
From heaven's throne descends God's Son
To join with fond elation
His Bride and congregation.

She is that great, unnumbered throng,
From all humankind elected,
The chosen Bride, for whom does long
The Bridegroom aye expected,
Before whom now all earth must bow,
As he appears with power
At God's appointed hour.
The virgins—they are that small band
That never ceases fighting
Till blessed redemption on each land
Descends, their faith requiting.
Their standing true makes all things new
From earth to highest heaven.
To them it will be given. (Dan 7:18; Luke 12:32)
They are the widow that persists (Luke 18:3)
Until the worn judge tires;
They are the chosen, who resist
As daring faith requires,
Who strive and fight by day and night
To show the dark accuser
That he must be the loser.
To their plea God inclines his ear;
He heeds their supplications
And soon will act to end all fear
Of Satan's depredations.
And yet, how can the Son of man
Return if so few greet him,
Prepare in faith to meet him! (Luke 18:8)
It is the virgins too who dare
To help where need is calling;
It is they who evade with care
The tempter's voice enthralling.
They shall be first to quench their thirst
And, festive garments wearing,
The wedding feast be sharing.
We are not told who else might be
The virgins in our story.
Theirs is a higher dignity
And great will be their glory.
With eager care they do declare
The Bridegroom's lofty station
And seek the Bride's salvation.
A warning does God for them sound
Lest they, too, grow halfhearted

And after faithful work be found
To have from love departed.
Such cannot stand with the virgins' band
When midst the wedding's splendors
The Bridegroom's praise it renders.

Next, a New Year's song (for the year 1877):

With fearful hearts people enter
Into the nascent year;
They worry lest their prayers
Might find no open ear.
Such trouble brought and heartache
The year that now has passed
That people's courage withered
Before the icy blast.
Wherever we are gazing,
Great sorrows people must bear;
Nor can hearts sad and weary
Find solace anywhere.
However good we have it,
Much pain does yet abide;
Our very noblest talents
Leave us unsatisfied.
One feels that Christ the Savior
Is missing everywhere
And that his absence from us
Is what we cannot bear.
It is not hard to fathom
Why here he will not stay;
The countless wrongs among us
Are what drives him away.
Should faith go forth to find him?
But faith does fade and flee.
Should love pursue and bind him?
But love fails wretchedly.
Would hope have strength to hold him?
Hope wilted long ago.
No wonder Satan's armies
Wield power here below!
How it should stir and grip us
To hear Christ's name ring out!
Were he to rule, how quickly
A change would come about!

The troubles that befall us
Would soon diminish then.
Oh, how it would enthrall us
If all were light again!
Yet is it not a token
That Christ's return is nigh,
When people's lives are so broken,
When masses groan and sigh?
When structures start to crumble
That once stood proud and tall,
And destined seems to tumble
What no one thought could fall.
In truth, the Lord is living
Who from the grave awoke!
All you that sigh and labor
Your necks bend to his yoke
And bind yourselves to serve him
With faith and courage true,
Until you, too, discover
How he makes all things new.
Does love burn low and feeble?
Let it shoot up in flame!
Is hope now deemed outmoded?
Then hope, nor mind the shame!
When once more we surrender
To faith and hope and love,
Will not the unlocked heavens
Rain healing from above?
Still, if you seek or leave him,
The Lord will not leave you!
You may not hope as bidden,
Yet will his light break through.
Though men take to their own selves
What rightly should be his,
It will yet be unfolded
How great his harvest is.
The Lord—this stands forever—
Was born and died for all,
Then raised to be enthroned
And rule in heaven's hall.
Therefore this generation,
Though faithless it may be,
Cannot delay much longer
God's year of jubilee.

Finally, the poem "The Transformation," based on 1 Corinthians 15:51–58:

We shall not all be fated
To leave this life and die,
But at the long awaited
Triumphant blast on high
We shall be changed completely
In a brief moment's time,
Quite suddenly and fleetly,
When sounds the trump sublime.
Then will the dead be rising
All incorruptible,
The living, changed, be loosened
From bonds terrestrial.
Thus dons the perishable
Imper'shability;
The mortal will be clothed
With immortality.
When incorruption graces
Perishability,
And what is mortal changes
To immortality,
Then is fulfilled the promise
Of prophets long ago,
For which the whole creation
Is waiting on tiptoe.
Grim death, we read, is swallowed
Up into victory!
How glorious is the downfall
Of this last enemy!
"Where, now that thou hast fallen,
Where, death, is thy dread sting?
Where, grave, is now thy triumph?"
Exultant voices ring.
The sting of death, 'tis written,
Has been men's grievous sin.
That sin might vanish wholly,
Christ Jesus did step in,
Who by his wounds did cancel
The law, which was our bane
And gave to sin its power;
Yet now its threat is vain.
Then will be manifested
The fruit Christ's cross has borne—

A fruit so long sought after
By men lost and forlorn.
Praise God, who has assured us
Of vict'ry in advance!
Soon you will see Christ rising
For our deliverance.
Therefore stand firm, my brothers!
Budge not, nor hold aloof!
And let God's work among you
Of growing love give proof!
We do not struggle vainly,
For God upholds our stand.
We know: our cause will triumph;
The great day is at hand.

By composing such songs, as well as the earlier songs based on psalms and prophecies, Blumhardt wanted to serve several purposes. In the first place, he hoped that putting these important Bible words into singable form would render them more accessible and impressive to some people, but besides that, he wanted to provide fresh material for singing. One has to sing these songs to discover their holy, quickening strength and to experience how such singing of unaltered biblical thoughts takes one back across the centuries into Bible times. Ultimately, though, the purpose these compositions served was a wistful one. Since Blumhardt yearned for fellowship with every fiber of his being, the awareness of standing alone with his clearest convictions and brightest hopes oppressed him all the more. In his loneliness these poetical endeavors served to comfort and strengthen him.

Hand in hand with Blumhardt's versifying went his composing. In his study he would use the time between one caller's departure and the entry of the next one to find a needed rhyme or to try out a musical passage on the piano. To him, new songs also meant new tunes. Most of the tunes he wrote in Möttlingen were in the style of our traditional church meters; they have a churchly character, at times reminiscent of the popular tone of our church melodies, even though here and there the motives are not interrelated with the same formal strictness as in the great classical melodies. In Boll he ventured into a new form, which was still more in keeping with his gifts and training, that of the motet; that is, he invented melodies for biblical texts. A motivating force here was his own dear grandchildren. Especially one little girl, barely three years old, kept begging him, "*Grosspapa*, we should also sing, 'Let all the children come unto me.'" "*Grosspapa*, we still can't sing the Hosanna!" As a result, two lovely compositions came into being. The first ("Let all the children") is like an enticing call, while the second ("All that hath life and breath") breathes a shy and holy joy such as naturally cannot be conveyed in words.

From there Blumhardt went on to greater works, trying his hand at presentations of biblical hymns of praise, a little reminiscent of oratorios. They were true expressions of the deepest and inmost need of his heart, of his holiest experiences and hopes. In particular, there were two such works. One is the triumph song based on Revelation 12:10–12, "Now the salvation and strength and the reign and the might of our God and of his Christ," a powerful song of victory for one, two, and four voices, interspersed with laments over still existent need. The other is the Virgin Mary's song of praise: "My soul doth magnify the Lord." If one has in one's ear Sebastian Bach's version of the same theme ("Magnificat") while listening to Blumhardt's composition, one cannot help feeling what an advantage it was for Bach that he unhesitatingly gave Mary's part now to soprano, now to tenor and even bass in turn, using from one to five voices. Blumhardt's historical conscientiousness kept him from being so audacious. In order to obtain more parts and an alternation of solos, duets, choir, and so on, he added to Mary some historically possible persons, such as Zechariah and Elizabeth and their servants, thus achieving a lovely and often elevating variety in the number and range of voices. So much about the outer frame of that work. When it comes to its inner content, I think it would have delighted Sebastian Bach's heart, in particular the soulful, jubilant thoughts it brings to expression.

Professional musicians found great joy in Blumhardt's original musical ideas and considered it an honor to examine and correct his sometimes rather bold settings. It contributed a great deal to the spiritual life in Bad Boll when such choral works were on occasion presented by musical members of the household.

It has been a joy for me to conclude the chapter with a discussion of the *Magnificat*, which we shall meet yet again as, one might almost say, Blumhardt's swan song.

Third Section

25

Pastoral Care in a Smaller Circle—Fresh Hopes

WE BROKE OFF OUR account of the little group that moved from Möttlingen to Bad Boll (see chapter 18) in order to devote this third part of our book mainly to a portrait of the "pastor of Bad Boll" and the impression of unchanging loveliness it left on visitors during the last three decades of his life. As we now focus once again on that central circle of Bad Boll, we want to trace at least the main lines of its inner history.

During the Möttlingen struggle and ever after, Blumhardt's family took an active part in his warfare against Darkness. As a result the members of his family were laid open to many serious onslaughts from that dark power. They would not have wanted it differently. For understandable reasons, in my account of that time I passed over the numerous strange attacks of illness, often aimed at precipitate death, that his family members—Gottliebin always most of all—were exposed to in Möttlingen, nor have I made mention of the always specially wonderful help that was given. Also, I related the unspeakable sufferings Gottliebin Brodersen underwent in Bad Boll much more briefly than Blumhardt himself does in his handwritten biography of Gottliebin. Hers was a steadfast, inconspicuous martyrdom, and it would serve no sensible purpose to publicize it.

Approximately one year after Gottliebin's death, attacks of the kind mentioned began to be concentrated on one person of that inner circle who did not belong to Blumhardt's own family. It was similar to the way it had been with Gottliebin in Möttlingen and demanded Blumhardt's special pastoral care to the same degree. Now, however, he was in possession of the fruit of victory, namely, a peace-imparting strength and an authority to speak out forgiveness—a gift disclosed and granted to him already in Möttlingen. That gave to his present struggle a peaceable and victorious character. It was uplifting and inspiring for Blumhardt to experience that the Savior is at the same time king and priest. But because his quiet labors were those of a counselor and, so to speak, father confessor, they evaded all publicity. It was noticeable, though, that Blumhardt now faced as a priest the foes he had formerly confronted as a warrior; that, too, committed him to absolute discretion.

All we could see was how remarkably these struggles affected Blumhardt's inner life in growing measure. The cloud of melancholy and wistfulness that darkened his sky until the early seventies and was noticed by those who saw deeper, disappeared more and more. There came a time when he seemed to grow younger every year. Each time I came back, he was even more lively, simple, joyful, and inwardly certain than the time before. His spirit seemed to grow more and more fertile, original, and luminous. Especially his hopes reached constantly new heights of clarity, breadth, assurance, and a kind of self-evidentness. It struck him as abnormal and irregular that forgiveness of sins in the name of Jesus has still not been given to the large majority of men—an anomaly that was bound to be set right in due time.[1] The Savior's love to all the lost, tender readiness to forgive, and peaceful heartiness came to him like a breath from heaven and streamed out from him to others. Indeed, in the marvelously liberating power that increasingly flowed from him to people's minds and hearts one could not help feeling the hand of the Lord himself, reaching out to the lost with mercy and power. If I were free to relate various instances of wolves changing into lambs (to use the prophet's picture) in the twinkling of an eye, it would show better than these inadequate words how the approach of an overwhelmingly great victory of grace could be sensed.

For a better appreciation of the clarity and certainty of Blumhardt's hopes we must remember their roots and foundations, that is, his constant concern for the lot of the whole human race. It is hard to form

---

1. In no way did his expectancy spring from an underestimation of sin. He could not imagine forgiveness for anybody except through earnest self-judgment, leading to deep remorse. That was precisely what he looked to for many, once the dark powers that harden people's hearts were broken.

an adequate idea of how heavily the distress of mankind, the wretchedness of its lost condition, weighed on his heart ever since his "struggle."
In the years between the late eighteen forties and the time we are now
concerned with, he shed many bitter tears because he saw no movement
toward what he hoped for. When it became more and more clear in the
mid-sixties that our generation would once again have to suffer the grim
scourge of war, he wept like a child. The renewed hopefulness we spoke
about helped Blumhardt's world-embracing vision to grow in conscious
strength and confidence. Wherever he sensed a danger to the whole
fabric of life, be it the plague, a false teacher, an epidemic of attempted
regicides, or even spiritualism, he took a stand with all the vigor of his
faith and did not rest until he felt reassured—often long before a turn for
the better was to be noticed on the surface of events.

Since the days of his "struggle" his sympathy and grief were no
longer confined to the living. The distress of the lost, which had been
going on day and night for centuries and millenniums, weighed heavily on his heart. His fifteen Advent sermons show how profoundly he
was stirred by the question: Is there any hope for them? He could not
turn away from the views he had expressed there. The proposition that
the lost would find salvation simply because philosophical necessity
required it continued to strike him as arbitrary and contrived. Yet in
that fresh struggle he was engaged in it seemed as if a new light of hope
and comfort was dawning on him. At least he gave the impression that
in his sympathy for the poor lost souls he saw himself far outstripped,
and indeed put to shame, by the Savior himself. He learned that Jesus as
the living One, the head of his Church on earth, is determined to seek
what is lost wherever he finds it, though it be in the deepest dungeons
of forsakenness. He also came to see that the Lord wants his authority to
forgive sins on earth understood in the widest possible sense, and that
one day the promise, "Everyone that calls upon the name of the Lord
will be saved" (Joel 2:32; Acts 2:21; Rom 10:13) will be fulfilled on a vast
scale. Blumhardt liked to say at that time, "I believe in Jesus Christ, who
will come from heaven to judge the living and the dead—but mark well:
not to execute them but to straighten them out!"

It was surely first from Holy Scripture that that light dawned on
him. As once before in his "struggle," need compelled him to search in it.
Timidly, hesitatingly he dared to conceive a thought in the above direction, to ponder it, and to let himself be guided by it. But his experience

resembled that of the men who with joyful abandon proclaimed the gospel also to the heathen (Acts 11:21) and of whom it says, "And the hand of the Lord was with them." Thus encouraged, he constantly obtained new light from Scripture; only so did what he hoped for become fully clear and understandable to him.

What would be the sense of expecting the most wonderful of all events for just the *last* generation of humanity? It would be an injustice to all preceding generations. Blumhardt began to see that the great promises will have a retroactive effect. Thus can come about what the last psalm calls for, "Let everything that has breath praise the Lord!" (Ps 150:6) and what Psalm 145 proclaims, "The Lord is good to all, and his compassion is over all that he has made" (Ps 145:9).

If the promise given to Abraham that through his offspring all nations on earth would be blessed (Gen 22:18) applies merely to "all nations" of some last and final generation and does not have retroactive power that would be but a parsimonious and inequitable fulfillment. And if Paul expresses the sure hope that "all Israel will be saved" (Rom 11:26), is some still-to-come generation of Jews "all Israel"? "No one thinks of the dead!" But if "all Israel," what is to become of the billions of men that died without a chance of hearing the Gospel? One of the first Bible passages to become important to Blumhardt in this context was Jesus' word, "But I, when I am lifted up from the earth, will draw all men to myself" (John 12:32). It is known too that Blumhardt saw in quite a new light the passage in Revelation 7:9–14 concerning the "great multitude that no one could count, from every nation, tribe, people, and language," who sing praises around the throne of God. About them the question is asked, "Who are they, and where did they come from?" and the answer given is, "These are they that have come out of the great tribulation; they have washed their robes and made them white in the blood of the Lamb." According to Blumhardt's interpretation (probably correct), this scene takes place *before* the final judgment, which is why the astonished question. What then is meant by the great tribulation? Blumhardt replies, "It is the unblessed state of those that died without knowing Christ."

Of still greater importance might be the passage, Isaiah 45:22–25, where the Lord cries: "Turn to me and be saved, all you ends of the earth, for I am God, and there is no other. By myself I swear; from my mouth goes forth a word of righteousness, which will not be revoked. To me every knee shall bow, every tongue shall confess, saying, 'In the Lord is my righteousness and strength.'" In Philippians 2:9–12 Paul interprets that passage as follows: "God has highly exalted Jesus and given him a name that is above every name, that at the name of Jesus every knee should bow, in heaven and on earth and under the earth, and every tongue confess that Jesus Christ is Lord, to the glory of God the Father." In Isaiah the confession reads, "The Lord is my righteousness and strength." As paraphrased by Paul—in a way that sees redemption as accomplished—that means, "Jesus Christ is Lord, to the glory of God the Father." Into whose mouth does Paul put that confession? Who is to avow it on bended knee? To the announcement that Isaiah hears—"To me every knee shall bow"—Paul adds an explanation to bring out the scope and extent of the event foretold. What unknown struggles and hardships the apostle must have been through! What secret connections, what threads running both upward and downward from earth, he must have experienced! What wishes and hopes he must have cherished to feel the need to thus expand on Isaiah's utterance! And in what way does he imagine that stupendous homage to take place, which all in heaven, on earth, and under the earth render to their king Jesus Christ? Afterward, is each throng to return to its respective place? If upward, that is conceivable, but downward as well?

To be sure, throughout this passage it is on the words "at the name of Jesus" that the main emphasis rests; nothing whatever will be of any avail for a soul's salvation but bowing before Jesus and confessing his name. On the other hand, it is noticeable how immensely wide are the circles to which Paul wants to proclaim the possibility of salvation. Now if there is a well-founded hope in the kingdom of heaven that the Lord's servants will rejoice one day in a harvest of undreamt-of magnitude, I do not find it hard to understand that in the Bible that hope is expressed in a very subdued manner—in a whisper, so to speak. What the Scripture brings home to us sinful, impudent, and stiff-necked men most loudly is the prospect nearest at hand—God's righteous judgment in all its grim earnestness. Nevertheless, only the above hope, so deeply anchored in the nature of the Savior as God's own Son, can give us full light on the work he is called to do. Indeed, that hope alone fully entitles us to believe in our own salvation, and it does find undeniable expression in prominent scriptural passages. One passage in particular has become important to me: "For in him all the fullness of God, by his own choice, came to dwell. Through him God chose to reconcile to himself all things, whether on earth or in heaven, by making peace through the shedding of his blood upon the cross" (Col 1:19–20). I am inclined to think with von Hofmann that "by the Lord Jesus' own choice" is meant, rather than "by God's own choice," as is usually assumed.[2] It makes no great difference, but the first interpretation does make it easier to understand the expression "all the fullness." The "fullness" would then include everything represented in verse 16 as "created in him," nothing less than "all things in heaven and on earth, visible and invisible, whether thrones or dominions or principalities or powers," that is, the whole spiritual world, whether it remained in him or turned away from him and against God. His longing is that everything might again come to dwell in him and be reconciled by him.[3]

The Bible passage known to express that hope most clearly is 1 Timothy 2:4–6: "God wants *all men* to be saved and to come to a knowledge of the truth. For there is one God and one mediator between God and men, the man Christ Jesus, who gave himself as a ransom for *all* men." Let us also think of 1 John 2:2: "Christ is the atoning sacrifice for our sins, and not only for ours but also for the sins of *the whole world*." Finally, there is the Lord's high-priestly prayer (John 17), where he asks the Father for all glory to be given him for the sake of his own, so that

2. Editors Note: The von Hofmann referred to here is J. C. K. von Hofmann (1810–1877), the leading representative of what eventually came to be called the Erlangen school or "mediating theology", a school of theology which, true to its name, sought to bring together multiple strands or schools of thought to form a mediating position.

3. I may be permitted to call to mind here the prophecy in Ezekiel 16:53, "I shall restore the fortunes of Sodom" and "Sodom with her daughters will return" (16:55), as well as Keil's fine discussion of that passage in his commentary. Keil also refers to the words of Jesus (which Blumhardt, too, found very important) that on the day of judgment it will be more bearable for Sodom than for Capernaum and concludes: "All pre-Christian judgments are not the final decision, a condemnation forever. Rather, they leave open the possibility of a later reprieve." Keil therefore conjectures that what is said in 1 Peter 3:12 and in 4:6 about a sermon preached to the victims of the Flood applies, according to the prophecy in Ezekiel, to the Sodomites too, and it may be assumed "also to all heathen peoples that either lived before Christ or otherwise departed this life without having heard of Christ." To be sure, Blumhardt, as far as I know, did not go so far as to regard the preaching of such a sermon in the afterlife as something to count on. For him the only legitimate soil for any further developments in the kingdom of God was the church of Christ here on earth. However, Keil and Blumhardt agree in neither discarding such prophecies as incompatible with received dogmas nor mistaking them for the false doctrine of restitution. [Editors' note: The Keil referred to here is Carl Friedrich Keil (1807–1888), a leading Old Testament scholar in the nineteenth century who with Franz Delitzsch (1813–1890), oversaw the publication of the multivolume *Commentary on the Old Testament*.]

the world may believe and know that the Father has sent him—in other words, that it *cease* being the world.

In Holy Scripture Blumhardt thus found expressed what his own experiences had dimly hinted at—expressed in a way that his misgivings about the doctrine of the restoration of all things could find no fault with. For one thing, he came to see all the Savior does as the free, un-coerced action of him to whom the Father has handed over judgment. For another, the limit of the Savior's all-embracing mercy—the willing-ness or unwillingness of the creature—was not done away with. "Jesus Christ has to be accepted as king; who is unwilling may have to face the abyss"—that statement defines Blumhardt's view.

In the light of these hopes Christ's incarnation and especially his crucifixion became more and more important to Blumhardt. Redemption is Jesus' way of "avenging" himself on all his enemies. All conceivable malice, from the invisible world as well, has been poured out on him, making itself guilty toward him; he has a right to avenge himself, and his vengeance is—forgiveness and redemption.

But it was not in a detached, contemplative way that this recog-nition lived in Blumhardt. The great developments his inner eye saw unfolding fairly made his heart burst with joy, longing, and hope. To conclude, let us hear what he had to say, at the end of 1878 or 1879, on the passage Isaiah 40:27–31, in particular about the words, "Those who wait on the Lord":

> To begin with, those who wait on the Lord bring it about that, very quietly and out of sight, our loving God does an immense amount of work. Down in the deepest, most hidden depths the eternal One is at work, all unnoticed by men, and what he does is so many-sided, great, and wonderful that, if our eyes were opened, we would be truly amazed.
>
> I have the impression that the last years, including the one now past, were years of grace in humankind's history—years to be remembered in eternity because of all that the Lord, through the waiting of "those who wait on the Lord," has secretly accom-plished with a view to the redemption to come. Don't believe it when you hear that the past year was again a year when very little happened and that things simply drag on in the same wretched old way. To be sure, on the surface it may almost look as if there were no God in heaven; however, no one is able to peer into the depths, and for the time being God doesn't *want* anyone to look into them either. But when we expect something to come—a new

time, a time of redemption, we mustn't think that it could simply come overnight, without any preparation. Still, until it actually breaks in on us, no human intellect could possibly grasp the amount of spadework our loving God has done in this past year in response to the groaning of all creation. If we knew everything God's wondrous hand has wrought in secret, we could perhaps—indeed, certainly—conclude this year with deep satisfaction.

All I want to say right now is: Believe in an eternal God in heaven who does an immense number of wonderful deeds in secret. It is written that he never wearies, that is: He needs no day of rest to strengthen and prepare himself for further labors and efforts the way we do. He just goes on working. Even when everything is at rest on the surface, he does *not* rest.

And our Lord Jesus Christ has exalted himself to God's right hand and governs until he has made all his enemies his footstool. Are you aware how he does it? Does it ever enter your mind? Or do you think that God would let you see how the Lord Jesus overcomes one enemy after the other, how he topples one principality and dominion of darkness after the other, and more and more brings all creatures in heaven and on earth to the point of confessing that Jesus Christ is the Lord, to the glory of God the Father? Or, just because you do not notice it happening, should it be written in vain, "He must reign till he has put all enemies under his feet" (1 Cor 15:25)?

To be sure, it also means that we must wait and that we implore, "Lord, up and arise! Lord, save us from our adversary!" This pleading is what matters; it rises up to God from many hearts these days, not least from us in our house too. Do you think those pleas just pass by God's countenance without leaving a trace, without meaning anything to him? Never! In response to those pleas he takes action! I am firmly convinced he has taken action and will do so. Suddenly, sooner or later, it will break in on us! Let us wait on the Lord, even when we see nothing. He goes on working like an army sapper, undermining the whole bulwark of Darkness until one day light will break in and God's glory be made manifest over Israel, which is now still in such misery and moans so pitifully. Suddenly it will see the light of day! May we cheerfully let our God go on laboring, sapping, and conquering. All at once his work will stand revealed, so that the whole creation will shout for joy at the greatness of its God. By restoring his creation he will wax even greater than he did by calling it into being with the command, "Let there be!"

26

Death

WE ARE NOW APPROACHING the end of this rich life—an end Blumhardt did not expect: his death. The wonderful time he was expecting was so close to him; he could already see it drawing so near that he really hoped to experience it. In his last years the yearning for it very nearly burst his heart. During the second half of the year 1879 he was in an increasingly elevated mood. His heart urged him to hymn the Lord's praise for the victories gained by His kingdom—victories Blumhardt regarded as already achieved or as imminent. Earlier on that mood had led him to set to music the victory song of Revelation 12, "Now the salvation and strength and the reign and the might of our God and of his Christ have come." He now busied himself in a similar way with the Magnificat, the song of the virgin Mary, in which he had once before, after the memorable victory in his Möttlingen struggle, poured out his gratitude. Exactly thirty-six years later, at Christmas 1879, he was able to listen to his own melodious setting of the Magnificat, deeply moved and secretly filled with feelings of victory much like those of that earlier time.

However, this Christmastide represented a high point and was followed by visible physical decline, even though Blumhardt himself would not admit to it. In the preceding Advent weeks he had been specially alert and elated inwardly. His son Theophil tells:

> Almost always, also when we relaxed with him in a familiar circle after dinner or in the evening, the conversation would turn either to some difficult Bible passage or to other spiritual subjects. Whenever it did *not* come to such an exchange, he felt dissatisfied

and would rather snooze quietly in his seat, while the company around him talked about outward matters. But as soon as the conversation returned to something of an inward nature, he would at once be all there again. Many friends who visited us recently can testify to the rich spiritual harvest to be garnered during those hours in the "smoke room," as he called it. Original thoughts kept gushing forth. Like so many lights they would illuminate much that seemed obscure and enigmatic. In particular the scriptural promises with their great hopes came up again and again, keeping his spirit fresh and lively and always providing it with new nourishment.

Death, the power from whose clutches, at Blumhardt's pleading, the Lord had snatched many a premature prey, was announcing its approach. To be sure, it was not the first time. For some years his body, grown very heavy and cumbersome, had been afflicted with ailments that made one wonder how he could remain so active and sprightly. He had, however, experienced such great things in his household as well as with others that he met any new assaults on his health with defiant valor and disregard. We must not find fault with him and his circle for a certain belligerent attitude toward death. How many graves in the cemetery of Bad Boll, e.g., those of Gottliebin, Julius Brodersen, Mina Braun, Nathanael's little son, and others are reminders of a fierce struggle for the life of each of those dear ones. Such struggles were always seen and waged within the context of the whole of life. Even though ending in outward defeat, they would each time afford hopeful glimpses of an ultimate victory. Hence, as mentioned, Blumhardt paid little—too little—heed to a fresh ailment—a cough of varying severity, which kept attacking him.

It is said to be a weakness of the elderly that they will not be talked into something. That applied to Blumhardt whenever he was expected to take it easy. There was nothing to be done against his firm determination to, say, go on holding the worship services himself. Thus he increasingly wore himself out but at the same time grew more and more active and industrious. His activity extended now to an area into which he had scarcely ventured before: With the help of a girl from his household he set out to examine and put in order everything in the way of books, writings, letters, etc. there was in his two studies. Cabinets containing letters and other documents accumulated over many years were gone through from top to bottom; all the contents were looked at and sorted out so that nothing would be left in disarray. "I must hurry to get it done," he often remarked, yet at the same time he remained most agreeably calm, serene, and genial, so that there seemed to be no reason for concern.

The approach of death was the last thing he would talk about; against the ominous cough he put up a valiant fight. Though he was apt to say, "I have the feeling that death is after me," he showed no signs of anxiety or worry that death might actually get the better of him. Rather, almost to the very end he expressed the hope that he might yet experience an approaching universal change for the better, though he often added, "If not I, then at least you."

After his death, it was wistfully touching to see that room, usually giving such a studious impression, so completely changed, that is, with everything in apple-pie order. What was behind that endeavor? Blumhardt was firmly convinced that he had completed the great task of his life and also that grave and possibly portentous events would come upon us in the very near future. He spoke in a very definite way of an imminent great shock that would hit everybody, including us, and had to be seen as the first sign of a new time. Once he said very seriously to one of his sons, "In the end it may be we who get hit the hardest." Yet, though he often expressed that foreboding, it did not grieve him at all, for he saw it as a step forward in the Lord's cause, to be followed by mercy. In a morning devotion he said, "You might feel scared, but don't let it frighten you, and remain of good cheer; it will be a shock, but wrapped up in it will be sheer grace. The shock will pass, but grace abides." He wished to be ready and prepared, the precious servant of the Lord. He wanted his Lord to find him not asleep and in disarray but awake and in readiness.

While thus engaged in setting things in order, he still continued his work of putting scriptural thoughts into verse. In particular, he very secretly put a series of expositions of important biblical passages into verse, hoping to one day surprise with it his two sons in the ministry. At the point where the pen was taken from his hand stands the stanza:

> Write this: Blest are the departed
> Who died trusting in the Lord.
> They, the faithful and wholehearted,
> Have passed on to their reward.
> From their labors now at rest,
> They shall evermore be blest.
> All their good deeds follow after
> To where Christ turns tears to laughter.

While thus "waiting and pressing forward," Blumhardt retained a lively concern for all who entered the house, as his son Theophil tells. He went out of his way to do good to everybody with friendly converse and would listen most sympathetically to all he met, even a beggar. In his very last days he still made many, indeed all who came close to him, happy by this kindness, which was truly illumined from heaven and rested on his countenance like rays of the sun. Persons who saw him and talked to him for just a few hours were so deeply impressed that they felt inwardly shattered by the tranquil power of his kindliness.

He also became increasingly punctual and meticulous in praying for those committed to him for intercession. More conscientiously than ever he noted on bits of paper the names of patients who had announced their coming, so that in the course of the day he and his sons could repeatedly bring them in prayer before the Lord. Requests for help, which kept arriving daily by telegram even from quite distant places, were always answered at once by a telegram conveying words of comfort. Often enough—toward the end almost regularly—the telegraph would presently also bring news of help received. One could only marvel at his eagerness to care for troubled souls, his sympathy for the sick, and his burning longing to obtain help for those entrusted to him for intercession.

However much he overcame himself, during the first weeks of the New Year his strength noticeably gave way under the attacks of his illness. On Sunday, February 15, 1880, a general day of repentance in the Protestant church of Württemberg, he preached in his beloved chapel his last sermon, basing it on the prescribed text: "My heart says to thee: Thou hast said, 'Seek ye my face!' Therefore thy face, Lord, do I seek" (Ps 27:8–9). He had also arranged for the Lord's Supper to be celebrated on this day, which was unusual. Both the sermon (published in the *Predigt-Blätter*, 1880) and the Lord's Supper celebration stood under such a blessing that Blumhardt afterward spoke again and again of how the Savior's special nearness had been felt.

The following week was a hard one. On Thursday he still worked until two o'clock in the morning on an exposition of Christ's footwashing for the Stuttgart Sunday paper, but in that night his illness took a very serious turn. On Saturday he developed pneumonia, but he still insisted on holding his beloved Saturday evening meeting, speaking on Psalm 46:2: "God is our refuge and strength, an ever present help in trouble." Though quite exhausted, he spoke very movingly and was able to finish his talk, but it soon became clear that he had gone beyond his strength. He was gripped by fever and from then on was a sick man struggling with death. He continued to live in his hopes. He would pray, "Thy kingdom come" or call out, "The Lord will lead his cause to a glorious end." A concern that had moved his heart deeply during the last years came very much to the fore in his brief prayers: that no one be lost and that a divine wrath blocking the way pass by. "Mercy, mercy!" he would implore, for himself and for those others. Once, when his sons entered the room, he raised himself from the chair with his last strength and cried, "The Lord will open his mild hand in mercy over all nations."

On the day he died—Wednesday, February 25, 1880—he lay on his bed as though fixed to it by his physical heaviness; there being no way of easing his position. In the course of a brief conversation on the struggle his life had been, his son Christoph said, "Papa, there is victory." Blumhardt replied, "I bless you for victory." With a last effort he laid his hand on Christoph's and afterward also on Theophil's head. At ten o'clock in the evening he still accepted a spoonful of wine but declined a second one. Then he passed into eternity.

During that whole time his wife had been so dangerously ill that she had to lie in a room at some distance from his own. Thus the two who had stood so faithfully by one another throughout their lives could not see each other during these serious days of parting. It was symbolic of the many renunciations that had been demanded of them in their family life.

The funeral took place on Saturday, February 28. The church service was conducted by the local minister, Pastor Schmid, who traced in delicate outlines the picture of the deceased. Others who spoke by the coffin were, as it happened, representative of the various circles hardest hit by this loss. Möttlingen was represented by the rector, Pastor Bunz; the Württemberg circles of believers, by Pastor Theurer, town minister of Stuttgart; the friends of Bad Boll, by me; the family, by Christoph Blumhardt. Blumhardt's song, "Jesus is victorious king" was sung; then the men from Möttlingen carried the coffin to the burial place, followed by children bearing palm branches.

27

Epilogue

A S WE STAND BY Blumhardt's grave, we once more survey his full life. All his friends testified that he was a man of *love*. That was what the friends of his younger years had said of him, and the last thirty-five years of his life attested to it in an amazing way. The present book actually gives but an inadequate impression of the tireless way he gave himself for others by day and night throughout that long time. Many who for weighty reasons despaired of themselves, were raised up again by the sheer power of his love. And how faithfully and meticulously was his intercessory love at work, continuing through decades and embracing children and children's children! This love sprang from a character that was absolutely true, as though woven of one and the same material throughout. Many a great man loses considerably in stature when experienced at close quarters. In Blumhardt's case, however, precisely those in a position to observe his life by day and night held him in such high regard as might hardly be understood if put into words.

But if what shone *out* from him, was mainly his love, that which above all shone *within* him was his *faith*. When a visitor told Gossner of blessed memory that he had just come from Blumhardt, Gossner replied, "From Blumhardt? That man has faith!" How humble, childlike, but at the same time how unrelenting was his faith! We know of the blessings it brought to others, but it also bore rich fruit for *him*—in particular the fruit of continual inner rejuvenation. Consider the transformations we have been able to observe in him—from the Schönthal student to the curate in Dürrmenz and assistant minister in Iptingen, then the fighting hero, the revival preacher, and finally the amiable housefather of Bad Boll. And how youthful he was even in his old age!

However, *hope* is the attribute for which his name may well be inscribed in heaven. After getting to know Blumhardt, not a few must have confessed, "Until now I thought I had love and faith, but only now do I see what real love and faith are." As regards hope, however, in the sense of a heart-lifting expectancy embracing all men and the whole of life, the same people might well discover they had not had the slightest trace of that before—not even a surrogate. After Blumhardt's death, he received praise from all sides for his faith and love, but his expectancy and hope was on the whole discreetly ignored. Yet, as we saw, it arose by an inner necessity from his faith and love, because both were directed to the universal.

There is a certain great man of our days who, constrained by his responsibilities as a ruler to apply Christian thinking to universal needs and the human condition as a whole, has left his name indelibly inscribed in the annals of history even while well advanced in years. In a popular girls' album of the year 1880 this man, in his own handwriting, laid the following motto on the heart of Germany's young people: In faith there is hope. No other word I know describes more fittingly the solid basis of Blumhardt's expectant attitude.

We should also remember that his expectancy was being fed by constant new experiences of the Lord's help. He was firmly convinced that these took place also for his own sake, to strengthen and reassure him. He saw them as friendly greetings, telling him from on high, "Just carry on! Keep on hoping! You are on the right track."

As can happen to any expectant man, however right and justified his hopes, Blumhardt was time and again mistaken as to the "when?" Understandably that did not discourage him. It may, however, provide a little justification for those of us who, to say the least, did not keep up with his soaring hopes. Mostly because of his solitary stand, maybe also as a result of physical exhaustion, toward the end Blumhardt's expectancy almost became a weakness—an impatience like that of a child crying for food. His heart just about burst with yearning and waiting, nourished on the one hand by the widespread distress, which lay heavy upon him, on the other hand and still far more by the radiant glory of what he saw approaching. These circumstances may perhaps give us a glimpse of the inner meaning of his passing. He worked himself into such an over-readiness—one might almost call it pushiness—that inevitably a wearying tension went out from him. And yet we know that whatever goes on in God's kingdom is of a spiritual, organic nature; hence it requires spirit, and therefore freedom, on the part of those involved and, just because of that, in one way also quiet and tranquility. So we who share Blumhardt's hopes may feel reassured by the knowledge that (as one letter of condolence puts it very fittingly) he is now no longer one of the expectant but one of the expected—that is, one of the throng of blessed souls and angels who will come with the Lord.

I am pleased to quote some excerpts from letters of condolence sent by other friends of Blumhardt. From a seaside town someone writes:

> Blumhardt was a sun among men—a sun that sent its kindly rays from Bad Boll far out into all lands. Wherever his influence made itself felt, his words of comfort carried light and peace into darkness and gloom. Just as all people are gladdened and enlivened by the sun, so Blumhardt's countenance was transfigured by the reflection of a spiritual and heavenly light. All that came to Bad Boll and were responsive to things divine rejoiced in it.

From a hilltop mansion of the aristocracy came the lament:

> Though I find myself far away and very low indeed, I still have to write. My heart is too full, and I feel like crying, "My father, my father! The chariots of Israel and its horsemen!" The faithful father has departed; the poor, suffering people's wall of prayer is gone; the crown has been snatched off your head, and blessed Boll has lost its center.

From the Cape of Good Hope an English archdeacon, who in his youth had been a guest in the Möttlingen rectory, wrote as follows:

> Mourning is sure to spread to all parts of the world, for he was known everywhere, not only because of his zealous missionary labors but also through the far-flung tidings of his work of faith. He did much for those around him and for his fatherland, but beyond that for the whole Christian world. He waged the struggle of faith against Satan, and the spirit filling him has surely been passed on to others also. Through him the whole fighting host of the faithful has, in part maybe unknowingly, been revitalized.

With surprising unanimity one thought recurs in most of the letters of condolence: Bad Boll remains what it is, a refuge for troubled souls in search of help. The thought, "Elijah's mantle has remained behind" is expressed again and again. That might seem strange to those not in close touch with Bad Boll, since God's kingdom knows no spiritual dynasties. But any reader of our "History of the House" and any visitor to Bad Boll during the last years will take such a continuity almost for granted. Because of Blumhardt's inner need for community he gradually evolved into something like a collective entity, in the sense that his wife and the small, quiet circle around him had grown to be one with him in his work. As we saw, his son Theophil had long acted as the father's spokesman among the reading public, while Christoph was his right-hand man in the Bad Boll household. When people spoke of the study they were so happy to visit, in the last years that almost referred more to Christoph's study than to his father's. For some time Christoph had also taken over the larger part of his father's correspondence. And in the same spirit in which his sons had thus worked as their father's assistants, they have gone on working. Blumhardt's family has been allowed to experience in rich measure the faithfulness of God, who has continued to shed blessings on their house, just as he did when the father was alive. To be sure, one misses at table the radiant figure of the Spirit-filled, highly cultured man, in whom everyone could sense the great things he had experienced. Thus, for those who wanted to get to know an interesting personality the great attraction is gone. Nevertheless, God has remained visibly close to the orphaned house. The Lord's blessed power to do good in body, soul, and spirit to those seeking help is active in Bad Boll to this day—if anything, more than before.

Today (Palm Sunday), as I put the finishing touches to this fourth edition, the above description of present-day Bad Boll still applies unchanged. In the meantime Theophil Blumhardt has become the rector in the village of Boll, while Christoph remains in sole charge of the household church in Bad Boll. In this way, Blumhardt's blessed twofold field of activity in Möttlingen—parish church and house church—has now been divided among his two minister sons.

In Hebrews 13:7–8 we are exhorted to consider, when remembering departed people of God, that the actual core and content of their being, Jesus Christ, remains with us, since he is the same yesterday and today and forever. That has been the experience also of our dear friends in Bad Boll.

I do think that in the life we have been considering, Jesus Christ has come to meet us in manifold ways and has let us see in a new light who he was, who he is, and who he will be. That was what Blumhardt gave his life to; it was what a hand from on high had intended it for. He was allowed to contribute greatly to the glorification of Jesus Christ, the Redeemer of the world for the salvation of the lost. When I concluded the first edition, I did so with the watchword for that day, "May the whole earth be filled with His glory. Amen and amen" (Ps 72:19). Blumhardt's life will continue to serve that goal and do its part in hastening on its fulfillment.

Scripture Index

Old Testament

Genesis
1:1	444
2:16	352
16	272
32:10	444

Exodus
10:26	9
15:26	244

Judges
6:13	260

1 Samuel
14:6	255, 325
17:24	136
17:28	140
17:46	137

Job
1:6	470
1:7	470
42:11	364

Psalms
2:11	63
6	77
14	260
18:3	228
19:7	451
19:8	457
22:3	330
22:23	330
25:3	451
25:16	448
27:8–9	523
32:1–4	172
32:3–5	192, 197
34:8	448
39:9	55
42:5	55–56
46:2	523
53	260
57:5–12	77
62:6–8	492
72:19	529
73:14	344
77:4–11	260
77:5	263
77:11	163
80	56
85:1	446
103	102
103:9	260
110:1	146
112:4	105
130	378
130:1–4	68
131	52
145:9	515
150:6	515

Proverbs
21:1	114
21:25	411

Isaiah

25:1   315
25:6–9 298, 315
25:7   297
25:8   316
25:8–9 319
40   273
40:1–11 378
40:3   269
40:5   269
40:27–31 518
44:1–5 298, 320
44:22–25 515
44:22   420
45:23–24 450
53:9   105
54:1ff 273
54:1   272
54:2–8 273
54:17   227
60:22   278
64:1   378

Jeremiah

9:1   258
3:25   142
23:5–6 449

Lamentations

3:58   452

Ezekiel

16:53   517
34   336
36:11   271
36:26   271
40–47   276

Daniel

7:18   506

Hosea

14:2   443
14:4   447

Joel

2:28   252, 317
2:28–32 263

2:31   269
2:32   269, 514

Micah

7:18–20 274

Habakkuk

2:3–4   141

Zechariah

8:13   271
8:23   173

Ecclesiasticus

2:1–8   136

New Testament

Matthew

5:3   443
5:14–16 308
5:43–48 46
5:45   257
5:46–47 48
6:7   231
6:9–13 313
6:21   445
7:11   202
7:13   289
7:15–16 453
9:1–8   238–45
9:35—10:1 258
10:20   266
11:3   185
11:6   185
11:25   231
12:32   145, 148
16:13   329
16:18   134, 145
16:19–20 200
16:19   190, 201
17:21   235
18:18   177, 190, 195, 201
21:29   431
24   277
24:14   113
24:21   276

24:24	280, 307
24:34	278
28:19	196
28:20	316

Mark

9:29	235
11:14	105
13:20	302
13:32	278

Luke

1:11–13	299
2:22–40	261
2:22–35	260
2:31–32	261
2:46–55	160
5:1–9	279
5:10	280
8:27–30	132
10:21	32
10:23–35	28–32
11:5–8	235
11:9–10	235
11:14–28	488ff
11:14	492
11:16	489
11:19	489
11:20	489
12:32	298, 506
12:35	289, 290, 302
13:3,5	365
13:16	470
16:23	145
16:26	142
18:1–8	236, 253
18:2–8	93
18:1	313
18:2	253
18:3	506
18:8	253, 323ff., 506
18:9	324
19:1–9	209
21:29–31	289
24:36	109

John

1:12	46
4:1–2	196
4:23–24	257
4:37–38	325
6:51–58	316
8:34	200
9:3	233
11:1–44	293
11:32–45	65
12:25	306
12:32	515
13:8	450
14:12	299
14:15–21	392
15:11	325
16:8	267
16:11	201, 291
16:24	445
17	517
17:22	292
19:26–27	160
20:21–23	195, 199
20:23	176, 190, 196, 243
20:25	251
21:11	279, 280

Acts

2:7	43, 174
2:16–21	263
2:21	514
2:16	268
2:38	267
2:39	267
3:10	174
3:19–20	289
5:11	174
8:14–17	267
10:38	257
10:44–48	187
11:21	5:15
19:14–16	216

Romans

8:19–23	145

1 Corinthians

4:20	204
6:11	196
7:23	473
7:31	354
9:27	480

1 Corinthians (*continued*)
10:14   470
11:30   199
13   71
15:21   292
15:25–26   250
15:25   251, 519
15:26   290
15:51–58   509
15:52–53   290
15:55   290

2 Corinthians
4:4   145, 291
5:20   234
8:23   418
12:8–9   471
12:8   232
12:17   470

Galatians
3:3   138, 345
3:13–14   266
3:26   345
3:29   272
4:22–31   272
4:24   272
4:29   273
6:7–8   345

Ephesians
1:18   22
2:2   145
3:19   250
4:28   173
6:7   368
6:13   136

Philippians
2:9–12   516
2:10   333
4:5   311

Colossians
1:13   200
1:19–20   517
2:15   297
2:16   367

1 Thessalonians
4:17   314

2 Thessalonians
2:11–12   307

1 Timothy
1:15   255
1:18   325
2:4–6   517
2:4   499

2 Timothy
2:3   64

Hebrews
2:14   292
6:5   145
8:11   394
10:13   251
12:4   480
12:6   471
13:7–8   528
13:8   259

James
1:6   235
2:16   235, 365
2:23   470
5:14   477
5:16   196, 478
5:17   478

1 Peter
1:5   290
1:7, 9   290
2:5   115
3:12   517
3:15–16   381
4:6   517
5:6   478

2 Peter
3:9   250, 281ff

1 John
1:9   193, 196
2:2   517

2:17	5
2:19	267
2:20	267
3:8	452
3:18	344

Revelation

1:14	448
1:16	446
3:7–8	162
3:12	115
3:17	237
3:20	129
7:9–14	515
12	520
12:10–12	511
13:10	471
14:12	231
21:5	445
21:6	452

Subject Index

Advent, 302ff., 501–2, 514
angel(s), 224, 259, 278, 299ff., 320, 335, 444
Apostolic age, apostles, xiii, 12, 128, 146, 158, 188, 196–97, 234, 237, 246, 252–69, 277, 280, 298–99, 309, 322, 455, 470, 479, 489
Arndt, Johann, 251
authority, spiritual, 93, 162, 171, 189–90, 194, 199–201, 242–43, 250, 258–59, 394, 454–55, 513–14

Bad Boll, xii, 173, 256, 333, 388–92, 405ff., 439ff
household, 409, 412ff., 419, 435
healings, 455ff., 481, 484–86
guests, 434ff., 455, 484
baptism, 196–97, 267–68, 320
Barth, Dr. Christian Gottlob, 11, 18, 38, 44, 59, 80–82, 95–100, 101–11, 115, 120, 153, 158, 166–68, 200, 207, 424
Basel Mission Society, 6, 9, 15, 35, 36–37, 41, 45, 101, 179, 184
Beatitudes, 41, 310
Bengel, J. A., 3–6
Bernese Evangelical Society, 42
Bible, 11–12, 36, 38–40, 45, 96, 102, 109, 132, 142, 144, 160, 198–99, 202, 230, 245, 248, 257, 276, 327, 351, 374, 377, 409, 418, 430, 437, 442–43, 453, 474, 478, 479, 487, 498, 502, 510, 520
Black Forest, xi, 91, 170, 179, 385, 496

Blätter aus Bad Boll, 132, 262, 263, 297, 345, 347, 363, 366, 369, 458
Blumhardt, Johann Georg, 9, 120
Christian Gottlieb, 9, 10, 37
Christoph Friedrich, ix, 11, 12, 401, 419–20, 432–34, 482–83, 524, 528
Karl, 35, 38, 44
Theophil, 432–34, 443, 503, 520, 524, 528
Brodersen, Gottlieben. See Dittus, Gottlieben
Brodersen, Theodor, 415, 434
Brunn, Nikolaus von, 37, 39

Calw, festival, 179–81, 495–98
Calw Publishing Association, 11, 33, 97, 100, 110–16, 380
Catholic Church, 189–91, 217, 286, 431
children, 28, 40, 61–62, 68, 78–80, 85, 108, 168–69, 182–86, 300, 328, 331, 332, 347–50, 431, 434–35, 465, 468, 471, 487
Christendom, 4, 252, 255–56, 266, 270–82, 303, 318, 370, 431, 479
Christliche Volksbote aus Basel, 180
Christ-Sarasin, Adolf, 37, 179–80, 186
Church, 93, 102, 213, 234–35, 253, 256, 259, 263, 266, 280, 286–87, 291–92, 335, 338, 369–70, 377, 505
confession of sin, 121, 163, 171, 181, 188–98, 204, 337
confirmation class, 55, 74, 78–79, 98, 109, 159–60, 167–68, 200

conscience, 59, 74, 130, 158, 163–75,
    183–95, 206, 227, 230, 238, 240,
    352–54, 366–70, 407, 423–25,
    426, 429, 436, 469, 492
conversion, 34, 35, 44, 99, 147, 173,
    175, 176–77, 209, 244–45, 287,
    346, 425, 427–29
correspondence, xii, 52ff., 104, 108,
    154–56, 168, 203, 341, 352,
    371–72, 419, 431–32, 545, 458,
    460–63, 468ff., 481, 491, 494,
    521, 528
cross, 61, 252, 283, 509, 516–17
counseling. *See* pastoral care

darkness. *See* evil
dead, spirits of the, 124, 132–34, 143–
    46, 293, 313, 472, 474
demon(s), demonic power, 94, 119,
    127, 132–36, 138, 140–43, 151,
    153, 216, 234–35, 248, 258, 283,
    297, 318, 472, 482, 488–92
depression, 210, 458, 469, 472
devil. *See* Satan
Dieterlen, Christoph, 202–3, 224, 391,
    425, 429, 431, 479
Dittus, Gottliebin, xii, 98, 117ff., 159,
    207, 219, 226, 231, 293, 373–76,
    388–90, 400, 412–16 418–24,
    457, 491, 512–13
    Andreas, 120, 412
    Johann Georg (Hans), 120, 125, 153,
        161–65, 210–12, 218, 220, 228,
        376, 412
    Katharina, 120, 150–53, 376, 412
Dürrmenz, 33ff., 52–54, 82–83, 178

Easter, 94, 182, 208, 217, 357, 374
education, 13–14, 329–31, 349ff.,
    431–32
emotionalism, 3–4, 172, 192, 198, 335,
    360, 467
eschatology. *See* Last Days
eternity, 120, 141, 416, 464, 467, 468
evil, 27, 74–75, 99, 134, 138, 145, 148,
    156, 180, 230, 232, 249, 257, 266–
    67, 275, 312–17, 376, 449, 489
Evil One. *See* Satan

faith, 11, 28, 30–31, 39, 46, 95, 128,
    138–39, 148–50, 176, 207, 215,
    225, 230–35, 242, 250–51,
    253–54, 284, 296–97 311–15,
    323–25, 345–46, 364, 417,
    427–29, 445, 448, 451, 470–72,
    491–92, 506, 526
Final Tribulation. *See* Last Days
forgiveness of sin, 68, 144–46, 166,
    171, 176, 194, 197, 204, 240–45,
    248–49, 256, 450
    absolution, 161–63, 171, 177–78,
        187, 190, 193, 196–99, 201, 204,
        217, 224, 513
    laying on of hands, 161–62, 178,
        181, 183, 199, 205, 219, 486
freedom, spiritual, 23, 177, 181, 201,
    243, 282, 284, 348, 351, 367,
    432, 473, 527

God
    God's love, 47–49, 71, 160, 249–50,
        256, 260, 295, 297, 329, 447,
        463–64, 492, 513
    judgment, 42, 94, 120, 141, 145–46,
        149, 159, 192, 249, 254–55, 264,
        307, 325, 365, 447–48, 471–72,
        515–18
    promises, 44, 102, 128, 139, 149,
        190, 200, 235, 243, 263–75,
        278–79, 281–82, 302–3, 314,
        317–18, 393, 395, 409, 428–29,
        451, 514–15
Goethe, Johann Wolfgang von, 15, 96,
    202, 423, 425
government authority, 217, 369–70
Gross, 95, 120, 166–67, 183, 200
Gundert, Hermann Dr., 11, 33, 42,
    496,

*Handbuch für Missionsgeschichte und
    Missionsgeographie*, 110, 113–15
*Handbüchlein für Weltgeschichte für
    Schulen und Familien*, 112, 115,
    501
Hauber, Dr. von, 15, 25, 111–12
healing(s), xii, 75, 132, 150, 176, 178,
    184, 205–7, 208, 210–16, 221–
    23, 224, 259, 334, 348, 352, 371,

healing(s) (*continued*)
    407, 415, 427–28, 439, 455, 462,
    477, 484, 485–86
Hegel, Georg Wilhelm Friedrich, 3,
    15, 23
history, 4–5, 31, 64, 97, 110, 112–15,
    194, 250, 277, 291–92, 296, 320,
    501
Hofacker, Wilhelm, 92, 228–29
Hoffmann, Wilhelm, 7–8, 15–16, 18–
    19, 22–24, 35, 37, 92, 159
holidays, religious, 355–61, 367–68
Holy Spirit, 83, 138, 176, 195, 218,
    282–85, 288, 317, 338, 345,
    392ff., 426, 440
    outpouring of, xi, 167, 179, 181,
        252–53, 263–70, 298, 319ff, 428
    power of, 195, 199–200, 504
    prayer for, 62–63, 94–95, 102
    divine powers, 162, 176, 199, 234,
        263, 265, 268, 427, 476, 479–80
hope, xii, 27, 68, 97, 107, 113, 128,
    136, 145, 157, 167, 173–75,
    188, 203, 233–35, 246ff., 298,
    313–15, 325, 338, 341, 377, 388,
    411, 445–46, 451, 454, 478–80,
    490–93, 499, 502, 507–8, 512ff.,
    521–22, 524, 526–27
humility, 25, 27, 188, 336, 421–22
hymn(s), compositions, 13, 93–95, 98,
    111–12, 225–26, 228, 330–32,
    377–79, 440, 435, 459, 497,
    504–11, 520

illness. *See* sickness

Jesus Christ
    savior, 28, 53, 57, 65, 94, 134,
        136–37, 146, 154–55, 176, 178,
        190, 193, 195, 202, 204, 206–7,
        238, 240, 250, 255, 275, 284,
        287–88, 308–9, 313, 325–26,
        345–46, 368, 427–28, 446–53,
        456, 513–14, 518
    victor, 95, 112, 119, 126, 128, 146,
        149, 151, 160, 174, 225, 227–28,
        231, 246, 249–50, 289–93, 330,
        377, 423, 480, 490, 520, 524
    redeemer, 240, 244, 291, 312

helper/healer, 394, 461–62, 465–69,
    474, 483, 485, 489–92
    blood of, 75–76, 95, 148, 201, 233,
        245, 254, 314, 316, 318, 324,
        452, 480, 515
    second coming. *See* Last Days
    resurrection of, 283, 290–92, 313
joy, 70, 76–77, 107, 136–37, 168–69,
    182, 185–86, 262, 271ff., 298ff.,
    317, 319, 325–26, 345, 390, 440,
    445
Jugendblätter, 115

Kerner, Justinus, 25
Kingdom of God, xi, xiii, 5–7, 14, 50,
    112, 128, 145, 146, 158, 195,
    204, 205, 250–51, 258, 270, 275,
    291, 296, 311, 411, 422–23, 436,
    489–91, 517, 527
Knapp, Albert, 92, 111, 158, 186,
    217–18, 377
Köllner (Blumhardt), Doris, 45ff.,
    59ff., 105, 155, 228–29, 399, 401
Korntal community, 6–7, 17, 45, 92
Korntal, festival, 136, 495
Krankheit und Heilung, 439, 456

Last Days, 146, 263, 265, 269, 308
    time of grace, 70, 282
    second coming, 44, 112, 128–29,
        249–50, 253, 262, 269, 275,
        277–78, 281ff., 303–13, 325,
        377, 444, 446, 450
law, 28, 32, 272, 299, 359, 367, 451,
    509
legalism. *See* law
Lord's Supper or Eucharist, 67, 69, 78,
    171, 175, 194, 199, 469, 523
Luther, Martin, 22, 34–35, 189, 281–92

Machtolf, Gottlieb Friedrich, 92–93,
    95, 120, 166, 186, 200, 376
magic, 75, 120, 126, 138, 143, 147–48,
    151, 154, 206, 209, 376, 470, 489
medicine. *See* medical science
medical science, 219, 221–23, 234–35,
    373, 390–91, 408–9, 468, 476,
    485, 495

mental illness, 134, 153, 210, 212–14, 234–35, 351–52, 373, 379, 408–9, 413, 456, 460–61, 466

miracle(s), 75, 93, 125, 152, 175, 183–84, 188, 205ff., 246–48, 259, 283, 292, 296, 299, 334, 424, 428, 446, 455, 458–60, 477, 479–81

mission, 44, 64, 80, 83, 96–97, 110, 112, 115, 155, 180, 370, 495–98, 501, 527

Monatsblätter für die Missionsstuden, 110, 116

morning devotions, 173, 185, 192, 254, 323ff., 333, 345, 374, 423, 434–35, 440–43, 458, 496, 502

music, 13, 23, 111, 357, 510, 511

Oetinger, Friedrich Christoph, 3–6, 66

pastoral care, xii, 33, 53, 67, 75ff., 109, 127, 135, 202, 213, 224, 234, 328, 331, 334ff., 342, 351, 362, 388, 455, 512ff

patience, 47, 77, 164, 245, 294, 313–14, 460, 464, 470–72, 498

Pentecost, 199, 252, 280, 322, 337–38

Pietism, 3–4, 97, 216, 251

pietists, 53, 54, 106, 340

piety, false, 65–66, 174, 179, 202, 214, 255–57, 310, 344, 347, 390, 423, 440

poem, poetry, 41, 98, 293–96, 378, 416–18, 504–7, 509–10

prayer, xii, 13, 75, 105, 138–40, 160, 164, 210, 215, 216, 231, 234, 240–45, 250ff., 257, 292, 313–15, 324–25, 335, 339, 366, 395, 445, 448, 474

  answered, 20, 72, 102, 155, 165, 176, 183–84, 188, 206, 211, 215, 228, 237, 407, 456–57, 461, 476ff., 490–92

  Blumhardt's practice, 77, 79, 92, 93ff., 109, 125, 127, 130–31, 135, 143, 161, 187, 213, 231–32, 235, 333, 336–37, 351, 418, 420–21, 428–29, 435, 440, 442, 459, 468, 523–24

preaching, 75, 83, 99, 103, 108, 166, 175–76, 210, 247–48, 258–59, 328–29, 331, 334, 392, 426–28, 479, 487ff., 495

Predigt-Blätter aus Bad Boll, 261, 281, 492, 523

principalities and powers, 75, 117, 137, 162, 174, 217, 246, 248, 258, 283, 297, 479, 488–91, 517

prophecy, 141, 263–69, 273, 275, 315–19, 428, 517

Protestant church, 3, 6, 15, 50, 91, 96, 189–90, 198, 277, 281–82, 285–87, 345–46, 431, 501

Rapp, George, 50

Rapp, Maria Magdalena, 222

Reformation, 22, 35, 176, 189–90, 270, 279–89, 426

religion, 113, 191, 202, 281, 291

repentance, xi, 158ff., 216, 240–41, 243, 245, 256, 259, 281, 285, 336, 345, 386, 425, 427–30

resignation, false, 221ff., 231–33

resurrection, 283, 290–92

revival, 92, 126, 158ff., 163, 172, 178, 191, 260, 278, 338, 340

revolution of 1848, 109, 383, 384

Sabbath, 356, 367, 424, 502

Satan, 93–95, 125–27, 131, 135, 138, 141–51, 154–55, 181, 201, 206, 215, 227, 236, 246, 249, 292, 312, 406, 450–52, 461, 470–71, 474, 480, 488–92, 505–7, 527

Schelling, Friedrich Wilhelm Josef, 15, 23

second coming of Christ. *See* Last Days

Sermon on the Mount, 41, 176, 308, 310, 428

sickness, 199, 213, 230–32, 234, 240, 243–44, 257, 258, 373, 439, 463, 468, 470, 477

sin, 27, 39, 53, 65, 74, 102, 145, 147–48, 161–62, 165–66, 175, 183, 190, 192–97, 200–201, 203–4, 230, 247–48, 314, 382, 444, 445, 471, 473

Society for Christianity, 36, 44
song, singing. *See* hymn(s)
Späth, Dr., 122, 123, 126
Spener, Philipp Jakob, 4, 251
Steinkopf, Dr., 36, 221–23
Strauss, David F., 23, 25, 42, 191
suffering, 47, 75–76, 136, 220–21,
    232–33, 240, 245, 252–53, 257,
    319, 321, 344, 407, 423, 448,
    466, 468, 471–72, 474, 480, 498
suicide, 191, 210, 212, 472
superstition, 138ff., 147–48, 206, 226,
    474, 489

Täglich Brod aus Bad Boll, 10, 105,
    173, 443, 503
theology, 14, 18, 21, 75ff., 296
tribulation. *See* suffering
Tübingen University, 14, 15, 20, 23, 37,
    40, 42, 111, 432

universalism, 46, 173, 249–50, 254,
    258, 288, 325–26, 341, 423, 502,
    514, 517–19
Unterhaugstett, 91, 98, 121, 160, 164,
    170, 228, 335

de Valenti, Dr. Ernst Josef Gustav, 40,
    234, 236, 379–82
*Vertheidigungsschrift gegen Herrn Dr.
    de Valenti*, 119, 125, 146, 196,
    197, 206, 221, 222, 232, 233,
    379, 381, 382

war, 112, 114, 277, 306, 314, 514
Werner, Karl, 38, 40, 101, 103–4

The Blumhardt Source Series

Johann Christoph Blumhardt
A Biography
Friedrich Zündel

The Gospel of God's Reign
Living for the Kingdom of God
Christoph Friedrich Blumhardt

Gospel Sermons
On Faith, the Holy Spirit, and the Coming Kingdom
Johann Christoph Blumhardt

Make Way for the Spirit
My Father's Battle and Mine
Christoph Friedrich Blumhardt

P. 145 — Death, another chance of forgiveness?

P. 175 — awakening, Preaching, sins and wrongs of people. Repentance

P. 232 — Patience in suffering

P. 238 — Jesus was a healer, helper and a remitter of sins

P. 287 — God's revelation, a preparation in deed and truth for the Lord's advent. Reformation as the model for spiritual renewal that must extend throughout the entire world.

9 780874 862416